CASES OF AMNESIA

In all cognitive domains, neuropsychological research has advanced through the study of individual patients, and detailed observations and descriptions of their cases have been the backbone of medical and scientific reports for centuries. *Cases of Amnesia* describes some of the most important single case studies in the history of memory, as well as new case studies of amnesic patients. It highlights the major contribution they make to our understanding of human memory and neuropsychology.

Written by world-leading researchers and considering the latest theory and techniques in the field, each case study provides a description of the patient's history, how their memory was assessed and what conclusions can be made in relation to cognitive models of memory.

Edited by Sarah E. MacPherson and Sergio Della Sala, *Cases of Amnesia* is a must read for researchers and clinicians in neuropsychology, cognitive psychology and cognitive neuroscience.

Sarah E. MacPherson is Senior Lecturer in the Department of Psychology, University of Edinburgh, UK. Her research focuses on the cognitive and neuropsychological investigations of executive abilities, memory and emotional and social functioning in healthy and pathological ageing and damaged brains.

Sergio Della Sala is Professor of Human Cognitive Neuroscience at the University of Edinburgh, UK. His research interests consider the relationship between brain and behaviour, including human memory from a neuropsychological perspective.

Frontiers of Cognitive Psychology
Series Editors
Nelson Cowan
University of Missouri-Columbia
David Balota
Washington University in St. Louis

Frontiers of Cognitive Psychology is a new series of cognitive psychology books, which aims to bring together the very latest research in the discipline, providing a comprehensive and up-to-date review of the latest empirical, theoretical and practical issues in the field. Each volume concentrates on a traditional core area of cognitive psychology, or an area which is emerging as a new core area for the future, and may include interdisciplinary perspectives from areas such as developmental psychology, neuroscience, evolutionary psychology, forensic psychology, social psychology, and the health sciences.

Published

Big Data in Cognitive Science
Michael N. Jones (Ed)

Network Science in Cognitive Psychology
Michael S. Vitevitch (Ed)

The Science of Expertise
Behavioral, Neural, and Genetic Approaches to Complex Skill
David Z. Hambrick, Guillermo Campitelli, Brooke N. Macnamara (Eds)

Forthcoming

New Methods in Cognitive Psychology
Daniel H. Spieler & Eric Schumacher (Eds)

For a full list of titles in this series, please visit https://www.routledge.com/Frontiers-of-Cognitive-Psychology/book-series/FCP

CASES OF AMNESIA

Contributions to Understanding Memory and the Brain

Edited by
Sarah E. MacPherson and Sergio Della Sala

NEW YORK AND LONDON

First published 2019
by Routledge
52 Vanderbilt Avenue, New York, NY 10017

and by Routledge
2 Park Square, Milton Park, Abingdon, Oxon, OX14 4RN

Routledge is an imprint of the Taylor & Francis Group, an informa business

© 2019 Taylor & Francis

The right of Sarah E. MacPherson and Sergio Della Sala to be identified as the authors of the editorial material, and of the authors for their individual chapters, has been asserted in accordance with sections 77 and 78 of the Copyright, Designs and Patents Act 1988.

All rights reserved. No part of this book may be reprinted or reproduced or utilised in any form or by any electronic, mechanical, or other means, now known or hereafter invented, including photocopying and recording, or in any information storage or retrieval system, without permission in writing from the publishers.

Trademark notice: Product or corporate names may be trademarks or registered trademarks, and are used only for identification and explanation without intent to infringe.

Library of Congress Cataloging-in-Publication Data
Names: MacPherson, Sarah E., editor. | Della Sala, Sergio, editor.
Title: Cases of amnesia : contributions to understanding memory and the brain / edited by Sarah E. MacPherson and Sergio Della Sala.
Description: New York, NY : Routledge, 2020.
Identifiers: LCCN 2018041516 | ISBN 9781138545557 (hardback) | ISBN 9781138545564 (paperback) | ISBN 9780429023880 (ebook)
Subjects: LCSH: Amnesia—Case studies. | Memory—Case studies.
Classification: LCC RC394.A5 C37 2020 | DDC 616.85/232—dc23
LC record available at https://lccn.loc.gov/2018041516

ISBN: 978-1-138-54555-7 (hbk)
ISBN: 978-1-138-54556-4 (pbk)
ISBN: 978-0-429-02388-0 (ebk)

Typeset in Bembo
by Apex CoVantage, LLC

To Sarah's husband Scott
To Sergio's nieces Caterina and Francesca and nephew Pietro

CONTENTS

Preface		*x*
Acknowledgements		*xiv*
List of Contributors		*xv*

1. The Single Case Study of Memory
   Tim Shallice — 1

2. The Earthquake that Reshaped the Intellectual Landscape of Memory, Mind and Brain: Case HM
   Donald G. MacKay — 16

3. The Case of YR: Selective Bilateral Hippocampal Lesions Can Have Quite Different Effects on Item Recognition, Associative Recognition and Recall
   Juliet S. Holdstock, Nicola M. Hunkin, Claire L. Isaac and Andrew R. Mayes — 40

4. Amnesic Patient VC: What Have We Learnt From Him?
   Carina Tudor-Sfetea and Lisa Cipolotti — 65

5. What Did Amnesic Actor AB Teach Us About Learning His Lines?
   Michael D. Kopelman and John Morton — 92

6   Cases of Hippocampal Memory Loss: Dr Z, the Engineer
    and the Glove Cutter   110
    Narinder Kapur and Steven Kemp

7   Persistent Déjà Vu, Recollective Confabulation and the
    Case of Patient AKP   131
    Chris J.A. Moulin

8   Case KC (Kent Cochrane) and His Contributions to
    Research and Theory on Memory and Related,
    Non-Memory Functions   156
    R. Shayna Rosenbaum and Morris Moscovitch

9   Right is Right for Episodic Memories in Two
    Contrasting Case Studies, CH and JR: Focal Retrograde
    Amnesia and Public Semantic Amnesia   187
    Liliann Manning

10 Sensory-Specific Visual Amnesia (Cases 1 and 2):
    An Acquired Visual-Limbic Disconnection Syndrome   203
    Elliott D. Ross

11 'Yes, I Remember'—Apparent Consolidation Under
    Conditions of Minimal Sensory Input in a Case of Severe
    Anterograde Amnesia: Case PB   220
    Michaela Dewar

12 VA: A Case Report of Transient Epileptic Amnesia   240
    John Baker, Sharon Savage and Adam Zeman

13 A "Purest" Impairment of Verbal Short-Term Memory.
    The Case of PV and the Phonological
    Short-Term Input Store   261
    Giuseppe Vallar

14 Semantic Short-Term Memory and its Role in Sentence
    Processing and Long-Term Memory: Evidence From
    Cases AB and ML   292
    Randi C. Martin

15 Interrelationship Between Semantic Memory and
   Personal Experience: Evidence From Semantic Dementia
   Patients KE and WM   315
   Julie Snowden

16 Iris Murdoch: Days Without Writing   336
   *Peter Garrard, John R. Hodges, Vijeya Ganesan and Karalyn
   Patterson*

17 The Wealth of Evidence From Brain Lesions Affecting
   Memory: How Should We Use It?   354
   Nelson Cowan and Candice C. Morey

18 Biases and Concerns With the Single Case Approach in
   the Neuropsychology of Memory   365
   Roberto Cubelli

19 The Case for Single Case Studies in Memory Research   377
   Simon Fischer-Baum and Yingxue Tian

20 Comments on the Single Case Approach to the Study of
   Memory and Other Domains of Cognition   389
   Max Coltheart

Index   *398*

PREFACE

The watercolour illustration on the cover of this book depicts a black swan, a metaphor for very rare events. The Roman poet Juvenal expressed it eloquently: "Rara . . . nigroque simillima cygno" ("rare . . . and very much like a black swan"). It winks both at Popper's Falsifiability epistemology and at Taleb's Black Swan Theory, postulating large unexpected effects from rare events. An exhaustive report of a neuropsychological single case is like a black swan; it offers a viewpoint which can modulate, change, or provide *Erschutterung* (shocks) to accrued theories of cognition. This important form of scientific reporting was on the verge of extinction, which would have deprived us of an important means to knowledge. Luckily, the pertinence of single cases in neuropsychology is being revalued; the black swan has offspring.

Single cases offer the possibility of detecting unforeseen symptoms or unpredicted patterns of spared and impaired abilities, hence anticipating and guiding further experimental investigations. In all cognitive domains, neuropsychological research has advanced through the study of exemplary individual patients. These include cases epitomising executive dysfunction, such as Phineas Gage, specific language or reading deficits such as Leborgne or Oscar C, praxis impairments, such as the Regierungsrat or visual agnosia, such as case HJA. Of course, early single cases also revealed specific memory deficits; for example, HM for long-term memory and PV for verbal short-term memory who both feature in this book. These cases are all mentioned in the *Cortex*, volume 97 editorial announcing the revamping of a section on single cases. Cortex is not the only outlet promoting the reappraisal of single cases; several other journals in our field, including *Cognitive Neuropsychology* and *Neurocase*, recognise their relevance in what Smalheiser and colleagues dubbed the "renaissance of the case report literature."

Detailed observations and descriptions of individual cases have been the backbone of medical and scientific reports for centuries. Several of them are beautifully summarised and commented upon in the two academic volumes on *Classic Cases in Neuropsychology* edited by Code, Joanette, Lecours, and Wallesch, but also popularised in anecdote-filled assemblages like Sam Kean's *The Tale of the Dueling Neurosurgeons*. Such cases also permeate the literature on memory. For example, in 1936, Gustav Störring described the case of Franz Breundl, known as Mr. B, a victim of carbon monoxide poisoning presenting with the inability to encode or retain any information (translated into English with a commentary in *Cortex*, volume 59). This and other beguiling cases were reported in excruciating detail but necessarily authors could not attempt to interpret the observed phenomena in terms of general cognitive theories. Claude Bernard (see Figure P1) was among the first to argue that the careful report of single cases might inform theories even more than group averages. In his *An Introduction to the Study of Experimental Medicine*, Bernard wrote that we "must never make average descriptions of experiments, because the true relations of phenomena disappear in the average.... Averages are applicable only to reducing very slightly varying numerical data about clearly defined and absolutely simple cases."

FIGURE P1 Claude Bernard and his pupils. Oil painting after Léon-Augus Lhermitte. From Wellcome Images, operated by Wellcome Trust. Licensed under the Creative Commons.

In the last decades, springing from the seminal articulations of Alfonso Caramazza, single case research in neuropsychology has contributed greatly to the development and testing of cognitive models. To appreciate how the reporting of single cases on specific memory deficits illuminates the cognitive neuroscience of memory, please see the recent review by Rosenbaum and colleagues in the Annals of the New York Academy of Sciences.

To obtain a sense of whether colleagues working in psychology and related disciplines believe that single cases *are* relevant and *should be* considered in the development of cognitive models of normal mind functioning, we devised an online survey. The survey was advertised and distributed via the Psychonomic Society and the Federation of European Societies of Neuropsychology, as well as social media outlets, such as Twitter and Facebook. Ninety-eight academic and clinical psychologists and neuropsychologists participated; individuals ranged in career from postgraduate student to full professor. The main point to emerge from our survey was the hiatus between the belief that single cases *should be* considered when developing cognitive models of normal function compared to the reality that they *are*. The majority of those who completed the survey (88%) stated that single cases should always be considered. However, fewer believed that evidence from the neuropsychology literature (39%) and single cases (33%) actually *are* considered, with most asserting that single cases are only somewhat considered in the development of cognitive models (63%).

In the '70s, Henri Hècaen maintained that "each observation of a patient potentially constitutes a privileged object of study." The overall aim of this book is to examine whether or not we should continue to care about these data in developing cognitive models of memory. In spite of more recent advances in neuroimaging techniques, single case studies remain an important methodology for understanding the architecture of human cognition. Memory, in particular, is an area of cognition that has benefited considerably through the study of single case amnesic patients. The focus of the book is to return to some of these earlier cases in the memory literature, as well as more recent or unpublished cases, and review their contribution in the light of current memory models.

Each chapter in this volume takes the form of a structured interview where the authors have been asked questions in relation to their study of single cases and models of memory. The interviews invited discussion from the authors about the patients' history, the assessments that were administered, any data that were not published but might now be of interest, the conclusions that were reached at the time of publication in relation to memory models, and whether or not these conclusions still hold today. Commentaries from additional authors and their interpretation of the findings in relation to current memory models enframe the content of the book. As with most collections, the case series presented in this volume is far from complete.

Other books are available that arouse our curiosity by telling the intriguing stories of individuals who lost their memory, such as patient HM (e.g., Corkin's

Permanent Present Tense: The Man with No Memory, and What He Taught the World) or Clive Wearing's story in *Forever Today: A Memoir of Love and Amnesia*. However, these tend to be biographical rather than academic in nature. Other volumes do focus on specific single cases in the memory literature, for instance the compelling collection edited by Campbell and Conway *Broken Memories: Case Studies in Memory Impairment*, or the fascinating *Case Studies in the Neuropsychology of Memory* by the late Alan Parkin, both now a little out of date. The present volume surfaces in their wake, in the hope to reconstruct the link between neuropsychological single case observations of specific memory loss and their meaning in terms of the cognitive architecture of memory in the healthy brain.

Sarah E. MacPherson and Sergio Della Sala,
Edinburgh, 12 June 2018

ACKNOWLEDGEMENTS

We are grateful to Nelson Cowan and Dave Balota for offering us the opportunity to edit a book in their *Frontiers in Cognitive Psychology* series, and to Paul Dukes, Claudia Bona-Cohen, Sophie Crowe, Ceri McLardy and Tina Cottone for their editorial assistance. We wish to thank Paolo Della Sala for drawing the cover illustration and all the authors for their contributions. We thank Steve Lewandowsky, Psychonomic Society, and Mervi Jehkonen, Federation of European Societies of Neuropsychology, for promoting our online survey to their societies' members. We are also thankful to Galit Rodin and the Wiley Agency (UK) Limited for granting permission to reproduce photographic material.

CONTRIBUTORS

John Baker—Cognitive Neurology Research Group, University of Exeter Medical School, Exeter, UK

Lisa Cipolotti—Department of Neuropsychology, National Hospital for Neurology and Neurosurgery, London, UK

Max Coltheart—Department of Cognitive Science and ARC Centre of Excellence for Cognitive Disorders, Macquarie University, Sydney, Australia

Nelson Cowan—Department of Psychological Sciences, University of Missouri, Columbia, MO, USA

Roberto Cubelli—Department of Psychology and Cognitive Sciences, University of Trento, Italy

Sergio Della Sala—Human Cognitive Neuroscience, Psychology, University of Edinburgh, UK

Michaela Dewar—Department of Psychology, School of Social Sciences, Heriot-Watt University, Edinburgh, UK

Simon Fischer-Baum—Department of Psychology, Rice University, Houston, TX, USA

Vijeya Ganesan—UCL-Great Ormond Street Institute of Child Health, London, UK

Peter Garrard—Molecular and Clinical Sciences Research Institute, St George's, University of London, UK

John R. Hodges—Brain & Mind Centre, University of Sydney, Australia

Juliet S. Holdstock—School of Psychology, University of Liverpool, UK

Nicola M. Hunkin—Department of Psychology, University of Sheffield, UK

Claire L. Isaac—Psychological Medicine, Oxford University Hospitals, UK

Narinder Kapur—University College London, London, UK

Steven Kemp—Leeds Teaching Hospitals NHS Trust, Leeds, UK

Michael D. Kopelman—Institute of Psychiatry, Psychology and Neuroscience, King's College London, UK

Donald G. MacKay—Psychology Department, University of California, Los Angeles, USA

Sarah E. MacPherson—Human Cognitive Neuroscience, Psychology, University of Edinburgh, UK

Liliann Manning—Psychology Department, Strasbourg University, and Cognitive Neuropsychology and Pathophysiology of Schizophrenia, INSERM U1114, Strasbourg, France

Randi C. Martin—Department of Psychological Sciences, Rice University, Houston, TX, USA

Andrew R. Mayes—School of Psychological Sciences, University of Manchester, UK

Candice C. Morey—School of Psychology, University of Cardiff, UK

John Morton—Institute of Cognitive Neuroscience, University College London, UK

Morris Moscovitch—Rotman Research Institute, Baycrest and Department of Psychology, University of Toronto, Toronto, Canada

Chris J.A. Moulin—LPNC CNRS UMR 5105, Université Grenoble Alpes, France

Karalyn Patterson—Department of Clinical Neurosciences and MRC Cognition & Brain Sciences Unit, University of Cambridge, UK

R. Shayna Rosenbaum—Department of Psychology and Vision: Science to Applications (VISTA) program, York University and Rotman Research Institute, Baycrest, Toronto, Canada

Elliott D. Ross—University of Oklahoma Health Sciences Center, Oklahoma City, Oklahoma, USA and University of Colorado School of Medicine, Denver, Colorado, USA

Sharon Savage—Cognitive Neurology Research Group, University of Exeter Medical School, Exeter, UK

Tim Shallice—Institute of Cognitive Neuroscience, University College London, London, UK and Cognitive Neuropsychology and Neuroimaging Lab, Scuola Internazionale Superiore di Studi Avanzati (SISSA), Trieste, Italy

Julie Snowden—Cerebral Function Unit, Neuroscience Centre, Salford Royal NHS Foundation Trust, UK and Division of Neuroscience and Experimental Psychology, School of Biological Sciences, University of Manchester, UK

Yingxue Tian—Department of Psychology, Rice University, Houston, TX, USA

Carina Tudor-Sfetea—Department of Neuropsychology, National Hospital for Neurology and Neurosurgery, London, UK

Giuseppe Vallar—Department of Psychology and Neuro-Mi, University of Milan-Bicocca, and Neuropsychological Laboratory, IRCCS Istituto Auxologico Italiano, Milan, Italy

Adam Zeman—Cognitive Neurology Research Group, University of Exeter Medical School, Exeter, UK

1
THE SINGLE CASE STUDY OF MEMORY

Tim Shallice

Introduction

This book is on a very important topic for scientific neuropsychology. It concerns the in-depth study of individual neurological patients with striking disorders in some aspect of the field of memory. Of all the areas of psychology, it is the area of memory, where in the last hundred years, the description of a surprising disorder in a single patient following a neurological intervention or disease that has had the most impact. Memory is a field where most of the greatest scientific advances from neuropsychological investigations have come from studies of a single patient, or less frequently, a few very similar patients, each treated as individuals. The seemingly more standard method of contrasting the average performance of large groups of patients has made much less of a splash. Interestingly, this is not true of all areas of psychology; executive functions are, for instance, a counterexample. However, for a variety of mainly bad reasons, the single case approach is currently being increasingly ignored across the board in favour of the seemingly more scientific, but actually less informative, study of the average performance of groups of patients. This book describes some of the most important single case studies in the history of memory. It shows the efficacy of the approach.

Descriptions of individual patients with selective disorders were a standard procedure in the late 19th century until the 1920s, and this was to become neuropsychological research. The approach reached its acme in the work of the diagram makers in language towards the end of the 19th century. In memory too, doctors working with neurological patients at that time were well aware of the existence of amnesia (i.e., the loss of the ability to retrieve information about one's personal past) (see, e.g., Chapter 6 this volume). Indeed, clinicians, such as Korsakoff, and in particular von Bekterew, associated amnesia with lesions to the diencephalon and even the hippocampus (Moscovitch, 2012).

However, in such work, descriptions of the cognitive state and behaviour of patients tended to be rather imprecise, non-quantitative and primarily the clinical interpretation of the investigator. So, in the 1920s and '30s, this method began to be seen as being insufficiently scientific. Aphasia researchers, such as Head (1926) and Weisenburg and McBride (1935), as well as Rylander (1939) who studied disorders of executive functions, introduced a more systematic and quantitative approach. This had two aspects. First, and very valuably, tests began to be standardised, or at least applied systematically, and with results reported quantitatively. Second, and less clearly beneficial, the performance of a series of patients selected using fairly wide criteria was reported, not just individual cases showing striking dissociations. Scientific neuropsychology was seen as embodying both aspects.

Human neuropsychological research at the time, however, had little impact on the scientific study of mental processes. This would, in any case, have been particularly difficult, especially in the field of memory. At a theoretical level, the doctrine of mass action (Lashley, 1929) was dominant. It viewed the effects of damage to the association cortex (i.e., the entire cortex except that devoted to perceptual or motor processing), as only a question of the amount of tissue loss; the specific location of the damage was held to be unimportant.

Milner on Selective Amnesia

Neglect of single-patient data and adherence to mass action ended dramatically following the publication of a number of papers in the late 1950s, in particular one reporting the memory disorder of HM (see Chapter 2 this volume) that occurred following bilateral medial temporal surgery aimed to reduce his epilepsy (Scoville & Milner, 1957). After his surgery, HM had a very severe amnesia, which meant he had virtually no conscious memory of what happened even minutes before. So, for example, the same joke could be told many times in an hour as he would not remember having told it before.

The dramatic change in impact resulting from the papers describing HM occurred for seven main reasons, six intellectual and one social:

1. HM's problems were restricted to memory; intelligence, for instance, was unaffected.
2. HM's difficulties were described clinically but also, critically, they were demonstrated quantitatively using the Wechsler Memory Scale and the Wechsler Adult Intelligence Scale.
3. The disorder was extremely severe. It was far from being a marginal effect.
4. Patient HM had been relatively normal as far as memory was concerned pre-surgically; the memory problems were clearly caused by the removal of a particular region of brain.
5. As far as the brain itself was concerned, the fact that the damage occurred as a result of neurosurgery meant that most unusually for neurological patients at that time, information about the localisation of damage was available prior to

post-mortem. Moreover, the lesions were relatively localised, being restricted to one part of the brain bilaterally; they were not diffuse. In other words, Lashley was wrong.
6. Similar memory problems were found in six other patients, whose difficulties were studied individually, not as a group. These six were, however, psychotic prior to their operations, as the neurosurgeon Scoville was a great proponent of prefrontal leucotomy (see Dittrich, 2016). Yet, similar, if somewhat milder, effects had been found by Milner and Penfield (1955) in two patients who underwent left medial temporal removal due to more conventional neurosurgery. Such memory deficits were unusual for unilateral patients, but were compatible with the findings on HM, if there had actually been damage in the other hemisphere which could not be detected given the methods available at the time. There was also a bilateral neurosurgical patient reported by Terzian and Dalle Ore (1955) who had similar memory problems to HM, together with features of the so-called Klüver-Bucy complex. This meant that HM was not a completely isolated unusual case.
7. Finally, from the important point of view of impact, the neurosurgeons Scoville and Penfield were very well known to the North American neuroscience community.

Milner followed up her original findings, by showing that there were aspects of memory which were still intact in HM (Milner, Corkin & Teuber, 1968). These, for instance, included his ability to learn procedural memory skills, such as mirror drawing. Warrington and Weiskrantz (1968), using a mixed individual case/group design, then found analogous preservation of perceptual learning; they averaged the performance of six patients, all of whom had a relatively pure amnesic syndrome.

An additional factor was soon to be added. Milner's studies do not appear to have been greatly influenced by the beginnings of cognitive psychology, which was occurring at much the same time. However, that was soon to change. Performance on another memory task found to be intact in HM was digit span, in which participants must immediately repeat back a string of digits presented at a rate of one per second. Similar preservation of span was found by Drachman and Arbit (1966) in five patients with severe amnesia following bilateral hippocampal removals. They interpreted this pattern of intact span in their amnesic patients in terms of preservation of short-term memory with impairment of long-term memory, a theoretical contrast which was being much investigated in normal subjects by cognitive psychologists at the time (e.g., Waugh & Norman, 1965; Glanzer & Cunitz, 1966).

Short-Term Memory

This link between cognitive psychology and neuropsychology led to experimental memory paradigms developed by cognitive psychologists being applied to the study of patients. Take the free recall paradigm developed by experimental psychologists in the 1950s (e.g., Deese & Kaufman, 1957). Participants are presented with a list of unrelated words at a fixed rate and have to recall as many words as they can at the end of the list in any order. The probability of an item being recalled is very dependent on the position in the list the word is presented. Moreover, this dependence has a very characteristic form. The first (primacy) and the last (recency) few items are better remembered than the items in the flat middle part of the so-called serial position curve. In addition, the length of the primacy and recency parts of the curve are independent of the overall length of the list (Murdock, 1962). However, other variables, such as rate of presentation or whether interfering material is presented before the recall attempt, lead to very different effects on the primacy and middle parts of the curve compared with the recency part. Glanzer and Cunitz (1966), who discovered these effects, argued that the items retrieved in the primacy and middle components of the serial position curve are held in long-term memory. By contrast, they maintained that items retrieved in the recency part of the curve were being held in short-term memory too.

When the free recall paradigm was used by Baddeley and Warrington (1970) with a small group of relatively pure amnesic patients using a mixed individual case/group design, it was found that their performance was essentially normal in the recency part of the curve. In contrast, performance on the middle part of the curve was completely at floor and greatly reduced on the primacy part. This is exactly what one would expect if one combined Glanzer and Cunitz's account of the free recall task with Drachman and Arbit's (1966) position that short-term memory was preserved in amnesia.

This perspective was supported by the discovery of patients with a second sort of memory problem, namely a specific difficulty in auditory-verbal short-term memory (see also Chapter 13 this volume). Warrington and Shallice (1969) described a patient, KF, suffering from a left temporo-parietal head injury who had a digit span of only 2.3. Words could be perceived normally at the one-per-second digit span presentation rate, and digit naming could be replaced by pointing to written digits without any improvement in span, suggesting that spoken production was not the problem. Moreover, when carrying out the free recall task, patient KF performed in an opposite fashion to Baddeley and Warrington's amnesics. Recency was restricted to a single item, instead of the normal five or so. Yet, the primacy and middle part of the curve were relatively intact (Shallice & Warrington, 1970).

Since the description of KF's short-term memory problem, about 20 similar cases have been described in the literature (see Vallar & Shallice, 1990 for the earlier ones). However, the syndrome is subtler clinically than the amnesic syndrome. As a result, like virtually all new forms of memory impairment described since HM, there have been critics of the claim that a new functional syndrome has been isolated. For instance, Buchsbaum and D'Esposito (2008, p. 773) argued, "The sheer rarity of the STM patient, for there are no more than 10–15 cases reported in the literature, might indicate that there is something out of the ordinary in the underlying neurobiology of these particular individuals". In fact, we do not know how rare the syndrome is, and indeed most patients with the classic clinical syndrome of conduction aphasia have short-term memory problems (Bartha & Benke, 2003; Gvion & Friedmann, 2012). Yet, they are not "pure" short-term memory cases; they have other problems too. I will return to this issue later.

The short-term memory patients were some of the main sources of evidence used by Baddeley and Hitch (1974) to support their model of working memory, which has become one of the most highly quoted in the area. In later versions of the model (e.g., Baddeley, 1986), the behaviour of these patients corresponds to an impairment of the phonological input buffer. Given the idea of a buffer as having two characteristics—the holding of information in the short term only and a dedicated procedure for retrieving that information—the idea of selective damage to buffers soon became productive. De Renzi and Nichelli (1975) briefly described two right hemisphere patients with scores on the non-verbal Corsi spatial scan test of 2.5, well below the normal range of 7. Both patients had perfect scores on a copy drawing test. Neither patient had neglect or any difficulty on a series of spatial perception tests. The problem would appear to be at the level of the visuo-spatial sketchpad component of the Baddeley-Hitch model (see also patients described by Farah, Levine & Calvanio, 1988 and Hanley, Young & Pearson, 1991). In contrast, Kinsbourne and Warrington (1962) have described four left hemisphere patients with difficulties reporting more than one visual item when more than one item is presented (see also Warrington & Rabin, 1971; Warrington & Shallice, 1980; see also Chapter 10).

Buffers are not only necessary parts of perceptual systems. They are also required in certain sorts of action systems. In support of this claim, Caramazza, Miceli and Villa (1986) and Caramazza, Miceli, Villa and Romani (1987) have described patients whose impairments correspond to damage to the phonological output buffer and graphemic output buffer, respectively, and these findings have been well replicated across other patients (see Shallice & Cooper, 2011, sections 7.5, 7.6 and 7.7).

Semantic Memory

Very soon after the double dissociation between disorders of short- and long-term memory was discovered, a second distinction derived from cognitive psychology led to the isolation of a new form of memory impairment. In a theoretical review article, Tulving (1972) drew a distinction between so-called episodic memory and semantic memory. Episodic memory, for him, was the system we use when we in some sense re-experience an event that has occurred to us in our past. Semantic memory, by contrast, is the organised knowledge one possesses of words and facts, and can be extended to apply to the significance of objects as known through the senses. Tulving's arguments for the distinction between these two systems did not include neuropsychological evidence. However, his theoretical characterisations were soon to be applied by neuropsychologists. Kinsbourne and Wood (1975) argued that the classical amnesic syndrome, of which HM is an example, corresponds to an impairment of episodic memory; semantic memory, in comparison, can be intact.

The complimentary syndrome was also soon-to-be reported. In the same year, Warrington (1975) described the neuropsychological characteristics of three patients, AB, EM and (less clearly) CR, whom she argued had a selective problem in the impairment of semantic memory. The patients had intact pre-semantic perception and intelligence. However, their knowledge of the meaning of words and of the significance of objects was severely degraded. The deficit seemed to involve all classes of concrete items. In contrast, clinically speaking, the three cases appeared have normal long-term recall of their lives. Moreover, in follow-up studies, Coughlan and Warrington (1981) investigated more formally the episodic memory of EM, the only patient of the three still available for testing. They found that when words still within her vocabulary were used, she was in the normal range in long-term recall of verbal material. These patients, then, represented the complimentary dissociation to amnesics, with episodic memory spared but semantic memory severely degraded (see also Chapter 14 for short-term memory cases).

Warrington's findings on selective impairment of semantic memory were confirmed and greatly extended to a sizeable subgroup of patients suffering from what is now known as semantic dementia by Snowden, Goulding and Neary (1989); Hodges, Patterson, Oxbury and Funnell (1992); and Patterson, Nestor and Rogers (2007) amongst others (see also Chapter 15 this volume). A computational theory of the organisation of semantic memory called the hub-and-spokes model, developed by Rogers et al. (2004), fitted their characteristics well (see also Patterson et al., 2007) with semantic dementia corresponding to damage to the hub component and the different dimensions of meaning corresponding to the spokes.

However, semantic dementia is not the only form of semantic memory impairment. In the late 1970s, acyclovir was discovered to be able to treat and arrest a form of encephalitis, herpes simplex encephalitis, a condition which prior to acyclovir was fatal in roughly 70% of cases. Yet, in practice, as the illness develops very rapidly, over a matter of days, even when acyclovir is administered in the acute phase, patients are often left with major neurological damage, particularly to the anterior temporal lobes. In the early 1980s, working with four patients who had been treated with acyclovir, JBR, SBY, KB and ING, Warrington and Shallice (1984) found that, in addition to a severe amnesia, the patients suffered from an impairment of semantic memory, which was much greater for some categories of knowledge than others. In particular, good knowledge of artefacts such as *tent, compass, wheelbarrow* and *submarine*, can be retained while knowledge of living things and foods is virtually at floor. A similar type of category specificity effect has been shown in a considerable number of patients with herpes simplex encephalitis; 27 are listed by Capitani, Laiacona, Mahon and Caramazza (2003).

Again, the complimentary pattern has been described in individual cases, initially by Warrington and McCarthy (1983) in a global aphasic patient, VER. Using five-alternative word-to-picture matching, VER was 88% correct with food names, but only 58% correct with object names. Animal names were similar to food names. By contrast, JBR, one of the herpes encephalitis patients, was nearly 100% accurate with object names, but around 60% to 70% correct with food and animal names. In their review, Capitani et al. (2003) listed 18 patients who showed some form of category specificity with knowledge of living things better preserved.

Unlike the short-term memory/long-term memory dissociations and the semantic memory/episodic memory dissociations, but like Milner's initial findings on amnesia, these category-specific phenomena were not prefigured in the theoretical framework of human experimental psychology. So, it is not surprising that they were initially fiercely contested as artefactual in the sense of being caused by factors unrelated to the neurological basis of semantic categories (e.g., Funnell & Sheridan, 1992; Stewart, Parkin & Hunkin, 1992; Gaffan & Heywood, 1993). For instance, Laws (2005) argued that the effects may be reducible to pre-morbid individual differences. However, such an account would not explain the gross differences across aetiology in the two complimentary category-specific effects. Thus, in Capitani et al.'s review of the 61 patients described in the literature showing a living things deficit, 44% had herpes simplex encephalitis. For the 17 patients with the complimentary pattern of artefact deficits, only one had had that illness.

More critically, when group studies were later carried out, there was a consistency of localisations of impairments across mixed aetiology groups (Damasio, Grabowski, Tranel, Hichwa & Damasio, 1996), dementing conditions (Brambati et al., 2006) and tumours (Campanella, Mondani, Skrap & Shallice, 2009). Living things deficits tend to be bilateral anterior medial inferior temporal. Artefacts deficits involve somewhat more posterior left superior temporal/inferior parietal regions. These localisations can hardly be due to pre-morbid individual differences. Thus, for category specificity, as for amnesia and semantic dementia, the reality of phenomena described in initial investigations of single cases were later supported in studies using group or case study procedures.

How can one explain the existence of these two forms of semantic memory deficit—semantic dementia and category specificity? Initially, when this type of category specificity was described—there are other forms—it was argued that sensory quality and functional (or characteristic action) aspects of meaning were stored separately in the brain. Is this compatible with the hub-and-spokes model? A promising possibility is the approach of Chen, Lambon Ralph and Rogers (2017), which uses a combination of meta-analysis of functional imaging studies, tractography and computational modelling to argue that category-specific effects arise from damage to spokes rather than the hub in the hub-and-spokes model. If this is the right approach, then the apparent inferential conflict between the two syndromes may be resolved.

Recollection, Familiarity and the Amnesic Syndrome

We had to wait another ten years for the next major set of memory dissociations to be described. Then two related syndromes were described. First, it had generally been believed that classical amnesic patients are impaired on both recall and recognition. Indeed, there has been intensive study of a number of patients of this type whose lesions from structural imaging appear to be restricted to the hippocampus (e.g., Reed & Squire, 1997; Cipolotti et al., 2001). Then, however, Vargha-Khadem et al. (1997) described three developmental patients with very early lesions to the hippocampus, who despite their very poor performance on recall tasks, were intact on recognition tasks. These findings were explained away by Manns and Squire (1999), who argued that the very early onset of the lesions could have allowed compensatory processes to occur, and so such results in developmental amnesia may not be relevant to patients where lesions occur in adulthood.

However, Mayes, Holdstock, Isaac, Hunkin and Roberts (2002) described a patient, YR, with bilateral hippocampal lesions possibly arising from an ischaemic incident, who was severely impaired on 34 recall tests—3.6 SDs below the control mean (see Chapter 3). Instead, on 42 different item recognition tests using a variety of materials, YR was much less impaired—0.5 SDs below the control mean. Similar patients have been described since (e.g., Bastin et al., 2004).

Mayes et al. explain the dissociation they found in YR using another conceptual framework derived from cognitive psychology. Mandler (1980) had argued that two separate processes underlie recognition—*recollection*, where one has a conscious experience of the event, and *familiarity*, where one has the feeling that a relevant event has occurred but no conscious memory of the event itself (see also Chapter 4). Recall, by contrast, is held to rely entirely on recollection. Mayes et al. use this dual-process distinction and argue that the recognition memory tests on which YR performs well are heavily loaded on familiarity.

This type of dual-process theory has, however, long been subject to the criticism that the memory traces underlying familiarity may not be qualitatively different from those underlying recollection but merely weaker (Wixted, 2007). What would be really strong evidence in favour of the dual-process approach would be selective impairments of the familiarity component following lesions to some region other than the hippocampus. Indeed, at least two cases have been described of this type—NB (Bowles et al., 2010) and (for faces only) OG (Edelstyn, Grange, Ellis & Mayes, 2016). NB had a large anterior left temporal lesion sparing the hippocampus but involving a large part of the left perirhinal cortex, the region most linked to familiarity in fMRI studies (Diana, Yonelinas & Ranganath, 2007). To complicate matters, though, OG had a lesion centred on the right mediodorsal thalamic nucleus, but this has been held by Aggleton, Dumont and Warburton (2011) to be part of the same network underlying familiarity. So, we have the beginnings of single case reports supporting the separable recollection/familiarity systems distinction, but further case descriptions are badly needed. Moreover, this leaves the conundrum of how to account for apparently selective hippocampal lesions affecting both recall and recognition to much the same extent in other patients. It is certainly possible that such patients have additional silent lesions, but this is very much an ad hoc account.

Further Striking Types of Impairment of Memory

Case studies of amnesic patients or studies of very small groups of "pure" patients of this type have produced a variety of phenomena relevant to memory theory. Take very long-term autobiographical memory (see Chapter 9). Amnesics produce very long-lasting retrograde amnesias, when appropriately tested (Sanders & Warrington, 1971), which provides strong support for the multiple-trace theory of hippocampal function (Nadel & Moscovitch, 1997). However, Graham and Hodges (1997) demonstrated a striking contrast between Alzheimer's disease patients (for a description see Chapter 16) and ones with semantic dementia in long-term recall of autobiographical events, including a detailed single case study of a semantic dementia patient, which seemed in conflict with this theory (Graham, 1999); in my view, though, their findings actually support it (see Shallice & Cooper, 2011, section 10.4).

At least three other striking phenomena have been obtained with studies of individual amnesic patients or very small groups (e.g., n = 3). One concerns the preservation of so-called fast mapping acquisition of semantic memories in amnesic patients (Sharon, Moscovitch & Gilboa, 2011). A second is that memory for scenes following selective hippocampal lesions is impaired but not memory for faces (Taylor, Henson & Graham, 2007). Then there are the strikingly beneficial effects of reduced retroactive interference in amnesics (Cowan, Beschin & Della Sala, 2004; Dewar, Garcia, Cowan & Della Sala, 2009; Chapter 11 this volume).

In some areas, though, we are in a situation somewhat similar to the dual process versus single process accounts of recognition in that there has yet to be an empirical resolution of apparently conflicting results across different amnesic patients. One such area is amnesics' acquisition of new semantic memories, where case studies do not seem to be consistent in their findings (e.g., Warrington & McCarthy, 1988; Verfaellie, Reiss & Roth, 1995; Verfaellie, Koseff & Alexander, 2000; Van der Linden, 2001). For a definitive review of single case studies relevant for memory theory, particularly with respect to classical pure amnesia, see Rosenbaum, Gilboa and Moscovitch (2014; Chapter 8 this volume).

There is, however, another type of phenomenon in the neuropsychology of memory. This is where findings have no obvious explanation within current memory theory at the time. The most obvious examples of this are Milner's original findings on patient HM, which were inexplicable given Lashley's mass action approach to memory. A second is category specificity. A third are represented by cases of accelerated forgetting (see Chapter 12 this volume).

Single case studies of memory include a fourth example of this type. This is confabulation, originally described as a sequela of alcoholism 130 years ago (Korsakoff, 1889), and later also associated specifically with ruptured aneurysms of the anterior communicating artery, amongst other aetiologies. The phenomenon is beautifully captured by Moscovitch's (1992) term "honest lying". In its more dramatic so-called spontaneous form, one has a "persistant, unprovoked outpourings of erroneous memories" (Kopelman, 2010, p. 15).

There is some disagreement over the empirical phenomena found in spontaneous confabulators (see Schnider, 2008 for a book-length review) but also much accord. The critical lesion location of inferior medial frontal lesions is widely agreed (Gilboa & Moscovitch, 2002; Schnider, 2003). So are some behavioural phenomena. For instance, Schnider, von Daniken and Gutbrod (1996) have shown that when asked to indicate the occurrence of repeated items in a sequence of picture stimuli, confabulators will incorrectly make false positives if there is a repeat of items presented an hour before. Classical medial lobe amnesics do not make such false positives (but see Gilboa et al., 2006).

However, to say that there is no agreement over why spontaneous confabulations occur would be a gross under-statement. Ideas vary enormously. Kopelman (2010) distinguishes four possible explanations. One is what he calls "context confusions", where the patient incorporates memories from one episode into another. A second is an impairment in the specification and verification of the appropriate memory trace. A third type is motivational, such as "to have a time of harmony and comfort rather than distress" (Conway & Tacchi, 1996, p. 333). A fourth possibility is a combination of a vivid imagination, an autobiographical memory impairment and inadequate monitoring. More recent ideas include the loss of a rapid reality checking system (Schnider, 2008), impairment in memory schema representation and instantiation (Ghosh, Moscovitch, Melo Colella & Gilboa, 2014) or gross damage to control systems which switch the hippocampus between encoding and retrieval (Shallice & Cooper, 2011, section 10.12). Whatever the eventual explanation of the confabulatory syndrome (or explanations), it seems unlikely to leave memory theory unchanged (see also Chapters 5 and 7 this volume).

Conclusions

In this chapter, it has been argued that single case studies of memory, or investigations in which a small number of very similar patients are studied, have been highly influential in shaping the history of ideas on memory. The theoretical relevance of phenomena found initially in a single case or multiple single cases has later been supported by other types of investigation, such as neuropsychological group studies, case series or functional imaging.

Yet, single case studies are not looked on with great favour in cognitive neuroscience at present. Journals like *Brain*, which have published many influential case studies in the past, no longer accept them (but see *Cortex*, for an exception). If asked to justify the downplaying of case studies, the argument is normally presented as that of Buchsbaum and D'Esposito (2008) given earlier, that individual cases may be atypical. Nonetheless, in the whole range of neuropsychological studies of individual cases, I know of only one example where theoretical inferences drawn from individual cases may not have been justified because the relevant patients were at the extremes of a distribution or otherwise atypical. This relates to the syndrome of "reading without semantics" (Woollams, Ralph, Plaut & Patterson, 2007, but see also Coltheart, Saunders & Tree, 2010).

In my view, the basic problem lies in the medicalisation of neuropsychology with sound treatment and science being held to be only based on results from groups and with cognitive frameworks and methodologies being considered unfashionable. In addition, there are the greater difficulties of actually carrying out single case studies because of the increased bureaucratic rigidity of current behavioural science and medical practice and the greater demands on the time of their practitioners. It does not lie in any inherent intellectual problem in single-case studies *per se* (see Shallice, 2015; Coltheart, 2017).

Of course, the potential atypicality of any patient whose difficulties are studied as an individual case cannot be ruled out a priori. However, let us return to the six intellectual reasons why Milner's findings on patient HM were influential. The more of these lines of support that are available, the less likely a striking phenomenon found in an individual case can be plausibly attributed to atypicality. More positively, the single case study can take one in novel directions because one is confronted by phenomena that are quite unexpected and demand an explanation. It is a royal road to serendipity, as the forthcoming chapters will underline.

Acknowledgements

I would like to thank Dr Sarah MacPherson for her great assistance in producing the final form of this chapter.

References

Aggleton, J. P., Dumont, J. R., & Warburton, E. C. (2011). Unraveling the contributions of the diencephalon to recognition memory: a review. *Learning & Memory, 18(6)*, 384–400.

Baddeley, A. D. (1986). *Working Memory*. Oxford: Oxford University Press.

Baddeley, A. D., & Hitch, G. J. (1974). Working memory. In G. A. Bower (Ed.), *Recent Advances in Learning and Motivation, Vol. 8*. New York: Academic Press, pp. 47–89.

Baddeley, A. D., & Warrington, E. K. (1970). Amnesia and the distinction between long- and short-term memory. *Journal of Verbal Learning & Verbal Behavior, 9(2)*, 176–189.

Bartha, L., & Benke, T. (2003). Acute conduction aphasia: an analysis of 20 cases. *Brain and Language, 85(1)*, 93–108.

Bastin, C., Linden, M., Charnallet, A., Denby, C., Montaldi, D., Roberts, N., & Andrew, M. (2004). Dissociation between recall and recognition memory performance in an amnesic patient with hippocampal damage following carbon monoxide poisoning. *Neurocase, 10(4)*, 330–344.

Bowles, B., Crupi, C., Pigott, S., Parrent, A., Wiebe, S., Janzen, L., & Köhler, S. (2010). Double dissociation of selective recollection and familiarity impairments following

two different surgical treatments for temporal-lobe epilepsy. *Neuropsychologia, 48(9)*, 2640–2647.
Brambati, S. M., Myers, D., Wilson, A., Rankin, K. P., Allison, S. C., Rosen, H. J., Miller, B. L., & Gorno-Tempini, M. L. (2006). The anatomy of category-specific object naming in neurodegenerative diseases. *Journal of Cognitive Neuroscience, 18(10)*, 1644–1653.
Buchsbaum, B. R., & D'Esposito, M. (2008). The search for the phonological store: from loop to convolution. *Journal of Cognitive Neuroscience, 20(5)*, 762–778.
Campanella, F., Mondani, M., Skrap, M., & Shallice, T. (2009). Semantic access dysphasia resulting from left temporal lobe tumours. *Brain, 132(Pt 1)*, 87–102.
Capitani, E., Laiacona, M., Mahon, B., & Caramazza, A. (2003). What are the facts of semantic category-specific deficits? A critical review of the clinical evidence. *Cognitive Neuropsychology, 20(3)*, 213–261.
Caramazza, A., Miceli, G., & Villa, G. (1986). The role of the (output) phonological buffer in reading, writing, and repetition. *Cognitive Neuropsychology, 3(l)*, 37–76.
Caramazza, A., Miceli, G., Villa, G., & Romani, C. (1987). The role of the graphemic buffer in spelling: evidence from a case of acquired dysgraphia. *Cognition, 26*, 59–85.
Chen, L., Lambon Ralph, M. A., & Rogers, T. T. (2017). A unified model of human semantic knowledge and its disorders. *Nature Human Behavior, 1*, 0039.
Cipolotti, L., Shallice, T., Chan, D., Fox, N., Schahill, R., Harrison, G., Stevens, J., & Rudge, P. (2001). Long-term retrograde amnesia: the crucial role of the hippocampus. *Neuropsychologia, 39*, 151–172.
Coltheart, M. (2017). The assumptions of cognitive neuropsychology: reflections on Caramazza (1984, 1986). *Cognitive Neuropsychology, 34(7–8)*, 397–402.
Coltheart, M., Saunders, S. J., & Tree, J. J. (2010). Computational modelling of the effects of semantic dementia on visual word recognition. *Cognitive Neuropsychology, 27(2)*, 101–114.
Conway, M., & Tacchi, P. (1996). Motivated confabulation. *Neurocase, 2*, 325–339.
Coughlan, A. K., & Warrington, E. K. (1981). The impairment of verbal semantic memory: a single case study. *Journal of Neurology, Neurosurgery and Psychiatry, 44*, 1079–1083.
Cowan, N., Beschin, N., & Della Sala, S. (2004). Verbal recall in amnesiacs under conditions of diminished retroactive interference. *Brain, 127(Pt 4)*, 825–834.
Damasio, H., Grabowski, T. J., Tranel, D., Hichwa, R. D., & Damasio, A. R. (1996). A neural basis for lexical retrieval. *Nature, 380(6574)*, 499–505.
Deese, J., & Kaufman, R. A. (1957). Serial effects in recall of unorganized and sequentially organized verbal material. *Journal of Experimental Psychology, 54(3)*, 180–187.
De Renzi, E., & Nichelli, P. (1975). Verbal and non-verbal short-term memory impairment following hemispheric damage. *Cortex, 11*, 341–354.
Dewar, M., Garcia, Y. F., Cowan, N., & Della Sala, S. (2009). Delaying interference enhances memory consolidation in amnesic patients. *Neuropsychology, 23(5)*, 627–634.
Diana, R. A., Yonelinas, A. P., & Ranganath, C. (2007). Imaging recollection and familiarity in the medial temporal lobe: a three-component model. *Trends in Cognitive Sciences, 11(9)*, 379–386.
Dittrich, L. (2016). *Patient HM: A Story of Memory, Madness and Family Secrets*. London: Random House.
Drachman, D. A., & Arbit, J. (1966). Memory and the hippocampal complex. II. Is memory a multiple process? *Archives of Neurology, 15*, 52–61.
Edelstyn, N. M., Grange, J. A., Ellis, S. J., & Mayes, A. R. (2016). A deficit in familiarity-driven recognition in a right-sided mediodorsal thalamic lesion patient. *Neuropsychology, 30(2)*, 213–224.

Farah, M. J., Levine, D. N., & Calvanio, R. (1988). A case study of mental imagery deficit. *Brain and Cognition, 8,* 147–164.

Funnell, E., & Sheridan, J. (1992). Categories of knowledge? Unfamiliar aspects of living and non-living things. *Cognitive Neuropsychology, 9,* 135–154.

Gaffan, D., & Heywood, C. (1993). A spurious category-spe- ciac visual agnosia for living things in normal human and nonhuman primates. *Journal of Cognitive Neuroscience, 5,* 118–128.

Ghosh, V. E., Moscovitch, M., Melo Colella, B., & Gilboa, A. (2014). Schema representation in patients with ventromedial PFC lesions. *Journal of Neuroscience, 34(36),* 12057–12070.

Gilboa, A., Alain, C., Stuss, D. T., Melo, B., Miller, S., & Moscovitch, M. (2006). Mechanisms of spontaneous confabulations: a strategic retrieval account. *Brain, 129(6),* 1399–1414.

Gilboa, A., & Moscovitch, M. (2002). The cognitive neuroscience of confabulation: a review and a model. In A. D. Baddeley, M. D. Kopelman & B. A. Wilson (Eds.), *Handbook of Memory Disorders,* 2nd edn. London: John Wiley and Sons, pp. 315–342.

Glanzer, M., & Cunitz, A. R. (1966). Two storage mechanisms in free recall. *Journal of Verbal Learning and Verbal Behavior, 5(4),* 351–360.

Graham, K. S. (1999). Semantic dementia: a challenge to the multiple-trace theory? *Trends in Cognitive Sciences, 3(3),* 85–87.

Graham, K. S., & Hodges, J. R. (1997). Differentiating the roles of the hippocampal complex and the neocortex in long-term memory storage: evidence from the study of semantic dementia and Alzheimer's disease. *Neuropsychology, 11(1),* 77–89.

Gvion, A., & Friedmann, N. (2012). Does phonological working memory impairment affect sentence comprehension? A study of conduction aphasia. *Aphasiology, 26(3–4),* 494–535.

Hanley, J. R., Young, A. W., & Pearson, N. A. (1991). Impairment of the visuo-spatial sketch pad. *Quarterly Journal of Experimental Psychology A, 43(1),* 101–125.

Head, H. (1926). *Aphasia and Kindred Disorders of Speech.* Oxford, England: Cambridge University Press.

Hodges, J. R., Patterson, K., Oxbury, S., & Funnell, E. (1992). Semantic dementia. Progressive fluent aphasia with temporal lobe atrophy. *Brain, 115(6),* 1783–1806.

Kinsbourne, M., & Warrington, E. K. (1962). A disorder of simultaneous form perception. *Brain, 85,* 461–486.

Kinsbourne, M., & Wood, F. (1975). Short term memory processes and the amnesic syndrome. In D. Deutsch & J. A. Deutsch (Eds.) *Short Term Memory.* New York: Academic Press, pp. 258–291.

Kopelman, M. D. (2010). Varieties of confabulation and delusion. *Cognitive Neuropsychiatry, 15(1),* 14–37.

Korsakoff, S. S. (1889). Étude medico-psychologique sur une forme des maladies de la memoire. *Revue Philosophie, 20,* 501–530.

Lashley, K. S. (1929). *Brain Mechanisms and Intelligence: A Quantitative Study of Injuries to the Brain.* Chicago, IL: University of Chicago Press.

Laws, K. R. (2005). "Illusions of normality": a methodological critique of category-specific naming. *Cortex, 41,* 842–851.

Mandler, G. (1980). Recognizing: the judgment of previous occurrence. *Psychological Review, 87(3),* 252–271.

Manns, J. R., & Squire, L. R. (1999). Impaired recognition memory on the doors and people test after damage limited to the hippocampal region. *Hippocampus, 9(5),* 495–499.

Mayes, A. R., Holdstock, J. S., Isaac, C. L., Hunkin, N. M., & Roberts, N. (2002). Relative sparing of item recognition memory in a patient with adult-onset damage limited to the hippocampus. *Hippocampus, 12*, 325–340.

Milner, B., Corkin, S., & Teuber, H.-L. (1968). Further analysis of the hippocampal amnesic syndrome: 14-year follow-up study of H.M. *Neuropsychologia, 6*, 215–234.

Milner, B., & Penfield, W. (1955). The effect of hippocampal lesions on recent memory. *Transactions of the American Neurological Association, 80*, 42–48.

Moscovitch, M. (1992). Memory and working-with-memory: a component process model based on modules and central systems. *Journal of Cognitive Neuroscience, 4(3)*, 257–267.

Moscovitch, M. (2012). Memory before and after HM: an impressionistic historical perspective. In A. Zeman, N. Kapur & M. Jones-Gotman (Eds.) *Epilepsy and Memory*. Oxford, UK: Oxford University Press, pp. 19–50.

Murdock, B. B., Jr. (1962). The serial position effect of free recall. *Journal of Experimental Psychology, 64(5)*, 482–488.

Nadel, L., & Moscovitch, M. (1997). Memory consolidation, retrograde amnesia and the hippocampal complex. *Current Opinions in Neurobiology, 7(2)*, 217–227.

Patterson, K., Nestor, P. J., & Rogers, T. T. (2007). Where do you know what you know? The representation of semantic knowledge in the human brain. *Nature Reviews Neuroscience, 8(12)*, 976–987.

Reed, J. M., & Squire, L. R. (1997). Impaired recognition memory in patients with lesions limited to the hippocampal formation. *Behavioral Neuroscience, 111*, 667–675.

Rogers, T. T., Lambon Ralph, M. A., Garrard, P., Bozeat, S., McClelland, J. L., Hodges, J. R., & Patterson, K. (2004). Structure and deterioration of semantic memory: a neuropsychological and computational investigation. *Psychological Review, 111(1)*, 205–235.

Rosenbaum, R. S., Gilboa, A., & Moscovitch, M. (2014). Case studies continue to illuminate the cognitive neuroscience of memory. *Annals of the New York Academy of Sciences, 1316*, 105–133.

Rylander, P. (1939). Personality changes after operations on the frontal lobes: clinical study of 32 cases. *Acta Psychiatrica Scandinavica, Suppl. 20*, 5–81.

Sanders, H., & Warrington, E. K. (1971). Memory for remote events in amnesic patients. *Brain, 94(4)*, 661–668.

Schnider, A. (2003). Spontaneous confabulation and the adaptation of thought to ongoing reality. *Nature Reviews Neuroscience, 4*, 662–671.

Schnider, A. (2008). *The Confabulating Mind: How the Brain Creates Reality*. Oxford: Oxford University Press. Schnider, A., von Daniken, C., & Gutbrod, K. (1996). The mechanisms of spontaneous and provoked confabulations. *Brain, 119*, 1365–1375.

Scoville, W., & Milner, B. (1957). Loss of recent memory after bilateral hippocampal lesions. *Journal of Neurology, Neurosurgery & Psychiatry, 20(1)*, 11–21.

Shallice, T. (2015). Cognitive neuropsychology and its vicissitudes: the fate of Caramazza's axioms. *Cognitive Neuropsychology, 32(7–8)*, 385–411.

Shallice, T., & Cooper, R. P. (2011). *The Organisation of Mind*. Oxford: Oxford University Press.

Shallice, T., & Warrington, E. K. (1970). Independent functioning of verbal memory stores: a neuropsychological study. *Quarterly Journal of Experimental Psychology, 22(2)*, 261–273.

Sharon, T., Moscovitch, M., & Gilboa, A. (2011). Rapid neocortical acquisition of long-term arbitrary associations independent of the hippocampus. *Proceedings of the National Academy of Sciences, USA, 108(3)*, 1146–1151.

Snowden, J., Goulding, P. J., & Neary, D. (1989). Semantic dementia: a form of circumscribed cerebral atrophy. *Behavioural Neurology, 2(3)*, 167–182.

Stewart, F., Parkin, A. J., & Hunkin, N. M. (1992). Naming impairments following recovery from herpes simplex encephalitis: category specific? *Quarterly Journal of Experimental Psychology, 44A*, 261–284.

Taylor, K. J., Henson, R. N. A., & Graham, K. S. (2007). Recognition memory for faces and scenes in amnesia: Dissociable roles of medial temporal lobe structures. *Neuropsychologia, 45(11)*, 2428–2438.

Terzian, H., & Dalle Ore, G. (1955). Syndrome of Klüver and Bucy, reproduced in man by bilateral removal of the temporal lobes. *Neurology, 5*, 374–380.

Tulving, E. (1972). Episodic and semantic memory. In E. Tulving & W. Donaldson (Eds.), *Organization of Memory*. New York: Academic Press, pp. 381–403.

Vallar, G., & Shallice, T. (1990). *Neuropsychological Impairments of Short-Term Memory*. Cambridge: Cambridge University Press.

Van der Linden, M., Cornil, V., Meulemans, T., Ivanoiu, A., Salmon, E., & Coyette, F. (2001). Acquisition of a novel vocabulary in an amnesic patient. *Neurocase, 7(4)*, 283–293.

Vargha-Khadem, F., Gadian, D. G., Watkins, K. E., Connelly, A., Van Paesschen, W., & Mishkin, M. (1997). Differential effects of early hippocampal pathology on episodic and semantic memory. *Science, 277*, 376–380.

Verfaellie, M., Koseff, P., & Alexander, M. P. (2000). Acquisition of novel semantic information in amnesia: effects of lesion location. *Neuropsychologia, 38(4)*, 484–492.

Verfaellie, M., Reiss, L., & Roth, H. L. (1995). Knowledge of New English vocabulary in amnesia: an examination of premorbidly acquired semantic memory. *Journal of the International Neuropsychological Society, 1(5)*, 443–453.

Warrington, E. K. (1975). The selective impairment of semantic memory. *The Quarterly Journal of Experimental Psychology, 27*, 635–657.

Warrington, E. K., & McCarthy, R. A. (1983). Category specific access dysphasia. *Brain, 106(Pt 4)*, 859–878.

Warrington, E. K., & McCarthy, R. A. (1988). The fractionation of retrograde amnesia. *Brain and Cognition, 7(2)*, 184–200.

Warrington, E. K., & Rabin, P. (1971). Visual span of apprehension in patients with unilateral cerebral lesions. *Quarterly Journal of Experimental Psychology, 23(4)*, 423–431.

Warrington, E. K., & Shallice, T. (1969). The selective impairment of auditory verbal short-term memory. *Brain, 92(4)*, 885–896.

Warrington, E. K., & Shallice, T. (1980). Word-form dyslexia. *Brain, 103(Pt 1)*, 99–112.

Warrington, E. K., & Shallice, T. (1984). Category specific semantic impairments. *Brain, 107(Pt 3)*, 829–854.

Warrington, E. K., & Weiskrantz, L. (1968). New method of testing long-term retention with special reference to amnesic patients. *Nature, 217(5132)*, 972–974.

Waugh, N. C., & Norman, D. A. (1965). Primary memory. *Psychological Review, 72(2)*, 89–104.

Weisenburg, T., & McBride, K. E. (1935). *Aphasia: A Clinical and Psychological Study*. Oxford, England: Commonwealth Fund.

Wixted, J. T. (2007). Dual-process theory and signal-detection theory of recognition memory. *Psychological Review, 114*, 152–176.

Woollams, A. M., Ralph, M. A., Plaut, D. C., & Patterson, K. (2007). SD-squared: on the association between semantic dementia and surface dyslexia. *Psychological Review, 114(2)*, 316–339.

2

THE EARTHQUAKE THAT RESHAPED THE INTELLECTUAL LANDSCAPE OF MEMORY, MIND AND BRAIN

Case HM

Donald G. MacKay

Please give our readers some background information about case HM

The currently ongoing revolution in the scientific understanding of memory, mind and brain began in 1953 with amnesic patient Henry Molaison, known widely only as HM until recently. To remedy life-threatening epilepsy at age 27, Henry underwent surgery that inadvertently destroyed brain structures in the medial temporal lobe, and he suffered catastrophic memory failures for the remaining 56 years of his life. He also experienced deficits in creating and expressing novel ideas, comprehending unfamiliar concepts and perceiving the unexpected in his visual world.

If Henry never had his 1953 operation, would the scientific community know as much about memory, mind and brain as it does now?

Case HM was a major earthquake that forever reshaped the intellectual landscape of memory, mind and brain. Scientific understanding of memory took off with this one case. Henry is the main reason we know that the hippocampal region is essential for forming new memories (see Figure 2.1). Case HM also helped the world understand what memories are and why the distinction between new versus old memories is so important.

Did serendipity play a role in your research with Henry, or could you have foreseen every step in the process?

Serendipity certainly contributed to my initial discoveries with Henry in 1966 (see MacKay, 1972). I was a 23-year-old graduate student at MIT. My mentor, Hans-Lucas Teuber (see Figure 2.2), introduced me to Henry and suggested that

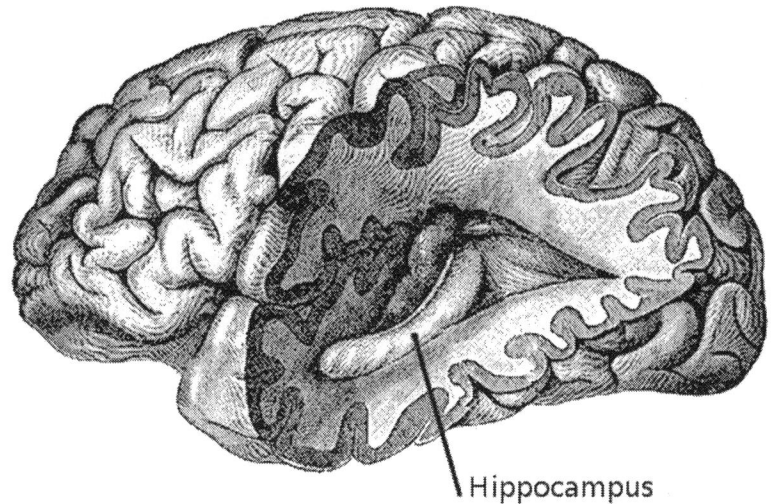

FIGURE 2.1 The human hippocampus in the medial temporal lobe next to the midbrain. Henry Gray (1918) *Anatomy of the Human Body*, Illustrated by Henry Vandyke Carter, 20th edition, Lea and Febiger, Philadelphia and New York, Plate 739.

FIGURE 2.2 Professor Hans Lucas Teuber, Chair of the MIT Psychology Department, circa 1969.

I test his language abilities using a sentence comprehension paradigm that I was developing at the time. It never crossed my mind that Henry's performance in my experiment would alter the direction of my research over the next half century.

Can you describe that first experiment?

It was 50 years ago, but I remember it vividly. I asked Henry to find and briefly describe the two meanings of 32 ambiguous sentences typed on index cards. An example sentence was, "I just don't feel like pleasing salesmen" and this is how the typical control participant described its two meanings: "I don't want to please salesmen, and I don't want agreeable salesmen around." Henry's response to the same sentence was different:

> The person doesn't like salesmen that are pleasing to him. Uh, and that personally he doesn't like them and and [*sic*] personally he doesn't like them [*sic*] and then I think of a phrase that he would say himself, he doesn't, uh, pleasing, as conglamo [*sic*], of all of pleasing salesmen.

The control participants detected the second meaning for all 32 sentences, whereas Henry detected almost none. And unlike the controls', Henry's meaning descriptions were usually inaccurate, incoherent, verbose and difficult to understand (see MacKay, 1972; also MacKay, Stewart & Burke, 1998).

FIGURE 2.3 Henry before his operation. Photo of Patient HM by Suzanne Corkin.
Copyright © Suzanne Corkin, 2013, used by permission of the Wylie Agency (UK) Limited.

FIGURE 2.4 Henry after his operation, around age 40. Photo of Patient HM by Suzanne Corkin.

Copyright © Suzanne Corkin, 2013, used by permission of the Wylie Agency (UK) Limited.

Did you encounter resistance to your initial findings with Henry or were they immediately accepted?

Resistance to my 1966 results was immediate and intense. Everybody believed that Henry's language use was normal. But here's this young graduate student telling the chair of the MIT Psychology Department and a distinguished international panel of visiting scientists, "No. Henry's sentence comprehension is inaccurate and abnormal. His sentence production isn't normal. He's incoherent and has word-retrieval problems." Virtually everyone viewed memory as synonymous with *event memory*, and because Henry couldn't recall recent events, they labeled him a pure memory case. They didn't understand that memory plays a role in comprehending and using language, and that event and language memories have equal status.

They thought of language and memory as separate?

Yes. However, my subsequent studies with Henry convinced me that memory is diverse in nature and integral to many aspects of cognition rather than separate and independent.

How do you mean diverse?

Different memory systems engage different types of units and rules. Let's compare verbal and event memories for a beautiful day. For the event memory, the hippocampal-region mechanisms link together at least four aspects of the event: *what* (aspects made the day beautiful), *when* (the day became beautiful), *where* (the beautiful day was experienced) and the *experiencer* (of the beautiful day). However, for the language memory, the hippocampal-region mechanisms link together, say, an adjective and a noun to form the noun phrase "beautiful day" for producing a sentence such as, "This is such a beautiful day." However, despite the surface differences in what gets linked to what, the same basic principles and processes underlie the formation of event memories and language memories (regardless of whether or not the speaker overtly expresses them).

Moreover, prevailing beliefs aside, event memories can be as complex as language memories. The simplest event memory (illustrated in the preceding example) links four features together (what happened to whom, where and when) and is no less complex than forming word memories. For example, when learning the word *ungentlemanliness*, hippocampal-region mechanisms also join together four aspects of the word: *un* + *gentleman* + *li* + *ness* (see MacKay, 2014).

Complex memory processes also underlie even the seemingly simple behavior of reading a familiar word aloud. This is because spelling doesn't unambiguously indicate how to pronounce most English words. For example, when reading the word *pedestrian* aloud, people must recall from memory the stress values of its syllables. Stress isn't in the letters, although it seems to be, because speakers retrieve the syllabic stress in familiar words extremely quickly during pronunciation.

My research with Henry revealed this surprising role of memory in word reading. As Henry grew older, his memory remained intact for the high-frequency words that he continued to use. However, with aging and disuse, his memories for words that he rarely used became degraded. Eventually, Henry couldn't read low-frequency words aloud without making spectacular errors. For example, he read the word *pedestrian* as "ped-AYE-ee-string." He stressed the wrong syllable in *pedestrian* and pronounced its second "e" as long (AYE and EE) rather than short. The reason is that Henry's degraded internal representation for the word *pedestrian* lacked those features (James & MacKay, 2001; MacKay & Hadley, 2009; MacKay, 2006).

Let's return to the opposition to your 1966 sentence comprehension results with Henry. How did you overcome that initial resistance?

By conducting six follow-up experiments that I reported in MacKay, James, Taylor and Marian (2007). One experiment ruled out forgetting as the basis for Henry's difficulties in comprehending ambiguous sentences. On each trial in that study, Henry and memory-normal controls saw a target sentence that was ambiguous, e.g., *When a strike was called, it surprised everyone*, typed above a single, simultaneously displayed interpretation that was either possible for that sentence, e.g., "The umpire unexpectedly called the pitch a strike," or impossible, e.g., "The umpire quickly called the coaches to the mound." The task was to say "yes" if the interpretation could fit the sentence, and "no" otherwise. Henry chose possible interpretations and rejected impossible ones reliably less often than the controls for *both* ways of interpreting the sentences. For example, Henry again responded incorrectly when a day later he saw the sentence, *When a strike was called, it surprised everyone*, coupled with its alternate interpretation, "The union workers unexpectedly went on a labour strike." This indicated that forgetting one interpretation after discovering the second cannot explain Henry's difficulties in comprehending ambiguous sentences.

Another follow-up experiment showed that Henry could accurately comprehend both meanings of ambiguous phrases and words, e.g., *strike*, presented in *isolation*, despite his inability to understand those ambiguous words in a sentence, such as, *When a strike was called, it surprised everyone*. The experimenter asked Henry and matched control participants to detect and describe the two meanings of ambiguous words, e.g., *tank*, and phrases, e.g., *on top of everything*, typed on cards. Here Henry discovered and correctly described both meanings of these ambiguous items without deficit, and memory load (defined as the number of words presented) had no effect on his performance. For example, Henry understood and described both meanings of long items such as *on top of everything* as readily as short ones such as *tank*. These findings suggested that Henry could use preformed internal representations in memory to comprehend familiar words and phrases presented in isolation. However, he couldn't comprehend the same ambiguous words in never previously encountered sentences because he couldn't integrate their multiple meanings with their novel sentential contexts.

Why not?

Because comprehending ambiguous words in sentences requires the formation of contrasting internal representations of who-did-what-to-whom in the sentence, and Henry had difficulty forming new internal representations. For example, comprehending *When a strike was called, it surprised everyone* to mean "All of the baseball fans were surprised when the umpire called a strike" requires one new who-did-what-to-whom representation, and comprehending the alternate meaning, "Workers and management were surprised when the union called a strike," requires another. However, presented in isolation, *strike* activates both its baseball meaning and its labour union meaning via internal representations that Americans (including Henry) formed during childhood. New context-dependent who-did-what-to-whom representations were unnecessary. We called this explanation the "new learning" hypothesis.

My lab then tested implications of this hypothesis. One was that Henry will have difficulty forming the new internal representations required to comprehend *either* meaning of a novel or never previously encountered ambiguous sentence.

The other was that Henry will have difficulty comprehending virtually *all* non-cliché sentences due to the ubiquity of ambiguity (see MacKay, 1966).

In one test, Henry and matched controls read unambiguous sentences, such as *The daughter that the mother adored fed her baby*, and answered a simultaneously presented multiple-choice question, here, *Who fed the daughter: the mother, the baby,* or *nobody?* Henry chose the wrong answer reliably more often than the controls, e.g., responding that "the mother" fed the daughter in *The daughter that the mother adored fed her baby* (the correct answer is "nobody").

Why?

Because Henry based his responses on familiar associations stored in memory without computing who-did-what-to-whom in these novel sentences. Henry incorrectly chose "mother" in the example sentence because preformed memory associations linked *mothers* but not *daughters* with *baby feeding*. However, asked whether the *mother* or the *young child* spilled water in *The mother that the young child loved spilled water,* Henry incorrectly responded "young child" because preformed memory associations linked *children* with spilling and *mothers* with mopping up. Henry's problem in understanding who-did-what-to-whom in sentences reflected difficulty in creating *new* internal representations, not difficulty in activating preformed associations in memory.

To determine what other relations besides who-did-what-to-whom were difficult for Henry to understand, we next presented Henry and closely matched controls with 62 novel sentences that were either grammatical or ungrammatical. The ungrammatical sentences violated rules governing many different types of conceptual relations, including time relations (e.g., *Yesterday he make it* violates a time relation but *Yesterday he made it* does not), number relations (e.g., *two horse* violates a number relation but *two horses* does not), reflexive gender relations (e.g., *She cut himself* violates a reflexive gender relation, but *She cut herself* does not) and simple reflexive relations (e.g., *They cut oneself with knives* violates a simple reflexive relation, but *They cut themselves with knives* does not). The task was to respond "yes" to grammatical sentences, e.g., *Sally and I are happy that you could make it*, and "no" to ungrammatical ones, e.g., *Sally and I am happy that you could make it*. Henry said "yes" to only 59% of the grammatical sentences, which was not significantly different from chance (50%), and reliably worse than the memory-normal controls.

Why?

Because Henry's hippocampal damage prevented him from forming new internal representations for comprehending many types of sentential relations besides who-did-what-to-whom.

Another experiment tested the "received wisdom" that Henry can comprehend novel metaphors. The basis for this claim was a famous anecdote repeated in Corkin (2013) and elsewhere: Seeing Henry working on a crossword puzzle, Corkin commented, "Henry, you're the puzzle king." To which Henry replied, "Yes, I'm puzzling," as if he fully understood Corkin's *puzzle king* metaphor and wanted to advance the conversation with a double reference to his crossword puzzle habit and his profound amnesia—an existential condition that puzzled him even in old age.

But Henry's "Yes, I'm puzzling" doesn't necessarily indicate that he comprehended *puzzle king* to mean "You are a king among solvers of crossword puzzles." Dominating at solving puzzles, being puzzling, and working on a puzzle represent distinct concepts. Distracted by his puzzle, Henry may have conflated the meanings of *puzzle* and *puzzling*—a type of conceptual confusion he frequently exhibited in my sentence comprehension experiments. Or maybe Henry *misheard* Corkin to say "puzzling" rather than "puzzle king"—in which case, his "Yes, I'm puzzling" is an appropriate response that makes perfect sense.

To obtain better data, my lab examined how Henry and matched controls comprehended short, never-previously encountered sentences from the metaphor subtest of the standardized Test of Language Competence (TLC). An example sentence was, *Maybe we should stew over his suggestion*. Their task was to choose among three alternative interpretations for the sentence. One was correct, e.g., *Let's think about it some more*, and two were incorrect interpretations, e.g., *Maybe we should put more meat into his suggestion*, and *Let's make sure to cook the stew long enough*.

Henry's score on this test (38% correct) was reliably worse than the controls' and not significantly different from random guessing (33% correct). This represented a serious cognitive deficit because metaphors are not just enjoyable—the stuff of poetry and great art. They are fundamental to everyday communication, thinking, learning and understanding—an important way of comprehending one type of concept in terms of another (see Lakoff & Johnson, 1980).

Henry's *incorrect* responses were also informative. He preferred wrong interpretations containing a word from the target sentence, here, *stew* in *Let's make sure to cook the stew long enough*, over wrong interpretations with no overlapping words, here, *Maybe we should put more meat into his suggestion*. This focus on lexical overlap between sentence and interpretation is consistent with Henry's ability to comprehend ambiguous words in isolation but not in sentences. Henry could understand familiar words and based his responses on word-level overlap without understanding either the target sentences or their possible interpretations *as sentence*s. Why? Because he couldn't integrate familiar word meanings with their sentence context to form novel internal representations—a creative process that yields different interpretations for *stew* in the contexts *stewing over a suggestion* (metaphoric) versus *cooking a stew* (literal).

Our conclusion? The same as for Henry's deficits in comprehending ambiguous sentences but not isolated ambiguous words. Comprehending familiar words *per se* involves routine processes that do not engage the hippocampal region. However, hippocampal-region mechanisms are essential for creating the new internal representations required to comprehend one kind of event—*taking the time to talk and think about something*—in terms of another—*slowly cooking, as with a stew* in sentences such as *Maybe we should stew over his suggestion*.

Simple reading tasks replicated and extended our observations on Henry's ability to comprehend sentential relations. In MacKay et al. (1998), participants read ambiguous and unambiguous sentences aloud, and Henry often omitted one or more words without correction. For example, he misread the ambiguous sentence *I just don't feel like pleasing salesmen* as "I don't like pleasing salesmen," omitting the words *just* and *feel*. The experimenter then asked Henry to read the sentence again. Henry's response: "I just don't like pleasing salesmen." Experimenter's feedback: "You're leaving out a word." Henry's response: "I just don't feel like pleasing, yep." The experimenter: "Read it again, then." Henry had to read one sentence six times before including each of its words.

Did forgetting cause Henry's reading mistakes?

No. The sentence to be read always remained in front of him, so nothing had to be remembered.

Did ambiguity contribute to his reading difficulties?

Perhaps. Because when Henry misread, he usually transformed ambiguous sentences into unambiguous ones. For example, Henry misread *John is the one to help today* as "John is the one that helped today"—eliminating the second interpretation, "John is the one for us to help today."

To address this issue, MacKay and James (2001) removed the ambiguities to determine whether Henry would misread relatively *unambiguous* sentences more often than normal. The task was to read each sentence aloud "as quickly as possible without making errors." The results indicated that Henry misread unfamiliar phrases, such as *golden urn*, more often than familiar ones, such as *hot dogs*, and he paused reliably longer-than-normal controls between the words in unfamiliar but not familiar phrases.

Why?

Because reading familiar phrases with preformed internal representations doesn't require hippocampal-region engagement. However, reading unfamiliar phrases requires hippocampal-region engagement to integrate the meanings of the words into new internal representations. This new learning hypothesis also explains why Henry paused abnormally when reading unpunctuated sentences, but not when reading sentences with commas marking the boundaries between major clauses (MacKay & James, 2001, 2002). Henry had learned in grade school about pausing after commas, but without punctuation to guide him after his lesion, he couldn't create novel internal representations of the major clauses between which to pause.

This pattern—longer-than-normal pauses between words in unfamiliar phrases and at major syntactic boundaries without commas, but not between words in familiar phrases or at major syntactic boundaries with commas—can't be explained as a timing disorder associated with Henry's cerebellar damage. Unlike Henry, patients with bilateral damage restricted to the cerebellum did not exhibit this pattern (see MacKay & James, 2001, 2002).

You argued in several other studies that Henry's language production was seriously impaired—which wasn't supposed to happen according to widely accepted wisdom. Where did this wisdom go astray?

The opinion that Henry's language skills were intact derived from informal interactions with Henry. These anecdotal impressions were misleading because Henry only became incoherent when forced to talk about something new. He was deficit-free when talking informally on topics of his own choosing.

Why is that?

Two reasons. First, when allowed to do so, Henry could communicate memories that he had acquired via massive repetition after his operation. Repetition is a slow and inefficient, but nonetheless effective, way of forming new internal representations without hippocampal engagement. Having participated in hundreds and perhaps thousands of experiments since his lesion, Henry learned their basic protocol. When experimenters repeatedly assured him that his participation helped others, Henry himself often repeated that he was "helping others." Via repeated media exposure after his lesion, Henry also learned to associate "Kennedy" with "death," although he didn't know whether Robert or John Kennedy was president (MacKay, Johnson, Fazel & James, 2013).

Second, Henry used clichés acquired before his operation, e.g., "in a way" and "the first thing I thought of," reliably more often than normal controls in open-ended conversations. This was because Henry was good at conjoining familiar clichés into sentences that were ungrammatical but nevertheless sounded coherent to naïve listeners.

Why?

Because people are skilled at interpreting ungrammatical sentences in grammatical ways (see Shafto & MacKay, 2010). During informal conversation, listeners used situational context to infer what Henry intended to say — and didn't notice his errors. In our studies, however, observers blind to speaker identity and without access to irrelevant context rated Henry's verbatim transcripts as reliably more ungrammatical and incoherent than those of memory-normal controls (MacKay et al., 1998).

Methodological flaws that favoured null results compounded the impression that HM was a "pure memory case." Some studies of Henry's visual cognition and language use lacked a control group. Others adopted control groups that were either methodologically unsound or otherwise inappropriate, e.g., unmatched on relevant dimensions such as age, education, IQ and background. For example, the control group in Schmolck, Stefanacci and Squire (2000) was so small and so heterogeneous or variable (some individuals were members of a University of California retirement community whereas others were not) that power was insufficient to reject the null hypothesis (no difference between Henry and the controls) (see MacKay, 2001). Even when control participants were matched appropriately, some studies failed to test for differences across relevant stimulus dimensions, e.g., familiar versus novel visual figures, and high versus low-frequency words (MacKay & James, 2009). When averaged across these stimulus dimensions, Henry's deficits became statistically undetectable because he only experienced difficulty when processing unfamiliar stimuli (see MacKay & Hadley, 2009).

So how did you ensure that information in your picture description experiments was unrehearsed and unfamiliar?

We had participants describe unfamiliar pictures in novel tasks. In one experiment (MacKay, James & Hadley, 2008), Henry and the controls had to include two or three pre-specified words in a single grammatical sentence that accurately described an unfamiliar picture. So here is a picture of a father and two little boys at a stoplight with a "Don't Walk" sign. You have to use the words "first," "cross" and "before" to describe the situation. What would a normal person like yourself say?

"Boys, you must look both ways first before you cross the street."

Excellent! You used all three words in a single grammatical sentence. The typical older adult, the same age as Henry at the time, said, "The father is telling his sons to look first before walking across the street." Henry said, "Before at first you cross across." He got all three words, but his sentence was ungrammatical.

So what was happening in his mind?

What he did is string together familiar words and phrases via free association: "*before*," "at *first*," "you *cross*" and "across," which is closely associated with "*cross*." The target words (in italics) triggered associated words in memory. He wasn't creating new representations for accurately and coherently describing the picture. He simply concatenated old or preformed memory associations. And the result was ungrammatical.

Could he sense he was doing it incorrectly?

That's what's really fascinating. He made spectacular errors but had no idea that he was making errors (see MacKay, James, Hadley & Fogler, 2011).

To him it made sense?

Well, I think he couldn't form a coherent representation against which to judge whether it made sense or not. When *you* make an error, you know it doesn't match what you intended to say. But he can't construct an internal representation of his initial intent in order to discover that he made an error (MacKay & Johnson, 2013).

I conducted several experiments to evaluate Henry's ability to detect errors. His error detection was extremely impaired, whether it was his own errors or errors that we built into pictures and sentences in our experiments.

Please describe some of those error detection experiments.

In some experiments, Henry and memory-normal controls (carefully matched for age, background, IQ, and education) saw sentences that were either error-free, e.g., *I helped myself to the birthday cake*, or erroneous, e.g., *I helped themselves to the birthday cake*. They responded "yes" if the sentence was error-free, but "no" if it contained an error, and then indicated which word was wrong. Henry produced reliably fewer correct responses than the controls, indicating an error detection deficit. And even when Henry correctly responded that a sentence contained an error, he was usually guessing because he couldn't specify what word was wrong (see MacKay & Johnson, 2013).

In another experiment, Henry and carefully matched memory-normal controls saw scenes depicting over 100 objects, some of which were "erroneous" or appeared in anomalous contexts, e.g., a classroom door with hinges on the same side as its doorknob. Their task was to circle as many erroneous objects as possible within a generous time limit. Henry circled reliably fewer erroneous objects than the controls, again indicating an error detection deficit.

Why couldn't he see that a door with same-side doorknob and hinges was anomalous?

Henry couldn't form internal representations (memories) for novel stimuli such as "impossible doors." This prevented him from detecting the anomaly because he couldn't compare his memory for normal doors with an internal representation (memory) of the impossible door (MacKay & James, 2009).

Let's return to the factors that led researchers astray. What else contributed besides methodological problems?

A firmly held theoretical framework that goes back to Descartes but is no longer tenable. Under the "stages of processing framework," human information processing begins with perception/comprehension and proceeds to memory storage, followed eventually by memory retrieval and, finally, action. Separate and independent systems perceive, store, retrieve and act on information, a way of thinking reflected in the DSM-V definition of amnesia, where patients are amnesic if and only if they have new learning deficits but relatively intact speech, visual cognition and language comprehension.

This widely accepted stages of processing framework faces many unsolved problems. One is the existence of "mirror neurons"—which engage in both action (e.g., reaching for an apple) and perception (e.g., seeing someone else reach for an apple). These perception-action units indicate that perception and action can be inseparable and non-sequential, contrary to the stages of processing framework.

My research with Henry also challenges the classic processing stages framework. Henry's deficits indicated that forming new internal representations (memories) is inherent to comprehending new linguistic information, creating novel speech and action plans and perceiving novel stimuli in the visual world, as well as to remembering personally experienced events. Contrary to the stages of processing framework, neither perception nor action are independent of the processes for forming and storing new memories or internal representations.

Nonetheless, firm belief in the stages of processing framework in the decades from 1960 to 1990 prevented researchers from accepting or even imagining that storage processes played a role in perception and action. Even today, some textbooks and general audience books (e.g., Corkin, 2013) continue to characterize Henry as having deficits in memory storage but not in perception, comprehension or action—a pure memory case.

Even though Henry had poor comprehension relative to matched controls, weren't his language impairments relatively minor in comparison with his memory impairments?

Which memory impairments are you referring to?

Henry's clearly deficient memory for events.

To compare Henry's ability to comprehend versus recall novel events, experiments must control for all other factors, including the event itself and the lag between occurrence and test. One can't validly compare comprehension of an ongoing event with recall of an otherwise identical event that happened long ago. Because such experimental controls have never been undertaken, the correct answer to your question is "Don't know." The claim that Henry's language impairments were minor relative to his "memory" impairments is speculation at best.

What's the bottom line for memory researchers? What do your observations with Henry imply for models of memory?

Despite the enormous impact of case HM on memory models over the past 50 years, observations with Henry, strictly speaking, only carry implications for models of *Henry's* memory. Generalizing to memory *per se* requires studies that compare Henry with otherwise similar memory-normal individuals in a wide range of identical tasks.

Now, for all of the tasks that my lab examined, Henry exhibited deficits when new memories (internal representations) were necessary to accomplish a task, but not when use of preformed internal representations sufficed. For example, *serial recall* of a list of familiar, unrelated words was more difficult for Henry than matched controls because the order or list context of the words lacks a preformed internal representation in Henry's brain. However, insert the same sequence of familiar words intermixed with non-words in a *lexical decision task*, and Henry will be deficit-free, responding "real word" as readily as controls. This is because activating pre-existing representations for the meanings of familiar words suffices to trigger the "real word" response, without forming new memory structures.

However, a caveat applies here: Preformed representations can become defunct or unusable due to aging, non-recent use and infrequent use over the lifetime. This caveat is essential for understanding the well-established link between anterograde amnesia and retrograde amnesia in amnesic patients. Recent evidence indicates that normal individuals, using their intact hippocampal mechanisms, can create new memory components to replace the long-established ones that non-recent use, infrequent use, and aging have damaged. After retrieval failures, normal older adults simply relearn completely forgotten information that they subsequently re-encounter in everyday life (see Figure 2.5).

However, Henry couldn't recover from retrieval failure as an older adult (see Figure 2.6). His hippocampal damage kept him from relearning forgotten information and restoring defunct memories, causing profound retrograde amnesia, i.e., inability to retrieve established memories (MacKay, 2014). Generalizing from case HM, anterograde amnesia (inability to form new memories) can cause retrograde amnesia (inability to retrieve existing memories) by preventing amnesics from relearning the information required to re-create degraded memories.

So here's the bottom line: hippocampal engagement is needed to create new cortical representations (memories) for comprehending and producing novel

How to Restore a Memory

Our memories gradually degrade over time if we do not use them. The hippocampus, which governs memory formation, is now thought to engineer the restoration of fading memories in response to experience. For example, if someone has not recently encountered the name of an object such as an abacus, that individual may not be able to recall that name—which had been stored in Broca's area, a region that houses names and labels—when she sees a picture of an abacus. But when she is told the name, the hippocampus swings into action to re-create its memory in Broca's area.

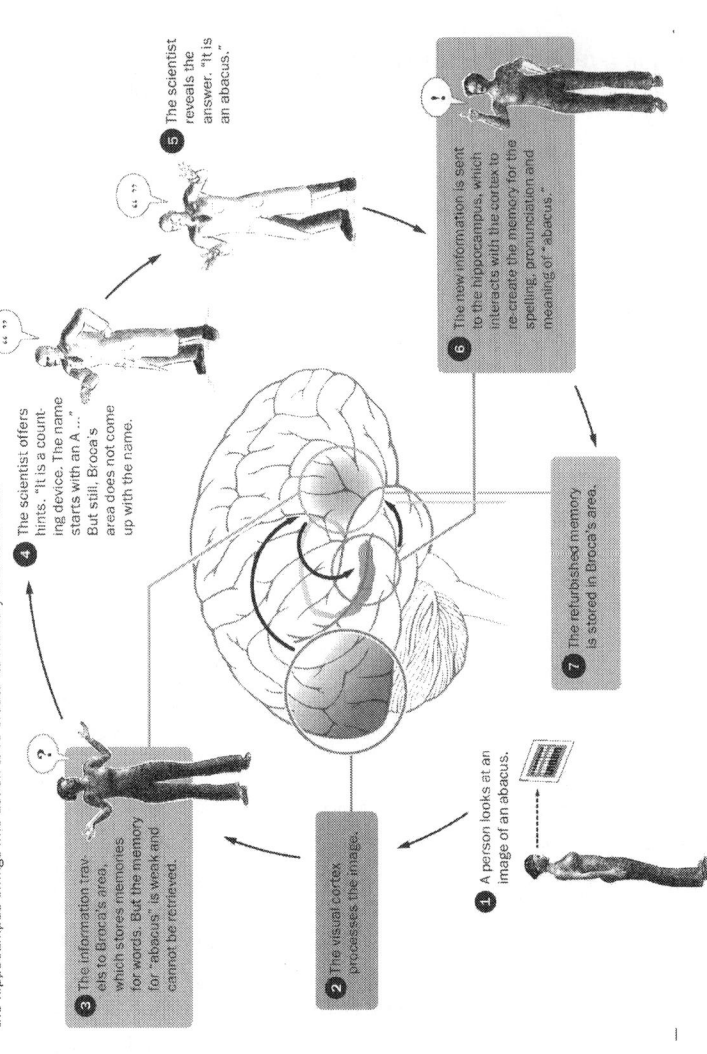

1. A person looks at an image of an abacus.
2. The visual cortex processes the image.
3. The information travels to Broca's area, which stores memories for words. But the memory for "abacus" is weak and cannot be retrieved.
4. The scientist offers hints. "It is a counting device. The name starts with an A ..." But still, Broca's area does not come up with the name.
5. The scientist reveals the answer. "It is an abacus."
6. The new information is sent to the hippocampus, which interacts with the cortex to re-create the memory for the spelling, pronunciation and meaning of "abacus."
7. The refurbished memory is stored in Broca's area.

FIGURE 2.5 How normal individuals restore broken memories.

Reproduced with permission. Copyright © (2014) Scientific American, Inc. All rights reserved.

FIGURE 2.6 Henry as an older adult around age 65.

Photo of Patient HM by Suzanne Corkin.

Copyright © Suzanne Corkin, 2013, used by permission of the Wylie Agency (UK) Limited.

concepts, including new representations that conjoin familiar concepts with their novel contexts in sentences, scenes and space-time episodes, as well as new memory components to replace ones that have become defunct due to aging, non-recent use and infrequent use over the lifespan. However, hippocampal engagement is unnecessary for using or activating memories in the cortex that are functional. Many observations with hippocampal amnesics (besides HM) support this contrast between new versus preformed internal representations (see, e.g., Barense, Gaffan & Graham, 2007; Hannula, Tranel & Cohen, 2006; Ranganath & D'Esposito, 2001; Warren, Duff, Tranel & Cohen, 2010).

Theories of *normal* memory also require the present distinction between processes for forming new memories versus for using (retrieving) established memories. For example, consider the counterintuitive fact that Americans use pennies countless times over their lifetime, but can't accurately draw a penny from memory. The conceptual representation of pennies in their brain, formed during childhood, consists of a small number of "distinctive features" (e.g., *round, copper-colored* and *engraved with the head of Abraham Lincoln*) that suffice to recognize and use pennies in everyday life (see Nickerson & Adams, 1979). However, this *canonical* penny memory is inadequate for accurately drawing a penny from memory. For this task, the hippocampal region must add many additional, never previously encoded features, e.g., the right-facing orientation for Lincoln's head.

So novel doesn't always mean "never-previously-encountered?"

Exactly. The theoretical distinction between new versus old or preformed internal representations is neither simple nor intuitively obvious. Whether a stimulus is novel or familiar depends on the task and the state of the perceiver's internal representations. Despite countless prior encounters with pennies, the rightward-facing orientation of Lincoln's head is novel for the many Americans who have never built this feature into their canonical penny representation. And even when their canonical penny representation contains that rightward-facing feature, subsequent disuse can render it defunct, unusable and novel in the task of drawing a penny from memory. Internal representations of familiar stimuli must be used in order to remain functional.

It is especially misleading to equate "novel" with "never previously encountered" when *familiar* aspects of a never-previously encountered stimulus suffice to carry out a task. For example, consider the "fragmented figure" task, where participants must identify familiar objects such as an elephant depicted with varying degrees of fragmentation or patchiness. In Milner (1970), Henry identified "fragmented elephants" as readily as normal controls, despite never having previously encountered a fragmented elephant stimulus *per se*. Patches containing an intact distinctive feature, say, the elephant's tusk, enabled Henry to identify the elephant based on his canonical memory for elephants formed as a child. Hippocampal-region engagement was unnecessary because performing this task did not require a new internal representation of the overall stimulus.

In several papers you reported parallel deficits and sparing in Henry's language, visual cognition and episodic memory. Can you illustrate some of those parallels?

Henry's errors in these domains illustrate the parallels. In sentence reading, spoken speech, visual cognition, semantic memory and episodic memory tasks, Henry produced only one type of error with reliably greater relative frequency than memory-normal controls: omission errors (as a percentage of all errors). For example, Henry tended to omit familiar words when reading never-previously encountered sentences aloud, e.g., misreading (without correction) the sentence *The boys who ate hot dogs got stomach aches* as *The boys ate hot dogs got stomach aches*.

Why were *omissions* so common?

Because Henry couldn't conjoin words into the novel phrases and propositions that he wanted to express. For example, when forming his plan or internal representation for reading aloud the sentence *The boys who ate hot dogs got stomach aches*, he couldn't conjoin the familiar word *who* with the verb phrase *ate hot dogs* to form the subordinate clause *who ate hot dogs*.

Omission errors also predominated in picture description and visual cognition tasks for the same reason. Henry tended to omit novel features in his perceptual representations of never-previously encountered visual objects and scenes. The impossible door seemed normal to Henry because he couldn't internally represent the novel relation between its hinges and the location of its doorknob. Omission errors likewise predominated in Henry's recall of novel events, an observation often mistakenly attributed to forgetting.

Why mistakenly?

Because the rate of forgetting over time is the same for Henry and normal controls when events have been encoded to the same criterion level (by giving Henry 20 times as many practice trials as the controls). Henry's problem is memory encoding, not memory retention.

So what do the parallels between Henry's deficits and sparing in sentence comprehension, sentence production, visual cognition and episodic memory imply for models of memory?

His deficits are parallel because the hippocampal region helps form new internal representations in the same way across these domains. And his sparing is parallel because the process of retrieving or activating preformed and functional internal representations is independent of the hippocampal region in all domains.

How exactly does the hippocampal region contribute to language memory?

Let's take a simple example: I recently learned the name *Sarah MacPherson*. How did I do that? I knew some people named *MacPherson* and others named *Sarah*, so my first step was to link those existing word units to a new or uncommitted unit in my cortex representing the unique conjunction *Sarah + MacPherson*. I then linked that *Sarah MacPherson* unit to the semantic information I discovered on the web about Sarah, e.g., what she looks like, her home university, what aspects of brain and memory she works on.

Not so fast. How did your hippocampal region link *Sarah* and *MacPherson* to a new cortical unit representing that particular combination of words?

The hippocampus is an activating mechanism that causes prolonged and extremely intense activity in connected units, in this case, the preformed units in my cortex that represent *Sarah* and *MacPherson*. Prolonged activation of these units over a period of seconds—which is an eternity in the brain—burned connections to a new cortical unit representing their conjunction. That's called binding. Newly bound units must soon get used or their connections will weaken and become defunct. However, if I continue to use my *Sarah MacPherson* unit, its connections will gain strength and become long-lasting —allowing me to retrieve the name *Sarah MacPherson* over an extended period.

Has your research with Henry affected how you perceive memory?

My view of memory has totally changed. My research with Henry showed that memory isn't just for events. There are encoding categories for visual memory and language memory, as well as for event memories (MacKay, Johnson & Hadley, 2013).

Can you illustrate what you mean by encoding categories for events?

Events such as meeting someone fall into one encoding category. The topics discussed in a conversation fall into another. Even after short delays, Henry couldn't recall events such as meeting someone at a particular time and place, but he could recall the general topics that were discussed, even after long interference-filled delays (e.g., 200 sec). This suggests that Henry's ability to encode new memories was impaired for some event categories (e.g., personal encounters) but not for others (e.g., topics of conversation).

How many encoding categories did your research with Henry reveal?

We discovered three types of encoding categories for events and many more encoding categories for language units, such as (adjective), (noun), (noun phrase), (given name), (family name) and (proper name). For example, English speakers create novel noun phrases, such as *neural politics* by combining lexical units in the encoding categories (adjective) + (noun), and they create novel proper names such as *Kennen MacKay* by combining units in the encoding categories (given name) + (family name).

Now, my research showed that Henry had difficulty combining some categories of units but not others when comprehending and producing novel phrases and sentences. For example, when combining nouns with pronouns, Henry often produced uncorrected errors, such as "wanted to see what *lady's* using to pull *himself* up besides *his* hands" (pronouns related to the noun *lady* are in italics). Here Henry combined a feminine noun, *lady*, with pronouns of the wrong gender (*himself* and *his*). However, Henry made no similar gender errors when combining *proper names* with visual referents. For example, in picture naming tasks, Henry often invented proper names, such as *David* and *Melanie* to describe people unknown to him, and gender always matched for the person depicted and Henry's made-up proper names. This observation suggests that Henry had intact hippocampal-region mechanisms for linking the encoding categories (proper name) and (person referent). And consistent with this hypothesis, Henry reliably *overused* proper names relative to normal controls, as if he was attempting to offset his difficulties in referring to people using pronouns and noun phrases such as *this lady* (MacKay, Johnson & Hadley, 2013).

So Henry used proper names to compensate for his difficulties in combining nouns with modifiers and pronouns?

Yes.

You noted earlier that Henry had difficulty creating fresh ideas. What are some theoretical implications of this problem?

Henry's deficit pattern in my research calls for refinement of recent indications that hippocampal region damage impairs the ability to imagine hypothetical states (e.g., Schacter, Addis & Buckner, 2007). Like comprehending and describing novel scenes, imagining novel situations requires hippocampal-region engagement to form new internal representations (see MacKay & Goldstein, 2016). However, just as Henry can use preformed internal representations to comprehend and describe *familiar* scenes and situations, amnesics should be able to use *preformed* internal representations to imagine solutions to *familiar* problems, such as how to circumnavigate an obstacle obstructing a walkway.

Henry's pattern of deficits also carries implications for theories of everyday creativity. Like creativity in general, everyday creativity requires the ability to form new concepts, images or internal representations that are useful or valuable in the real world, as when people accurately communicate novel information that helps a listener solve real-world problems.

To examine relations between everyday creativity and the hippocampal region, MacKay and Goldstein (2016) compared how Henry and memory-normal individuals responded to questions in real-world interviews. The results indicated deficits in Henry's everyday creativity. Unlike the normal interviewees, Henry answered in ways that disrupted ongoing communication. Why? Because he couldn't understand *novel* aspects of his interviewer's questions.

So constructive communication in the real world may require hippocampal region engagement, but for most people, doesn't creativity imply a *product*, a valuable artwork, say, or an invention adopted in the real world?

True. But ordinary people also form and communicate new and useful concepts that represent a type of creative product.

If creativity can be intangible, what's the difference between creativity and imagination?

Creative products are *useful*, whereas imaginative products may be useless or *counterproductive*, like those often generated by hypochondriacs, schizophrenics and psychotics. Imagining must have beneficial effects in the real world to count as *creative*.

What implications do Henry's linguistic deficits carry for theories of language use?

Theories developed since Broca and Wernicke have focused on effects of *cortical* damage on language use. My results with Henry suggest a new role for the hippocampal region in theories of language and brain.

What's the new role of the hippocampus?

To form novel internal representations when comprehending and producing discourse. This supplements the obvious role of the hippocampal region in learning what novel words and phrases mean and how they're pronounced.

Would you expect other patients with severe amnesia to exhibit the same language deficits and sparing as Henry?

Yes and no. I would expect Henry's pattern of sparing and deficits in amnesics with *hippocampal-region damage* resembling Henry's, but not in amnesics with diffuse *cortical damage* (which can alone cause both aphasia and retrograde amnesia).

Is case HM still relevant to the cognitive and brain sciences now, almost ten years after Henry's death?

After shocks from Earthquake HM persist to this day. The field is still processing the new ideas in recently published studies with Henry. New data are being analyzed. New books about Henry are in press (see Dittrich, 2017; MacKay, in press). Case HM will undoubtedly continue to reshape the intellectual landscape of memory, mind and brain for years to come.

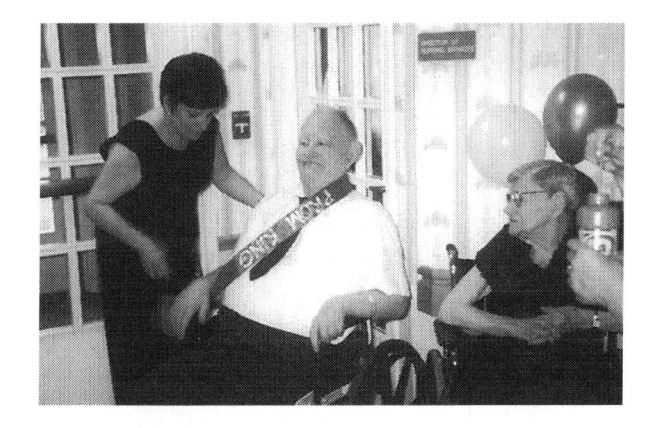

FIGURES 2.7A AND 2.7B Henry in the period before his death at age 82.

Photos of Patient HM by Suzanne Corkin. Copyright © Suzanne Corkin, 2013, used by permission of the Wylie Agency (UK) Limited.

References

Barense, M. D., Gaffan, D., & Graham, K. S. (2007). The human medial temporal lobe processes online representations of complex objects. *Neuropsychologia, 45,* 2963–2297.
Corkin, S. (2013). *Permanent Present Tense: The Unforgettable Life of the Amnesic Patient, H.M.* New York: Basic Books.
Dittrich, L. (2017). *Patient H.M.: A Story of Memory, Madness, and Family Secrets,* 2nd Edition. New York: Random House.
Hannula, D., Tranel, D., & Cohen, N. J. (2006). The long and the short of it: relational memory impairments in amnesia, even at short lags. *Journal of Neuroscience, 26,* 8352–8259.
James, L. E., & MacKay, D. G. (2001). H.M., Word knowledge and aging: support for a new theory of long-term retrograde amnesia. *Psychological Science, 12,* 485–492.
Lakoff, G., & Johnson, M. (1980). *Metaphors We Live By.* Chicago: University of Chicago Press.
MacKay, D. G. (1966). To end ambiguous sentences. *Perception and Psychophysics, 1,* 426–436.

MacKay, D. G. (1972). The search for ambiguity by an amnesic patient: implications for the theory of comprehension, memory and attention. Unpublished manuscript, Psychology Dept., University of California Los Angeles. Also available at http://mackay.bol.ucla.edu/publications.html.

MacKay, D. G. (2001). A tale of two paradigms or metatheoretical approaches to cognitive neuropsychology. Did Schmolck, Stefanacci, and Squire demonstrate that "Detection and explanation of sentence ambiguity are unaffected by hippocampal lesions but are impaired by larger temporal lobe lesions"? *Brain and Language, 78,* 265–272.

MacKay, D. G. (2006). Aging, memory and language in amnesic H.M. *Hippocampus, 16,* 491–495.

MacKay, D. G. (2014). The engine of memory: even after his death, the famous amnesic H.M. is revolutionizing our understanding of how memory works and how we maintain it as we age. *Scientific American Mind, 25,* 30–38. Also available at http://mackay.bol.ucla.edu/publications.html.

MacKay, D. G. (in press). *Remembering: What Fifty Years of Research with Famous Amnesia Patient H.M. Can Teach Us About Memory and How It Works.* New York: Prometheus Books.

MacKay, D. G., Burke, D. M., & Stewart, R. (1998). H.M.'s Language production deficits: implications for relations between memory, semantic binding, and the hippocampal system. *Journal of Memory and Language, 38,* 28–69.

MacKay, D. G., & Goldstein, R. (2016). Creativity, comprehension, conversation and the hippocampal region: new data and theory. *AIMS Neuroscience, 3(1):* 105–142. doi: 10.3934/Neuroscience.2016.1.105. Available at www.aimspress.com/journal/neuroscience.

MacKay, D. G., & Hadley, C. (2009). Supra-normal age-linked retrograde amnesia: lessons from an older amnesic (H.M.). *Hippocampus, 19,* 424–445.

MacKay, D. G, & James, L. E. (2001). The binding problem for syntax, semantics, and prosody: H.M.'s selective sentence-reading deficits under the theoretical-syndrome approach. *Language and Cognitive Processes, 16,* 419–460.

MacKay, D. G., & James, L. E. (2002). Aging, retrograde amnesia, and the binding problem for phonology and orthography: a longitudinal study of "hippocampal amnesic" H.M. *Aging, Neuropsychology and Cognition, 9,* 298–333.

MacKay, D. G., & James, L. E. (2009). Visual cognition in amnesic H.M.: selective deficits on the What's-Wrong-Here and Hidden-Figure tasks. *Journal of Clinical and Experimental Neuropsychology, 31,* 769–789.

MacKay, D. G., James, L. E., & Hadley, C. (2008). Amnesic H.M.'s performance on the test of language competence: parallel deficits in memory and sentence production. *Journal of Experimental and Clinical Neuropsychology, 30,* 280–300.

MacKay, D. G., James, L. E., Hadley, C. B., & Fogler, K. A. (2011). Speech errors of amnesic H.M.: unlike everyday slips-of-the-tongue. *Cortex; 47,* 377–408.

MacKay, D. G., James, L. E., Taylor, J. K., & Marian, D. E. (2007). Amnesic H.M. exhibits parallel deficits and sparing in language and memory: systems versus binding theory accounts. *Language and Cognitive Processes, 22(3),* 377–452.

MacKay, D. G., & Johnson, L. W. (2013). Errors, error detection, error correction and hippocampal-region damage: data and theories. *Neuropsychologia, 51(13),* 2633–2650. doi: 10.1016/j.neuropsychologia.2013.08.009.

MacKay, D. G., Johnson, L. W., Fazel, V., & James, L. E. (2013). Compensating for language deficits in amnesia I: H.M.'s spared retrieval categories. *Brain Sciences, 3(1),* 262–293. doi:10.3390/brainsci 3010262.

MacKay, D. G., Johnson, L. W., & Hadley, C. (2013). Compensating for language deficits in amnesia II: H.M.'s spared versus impaired encoding categories. *Brain Sciences, 3(2)*, 415–459. doi:10.3390/brainsci3020415.

MacKay, D. G., Stewart, R., & Burke, D. M. (1998). H.M. revisited: relations between language comprehension, memory, and the hippocampal system. *Journal of Cognitive Neuroscience, 10*, 377–394.

Milner, B. (1970). Memory and the temporal regions of the brain. In K. H. Pribram & D. E. Broadbent (Eds.), *Biology of Memory*. New York: Academic Press.

Nickerson, R. S., & Adams, M. J. (1979). Long-term memory for a common object. *Cognitive Psychology, 11*, 287–307. doi:10.1016/0010-0285(79)90013-6.

Ranganath, C., & D'Esposito, M. (2001). Medial temporal lobe activity associated with active maintenance of novel information. *Neuron, 31*, 865–873.

Schacter, D. L., Addis, D. R., & Buckner, R. L. (2007). Remembering the past to imagine the future: the prospective brain. *Nature Review Neuroscience, 8*, 657–661.

Schmolck, H., Stefanacci, L., & Squire, L. R. (2000). Detection and explanation of sentence ambiguity are unaffected by hippocampal lesions but are impaired by larger temporal lobe lesions. *Hippocampus, 10*, 759–770.

Shafto, M. A., & MacKay, D. G. (2010). Miscomprehension, meaning and phonology: the unknown and phonological Armstrong illusions. *European Journal of Cognitive Psychology, 22*, 529–568.

Warren, D. E., Duff, M. C., Tranel, D., & Cohen, N. J. (2010). Medial temporal lobe damage impairs representation of simple stimuli. *Frontiers in Human Neuroscience, 4*, 35. doi: 10.3389/fnhum.2010.00035.

3

THE CASE OF YR

Selective Bilateral Hippocampal Lesions Can Have Quite Different Effects on Item Recognition, Associative Recognition and Recall

Juliet S. Holdstock, Nicola M. Hunkin, Claire L. Isaac and Andrew R. Mayes

Why are neuropsychological cases important for informing our understanding of the normal mind?

There are two kinds of neuropsychological single case studies. The first kind, in which we are interested, is the study of a patient who has a selective and accurately localized lesion in a brain region of theoretical interest, and which aims to determine his/her pattern of memory/cognitive performance relative to suitably matched controls. Study of such single cases aims to advance knowledge in two ways: It aims to identify precisely what deficits relatively selective damage/dysfunction of a specific structure causes and, by appropriately qualified inference, it aims to identify what the cognitive functions of the critical structure are when it is working properly. Single cases like these differ radically from the second kind of single case study where the sole interest is to find behavioural dissociations in order to determine how the normal human mind is functionally organized. Knowledge of the precise location of brain damage is usually unnecessary and of little relevance for this second kind of single case study.

In the mid-1990s, it had only been possible to accurately image lesion location in human brains using MRI for a few years. Very few patients with organic amnesia had had the location of their lesions precisely identified. When this had been done it usually depended upon post-mortem histology as with the hippocampal lesion case, RB (Zola-Morgan, Squire & Amaral, 1986). Much research aimed at determining the neural structures underlying memory had used animal lesion research with monkeys and rodents, where lesions could be created with much greater accuracy and specificity than typically occurred adventitiously in humans. Despite its major advantage, this kind of research faced two problems. First, it was hard to be confident that the same kinds of memory were being tapped in animal models and human amnesics. Second, it was also hard to be sure how similar human, primate and rodent brains were structurally and, hence, how accurate the view was of organic amnesia and the neural organization of memory in humans, based on these animal models.

Like other forms of cognition, memory almost certainly depends on the interaction of a number of processes, each mediated by distinct brain regions. If, as much evidence indicates, organic amnesia can be caused by damage to any one of a number of distinct brain regions, then amnesic disorders should fractionate to reflect the disruption of different memory-supporting processes. By the mid-1990s, it was notable that, unlike organic disorders of perception, movement and language, and apart from material-specific disorders of memory linked to hemispheric differences, functional fractionations of amnesia had not been convincingly demonstrated. Although this may have been partly due to lesions at one site disrupting normal function at connected sites, even if these are structurally intact, the most likely reason why functional fractionation had not been found was because most lesions extended across functional brain zones.

Finding amnesic patients with very selective lesions was, and still is, therefore very important because, with appropriate reservations, they allow inferences to be made about what the likely functions of the damaged structures would have been if they had not been damaged. But patients with even relatively selective damage to structures, such as the hippocampus, fornix and memory-related nuclei or fibre tracts in the midline diencephalon, are extremely rare and can only properly be identified with high-resolution MRI scans. Assembling case series of such rare patients will minimally take several years, as care needs to be taken to ensure close similarity of key factors, such as their extent and location of brain damage/dysfunction and functional reorganization. Consequently, initial inferences might have to depend on a single case study.

In the early 2000s, you reported a series of studies with case YR who demonstrated impaired recall, preserved item recognition but impaired recognition memory for associations. First of all, can you provide us with some background information about YR?

Our first contact with YR was in 1995 when she approached us to volunteer to take part in our memory research. Her memory impairment had started in 1986 when she was 49 years old, following an incident in which opiate drugs were administered intravenously to relieve severe back pain. This may have triggered a hypoxic episode, because a few hours after the administration of these drugs, she was found in a confused state by her sister and admitted to hospital. She underwent a number of examinations, including EEG but no definite cause for her confusion could be found, although the staff believed that she may have suffered an ischemic infarct. Her confusion gradually resolved but she was left with a moderate memory impairment. After the incident, she successfully returned to her full-time clerical job but, when she was later allocated a new role, she began to struggle because of her memory problems, and was made redundant. Her memory impairment appeared to have remained stable from the initial incident to the time at which we tested her (1995–1999). Around 2000, YR's performance on several perception, intelligence and memory tests showed deterioration, and she no longer showed the consistent behavioural pattern that she had shown from 1995 to 1999 and which we report next. It was suspected that at that time she had started to develop a dementing illness, but as she did not wish to undergo further MRI scanning, confirmation of this could not be obtained.

How did you first realize that this case was interesting?

We tested YR on a range of standardized neuropsychological tests, which confirmed that she had a selective memory impairment in the face of preserved intelligence and other cognitive functions (Holdstock et al., 2000). What was rapidly apparent and struck us as of critical importance was YR's pattern of performance on the standardized recognition and recall tests. Thus, on the Warrington Recognition Memory Test and the recognition subtests of the Doors and People Test, she was unimpaired (50th percentile and above), whereas her performance on the recall subtests of the WMS-R and Doors and People Test was impaired (ranging from less than the 1st percentile to the 5th percentile). She therefore appeared to have impaired recall but preserved recognition, according to these standardized tests (see Table 2, Holdstock et al., 2000). MRI revealed an unusually selective bilateral lesion of the hippocampus.

The reason we became very excited with this pattern of memory performance was because her preserved item recognition presented a challenge for the long-held, prevailing view that the hippocampus supports both recall and item recognition, such that damage to this structure will impair both these aspects of memory (e.g., Squire & Zola, 1998). Indeed, in 1995, the general view was that, although organic amnesia might differ in severity and in the locus of its underlying lesions, it was always characterized by similar recognition and recall impairments.

However, this view was not quite universal because seven years previously, Hirst et al. (1986, 1988) had found that recall was more impaired than recognition in a mixed group of organic amnesics. They demonstrated this by giving the patients longer study exposures to stimuli or testing them after shorter delays so that recognition was matched to that of a control group, but recall remained impaired under the same conditions. They also showed that, in the non-Korsakoff patients, this deficit pattern was not associated with dysexecutive function. This was important because, at the time, it was believed that frontal damage could impair recall, leaving recognition entirely intact (see Mayes,

1988). However, the use of a matching procedure to demonstrate this dissociation between recall and recognition was problematic because it was difficult to rule out the possibility that the matching procedure itself had a differential effect on the two types of task. Thus, the identification of a patient who showed a more complete dissociation that was detectable without the need for a matching procedure was of clear importance, especially as YR had no problems with executive functions.

The year after we first met YR, a meta-analysis of published literature looking at recall and recognition performance on standardized tests of amnesics with several aetiologies indicated that recognition was often preserved relative to recall (Aggleton & Shaw, 1996). The authors argued that such preservation seemed to be most obviously apparent in patients with more selective lesions of the hippocampus whereas recognition deficits became more apparent when damage included the perirhinal cortex and/or dorsomedial nucleus of the thalamus. These findings subsequently led to the development of Aggleton and Brown's (1999) well-known, dual-process theory of anterograde amnesia, according to which two kinds of memory contribute to explicit or declarative memory: recall, including a form of cued recall called recollection that contributes to recognition memory, and familiarity, with the former but not the latter dependent on the hippocampus (see also Aggleton et al., 2000).

Can you summarize the main neurological features of this case?

YR had an unusually selective and symmetrical lesion of the hippocampus. Volumetric analysis of her 3D T1-weighted radiofrequency spoiled gradient echo (SPGR) MRI scan showed that there was a 50% reduction in the volume of her hippocampus bilaterally, which extended uniformly along the anterior to posterior extent of the structure (see Figure 3.1). In contrast, her amygdalae, although small, appeared structurally intact. Brain damage, as indicated by volume reduction, did not encroach on her neocortical medial temporal lobe regions (Holdstock et al., 2000; Mayes et al., 2001; Mayes, Holdstock, Isaac, Hunkin & Roberts, 2002), including her perirhinal cortex (Mayes et al., 2004). The volumes of her temporal lobes (Mayes et al., 2004), and grey and white matter of the frontal lobes and parietal cortex, were all within the normal range (Holdstock et al., 2000; Mayes et al., 2001, 2002).

What was this case's pattern of spared and impaired memory abilities?

The initial pattern of YR's performance on standardized tests (i.e., impaired recall, spared recognition) prompted us to investigate YR's recall and recognition memory in more detail.

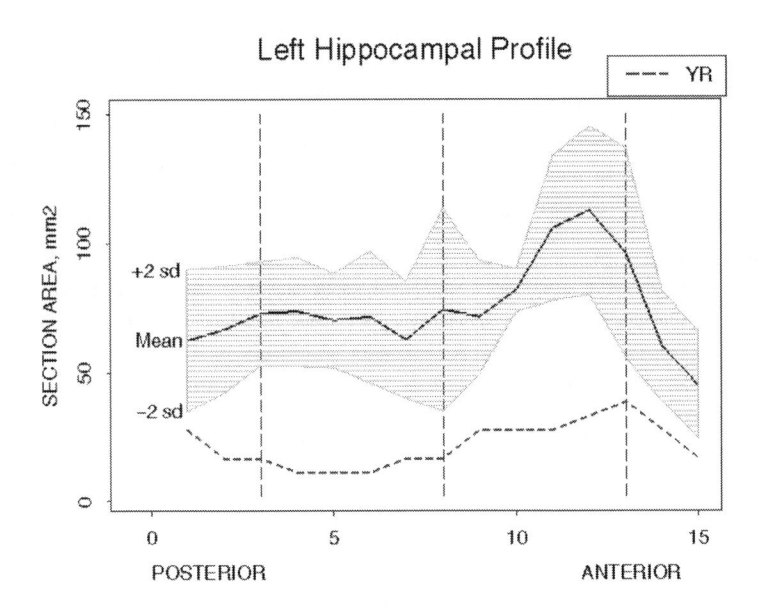

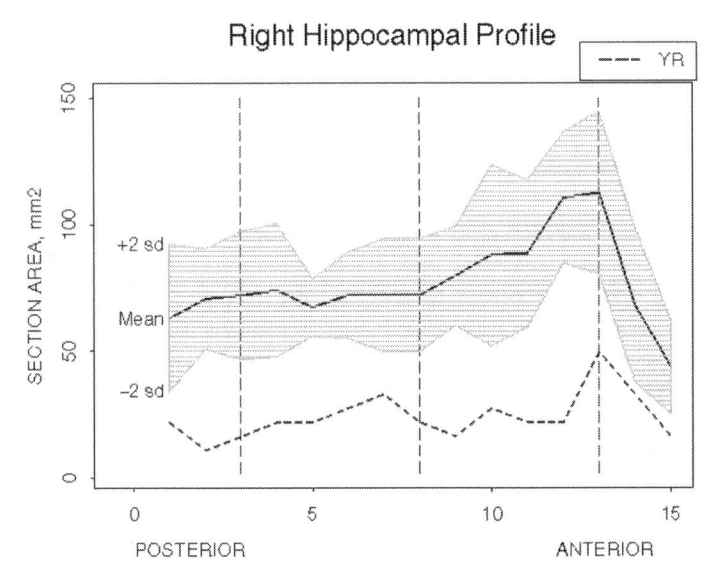

FIGURE 3.1 Hippocampal section area for YR (dashed line), and the mean section area for eight age and sex matched healthy controls (solid line), is plotted as a function of section position through slices 1–15. The shaded region extends between 2SDs above and below the mean for controls. Reprinted from Hippocampus, 14, Mayes et al., Associative recognition in a patient with selective hippocampal lesions and relatively normal item recognition, 763–784,

Copyright (2004), with permission from John Wiley & Sons.

Spared Item Recognition Versus Impaired Recall

We tested YR and a group of age- and IQ-matched female controls on 43 item recognition tests that assessed forced-choice and yes/no recognition for individual items such as faces, pictures of objects, patterns, words, names and facts over retention intervals which ranged from immediate test, through intermediate delays of seconds and minutes to long delays of up to 30 days. YR and her controls were also tested on 34 recall tests for visual/visuospatial and verbal material which used a similar range of delays. The recognition and recall tests comprised both standardized neuropsychological tests and specific tests that we constructed for experimental purposes. Our results showed a striking dissociation between YR's recall, which was clearly impaired (3.6 SD below the control mean), and her item recognition, which was just 0.5 SD below the control mean and actually at or above the control mean on a third of the tests (see Figure 3.2). This relative sparing of item recognition in YR was not significantly influenced by whether tests tapped visual or verbal materials, had a yes/no or forced-choice format, contained few or many items, had one or several foils per target item, used short or very long

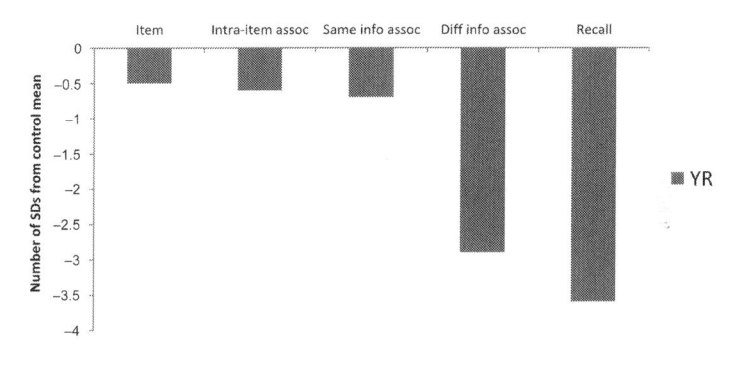

Key

Item = mean performance on 43 item recognition tests (data from Mayes et al., 2002)

Intra-item assoc= mean performance on three tests of recognition of associations between elements of items (e.g. composite words such as "earthquake" and "silkworm", which at test had to be distinguished from recombination foils, such as "earthworm") (data from Mayes et al., 2004)

Same info assoc = mean performance on four tests of recognition of associations between same types of information (e.g. word pairs and face pairs) (data from Mayes et al., 2004)

Different info assoc = mean performance on 18 tests of recognition of associations between information of different kinds (data from Mayes et al., 2004)

Recall = mean performance on 34 recall tests (data from Mayes et al., 2002)

FIGURE 3.2 YR's performance plotted as the number of standard deviations from the control mean on tests of item recognition, intra-item associative recognition, recognition of associations between information of the same kind, recognition of associations between information of different kinds and recall.

delays or were difficult or easy for normal subjects (Mayes et al., 2002). (Difficulty was defined by where the control mean score on a test fell between chance and a perfect score, using a standardized scale.)

Spared Item Familiarity Memory

The dominant view of item recognition memory is that it depends on item familiarity and a form of cued recall known as recollection. During recollection, the target item acts as a cue for the recall of details associated with that item from when it was previously encountered in a study context (Mandler, 1980; Jacoby, 1991; for review, see Yonelinas, 2002). In contrast, familiarity is a feeling that re-encountered information has been experienced previously and which occurs in the absence of any recall (see Norman & O'Reilly, 2003; Brown & Aggleton, 2001). The relative contribution of these two kinds of memory to recognition will depend on the features of the recognition test as well as other factors, such as depth of encoding and strategy.

Operationally, recollection and familiarity can be differentiated by the Remember/Know technique. When an individual makes a positive recognition response, they are asked whether they "remember" that item (i.e., they can recall specific contextual details encoded when the item was studied) or whether they just "know" that they had seen the item before (i.e., they have a feeling that the item is familiar but are unable to retrieve any contextual details about that item from the study episode).

YR's performance on eight Remember/Know item recognition tests suggested that her familiarity memory was unimpaired (Holdstock et al., 2002b). This clear impression from the "Remember/Know" procedure of normal familiarity in YR was consistent with observations of her memory in daily life, which showed that her recall was poor, but that after she had encountered objects and other items (e.g., people's faces), subsequent encounters produced a clear sense of familiarity.

Assessments of YR's recollection using the Remember/Know procedure were problematic, however, because her grasp of the concept of recollection was poor. For example, when she confidently felt that she had previously seen an item on a screen, she tended to report it as remembered even though questioning indicated that she recalled no specific information. Although this problem may be worse in amnesic patients, it also exists with normal participants unless particular care is taken with the way in which the Remember/Know procedure is given (see Migo et al., 2012 for a discussion). When YR and her controls were asked to justify their remember responses by, for example, reporting their item-specific thoughts during encoding and indicating approximately where in the list the item occurred, YR's recollection was impaired (see Mayes et al., 2004).

Indirect evidence of normal familiarity but impaired recollection in YR was provided by a forced-choice recognition test of faces which used immediate and repeated testing (Mayes et al., 2004). Using the procedure of Aggleton et al. (2000), a face recognition test similar in format and difficulty to the Warrington Recognition Memory Test was completed with memory being tested immediately after presentation and again, using the same test materials, after a 5-minute delay. During the immediate recognition test, relative familiarity can be used to distinguish between targets and foils because only one of each test pair has been studied, and YR's performance was close to the control mean. In the delayed tests, targets and foils had overlapping levels of familiarity so that subjects' accurate recognition responses depended upon recollecting face-study context associations. YR showed a much larger drop in performance from the immediate to repeat test than her controls (2.4 SDs larger) (Mayes et al., 2004), consistent with a deficit in the recollective aspect of recognition.

Spared Forced-Choice but Impaired Yes/No Item Recognition When Targets and Foils Were Very Similar

The finding that YR had intact item familiarity but impaired recollection predicted that her item recognition would be impaired on specific item recognition tests that rely heavily on recollection. One such test is a yes/no item recognition test in which targets are very similar to their corresponding foils. Norman and O'Reilly (2003) argued that neocortical regions that support familiarity assign overlapping representations to similar stimuli. Thus, foils will have similar levels of familiarity to their corresponding targets, making it difficult to accurately distinguish between targets and foils when they are presented individually as in a yes/no paradigm. Under these circumstances, Norman and O'Reilly argued that accurate recognition relies on recollection mediated by the hippocampus. In contrast, they argued that in a forced-choice paradigm, targets can be accurately selected from amongst very similar corresponding foils at test on the basis of familiarity alone. This is because, although the target/foil familiarity differences are small, the familiarity of targets is reliably higher than that of their similar foils.

We tested YR's ability to differentiate targets from highly similar foils in recognition tests using line drawn objects (see Figure 3.3). Consistent with Norman and O'Reilly's (2003) predictions, we found that YR's performance was only impaired on yes/no recognition; on forced-choice tests, her recognition performance was unimpaired and slightly better than the control mean (Holdstock et al., 2002b). This was the case even though, for control subjects, the tasks were of comparable difficulty. Similarly, Mayes et al. (2001) found that YR's forced-choice recognition of words that were presented amongst semantically related foils was unimpaired, whereas her yes/no recognition of words was impaired under the same circumstances. This pattern did not, however, reflect a general impairment in yes/no item recognition, as YR performed well on other yes/no item recognition tests which used *dissimilar* targets and foils (Mayes et al., 2002).

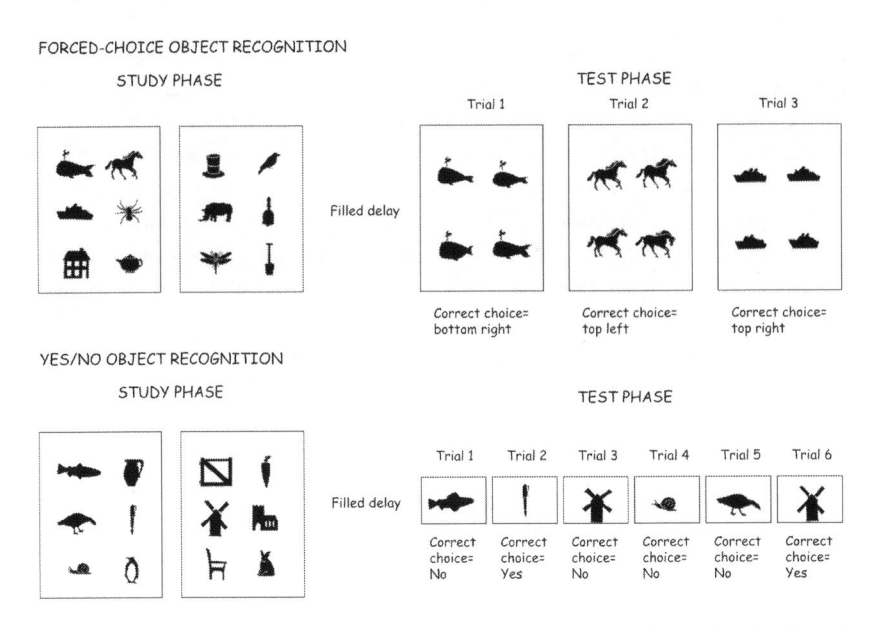

FIGURE 3.3 Schematic diagram illustrating the study and test phases for the forced-choice object recognition test (top half) and the yes/no object recognition test (lower half), which used very similar targets and corresponding foils. For the forced-choice object recognition test, a set of 12 study items are shown along with the stimuli presented on the first 3 test trials. The correct choice for each test trial is indicated in each case. For the yes/no object recognition test, a set of 12 study items are shown along with the stimuli presented on the first 6 test trials. Again, the correct response is indicated for each test trial. Reprinted from Hippocampus, 12, Holdstock et al., *Under What Conditions Is Recognition Spared Relative to Recall After Selective Hippocampal Damage in Humans?*, 341–351.

Copyright (2002) with permission from John Wiley & Sons.

Accelerated Forgetting of Information When Assessed by Recall but Not by Forced-Choice Item Recognition

If information is forgotten at an accelerated rate following learning when rehearsal is prevented, it is likely that early consolidation into long-term memory is not occurring normally. On item recognition tests, YR did not forget at an accelerated rate. Her performance relative to the control mean did not differ significantly over delays of less than 1 minute, 1 minute to 1 hour and 1 hour to 30 days. In contrast, YR's recall was impaired even on immediate testing, which made it impossible to look at whether she forgot information at an accelerated rate over longer delays in the full battery of tests. However, when YR was given greater exposure to match her story recall to that of controls at a filled 20 second delay, she forgot matched, different stories significantly faster than control participants over completely filled 1, 2, 5 and 10 minute delays (see Isaac & Mayes, 1999; Mayes et al., 2002).

Spared Recognition of Intra-Item Associations and Recognition of Associations Between Information of the Same Kind Versus Impaired Recognition of Associations Between Information of Different Kinds

YR and matched control participants were tested on 25 associative recognition tests. To create foils, the components of a subset of the studied associations were recombined to create novel (unstudied) associations. Correct recognition therefore required memory for the studied associations and could not merely be based on the familiarity of the individual components (all components had been studied and were therefore familiar). Three of the tests involved intra-item associations and used as stimuli either (1) composite words, such as "earthquake" and "silkworm", which at test had to be distinguished from recombination foils, such as "earthworm" or (2) faces which at test had to be distinguished from foil faces that were created by recombining the features of the other studied faces. Four of the tests involved associations between items of the same kind, and included recognition of word pairs, word triplets and face pairs. The remaining 18 tests involved associations between information of different kinds and included tests of the spatial position and temporal order of words and pictures, picture and auditory associations, picture and visually presented word associations (e.g., face-occupation pairings), and associations between orthographic strings and meaning (e.g., learning the meanings of unfamiliar words).

YR was unimpaired on the intra-item associative recognition memory tests, with her performance on these tests being at a comparable level to her old/new item recognition performance (Mayes et al., 2004). Her recognition memory for associations between similar kinds of items was also unimpaired and as good as her item recognition (see Figure 3.2).

In contrast, her recognition memory for associations between different kinds of information was impaired and often at or around chance levels (see Figure 3.2). YR was significantly more impaired at this form of associative recognition memory than she was at either item recognition memory or recognition memory for associations between items of the same kind (Mayes et al., 2004). This difference between performance on item and "different information" associative recognition tests was maintained even when these tests were closely matched on a variety of variables, such as difficulty and paradigm type (Mayes et al., 2001; Holdstock, Mayes, Isaac, Gong & Roberts, 2002a, 2002b, Mayes et al., 2004).

Impaired Memory for Spatiotemporal Information

YR's impairment in associative recognition of information of different kinds included memory for the spatial position and temporal order of words and pictures (Mayes et al., 2001; Holdstock et al., 2002b; Mayes et al., 2004). There had long been an emphasis on the role of the hippocampus in memory for spatiotemporal information. A key role for this structure in spatial memory was proposed within the cognitive mapping hypothesis (O'Keefe & Nadel, 1978). According to this hypothesis, the hippocampus is critical for forming a representation of a place in the environment when this is identified by the relative position of an array of external stimuli or landmarks (i.e., using an allocentric frame of reference). In contrast, it is proposed that the hippocampus is not critical when the location can be identified by its relative position to the observer (i.e., egocentric frame of reference). We tested this hypothesis by asking YR and her matched controls to remember the position of a light on a large board under two conditions. In the allocentric condition, which was conducted with the room lights on, the participants viewed the light and then moved to a new position around the board before making their memory judgement about the light's position. In the egocentric condition, the participants viewed the light in the dark and then made their memory judgement in the dark from the position they had been in at study. Consistent with the theory's predictions, we found that, after a 60 s retention interval, YR was more impaired at recalling allocentric than egocentric information and was also impaired at recognizing allocentric spatial information (Holdstock et al., 2000).

We found that YR was also clearly impaired at two kinds of temporal memory: one involved identifying which list an item came from when the lists could only be distinguished by *when* they occurred (between-list discrimination) and the other involved recalling the temporal order in which items had been presented within a list (within-list discrimination) (Mayes et al., 2001). Interestingly, her ability to recognize both the temporal and spatial relationships between two words were impaired, even though her word pair recognition was close to the mean of her matched control group.

However, it was notable that YR's associative recognition was not restricted to recognition of item-spatial and temporal location associations. Her recognition of associations between different kinds of information where spatiotemporal differences played no obvious role was also impaired. For example, she was very impaired at recognizing associations between specific faces and the specific voices in which a sentence (which was always the same) was spoken. The studied face-voice associations almost certainly could not have been identified by distinctive spatiotemporal features.

Summary

When responses could be made on the basis of familiarity, YR was unimpaired at item recognition, recognition of intra-item associations and recognition of associations between items of the same kind. In contrast, when successful performance required the use of recollection, her item recognition was impaired (i.e., yes/no recognition using foils that were very similar to their corresponding targets). She was also impaired on tests of recall, recollection and recognition of associations between information of different kinds, which included, but was not restricted to, spatial and temporal associations. She showed accelerated forgetting when her memory was tested by recall but not by item recognition.

Can you specify why this case was relevant in relation to the knowledge at the time?

YR's preservation of item recognition and item familiarity but impaired recall and recollection was consistent with Aggleton and Brown's (1999) dual-process theory of anterograde amnesia (see also Aggleton et al., 2000). This holds that while recall and recollection are dependent on the hippocampus, item familiarity, which can often successfully support item recognition, does not depend on this structure but instead is mediated by a circuit that includes the perirhinal cortex and dorsomedial nucleus of the thalamus.

It has long been argued that the neocortex and hippocampus represent information neurally in different ways. The neocortex learns more slowly and processes its inputs so as to make them neurally more similar to other inputs in order to extract common features. Such neural representations support familiarity through a matching process but do not support recollection/recall. In contrast, the hippocampus processes and stores its inputs sparsely so as to make even similar inputs have neurally distinct and non-overlapping representations (pattern-separated). Such neural representations support recollection/recall through a process of pattern completion in which partial cues lead to the reactivation of the full representation (Norman & O'Reilly, 2003). Pattern-separated representations are, however, very poor at supporting the matching process essential for familiarity (Norman & O'Reilly, 2003). It has been argued that because hippocampal representations are pattern-separated, the hippocampus can learn rapidly without suffering from catastrophic interference (McClelland et al., 1995). This model therefore predicts that hippocampal damage will impair recollection/recall, as this is dependent on the hippocampus, but good item recognition performance will be maintained because studied items tend to trigger a stronger familiarity signal in the medial temporal lobe cortices than do foils. YR's good item recognition relative to her clearly impaired recall following selective bilateral hippocampal damage was therefore exactly the pattern predicted by this model (Mayes et al., 2002). Also, as predicted by this model, YR's yes/no recognition, but not her forced-choice recognition, of line drawn objects was impaired when the foils were physically very similar to their targets (Holdstock et al., 2002b). Norman and O'Reilly (2003) have argued that, with the forced-choice task, targets can be accurately selected from amongst very similar corresponding foils on the basis of familiarity alone whereas successful yes/no recognition under these conditions has to rely largely on recollection. Further evidence for these claims has been subsequently found by Migo et al. (2009) by using more elaborated versions of the Remember/Know procedure.

Our finding that YR's recognition memory for intra-item associations and associations between arbitrarily linked items of the same kind was equivalent to her item recognition memory suggested that familiarity could be based not only on individual item features but also on specific combinations of features that compose an item (e.g., a specific combination of facial features) and on associations between arbitrarily linked items of the same kind (e.g., pairs of faces). Other views at that time allowed that there may be familiarity memory only for unitized items. Consequently, the proposal that YR's good recognition of word pairs and face pairs was mediated by familiarity provided a challenge for these views (e.g., see Yonelinas, 2002) because such pairs are unlikely to become unitized, merely directly linked.

YR's impaired recognition of associations between different kinds of information suggested that recognition of this kind of associative information was dependent on the hippocampus. We proposed that this was the case because different domain-specific processing streams do not fully converge in the medial temporal lobe cortices but only in the hippocampus. Consequently, only the hippocampus can rapidly form arbitrary associative memories across these processing streams (Mayes et al., 2004). As a result, little or no medial temporal cortex-mediated associative familiarity memory can be created to support recognition of associations between different types of information after only one or two study trials, so accurate responses must rely on recall/recollection (Mayes et al., 2004).

We found that YR's recognition was impaired for all arbitrary associations between different types of information. This included, but was not limited to, associations between items and spatial or temporal information. It also included associations between, for example, faces and voices, and pictures and names as well as the learning of new semantic information, such as the definitions of novel words. This challenged existing views that hippocampal damage disrupts acquisition of episodic, but not semantic, memories (Vargha-Khadem et al., 1997; Baddeley, Vargha-Khadem & Mishkin, 2001; Kesner, 1998) or specifically disrupts spatial or spatiotemporal memories (Burgess, Maguire & O'Keefe, 2002; Kesner, 1998). Rather we proposed that hippocampal damage impaired the acquisition of *all* arbitrary associations when the information that needs to be associated is represented in distinct medial temporal neocortical regions and only fully converges in the hippocampus. This does not, however, preclude the possibility that the hippocampus creates all associative memories within a spatiotemporal framework even when the spatiotemporal information provides no useful discriminative information.

Others have argued that the hippocampus facilitates the formation of flexible associations between item and contextual information such that the elements can be individually accessed in different contexts, and that this makes it critical for recollection but not familiarity (Eichenbaum & Bunsey, 1995; see Eichenbaum,

Yonelinas & Ranganath, 2007 and Diana, Yonelinas & Ranganath, 2007 for reviews). In contrast, the parahippocampal cortex can represent associations, for example, between elements of a scene, but it forms unitized representations where the different elements of these representations cannot be attended to separately. We tested the predictions of this model using the visual paired comparison task. This task exploits the natural tendency for individuals to look at a novel stimulus preferentially over a familiar stimulus. Thus, the task provides an indirect measure of recognition. YR and matched control participants viewed a picture of an object on a coloured background and then immediately afterwards, this familiar object was shown again, this time paired with a novel object. Consistent with the predictions of the model, all participants displayed a novelty preference, provided the background on which the old and new objects were shown was the same as the one used during the learning phase. When the background of the familiar object was changed between initial familiarization and test, only the control participants showed a novelty preference; YR showed no preference between novel and familiar stimuli (Pascalis, Hunkin, Bachevalier & Mayes, 2009).

Pascalis et al. argued that YR's hippocampal damage meant that she could only form unitized object-context associative memory representations and, because the different elements of such scene- or context-like representations are not automatically attended to separately, she experienced a familiar object in a new context as a novel object-context or scenic whole. In contrast, control participants, who can form more flexible object-context associative representations, experience a familiar object in a new context as old. These flexible object-context associative representations, which are available to the control participants but not YR, are likely to be the rich flexible associations that are mediated by the hippocampus and support recollection. The hippocampus is very good at rapidly forming associations between previously unconnected stimulus components and detailed aspects of the context in which they are encountered that are neurally distinct even from similar associations. This enables flexible recall/retrieval of parts of the whole association from multiple componential cues.

In summary, our findings concerned with the recognition of information of different kinds suggested that, although YR could not form rich flexible associative connections between objects and scenes/contexts (Mayes et al., 2004), she could form unitized object-context associations (Pascalis et al., 2009). The circumstances under which she is able to do this remain to be fully determined, but appear to include the situation in which a prominent object is completely surrounded by a scene or context.

Given our current knowledge, would this case still be relevant today?

In brief, in our current state of knowledge with many issues still unresolved, it remains critically important to test as many patients as possible with selective hippocampal damage, like YR. After YR ceased to be available for testing, we further developed our interpretation of her pattern of memory loss in the Convergence, Recollection and Familiarity Theory (CRAFT) (Montaldi & Mayes, 2010, see also Mayes et al., 2007). According to this theory, the perirhinal cortex rapidly processes its item/object inputs so as to create memory representations with little pattern separation, such representations support item familiarity well but not item-cued recall/recollection. This region can form unitized intra-item associations between components of items (e.g., features of a face) but can also form non-unitized direct inter-item associations between items of the same kind that converge in that region (e.g., two faces are directly linked rather than being linked by an intermediary such as an aspect of the context) enabling associative familiarity (the feeling that the two items have appeared together in the past). Although both unitized and direct associations support familiarity, only unitized associations are inflexible, leading to poor recognition of isolated components (e.g., a mouth) which will worsen as unitization strengthens. This possibility remains to be fully tested. Following Diana et al. (2007), the theory proposes that contextual information (visual, spatial, semantic and gist/schematic information that is peripheral to the items that lie at the focus of attention) converges on the parahippocampal cortex. Given the similar neocortical cytoarchitectonic structure to that of the perirhinal cortex, the theory argues that the parahippocampal cortex represents information in a similar way to the perirhinal cortex, although the type of information it represents is different. According to CRAFT, the parahippocampal cortex rapidly forms poorly pattern-separated memory representations of intra-context associations and non-unitized, but direct context-context associations that support familiarity memory for the context well but support context-cued recall/recollection poorly. The hippocampus is viewed as lying at the top of the medial temporal lobe hierarchy, and CRAFT proposes that different (between domain) inputs only converge for memory processing in this structure. Its mainly archicortical cytoarchitecture enables it to form pattern-separated object/item-context associative representations that support cued recall/recollection memory through pattern completion. Such memories can be flexibly accessed using many different cues.

One unresolved issue is what kinds of different information only converge in the hippocampus so that they are only supported by recollection and what kinds of different information can converge in neocortical medial temporal lobe structures and support associative familiarity. While it has been argued that context information is projected to parahippocampal cortex, whereas item/object information is projected to the perirhinal cortex (see Montaldi & Mayes, 2010), it is well known that there are reciprocal connections between the two that may enable convergence of item and context information within these neocortical medial temporal lobe regions. Furthermore, in a recent unpublished study, we have found fMRI evidence that indicates object and scene familiarity each influence both the perirhinal and the parahippocampal cortices. However, these influences were not overlapping and were qualitatively different. Thus, it is unclear how similar our scenes were to "contextual" information. Nevertheless, the potential for convergence of object information from perirhinal cortex and context information from parahippocampal cortex could account for our finding that YR was sometimes able to form unitized object-context associations whilst being unable to form rich flexible associations that support recollection (Pascalis et al., 2009). Another possibility is that an object in a surrounding background, as in the study of Pascalis et al. (2009), might be processed as a unitized scene by the parahippocampal cortex in patients like YR, rather than an association between two independent components, one of which is an object (processed by perirhinal cortex) and the other of which is a background (processed by parahippocampal cortex). Scene familiarity would successfully support recognition and novelty preference, as long as the object is presented in the background within which it was studied. Considerable further research is clearly needed to explore these possibilities.

Although CRAFT provides what we consider to be currently the most likely explanation of the relative roles of medial temporal lobe structures in familiarity and recall/recollection, others have proposed alternative views and the issue is far from resolved (see Montaldi & Mayes, 2010, for discussion). It is critical, therefore, to collect more data from patients like YR, along with conducting complementary functional imaging studies of healthy individuals and animal studies, to advance our understanding of the memory functions of the hippocampus and connected structures.

Another unresolved issue concerning hippocampal function that would benefit from further testing of patients like YR, is whether hippocampal involvement is limited to long-term declarative memory, whether it is also necessary for maintaining certain kinds of associative information representations over very short delays, or even perceptually representing such information normally in the first place. Recent findings (e.g., Hannula, Tranel & Cohen, 2006; Olson, Page, Moore, Chatterjee & Verfaellie, 2006) have demonstrated hippocampal involvement in relational memory at short lags and in processing scenes (Mullally, Intraub & Maguire, 2012). YR was impaired at recognition of associations between different kinds of information, such as pictures of faces and auditorily presented names, and recall of a wide variety of information even at unfilled delays of a few seconds. This would be consistent with impairments in recall and associative recognition of information held in immediate memory. Our work on YR's novelty preference impairment for object-context compounds suggested that not only was her immediate memory for this kind of association impaired, but so perhaps was her ability to represent it in the first place. When the background context was unchanged between study and test, she showed normal novelty preference for unstudied, relative to studied, objects against that same background. However, she showed no preference for unstudied, relative to studied, objects when both were set against a different background context from the one used immediately before for the studied object (Pascalis et al., 2009). We argued that this pattern could be explained by proposing that YR represented the object-context associations in a different way to her controls. In the case of YR, we argued that she formed only unitized object-context associative representations, the parts of which she probably failed to identify effectively. This enabled novelty detection on the basis of familiarity when the object was presented against the same background as at study but not when it was presented against a new background. For YR's controls, when objects were paired with new background contexts, novelty detection may largely have depended on rich flexible object-context associations, mediated by the hippocampus, that supported recollection. This is usually regarded as a long-term memory function, but it appears to have been absent in YR even when there was close to no delay at all. This indicates that her immediate recollection was disrupted, implying she had a short-term/working memory recall deficit for these kinds of association and suggests that this might have been caused by her inability to represent this information at input in the way that normal people do. These data imply that the hippocampus is necessary for not only long-term recollection/recall but also immediate recollection/recall and even appropriately flexible processing and representation of certain inputs. This needs confirming and extending by work on patients who show YR's pattern of preserved familiarity and impaired recollection/recall, particularly as YR's impaired novelty preference for single unstudied versus studied faces at almost immediate delay is very hard to reconcile with her completely normal face recognition under much harder conditions and longer delays (Pascalis et al., 2004; Mayes et al., 2002).

A further set of unresolved issues concerns whether the hippocampus is not only critical for consolidating rich flexible long-term associative memories from close to input up to some minutes following this, but over a longer period running from around a day to weeks or longer. Although YR's item recognition memory declined at a normal rate, the rate at which her recall of short stories and word lists declined was pathologically accelerated so that little recall remained at ten minutes (Mayes et al., 2002). We need further information about this from additional hippocampal patients. If we can match recall to control levels at ten minute delays, we can discover whether these patients show a normal or abnormal rate of forgetting over longer delays.

Do you think that there is anything unique that the reports of this case added to our knowledge?

Patients with selective hippocampal lesions are rare and yet extremely important for advancing knowledge of the mnemonic role of the human hippocampus. The opportunity to study such a patient in considerable depth is very unusual. A unique aspect of our work with YR was the very extensive battery of memory tests that we administered, which we developed to systematically explore her recall and recognition memory. This allowed a comparison of her item recognition, recall and associative recognition using the same materials and using tests matched for difficulty for control subjects. Thus, we could demonstrate the consistency of the pattern of YR's memory performance and draw more reliable conclusions than we would have been able to on the basis of a small number of tests.

YR was the first patient with adult-onset selective hippocampal lesions shown to have sparing of item recognition, recognition of intra-item associations and recognition of associations between items of the same kind for both visual and verbal material but clearly impaired recall and recognition of associations between different types of information. Although a similar pattern had been reported in young patients who suffered selective hippocampal damage during early childhood (Vargha-Khadem et al., 1997), the early age of onset of their damage meant that the possibility that some aspects of their memory were spared because of reorganization of function could not be ruled out. Evidence consistent with this argument was presented at a later time for one of these patients (Maguire, Vargha-Khadem & Mishkin, 2001). The late age of onset of YR's hippocampal damage meant that her spared item recognition, recognition of intra-item associations and recognition of associations between items of the same kind can be much less easily explained by the development of compensatory mechanisms. YR's data therefore strongly suggested that these three aspects of memory are not dependent on the hippocampus.

What are the shortcomings of this case?

The potential weakness is that YR was a single case, and the pattern of spared and impaired memory has varied enormously between patients with hippocampal damage. While a number of patients with hippocampal damage have now shown a pattern similar to YR (Vargha-Khadem et al., 1997; Henke et al., 1999; Mayes et al., 2002; Bastin et al., 2004; Turriziani, Fadda, Caltagirone & Carlesimo, 2004; Aggleton et al., 2005; Barbeau et al., 2005; Holdstock, Mayes, Gong, Roberts & Kapur, 2005), others have shown no memory deficit (Holdstock et al., 2008), consistently impaired recall but variable recognition memory (Holdstock et al., 2008) and clearly impaired recall and recognition memory (Kartsounis, Rudge & Stevens, 1995; Reed & Squire, 1997; Cipolotti et al., 2001; Stark, Bayley & Squire, 2002; Stark & Squire, 2003; Cipolotti et al., 2006; Gold, Hopkins & Squire, 2006). It has been suggested that these memory differences may reflect patient differences in the exact location of their hippocampal damage, residual hippocampal function, reorganization of function and extension of damage/dysfunction to familiarity-mediating regions outside the hippocampus (see Holdstock et al., 2008 and Montaldi & Mayes, 2010). The imaging data available for YR and the other patients with adult-onset hippocampal lesions in the literature do not allow these issues to be fully explored. Structural scanning in the 1990s lacked the precision to determine the precise location and selectivity of lesions to the hippocampus. Functional imaging studies of single patients were tricky and not generally conducted, and these are important because they enable us to address questions, such as whether any remaining hippocampal tissue is functional, whether brain dysfunction is present outside the hippocampus and whether there has been any reorganization of brain function (see Holdstock et al., 2008 for a discussion of these issues). Unfortunately, we were unable to conduct functional imaging studies of YR because she declined all further scanning.

Recollection usually leads to more accurate recognition than familiarity so some have argued that recollection and familiarity are confounded by recognition strength (see Montaldi & Mayes, 2010). Consistent with this argument, YR's data could be interpreted as loss of strong but preservation of weak memories rather than loss of recollection and preservation of familiarity. However, recent evidence from intracranial electrographic recordings from the human hippocampus and perirhinal cortex has provided strong evidence against the memory strength view, and instead has suggested that these regions support at least two qualitatively different functions during recognition memory (Staresina, Fell, Dunn, Axmacher & Henson, 2013). Furthermore, the opposite pattern to that seen in YR, spared recollection but impaired familiarity, has now been reported that was related to volume reduction in left perirhinal cortex (Bowles et al., 2007), both bilateral (Yonelinas et al., 2007) and left entorhinal cortex (Brandt, Eysenck, Nielsen & von Oertzen, 2016) and the combined neocortical medial temporal lobe regions (Wolk, Dunfee, Dikerson, Aizenstein & DeKosky, 2011), which cannot be easily explained by the strength view.

In our analysis of YR's item recognition performance, we explored the effect of a number of test characteristics, including whether the tests were verbal or nonverbal, and found that they had no significant effect on her performance. We did not, however, look at the effect of specific test materials, leaving open the possibility that her item recognition may be preserved more for some specific types of stimuli than others. Indeed, it has since been found that YR performed significantly better on face recognition than word recognition (Chris Bird, personal communication) consistent with the findings of a meta-analysis of her and nine other hippocampal patients' word and face recognition on the Warrington Recognition Memory Test (Bird & Burgess, 2008). This difference in performance may relate to the fact that the words were highly familiar prior to study, whereas the faces were unfamiliar which would make it harder to make item recognition decisions on the basis of item familiarity for the words than the faces.

Are there any assessments/paradigms that you would administer now to this individual if she was available?

If YR was still available, we would perform many investigations with her and other patients with relatively selective hippocampal damage, as well as matched controls, of which some examples are given next.

First, we would take advantage of advances in MRI research since the 1990s (e.g., in measuring fibre tracts) to gain a more detailed characterization of brain damage/dysfunction in YR and patients like her to help explain why "hippocampal" patients have shown unexplained differences in their pattern of memory breakdown. We strongly suspect that the hippocampus mediates recollection but not familiarity memory (because the bulk of the fMRI evidence suggests that the hippocampus plays no role in familiarity). Our suspicions have two important implications. (1) "Hippocampal" patients impaired at familiarity as well as recollection will have damage/dysfunction that extends into non-hippocampal medial temporal lobe and/or extra-medial temporal lobe regions that mediate familiarity memory in probably all healthy people. (2) YR and patients like her who have preserved familiarity memory will not have damage/dysfunction in these regions, will show no familiarity function in any residual hippocampus and will not show signs of functional reorganization with respect to familiarity processing.

Structural and functional imaging improvements would help us check whether these suspicions are correct. For example, systematic fMRI would determine whether any healthy normal people show hippocampal activity modulation when familiarity memory is present or being created, taking particular care that apparent familiarity is not accompanied by undetected recollection. Then, structural and functional imaging would be able to identify whether, relative to patients with preserved familiarity, patients with familiarity deficits show more grey matter, fibre tract and resting state fMRI abnormalities in non-hippocampal regions that the systematic fMRI in healthy people has related to the mediation of familiarity.

Second, we would conduct further studies of familiarity and recollection using a greater variety of stimuli, and matching confident familiarity with recollection for recognition accuracy/strength. This matching procedure addresses the argument that spared familiarity after hippocampal damage reflects spared weaker recognition memories. We would also administer further associative recognition tests to confirm that the hippocampus is involved in recognition of both spatiotemporal and non-spatiotemporal associative information. We would examine recollection and associative familiarity for this material with a particular interest in whether or not associative familiarity would be preserved following hippocampal damage. We would also examine whether YR and patients like her are impaired at recall-like, but not familiarity-like associative priming. Finally, we would check whether patients like YR can learn and retain over at least one week novel associative memories (names of objects) normally, when using a fast mapping procedure in which an association between a new word and concept is learnt incidentally in a single trial (e.g., in the fast mapping procedure used by Sharon, Moscovitch and Gilboa (2011) participants were shown a picture of a common item (e.g., dog) and an uncommon item (e.g., numbat) and were given an instruction that referred to the name of the uncommon item, for example, "click on the numbat"). It has been recently claimed that fast mapping is intact in patients with hippocampal damage (Sharon et al., 2011).

Third, we would examine whether YR and patients like her have problems, processing and representing spatiotemporal associative inputs and whether they show working (immediate) memory problems for these associations because of this. This follows from recent proposals that the hippocampus is involved in constructing mental images (Hassabis & Maguire, 2007), processing scenes (Mullally et al., 2012) and short-term as well as long-term associative memory (Hannula et al., 2006; Olson et al., 2006).

Fourth, we would explore memory consolidation over time scales ranging from seconds to minutes and from hours to days/weeks/months/years/decades in YR and patients like her. Consolidation/maintenance of older memories can be addressed by examining retrograde amnesia for episodic memory and matching semantic memories with varying amounts of spatiotemporal content to see whether such memories become independent of the hippocampus over time (e.g., Squire & Alvarez, 1995). Some of this work could involve testing recall of pre- and post-morbid episodic and semantic memories involving spatial layouts, acquired at different times, such as memories of the layout of previous houses and their local environment, and episodes associated with these. How strongly memories of different pre- and post-morbid ages correlate with each other would also be explored to determine whether the neural bases of memory changes as it ages and whether brain function was or was not normal when they were acquired.

Over a shorter time scale of hours, days or weeks, we would address the issue of whether hippocampal amnesics show a normal forgetting rate if their initial level of performance is boosted. If this is found to be the case, we could conclude that the apparent increased forgetting rate observed in these patients is the result of an initial consolidation problem. In contrast, patients with accelerated long-term forgetting show normal recall over delays of minutes and hours following learning, but accelerated forgetting over delays of 24 hours or more (e.g., Mayes et al., 2003). It is controversial whether these patients have a neurally distinct consolidation impairment from hippocampal patients. We would attempt to address this issue by minimizing interference for ten minutes or so after learning by putting learners in a darkened room with relaxation instructions as done by Della Sala and colleagues (e.g., Dewar, Fernandez Garcia, Cowan & Della Sala, 2009). If the hippocampal patients' free recall approaches normal levels when this is done, we would test whether forgetting over a week is still accelerated or whether it occurs at a normal rate. A finding that it occurs at a normal rate would suggest that accelerated forgetting over a scale of minutes is caused by disruption of a different consolidation/maintenance mechanism from that underlying the accelerated forgetting over a scale of hours to weeks that is found in accelerated long-term forgetting patients.

Conclusions

Our extensive studies of patient YR have shown that damage to the hippocampus impairs recall, recollection and recognition of associations between information of different kinds but can spare recognition memory when this can be based on a feeling of familiarity. This has led to the development of CRAFT, which argues that the hippocampus and medial temporal cortex represent information in different ways such that the hippocampus can support recollection/recall and form flexible associations between information of different kinds, whereas the medial temporal cortex can support familiarity for individual items, intra-item associations and associations between items of the same kind. The data from Pascalis et al. (2009) suggest that the medial temporal cortex can also form unitized object-context associations on which familiarity decisions can be based. Future work will need to determine under what particular conditions recognition of associations between information of different kinds can be supported by medial temporal cortex, whether the hippocampus is necessary for processing/representation, as well as memory of, associative information and over what time scale it is needed for memory consolidation.

References

Aggleton, J. P., & Brown, M. W. (1999). Episodic memory, amnesia, and the hippocampal-anterior thalamic axis. *Behavioural and Brain Science*, 22, 425–489.

Aggleton, J. P., McMackin, D., Carpenter, K., Hornak, J., Kapur, N., Halpin, S., Wiles, C. M., Kamel, H., Brennan, P., Carton, S., & Gaffan, D. (2000). Differential cognitive effects of colloid cysts in the third ventricle that spare or compromise the fornix. *Brain*, 123, 800–815.

Aggleton, J. P., & Shaw, C. (1996). Amnesia and recognition memory: a re-analysis of psychometric data. *Neuropsychologia*, 34, 51–62.

Aggleton, J. P., Vann, S. D., Denby, C., Dix, S., Mayes, A. R., Roberts, N., & Yonelinas, A. P. (2005). Sparing of the familiarity component of recognition memory in a patient with hippocampal pathology. *Neuropsychologia*, 43, 1810–1823.

Baddeley, A., Vargha-Khadem, F., & Mishkin, M. (2001). Preserved recognition in a case of developmental amnesia: implications for the acquisition of semantic memory? *Journal of Cognitive Neuroscience*, 13, 357–369.

Barbeau, E. J., Felician, O., Joubert, S., Sontheimer, A., Ceccaldi, M., & Poncet, M. (2005). Preserved visual recognition memory in an amnesic patient with hippocampal lesions. *Hippocampus*, 15, 587–596.

Bastin, C., Van der Linden, M., Charnallet, A., Denby, C., Montaldi, D., Roberts, N., & Mayes, A. R. (2004). Dissociation between recall and recognition memory performance in an amnesic patient with hippocampal damage following carbon monoxide poisoning. *Neurocase*, 10, 330–344.

Bird, C. M., & Burgess, N. (2008). The hippocampus supports recognition memory for familiar words but not unfamiliar faces. *Current Biology*, 18, 1932–1936.

Bowles, B., Crupi, C., Mirsattari, S. M., Pigott, S. E., Parrent, A. G., Pruessner, J. C., Yonelinas, A. P., & Köhler, S. (2007). Impaired familiarity with preserved recollection after anterior temporal-lobe resection that spares the hippocampus. *Proceedings of the National Academy of Sciences*, 104, 16382–16387.

Brandt, K. R., Eysenck, M. W., Nielsen, M. K., & von Oertzen, T. J. (2016). Selective lesion to the entorhinal cortex leads to an impairment in familiarity but not recollection. *Brain and Cognition*, 104, 82–92.

Brown, M. W., & Aggleton, J. P. (2001). Recognition memory: what are the roles of the perirhinal cortex and hippocampus? *Nature Reviews Neuroscience, 2*, 51–61.

Burgess, N., Maguire, E. A., & O'Keefe, J. (2002). The human hippocampus and spatial and episodic memory. *Neuron, 35*, 625–641.

Cipolotti, L., Bird, C., Good, T., Macmanus, D., Rudge, P., & Shallice, T. (2006). Recollection and familiarity in dense hippocampal amnesia: a case study. *Neuropsychologia, 44*, 489–506.

Cipolotti, L., Shallice, T., Chan, D., Fox, N., Scahill, R., Harrison, G., Stevens, J., & Rudge, P. (2001). Long-term retrograde amnesia . . . the crucial role of the hippocampus. *Neuropsychologia, 39*, 151–172.

Dewar, M., Fernandez Garcia, Y., Cowan, N., & Della Sala, S. (2009). Delaying interference enhances memory consolidation in amnesic patients. *Neuropsychology, 23*, 627–634.

Diana, R. A., Yonelinas, A. P., & Ranganath, C. (2007). Imaging recollection and familiarity in the medial temporal lobe: a three-component model. *Trends in Cognitive Sciences, 11*, 379–386.

Eichenbaum, H., & Bunsey, M. (1995). On the binding of associations in memory: clues from studies on the role of the hippocampal region in paired-associate learning. *Current Directions in Psychological Science, 4*, 19–23.

Eichenbaum, H., Yonelinas, A. P., & Ranganath, C. (2007). The medial temporal lobe and recognition memory. *Annual Review of Neuroscience, 30*, 123–152.

Gold, J. J., Hopkins, R. O., & Squire, L. R. (2006). Single-item memory, associative memory and the human hippocampus. *Learning and Memory, 13*, 644–649.

Hannula, D. E., Tranel, D., & Cohen, N. J. (2006). The long and the short of it: relational memory impairments in amnesia, even at short lags. *The Journal of Neuroscience, 26*, 8352–8359.

Hassabis, D., & Maguire, E. A. (2007). Deconstructing episodic memory with construction. *Trends in Cognitive Sciences, 11*, 299–306.

Henke, K., Kroll, N. E. A., Behniea, H., Amaral, D. G., Miller, M. B., Rafal, R., & Gazzaniga, M. S. (1999). Memory lost and regained following bilateral hippocampal damage. *Journal of Cognitive Neuroscience, 11*, 682–697.

Hirst, W., Johnson, M. K., Kim, J. K., Phelps, E. A., Risse, G., & Volpe, B. T. (1986). Recognition and recall in amnesia. *Journal of Experimental Psychology: Learning Memory, & Cognition, 12*, 445–451.

Hirst, W., Johnson, M. K., Phelps, E. A., & Volpe, B. T. (1988). More on recognition and recall in amnesics. *Journal of Experimental Psychology: Learning, Memory, & Cognition, 14*, 758–762.

Holdstock, J. S., Mayes, A. R., Cezayirli, E., Isaac, C. L., Aggleton, J. P., & Roberts, N. (2000). A comparison of egocentric and allocentric spatial memory in a patient with selective hippocampal damage. *Neuropsychologia, 38*, 410–425.

Holdstock, J. S., Mayes, A. R., Gong, Q. Y., Roberts, N., & Kapur, N. (2005). Item recognition is less impaired than recall and associative recognition in a patient with selective hippocampal damage. *Hippocampus, 15*, 203–215.

Holdstock, J. S., Mayes, A. R., Isaac, C. L., Gong, Q., & Roberts, N. (2002a). Differential involvement of the hippocampus and temporal lobe cortices in rapid and slow learning of new semantic information. *Neuropsychologia, 40*, 748–768.

Holdstock, J. S., Mayes, A. R., Roberts, N., Cezayirli, E., Isaac, C. L., O'Reilly, R. C., & Norman, K. A. (2002b). Under what conditions is recognition spared relative to recall after selective hippocampal damage in humans? *Hippocampus, 12*, 341–351.

Holdstock, J. S., Parslow, D. M., Morris, R. G., Fleminger, S., Abrahams, S., Denby, C., Montaldi, D., & Mayes, A. R. (2008). Two case studies illustrating how relatively selective hippocampal lesions in humans can have quite different effects on memory. *Hippocampus, 18*, 679–691.

Isaac, C. L., & Mayes, A. R. (1999). Rate of forgetting in amnesia I: recall and recognition of prose. *Journal of Experimental Psychology: Learning Memory and Cognition, 25*, 942–962.

Jacoby, L. L. (1991). A process dissociation framework: separating automatic from intentional uses of memory. *Journal of Memory and Language, 30*, 513–541.

Kartsounis, L. D., Rudge, P., & Stevens, J. M. (1995). Bilateral lesions of CA1 and CA2 fields of the hippocampus are sufficient to cause a severe amnesic syndrome in humans. *Journal of Neurology, Neurosurgery and Psychiatry, 59*, 95–98.

Kesner, R. P. (1998). Neurobiological views of memory. In J. Martinez & R. Kesner (Eds.), *Neurobiology of Learning and Memory*. San Diego, CA: Academic Press, pp. 361–416.

Maguire, E. A., Vargha-Khadem, F., & Mishkin, M. (2001). The effects of bilateral hippocampal damage on fMRI regional activations and interactions during memory retrieval. *Brain, 124*, 1156–1170.

Mandler, G. (1980). Recognizing: the judgement of previous occurrence. *Psychological Review, 87*, 252–271.

Mayes, A. R. (1988). *Human Organic Memory Disorders*. Cambridge: Cambridge University Press.

Mayes, A. R., Holdstock, J. S., Isaac, C. L., Hunkin, N. M., & Roberts, N. (2002). Relative sparing of item recognition memory in a patient with adult-onset damage limited to the hippocampus. *Hippocampus, 12*, 325–340.

Mayes, A. R., Holdstock, J. S., Isaac, C. L., Montaldi, D., Grigor, J., Gummer, A., Cariga, P., Downes, J. J., Tsivilis, D., Gaffan, D., Gong, Q., & Norman, K. A. (2004). Associative recognition in a patient with selective hippocampal lesions and relatively normal item recognition. *Hippocampus, 14*, 763–784.

Mayes, A. R., Isaac, C. L., Downes, J. J., Holdstock, J. S., Hunkin, N. M., Montaldi, D., MacDonald, C., Cezaryirli, E., & Roberts, J. N. (2001). Memory for single items, word pairs, and temporal order in a patient with selective hippocampal lesions. *Cognitive Neuropsychology, 18*, 97–123.

Mayes, A. R., Isaac, C. L., Holdstock, J. S., Cariga, P., Gummer, A., & Roberts, N. (2003). Long-term amnesia: a review and detailed illustrative case study. *Cortex, 39*, 567–603.

Mayes, A., Montaldi, D., & Migo, E. (2007). Associative memory and the medial temporal lobes. *Trends in Cognitive Sciences, 11*, 126–135.

McClelland, J. L., McNaughton, B. L., & O'Reilly, R. C. (1995). Why there are complementary learning systems in the hippocampus and neocortex—insights from the successes and failures of connectionist models of learning and memory. *Psychological Review, 102*, 419–457.

Migo, E., Montaldi, D., Norman, K. A., Quamme, J., & Mayes, A. R. (2009). The contribution of familiarity to recognition memory is a function of test format when using similar foils. *Quarterly Journal of Experimental Psychology, 62*, 1198–1215.

Migo, E. M., Mayes, A. R., & Montaldi, D. (2012). Measuring recollection and familiarity: improving the remember/know procedure. *Consciousness and Cognition, 21*, 1435–1455.

Montaldi, D., & Mayes, A. R. (2010). The role of recollection and familiarity in the functional differentiation of the medial temporal lobes. *Hippocampus, 20*, 1291–1314.

Mullally, S. L., Intraub, H., & Maguire, E. (2012). Attenuated boundary extension produces a paradoxical memory advantage in amnesic patients. *Current Biology, 22*, 261–268.

Norman, K. A., & O'Reilly, R. C. (2003). Modeling hippocampal and neocortical contributions to recognition memory: a complementary learning systems approach. *Psychological Review, 110*, 611–646.

O'Keefe, J., & Nadel, L. (1978). *The Hippocampus as a Cognitive Map*. Oxford: Clarendon Press.

Olson, I. R., Page, K., Moore, K. S., Chatterjee, A., & Verfaellie, M. (2006). Working memory for conjunctions relies on the medial temporal lobe. *The Journal of Neuroscience, 26*, 4596–4601.

Pascalis, O., Hunkin, N. M., Bachevalier, J., & Mayes, A. R. (2009). Change in background context disrupts performance on visual paired comparison following hippocampal damage. *Neuropsychologia, 47*, 2107–2113.

Pascalis, O., Hunkin, N. M., Holdstock, J. S., Isaac, C. L., & Mayes, A. R. (2004). Visual paired comparison performance is impaired in a patient with selective hippocampal lesions and relatively intact item recognition. *Neuropsychologia, 42*, 1293–1300.

Reed, J. M., & Squire, L. R. (1997). Impaired recognition memory in patients with lesions limited to the hippocampal formation. *Behavioral Neuroscience, 111*, 667–675.

Sharon, T., Moscovitch, M., & Gilboa, A. (2011). Rapid neocortical acquisition of long-term arbitrary associations independent of the hippocampus. *Proceedings of the National Academy of Sciences, 108*, 1146–1151.

Squire, L. R., & Alvarez, (1995). Retrograde amnesia and memory consolidation: a neurobiological perspective. *Current Opinion in Neurobiology, 5*, 169–177.

Squire, L. R., & Zola, S. M. (1998). Episodic memory, semantic memory, and amnesia. *Hippocampus, 8*, 205–211.

Staresina, B. P., Fell, J., Dunn, J. C., Axmacher, N., & Henson, R. N. (2013). Using state-trace analysis to dissociate the functions of the human hippocampus and perirhinal cortex in recognition memory. *Proceedings of the National Academy of Sciences, 110*, 3119–3124.

Stark, C. E. L., Bayley, P. J., & Squire, L. R. (2002). Recognition memory for single items and for associations is similarly impaired following damage to the hippocampal region. *Learning and Memory, 9*, 238–242.

Stark, C. E. L., & Squire, L. R. (2003). Hippocampal damage equally impairs memory for single items and memory for conjunctions. *Hippocampus, 13*, 281–292.

Turriziani, P., Fadda, L., Caltagirone, C., & Carlesimo, G. A. (2004). Recognition memory for single items and for associations in amnesic patients. *Neuropsychologia, 42*, 426–433.

Vargha-Khadem, F., Gadian, D. G., Watkins, K. E., Connelly, A., Van Paesschen, W., & Mishkin, M. (1997). Differential effects of early hippocampal pathology on episodic and semantic memory. *Science, 277*, 376–380.

Wolk, D. A., Dunfee, K. L., Dikerson, B. C., Aizenstein, H. J., & DeKosky, S. T. (2011). A medial temporal division of labor: insights from memory in aging and early Alzheimer disease. *Hippocampus, 21*, 461–466.

Yonelinas, A. P. (2002). The nature of recollection and familiarity: a review of 30 years of research. *Journal of Memory and Language, 46*, 441–517.

Yonelinas, A. P., Widaman, K., Mungas, D., Reed, B., Weiner, M. W., & Chui, H. C. (2007). Memory in the aging brain: doubly dissociating the contribution of the hippocampus and entorhinal cortex. *Hippocampus, 17*, 1134–1140.

Zola-Morgan, S., Squire, L. R., & Amaral, D. G. (1986). Human amnesia and the medial temporal region: enduring memory impairment following a bilateral lesion limited to field CA1 of the hippocampus. *Journal of Neuroscience, 6*, 2950–2967.

4

AMNESIC PATIENT VC

What Have We Learnt From Him?

Carina Tudor-Sfetea and Lisa Cipolotti

Fifteen years ago, you and your colleagues reported a detailed investigation of VC, a patient with severe anterograde and retrograde amnesia. Despite his amnesia, a few years later, you report that his recollective- and familiarity-based recognition processes were spared for unknown faces. First of all, can you provide us with some background information about VC?

VC was a retired chief engineer in large ships such as liners who became profoundly amnesic at the age of 67 following a tachyarrhythmia requiring cardioversion. His wife and his colleagues reported that pre-morbidly he used to have excellent memory and was able to function at a high level in his highly responsible job. The **neurological examination** revealed a profound amnesia which affected both retrograde memory for personal and non-personal memories and anterograde memory for verbal and topographical material. Anecdotally, it was observed that VC appeared to have a very sparse recollection of events in his life. For instance, he could not remember the death of his wife or attending her funeral even days after these events. Another striking observation was that he never recognized the experimenters during the seven years of testing, despite having spent prolonged periods of time with them. However, despite this grave memory impairment, VC had no other cognitive abnormalities. One of VC's first **clinical MRI** scans documented an increased signal return throughout the length of both hippocampi. Both hippocampi were severely atrophied. Figure 4.1 depicts VC's severely atrophied left hippocampus and, for comparison, the left hippocampus of an age-matched healthy control. VC was first assessed in the Neuropsychology Department of the National Hospital for Neurology and Neurosurgery in September 1993. He was subsequently reassessed over a seven-year period on

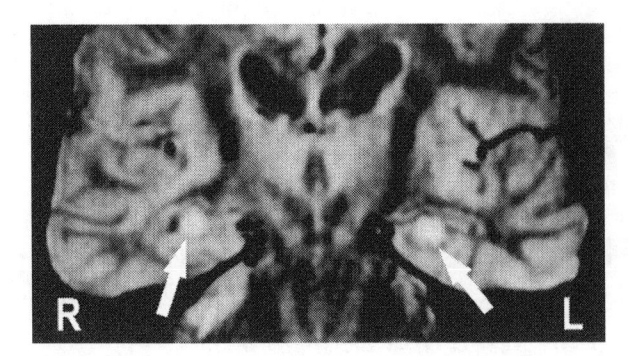

FIGURE 4.1 Coronal sections through temporal lobe at the level of the body of the hippocampus. High signal return seen in each hippocampus (TR 2000/TE30 ms and 5mm thick). Reprinted from Neuropsychologia, 44, Cipolotti, Bird, Good, Macmanus, Rudge, & Shallice, Recollection and familiarity in dense hippocampal amnesia: a case study, 489–506,

Copyright (2006), with permission from Elsevier.

a considerable number of clinical and experimental tasks designed to assess his retrograde and anterograde memory.

How did you first realize that this case was interesting?

We first realized that VC was an interesting case during a clinical case demonstration which I (LC) ran at the National Hospital for Neurology and Neurosurgery. It became apparent that VC had a striking dissociation between a profoundly impaired anterograde and retrograde episodic memory and otherwise well-preserved memory for events that were semantic in nature. For instance, he was unable to remember whether his mother, who had lived with him and his wife and had died approximately 20 years before, was still alive or not. At the same time, he had no difficulties in remembering facts such as the circumstances surrounding Rasputin's death. I thought that VC was an excellent example of pure amnesia. Despite the large number of patients I saw over the years, I encountered very few pure amnesic patients. So, VC was a good example of the rare pure amnesic syndrome. Moreover, at the case demonstration, Dr Peter Rudge, a knowledgeable neurologist with great experience in interpreting neuroimaging findings, discussed VC's MRI scans. Dr Rudge simply could not stress enough how highly selective VC's bilateral hippocampal damage was. Together with Luke Kartsounis and other colleagues, he had previously conducted an investigation on VC documenting that damage to the CA1 and CA2 fields of the hippocampus was associated with severe amnesia (Kartsounis, Rudge & Stevens, 1995). So, VC's amnesia was associated with a highly selective lesion. Shortly after the case demonstration,

I had the privilege to discuss some of our preliminary findings with Professor Tim Shallice, who emphasized how further investigation of patient VC could contribute to the theoretical discussions regarding the role of the hippocampus in memory. Thus, we realized the investigation of VC's amnesia could allow us to further our understanding of the neurocognitive architecture of memory functions.

Can you summarize the main features of this case?

VC had a remarkably extensive and ungraded retrograde amnesia which affected both personal (autobiographical) and non-personal (public events and figures) memories. He also showed a severe pervasive impairment of anterograde memory encompassing recognition and recall of verbal and non-verbal memoranda, with one notable exception (see the following). In stark contrast, VC had normal IQ and intact performance on standard perception, executive function and language tests. His pre-morbid general semantic knowledge was also preserved as shown by his intact performance on a range of naming, vocabulary, fluency and comprehension tests. VC's normal general neuropsychological profile was stable over the experimental period of seven years, suggesting no progressive cognitive decline over this period (see Table 4.1). Extensive neuroradiological investigations using a variety of different qualitative and quantitative methods provided converging evidence of focal bilateral hippocampal damage. The hippocampi were reduced

TABLE 4.1 VC's performance on a series of cognitive tasks

Cognitive domain and test	Mean performance over five assessments (September 1993 to April 2000)
Verbal and performance IQ	
Wechsler Adult Intelligence Scale-Revised; WAIS-R (Wechsler, 1981)	VIQ: 104/PIQ: 129
Nominal skills	
Graded Difficulty Naming Test; GNT (McKenna & Warrington, 1980)	50th – 75th percentile
Visuoperceptual and visuospatial skills	
Incomplete Letters	Above 5% cut-off
Cube Analysis	Above 5% cut-off
Object Decision	Above 5% cut-off
(Visual Object and Space Perception battery, VOSP, Warrington & James, 1991)	
Frontal lobe (executive) function	
Weigl Sorting Test (Weigl, 1941)	Passed
Cognitive Estimates Test (Shallice & Evans, 1978)	Passed
Modified Wisconsin Card Sorting Task (Nelson, 1976)	Passed
Hayling Test (Burgess & Shallice, 1997)	Scaled score: 6 (average)

in volume by 47% on the left and 44% on the right, with no evidence that the residual hippocampal tissue was functional.

What was this case's pattern of spared and impaired cognitive abilities?

Standard Clinical Memory Tests

Standard clinical memory tests revealed the presence of a severe anterograde memory impairment affecting both recognition and recall, which remained static over the seven-year testing period (Cipolotti et al., 2001, 2006). A break down of VC's mean performance on standard clinical memory tests is shown in Table 4.2. Grave verbal and topographical recognition and recall impairments were documented. For example, on the delayed condition of the AMIPB Story, he was not able to remember that the story had ever been read to him. Strikingly, VC was found to have spared visual recognition memory for unfamiliar faces, as assessed by the Recognition Memory Test for Faces (RMT-F, Warrington, 1984).

TABLE 4.2 VC's performance on standard clinical memory tests

Memory domain and test	Performance
Short-term memory	
Digit Span Subtest (WAIS-R; Wechsler, 1981)	6
Short-term Topographical Memory Test with 2s delay (Hartley et al., 2007)	<1st percentile
Verbal recognition	
Recognition Memory Test for Words (Warrington, 1984)	Always <10th percentile
Visual recognition	
Recognition Memory Test for Faces (Warrington, 1984)	At or >25th percentile
Topographical Memory Test of Outdoor Scenes (Warrington, 1996)	Always <10th percentile
Verbal recall	
Story recall	Always <5th percentile
Immediate	Always 0
Delay	<5th percentile
List learning	
(Adult Memory and Information Processing Battery; AMIPB; Coughlan & Hollows, 1985)	
Paired Associates Learning test (Warrington, 1996)	
T1	Always at or <5th percentile
T2	Always at or <5th percentile
Visual recall	
Rey-Osterreith Complex Figure (Osterrieth, 1944)	
Delay	Always <5th percentile

Memory domain and test	Performance
Parallel recognition and recall based tests of verbal and non-verbal memory	
The Doors and People Test (Baddeley et al., 1994)	
Names test	
Immediate verbal recall	Always <1st percentile
Delayed verbal recall	Mean score: 3.5/12
Verbal recognition test A	Always <1st percentile
Verbal recognition test B	Always <1st percentile
Doors visual recognition test	
Test A	Always <1st percentile
Test B	Always <1st percentile
Shapes test	
Immediate visual recall	Always <1st percentile
Delayed visual recall	Mean score: 4/12

Short-Term Memory

Certain aspects of VC's short-term memory functions were normal while others were impaired. VC's auditory verbal short-term memory was normal, as assessed by the Digit Span Subtest of the WAIS. In contrast, on a topographical memory test involving a four-alternative delayed match to sample (delay = 2s), VC was significantly impaired, scoring below the first percentile (Hartley et al., 2007) (see Table 4.2).

Semantic Memory

Similar to his short-term memory, certain aspects of VC's semantic memory were also normal. VC's semantic knowledge of vocabulary from the retrograde period was intact, as shown by his high average performance on the Vocabulary subtest of the WAIS-R. VC also performed well on picture naming, category-specific names and category fluency tests, as well as on three tests of comprehension. In contrast, he was unable to acquire new vocabulary which had entered the British lexicon subsequent to his becoming amnesic (see Table 4.3). Therefore, his inability to update his vocabulary reflects a remarkable degree of impairment in comparison with his excellent lexical-semantic knowledge from his pre-morbid period.

Episodic Memory

Retrograde Memory for Non-Personal Events

To assess non-personal retrograde memory, VC was tested using a variety of experimental tasks such as: the dead or alive test, the famous public events questionnaire, the famous faces and names familiarity tests. VC's performance was

TABLE 4.3 VC's semantic memory test scores

Test		
Retrograde semantic memory	*VC's performance/no. correct*	
Vocabulary subtest of WAIS-R	Scaled score: 12 (high average)	
Cambridge new naming test (Bozeat et al., 2000)	63/64	
Living items	31/32	
Man-made items	32/32	
Category-specific naming test (Bozeat et al., 2000)		
Animals	23/30	
Fruit	18/30	
Small manipulable objects	20/30	
Large objects	20/30	
Category fluency (1 min)		
Animals	14	
Birds	10	
Dogs	7	
Household	16	
Vehicles	13	
Tools	8	
Fruits	10	
Boats	8	
F	15	
A	18	
S	17	
Graded synonyms test (Warrington et al., 1998)	46/50 (75th percentile)	
Camel and cactus test (Bozeat et al., 2000)		
Words	62/64	
Pictures	61/64	
Cambridge comprehension test (Hodges and Patterson, 1995)		
Living	32/32	
Non-living	32/32	
Anterograde semantic memory	**VC**	**Healthy controls mean (SD)**
New vocabulary test		
Recall	4/20	14.9 (2.08)
Recognition	12/20	18.0 (1.15)

found to be globally impaired on all these tests with no sparing of remote memories. To illustrate this, let us consider his performance on the famous public events questionnaire and famous faces tests. These two tests were developed following the procedure used by Sanders and Warrington (1971). They were designed to assess memory for public events and famous people which were deemed to be of major importance between 1960 and 1988, whereby an effort was made to avoid events subject to repeated review in the media, films or books. This resulted in tasks of non-personal memory with a strong episodic component, as the items were associated with a restricted context at a given point in time. Healthy controls performed more poorly on questions referring to people or events that belonged to more remote periods in time, suggesting that the selection criteria for the construction of the tasks were methodologically sound and the questions for the different time periods were balanced. Other similar tests of remote memory might use events and people from a given period, but their extended notoriety would have effectively made them part of general knowledge and thus more "semantic". This is shown by the finding that healthy controls exhibit no significant differences in performance on questions referring to people or events more remote in time compared to more recent ones (e.g., Cohen & Squire, 1981; Rempel-Clower, Zola, Squire & Amaral, 1996). These memories would thus be less vulnerable to hippocampal lesions. VC's performance was very poor on the public events and famous people tests. His scores were in the severely impaired range compared to age- and education-matched healthy control participants. For some decades, his performance was even at chance (see Table 4.4; raw scores were converted due to skewed distributions). Importantly, these results indicated that VC suffered from an extensive and ungraded retrograde amnesia. Remote memories for non-personal events were not spared or less impaired than more recent memories in VC.

Retrograde Memory for Personal Events

VC was administered the autobiographical memory interview (Kopelman, Wilson & Baddeley, 1989). The results indicated that VC was completely unable to recall autobiographical episodes from his recent life and almost completely unable to recall autobiographical episodes from childhood and early adult life. He scored in the abnormal range for all three periods of life (see Table 4.5). This shows that he had severe impairment of autobiographical memories from his childhood, early adult life and recent life. Thus, there was also no indication of a temporal gradient in VC's autobiographical memory.

Anterograde Memory

Five new experimental verbal and non-verbal recognition memory tests were administered to investigate the relative contribution of recollection and familiarity to VC's residual recognition skills. These involved verbal (words), as well

TABLE 4.4 VC's performance in comparison to healthy controls on three retrograde memory experimental tests

Test	VC	Healthy controls
Famous public events questionnaire test	**Percentage score**	**Mean percentage score**
Recall	(sqrt transformation)	(sqrt transformation)
1960s	3.3	42
1970s	3.3	28
1980s	0	47
1990s	3.3	53
Multiple-choice recognition	(arcsin transformation)	(arcsin transformation)
1960s	50	67
1970s	30	54
1980s	43	81
1990s	56	84
Famous faces test	**Percentage score**	**Mean percentage score**
Recall	(sqrt transformation)	(sqrt transformation)
1960s	6	27
1970s	0	18
1980s	0	40
1990s	5	50
Multiple-choice recognition	(arcsin transformation)	(arcsin transformation)
1960s	54	70
1970s	56	64
1980s	65	82
1990s	46	85

TABLE 4.5 VC's autobiographical memory performance

Autobiographical memory interview	Number correct	Comment
Childhood	1/9	Definitely abnormal
Early adult life	2/9	Definitely abnormal
Recent life	0/9	Definitely abnormal

as non-verbal (faces, buildings and landscapes) memoranda. Based on the dual-process theory, according to which recognition reflects the contribution of two independent processes, recollection and familiarity (e.g., Jacoby, 1991; Yonelinas, 1994; Aggleton & Brown, 1999; Kelley & Wixted, 2001; for a review, see Yonelinas, Aly, Wang & Koen, 2010), a receiver-operating characteristics (ROC) analysis was adopted (Ratcliff, Sheu & Gronlund, 1992; Yonelinas, Kroll, Dobbins, Lazzara & Knight, 1998). VC's and healthy controls' sensitivity was calculated using standard signal-detection theory methodology (Macmillan & Creelman, 2005). A comparison was made following the procedure of Crawford and Garthwaite (2002).

TABLE 4.6 VC's sensitivity and relative sensitivity (recollection/familiarity) in comparison to healthy controls on five experimental recognition memory tests

Process/type of memoranda	VC	Healthy controls mean (SD)
Words	0.65	1.65 (0.27)
Buildings	0.41	1.61 (0.44)
Landscapes	0.54	1.72 (0.50)
Faces	1.55	1.73 (0.51)
Recollection		
Words	0	0.38 (0.14)
Buildings	0.025	0.44 (0.09)
Landscapes	0.05	0.44 (0.13)
Faces	0.21	0.36 (0.18)
Familiarity		
Words	0.63	1.24 (0.32)
Buildings	0.45	1.19 (0.38)
Landscapes	0.43	1.18 (0.43)
Faces	1.28	1.27 (0.36)

As shown in Table 4.6, VC was significantly impaired on the two verbal recognition memory tests. Similarly, his performance was also significantly impaired on the two memory tests employing topographical memoranda (buildings and landscapes). Although markedly impaired, VC's performance on these two topographical tasks was nevertheless above chance. Strikingly, VC's performance was normal on the memory test using unfamiliar faces. These results confirm previous findings, indicating that VC's verbal and topographical recognition memory was severely impaired. However, they also suggest the remarkable and selective preservation of a particular type of non-verbal memory dedicated to faces.

To clarify the relative contribution of recollection and familiarity to VC's residual recognition skills, a ROC analysis was carried out. VC's recollection and familiarity processes for unfamiliar faces were well preserved. In contrast, recollection for verbal and topographical material was at floor. Familiarity was also impaired, significantly below controls for verbal and topographical stimuli. Familiarity was significantly impaired, significantly below controls, for verbal and buildings, although it did not reach significance for landscapes. These results suggest that the hippocampus is involved in recollection of verbal and topographical material. It also plays an appreciable role in familiarity processes for these stimuli. However, recollection and familiarity of human faces appear not to depend on this region.

What were the imaging findings in VC's case?

Converging evidence from a variety of different neuroimaging methods confirmed selective damage to the hippocampi. **Structural MRI** findings consistently found selective bilateral hippocampal damage. Abnormal signal return from the left amygdala was also found, with no evidence of abnormal signal return from any other part of the brain. In particular, both thalami and parietal lobes were normal, as well as the temporal poles, anterior middle temporal gyri and anterior parahippocampal gyri on both sides, with some reduced white matter layer of the parahippocampal gyrus.

Detailed *volumetric MRI* measurements (based on region of interest—ROI—metrics) revealed gross abnormalities in both hippocampi, which were markedly shrunken (left hippocampus: between 5 and 6 SDs; right hippocampus: between 4 and 5 SDs below the control mean). In contrast, the volumes of both entorhinal cortices were entirely normal. The volumes of both left and right temporal lobes and temporal gyri were also within normal limits. There were no obvious morphological abnormalities of the grey matter of the parahippocampal gyri, but the white matter layer was noted to be somewhat reduced in size (left: between 2 and 3 SDs below the control mean; right: less than 1 SD below the control the mean). This mild degree of volume loss in the parahippocampal gyrus was clearly much less than that noted for the hippocampi and was attributed to the reduced size of the white matter layer.

Voxel-based morphometry (VBM) revealed grey matter atrophy in the head and body of both hippocampi, particularly medially (see Figure 4.2). This atrophy was significant on the right and just failed to reach significance on the left. Importantly, there were no grey matter differences in the bulk of the entorhinal cortex between VC and controls. Furthermore, no grey matter atrophy was detected in

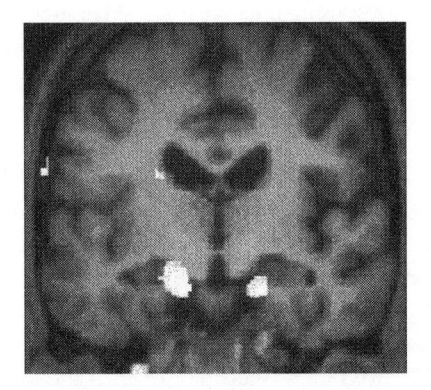

FIGURE 4.2 VBM results. Atrophy in the medial aspects of both hippocampi, bordering on the upper margin of entorhinal cortex bilaterally can be seen (the images are presented at the threshold of P < 0.001 for display purposes and clarity). Reprinted from Neuropsychologia, 44, Cipolotti, Bird, Good, Macmanus, Rudge, & Shallice, Recollection and familiarity in dense hippocampal amnesia: a case study, 489–506,

Copyright (2006), with permission from Elsevier.

the perirhinal cortex, in the temporal lobes or elsewhere in the cortex. The only area of white matter atrophy detected was adjacent to the lateral border of the right hippocampus.

An *fMRI* experiment using retrieval of basic autobiographical facts and general knowledge revealed that VC was able to successfully retrieve these facts as well as healthy controls. However, his hippocampi did not show any changes in activity during the task, unlike controls (see Figure 4.3). In contrast, he activated medial frontal, retrosplenial, temporoparietal junction, lateral temporal cortices, temporal pole and the left parahippocampal gyrus the same as controls.

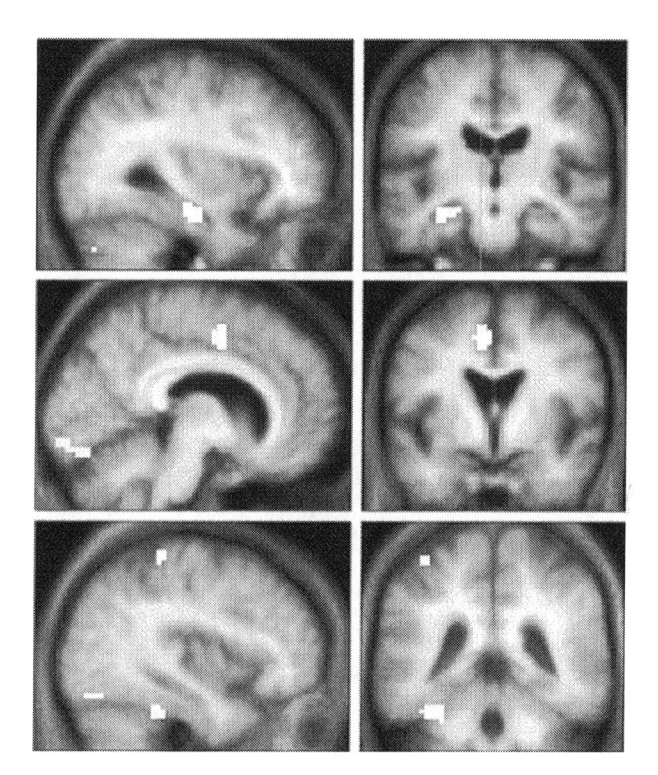

FIGURE 4.3 Brain areas more active in control subjects. Sagittal (left panels) and coronal (right panels) sections through the averaged structural MRI scan of the healthy controls. The areas in white are those more active for the control subjects compared with VC for the contrast of general knowledge—control task. These include the left hippocampus, left retrocalcarine cortex, mid-cingulate gyrus, left post-central gyrus, and left posterior parahippocampal gyrus. Reprinted from Neuroimage, 27, Maguire, Frith, Rudge, & Cipolotti, The effect of adult-acquired hippocampal damage on memory retrieval: an fMRI study, 146–152, Copyright (2005), with permission from Elsevier.

MR spectroscopy (¹H MRS) showed neuronal integrity in VC's frontal, medial and lateral temporo-occipital regions as well as the thalami, but not in VC's hippocampi.

Thus, a variety of different and independent quantitative neuroradiological methods provided converging evidence of severe hippocampal damage. To our knowledge, no other amnesic patient has been so extensively studied using such a variety of different neuroradiological investigations.

Do you think this case contributes to our understanding of how the normal mind works and do you think that there is anything unique that the reports of this case added to our knowledge?

The investigation of VC represents one of the few instances in the literature where the involvement of key anatomical structures in the storage and retrieval of mnestic traces was quantitatively verified with a variety of neuroimaging paradigms and extensive theoretically motivated tests. Our findings re-opened the intense debate about the role of the hippocampus in remote memory, recollection and familiarity and semantic memory (for discussion see Nadel & Moscovitch, 2001).

The Role of the Hippocampus in Remote Memory

VC had lesions principally restricted to the hippocampus yet showed extensive and ungraded remote memory impairment for famous public events spanning over four decades of his lifetime. Similarly, VC's autobiographical memories were equally affected for all the periods of his life spanning from very recent times to his childhood. These findings suggest that the role of the hippocampus is unlikely to be restricted only to the temporary consolidation of memory traces, as assumed by a variety of influential memory models, such as the Standard Consolidation Theory (Squire, 1992). The findings on VC support models, such as the Multiple Trace Theory and the Transformation Theory (Winocur, Moscovitch & Bontempi, 2010; Winocur & Moscovitch, 2011). The Multiple Trace Theory assumes that when a memory trace is reactivated, a new hippocampal trace is created, thus forming a multiple trace for each memory. These memory traces are not transferred from the hippocampus to the neocortex. Rather, the model postulates that episodic memory always depends on the hippocampal system, which provides the necessary contextual information. The Transformation Theory suggests that changes in neural representation in systems consolidation are accompanied by corresponding changes in the nature of the memory. Thus, hippocampally dependent, episodic or context-specific memories transform into semantic, or gist-like versions that are represented in extra-hippocampal structures. To the extent that episodic memories are retained, they will continue to require the hippocampus, but the hippocampus is not needed for the retrieval of semantic memories. Patient VC added to our knowledge in so far as the pattern of obtained results suggests that the hippocampus is critical for effective retrieval of remote episodic memories, and it may provide a form of representation which is not available to the neocortex.

The Role of the Hippocampus in Recollection and Familiarity

VC's recollection and familiarity processes for words and topography were severely impaired, yet several neuroimaging investigations suggested that VC's perirhinal and entorhinal cortices were spared. These findings are difficult to accommodate with the view that normal recognition memory is subserved by two functionally and anatomically distinct processes (e.g., Jacoby, 1991; Yonelinas, 1994). In particular, it has been suggested that only recollection is subserved by the hippocampus whilst familiarity is underpinned by perirhinal and entorhinal cortices (e.g., Brown & Aggleton, 2001; Aggleton & Brown, 1999). Instead, our findings suggest that the hippocampus is critically involved in both recollective and familiarity processes. Perirhinal and/or entorhinal cortex may play some role in familiarity. However, this is not sufficient to sustain effective recognition memory processes. In accordance with this, Manns, Hopkins, Reed, Kitchener and Squire (2003) reported patients with bilateral hippocampal damage, impaired on both recollection and familiarity. Furthermore, Kirwan, Wixted and Squire (2010) found that patients with circumscribed hippocampal damage showed no increased likelihood of experiencing high-confidence, familiarity-based recognition in the absence of recollection, compared to healthy controls. This would be explained by the idea that hippocampal damage does not selectively impair recollection.

The Role of the Hippocampus in Different Types of Visual Memoranda

The study of VC's anterograde memory highlighted for the first time that the hippocampus is not involved in the recollection and familiarity of unfamiliar faces. This finding coupled with findings in patients who showed topographical memory impairment but spared recognition memory for faces (e.g., Cipolotti & Maguire, 2003) suggests that there may be different types of visual memory subserved by different neuronal structures (see also Lee et al., 2005b; Smith et al., 2014). More precisely, what becomes apparent is a dissociation between the perception of faces and scenes, and their respective neural underpinnings, with the hippocampus being critical only for the latter (Bird et al., 2007; Bird & Burgess, 2008). Indeed, other case studies have reported selective sparing of recognition memory for faces in patients with focal bilateral hippocampal damage (Carlesimo, Fadda, Turriziani, Tomaiuolo & Caltagirone, 2001; Taylor et al., 2007). This has further been confirmed by lesion and neuroimaging studies having reported an area in the fusiform gyrus which has been identified as a key area for face processing (Fusiform Face Area, FFA; e.g., Kanwisher, McDermott & Chun, 1997; Maguire, Frith & Cipolotti, 2001a). Perhaps this area, alongside face-selective patches in the ventral anterior temporal lobes interconnected with it and with the occipital face area (Collins & Olson, 2014), may underpin VC's spared recollection and familiarity for faces. Similarly, an area in the parahippocampal cortex has been identified as being critically involved in perception of scenes depicting places (Parahippocampal Place Area, PPA; Epstein & Kanwisher, 1998).

The Role of the Hippocampus in Semantic Memory

VC's knowledge of semantic information from the pre-morbid period was intact. However, he was unable to acquire new semantic knowledge in the post-morbid period. This dissociation hints to a role for the hippocampus in semantic learning, but not in retrograde semantic memory. Evidence of no new vocabulary acquisition has previously been reported in long-standing amnesia (e.g., Gabrieli, Cohen & Corkin, 1988). VC, together with patient LJ reported by Reed and Squire (1998), were amongst the first cases in which impaired vocabulary acquisition was established following damage restricted to the hippocampus, thus providing causal evidence suggesting that new fact learning is impaired by hippocampal pathology. A possible explanation for the restricted semantic learning observed in hippocampal amnesic patients may be that in the absence of a functioning hippocampal system the neocortex can learn (albeit slowly), in isolation, through repeated exposure to the information, as suggested for example by McClelland, McNaughton, and O'Reilly's (1995) computational model. In this context, it is possible that VC's seven-year, post-morbid testing period was not long enough to allow for such a learning process.

Notably, patients with developmental amnesia caused by early hippocampal damage, comparable to that of VC, have been documented as being able to acquire new semantic memories (Vargha-Khadem et al., 1997). Interestingly, at least one of these developmental amnesic patients, Jon, has been shown to show some activation in the damaged hippocampal tissue during personal and general fact retrieval (Maguire et al., 2001c). However, in VC's case, when using an identical fMRI paradigm, no activation changes were found in his residual hippocampal tissue, despite the fact that his behavioural performance and reaction times were comparable to age-matched healthy controls (Maguire, Frith, Rudge & Cipolotti, 2005). One might thus speculate that the developmental amnesic patient's successful acquisition of semantic memories may be in part related to the residual hippocampal contribution.

Do you think this case has been considered by people who develop theories of the normal mind? If yes, how? If no, should he?

The investigation of patient VC has been considered by theoreticians in the field. Our studies on VC were cited over 500 times by subsequent studies in the field. Notably, VC's case was the main subject of a piece by Nadel and Moscovitch

(2001), arguing that "this report (i.e., Cipolotti et al., 2001), along with other recent findings, re-opens the debate about the role of these medial temporal lobe structures, indicating that their role extends much further than traditional theory had suggested" (p. 228). The findings on patient VC were taken into consideration as part of the debate between contrasting theoretical models such as the Standard Consolidation Theory (Squire, 1992) and the Multiple Trace Theory (Nadel & Moscovitch, 1997). For example, Winocur and colleagues (2010) cited VC as providing evidence in favour of the Multiple Trace Theory and subsequent Transformation Theory. Notably, the findings on VC were also investigated by computational neuroscientists attempting to clarify the use of Hebbian learning rules to model aspects of learning. Thus, McClelland (2006) considered findings on VC to explore failures of learning in relatively pure cases of amnesia and attempted to clarify the process of strengthening responses made to an input. McClelland concluded that there seem to be processes at work strengthening the response a person makes to an input, even when that response is incorrect. This may explain cases of failure to learn if circumstances lead to the production of incorrect or unhelpful responses instead of correct or helpful ones (McClelland, 2006). More recently, Clark and Maguire (2016) used VC's case to illustrate cases of patients suffering complete loss of autobiographical memories across all time points—recent and remote—to readdress the issue of whether the hippocampus is required for recalling remote autobiographical memories, which is still hotly debated.

Can you specify why this case was relevant in relation to the knowledge at the time and would he still be relevant to the knowledge of today?

The seminal work of Brenda Milner on the famous case of HM (Scoville & Milner, 1957) highlighted for the first time the critical role of the hippocampal formation and related structures such as the enthorinal, perirhinal and parahippocampal cortices in memory. Some years later, Sanders and Warrington (1971) suggested that the medial temporal lobe was implicated in the retrieval of all remote memories. However, the exact nature of the hippocampal and related structures' role in memory was still hotly debated in the early 2000s. The leading theory at the time suggested that the hippocampus was critical for memory encoding and for the consolidation of memory traces only for a limited period, but not for the permanent storing of memory itself (e.g., Squire, 1992). However, in the early 2000s, some studies started to challenge this dominant view. For example, fMRI studies reported that hippocampal activation was as strong for remote memory retrieval as it was for recent memory retrieval (e.g., Maguire, Henson, Mummery & Frith, 2001b; Ryan et al., 2001). Lesion studies reported patients with medial temporal lobe damage whose retrograde amnesia lasted for decades (e.g., Damasio, Eslinger, Damasio, Van Hoesen & Cornell, 1985; Tulving, Schacter, McLachlan & Moscovitch, 1988; Warrington & McCarthy, 1988; Kopelman, Stanhope & Kingsley,

1999; Chan, Henley, Rossor & Warrington, 2007). As discussed earlier, patient VC had sparing of the enthorinal and adjacent temporal cortex, and had damage almost completely restricted to the hippocampus. He had a profound and long-lasting retrograde amnesia for a period of over 40 years. These patterns of results support the notion that the hippocampus is important for the retrieval of remote episodic memories. As such, the findings in VC's case "raised the possibility that the standard model of hippocampal function, one that posits a relatively restricted time-limited role in episode memory, is in need of modification" (Nadel & Moscovitch, 2001, p. 229).

Moreover, at the time, the role of the hippocampus in semantic memory as well as in familiarity-based recognition was also subject of intense debate. For example, the influential proposal put forward by Squire and colleagues suggested that both episodic and semantic memory were impaired in hippocampal amnesia (e.g., Squire & Alvarez, 1995). Indeed, impaired semantic learning had been found in several cases, such as HM (Gabrieli et al., 1988) and GD (Shimamura & Squire, 1987). This was also the case for VC (Cipolotti et al., 2001). However, the role of the hippocampus in pre-morbidly acquired semantic knowledge was unclear, as it was under debate whether episodic memory was substantially more affected by amnesia than semantic memory (e.g., Mishkin, Vargha-Khadem & Gadian, 1998). VC's performance on tests of remote semantic memory was intact. This supported the idea that the hippocampus might play a role in consolidating semantic information in other structures, but not in retaining or retrieving them once consolidation is complete (Nadel & Moscovitch, 1997).

In terms of recognition memory, the dominant view was based on the dual-process theory, with one camp arguing that the hippocampus was involved in recollection of the context of events, but not for familiarity-based recognition (Aggleton & Brown, 1999), while others suggested that recognition memory as a whole depended on the hippocampus (e.g., Reed & Squire, 1997; Spiers, Maguire & Burgess, 2001). However, the difference between types of memoranda and, more precisely, between types of visual memoranda, had scarcely been explored. VC's performance on recollection-based and familiarity-based processes was completely at floor both for words and topographical memoranda. In striking contrast, recollection-based and familiarity-based processes were spared for unfamiliar faces, with VC's familiarity estimates being indistinguishable from the controls. This not only suggested that the hippocampus was completely critical for recollection and that it contributed, although not exclusively, to familiarity but also brought to light, for the first time, a dissociation between verbal and topographical memoranda on the one hand, and unfamiliar faces memoranda on the other hand. The role of the hippocampus in the two subprocesses of recognition memory, recollection and familiarity, is also still under investigation. It remains unclear whether the hippocampus is required for both subprocesses (e.g., Merkow et al., 2015), or only for recollection, with familiarity depending on extra-hippocampal structures (e.g., Sadeh, Ozubko, Winocur & Moscovitch, 2014).

Today, the issue of what types of memory are dependent exclusively on the hippocampus is still debated. The Standard Consolidation Theory (Squire, 1992) still has its proponents despite accumulating evidence in favour of the Multiple Trace Theory (Nadel & Moscovitch, 1997) and the Transformation Theory (Winocur et al., 2010; Winocur & Moscovitch, 2011). To account for such findings, especially those using fMRI, supporters of the Standard Consolidation Theory have argued that the hippocampal activity registered during recall of remote memories is due to the re-encoding of memories retrieved from the neocortex rather than due to the memories themselves (Squire & Wixted, 2011). While this interpretation is rather difficult to refute, it may also prove too simple given recent evidence of different patterns of hippocampal activation for recent and more remote memories (Bonnici et al., 2013, as cited in Moscovitch, Cabeza, Winocur & Nadel, 2016).

Were there any relevant data that you did not manage to publish on this case?

At the time, we were investigating the memory functions of patient VC, we also completed a separate investigation on a patient who, following a right frontal lesions, developed "acquired sociopathy", characterized by high levels of aggression and callous disregard for others (Blair & Cipolotti, 2000). A detailed investigation of theory of mind functions was carried out on the "acquired sociopathic" patient. We decided to administer some of the theory of mind tasks used with the "acquired sociopathic" patient to VC. Clinically, VC appeared to be able to understand the intentions of others and respond to their needs, at least in the present moment. At the time, we thought it could be of interest to document these abilities formally. We therefore administered an advanced theory of mind task to VC, which required him to read 24 stories describing a naturalistic social situation and answer questions on why the characters behaved as they did (Happé, 1994). Three scores were generated from VC's performance. The first, total score indexed VC's comprehension of the situation; the other two scores referred to the justification of VC's answers when interpreting the characters' behaviour, more precisely reference to either the characters' mental states or physical information. VC's performance on the advanced theory of mind task was unimpaired (his total score was flawless). An analysis of his responses revealed that he was able to use mental state justification correctly. These results indicated that VC did not have a theory of mind impairment. At the time, we did not fully understand the importance of publishing these data. Fortunately, a few years later, Rosenbaum and colleagues (2007) conducted a formal investigation of theory of mind abilities in patients with episodic memory impairment. Similar to our unpublished findings on VC, the authors reported that theory of mind is spared in patients with episodic memory impairment. These findings furthered our understanding of the role of the medial temporal structures in episodic memory and theory of mind. They suggested that theory of mind can function independently of episodic memory. In line with this, some neuroimaging findings showed both common and unique neural correlates of autobiographical memory and theory of mind (Rabin, Gilboa, Stuss, Mar & Rosenbaum, 2010).

What are the shortcomings of this case?

Testing over a longer period of time (i.e., over the seven-year period we had available) may have helped clarify issues regarding the role of the hippocampus and/or neocortex in learning. For example, models such as those postulated by McClelland et al. (1995) asssume that hippocampal amnesic patients may still be able to learn new semantic information albeit slowly, through repeated exposure. In line with this, patient RS was able to acquire semantic information about famous people and public events, as well as new vocabulary, in the 13-year post-morbid period (Kitchener, Hodges & McCarthy, 1998). However, VC was unable to acquire new semantic information, more precisely, vocabulary which had entered the British lexicon subsequent to his becoming amnesic. Given the unspecified "slow" interval of time necessary for learn to take place, it is may well be possible that VC's 7-year post-morbid testing period was not of sufficient length to allow for a learning process to occur, while RS' significantly longer 13-year period might have allowed the slow learning of vocabulary and semantic facts.

Furthermore, carrying out an autopsy on VC's brain after his death may also have brought invaluable information. More precisely, it may have clarified issues regarding gross pathology, but also histopathology, which would have been impossible to examine, as in the case of Warrington and Duchen's (1992) investigation of amnesic patient NT. Importantly, an autopsy would have helped settle any outstanding issues regarding any hidden pathology that VC was suspected to have by some experts in the field who reviewed our work.

Do you remember whether you had difficulty publishing your work with VC? If so, what was this difficulty? Were there any issues that reviewers were particularly blunt about?

Our papers on patient VC were indeed rather difficult to publish. They were rejected by some of the most influential journals in the field and heavily criticized by the reviewers. Some of our findings on patient VC made new original contributions that went against 'traditional wisdom' in the field. As such some reviewers were sceptical of our results and preferred to interpret them as due to causes other than VC's obvious hippocampal impairment.

Reviewers often argued that hidden pathology may have been at the root of VC's extensive memory impairment. More precisely, they claimed that a cortical deficit resulting from hidden pathology may not show up on MRI or comprehensive cognitive testing. For example, Markowitsch and colleagues (1997) reported an amnesic patient whose PET investigation revealed wide-spread regions of hypo-activity that, according to the authors, could not be predicted from the MRI scans. However, this patient, who was often quoted as an example of hidden pathology, was in a coma for 14 days, had non-specific cortical/subcortical atrophy on the MRI and had deficits in general intelligence, and on attention and concentration tests. In contrast, VC's MRI showed no atrophy compared with intact age-matched healthy controls, was not in a coma and, apart from the episodic memory abnormality, his performance on a series of cognitive tests was in the expected average/high average range.

The reviewers were also often sceptical of our MRI findings. For example, they suggested that our MRI findings were of "poor quality and partly non-interpretable", and that we failed to "evaluate possible thalamic dysfunction". This was despite the fact that the resolution of our images of VC's hippocampus was below 1 mm, and we could not find abnormal signal return from any other part of the brain except the hippocampus and the left amygdala. Importantly, as we specifically reported, both thalami were normal.

VC's grave amnesia was also attributed by the referees to his "history of epilepsy . . . tachyrhythmia . . . migraine and alcohol excesses". However, VC did not have epilepsy and his tachyrhythmia was short-lived and was the cause of the sudden onset of his amnesia. VC did have migraine, in common with 10% of the rest of the population. Additionally, VC had not drunk alcohol in excess for many years; his consumption was within medical guidelines. Crucially, his performance on tests tapping into all other cognitive functions apart from memory was entirely in keeping with his estimated pre-morbid functioning. Importantly, VC's age was almost the same as HM (who did have intractable epilepsy) who was considered one, if not the best, example of amnesic patient reported in the literature.

We were also criticized on the grounds that the neuropsychological data were "incomplete for a severely amnesic patient of this kind and reported superficially". The fact that we did not test in detail VC's attention was considered a serious shortcoming. Admittedly, we did not directly test VC's attention and concentration, since we felt this was unnecessary in light of his performance IQ of 140. Moreover, our cognitive baselines were far more detailed than the comparable papers (e.g., Kapur & Brooks, 1999), and entirely comparable to those of patient HM.

One particularly memorable comment was related to the fact that we did not discuss "the possible mix of psychogenic retrograde amnesia". We obviously felt that it was somewhat bizarre to discuss the possibility of a functional overlay in a patient with lesions in an area known to be critically involved in a particular cognitive function and who presented in many respects the expected type of impairment following such damage.

Are there any assessments/paradigms that you would administer now to this individual if he was available?

Imaging techniques have made considerable advances since our original studies on VC. In particular, diffusor-tensor imaging (DTI) can reveal unique information about brain network connectivity (Soares, Marques, Alves & Sousa, 2013). Of course it would have been invaluable to have the opportunity to investigate the connections between hippocampus and cortical areas in VC's brain using this technique. Also we would like to have further investigated aspects of VC's perception and the ability to imagine future scenarios.

VC's perceptual skills were found intact when assessed by standard neuropsychological tests (Incomplete Letters, Cube Analysis, Object Decision from the Visual Object and Space Perception Battery; VOSP, Warrington & James, 1991 and the copying condition of the Rey-Osterreith Figure, Osterrieth, 1944). However, it may be possible that these tests are not sensitive enough, as they do not involve complex object or spatial scene perception (such as the VOSP tests), or because they can be solved on a feature-by-feature basis (such as the Rey-Osterreith Figure), and thus are not dependent on processing conjunctions of features (Lee, Barense & Graham, 2005a). Lee and colleagues (2012) suggested that the hippocampus was involved in higher-order spatial perception. More precisely, this structure seems critical for the discrimination of simultaneously presented complex spatial scene stimuli, but not faces, objects, abstract art or colour (e.g., Lee et al., 2005c). To further evaluate this proposal, we would have liked to test patient VC using paradigms including complex visual discrimination of morphed pairs of images whereby one has to distinguish which of the two images is more similar to a third image, which had originally been used to create the morphed stimuli (e.g., Lee et al., 2005c). Another paradigm could be an oddity judgement task, whereby participants have to select the odd-one-out from an array of simultaneously presented stimuli (e.g., Lee et al., 2005b). This may provide more evidence for the role of the hippocampus in spatial perception *per se*.

The role of the hippocampus in imagining future scenarios has also been subject to intense debate. Thus, Hassabis and colleagues (2007) reported that hippocampal amnesic patients were markedly impaired in constructing new imagined experiences in response to short verbal cues, compared to matched healthy controls. The authors documented that the patients' imagined experiences lacked spatial coherence of an environmental setting and only comprised fragmented images. These findings led to the suggestion that the hippocampus may provide the spatial context of imagined experiences, which may also be reflected in hippocampal amnesic patients' impairment in re-experiencing past events. In contrast, Squire and colleagues (2010) reported five patients with bilateral hippocampal damage who showed a spared capacity to imagine future events. Based on their results, the authors claimed that the ability to imagine future scenarios is independent of the hippocampus. Notably, a recent review revealed that fMRI results in tasks requiring events to be imagined, all of which included naturalistic scenes, consistently reported activation of the anterior hippocampus, more precisely, the medial bank of the anterior hippocampus (Zeidman & Maguire, 2016). VC's hippocampal lesions involved the anterior as well as the posterior hippocampus. Thus, his performance on tasks such as those used by Hassabis and colleagues (2007) and Squire and colleagues (2010) may have contributed to this debate.

In general, do you think that neuropsychology cases could contribute to our understanding of the normal mind? Should these data be considered and if so why?

The contributions of neuropsychology single case studies to the understanding of the mind and brain have been the subject of much discussion, particularly with the development of new, more advanced methodologies. It has been argued that single case studies may not be valuable for generalization to the general population. However, it has also been argued that single case studies or studies carried out on a very small number of patients considered functionally similar may provide experimental evidence against which a variety of classical modular as well as computational models can be tested (Shallice, 2015). This was indeed the case for VC, whose case contributed to challenging the Standard Consolidation Theory (Squire, 1992). Notably, for the memory domain, it has been elegantly argued that revealing single cases of amnesic patients can provide material for "a clear theory that can cultivate and cast light on what is observed, together with an individual with a clear pattern of spared and impaired abilities who, in turn, casts a long shadow over the field" (Rosenbaum, Gilboa & Moscovitch, 2014, p. 105). In-depth investigations of an individual's pattern of spared and impaired abilities may allow for the uncovering of dramatic and stark deficits that are not so easy to detect in group studies. Thus, in-depth single case studies may be valuable starting points for establishing the characteristics of a putative functional syndrome which may in turn lead to making inferences regarding normal function (Shallice, 2015). Last but not least, the value of single case studies also lies in engaging interest and, by doing so, also stimulating further research. Importantly, as shown by the fascination with such cases as HM who continue to inspire researchers and debate (for examples, see Corkin, 2013; Dittrich, 2016), the focus on the individual and the effects of his/her specific injury on his/her behaviour spark interest in the function of the damaged region of the brain more than group studies and statistics. Thus, as elegantly put by Rosenbaum and colleagues "single-case studies stimulate interest, involvement, and sustain commitment to research and clinical applications. They engage the heart as well as the mind" (Rosenbaum et al., 2014, p. 126).

We are now living in an era where ethics committees would like to foresee every step. How much serendipity was involved in your assessment?

We were very lucky at the time of studying VC's case. First of all, VC greatly enjoyed taking part in the experimental investigations. He loved having us visit him at his home; he also liked coming to the department and participating in case demonstrations with students. The testing's sessions never distressed him or tired him in any way. We also had a combination of favourable circumstances that allowed us to have rapid exchanges of ideas between clinicians and researchers with different expertise. We were also working in a climate when the ethical requirements were not as regimented as nowadays. This allowed us to extensively investigate VC's case and to develop and modify our research protocols on the basis of the results we were obtaining. Potentially interesting single cases are not predictable in advance and they need to be investigated with a flexible approach. Instead, nowadays, ethics committees strive to foresee various steps of investigation. In our view this has the consequence of losing out in flexibility and serendipity (for further discussion, see Shallice, 2015). Without any doubt we would have significantly more difficulties in pursuing a study such as the one conducted on VC in the current climate.

References

Aggleton, J. P., & Brown, M. W. (1999). Episodic memory, amnesia, and the hippocampal-anterior thalamic axis. *Behavioral and Brain Sciences, 22*, 425–489.

Bird, C. M., & Burgess, N. (2008). The hippocampus supports recognition memory for familiar words but not unfamiliar faces. *Current Biology, 18*, 1932–1936.

Bird, C. M., Shallice, T., & Cipolotti, L. (2007). Fractionation of memory in medial temporal lobe amnesia. *Neuropsychologia, 45*, 1160–1171.

Blair, R., & Cipolotti, L. (2000). Impaired social response reversal. A case of "acquired sociopathy". *Brain, 123 (Pt 6)*, 1122–1141.

Bonnici, H. M., Chadwick, M. J., & Maguire, E. A. (2013). Representations of recent and remote autobiographical memories in hippocampal subfields. *Hippocampus, 23*, 849–854.

Bozeat, S., Lambon Ralph, M. A., Patterson, K., Garrard, P., & Hodges, J. R. (2000). Non-verbal semantic impairment in semantic dementia. *Neuropsychologia, 38*, 1207–1215.

Brown, M. W., & Aggleton, J. P. (2001). Recognition memory: what are the roles of the perirhinal cortex and hippocampus? *Nature Reviews Neuroscience, 2*, 51–61.

Burgess, P. W., & Shallice, T. (1997). *The Hayling and Brixton Tests*. Bury St. Edmunds, UK: Thames Valley Test Company.

Carlesimo, G. A., Fadda, L., Turriziani, P., Tomaiuolo, F., & Caltagirone, C. (2001). Selective sparing of face learning in a global amnesic patient. *Journal of Neurology, Neurosurgery, & Psychiatry, 71*, 340–346.

Chan, D., Henley, S. M. D., Rossor, M. N., & Warrington, E. K. (2007). Extensive and temporally ungraded retrograde amnesia in encephalitis associated with antibodies to voltage-gated potassium channels. *Archives of Neurology 64*, 404–410.

Cipolotti, L., Bird, C., Good, T., Macmanus, D., Rudge, P., & Shallice, T. (2006). Recollection and familiarity in dense hippocampal amnesia: a case study. *Neuropsychologia, 44*, 489–506.

Cipolotti, L., & Maguire, E. A. (2003). A combined neuropsychological and neuroimaging study of topographical and non-verbal memory in semantic dementia. *Neuropsychologia, 41,* 1148–1159.

Cipolotti, L., Shallice, T., Chan, D., Fox, N., Scahill, R., Harrison, G., Stevens, J., & Rudge, P. (2001). Long-term retrograde amnesia . . . the crucial role of the hippocampus. *Neuropsychologia, 39,* 151–172.

Clark, I. A., & Maguire, E. A. (2016). Remembering preservation in hippocampal amnesia. *Annual Review of Psychology, 67,* 51–82.

Cohen, N. J., & Squire, L. R. (1981). Retrograde amnesia and remote memory impairment. *Neuropsychologia, 19,* 337–356.

Collins, J. A., & Olson, I. R. (2014). Beyond the FFA: the role of the ventral anterior temporal lobes in face processing. *Neuropsychologia, 61,* 65–79.

Coughlan, A. K., & Hollows, S. K. (1985). The Adult Memory and Information Processing Battery (AMIPB). Leeds, UK: St. James's University Hospital.

Corkin, S. (2013). *Permanent Present Tense: The Unforgettable Life of the Amnesic Patient, H.M.* New York: Basic Books.

Crawford, J. R., & Garthwaite, P. H. (2002). Investigation of the single case in neuropsychology: confidence limits on the abnormality of test scores and test score differences. *Neuropsychologia, 40,* 1196–1208.

Damasio, A. R., Eslinger, P. J., Damasio, H., Van Hoesen, G. W., & Cornell, S. (1985). Multimodal amnesic syndrome following bilateral temporal and basal forebrain damage. *Archives of Neurology, 42,* 252–259.

Dittrich, L. (2016). *Patient H.M.: A Story of Memory, Madness, and Family Secrets.* London: Chatto & Windus.

Epstein, R., & Kanwisher, N. (1998). A cortical representation of the local visual environment. *Nature, 392,* 598–601.

Gabrieli, J. D. E., Cohen, N. J., & Corkin, S. (1988). The impaired learning of semantic knowledge following bilateral medial temporal-lobe resection. *Brain and Cognition, 7,* 157–177.

Happé, F. G. E. (1994). An advanced test of theory of mind: understanding of story characters' thoughts and feelings by able autistic, mentally handicapped, and normal children and adults. *Journal of Autism & Developmental Disorders, 24,* 129–154.

Hartley, T., Bird, C. M., Chan, D., Cipolotti, L., Husain, M., Varga-Khadem, F., & Burgess, N. (2007). The hippocampus is required for short-term topographical memory in humans. *Hippocampus, 17,* 34–38.

Hassabis, D., Kumaran, D., Vann, S. D., & Maguire, E. A. (2007). Patients with hippocampal amnesia cannot imagine new experiences. *Proceedings of the National Academy of Sciences, USA, 104,* 1726–1731.

Hodges, J. R., & Patterson, K. (1995). Is semantic memory consistently impaired early in the course of Alzheimer's disease? Neuroanatomical and diagnostic implications. *Neuropsychologia, 33,* 441–459.

Jacoby, L. L. (1991). A process dissociation framework: separating automatic from intentional uses of memory. *Journal of Memory and Language, 30,* 513–541.

Kanwisher, N., McDermott, J., & Chun, M. M. (1997). The fusiform face area: a module in human extrastriate cortex specialized for face perception. *Journal of Neuroscience, 17,* 4302–4311.

Kapur, N., & Brooks, D. J. (1999). Temporally-specific retrograde amnesia in two cases of discrete bilateral hippocampal pathology. *Hippocampus, 9,* 247–254.

Kartsounis, L. D., Rudge, P., Stevens, J. M., 1995. Bilateral lesions of CA1 and CA2 fields of the hippocampus are sufficient to cause a severe amnesic syndrome in humans. *Journal of Neurology, Neurosurgery, & Psychiatry, 59*, 95–98.

Kelley, R., & Wixted, J. T. (2001). On the nature of associative information in recognition memory. *Journal of Experimental Psychology: Learning, Memory, and Cognition, 27*, 701–722.

Kirwan, C. B., Wixted, J. T., & Squire, L. R. (2010). A demonstration that the hippocampus supports both recollection and familiarity. *Proceedings of the National Academy of Sciences, USA, 107*, 344–348.

Kitchener, E. G., Hodges, J. R., & McCarthy, R. (1998). Acquisition of post-morbid vocabulary and semantic facts in the absence of episodic memory. *Brain, 121*, 1313–1327.

Kopelman, M. D., Stanhope, N., & Kingsley, D. (1999). Retrograde amnesia in patients with diencephalic, temporal lobe or frontal lesions. *Neuropsychologia, 37*, 939–958.

Kopelman, M. D., Wilson, B. A., & Baddeley, A. D. (1989). The autobiographical memory interview: a new assessment of autobiographical and personal semantic memory in amnesic patients. *Journal of Clinical and Experimental Neuropsychology, 11*, 724–744.

Lee, A. C. H., Barense, M., & Graham, K. (2005a). The contribution of the human medial temporal lobe to perception: bridging the gap between animal and human studies. *Quarterly Journal of Experimental Psychology, Section B, 58*, 300–325.

Lee, A. C. H., Buckley, M. J., Pegman, S. J., Spiers, H., Scahill, V. L., Gaffan, D., Bussey, T. J., Davies, R. R., Kapur, N., Hodges, J. R., & Graham, K. S. (2005b). Specialization in the medial temporal lobe for processing of objects and scenes. *Hippocampus, 15*, 782–797.

Lee, A. C. H., Bussey, T. J., Murray, E. A., Saksida, L. M., Epstein, R. A., Kapur, N., Hodges, J. R., & Graham, K. S. (2005c). Perceptual deficits in amnesia: challenging the medial temporal lobe "mnemonic" view. *Neuropsychologia, 43*, 1–11.

Lee, A. C. H., Yeung, L.-K., & Barense, M. D. (2012). The hippocampus and visual perception. *Frontiers in Human Neuroscience, 6*, 91.

Macmillan, N. A., & Creelman, C. D. (2005). *Detection Theory: A User's Guide, Detection Theory: A User's Guide* (2nd ed.) Mahwah, NJ, US: Lawrence Erlbaum Associates Publishers.

Maguire, E. A., Frith, C. D., & Cipolotti, L. (2001a). Distinct neural systems for the encoding and recognition of topography and faces. *Neuroimage, 13*, 743–750.

Maguire, E. A., Frith, C. D., Rudge, P., & Cipolotti, L. (2005). The effect of adult-acquired hippocampal damage on memory retrieval: an fMRI study. *Neuroimage, 27*, 146–152.

Maguire, E. A., Henson, R. N., Mummery, C. J., & Frith, C. D. (2001b). Activity in prefrontal cortex, not hippocampus, varies parametrically with the increasing remoteness of memories. *Neuroreport, 12*, 441–444.

Maguire, E. A., Vargha-Khadem, F., & Mishkin, M. (2001c). The effects of bilateral hippocampal damage on fMRI regional activations and interactions during memory retrieval. *Brain, 124*, 1156–1170.

Manns, J. R., Hopkins, R. O., Reed, J. M., Kitchener, E. G., & Squire, L. R. (2003). Recognition memory and the human hippocampus. *Neuron, 37*, 171–180.

Markowitsch, H. J., Weber-Luxemburger, G., Ewald, K., Kessler, J., & Heiss, W. D. (1997). Patients with heart attacks are not valid models for medial temporal lobe amnesia. A neuropsychological and FDG-PET study with consequences for memory research. *European Journal of Neurology, 4*, 178–184.

McClelland, J. L. (2006). How far can you go with Hebbian Learning, and when does it lead you astray? In Y. Munakata & M. H. Johnson (Eds.), *Processes of Change in Brain and Cognitive Development: Attention and Performance*. Oxford: Oxford University Press, pp. 33–69.

McClelland, J. L., McNaughton, B. L., & O'Reilly, R. C. (1995). Why there are complementary learning systems in the hippocampus and neocortex. *Psychological Review, 102*, 419–457.

McKenna, P., & Warrington, E. (1980). *The Graded Naming Test.* Windsor: NFER-Nelson.

Merkow, M. B., Burke, J. F., & Kahana, M. J. (2015). The human hippocampus contributes to both the recollection and familiarity components of recognition memory. *Proceedings of the National Academy of Sciences, 112*, 14378–14383.

Mishkin, M., Vargha-Khadem, F., & Gadian, D. G. (1998). Amnesia and the organization of the hippocampal system. *Hippocampus, 8*, 212–216.

Moscovitch, M., Cabeza, R., Winocur, G., & Nadel, L. (2016). Episodic memory and beyond: the hippocampus and neocortex in transformation. *Annual Review of Psychology, 67*, 105–134.

Nadel, L., & Moscovitch, M. (1997). Memory consolidation, retrograde amnesia and the hippocampal complex. *Current Opinion in Neurobiology, 7*, 217–227.

Nadel, L., & Moscovitch, M. (2001). The hippocampal complex and long-term memory revisited. *Trends in Cognitive Sciences, 5*, 228–230.

Nelson, H. E. (1976). A modified card sorting test sensitive to frontal lobe defects. *Cortex, 12*, 313–324.

Osterrieth, P. A. (1944). Le test de copie d'une figure complexe: Contribution à l'étude de la perception et de la mémoire. *Archives de Psychologie, 30*, 206–353.

Rabin, J. S., Gilboa, A., Stuss, D. T., Mar, R. A., & Rosenbaum, R. S. (2010). Common and unique neural correlates of autobiographical memory and theory of mind. *Journal of Cognitive Neuroscience, 22*, 1095–1111.

Ratcliff, R., Sheu, C., & Gronlund, S. D. (1992). Testing global memory models using ROC curves. *Psychological Review, 99*, 518–535.

Reed, J. M., & Squire, L. R. (1998). Retrograde amnesia for facts and events: findings from four new cases. *Journal of Neuroscience, 18*, 3943–3954.

Reed, J. M., & Squire, L. R. (1997). Impaired recognition memory in patients with lesions limited to the hippocampal formation. *Behavioral Neuroscience, 111*, 667–675.

Rempel-Clower, N. L., Zola, S. M., Squire, L. R., & Amaral, D. G. (1996). Three cases of enduring memory impairment after bilateral damage limited to the hippocampal formation. *Journal of Neuroscience, 16*, 5233–5255.

Rosenbaum, R. S., Gilboa, A., & Moscovitch, M. (2014). Case studies continue to illuminate the cognitive neuroscience of memory. *Annals of the New York Academy of Sciences, 1316*, 105–133.

Rosenbaum, R. S., Stuss, D. T., Levine, B., & Tulving, E. (2007). Theory of mind is independent of episodic memory. *Science, 318*, 1257.

Ryan, L., Nadel, L., Keil, K., Putnam, K., Schnyer, D., Trouard, T., & Moscovitch, M. (2001). Hippocampal complex and retrieval of recent and very remote autobiographical memories: evidence from functional magnetic resonance imaging in neurologically intact people. *Hippocampus, 11*, 707–714.

Sadeh, T., Ozubko, J. D., Winocur, G., & Moscovitch, M. (2014). How we forget may depend on how we remember. *Trends in Cognitive Sciences, 18*, 26–36.

Sanders, H. I., & Warrington, E. K. (1971). Memory for remote events in amnesic patients. *Brain, 94*, 661–668.

Scoville, W. B., & Milner, B. (1957). Loss of recent memory after bilateral hippocampal lesions. *Journal of Neurology, Neurosurgery, & Psychiatry, 20*, 11–21.

Shallice, T. (2015). Cognitive neuropsychology and its vicissitudes: the fate of Caramazza's axioms. *Cognitive Neuropsychology, 32*, 385–411.

Shallice, T., & Evans, M. E. (1978). The involvement of the frontal lobes in cognitive estimation. *Cortex, 14*, 294–303.

Shimamura, A. P., & Squire, L. R. (1987). A neuropsychological study of fact memory and source amnesia. *Journal of Experimental Psychology: Learning, Memory, and Cognition, 13*, 464–473.

Smith, C. N., Jeneson, A., Frascino, J. C., Kirwan, C. B., Hopkins, R. O., & Squire, L. R. (2014). When recognition memory is independent of hippocampal function. *Proceedings of the New York Academy of Sciences, 111*, 9935–9940.

Soares, J. M., Marques, P., Alves, V., & Sousa, N. (2013). A hitchhiker's guide to diffusion tensor imaging. *Frontiers in Neuroscience, 7*, 31.

Spiers, H. J., Maguire, E. A., & Burgess, N. (2001). Hippocampal amnesia. *Neurocase, 7*, 357–382.

Squire, L. R. (1992). Memory and the hippocampus: a synthesis from findings with rats, monkeys, and humans. *Psychological Review, 99*, 195–231.

Squire, L. R., & Alvarez, P. (1995). Retrograde amnesia and memory consolidation: a neurobiological perspective. *Current Opinions in Neurobiology, 5*, 169–177.

Squire, L. R., van der Horst, A. S., McDuff, S. G. R., Frascino, J. C., Hopkins, R. O., Mauldin, K. N., 2010. Role of the hippocampus in remembering the past and imagining the future. *Proceedings of the New York Academy of Sciences, 107*, 19044–19048.

Squire, L. R., & Wixted, J. T. (2011). The cognitive neuroscience of human memory since H.M. *Annual Review of Neuroscience, 34*, 259–288.

Taylor, K. J., Henson, R. N. A., & Graham, K. S. (2007). Recognition memory for faces and scenes in amnesia: dissociable roles of medial temporal lobe structures. *Neuropsychologia, 45*, 2428–2438.

Tulving, E., Schacter, D. L., McLachlan, D. R., & Moscovitch, M. (1988). Priming of semantic autobiographical knowledge: a case study of retrograde amnesia. *Brain and Cognition, 8*, 3–20.

Vargha-Khadem, F., Gadian, D. G., Watkins, K. E., Connelly, A., Van Paesschen, W., & Mishkin, M. (1997). Differential effects of early hippocampal pathology on episodic and semantic memory. *Science, 80(277)*, 376–380.

Warrington, E. K. (1984). *Recognition Memory Test*. Windsor, UK: NFER Nelson Publishing Co. Ltd.

Warrington, E. K. (1996). *The Camden memory tests*. Hove, UK: Psychology Press.

Warrington, E. K., & Duchen, L. W. (1992). A re-appraisal of a case of persistent global amnesia following right temporal lobectomy: a clinico-pathological study. *Neuropsychologia, 30*, 437–450.

Warrington, E. K., & James, M. (1991). *The Visual Object and Space Perception Battery*. Bury St. Edmunds, UK: Thames Valley Test Company.

Warrington, E. K., & McCarthy, R. A. (1988). The fractionation of retrograde amnesia. *Brain and Cognition, 7*, 184–200.

Warrington, E. K., McKenna, P., & Orpwood, L. (1998). Single word comprehension: a concrete and abstract word synonym test. *Neuropsychological Rehabilitation, 8*, 143–154.

Wechsler, D. (1981). *Manual for the Wechsler Adult Intelligence Scale—Revised*. New York: Psychological Corporation.

Weigl, E. (1941). On the psychology of so-called processes of abstraction. *The Journal of Abnormal and Social Psychology, 36*, 3–33.

Winocur, G., & Moscovitch, M. (2011). Memory transformation and systems consolidation. *Journal of the International Neuropsychological Society, 17*, 766–780.

Winocur, G., Moscovitch, M., & Bontempi, B. (2010). Memory formation and long-term retention in humans and animals: convergence towards a transformation account of hippocampal-neocortical interactions. *Neuropsychologia, 48*, 2339–2356.

Yonelinas, A. P. (1994). Receiver-operating characteristics in recognition memory: evidence for a dual-process model. *Journal of Experimental Psychology: Learning, Memory, and Cognition, 20*, 1341–1354.

Yonelinas, A. P., Aly, M., Wang, W.-C., & Koen, J. D. (2010). Recollection and familiarity: examining controversial assumptions and new directions. *Hippocampus, 20*, 1178–1194.

Yonelinas, A. P., Kroll, N. E., Dobbins, I., Lazzara, M., & Knight, R. T. (1998). Recollection and familiarity deficits in amnesia: convergence of remember-know, process dissociation, and receiver operating characteristic data. *Neuropsychology, 12*, 323–339.

Zeidman, P., & Maguire, E. A. (2016). Anterior hippocampus: the anatomy of perception, imagination and episodic memory. *Nature Reviews Neuroscience, 17*, 173–182.

5

WHAT DID AMNESIC ACTOR AB TEACH US ABOUT LEARNING HIS LINES?

Michael D. Kopelman and John Morton

You recently reported the case of an actor, case AB, affected by severe autobiographical amnesia who nonetheless could learn new plays or recite old ones. One of the features of his performance was that he was impaired at the first learning trial, but then showed a learning curve similar to people without memory problems. Can you provide us with some background information about these cases?

AB was an actor of considerable accomplishment. Since coming to prominence in the 1960s, he had appeared in very many stage plays, films for the cinema, and television programmes. He was perhaps best known for his English stage performances, encompassing Shakespeare and the 'classics' as well as modern theatre. There had been a relative lull in his career in middle years, when he had been distracted by other activities, but he remained acting throughout the decades, making a significant comeback in the last decade of his career, during which he received many outstanding notices and reviews for his performances of major theatrical roles.

AB was a highly literate man of wide reading who, in his youth, had studied English literature under the tutelage of F. R. Leavis. He had published a biography of a family member. He wrote poetry, and he was an able pianist. He was also known for his strong political views; he was a pacifist, and he campaigned on many issues, including nuclear disarmament, international peace, and human rights. He was happily married with four adult children.

AB was 66 at the time of his illness and at the pinnacle of his career. In June 2005, AB was speaking at a public meeting, when he suffered a cardiac arrest. He was resuscitated by people present at the scene, including the police, and then by ambulance personnel. The medical records noted five minutes' 'down time' until he was resuscitated. He was taken by ambulance to the local hospital, and then transferred to the intensive care unit of a major acute hospital in London. Two coronary stents were inserted, and later a cardioverter defibrillator was implanted.

AB's recovery was slow. He was initially very confused, disorientated in time and place, and frequently confabulating, often with a grandiose flavour to the confabulations. He was profoundly amnesic, and it was noted that he had very little awareness of the severity of his amnesia. He alternated between intense irritability and apathy. It took two months before he was "beginning to recognise family members". He was transferred to a major Rehabilitation Unit near his home, first as an inpatient, and then as an outpatient. He had to be briefly readmitted to a local hospital when he became very confused again.

AB was first seen by one of us five months after his initial illness. At this stage, he was partially orientated, and confabulating less frequently, but he was still severely amnesic. He was completely unaware of his heart attack or cardiac arrest. He reported that his main problem was "fatigue", and he said that his main goal was to return to work as soon as possible. (At that stage, this was completely out of the question). He thought that there was a current war being fought in the Balkans, as had been the case ten years earlier, but he was unaware of current wars in Iraq or Afghanistan. Ten minutes after discussing the family biography that he had written, AB did not have any recall of this conversation, nor of the fact that he had just been told by the clinician that he (the clinician) had read this book. Examples of AB's confabulations were that he should be performing in a theatre that evening; that he was supposed to be at a centre where he used to work; that he had to attend a Court case, which had occurred 20 years earlier; that he was in foreign city (where he had spent considerable time); and that his (deceased) mother had accompanied him to another medical appointment. AB's wife reported that, at home, he had sometimes been very agitated about these confabulations, wanting to act on them.

Over the course of the next six months, AB's confabulations gradually subsided, but he remained profoundly amnesic. Our experimental studies were conducted in August and September 2006, when AB was still severely memory impaired, but no longer confabulating (Kopelman & Morton, 2015).

AB was followed up over the course of the next four years until his sudden death. On the one hand, AB showed a slow but definite clinical improvement during that time (see the following). Despite his severe memory impairment, AB was able to give acting performances on radio, some quite lengthy, and on film for television or cinema, where he was able to overcome his handicap by either reading the script or by a series of prompts. Remarkably, in the last year of his life, AB even performed on the stage in a part that he had performed before his illness and in which it was possible to have the script in front of him as a prompt. His performance was witnessed by both of the present authors; he certainly did not give the appearance of reading, but performed with great fluency, and he was given a standing ovation by the audience.

On the other hand, AB did not react well to his illness. As his memory very slowly improved, so did his awareness of his handicap. At times, he appeared depressed, irritable, and very apathetic, getting up late in the morning, and having to be encouraged to carry out his personal hygiene. He resumed heavy smoking, having given up cigarettes some years before his illness, and he increased his intake of alcohol, worrying in view of his cardiovascular history. He was given various forms of psychological and psychiatric support. His sudden death was caused by a cerebral haemorrhage, said to be the result of a cerebral aneurysm.

It had been a pleasure to know AB. He was a highly intelligent man of considerable accomplishments and of great charm, when not weighed down psychologically by his illness. Both authors were struck by his immense skills (see the following). After reading silently through a passage of difficult verse or prose, sometimes with complex syntax and semantics, AB would then read it aloud with perfect parsing, fluency, and emphasis, even if it were a passage that he had never read before.

AB underwent a CT brain scan in November 2006 (his defibrillator prevented our carrying out an MRI). Although not of terribly good quality, this 3-D CT scan showed widening of the fronto-temporal sulci and the anterior horns of the lateral ventricles. Coronal slices showed enlargement of the temporal horns, consistent with medial temporal lobe atrophy. An 18 fluoro-deoxy-glucose positron emission tomographic (PET) scan was also carried out in November 2006, and this was compared with the findings from 20 healthy volunteers from Toosy et al.'s (2008) study. AB showed reduced metabolism (glucose uptake) in the thalamus bilaterally, as well as in the medial and ventro-medial frontal and retrosplenial regions (see Figure 5.1). Reduced thalamic and retrospenial glucose uptake in hypoxic-ischaemic brain damage following cardiac arrest had previously been reported by Markowitsch, Weber-Luxenburger, Ewald, Kessler and Heiss (1997) and by Reed et al. (1999).

How did you first realise that this case was interesting?

In the clinic, AB's wife would tell anecdotes emphasising the profundity of AB's amnesia. For example, whilst still in hospital, AB had asked whether his mother would be visiting that day. When his wife replied, "No", AB asked, "Why not?" Mrs AB had to tell AB that his mother had died a couple of years earlier. AB burst into tears, crying "piteously", and this episode was repeated every time that AB was told about his mother's death. In this, AB was re-enacting the experience,

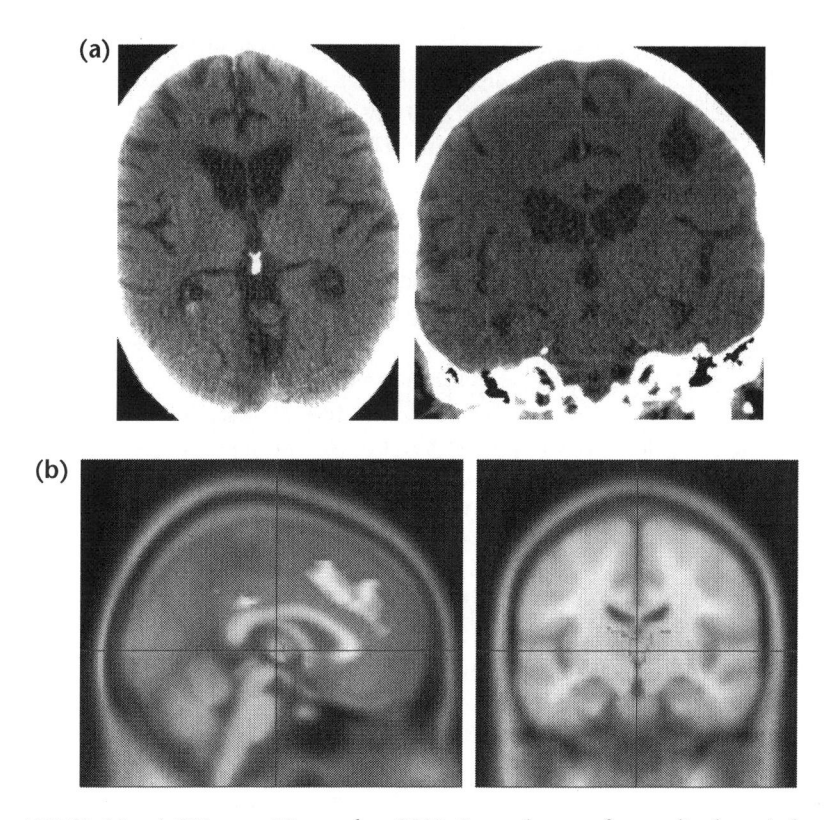

FIGURE 5.1 a) **CT scan, November 2006.** Some degree of generalised cortical atrophy and evidence of bilateral medial temporal lobe atrophy. b) **(Quantified) FDG-PET hypometabolism**. PET scan November 2006 showing reduced glucose uptake, relative to 20 healthy controls (P < 0.001, uncorrected). Reprinted from Kopelman & Morton, Amnesia in an actor: learning and re-learning of play passages despite severe autobiographical amnesia, Cortex, 67, 1–15, 2015.

Copyright (2015), with permission from Elsevier.

described by Milner (1966), of the famous amnesic patient, HM, who cried afresh every time he was told that his uncle had died.

What particularly struck us was something else that Mrs AB told us. AB had been listening on the radio to his own performance (a few years previously) of the principal figure in a classic Shakespearean tragedy. Mrs AB reported that he looked perplexed: "Who has written this?" He did not appear to recognise any of the text. Later, Mrs AB found his copy of the play, and he read it for a while, saying that it looked "more familiar", but he still did not know what play it was. We asked whether AB was better at recognising plays that he had performed earlier in his life than more recently, wondering about a temporal gradient; Mrs AB was not sure, and it was difficult to obtain a clear answer from AB himself. On the other hand, Mrs AB also reported that AB occasionally surprised her by producing correct factual information about members of the family.

Consequently, it occurred to us that it would be very interesting to explore further AB's autobiographical and personal semantic knowledge, not only about general, personal events and facts that had occurred across his life, but more specifically with respect to his autobiographical and factual recollection of plays he had performed in. Moreover, as his stated ambition was to get back to his acting career as soon as possible, we decided to examine his ability to learn passages from plays that he had not performed, as well as his ability to re-learn plays that he had performed at different points in his past. Aware of the literature that new semantic learning might be possible within neocortical brain structures, even when rapid episodic learning has been disrupted by damage to the hippocampal system (Marr, 1971; McClelland, McNaughton & O'Reilly, 1995), we thought that this would be an opportunity to explore this hypothesis in a unique fashion.

Can you summarise the main features of this case?

We found that AB's performance on standard episodic memory tests, and on measures of retrograde amnesia including autobiographical memory, was severely impaired. Moreover, when presented with passages from plays he had not appeared in, AB showed a severe impairment at the first learning trial. However, at subsequent learning trials, he showed a 'normal' learning curve for this semantically and syntactically complex material. On being presented with passages of plays he had performed in the past, AB did not show any recognition of them whatsoever, as one might expect from his severe episodic memory impairment. However, AB showed a striking benefit (savings score) in re-learning passages he had previously performed, compared with new passages, despite not having any autobiographical recall of having performed the re-learned passages before. Moreover, although his initial recall performance in learning these passages was impaired, compared with healthy control actors of similar age and experience, AB demonstrated the same incremental learning rate on subsequent learning trials of the passages as did the controls. An interesting observation was that, when we compared AB's performance on Shakespearean versus non-Shakespeare passages, he showed superior performance on the Shakespeare passages (in terms of percent correct scores), whereas the controls showed identical performance (in terms of percent correct) on Shakespeare versus non-Shakespeare passages. We concluded that, although severely impaired at the first learning trial (on both 'new' and 'old' passages), AB was able to employ his long-established semantic and procedural skills in attempting the task (perhaps especially so on the Shakespeare passages), and that thereafter he showed a 'normal' rate of incremental learning from a lower baseline (Kopelman & Morton, 2015).

What were the case's patterns of impaired and spared abilities?

Design and Methods

The design of this experiment was quite intricate. In order to assess AB's re-learning of passages from plays he had performed, we obtained from his wife a copy of his theatrical curriculum vitae, running from performances in the 1960s (when he was in his 20s) until the time of his illness in 2005 (when he was in his mid-60s). We selected two passages from each of 16 plays he had performed across that period, giving 32 passages in total. We also selected 22 passages from 'control' plays, which he had not performed. These were selected to 'match' as closely as possible the plays which he had performed. Twenty-two of AB's passages were from Shakespeare, and 32 were not from Shakespeare. Passages were selected so that there were no direct clues to their origin, such as proper names or well-known quotations. The mean length of these passages was 46.4 words (± 6.2).

In addition, we developed a Personal Semantic/Autobiographical Memory Questionnaire, related to these passages. After reading each passage aloud, and turning over the sheet on which it was presented so that he could no longer see it, AB was asked a series of questions: Whether the passage was familiar? Who was the author? The name of the play? The character? He was asked whether he had performed this role (1 point). If he said yes, he had performed the role, he was then asked a series of context questions concerning personal semantic facts: when he had performed it (1 point), where he had performed it (2 points), who had directed him (1 point), any memories of the director's style (2 points), and he was asked to name three other people in the cast (3 points). There was a total of 10 points for these items.

Immediately after responding to these items, AB was asked to retrieve two autobiographical memories for events and to describe them in as much detail as possible: one relating to an incident which occurred during a performance of the play (prompt = to do with other players/the audience) and one relating to another incident around that time (prompt = involving relationships, family, or work). If he did not respond immediately, he was given the appropriate prompt. Autobiographical event memories were scored on a 0–3 scale (half-points were allowed) in terms of their descriptive richness and specificity in time and place (compare the scoring procedure for the Autobiographical Memory Interview; Kopelman, Wilson & Baddeley, 1990). In addition, autobiographical memory responses were then re-scored for only 'pure episodic' memories (scores of 3.0 or 2.5 per memory), and, in this instance, scores of 2 or less were re-coded as 0.

In terms of learning or re-learning the new (not performed) or old (previously performed) passages, AB was then shown the passage again, asked to read the passage aloud once more, and then the sheet was turned over face down. He was invited to recite the passage from memory as best he could, and his response was recorded manually and on an audiotape. He then read the passage once more, after which he was asked to recall it again. He was given a maximum of five learning trials (T1 to T5). Alternatively, the trial was ended after perfect recall. These responses were scored in terms of their number of words correct, and then converted to percent correct scores.

After the learning trials were completed, AB was given the name of the play (not having identified any of them correctly before). He was then asked again whether he had performed it in the past. If the answer was now, "Yes", the personal semantic and autobiographical event memory questions were asked again ('post-prompting').

Finding suitable control participants was something of a challenge. They needed to be professional actors, lacking any brain disease, but of equivalent age, eminence, and stage experience. In the end, we obtained three male and two female actors, mainly through AB's contacts and family, who were of similar age (mean = 65.40 ± 3.65). Again, there was substantial preparatory work. We obtained the theatrical CVs from each of these actors, selecting plays that they had performed between the 1960s and 2000s, as well as comparable 'control' plays. As with AB, we selected a mixture of Shakespeare, classical, and more modern plays, sometimes using plays that AB had performed as 'control' plays for the control participants. We then selected passages to administer to each of the controls in the same way as we had done with AB. The overall mean length of the control passages was 47.5 words (± 5.5), which did not differ significantly from the length of AB's passages. The procedure was the same as for AB.

AB's Impaired Abilities

In terms of background neuropsychological tests, AB showed relatively preserved verbal IQ (115), but impaired performance IQ (89) as a result of his cognitive slowing. He showed severe impairment of verbal and visual recall memory and visual recognition memory (all below the fifth percentile) with slightly better performance on verbal recognition memory. He was also impaired on three tests of executive function. On measures of retrograde memory, AB was severely impaired in identifying famous faces from the 1970s to the 2000s with a 'flat' temporal gradient. On the Autobiographical Memory Interview, AB showed impairments across all time periods, but with a fairly pronounced 'temporal gradient' for both personal semantic facts and autobiographical events.

With regard to the experimental tests, AB said, "No", to all passages when asked whether he had performed the play from which each was taken, obtaining zero hits and 100% false negatives. By contrast, the control actors obtained 88.6% hits and 11.4% false negatives for the plays that they had performed. After being told the name of the play, AB obtained 80% correct hits and 20% false negatives, whereas the controls now obtained 100% hits. In brief, before prompting, AB had not identified any of the passages as familiar, and so concluded he had not appeared in the plays from which the passages were taken. The control participants, on the other hand, recognised the vast majority of their passages.

Furthermore, AB could not recall any personal semantic/context details before being prompted with the names of the plays from which the passages were taken. Even after prompting with the name of the play, his mean score (for the passages he had performed) was only 3.53 (± 2.82) out of 10. By contrast, the controls scored a mean of 7.33 (± 3.42) pre-prompting, and 8.60 (± 1.23) after prompting for plays they had performed.

AB was unable to give any autobiographical memories before being told the name of the play (Figure 5.2). Mean scores for controls were 4.17 (± 2.28) for total autobiographical memory, and 3.75 (± 2.38) for 'pure' episodic memories. After prompting with the names of the plays, AB still showed very few responses: his mean autobiographical memory score was 1.25 (± 1.47) versus the controls' mean of 4.94 (± 1.42) (t (58) = 8.83, p < 0.001). Moreover, most of his memories came from the 1960s to 1980s, whereas the controls showed a fairly uniform level of performance from the 1960s to the 2000s. For 'pure episodic' memories, AB's mean score was only 0.37 (± 1.02): he gave only two such responses. The control mean (4.44 ± 1.89) remained significantly higher than AB's (t (58) = 8.15, p < 0.001). In short, AB could not remember any autobiographical memories related to the time when he had performed these plays and, even after being

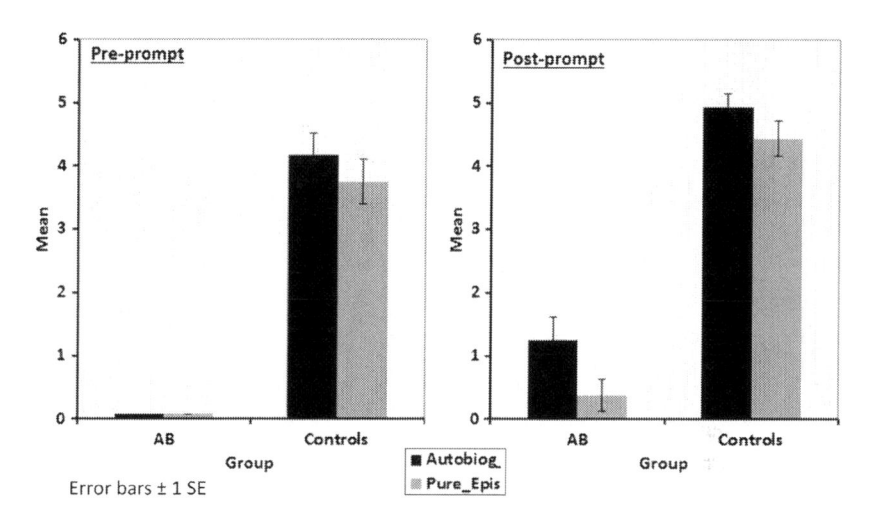

FIGURE 5.2 Autobiographical memory. Autobiographical memory scores (out of 6) and 'purely episodic' autobiographical memory scores pre- and post-prompt (i.e. being given the name of the play). Reprinted from Kopelman & Morton, Amnesia in an actor: learning and re-learning of play passages despite severe autobiographical amnesia, *Cortex*, 67, 1–15, 2015. Copyright (2015), with permission from Elsevier.

prompted with the names of the plays, he could give only very minimal autobiographical memories. By contrast, all five of the control participants showed rich autobiographical memories for facts and events, occurring at the times that they had performed their plays.

In terms of learning or re-learning the passages from the plays, AB showed a severe decrement in performance at the first learning trial, relative to the healthy control actors (Figure 5.3). For the 'new' passages, AB differed significantly from the controls on the first trial (Crawford & Howell, $t = -2.53$, $p = 0.032$; Anova $F(5, 77) = 14.62$, $p < 0.001$, Dunnett post hocs, $p = 0.027$ to < 0.001). For re-learned lines at the first trial, AB was again significantly impaired, relative to controls (Crawford & Howell, $t = -2.52$, $p = 0.033$; Anova $F(5, 98) = 8.30$, $p < 0.001$).

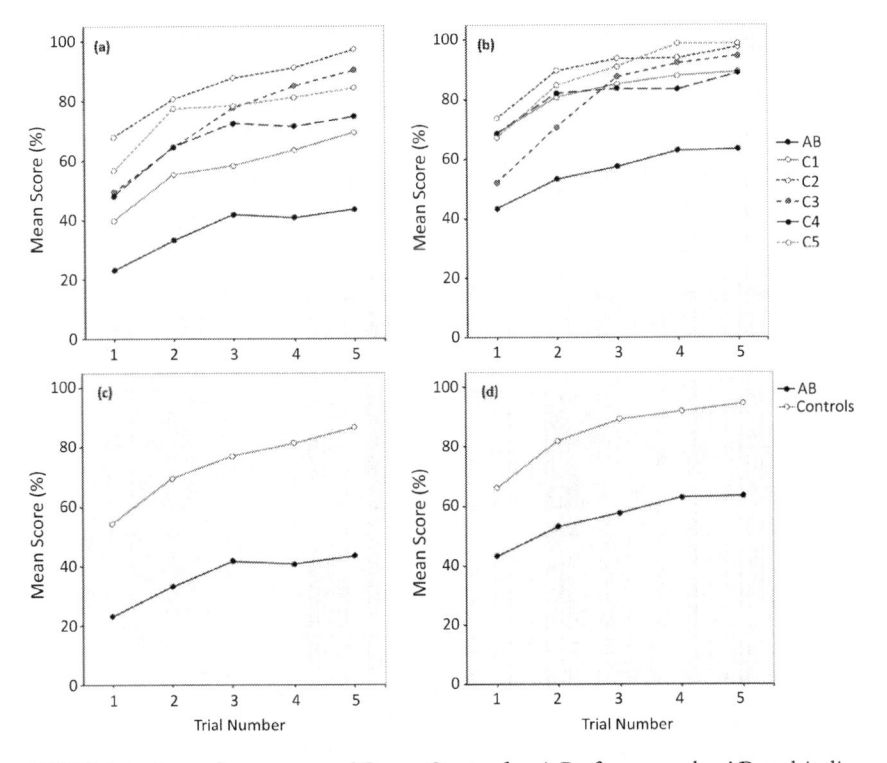

FIGURE 5.3 **Learning curves: AB vs. Controls.** a) Performance by AB and individual controls on learning 'new' passages. b) AB vs individual controls: 'old' (re-learned) passages. c) AB vs control means: new passages. d) AB vs control means: old (re-learned) passages. Reprinted from Kopelman & Morton, Amnesia in an actor: learning and re-learning of play passages despite severe autobiographical amnesia, *Cortex*, 67, 1–15, 2015.

Copyright (2015), with permission from Elsevier.

AB's Spared Abilities

By contrast, Figure 5.3 shows that, after the first trial, AB's incremental learning from the first to the fifth trial was closely in parallel to those of the other actors, and their mean curve, both for new and re-learned lines. We examined the slopes of the learning curves (Trials 1–5) by determining the Beta values of the linear regression for each passage, and then comparing each participant's mean Beta value on a one-way ANOVA with Dunnett post-hoc tests (AB vs each control). We found a significant difference between the participants for new lines ($F (5, 77) = 3.30, p < 0.01$) but, on Dunnett post hoc tests, this was accounted for purely by a difference between one control and AB. Differences between the other controls and AB were minimal and non-significant. Omitting the one control, there were no significant differences between the participants in their learning slopes. On examining Beta values between T1 and T5 for re-learned lines, there was again a significant difference between participants ($F (5, 96) = 4.85, p = 0.001$), accounted for by a difference (on a Dunnett post hoc test) between the same one control and AB; differences between AB and the other participants were negligible and non-significant. Omitting this control, there were no significant differences between the participants ($F (4, 79) = 0.74, p = 0.57$).

When comparing AB's performance on re-learned passages, compared with the new or novel passages, Figure 5.4 shows a significant difference in AB's

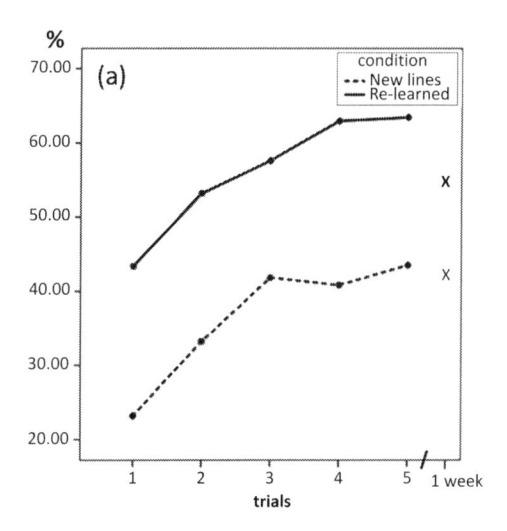

FIGURE 5.4 **AB's learning curves: old vs new passages.** AB's performance in learning 'old' (re-learned) and 'new' passages over five trials and a subset of 1 week's delay. Reprinted from Kopelman & Morton, Amnesia in an actor: learning and re-learning of play passages despite severe autobiographical amnesia, *Cortex*, 67, 1–15, 2015.

Copyright (2015), with permission from Elsevier.

performance at trial 1 (t (52) = 3.70, p = 0.001). In other words, AB showed a significantly better performance in the recall of lines he had previously performed, despite not recognising the lines, the plays that they had come from, or whether or not he had previously performed these lines. In other words, there was an 'implicit' benefit from his having performed these lines before in the absence of conscious awareness of having done so. However, inspection of the curves in Figure 5.4 appears to show similar rates of learning for the 'new' and 'old' lines with relatively good retention after a week. There was a significant main effect of condition (F (1, 52) = 13.28, p = 0.001) and a significant effect of learning trial (F (4, 49) = 15.30, p < 0.001). Yet, there was no significant condition by trial interaction (F (4, 49) = 0.43, p = 0.79), consistent with equivalent learning rates.

We also compared AB's performance on Shakespeare versus non-Shakespeare passages, and we did this also in the controls. Figure 5.5a shows that AB performed significantly better at his Shakespearean passages than his non-Shakespearean ones (F (1, 52) = 11.17, p = 0.002) although, again, there was no difference in the slopes of his learning curves. By contrast, Figure 5.5b shows that the controls performed almost identically on their Shakespearean and non-Shakespearean passages. AB's advantage for Shakespearean passages was virtually the same for 'new' and re-learned passages.

Finally, we gave AB a series of culturally highly familiar quotations ("Once more unto the breach, dear friends, once more"; "Tomorrow, and tomorrow, and tomorrow"; "To be, or not to be: that is the question"; "Now is the winter of our discontent"). Asked to identify the play from which each came, AB did so correctly for 10 out of 16 such lines, and he correctly identified the character for 8 of them. He produced the continuation line on 5 out of 16 occasions and, when cued with the beginning of the next line, he produced the appropriate response in a further 5 out of 8 trials. Moreover, in many cases, AB also volunteered information about whether or not he had performed the role. Tested in the same way, a single control identified all 16 plays correctly, but provided the next line without error in only three cases. In other words, although AB had been unable to identify less familiar passages, or know whether he had performed them, he could recognise and place these culturally much more familiar passages, such as "To be, or not to be".

Do you think that there is anything unique that the report of this case added to our knowledge?

Marr (1971) postulated the notion that a 'sparse' hippocampal system encodes episodic memories, but that slower learning (particularly perhaps of semantic information) can occur within the neocortical system. This hypothesis was later incorporated into McClelland, McNaughton and O'Reilly's (1995) connectionist model of complementary learning systems in the hippocampus and neocortex. As a result, there have been various attempts to show new semantic learning

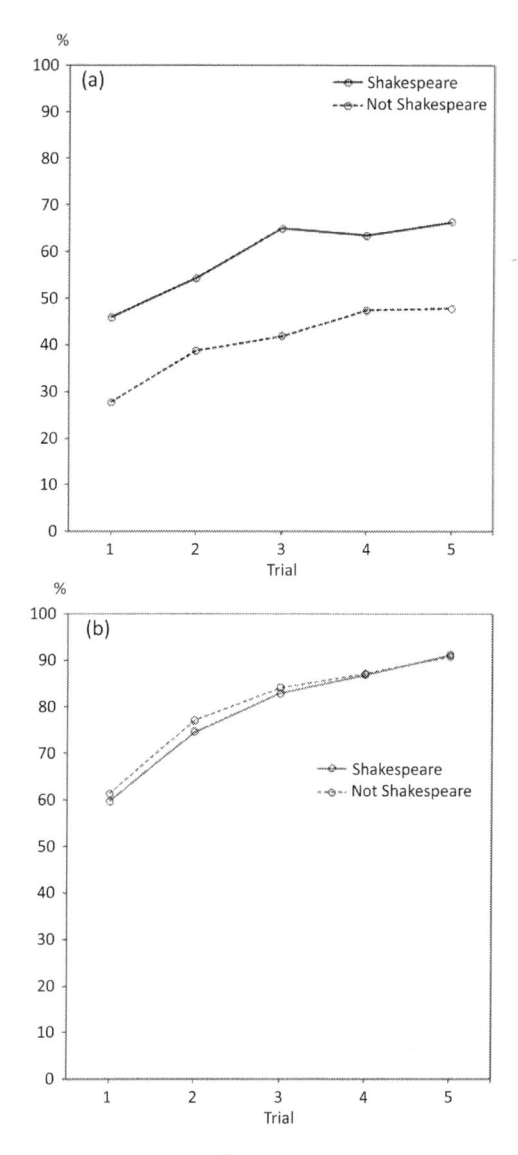

FIGURE 5.5 **Shakespeare vs non-Shakespeare passages.** a) AB. b) Controls. Reprinted from Kopelman & Morton, Amnesia in an actor: learning and re-learning of play passages despite severe autobiographical amnesia, *Cortex*, 67, 1–15, 2015.

Copyright (2015), with permission from Elsevier.

in amnesic patients with extensive bilateral hippocampal or medial temporal lobe damage, but these have mostly employed rather simple tasks, such as learning novel three-word sentences (Tulving, Hayman & Macdonald, 1991; Bayley & Squire, 2002; Stark, Stark & Gordon, 2005, 2008; Sharon, Moscovitch & Gilboa, 2011). Other investigators have examined whether new semantic knowledge has been acquired by amnesic patients since the onset of their disorder (e.g., Verfaellie, Koseff & Alexander, 2000; Westmacott & Moscovitch, 2001; O'Kane, Kensinger & Corkin, 2004; McCarthy, Kopelman & Warrington, 2005). However, these investigations have either examined the acquisition of semantic knowledge using very simple tasks (e.g., three-word learning), and/or they have demonstrated the acquisition of such knowledge by using familiarity judgements, forced-choice recognition, or (occasionally) cued recall, rather than by free recall techniques.

In our investigation, we demonstrated new semantic learning of material that was both longer and more syntactically and semantically complex than that which has been used in previous such studies. A potential explanation of the findings is that we have demonstrated residual 'semantic' learning by a neocortical route. However, AB's learning was not 'slow' insofar that his learning rate (after the first trial) was the same as the mean of the controls. There is no doubt that AB had a severe episodic memory impairment, as demonstrated on his background neuropsychological tests and in terms of his autobiographical memory performance. Our evidence points to a dissociation between episodic and semantic systems as well as between the critical brain structures (hippocampal, neocortical) which underlie such learning.

The findings also point to a pronounced dissociation between autobiographical recollection and personal semantic knowledge, on the one hand, and implicitly stored learning, on the other. This was exemplified by the striking benefit to AB in re-learning verse or prose passages (at least at the first learning trial), relative to his performance on novel or 'new' passages. This benefit or 'sparing' in re-learning 'old' passages was in stark contrast to AB's failure to recognise the re-learned passages as familiar, to know whether he had performed them in the past or not, to be able to recollect aspects of (personal semantic) contextual memory relating to his performance, or to be able to retrieve any autobiographical events from that time.

We were both very struck by AB's ability to read, parse, and extract meaning on the first run-through of even the most complex 'novel' passages, presumably using his long-established actorly procedural and semantic skills. Consistent with this, we noted AB's superior performance on Shakespearean passages, relative to the other play passages he was given, a phenomenon which was not seen in the other actors that we tested. We postulated that AB's exceptional semantic and procedural skills in verse and prose reading may have permitted him to 'chunk' the material skilfully, according to pre-existing schema (Ghosh & Gilboa, 2014). His anterograde memory deficit was evident at the first learning trial, where he consistently performed worse than controls but, thereafter, he was able to learn and retain (for use at subsequent learning trials) longer and much more complex material (in terms of syntax and semantics) than has been demonstrated previously. On top of this, his 'implicit' knowledge of the material, originally embedded in an autobiographical context no longer available to him, further facilitated his performance of previously performed passages. Greenberg and Verfaellie (2010) have reviewed how past autobiographical knowledge can facilitate subsequent semantic learning and retrieval, just as semantic memory can facilitate new episodic learning.

We feel it is worth emphasising that, although the first learning trial unambiguously reflected a number of variables—AB vs control, old vs new, Shakespeare vs other [for AB]—subsequent learning trials proceeded along similar lines for all cases. This suggests that, for AB and controls, after the first learning trial, the prior (implicit) knowledge was no longer used, and learning proceeded simply from the interaction of the trace of the previous trial with the repeated stimulus.

In summary, our study shows: (i) a clear difference between performance on the first learning trial, where AB was impaired, and subsequent incremental learning where he showed a performance comparable to controls, and (ii) a pronounced contrast between his 'implicit' knowledge of plays he had performed in the past, where his use of implicit information was equal to that of the controls, compared with his severely deficient explicit or autobiographical awareness of these performances. We have suggested that this results from AB's long-established semantic and procedural skills, allowing him to 'chunk' the material according to pre-existing schema. What is exceptional about this case is the complexity of the learning that we have demonstrated in a severely amnesic and brain-damaged patient. Further examination of complex learning in amnesic patients, perhaps particularly in those with unusual skills, would be highly relevant to corroborating these findings.

Were there any relevant data that you did not manage to publish on this case?

AB was tested five times between July 2005 and February 2007. He was booked for re-testing at the time of his death (five years after his initial illness), and unfortunately this never happened. However, in the meantime, there had been noticeable clinical improvement in that he was able to report more about recent everyday activities, and he even managed a stage performance with the text in front of him. This took place approximately eight months before his death, and AB talked about his preparation. He said that he practised for approximately an hour to an hour and a half each day. He did not commit all the lines to memory, and did not carry out word-by-word learning. Instead, he said that he "thinks about the performance ... how it will work best. ... By reading aloud, I work on it". Despite this, AB still had a severe amnesia in everyday life: for example, he could not recall at all a therapist whom he had met on approximately 12 occasions previously, and he had only vague recollection about another therapist, whom he had met on more than 20 occasions.

What are the shortcomings of this case?

We were unable to obtain a good quality MRI, because AB had had a defibrillator inserted. We consulted the cardiologist about whether this particular defibrillator would be compatible with an MRI, and she advised caution, so we did not carry it out. A three-dimensional CT scan and a quantified FDG-PET scan carried out in 2006 showed the changes mentioned earlier, indicative of medial temporal lobe atrophy on CT scan, and thalamic and retrosplenial hypometabolism bilaterally on PET. In other words, there was evidence of damage in at least three structures within the limbic circuitry, consistent with AB's severe amnesia. Likewise, the medial and ventro-medial frontal changes on PET may well have accounted for the behavioural changes observed—AB's initially severe spontaneous confabulation and his more persistent irritability and apathy.

Do you remember whether you had any difficulty publishing this report? Or whether there were any issues that reviewers were particularly blunt about?

In general, the reviewers were very constructive and helpful. One reviewer asked whether there was any evidence about AB's learning rate on test material which was not based on passages from plays. We produced data from the verbal recall component of the Doors and People Test, which showed a similar pattern to AB's performance on the play passages—namely, severely impaired initial recall performance with subsequent incremental learning that paralleled that of healthy controls.

The main issue raised concerned the statistical analyses for comparing the slopes of the learning curves in AB, relative to a small group of controls. We had consulted John Crawford (personal communication), who suggested three possible methods: (i) his Singslope method to determine the slope of a patient's regression line in comparison to that of controls, (ii) his Bayesian Standardised Difference Test (BSDT) to compare performance on the initial trials with the final trials in the case and controls, and (iii) his Intra-Individual Measure of Association (IIMA) to examine whether the correlation between AB's performance at trial 1 and trial 5 differed significantly from the correlation in controls (Crawford, Garthwaite, Howell & Venneri, 2003; Crawford & Garthwaite, 2004). He warned us that the first two programs might not run if the assumption of equal variance amongst the controls was violated, and this was the case. Consequently, we ran IIMA but a referee was uncomfortable with this method. We had also compared the beta values for the learning slopes (between T1 and T5) of each participant using a one-way Anova, and this is what we published. The findings were essentially the same.

One reviewer also queried whether we had protected the patient's identity sufficiently. This was a very reasonable question to raise, and was particularly difficult, given that the actor was well known. The actor knew that we were carrying out the study with a view to publication. The manuscript was sent to, and approved by, his widow and daughter before submission, and some very minor changes were made at this point. After receiving the reviewers' comments, we omitted a couple more minor details, which might have led to identification. However, newspaper articles and a book have since been published about this person's amnesia, and consequently it may not be very difficult to identify him, but we have family approval for what we have published. These same issues about confidentiality arise, of course, in connection with the present article.

Scientific journals are making it increasingly difficult to publish single cases, and they often want details changed, and no longer allow the use of real initials (such as HM). There is a danger that changing too many details detracts from the overall veracity of a case description. On the other hand, television documentaries commonly drive a ramrod into issues of confidentiality; and medical and psychologist experts can be seen describing the small details of patients' disorders with frank abandon, often including the name of the patient. Whilst this latter trend is to be deplored, we feel strongly that sober and anonymised scientific reports should not be prevented, if suitable precautions have been taken.

Are there any assessments/paradigms that you would administer now to this individual if he were available?

We would have liked to have tested him on other forms of complex learning, involving both episodic memory tasks and skill acquisition. AB was a reasonably accomplished pianist, and he prided himself on his fencing skills, which had been put to good use in theatrical performances. With some ingenuity, we might have been able to examine his learning and re-learning across a range of skills and expertise.

Do you think this case has been considered by people who developed theories of the normal mind? If yes, how? If no, should they?

Probably not yet, and yes of course they should! The study has shown a dissociation between autobiographical/episodic memory and new semantic learning, but it has also indicated how various skills (such as established semantic and procedural skills and chunking) may interact in learning. This is important for understanding normal memory. Moreover, models of normal memory need to allow for the manner in which highly specific cognitive deficits unfold in brain damage.

In general, do you think that neuropsychology cases could contribute to our understanding of the normal mind? Should these data be considered, and if so, why?

'Normal' psychology needs to set up cognitive models, which are compatible, as just stated, with the manner in which specific deficits arise in brain damage.

Neuropsychological information, particularly from single cases, plays an important role in contributing to that understanding. Moreover, the pattern of cognitive performance may vary across individuals, and there is change through time following brain damage, both of which should be allowed for in our models. The danger of single case accounts is in generalising unduly from individuals (e.g., "Surface dyslexics do this". "Deep dyslexics do that".). However, models of memory or other cognitive function, derived from functional imaging in normals, are vulnerable to many artefacts (e.g., changing of filters, selective reporting of findings), and there is an urgent need to test these models and their predictions against what actually happens to cognitive function in brain damage.

We are now living in an era where ethics committees would like to foresee every step. How much serendipity was involved in your assessment?

Serendipitous was the fact that the patient was seen by the first author, because he had been involved in medico-legal cases with AB's son-in-law, a prominent human rights lawyer. As mentioned earlier, the study partly arose because of comments made by AB and, more particularly, his wife, during clinical sessions when his amnesia was being assessed. The study would have been much more difficult, had the first author complied with the prevalent NHS philosophy of assessing and then discharging patients as rapidly as possible.

The construction of our test material, both for AB himself, and the individual controls, would have been impossible, had we been required to produce all our test material in advance to an Ethics Committee. The modern approach of Ethics Committees, requiring researchers to foresee every step in conducting a study, would have made the present investigation impossible.

References

Bayley, P. J., & Squire, L. R. (2002). Medial temporal lobe amnesia: gradual acquisition of factual information by nondeclarative memory. *Journal of Neuroscience*, 22, 5741–5748.

Crawford, J. R., & Garthwaite, P. H. (2004). Statistical methods for single-case studies in psychology: comparing the slope of a patient's regression line with those of a control sample. *Cortex*, 40, 533–548.

Crawford, J. R., Garthwaite, P. H., Howell, P. H., & Venneri, A. (2003). Intra-individual measures of association in neuropsychology: inferential methods for comparing a single-case with a control or normative sample. *Journal of the International Neuropsychological Society*, 9, 989–1000.

Ghosh, V. E., & Gilboa, A. (2014). What is a memory schema? A historical perspective on current neuroscience literature. *Neuropsychologia*, 53, 104–114.

Greenberg, D. L., & Verfaellie, M. (2010). Interdependence of episodic and semantic memory: evidence from neuropsychology. *Journal of the International Neuropsychological Society*, 16, 748–753.

Kopelman, M. D., & Morton, J. (2015). Amnesia in an actor: learning and re-learning of play passages despite severe autobiographical amnesia. *Cortex*, 67, 1–15.

Kopelman, M. D., Wilson, B. A., & Baddeley, A. D. (1990). *The Autobiographical Memory Interview*. Bury St Edmunds: Thames Valley Test Company.

Markowitsch, H. J., Weber-Luxenburger, G., Ewald, K., Kessler, J., & Heiss, E.-D. (1997). Patients with heart attacks are not valid models for medial temporal lobe amnesia. A neuropsychological and FDG-PET study with consequences for memory research. *European Journal of Neurology, 4*, 178–184.

Marr, D. (1971). Simple memory: a theory for archicortex. *Philosophical Transactions of the Royal Society B Biological Sciences, 262*, 23–81.

McCarthy, R. A., Kopelman, M. D., & Warrington, E. K. (2005). Remembering and forgetting of semantic knowledge in amnesia: a sixteen-year follow-up investigation of RFR. *Neuropsychologia, 43*, 356–372.

McClelland, J. L., McNaughton, B. L., & O'Reilly, R. C. (1995). Why there are complementary learning systems in the hippocampus and neocortex: insights from the successes and failures of connectionist models of learning and memory. *Psychological Review, 102*, 419–457.

Milner, B. (1966). Amnesia following operation on the temporal lobes. In C. W. M. Whitty & O. L. Zangwill (Eds.), *Amnesia* (1st ed.). London: Butterworths, pp. 109–133.

O'Kane, G., Kensinger, E. A., & Corkin, S. (2004). Evidence for semantic learning in profound amnesia: an investigation with patient H.M. *Hippocampus, 14*, 417–425.

Reed, L. J., Lasserson, D., Marsden, P., Lewis, P., Stanhope, N. Guinan, E., & Kopelman, M. D. (1999). FDG-PET analysis and findings in amnesia resulting from hypoxia. *Memory, 7*, 599–612.

Sharon, T., Moscovitch, M., & Gilboa, A. (2011). Rapid neocortical acquisition of long-term arbitrary associations independent of the hippocampus. *Proceedings of the National Academy of Sciences USA, 108*, 1146–1151.

Stark, C. E. L., Stark, S. M., & Gordon, B. (2005). New semantic learning and generalization in an amnesic patient. *Neuropsychology, 19*, 139–151.

Stark, S., Gordon, B., & Stark, C. (2008). A case study of amnesia: exploring a paradigm for new semantic learning and generalization. *Brain Injury, 22*, 283–292.

Toosy, A. T., Burbridge, S. E., Pitkanen, M., Loyal, A. S., Akanuma, N., Laing, H., Kopelman, M. D., & Andrews, T. C. (2008). Functional imaging correlates of fronto-temporal dysfunction in Morvan's syndrome. *Journal of Neurology, Neurosurgery and Psychiatry, 79*, 734–735.

Tulving, E., Hayman, C. A., & Macdonald, C. A. (1991). Long-lasting perceptual priming and semantic learning in amnesia: a case experiment. *Journal of Experimental Psychology: Learning, Memory, & Cognition, 17*, 595–617.

Verfaellie, M., Koseff, P., & Alexander, M. P. (2000). Acquisition of novel semantic information in amnesia: effects of lesion location. *Neuropsychologia, 38*, 484–492.

Westamacott, R., & Moscovitch, M. (2001). Names and words without meaning: incidental postmorbid semantic learning in a person with extensive bilateral medial temporal damage. *Neuropsychology, 15*, 586–596.

6

CASES OF HIPPOCAMPAL MEMORY LOSS

Dr Z, the Engineer and the Glove Cutter

Narinder Kapur and Steven Kemp

This chapter discusses three cases of major memory disorder associated with hippocampal pathology. In all three cases, the clinical picture was initially a diagnostic puzzle that was only solved when the cases came to post-mortem, where the location of pathology was confirmed as the medial temporal lobe. Two articles by Hughlings-Jackson (Hughlings-Jackson, 1888; Hughlings-Jackson & Coleman, 1898) mainly deal with a patient who was variably referred to as Dr Z or Quaerens, but these were in fact one and the same person, a Dr Arthur Myers (Taylor & Marsh, 1980; Critchley & Critchley, 1998). Dr Myers originally wrote up his own case under the pseudonym Quaerens ('The Seeker') in the 1870 issue of the medical journal *The Practitioner* (Quaerens, 1870). The case of Dr Myers (whom we will refer to as Dr Z) is a fascinating account of the subtle cognitive manifestations of epileptiform activity.

Can you provide some background to this case?

On January 10, 1894, a distinguished doctor in London, Dr Anthony Myers, was found dead, having apparently committed suicide with a drug overdose. He lived at 2 Manchester Square, London, and his next-door neighbour at 3 Manchester Square was an eminent neurologist who had been looking after him for many years. That neurologist was none other than Dr Hughlings-Jackson. In an article published in Brain in 1888, Dr Hughlings-Jackson had meticulously described the transient episodes of 'confusion' which had characterised the temporal lobe epilepsy with which Dr Myers (who we will refer to as Dr Z) suffered. Dr Hughlings-Jackson was present at the post-mortem where his colleague, Dr Walter Colman, found a discrete area of softening in the medial part of the left temporal lobe. This post-mortem finding was outlined in a publication by

Hughlings-Jackson and Coleman ten years later. Although other cases of epileptic seizures associated with anomalous experiences had been described in previous years (see Taylor & Marsh, 1980), what made this case all the more remarkable were both the focal lesion found at post-mortem and the detailed documentation of the transient episodes of memory loss, both by the patient himself with all his medical insights, and by Hughlings-Jackson, with whom he was closely acquainted.

Can you summarise the main features of this case?

This was the case of a physician who suffered from what appeared to be temporal lobe seizures since the age of 20 years. These seizures continued till his death, 27 years later. In addition to classic features, such as bucco-facial manifestations that included involuntary salivation or biting of his tongue, Dr Z also suffered from transient disturbances of memory, which would sometimes occur in isolation. A number of the seizure events occurred during the night, and this nocturnal feature has been noted in cases of transient epileptic amnesia, where amnesia on awakening is found in 70% of cases (Zeman & Butler, 2010). His ictal memory episodes would include strong feelings of déjà vu and periods of time for which he would have amnesia, but when he appeared to be functioning normally. It is these latter transient amnesic episodes which presaged the characterisation of the condition that was later coined, 'transient epileptic amnesia' (Kapur, 1990). The wealth of documentation of the transient amnesic episodes, both by Dr Z himself and by Hughlings-Jackson, as well as the subsequent focal left medial temporal lobe lesion found at post-mortem, helped to make this case unique.

What was the pattern of spared and impaired abilities in this case?

Detailed neuropsychological testing was of course not available for this case when it was reported in the 1880s, but the written reports suggest that most of the individual's cognitive functions were relatively spared. Dr Z continued practising as a doctor, and there was no evidence that he suffered from major anterograde memory difficulties in his everyday life. He did not appear to show any evidence of a language disorder. While his subsequent suicide suggests he had been suffering from a depressive disorder at some point in time, major mood changes were not documented either by the patient himself or by Hughlings-Jackson. His impaired abilities were primarily those that were manifest during the ictal events—false recollection when he suffered déjà vu episodes, and major subclinical consolidation failure for new memories during the amnesic episodes. The false recollection was, for example, evident in an episode when Dr Z was on a train, at the second station of four station stops, and when he felt that the conversation he was over-hearing from two strangers was somehow familiar and related to a past recollection. The subclinical consolidation failure was evident by the fact that his next memory was when he arrived at a house half a mile from the fourth station. Dr Z noted,

> I searched my pockets for the ticket, which was to the fourth station, found it gone, and concluded that I must have passed the third station, got out at the fourth, given up my ticket and walked on as I had previously intended, though I had no memory of anything since the second station came ten or twelve minutes previously. I imagine that I had carried out my intention automatically and without memory.
>
> (Hughlings-Jackson, 1888, p. 205)

Do you think this case contributes to our understanding of how the normal mind works?

It is widely believed that memory for facts ('semantic memory'), memory for how to carry out procedures ('procedural memory') and memory for events ('episodic memory') can be dissociated. Since Dr Z could see and examine a patient, yet had no memory for having done so, the case helps to reinforce a view of how memory operates in the normal brain, with discrete episodic memory disturbance being dissociable from other aspects of memory, such as semantic memory, working memory and procedural memory.

Do you think there is anything unique that the report of this case adds to our knowledge?

The main unique contribution of Dr Z is the documentation of transient epileptic amnesia episodes, a number of them subclinical at the time of occurrence. The other contributions are the occurrence of false recollection in his déjà vu episodes, and the fact that the lesion was adjacent to the hippocampus, as confirmed at post-mortem. In the case of subtle episodes of transient epileptic amnesia, which entailed an abnormal state of consciousness that was followed by memory loss for the event, Dr Z's account of one such episode was that in 1871 he was standing at the foot of a college staircase when, 'my attention was suddenly absorbed in my own mental state, of which I know no more than that it seemed to me to be a vivid and unexpected 'recollection'—of what, I do not know'. In the case of his déjà vu episodes, these are exemplified by the one referred to earlier when Dr Z had a strong illusory feeling of familiarity while on a train journey.

Can you specify why this case relevant to the knowledge at the time and would it still be relevant to the knowledge of today?

In the latter part of the 19th century, the characterisation of seizures was still a work in progress, and the association between memory disturbance and the temporal lobes was still a matter of conjecture. Therefore, the anatomo-clinical correlation that emanated from Dr Z's post-mortem was in some respects a major step forward in the documentation of temporal lobe epilepsy and the anatomical basis of human memory. This case remains relevant today, as both false recollection and transient epileptic amnesia (TEA) remain active areas of research. For example, one of the issues in current research is whether instances of loss of autobiographical memory or instances of accelerated long-term forgetting may be due to the presence of subclinical seizures or whether they represent the consequences of a structural abnormality to medial temporal lobe structures (Ricci, Mohamed, Savage, Boserio & Miller, 2015). The detailed characterisation of Dr Z's episodes suggests that subclinical seizures may commonly exist and represent one of the mechanisms underlying memory loss in TEA. When patients present with discrete episodes of autobiographical memory loss, similar to what Dr Z reported, with no obvious psychological explanation, can we speculate—as was the case with Dr Z—that these patients have experienced subclinical memory consolidation failure that has resulted in gaps in their memory and a sense of bewilderment that they cannot remember an episode during which, to themselves and to others, they were behaving perfectly normally (Kapur et al., 1997; Hornberger et al., 2010)?

There are a number of issues raised by this case, and we will consider each of the issues in turn in the light of research findings. These issues relate to (1) déjà vu episodes, (2) transient amnesic episodes, (3) clinical/diagnostic issues and (4) awareness of memory loss.

a. Déjà Vu Episodes

Memory loss or distortions in memory, as often seen in epilepsy, which may also be induced by electrical stimulation of areas in the temporal lobes, are now accepted as reflecting abnormal discharges from the hippocampus, amygdala and related structures (Halgren Walter, Cherlow & Crandall, 1978; Fish, Gloor, Quesney & Oliver, 1993), rather than the neocortex, as originally proposed by Penfield (Penfield & Perot, 1963; cf. Hogan & English, 2012). A number of the 'dreamy states' or 'intellectual aura' described by Dr Z and discussed by Hughlings-Jackson across a series of cases were characterised by feelings of déjà vu—in this case, they were feelings of

> realising that what is occupying the attention is what has occupied it before, and indeed has been familiar, but has been for a time forgotten, and now is recovered with a slight sense of satisfaction as if it had been sought for.
> *(1888, p. 202)*

It is of note that Fish et al. (1993) found a greater right hemisphere focus for déjà vu episodes, and Kovacs et al. (2009) reported right hippocampal hyperperfusion during déjà vu episodes. However, Heydrich, Marillier, Evans, Blanke and Seeck (2015) reported that déjà vu could occur in cases of both right and left temporal lobe epilepsy, and Takeda et al. (2011) found that in an epileptic patient with persistent déjà vu, a déjà vu episode was associated with hyperperfusion in the left medial temporal lobe. It is of note that Dr Z's lesion was in the left uncus— 'a small cavity, collapsed and almost empty, with indefinite walls, situated in the uncinated gyrus, five-eighth inch below the surface just in front of the recurved tip of the uncus' (1898, p. 587). The right hemisphere activation may be explained by the fact that the actual subjective experience of déjà vu may take the form of familiarity misrecognition for the visual environment, or it may have a more general/verbal nature. In the case of the Fish et al. (1993) study, the emphasis was probably on the visual manifestations of déjà vu, whereas for patient Z, the content of the déjà vu experience seemed to be related to thoughts and verbal statements (e.g., when he was reading poetry and found lines to be familiar).

Patient Z's illusion of familiarity was quite often dramatic: 'The line I am reading or just going to read seems somehow familiar, or just what I was trying to recollect, though I may never have seen or heard it before' (1888, p. 203). While such phenomena have frequently been described in cases of temporal lobe epilepsy, both in terms of spontaneous experiences and those induced by brain stimulation, there appears to have been little attempt to dissect the cognitive components of such experiences. An interesting, related observation that has been reported in the experimental psychology field is that of false memories—these are induced by asking subjects to recall word lists where a target word (e.g., sleep) is missing, but their high-associated words (e.g., bed, rest, awake) are present (Roediger & McDermott, 1995; Jou & Flores, 2013). In the laboratory setting, participants will not only sometimes recall the target lure word in a free recall task (in this case 'sleep'), but more commonly in recognition memory tests, they will make false-positive responses to these target lure words, indicating that they were present in the original word list. It would be interesting to see if patients with temporal lobe epilepsy, who may be susceptible to feelings of déjà vu, and those amnesic patients who show an increased tendency to produce confabulatory responses, would demonstrate a greater degree of false-familiarity effects in paradigms such as those used by Roediger and McDermott. If so, this may point to whether there are distinct or overlapping mechanisms underlying false recollection in laboratory and in everyday settings. Such findings would be additionally informative in the context of a report of reduced false recollection of lure items in patients with a bilateral hippocampal and a right hippocampal focus to their temporal lobe epilepsy (Chiu et al., 2010).

b. Transient Amnesic Episodes

The term 'transient epileptic amnesia' (TEA) (Kapur, 1990) was introduced to describe episodes of memory loss which may be the sole or predominant manifestation of seizure activity. The term may usefully classify some of the attacks shown by Dr Z and described earlier, especially those that were observed by colleagues

Cases of Hippocampal Memory Loss 115

and where no abnormality of behaviour was apparent apart from memory loss. One such episode, called a 'petit mal' by Dr Z, is described as follows,

> In the same way a petit mal when I was playing lawn tennis did not in the opinion of my adversary make my strokes or judgement of pace and position of balls to be struck any worse than normal. I had no recollection of the strokes during a minute or two.
>
> *(Hughlings-Jackson, 1888, p. 204)*

As outlined in Figure 6.1, it is important to distinguish such episodes from post-ictal confusional states that follow classical temporal lobe seizures where there is loss of consciousness, where behaviour may appear to be quite normal for a period of time and where there is no subsequent recollection of the behaviour in question—it is quite possible that the epileptic event of Dr Z that was observed in detail by Hughlings-Jackson himself (Hughlings-Jackson & Coleman, 1898, p. 582) did represent a case of post-ictal confusion or 'unconsciousness' after an attack, the term 'unconsciousness' being one adopted by Hughlings-Jackson. Hughlings-Jackson makes the interesting comment: 'On another occasion, there were post-epileptic actions by Z during "unconsciousness", of a kind which in a man fully himself would be criminal, and must have led to very serious consequences had not, fortunately, his condition be known' (Hughlings-Jackson & Coleman, 1898 p. 584).

Cases of TEA may be manifest in a variety of forms, but typically the episodes are shorter and more frequent than transient global amnesia. The degree of anterograde memory impairment (inability to retain new information) is more variable than in transient global amnesia, and with some cases only manifesting some degree of retrograde amnesia (inability to recall events before the onset of

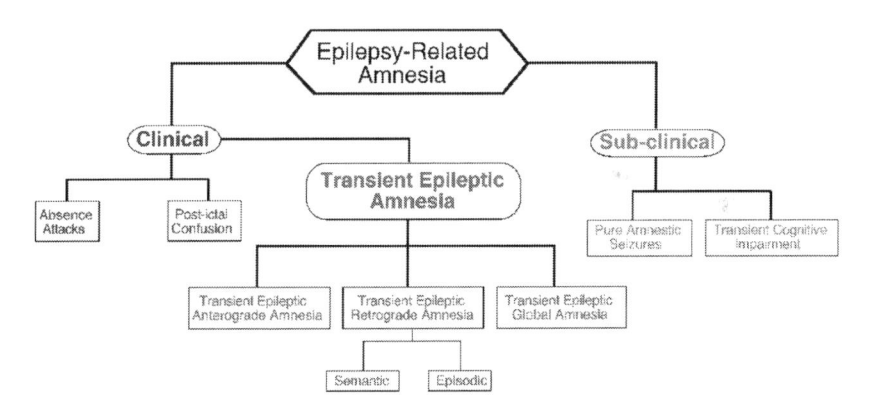

FIGURE 6.1 A schematic representation of the various forms of acute memory loss associated with epilepsy.

an insult to the brain). There is also a tendency for TEA attacks to occur more frequently in the morning. Although one of us found (Kapur, 1990) that in three cases of TEA, out of a sample of four cases, there was a greater left temporal lobe focus to the EEG abnormality, bilateral medial temporal lobe abnormality has also been implicated in these types of amnesia (Palmini, Gloor & Jones-Gotman, 1992; Butler et al., 2013). Here again, it is of interest that the abnormal focus in Dr Z was found in the left uncus. It needs to be borne in mind that more sophisticated neuropathological examination might have yielded evidence of right hippocampal/parahippocampal abnormality and that in any case spread of seizure discharge to contralateral medial temporal lobe structures may have resulted in effective bilateral abnormality (Halgren et al., 1991).

TEA itself is best conceived of as a term to describe a type of attack that may occur in temporal lobe epilepsy, rather than a disease classification. It is therefore important to be sure that the amnesic episodes are not post-ictal confusional states related to complex partial seizures, and that they do not reflect petit-mal/'absence' attacks. The following format may be of practical help in the diagnosis of the condition. Where transient amnesic episodes may be classified as TEA, the clinician should ask the following questions:

1. Are there instances of loss of established memories (facts, personally experienced events, etc) or of retaining new information? Dr Z refers to episodes where he noticed a 'temporary loss of memory for habitually familiar names or faces' (Hughlings-Jackson, 1888, p. 203). In the case of past memory loss ('retrograde amnesia'), it is useful to note the temporal features of any such amnesia (how far did it go back?), together with information on how quickly this amnesia resolved or 'shrunk'.
2. Apart from the memory loss, was the behaviour of the patient abnormal during the episode? Important features include any disorganised behaviour, incoherent or repetitive speech, etc. Dr Z clearly had some abnormality in behaviour during certain episodes for which he had complete amnesia (e.g., there were errors in his written notes made during a consultation, for which he subsequently had amnesia. Thus, he made word substitution errors, initially writing 'years' when he meant 'weeks' and writing 'legs' when he meant 'arms' (Jackson & Coleman, 1898, p. 584).
3. Are there witnessed descriptions of the amnesic attacks? Witnessed information is important in order to get an accurate description of the behaviour of the patient during the attack, and in particular to confirm the absence of motor or any other physical manifestations of epilepsy. In the case of Dr Z, some attacks were witnessed, although the only witnessed account appears to be that relating to Hughlings-Jackson's own observations. Hughlings-Jackson (1898) notes that a number of Dr Z's attacks were witnessed, some of them, 'by a highly accomplished medical man' (presumably another doctor), and that this particular observer did not find evidence of minor changes (grunt

sounds, lip-smacking movements) that might accompany the episodes of acute memory disturbance.
4. Does the patient have subsequent amnesia for the episode in question? It is important to realise that in some cases of epilepsy-related transient amnesic attacks, the behaviour of the patient may have been quite normal during the episode in question, without any abnormal behaviour or impairment in recalling old memories/retaining new memories, but at a subsequent time, the patient will show amnesia for the period in question (Palmini et al., 1992; Kapur, 1990). In some cases, the patient will suddenly find himself/herself in a different location and realise that there is a gap in his/her past that he/she cannot account for. However, in other cases, there may be no spontaneous awareness of an episode of amnesia. Such episodes of 'subclinical amnesia' may never come to the notice of the patient or anyone else, unless a subsequent discussion or event somehow relies on the memory of this 'missing period'. By their very nature, these particular episodes are notoriously difficult to document.
5. Is there evidence of an epileptogenic lesion—classical epileptic seizures, spike waves on EEG recording, brain imaging evidence of temporal lobe pathology, or reduction of frequency/severity of attacks after the introduction of anti-convulsant medication? Some form of transient epileptic amnesia could be seen to be a type of 'Todd's paralysis' (Morrell, 1980). (In Todd's paralysis, a minor seizure involving the motor cortex results in transient motor weakness.) One might argue that, where the clinical manifestations of a complex partial seizure are very subtle, it may never be possible, without depth electrode recordings from limbic structures and video monitoring, to be certain that a case of TEA was not one of post-ictal amnesia.

Where there is no witnessed information, or where there is no firm evidence of an epileptogenic lesion, but where the attacks are strongly suspected of being instances of TEA, then we would recommend a diagnosis of *possible TEA* be made. Where there is a wide range of supportive evidence, including witness information, then we would suggest that a diagnosis of *probable TEA* be made.

c. Clinical/Diagnostic Issues

The feeling of dread noted by Dr Z (Jackson & Coleman, 1898, p. 582) is often found in temporal lobe epilepsy, and probably relates to the involvement of the amygdala (Fish et al., 1993), which presumably in the case of Dr Z resulted from after-discharges from the uncus lesion. Dr Z uses the term 'petit mal' to describe some of his attacks, but they would probably be classified as 'simple partial seizures' in current terminology, since both are largely synonymous and refer to clinical seizure activity without loss of consciousness.

From a clinical point of view, some of the attacks that Dr Z suffered vividly bring home the diagnostic dilemma when a clinician is faced with minor behavioural changes, but where there is no physical or laboratory evidence of structural brain abnormality. When he first experienced his attacks, Dr Z, 'regarded the matter playfully and as of no practical importance' (Hughlings-Jackson, 1888, p. 184). This was three years before he had his first grand mal seizure (what Hughlings-Jackson calls a 'haut mal'). Just as Alzheimer's disease is often a purely neuropsychological diagnosis, with no reliable biological marker currently available to help in the clinical decision process, in a similar fashion, some forms of epilepsy can only be diagnosed on the basis of careful neuropsychological assessment. This needs to include, if possible, assessment of very long-term retention and performance on tests of retrograde memory (cf Kapur et al., 1997).

d. Awareness of Memory Loss

From a theoretical point of view, transient amnesic episodes, such as those experienced by Dr Z, provide a dramatic illustration of the disconnection that may occur at different levels of the memory awareness system. Purposeful, coherent activity may appear to take place—with no awareness of any abnormality on the part of the patient or a close observer—but significant errors may be present in parts of the performance of the individual (e.g., Dr Z during his consultation with one of his patients, where his subsequent notes were found to contain semantic/grammatical errors). At a further level, normal activity may appear to take place, this time without evidence of any performance errors, but the individual may have no subsequent recollection of the period in question. In a sense, this is little different from what may pertain for a number of sample behaviours of a patient with a classical amnesic syndrome—it may be possible to have a normal conversation with the individual or for that person to perform a number of everyday tasks without error, but there will be no subsequent recall of events that took place during that period of time. In one form of these attacks of 'subclinical amnesia', the dissociation between awareness and amnesia is complete and absolute, with the individual having no conscious awareness that memory processes have returned to normal or even that anything abnormal ever took place. In another form of the attacks, there may be a sudden realisation of a memory gap—this may be precipitated by, for example, the individual finding himself/herself in a different location to one where he/she was at the beginning of the period of subclinical amnesia. In this case, there is an awareness that the 'stream of consciousness' has been broken. At each of these levels of awareness and disconnection, it would seem that normal neural feedback/loop mechanisms are at fault—this may be due to disturbance of an overall executive/control mechanism, perhaps located in the frontal lobes, or it may represent the involvement of one or more connections between discrete processing which give the individual continuous feedback with regard to integrity of cognitive functioning. If one postulates that there are at least two universal, continuous 'streams of consciousness', one for awareness of time and the other for awareness of place, then the evidence from phenomena such as those shown by Dr Z would seem to suggest these levels of consciousness can be disconnected from the mechanisms governing the consolidation of more discrete events into long-term retention (see also case 2 of Palmini et al., 1992). This level of disconnection is seldom seen in the classical amnesic syndrome, and TEA episodes may be one of the few handles with which to examine such dissociations.

What are the shortcomings of this case?

The main shortcomings of this case are, of course, the absence of data that we currently take for granted—a detailed neuropsychological profile, brain imaging and EEG recordings.

Are there any assessments/paradigms that you would administer now to this individual if they were available?

We would certainly carry out detailed testing of autobiographical and public events memory, in addition to conducting a comprehensive neuropsychological assessment. We would also administer paradigms such as the Deese-Roediger-McDermott paradigm to examine false recollection in order to see if the mechanisms underlying the two forms of false memories are similar. We would use a long-term accelerated forgetting paradigm to determine whether there was rapid forgetting over longer intervals. In addition to MR imaging, we would arrange for video telemetry in an attempt to capture some of his ictal amnesic episodes in vivo.

Do you think this case is still informative now? Are we now better able to interpret the patterns of spared and impaired abilities? If so, in what way?

The case remains informative, mainly in the context of the characterisation of transient epileptic amnesia episodes. With a multiple-systems view of memory, and our knowledge of subclinical seizures from depth electrode in vivo EEG recordings, we are now better able to understand the episodes of memory disturbance that at the time appeared quite peculiar. The case is also significant in generally teaching clinicians about the importance of careful observations and documentation of clinical features and the importance of subtle symptoms, as noted by Compston in his commentary on Hughlings-Jacksons' papers on Dr Z (Compston, 2007).

Are you aware of other historical cases who add to our understanding of memory loss?

In what follows, we present two patients with temporal lobe epilepsy who underwent respective surgery, with detailed outcome data that influenced the contemporary understanding of human memory and modern epilepsy surgery.

After his retirement in 1974, Wilder Penfield published a paper (Penfield & Mathieson, 1974) setting out the case history of two patients that were first published by Penfield and Brenda Milner in the Archives of Neurology in 1958. Through careful neuropsychological testing, Milner had already shown that unilateral temporal lobectomy for the relief of epilepsy did not result in dense anterograde amnesia, but that verbal memory decline could occur following left resective surgery. Penfield's (1958) paper post-dated Scoville and Milner's (1957) publication showing that removing bilateral hippocampal zones had an ill-fated neuropsychological outcome. Penfield's (1958) contribution to the literature was that, in a few rare cases, partial left temporal lobectomy can result in a catastrophic memory outcome. The original 1958 and further 1974 papers were reflections on how this can happen, with post-mortem findings documented in 1974. Here we would like to offer further reflections on Penfield's two classic case studies reported in the 1974 paper in the context of the current literature.

Can you provide some background to these cases?

Patient 1, a civil engineer, developed seizures in 1940 that became more frequent and severe, resulting in admission to the Montreal Neurological Institute in 1946. Seizure semiology included a staring appearance of the eyes, followed by head turning usually to the right, and motor and oro-alimentary automatisms. He did not suffer generalised convulsions. EEG showed slow and sharp waves localised in the left temporal region. A 'pneumoencephalogram' (CT scanning was not introduced until 1972) showed moderate ventricular enlargement, but no focal deformity of either lateral ventricle. Patient 1 was concerned about losing his job and was amenable to surgery. He underwent two neurosurgical procedures. In 1951, 4cm of his left lateral temporal lobe was removed, leaving the hippocampus and uncus intact for fear of leaving the patient aphasic. He made a good recovery and had several years of reduced seizure frequency, but in 1951, his seizure control deteriorated. Therefore, Patient 1 underwent a second craniotomy, this time with the removal of the uncus and anterior half of the left hippocampus. In spite of pre-operative evidence of left temporal lobe epilepsy, his seizures continued and EEG during a seizure showed a right temporal lobe abnormality, spreading to the left. Following the second operation, the Montreal team were shocked to discover that Patient 1 had persisting severe anterograde amnesia together with a marked retrograde amnesia, which improved. Brenda Milner carried out extensive neuropsychological testing and found that speech, perception, procedural memory and general cognitive functioning were preserved. The team suspected latent pathology in contralateral right temporal lobe structures and when Patient 1 died of a pulmonary embolism, post-mortem confirmed a pale and shrunken right hippocampus consistent with hippocampal sclerosis. Excision of the left hippocampus extended back to leave 22 mm of its posterior portion intact. The team concluded that Patient 1's memory deficit was due to the removal of functional left hippocampal structures in a patient with minimal right hippocampal function.

Patient 2 reported by Penfield and Milner (1958) and Penfield and Mathieson (1974) was a glove cutter by trade and underwent a left temporal lobectomy in 1952 including excision of the whole left hippocampal zone (more extensive than Patient 1). Following surgery, he was left with similar memory deficits to Patient 1, but his retrograde memory loss was more extensive and improved little over time.

Although markedly compromised by their severe memory loss, both the civil engineer and the glove cutter were able to continue to earn a living. Brenda Milner commented that each 'had preserved memory of his special skills' (Penfield & Mathieson, 1974, p. 148). The engineer continued to produce complex drawings, but if distracted, he would forget what he had drawn. The glove cutter was still a proficient glove cutter.

Have these two cases added to our knowledge?

There are many lessons to be learnt from these two patients and they serve as a reminder of how studying brain lesions and reporting negative results (i.e., memory deficits following unilateral temporal excisions) can advance thinking and improve treatment for patients. In carefully assessing and reporting their surgical and neuropsychological outcomes, Penfield and Mathieson acted as exemplary academic clinicians. It is right to acknowledge their significant contribution to epilepsy surgery and neuropsychological function and to pick up this story from where they left off.

Mesial temporal lobe epilepsy with hippocampal sclerosis is now a well-characterised disorder. The typical clinical history is early febrile convulsions, followed by a latent period, with seizure occurrence in mild to late childhood, and seizures becoming refractory to antiepileptic drugs (Baulac, 2015). Seizures have characteristic temporal lobe semiology. Auras are common, typically an ascending epigastric sensation sometimes accompanied by fear. Mental hallucinations such as déjà vu often occur. Consciousness becomes impaired, with staring or motor features and automatisms, which are typically oro-alimentary (lip-smacking) or gestural (fiddling or picking). Dysphasia is common with seizures that occur in the left hemisphere. There is usually a period of post-ictal confusion/disorientation. MRI (brain) scanning is a key diagnostic procedure, with hippocampal sclerosis usually visible on coronal slices. There are also characteristic EEG and neuropsychological features. Due to reorganisation of function, the neuropsychological profile is not always lateralised (Gargaro et al., 2013).

Ictal head turning was a feature of significance in Penfield's (1974) paper. Rémi et al. (2011) report both contralateral and ipsilateral head turning in temporal lobe epilepsy, with ipsilateral head turning generally preceding contralateral head turning in temporal lobe epilepsy, whereas all patients with frontal lobe epilepsy displayed contralateral head turning. It is now understood that hippocampal sclerosis is unilateral in about 80 per cent of neurosurgical cases (Panayiotopoulos, 2005)—therefore it is only in a significant minority of cases that hippocampal sclerosis is a bilateral disease.

What techniques were developed to safeguard against poor memory outcomes following epilepsy surgery?

In 1960, Wada and Rasmussen developed the amobarbital test (commonly known as the Wada test) to help safeguard against poor neuropsychological outcomes. The basis of the test was that by 'shutting down' one hemisphere using a drug, the viability of the other hemisphere could be tested, and side of pathology delineated. The procedure is repeated on the opposite hemisphere and surgery avoided when both temporal lobes are deemed to be nonviable. Although originally developed to lateralise language, the intracarotid amobarbital procedure or Wada test was later adapted to establish that the not-to-be-operated hemisphere of the brain could support memory (Loring, Meador, Lee & King, 1992).

There is no standardised procedure for the Wada test and individual centres tend to use their own variation on the procedure. However, the technique follows the basic principle of transiently anaesthetising each hemisphere of the brain, ipsilateral and then contralateral to the lesion (usually with sodium amytal) and before the effect wears off, testing language and presenting material-to-be-remembered. Recall is then tested once the EEG has returned to normal, with encoding having taken place in just one hemisphere. This became the standard technique to determine which hemisphere of the brain is eloquent and whether the hemisphere contralateral to the lesion to be resected can support memory prior to unilateral epilepsy surgery involving temporal lobe structures.

The Wada test has gone through three phases. First, as a standard pre-surgical investigation. Second, falling out of favour as people began to question how well it predicted post-operative memory functioning and as functional imaging, mainly fMRI and to a lesser extent magnetoencephalography (MEG), became available clinically. Third, and most recently, there has been a slight reversal in this trend, with many surgery centres selectively using the Wada test in complex cases and there being an increasing appreciation that the Wada test and functional imaging are not directly competing technologies. The arguments for and against Wada testing continue to be presented and debated at most international epilepsy conferences and Sharan, Ooi, Langfitt and Sperling (2011) published such a debate from a meeting of the American Epilepsy Society.

Today, clinicians and neurosurgeons anxious not to surgically treat epilepsy at the expense of functional memory loss have the Wada test and fMRI at their disposal, as well as more advanced neuropsychological assessment. Current thinking is that whilst fMRI and Wada test findings are generally in good agreement for language laterality, fMRI memory paradigms have been slow to develop and concordance rates for fMRI memory activation and Wada test findings are not always high (Bauer, Reitsma, Houweling, Ferrier & Ramsey, 2014; Dupont et al., 2010). Although fMRI is on the ascendant, current thinking is to view fMRI and Wada as complementary approaches to predicting neuropsychological risk. This is a luxury that Penfield and his colleagues did not have.

Have these cases added to our knowledge of human memory?

Yes—the pioneering work of Scoville and Milner (1957) and Penfield and Milner (1958) on temporal lobectomy resulted in a period of great learning about human memory, with the dominant paradigm being the model of material specificity. The notion that left and right temporal lesions predominantly affect verbal and non-verbal memory respectively remains a key principle in pre-epilepsy surgery work-up and risk appraisal. In spite of the influence of this model and its parsimonious pragmatism, it is increasingly coming under pressure. Baxendale (2008) points out that, on a testing level, the logic is challengeable because neuropsychological tests and individuals differ in the ability to verbalise non-verbal tests and use imagery for verbal tests. Hence, there is not a straightforward verbal route to performance on verbal tests and not a straightforward visual route to performing well on non-verbal tests. A more theoretical and fundamental challenge to the model of material specificity comes from Saling (2009). This detailed paper sets out challenges to the key assumptions of the model of material specificity and argues that performance is task-specific rather than strongly and literally lateralised along verbal and non-verbal lines. Saling argues that left mesial temporal lesions can affect aspects of non-verbal as well as verbal memory and right mesial temporal lesions can affect verbal memory. There is, then, emerging evidence that the original ideas of material specificity have become too restrictive and a more neuropsychologically nuanced understanding is warranted.

Have these cases contributed to our understanding of specific memory systems?

In spite of severe anterograde amnesia, both of Penfield's patients could continue in their respective professions, one as a glove cutter and the other producing engineering drawings, and neither patient appeared to report deterioration of pre-existing skills.

The dissociation of episodic memory and procedural memory is now well established. One well-known and dramatic example of this is Clive Wearing, an accomplished musician who suffered herpes simplex encephalitis (Wearing, 2005). Wearing was left with a profound amnesia and unable to form any new memories and lived in a constant state of thinking he had recently woken up, without recall of recent past events. He is also reported as having significant retrograde amnesia. Yet, Wearing could still play the piano and conduct a choir in spite of having no knowledge of how he acquired these skills. A more recent case of preserved procedural memory is reported by Wilson and Hughes (1997). Patient JC was a young man who became amnesic following a ruptured left posterior cerebral artery aneurysm. Neuropsychological assessment showed the features of a pure amnesic syndrome, with severe anterograde amnesia and intact higher neurocognitive functions. Performance on forced-choice recognition memory tests was at chance. In spite of a dense amnesia, JC was able to learn how to type and he learnt how to restore furniture at college. He was not consciously aware of how he acquired these skills. He was able to apply these newly acquired skills and work successfully as a furniture restorer. With guidance from Wilson and her team, JC was able to compensate for his dense anterograde amnesia via external and internal compensation strategies. Imaging data from healthy individuals show that skill acquisition and procedural memory are mediated by the basal ganglia, cerebellum, prefrontal cortex and supplementary motor area (Wolk & Budson, 2010; Mochizuki-Kawai, 2008; Halsband & Lange, 2006), areas that were largely spared both in the case of JC and Clive Wearing.

These cases show that procedural memory can be relatively preserved following damage to classic limbic system structures involved in episodic memory, but what about remote memory?

The balance of evidence shows that temporal lobe epilepsy and resective surgery can to some degree affect remote memory in the form of memory for public events and autobiographical memory (Bergin, Thompson, Baxendale, Fish & Shorvon, 2000; McAndrews & Cohn, 2012), with particularly prominent loss of remote memory found in TEA (Butler & Zeman, 2008). Compared to work on episodic memory, research on remote memory has progressed slowly and has shown that temporal lobe epilepsy patients frequently report poor recall for past public events or loss of vividness for past personal events. The association between temporal lobe epilepsy and remote memory is of theoretical and clinical importance. The two influential theoretical positions on this topic are consolidation theory, i.e., that limbic structures are involved in the formation of new memories and thereafter long-term storage is neocortical (Squire & Alvarez, 1995) and multiple-trace theory (Moscovitch et al., 2005), which holds that the involvement of limbic system structures in long-term retention is of a more permanent nature. Data accrued over the past decade appear mixed, confirming and contradicting predictions of both the standard consolidation position and multiple-trace theory (Noulhiane et al., 2007; Meeter & Murre, 2004; Piolino et al., 2003).

Functional imaging studies using multi-voxel pattern analysis (Bonnici, Chadwick & Maguire, 2013; Maguire, 2014) report findings that support the continued role of the hippocampus in autobiographical memory. Further, an anterior–posterior distinction emerged from these data, with the posterior hippocampus being involved in the retention of more remote autobiographical memories. The anterior hippocampus contained information about recent (2 weeks old) and remote (10 years old) autobiographical memories. Penfield and Mathieson (1974) comment on this anterior–posterior distinction in the discussion of their paper.

What have we learnt about the psychosocial aspects of epilepsy surgery?

In a series of well-reasoned phenomenological writings, Wilson, Bladin, and Saling (2001, 2004; Wilson, Frazer, Lawrence & Bladin, 2007) coined the term 'the burden of normality' to refer to the potential psychological challenges facing epilepsy surgery patients in the transition from intractable seizures to remission. The basic premise here is that the transition from chronic illness (i.e., epilepsy) to improved seizure control or seizure freedom can present unique coping and psychosocial challenges with outcomes that can, at face value, seem counter-intuitive. Post-surgery patients can struggle to cope with seizure freedom because living with epilepsy hinders the development of independent living skills and creates psychological difficulties that do not quickly dissipate. These papers are important for a number of reasons. First, they show that psychosocial outcomes can be complex and determined by multiple interacting pre- and post-surgery factors. It is not simply that a good psychological outcome follows a good seizure outcome. Second, awareness that, for some patients, psychosocial outcome can be paradoxical with impaired psychosocial functioning in spite of seizure freedom. Third, these papers invite a psychological understanding of the process of change post-surgery and, with it, the potential to identify pre-surgical psychological factors that could be targeted, so as to prevent or ameliorate adverse outcomes. In an attempt to operationalise the concept of burden of normality and identify at-risk patients as possible candidates for pre-surgery ameliorative approaches, our own research group recently published data showing the certain positive pre-surgery psychological coping styles (i.e., being able to make the best of a situation and see challenges in a positive light) predicted a favourable psychosocial adaptation to epilepsy surgery (Kemp et al., 2016). We present these data as contributing to the small and important literature on pre-surgery determinants of post-surgery quality and the identification of potential 'red flags' for adjustment difficulties as potential targets for ameliorative psychological techniques that could be carried out pre-surgery.

What does this past work mean for what we tell epilepsy surgery patients today?

In a young and developing science such as neuropsychology, much has happened in the 60 years since the time that Penfield and Milner reported patients with poor memory outcome following epilepsy surgery. This brief section has attempted to reflect on these two seminal case studies and place them in the context of subsequent developments in investigative techniques, neuropsychological theory and rehabilitation approaches. In our own epilepsy surgery clinics, patients often ask us if the operation is new and how long it takes. We tell them that the operation has been around for years and that it is not new or radical. We tell patients and families that we have got better at the various tests that guide us in achieving a good outcome, at measuring thinking skills and at supportive approaches after surgery. Patients are generally reassured, to a point, but there is always that unspoken leap of faith into the operating theatre.

Do you think these cases have been considered by people who develop theories of the normal mind? If yes, how? If no, should they?

In general, clinical neuropsychological cases have now been embedded in the development of theories of the normal mind, and this applies of course to classic amnesic patients. Until recently, cases of transient amnesia in general, and transient epileptic amnesia in particular, have featured less in the development of theories of normal cognitive functioning, partly because they are relatively rare or are only now being well documented. There is no good reason why such phenomena should not be more actively considered in both theories of human cognitive function, in our understanding of brain structures and networks, and in pathophysiological models relating to the initiation, propagation and termination of epileptic seizures.

In general, do you think that neuropsychology cases could contribute to our understanding of the normal mind? Should the data from these cases be considered, and if so why?

In general, we do think that neuropsychology cases could contribute to our understanding of the normal mind, especially where they provide observations that refute or confirm predictions of a model or theory of how the human mind works. These historical cases do harmonise with current thinking relating to the fractionation of human memory and the key role of hippocampal and related structures in memory consolidation and retrieval.

Acknowledgements

A version of parts of the article on Dr Z appeared in Kapur, N. (Ed.), 1997. *Injured Brains of Medical Minds: Views from Within*. Oxford: Oxford University Press.

References

Bauer, P. R., Reitsma, J. B., Houweling, B. M., Ferrier, C. H., & Ramsey, N. F. (2014). Can fMRI safely replace the Wada test for preoperative assessment of language lateralisation? A meta-analysis and systematic review. *Journal of Neurology, Neurosurgery, and Psychiatry, 85(5)*, 581–588.

Baulac, M. (2015). MTLE with hippocampal sclerosis in adult as a syndrome. *Revue Neurologique, 171(3)*, 259–266.

Baxendale, S. (2008). The impact of epilepsy surgery on cognition and behavior. *Epilepsy & Behavior, 12(4)*, 592–599.

Bergin, P. S., Thompson, P. J., Baxendale, S. A., Fish, D. R., & Shorvon, S. D. (2000). Remote memory in epilepsy. *Epilepsia, 41(2)*, 231–239.

Bonnici, H. M., Chadwick, M. J., & Maguire, E. A. (2013). Representations of recent and remote autobiographical memories in hippocampal subfields. *Hippocampus, 23*, 849–854.

Butler, C., van Erp, W., Bhaduri, A., Hammers, A., Heckemann, R., & Zeman, A. (2013). Magnetic resonance volumetry reveals focal brain atrophy in transient epileptic amnesia. *Brain, 28*, 363–369.

Butler, C. R., & Zeman, A. Z. (2008). Recent insights into the impairment of memory in epilepsy: transient epileptic amnesia, accelerated long-term forgetting and remote memory impairment. *Brain, 131(Pt 9)*, 2243–2263.

Chiu, M. J., Lin, C. W., Chen, C. C., Chen, T. F., Chen, Y. F., Liu, H. M., Chu, C. P., Liou, H. H., & Hua, M. S. (2010). Impaired gist memory in patients with temporal lobe epilepsy and hippocampal sclerosis. *Epilepsia, 51*, 1036–1042.

Compston, A. (2007). From the archives. *Brain, 130*, 1712–1714.

Critchley, M., & Critchley, E. (1998). *John Hughlings-Jackson: The Father of English Neurology*. Oxford: Oxford University Press.

Dupont, S., Duron, E., Samson, S., Denos, M., Volle, E., Delmaire, C., Navarro, V., Chiras, J., Lehéricy, S., Samson, Y., & Baulac, M. (2010). Functional MR imaging or Wada test: which is the better predictor of individual postoperative memory outcome? *Radiology, 255(1)*, 128–134.

Fish, D. R., Gloor, P., Quesney, F. L., Oliver, A. (1993). Clinical responses to electrical brain stimulation of the temporal and frontal lobes in patients with epilepsy. *Brain, 116*, 397–414.

Gargaro, A. C., Sakamoto, A. C., Bianchin, M. M., Geraldi Cde, V., Scorsi-Rosset, S., Coimbra, E. R., Carlotti, C. G. Jr, Assirati, J. A., & Velasco, T. R. (2013). Atypical neuropsychological profiles and cognitive outcome in mesial temporal lobe epilepsy. *Epilepsy & Behaviour, 27*, 461–469.

Halsband, U., & Lange, R. K. (2006). Motor learning in man: a review of functional and clinical studies. *Journal of Physiology, 99(4–6)*, 414–424.

Halgren, E., Stapleton, J., Domalski, P., Swartz, B. E., Delgado-Escueta, A.V., Walsh, G. O., Mandelkern, M., Blahd, W., & Ropchan, J. (1991). Memory dysfunction in epilepsy patients as a derangement of normal physiology. *Advances in Neurology*, *55*, 385–410.

Halgren, E., Walter, R. D., Cherlow, D. G., & Crandall, P. H. (1978). Mental phenomena evoked by electrical stimulation of the human hippocampal formation of amygdala. *Brain*, *101*, 83–117.

Heydrich, L., Marillier, G., Evans, N., Blanke, O., & Seeck, M. (2015). Lateralising value of experiential hallucinations in temporal lobe epilepsy. *Journal of Neurology, Neurosurgery and Psychiatry*, *86*, 1273–1276.

Hogan, R., & English, E. (2012). Epilepsy and brain function: common ideas of Hughlings-Jackson and Wilder Penfield. *Epilepsy and Behavior*, *24*, 311–313.

Hornberger, M., Mohamed, A., Miller, L., Watson, J., Thayer, Z., & Hodges, J. R. (2010). Focal retrograde amnesia: extending the clinical syndrome of transient epileptic amnesia. *Journal of Clinical Neuroscience*, *17*, 1319–1321.

Hughlings-Jackson, J. (1888). On a particular variety of epilepsy ('Intellectual aura'), one case with symptoms of organic brain disease. *Brain*, *11*, 179–207.

Hughlings-Jackson, J., & Coleman, W. (1898). Case of epilepsy with tasting movements and 'dreamy state'—very small patch of softening in the left uncinated gyrus. *Brain*, *21*, 580–590.

Jou, J., & Flores, S. (2013). How are false memories distinguishable from true memories in the Deese-Roediger-McDermott paradigm? A review of the findings. *Psychological Research*, *77*, 671–686.

Kapur, N. (1990). Transient epileptic amnesia: a clinically distinct form of neurological memory disorder. In H. J. Markowitsch (Ed.), *Transient Global Amnesia and Related Disorders*. New York: Hogrefe and Huber, pp. 140–151.

Kapur, N., Millar, J., Colbourn, C., Abbott, P., Kennedy, P., & Docherty, T. (1997). Very long-term amnesia in association with temporal lobe epilepsy; Evidence for multiple-stage consolidation processes. *Brain and Cognition*, *35*, 58–70.

Kemp, S., Garlovsky, J., Reynders, H., Caswell, H., Baker, G., & Shah, E. (2016). Predicting the psychosocial outcome of epilepsy surgery: a longitudinal perspective on the 'burden of normality'. *Epilepsy & Behavior*, *60*, 149–152.

Kovacs, N., Auer, T., Balas, I., Karadi, K., Zambo, K., Schwarcz, A., Klivenyi, P., Jokeit, H., Horvath, K., Nagy, F., & Janszky, J. (2009). Neuroimaging and cognitive changes during déjà vu. *Epilepsy & Behavior*, *24*, 190–196.

Loring, D. W., Meador, K. J., Lee, G. P., & King, D. W. (1992). *Amobarbital Effects and lateralised Brain Function: The Wada Test*. New York: Springer-Verlag.

Maguire, E. (2014). Memory consolidation in humans. New evidence and opportunities. *Experimental Physiology*, *99*, 471–486.

McAndrews, M. P., & Cohn, M. (2012). Neuropsychology in temporal lobe epilepsy: influences from cognitive neuroscience and functional neuroimaging. *Epilepsy Research and Treatment*, 925238.

Meeter, M., & Murre, J. M. (2004). Consolidation of long-term memory: evidence and alternatives. *Psychological Bulletin*, *130(6)*, 843–857.

Mochizuki-Kawai, H. (2008). Neural basis of procedural memory. *Brain Nerve*. *60(7)*, 825–832.

Morrell, F. (1980). Memory loss as Todd's paralysis. *Epilepsia*, *21*, 185.

Moscovitch, M., Rosenbaum, R. S., Gilboa, A., Addis, D. R., Westmacott, R., Grady, C., McAndrews, M. P., Levine, B., Black, S., Winocur, G., & Nadel, L. (2005). Functional neuroanatomy of remote episodic, semantic and spatial memory: a unified account based on multiple trace theory. *Journal of Anatomy*, *207(1)*, 35–66.

Noulhiane, M., Piolino, P., Hasboun, D., Clemenceau, S., Baulac, M., & Samson, S. (2007). Autobiographical memory after temporal lobe resection: neuropsychological and MRI volumetric findings. *Brain, 130(Pt 12)*, 3184–3199.

Palmini, A. L., Gloor, P., & Jones-Gotman, M. (1992). Pure amnestic seizures in temporal lobe epilepsy. *Brain, 115*, 749–769.

Panayiotopoulos, C. P. (2005). *The Epilepsies: Seizures, Syndromes and Management*. Oxfordshire, UK: Bladon Medical Publishing.

Penfield, W., & Perot, P. (1963). The brain's record of auditory and visual experience: a final summary and discussion. *Brain, 86*, 595–596.

Penfield, W., & Mathieson, G. (1974). Memory. Autopsy findings and comments on the role of hippocampus in experiential recall. *Archives of Neurology, 31(3)*, 145–154.

Penfield, W., & Milner, B. (1958). Memory deficit produced by bilateral lesions in the hippocampal zone. *AMA Archives of Neurology and Psychiatry, 79(5)*, 475–497.

Piolino, P., Desgranges, B., Belliard, S., Matuszewski, V., Lalevée, C., De la Sayette, V., & Eustache, F. (2003). Autobiographical memory and autonoetic consciousness: triple dissociation in neurodegenerative diseases. *Brain, 126(Pt 10)*, 2203–2219.

Quaerens. (1870). A prognostic and therapeutic indication in epilepsy. *The Practitioner, 4*, 284–285.

Rémi, J., Wagner, P., O'Dwyer, R., Silva Cunha, J. P., Vollmar, C., Krotofil, I., & Noachtar, S. (2011). Ictal head turning in frontal and temporal lobe epilepsy. *Epilepsia, 52(8)*, 1447–1451.

Ricci, M., Mohamed, A., Savage, G., Boserio, J., & Miller, L. A. (2015). The impact of epileptiform abnormalities and hippocampal lesions on retention of recent autobiographical experiences: adding insult to injury? *Neuropsychologia, 66*, 259–266.

Roediger, H. L., & McDermott, K. B. (1995). Creating false memories: remembering words not presented in lists. *Journal of Experimental Psychology: Learning. Memory and Cognition, 21*, 803–814.

Saling, M. M. (2009). Verbal memory in mesial temporal lobe epilepsy: beyond material specificity. *Brain, 132(Pt 3)*, 570–582.

Scoville, W. B., & Milner, B. (1957). Loss of recent memory after bilateral hippocampal lesions. *Journal of Neurology, Neurosurgery, and Psychiatry, 20(1)*, 11–21.

Sharan, A., Ooi, Y. C., Langfitt, J., & Sperling, M. R. (2011). Intracarotid amobarbital procedure for epilepsy surgery. *Epilepsy and Behavior, 20(2)*, 209–213.

Squire, L. R., & Alvarez, P. (1995). Retrograde amnesia and memory consolidation: a neurobiological perspective. *Current Opinion in Neurobiology, 5(2)*, 169–177.

Takeda, Y., Kurita, T., Sakurai, K., Shiga, T., Tamaki, N., & Koyama, T. (2011). Persistent déjà vu associated with hyperperfusion in the entorhinal cortex. *Epilepsy and Behavior, 21*, 196–199.

Taylor, D. C., & Marsh, S. M. (1980). Hughlings-Jackson's Dr Z: the paradigm of temporal epilepsy revealed. *Journal of Neurology, Neurosurgery and Psychiatry, 43*, 758–767.

Wearing, D. (2005). *Forever Today: A Memoir of Love and Amnesia*. Corgi.

Wilson, B. A., & Hughes, E. (1997). Coping with amnesia: the natural history of a compensatory memory system. *Neuropsychological Rehabilitation, 7(1)*, 43–56.

Wilson, S. J., Bladin, P. F., & Saling, M. M. (2001). The "burden of normality": concepts of adjustment after surgery for seizures. *Journal of Neurology, Neurosurgery and Psychiatry, 70*, 649–656.

Wilson, S. J., Bladin, P. F., & Saling, M. M. (2004). Paradoxical results in the cure of chronic illness: the "burden of normality" as exemplified following seizure surgery. *Epilepsy and Behavior, 5*, 13–21.

Wilson, S. J., Frazer, D. W., Lawrence, J. A., & Bladin, P. F. (2007). Psychosocial adjustment following relief of chronic narcolepsy. *Sleep Medicine, 8*, 252–259.

Wolk, D. A., & Budson, A. E. (2010). Memory systems. *Behavioral Neurology, 16(4)*, 15–28.

Zeman, A., & Butler, C. (2010). Transient epileptic amnesia. *Current Opinion in Neurology, 23*, 610–616.

7

PERSISTENT DÉJÀ VU, RECOLLECTIVE CONFABULATION AND THE CASE OF PATIENT AKP

Chris J.A. Moulin

A decade ago, you and your colleagues reported on two cases, AKP and MA, who presented with constant déjà vu and a high level of false recognition. You termed their memory disorder "recollective confabulation". Can you provide us with some background information about these cases?

In 2005, we presented the case reports of two patients, AKP and MA, and described their experience of recollective confabulation (Moulin, Conway, Thompson, James & Jones, 2005). At the time I met these two patients, I was working in a memory clinic, and unlike most of our patients, who presented with forgetfulness, these patients presented with what their GPs and carers described as constant déjà vu. In essence, these patients continually claimed that a current experience had already taken place when in fact it had not. These feelings were particularly pronounced for media content: these two people withdrew from watching the television or reading newspapers because they claimed to have encountered all of their content before. Even when not at home, the events that happened and things that they experienced were described as repetitions of previous events (e.g., *that bird is always singing the same tune in the same tree*). The constant complaint that they had already done everything before was tiresome for the carers and at times distressing for the patients.

Most strikingly, these patients did not merely report finding things familiar, but they also recollected details to justify their feelings: they 'remembered' non-existent previous episodes, such as having already read the newspaper and providing an account of how they had woken up early and secretly gone to read the newspaper as it was being unloaded from the lorry in the village. It was this tendency to generate false supporting information in the form of confabulations that led us to label their behaviour as *recollective confabulation*. In early articles, and in the media, we also referred to this symptom as *déjà vécu*, which in retrospect was ill-advised—I will explain why next.

In short, these patients with recollective confabulation seem to be 'stuck in a time loop'. As far as we can tell, this feeling is constant. It leads to the patients reporting their experience of the present moment as if it is a memory, describing the current situation as if it is proof that what they are encountering now, they have encountered before. For example, in this quote, AKP is describing in a radio interview how he can be certain that the same radio journalist had already interviewed him:

> The surroundings are the same, and that without being offensive your sight against the filing cabinets and so on, and the heater, it looks familiar. Since then, [my] memory got slightly worse, that's all. Besides, you asked the same questions. Why I remember them, and whether they are really the same, I don't know, but it seems like it.

In fact, it was a very novel and distinctive event for AKP—the BBC—or any radio journalist, had never interviewed him before.

In the 2005 article, we presented two cases. The original and most detailed case presentation was AKP. MA was added after. With AKP, I had imagined that perhaps these problems were underreported, due to them being bizarre or difficult to explain. We found that if we asked for people's experiences of déjà vu in the dementia clinic, we identified a handful of patients per year with similar problems; MA was one such patient. Subsequently, I have published a case series of 12 similar patients including AKP (Moulin, 2013). Although I have found some overlap in terms of symptoms and recollective confabulation, the patients have turned out to be heterogeneous in terms of aetiology, severity, neuroimaging findings, intelligence level, and even performance on memory tests. All the patients have had mild memory problems, however, and all of them have been older adults. Most of them have had a diagnosis of dementia. Since AKP was our first and most important case, I shall focus this chapter on discussing his case.

How did you first realise that these cases were interesting?

I met AKP during my postdoc period, and at the time, whilst I worked in Bristol, the lab was full of memory experts and their visitors. Just in sharing the case over coffee with Alan Baddeley, Martin Conway, and Malcolm Brown amongst others, it was clear that this presentation was unusual. Visitors to Bristol, such as Nelson Cowan, were also fascinated by the case. Most critically, Gus Craik, whilst spending some time in the department at Bristol, said that he had once seen a similar case, and he compared notes with me. I'm pleased to say that later, he eventually published this case, co-authored by one of my PhD students (Craik et al., 2014). That case (VL) is very important for this work, because it is the first case with detailed neuroimaging findings, and perhaps reassuringly, this case was observed in a different lab.

We were all using the term 'déjà vu' to describe AKP's problems at this point, and I found very little on déjà vu in general in handbooks. I very quickly learned that déjà vu was a stereotypical symptom of temporal lobe epilepsy, but AKP clearly did not have epileptic symptoms, and the déjà vu was not fleeting and temporary as in epilepsy (for a review of déjà vu in epilepsy see Illman, Butler, Souchay & Moulin, 2012).

At the time, I did not find any cases that were similar to AKP, although we have recently translated a French case from 1896 that appears rather similar (Bertrand, Martinon, Souchay & Moulin, 2017). The issue was not so much whether the case was interesting or not, but what it meant for theories of memory and how to explain it. I felt an immense pressure to make sense of AKP's behaviour and integrate it into models of memory function. Everybody found the case interesting, and unusual, but what was its value to the scientific community?

In Bristol, I spent a lot of time discussing the case—and case studies more generally—with Iain Gilchrist, who had just taken up his first lectureship in Bristol. He worked with Tom Troscianko on vision and together they had experience in publishing single case reports. Iain had published an article (Gilchrist, Brown, Findlay & Clarke, 1998) in the Proceedings of the Royal Society on the case of AI, a patient with total ophthalmoplegia, which resulted in a lack of eye movements. Critically for theories of active vision, she samples the environment with head movements that are qualitatively similar to the eye-based orientating of healthy controls. Iain modestly asserted that the article and resulting theoretical insight was pretty much just serendipity: he was lucky that AI walked into his lab. I now realise after years of hard work publishing single cases that although serendipity is a major factor, making sense of the unusual or uncommon, using the interesting case to vet accrued knowledge is the real hard part. I still wonder whether I have managed to generate a sensible, impactful contribution, or whether the work is just published because it is inherently interesting.

Can you summarise the main features of AKP?

AKP was referred to the memory clinic via his family doctor. At the time, he was 80 years old. When it was suggested that he attend the memory clinic, he told his doctor that he had already been (which was not in fact possible). AKP's wife believed that the patient's sensation of life repeating was practically constant. She also told me that she thought the experience was more frequent and more intensely felt for more novel, remarkable aspects of daily life (such as people calling at the door, going to new places). The sensation was so strong that it influenced AKP's daily activities. It was extremely prominent when he went for a walk; AKP read car number plates and stated that the drivers must have had very regular habits, always passing by at the exact same time every day. When shopping, AKP would state that it was unnecessary to purchase certain items because he had bought the items the day before. There were also occasional autobiographical confabulations, including the belief that he had been married three times to the same woman, with three separate, repeated ceremonies around Europe. AKP was somewhat insightful about his difficulties: when he said he had seen a programme before and his wife asked him what happened next, he replied, 'How should I know, I have a memory problem!'

In terms of the brain, structural MRI showed atrophy in the temporal lobes and hippocampus. There was some asymmetry, with more cell loss on the left. There was no atrophy of the frontal lobes. SPECT showed reduced perfusion to the medial cortex of both temporal lobes and to the visual cortex in both hemispheres. Perfusion to the frontal lobes was well within normal limits. An awake EEG was also within normal limits, with no focal or epileptiform features. Unfortunately, I never saw the scans directly; but relied on the summary reports written by the radiologists. Specific research scans were not carried out.

AKP was Polish—English bilingual. He was trained to master's level in the UK and was a retired engineer. On standardised tests, he had an above-average IQ according to his performance on the National Adult Reading Test (Nelson & Willison, 1991). On the WAIS, he scored in the 91st percentile for digit span, 75th percentile for similarities and in the 99th percentile for picture completion. He had a Mini-Mental State Examination score (MMSE; Folstein, Folstein & McHugh, 1975) on initial testing of 26/30 and this remained stable during the period he was assessed and 13 months later it was still 26/30.

AKP had impaired recall and recognition. On the story recall test from the Adult Memory and Information Processing Battery (Coughlan & Hollows, 1985), he had below average immediate recall (10th percentile) and after a 20 min delay, delayed recall was zero. On the Hopkins Verbal Learning Test (HVLT; Brandt, 1991) immediate recall was abnormal, he also made three intrusion errors—one prior test item, and two semantically related words. On recognition, AKP scored 12 hits, but also made 8/12 false-positive errors. On tests of executive function, he showed a mixture of spared and impaired performance. Verbal fluency was low normal (30 items generated to F.A.S., 11th–22nd percentile), but English was not AKP's native language. The Hayling Sentence Completion task (Burgess & Shallice, 1996) showed significant executive deficits. AKP finished sentences with connected completions in the unconnected condition, (e.g., 'Most cats see very well at ... night'.) On the Trail Making Task (Reitan, 1992); however, he showed no impairment and completed Part A in 70 seconds, and Part B in 166 seconds.

Our research testing work focussed on recognition memory (see Figures 7.1 and 7.2 for a photograph of some of the original materials). His particular problem was that he made a lot of false-positive errors. This was particularly severe on tests of continuous recognition: a task where participants are shown a series of stimuli, some of which repeat and the task is to report whether they have seen the items before. On such a task using faces, AKP had a z-score of 22.27 for his false positives: he believed that nearly all the faces were repetitions of those he had seen earlier within the task, but they were not.

What was AKP's pattern of spared and impaired abilities?

It is always critical to set such impairments against spared abilities—for this purpose we tested AKP's ability to discriminate two morphed faces in a task where he had to merely report whether the faces were identical or not. Due to space

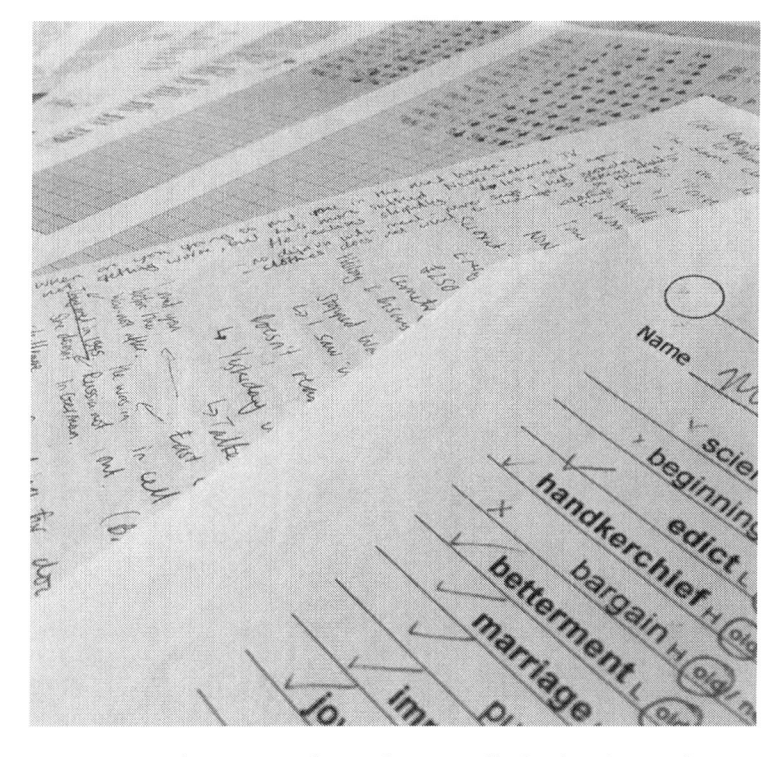

FIGURE 7.1   Research assessment focussed on specially developed tests of recognition memory, especially for high and low-frequency words, some of which are shown here. Many more tests were devised and carried out than appeared in the final paper.

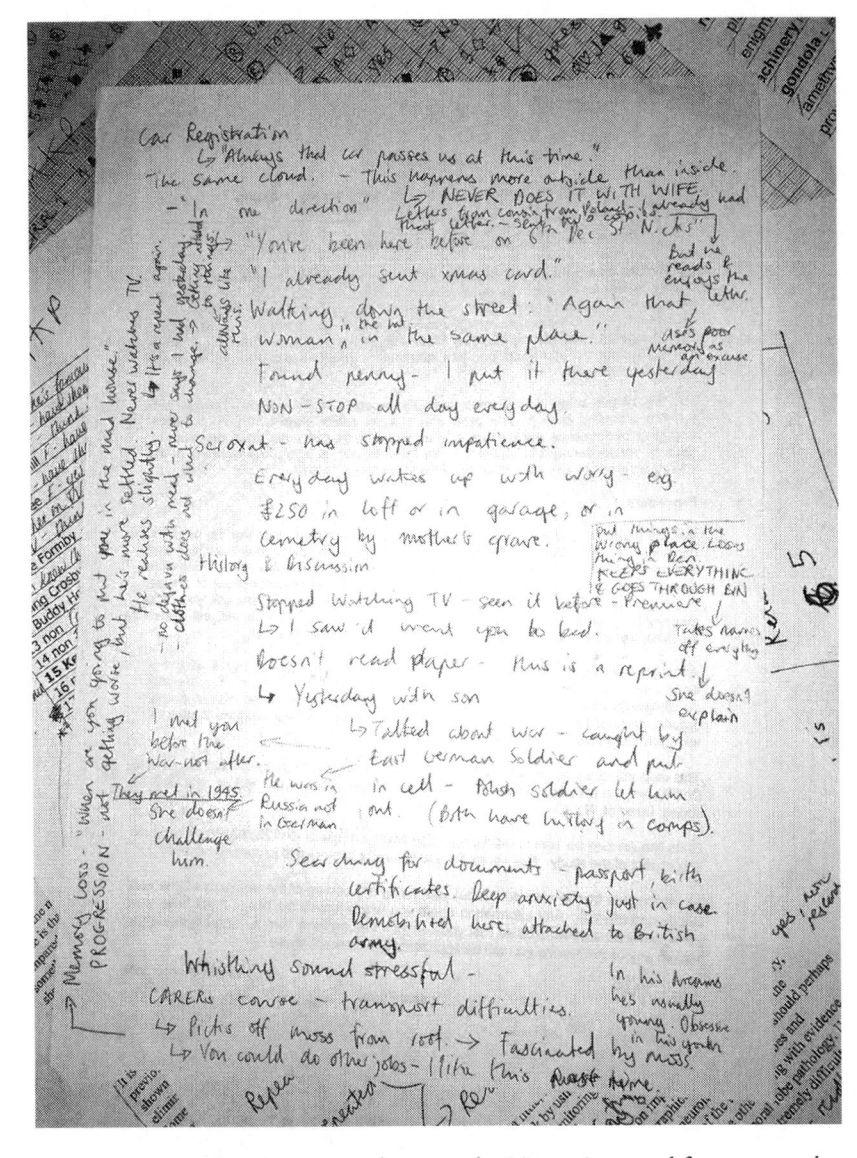

FIGURE 7.2 Extensive notes were taken at each visit—as is normal for neuropsychological casework. The original accounts of what the patient had said were invaluable, especially when asked for further detail in accounts of AKP in the media. The page shown here is from the first visit: 'You've been here before on the 6th Dec'.

constraints in the original article, we did not present these data, but the critical issue was that he had completely normal performance in this regard: he was able to differentiate faces to the same degree as healthy age-matched controls. In any case, AKP's poor performance on the continuous recognition task described earlier did not seem to spring merely from confusion or a failure to discriminate faces, since he justified—spontaneously—his false-positive responses with recollective confabulations, such as 'seen before, I know because his tie is lower than it should be. Does he wear artificial hair now and then?'

A further worry was that his high levels of false alarms were merely to do with a bias to responding 'yes' in tests of recognition memory. It was possible that AKP was merely perseverating in his responses. This seems unlikely given that he spontaneously justified his false alarms with recollective confabulations, but on the other hand, the justifications may just be post hoc rationalisations used to validate his inappropriate judgements. To set the problem with false positives in some kind of context, we measured AKP's general knowledge. His wife had reported that he did not claim to know facts that he could not have known. In talking with AKP, his problem seemed to be limited to life events, daily activities, and in general, we thought his problem with false positives was limited to episodic memory.

We thus administered a general knowledge test, whereby we asked questions such as: *What is the holy city of Islam called?* We used a feeling-of-knowing (FOK) paradigm (e.g., Wojcik, Moulin & Souchay, 2013). In a first phase, all participants were instructed not to guess, and to recall the correct answer. On this part, AKP had 69% correct recall compared to the controls' 80% (a z-score of -2.12), suggesting that he did actually volunteer answers for recall that were incorrect to a different extent than controls. In this first phase, if the participant could not recall the correct answer, they were asked to predict their response on an upcoming recognition test on a three-point scale (ranging from being certain to guessing). Critically, AKP did not report guessing any more than the controls. In the second phase, a recognition test was carried out using the same questions again, but with a four-alternative choice recognition methodology; the participants had to choose between *Mecca, Jerusalem, Amman* or *Jericho*, for example. AKP's correct recognition was somewhat worse than controls ($z = -1.39$) but importantly, he showed the appropriate relationship between his evaluations of his performance and his actual performance: he was not guessing on this task believing himself to be correct, and he did not confabulate any responses or justifications. The proportion of incorrect answers for which he was certain they were correct was actually lower than controls ($z = -0.60$). In sum, whilst it might be difficult to argue that his semantic memory (as reflected in this general knowledge task) was intact, there was certainly some difference between his difficulties on episodic recognition and semantic recognition tasks. At least we were confident that AKP's awareness of his retrieval of general knowledge was not dysfunctional in the same way as for the episodic tasks. Plus, he did not *always* offer a response and did not seem to perseverate on these semantic tasks.

In general, AKP had relatively spared semantic memory, could make appropriate perceptual judgements about complex stimuli using 'yes' and 'no' answers, and performed normally on some executive tests. However, it is difficult to talk about spared and impaired abilities since AKP had an atypical dementia profile with a progressive alteration of several cognitive abilities. At first, he was articulate and lucid, but very confused about his memory function, and I would say that he only had a very specific memory deficit. But with time, the delusions about his memory spread to autobiographical beliefs and he showed more typical symptoms of dementia, including getting lost in familiar environments. Towards the end of my time working with him, his wife described how she had found him in the kitchen boiling water in a frying pan without a lid in order to make a cup of tea. This cognitive failure was striking for her since she described how he would always discuss scientific principles in daily life: the lack of a lid and the shape of the pan are not ideal for boiling water—and in any case, he had overlooked using the electric kettle. Thus, one aspect of the original presentation which is missing (because any case study is usually only a snapshot in time) is that AKP showed cognitive decline and some delusional behaviour in other aspects of his mental and daily life that were not present at the time of the initial memory testing or at the onset of the recollective confabulation.

How did you set about researching AKP's experiences?

Our novel experimental work focussed on the recollective experience paradigm. This paradigm is used to measure the relative contributions of recollection and familiarity to recognition memory decision making. Tulving (1985) argued that it was possible to classify different memory systems on the basis of subjective experience. In the recollective experience paradigm, participants report their subjective experience or sensations attached to the retrieval of an item from memory. Basically, it allows us to distinguish between sensations of 'remembering' and 'finding familiar' experiences. Remembering is the act of bringing something to mind with recollective experience: It includes a subjective state of pastness and knowledge about the memory's context and source. On the other hand, when we find something familiar, there is no rich contextual information, or a sense of pastness, we just know the information that we have retrieved. Our participants (AKP, MA and controls) made subjective evaluations based on the definitions given in Table 7.1 (Moulin et al., 2005, p. 1369).

Participants were introduced to recollection and familiarity through the use of a vignette about encountering a person on the street. For recollection, they were told that they can sometimes remember a lot about someone when they see them on the street: who they are, where they work, when they last saw them, how they felt when they last saw them. It was also explained that on other occasions, we merely know that we recognise the person, but we are not sure where from or who they are. This is familiarity. Whenever they said they remembered something,

TABLE 7.1 The definitions for remember, familiar, guess and new responses presented to participants.

Remember	This is one of the words I saw/heard before. I can remember hearing it. It has a feeling of pastness. I can remember something about it when it was presented before
Familiar	This is one of the words I saw/heard before; it seems familiar to me
Guess	This is one of the words I heard before, but I'm guessing
New	This is a word I did not see before

TABLE 7.2 The justifications for remember and familiar responses made by AKP and MA. Reprinted from Neuropsychologia, 43, Moulin, Conway, Thompson, James & Jones, Disordered memory awareness: recollective confabulation in two cases of persistent déjà vécu, 1362–1378,

Word	Status	Subjective Judgement	Justification
Edict	Target	Familiar	Just a feeling
Modernist	Target	Familiar	It's vague, I think I saw it before
Handkerchief	Target	Remember	Because I have not got one on me, I always forget it
Gondola	Target	Remember	I remember seeing this at the beginning
Polka	Target	Remember	Polka is Polish for female
Employment	Target	Remember	It's very long, one of the longest you showed me
Science	Distracter	Familiar	Just rings a bell, a familiar word
Bargain	Distracter	Familiar	I just feel I saw it, what else can one say?
Puck	Distracter	Remember	By association—change the first letter
Plaza	Distracter	Remember	Polish is the same, it means beach
Enigma	Distracter	Remember	Enigma variations, it sticks in the mind
Abode	Distracter	Remember	It just seems like I remember it. I cannot explain, except the symmetry at presentation

Copyright (2005), with permission from Elsevier.

we also asked them to make justifications, examples of which are presented in Table 7.2. There is a large literature on these two types of recognition memory decisions and they relate to healthy memory and their location in the brain (for reviews see Yonelinas, 2002; Mandler, 2008; Moulin, Souchay & Morris, 2013).

In the two experiments reported in the original article, we found that AKP had a normal pattern of recollection and familiarity for his correct recognition responses. Unusually, but as we might expect from the quote about the radio journalist noted earlier, he also made a lot of false positives which he claimed to remember from encoding, and even generated plausible justifications. Thus, these simple tasks that ask for subjective reports, were suitable for exploring and quantifying AKP's subjective experience. Bear in mind that it is unusual for healthy people to make false positives on the basis of recollection: one cannot retrieve specific information from the encoding episode of a word that was never presented in the study phase. However, 57% of all AKP's false-positive errors were experienced as 'remembering'. In terms of a z-score, this is 14.55—AKP 'remembered' many more false positives than controls. In a second experiment, we replicated this pattern and gathered justifications for his recollective responses (Table 7.2) that corroborated our hypothesis of recollective confabulation.

Do you think these cases contribute to our understanding of how the normal mind works?

We have drawn several new theoretical insights from AKP, but mostly we have used the case to underline how memory retrieval is guided by subjective sensations and justifications, which are separate from the contents and the act of retrieval itself. The fact that people can have such a strange false-memory problem which impacts on their daily activities and their mood suggests that the mind can generate strong sensations which it then justifies against all rational possibilities rather than rejecting them as false. We have tried to generate a debate and a theoretical framework to consider such feelings in daily life and in healthy people (e.g., Moulin & Souchay, 2013). In such work, we discuss 'epistemic feelings'; the sensations generated by the cognitive system to guide processing. These include the feeling of familiarity and the experience of remembering, and other such subjective states. We think that recollective confabulation is evidence for the existence of an epistemic feeling of familiarity which, when it is dysfunctional or constant (as in these cases), can be erroneously interpreted as being the mental reliving or recollection of a previous event.

We have, perhaps more ambitiously, also used the patients to make neuroscientific claims about the role of the hippocampus in encoding and retrieval (e.g., O'Connor, Lever & Moulin, 2010) because one interpretation of recollective confabulation is that encoding of information is misinterpreted as retrieval. Within this context, the work with these patients interested me personally in the relationship between novelty and familiarity, although our speculative ideas about what these patients tell us about novelty and memory encoding need development. In short, we argued that patients such as AKP are more likely to experience novel stimuli as having been encountered before. Our impression was that whenever attention was engaged by an arousing or novel stimulus, there was accompanying familiarity and subsequent recollective confabulation. We argued novelty detection is a key step in a process by which attention is orientated towards encoding a stimulus (e.g., Tulving, Markowitsch, Craik, Habib & Houle, 1996). In such situations, the memory system should be working to encode such features for future reference, but AKP misinterpreted such contextual and perceptual information as retrieval from memory. In fact, the empirical evidence for this is lacking. Carers of multiple cases highlighted that the recollective confabulation was worse in novel contexts, and AKP's wife also spontaneously mentioned this—saying that the symptoms were worse outside the house than in it. However, a priority is to examine whether novelty and distinctiveness contribute false recognition in these patients in laboratory tasks.

We focussed on an interesting idea that encoding-related activity could be misinterpreted as retrieval-related. This proposal rests on the idea that the hippocampus supports novelty detection as well as recollection, and that recollection normally involves a transient and distinct theta-based coupling between the hippocampus and other regions that receive information from the hippocampus. Our account assumes that the hippocampus is crucial for reactivating the context associated with an event, and thus for episodic recollection. It also assumes that various neocortical areas (e.g., medial parietal, visual) are involved in recreating the specific contents of the event being recollected. Another assumption is that a third region, such as the medial prefrontal cortex or retrosplenial cortex, is associated with the subjective, conscious experience that these contents evoke, resulting in recollection of one's own past. The general idea was that exactly the same network is involved in novelty detection as in recollection, but that higher-order structures are required to interpret theta phase in the hippocampus (which shifts according to retrieval or novelty detection activity, e.g., Hasselmo, Bodelón & Wyble, 2002). Thus, patients such as AKP might be able to contribute something to the understanding of the conundrum of how the hippocampus seems to underpin two seemingly paradoxical functions: retrieving prior occurrences and encoding new ones (e.g., Barbeau, Chauvel, Moulin, Regis & Liégois-Chauvel, 2017). However, to test this idea, we would need to know much more about these patients at a microscopic, neuroscientific level.

What does AKP tell us about the déjà vu experience?

Recollective confabulation makes a critical point that helps us understand better healthy déjà vu: AKP is unaware that the false familiarity is indeed false. AKP acted on his familiarity, refusing to watch the TV or read the newspaper, and confabulated justifications of prior events that never happened in order to support the sense that his life was repeating. From the outside, this must seem like being trapped in a permanent déjà vu experience. We argue though, that the very awareness of the familiarity being false is the defining characteristic of déjà vu. AKP's false familiarity is not corrected or acknowledged as false as it would be in healthy (or even epileptic) déjà vu. Healthy déjà vu could not be more different: in healthy déjà vu, we likewise have a strong sense of familiarity, but at the same time, we are aware that this is a false sensation (Moulin, 2013; Bertrand, Martinon, Souchay & Moulin, 2017).

Unlike people with recollective confabulation, we do not act on our feelings when we have déjà vu. It is possible to visit New York for the first time in our lives but to find it eerily familiar. However, we do not—exactly as one of our patients *has* done—go back to our hotel and refuse to come out saying we have done it all before (see O'Connor, Lever & Moulin, 2010).

A further difference is that healthy déjà vu experiences are always short-lived—probably because we can 'resist' the feeling of familiarity and generate information to counteract it. The fact that we are aware of it, is probably what stops the sensation developing. For research into healthy déjà vu, then, the chronic problems of our patients emphasise that part of the healthy experience is a form of conflict in mental evaluations derived from a metacognitive awareness of the memory system. This awareness is deficient in cases like AKP. Thus, healthy déjà vu is characterised as a temporary clash in two opposing mental evaluations (see O'Connor & Moulin, 2010). There was no such clash in evaluations in AKP—he did not know that he actually had not seen a TV programme before, even if he felt he had.

Some of this thinking about the relationship between déjà vu and recollective confabulation was not developed until later work, as I describe next. At the time we published the original article, we were focussed on recollection and the idea that that AKP was falsely *recollecting* information, not merely finding information familiar. We used this false recollection to develop a more general theory about differences between false familiarity (in déjà vu) and false recollection (in déjà vécu). I explain this idea next. Perhaps most importantly, I was not engaged in researching déjà vu when I met AKP. Rather, it was working with him that inspired other projects and experiments relating to déjà vu in healthy groups and clinical populations.

Do you think that there is anything that the report of these cases has added to our understanding of pathological states and memory dysfunction?

I think they have supported and extended existing theories of dysfunction. For instance, recollective confabulation could be described as a delusional belief, akin to reduplicative paramnesia. Reduplicative paramnesia is an infrequent disorder characterised by the subjective conviction that a place, person or event is duplicated (Pisani, Marra & Silveri, 2000). Feinberg and Shapiro (1989, p. 40) describe a form of reduplication where '*the patient maintains that his current experiences are a repeat of past experiences*'. They suggest that reduplicative syndromes occur where an unfamiliar environment or event appears in a 'pathologically familiar form', such as when a hospital room is mistaken for a patient's home; they even specify that reduplicative paramnesia can resemble déjà vu.

Our 'unique' cases resemble previously published cases of reduplicative paramnesia in dementia. Mendez (1992) reports seven cases of dementia with delusional misidentification syndromes, where the focus is on misidentification of people (Capgras' delusion). Of these seven cases, two present with reduplications that involve time. Case 4 was an 83-year-old who claimed that her nurse had been replaced by a substitute who intended to harm her. In addition, she 'had episodes of déjà vu, e.g. saw a person on a bicycle and claimed, "I have seen all this before"' (p. 415). Case 6, an 88-year-old woman, denied the identity of her daughter and claimed there was a good and a bad version of her. In addition, 'She had episodes of unfamiliar events appearing familiar, e.g. driving on unfamiliar streets she said "that car is always here every time we go by here"' (p. 415). She also had visual hallucinations of familiar persons.

There are thus considerable overlaps between our concept of recollective confabulation and temporal reduplication, although AKP (like my other recollective confabulation patients) did not have hallucinations or other forms of reduplicative paramnesia. Interestingly, reduplicative paramnesias are thought to arise due to a misconnection or disruption to fronto-temporal circuits, particularly following damage to right frontal areas. Feinberg and Shapiro (1989) specify that a right frontal disruption leads to a disturbance of familiarity and that this leads to a confabulation of why the 'familiar is experienced as strange or vice versa' (p. 46). Critically, these delusional misidentifications of people, places and time, have all been hypothesised as stemming from memory-like disruptions to feelings of familiarity (Feinberg & Roane, 2005). According to Pisani, Marra, and Silveri (2000), reduplicative paramnesia is caused by 'difficulties in organizing, in the right space and time, memories that are similar and can be distinguished only by a correct contextual analysis and encoding' (p. 327).

This notion has some parallels with how recollection and familiarity are suggested to operate together in the healthy memory system. Familiarity operates as a mechanism by which the intensity of memory can be gauged. An initial assessment of familiarity is used to rapidly assess memory and to trigger other more effortful, strategic retrieval processes that can possibly pinpoint the source of the familiarity and retrieve contextual specifics (e.g., Mandler, 2008; Moulin, 2013). Reduplicative paramnesia may arise, therefore, when memory mechanisms are faulty: firstly, there is excess familiarity; secondly, there is a failure to pinpoint the source of this familiarity or reject it, confusing two places, or people that are similar.

Finally, there is a similarity between the justifications of our patients and those of patients with reduplicative paramnesias. Kapur, Turner and King (1988) report a case of reduplicative paramecia where the patient

> continued to insist that the house was not his 'real' house and remarked on how striking it was that the owners of this house had the same ornaments as he had in 'his' house and on what a coincidence it was that there were similar items beside the bed as there were in 'his' house.
>
> (p. 579)

These perceptual details used as justification seem like those in AKP's quote noted earlier, using such details to support the delusion of repetition, rather than to reject it.

Can you specify why AKP was relevant in relation to the knowledge at the time and would the case still be relevant to the knowledge of today?

At the time of writing the article, it was difficult to know to which literature to appeal to. We were excited to use the AKP case to illuminate our understanding of déjà vu and to recapture the study of déjà vu for cognitive psychology rather than parapsychology. In this regard, we were scooped, because Brown's excellent book on déjà vu (Brown, 2004) and the associated review of the literature (Brown, 2003) came out before our article was ultimately accepted. The déjà vu literature at the time was lacking in theoretical structure, without any concrete proposals as to how it was formed either cognitively or neuroanatomically (except from some excellent work using stimulation of the cortex by Patrick Chauvel and colleagues; e.g., Bancaud, Brunet-Bourgin, Chauvel & Halgren, 1994). In the end, in the 2005 AKP article, we based our ideas about dysfunctional recollection (déjà vécu) and familiarity (déjà vu) on a very obscure source that Martin Conway (one of the co-authors) had found (Funkhouser, 1995). Funkhouser, a psychoanalyst, had claimed that déjà vu could be separated into different types: déjà vécu, déjà senti, and déjà visité. Funkhouser's fractionation of déjà vu states is drawn from scientific works and literature. To describe déjà vécu, he uses a passage from Charles Dickens' David Copperfield:

> We have all some experience of a feeling, that comes over us occasionally, of what we are saying and doing having been said and done before, in a remote time of our having been surrounded, dim ages ago, by the same faces, objects, and circumstances of our knowing perfectly what will be said next, as if we suddenly remember it!
>
> *(Dickens, 1850/1869, Chapter 39)*

This description stresses contextual details and associated feelings and thoughts. As such, it parallels the experience of remembering. We thought that this notion of reliving, re-experiencing and falsely recollecting the past was a lot like AKP's experience. From there, we made the case that déjà vu experiences could be separated into false familiarity (déjà vu) or false recollection (déjà vécu). In honesty, this is something that still needs empirical support. But at the time, it was important to try to develop some concrete proposals about how we might go about researching déjà vu. I thought that cases like AKP might enable us to study the mechanisms in déjà vu that are usually so unpredictable and short-lived. I think the paper has had some impact in this regard, but more in terms of launching my research interests in déjà vu as credible and publishable. The paper itself does not offer a very conclusive account of déjà vu.

When testing and later writing up AKP's case, I felt considerable pressure to develop a theory of his problem, and in particular, to use this strikingly unusual case to say something about the memory system. I am not sure that this pressure is such a good thing—it led to some rather grandiose and speculative material in the original paper, which was not supported in the later case series where more patients were included and better statistical analysis was possible (Moulin, 2013). I now firmly believe that publishing in high-impact prestigious journals should not necessitate that we make big claims about theories and overturn models with case studies, though that is indeed possible. It should be possible to publish interesting but unusual, or difficult to explain cases in prominent places so that the scientific and clinical community can share the information, but not to offer a theoretical account—or at least to remain neutral or perplexed by the case. The most important aspect of the initial paper, now and at the time, was to merely document that such problems do exist, and how we might tackle them scientifically. I know from working with patients and carers that this is very reassuring, and I see it as the most important part of publishing such cases.

What are the shortcomings of this case report?

It was a great shame not to have any high-resolution magnetic resonance imaging of AKP's brain. In fact, we have not had detailed neuroimaging for any of the cases of recollective confabulation we have published (but see Craik et al., 2014), and so we have had to go on CT and SPECT scans and the results of neuropsychological testing. In this way, our capacity to pinpoint cerebral networks involved in this problem has been lacking.

Do you remember whether there were any issues that reviewers were particularly blunt about?

We did not have a tricky amount of toing and froing with our reviewers. I think the novelty of the case and the fact that we presented a number of experimental tasks in the original submission helped us greatly and, the fact that déjà vu had not been much researched also helped.

Are there any assessments/paradigms that you would administer now to these people if they were available?

As noted earlier, some high-resolution structural neuroimaging would have been helpful to identify the particular temporal lobe atrophy—perhaps even with a volumetric analysis of key structures. For instance, it is still not known to what extent the atrophy is in the hippocampal (recollection) or parahippocampal (familiarity) areas and, structural imaging might have shown some clearer frontal atrophy. Craik et al.'s patient VL (published in 2014) showed both hippocampal and parahippocampal atrophy confirmed by a volumetric analysis. Moreover, they were able to pinpoint lateral frontal atrophy. In terms of looking at the brain processes in recognition memory, it would have been great to use EEG, which is well suited to recognition paradigms (e.g., Wilding, 2000). Using an ERP design, the specific neural signature differences between hits and false positives could have been examined, with particular reference to the P600 effect (e.g., Curran, 1999) which is proposed to index recollection processes.

Otherwise, one regret is that with all my research involving these types of patients, I have been over-reliant on tasks that involve subjective reports. Clearly, such patients have a dysfunctional awareness of what is novel and what is repeating, and this evident in their subjective reports. As such, asking them to judge and justify the basis of their recognition memory decisions is pertinent but perhaps contaminated by their difficulties generally. That is, I wonder whether the subjective categories of responding to words in a recognition memory test can be biased by people's general disposition and optimism. Some people will say they remember seeing an item, and justify why, whereas others may be more cautious. Some people may say that they feel like they've seen everything before, and respond 'yes' to everything, whereas others, more insightfully, may say that it is impossible to carry out the test because they have a problem with their memory and therefore report 'no' to every item. This problem is magnified for reporting subjective experiences during recollection: people's understanding of the terms 'remembering' and finding 'familiar' may vary, and people may feel more or less confidence and use different levels of information to make their decisions, or even use different strategies to make their evaluations. This is an age-old problem in psychology: being over-dependent on subjective evaluations.

Of course, we used objective variables—such as word frequency—to corroborate the patients' responses. For his hits, AKP made more remember responses for his correct recognition for low-frequency words (77%) than for high-frequency words (46%). This shows to an extent that his subjective evaluations are based on commonly found patterns of performance in healthy populations. Low-frequency words such as *Gondola* are more distinctive and it is thus more likely to be able to recall something about encountering this word on the study list when compared to words such as *Preference*, which may merely appear familiar or could be confused with other familiar words and concepts not seen on the study list.

However, for the next patient like AKP whom I will assess, I would like to use more objective indices of recollection and familiarity, and this will be a priority for future research in this group. We now suspect that AKP and other recollective confabulators generate familiarity almost constantly, and find everything familiar. They then generate recollective justifications for this false familiarity, not understanding that the familiarity is false. This is a two-factor account—there's a lower level memory problem (false familiarity) combined with a higher-order failure to correctly interpret/control/reject the feeling of false familiarity (which leads to the recollective confabulations). According to this hypothesis, patients like AKP should show difficulty on tasks that rely on recollection mechanisms to gate or control familiarity decisions. A perfect, more objective, method for achieving this would be Jacoby's process dissociation procedure (e.g., Jennings & Jacoby, 1997). In this paradigm, participants complete two versions of a recognition memory test with repeating distracter items. It follows the standard format of a yes/no recognition memory test except that the distracter items in the test phase repeat. In one version of the task (i.e., the inclusion condition), participants have to respond 'yes' all items that they judge as old. That means they endorse having seen both the targets seen in the study phase and the repeating distracters. In this version of the task, anything that is familiar to them, for any reason, should be endorsed as old. In the other version of the task (i.e., the exclusion condition), recollection is required to overcome the familiarity of the repeating distracters. In this version, the task for participants is only to endorse as having seen before the targets from the original study phase. The repeating distracters will be familiar to them, but they need to be able to 'recollect to reject' (cf. Brainerd, Reyna, Wright & Mojardin, 2003) in order to distinguish the original targets from the repeating foil. Given that we think the problem lies with using metacognitive control processes to overcome the false familiarity, we should find that the patients would show very low performance on the version for the task where they are required to use recollection to overcome familiarity. Although the patients would be reporting 'yes' and 'no' to items in a test (which is subjective), we are not reliant upon subjective report to distinguish familiarity from recollection.

Finally, I now regret not using a different kind of proportional analysis in the original 2005 paper. One way of considering whether the subjective evaluations are appropriate or in line with theoretical considerations is to consider the proportions correct for each type of subjective report: that is, if someone says that they 'remember' seeing a word, what is the probability that they will be correct? In the paper, we only reported the other proportion: if someone correctly recognises something, what is the probability that they will report as 'remembered'. Because recollection, 'remembering', is typically less prone to false alarms and requires a higher level of evidence than familiarity, we expect performance to be higher for 'remembering' as compared to finding familiar. In fact, this analysis, which I did carry out in a subsequent study, yielded results that helped us understand recollective confabulation, which I elucidate next.

These cases were reported in 2005. Do you think these cases are still informative now? Are we now better able to interpret these patterns of spared and impaired abilities? If so, in what way?

Since 2005, we have a better idea of the neurological underpinning of these recollective confabulation problems. The neuroimaging study by Craik et al. (2014) on case VL, supports our speculations about frontal/executive processes. They state,

> We suggest that owing to binding failures in MTL [medial temporal lobe] regions, VL's recognition processes were forced to rely on earlier than normal stages of analysis. Environmental features on a given recognition trial may have combined with fragments persisting from previous trials resulting

in erroneous feelings of familiarity and of recollection that were not discounted or edited out, due to her impaired frontal processes.

(Craik et al., 2014, p. 367)

My own work since the original case has moved the emphasis away from a disorder of recollection towards the idea that the false recognition is based on elevated familiarity that is then interpreted as being recollection; which is a subtle difference from the original presentation. This change in emphasis came about because over time we accumulated enough cases (12) that were similar to AKP to run a group analysis with a relatively large set of controls (Moulin, 2013). I repeated exactly the same set of recognition memory tasks that we had conducted with AKP, and found the same patterns of performance. However, as described earlier, I also considered the proportion correct for the remember and familiar judgements separately. With this analysis, and with the ability to test with standard group level inferential statistics, it became clear that when the recollective confabulators reported 'remembering' something, they were actually, on the whole, fairly accurate. This suggested that the problem did not lie with recollection mechanisms. On the other hand, if we showed patients a high-frequency word at test, they were no better than chance in their recognition, regardless of the subjective evaluation that they gave it. They responded appropriately to the distinctiveness of the low-frequency words, but they could not discriminate targets from distracters for the high-frequency words, and their subjective evaluations of remember and familiar were not diagnostic of their performance.

In a second experiment (Moulin, 2013), I showed that the recollective confabulators were inappropriately overconfident in their recognition memory—even more confident than a group of patients with dementia but without recollective confabulation. What set apart the recollective confabulators from the non-confabulating dementia patients was their metacognition: the recollective confabulation group had very inaccurate, overconfident evaluations of their memory function. My hypothesis now is that recollective confabulation is caused by erroneous familiarity generated in the MTL which is combined with a metacognitive failure: the high level of familiarity is interpreted as indicating having experienced an event before. Instead of metacognitively correcting this false impression, the recollective confabulation patient, such as AKP, generates false information to support their delusional belief of prior occurrence. Thus, in conclusion, if one is to understand these patients better, I think it better to refer to the subsequent work rather than the original paper.

Do you think these cases have been considered by people who develop theories of the normal mind? If yes, how? If no, should they?

Once a paper is published, it is always interesting to see how it is received and cited; this might be the most concrete response to how relevant the case is. At the time of writing, the case report has only been modestly cited (68 according to Google Scholar). There has been more media interest than scientific interest. Undoubtedly, where the case has had the most impact on theories of the healthy mind is in research into déjà vu in healthy groups, as explained earlier, even though it does not really make a direct contribution. The case has been cited in philosophical works (e.g., de Sousa, 2009; Brun et al., 2008; Arango-Munoz, 2014; Bortolotti, 2010; Gerrans, 2014). These works draw upon AKP's particular cognitive difficult to illustrate how false memories are generated, and that they can be strongly held delusional beliefs. Perhaps most reassuringly for me given my own theoretical viewpoint, these philosophical works claim that these patients provide evidence that epistemic feelings in the cognitive system guide complex behaviours and mental attributions. It is rare to see such specific disorders in the feelings of familiarity and recollection, but when they go wrong, such as in AKP, a striking and unusual form of memory impairment is created.

Apart from the interest from philosophers, the work has been cited as a general reference to show how memory can be thought of as reconstructive and based on how things feel during retrieval. For instance, Schacter and Addis (2007) cite the paper as part of a set of various studies into confabulation which indicates that memory is fundamentally constructive. Conway (2005) cites the case in detail, using it as an example of how recollective experience 'signals' to the experient the status of the self-memory system. The fact that AKP's erroneous feelings cause him to act in particular ways suggests that the feeling of recollection is not a mere epiphenomenon—it guides our memory retrieval processes and actions. If we feel we have watched a TV programme before, this feeling is enough to stop us from watching it again—as was the case with AKP. Conway (2005, p. 616) concludes:

> More generally this account [AKP] of a malfunction of autonoetic consciousness is consistent with current thinking about one possible the function of consciousness, namely Baars's (2002) conscious access hypothesis. The suggestion is that consciousness serves an integrative function and acts to temporally bind together networks that operate nonconsciously, separately, and independently.

AKP's particular deficit is therefore perhaps evidence that there exists a special system that acts to bind together and interpret memory experiences and allows them to be experienced as such. Conway (2005, p. 615) placed a strong emphasis on the idea that 'AKP experienced the present as the past'.

Finally, a relevant point which I think has not been picked up as well as it might, is that perhaps all 'remembering' in terms of generating material from previous study episodes is re-created post hoc in order to justify the feeling, not the other way around. It is so clear from the justifications given in Table 7.2 that our patients generate plausible supporting material for their false positives. Perhaps this is all any of us do when recollecting something—bring to mind something to support our feeling of remembering. AKP has a metacognitive inhibitory control problem, but otherwise, his post hoc rationalisations of his memory experience might be exactly like those healthy people generate for true recognition.

In general, do you think that neuropsychology cases could contribute to our understanding of the normal mind? Should this data be considered and if so why?

I think that single cases continue to be extremely important in memory research. Data from single cases with neurological damage can test and refine models in ways that we cannot do with neuroimaging. I very much see single case research as opportunism, the 'naturally occurring experiment'. When our patients are motivated and generous enough to help us with our research, we can use their data to better understand their condition but also test otherwise difficult-to-test hypotheses. Plus, these single cases are often—as with the science of the 19th century—curios which demand our explanation. This can be a refreshing way to work: responding to an unusual symptom, such as recollective confabulation, and seeing how we can incorporate it into existing models. In this way, this kind of research is about data coming to find us, rather than us going in search of data according to the hypothetico-deductive tradition. What is clear to me is that we need to consider carefully both neuroimaging and classical neuropsychological data together—and whereas neuroimaging is in its infancy, single cases have been around for more than a hundred years. Finally, research is also about the transmission of new ideas and the diffusion of information. To clinicians and students alike, single cases are often extremely instructive and inspirational illustrations of a particular cognitive or neuropsychological phenomenon.

In sum, I am wholly in support of single cases informing theory and debate in cognitive neuropsychology. But I also feel we have learned most about recollective confabulation from the group study of the similar patients than from the initial single cases. At the time I assessed AKP and MA, we understood it to be much rarer than it turned out to be. In any case, the group study would never have occurred without the initial casework.

We are now living in an era where ethics committees would like to foresee every step. How much serendipity was involved in your assessment?

From Roy Jones, the senior clinician on the original article, I learned that with each individual person, if we want to really discover and treat their difficulties, the distinction between research and clinical practice is necessarily blurred. This is often the case with neuropsychology, where the psychologist 'follows their nose' in order to pinpoint a particular disorder (at the same time avoiding administering behavioural tasks which are harmful or superfluous). Thus, when trying to explore in detail a clinical finding in order to better understand and treat someone, we end up doing things that are novel and tailor-made. Even with more medical interventions, what may be done experimentally on a clinical basis, trying to heal someone with the new use of an already licenced medication, seems to straddle attentive, person-centred care and research. It often seems to me like our actions can be the same—interviewing, testing, designing new tasks, re-interviewing, re-testing, and so on, but at some point, when we start to talk about publication and dissemination, this becomes research, whereas before it was just clinical practice. Moreover, if we learn something whilst doing something new, I think we have a moral obligation to publish our findings for others.

Naturally, I had NHS ethical approval for carrying out ad hoc neuropsychological tests (for research purposes) on people with dementia and those who frequented the memory clinic, and I abided by the guidelines set out by the British Psychological Society and the NHS. At the same time, I did not re-write an application specifically for each hypothesis and each memory test I developed for AKP. Personally, I think ethical standards in research are of paramount importance, but what is critical is to have well-motivated and ethically trained researchers working with good intentions. This is not necessarily achieved by cumbersome bureaucracy which could unintentionally kill off the kind of exploratory testing and interviewing which is in the DNA of neuropsychology. It will though always be important for neuropsychological research to be overseen by ethics committees—we are in the privileged position of working closely with people who may not be able to always make their own ethical decisions.

This research work on recollective confabulation and related problems (such as psychogenic déjà vu, see the following) is completely serendipitous. I have no formal research programme on déjà vu, taking my work one case at a time—the aim is to meet and test people's memory. This kind of case-by-casework is difficult sometimes to explain to managers and university staff who are not familiar with case study work: it is more difficult, if not impossible, for example, to apply for research grants to carry out this kind of responsive research. Thus I am grateful to have had the kinds of employment where I had enough freedom and resources to follow these patients and to bring their stories to the scientific literature, even if they were not going to land the university a large international grant.

How have the déjà vu research and the recollective confabulation cases been received in the media?

On February 2, 2006, the Press Office at the University of Leeds press-released an account of the article describing AKP. It was an accidental stroke of genius. Thanks to it being Groundhog Day, the world's press had even more of an excuse to print an account of the 'world's first study' of a case of pathological déjà vu, or what many described as a real-life Groundhog Day: a reference to the great Harold Ramis film, where Bill Murray plays a character stuck in a time loop living the same day over and over. There was a wave of press interest in my work on déjà vu that culminated in a *New York Times* feature, and a slot on BBC Radio Four's PM programme: a piece about déjà vu that was played twice. Endel Tulving told me in Sydney at the International Conference on Memory in 2006 that he'd read about my work in the *New York Times*.

Ever since my research in recollective confabulation has had something of an ongoing symbiosis with press coverage. My work has been sustained by media interest. Each new case reported in the news leads to another ten or so people contacting me to describe their own situation. Each of which is equally striking, subtly different, and often as sad as it is bewildering. I have been amazed by the ability of the press to recreate—over and over again—interest in the same topic, always finding a novel angle for the same basic story: déjà vu gone wrong, lives lived in a loop, what we can understand about 'healthy' déjà vu from studying such chronic cases of recollective confabulation. Most strikingly, however, is the extent to which the media has made me realise how some psychological concepts are very well depicted in artistic works, and I do not think that the comparison with the film Groundhog Day is altogether unhelpful.

As one example, recollective confabulation tends to result in a kind of apathetic, resigned withdrawal which appears a bit like depression (although there is rarely low mood in my experience). Ramis got this idea exactly right in Groundhog Day. In a bar in a bowling alley, a forlorn Bill Murray (Phil) asks a fellow drinker:

PHIL: What would you do if you were stuck in one place and every day was exactly the same, and nothing that you did mattered?
RALPH: That about sums it up for me.

This is a clip I show to my class in my lectures on memory: it sums up one of the functions of the memory system; to encode and appreciate novelty. AKP was possibly completely unable to appreciate novelty.

The media has also shaped this research with AKP by having directly interacted with him. As journalists can often do as well as, if not better than psychologists, an insightful and direct question can elegantly expose the underlying cognitive processes in the problem. The question, 'I suppose you've been interviewed by me before?' provoked AKP into justifying his present moment: he had been interviewed on the radio before because everything then was as it is now. His description of the present moment was a reduplication of a confabulated past: this directly inspired our choice to start measuring recollective experience.

Immediately after the first wave of newspaper articles, TV documentaries and radio pieces, a different type of patient started contacting me themselves, as well as the carers and family members of people with recollective confabulation. These cases were striking because they contacted me claiming that they themselves had what I had been describing in the media: permanent déjà vu. This has turned out to be an even more perplexing and rare problem. These people appear to have déjà vu like you and I would have it, but they are constantly fighting with the feeling that their life is in a time loop, and that their memory system is playing tricks upon them. They feel stuck in a terrifying recursive loop. Again, this work (Wells et al., 2014) has involved researching and publishing a single case, and little else (for now).

Our patient was greatly distressed by his feelings of repetition, and struggled in daily life, even though he was aware of the déjà vu and the fact that it was an erroneous sensation. We think that this type of problem is related to an anxiety disorder, and perhaps the feelings of déjà vu trigger feelings of anxiety that causes a feedback loop aggravating the feeling of familiarity. We called this presentation psychogenic déjà vu, as examination revealed no organic cause.

I remain indebted to people like AKP, and those who contact me to share their experiences, and feel frustrated that I cannot do more to help. There is a great value in research which validates and classifies people's experiences, especially when so many people contact me to say that medical professionals have not taken their condition seriously, or have not known what to make of it.

References

Arango-Muñoz, S. (2014). The nature of epistemic feelings. *Philosophical Psychology, 27(2),* 193–211.
Baars, B. J. (2002). The conscious access hypothesis: origins and recent evidence. *Trends in Cognitive Sciences, 6(1),* 47–52.
Bancaud, J., Brunet-Bourgin, F., Chauvel, P., & Halgren, E. (1994). Anatomical origin of déjà vu and vivid "memories" in human temporal lobe epilepsy. *Brain, 117(1),* 71–90.
Barbeau, E. J., Chauvel, P., Moulin, C. J. A., Regis, J., & Liégeois-Chauvel, C. (2017). Hippocampus duality: memory and novelty detection are subserved by distinct mechanisms. *Hippocampus, 27,* 405–416.
Bertrand, J. M., Martinon, L. M., Souchay, C., & Moulin, C. J. (2017). History repeating itself: Arnaud's case of pathological déjà vu. *Cortex, 87,* 129–141.
Bortolotti, L. (2010). Agency, life extension, and the meaning of life. *The Monist, 93(1),* 38–56.
Brainerd, C. J., Reyna, V. F., Wright, R., & Mojardin, A. H. (2003). Recollection rejection: false-memory editing in children and adults. *Psychological Review, 110(4),* 762.
Brandt, J. (1991). The Hopkins Verbal Learning Test: development of a new memory test with six equivalent forms. *The Clinical Neuropsychologist, 5(2),* 125–142.
Brown, A. S. (2003). A review of the déjà vu experience. *Psychological Bulletin, 129(3),* 394–413.
Brown, A. S. (2004). *The Déjà Vu Experience.* Hove, UK: Psychology Press.
Brun, G., Doğuoğlu, U., & Kuenzle, D. (Eds.). (2008). *Epistemology and Emotions.* Aldershot, UK: Ashgate Publishing, Ltd.
Burgess, P. W., & Shallice, T. (1996). Response suppression, initiation and strategy use following frontal lobe lesions. *Neuropsychologia, 34(4),* 263–272.
Conway, M. A. (2005). Memory and the self. *Journal of Memory and Language, 53,* 594–628.
Coughlan, A. K., & Hollows, S. E. (1985). *The Adult Memory and Information Processing Battery (AMIPB): Test Manual.* AK Coughlin, Leeds, UK: Psychology Department, St James' Hospital.

Craik, F. I., Barense, M. D., Rathbone, C. J., Grusec, J. E., Stuss, D. T., Gao, F., . . ., & Black, S. E. (2014). VL: a further case of erroneous recollection. *Neuropsychologia, 56,* 367–380.

Curran, T. (1999). The electrophysiology of incidental and intentional retrieval: ERP old/new effects in lexical decision and recognition memory. *Neuropsychologia, 37(7),* 771–785.

de Sousa, R. (2009). Epistemic feelings. *Mind & Matter, 7(2),* 139–161.

Dickens, C. (1850/1869). *David Copperfield.* The Charles Dickens Edition. Imprint, 1869. New York: D. Appleton & Co.

Feinberg, T. E., & Roane, D. M. (2005). Delusional misidentification. *Psychiatric Clinics, 28(3),* 665–683.

Feinberg, T. E., & Shapiro, R. M. (1989). Misidentification-reduplication and the right hemisphere. *Neuropsychiatry, Neuropsychology, & Behavioral Neurology, 2(1),* 39-48.

Folstein, M., Folstein, S., & McHugh, P. (1975). 'Mini mental' state: a practical method for grading the cognitive state of patients for the clinician. *Journal of Psychiatric Research, 12,* 189–198.

Funkhouser, A. (1995). Three types of déjà vu. *Scientific and Medical Network Review, 57,* 20–22.

Gerrans, P. (2014). Pathologies of hyperfamiliarity in dreams, delusions and déjà vu. *Frontiers in Psychology, 5,* 97.

Gilchrist, I. D., Brown, V., Findlay, J. M., & Clarke, M. P. (1998). Using the eye—movement system to control the head. *Proceedings of the Royal Society of London B: Biological Sciences, 265(1408),* 1831–1836.

Hasselmo, M. E., Bodelón, C., & Wyble, B. P. (2002). A proposed function for hippocampal theta rhythm: separate phases of encoding and retrieval enhance reversal of prior learning. *Neural Computation, 14(4),* 793–817.

Illman, N. A., Butler, C. R., Souchay, C., & Moulin, C. J. A. (2012). Déjà experiences in Temporal Lobe Epilepsy. *Epilepsy Research and Treatment.* doi:10.1155/2012/539567.

Jennings, J. M., & Jacoby, L. L. (1997). An opposition procedure for detecting age-related deficits in recollection: telling effects of repetition. *Psychology and Aging, 12(2),* 352–361.

Kapur, N., Turner, A., & King, C. (1988). Reduplicative paramnesia: possible anatomical and neuropsychological mechanisms. *Journal of Neurology, Neurosurgery, and Psychiatry, 51,* 579–581.

Mandler, G. (2008). Familiarity breeds attempts: a critical review of dual-process theories of recognition. *Perspectives on Psychological Science, 3(5),* 390–399.

Mendez, M. (1992). Delusion misidentification of persons in dementia. *British Journal of Psychiatry, 160,* 414–446.

Moulin, C. J. A. (2013). Disordered recognition memory: recollective confabulation. *Cortex, 49(6),* 1541–1552.

Moulin, C. J. A., Conway, M. A., Thompson, R. G., James, N., & Jones, R. W. (2005). Disordered memory awareness: recollective confabulation in two cases of persistent Déjà vécu. *Neuropsychologia, 43,* 1362–1378.

Moulin, C. J. A., & Souchay, C. (2013). Epistemic feelings and memory. In T. Perfect & S. Lindsay (Eds.), *Sage Handbook of Applied Memory.* Thousand Oaks, CA: Sage Publications, pp. 520–539.

Moulin, C. J. A., Souchay, C., & Morris, R. G. (2013). The cognitive neuropsychology of recollection. *Cortex, 49(6),* 1445–1451.

Nelson, H., & Willison, J. (1991). *The Revised National Adult Reading Test—Test Manual.* Windsor, UK: NFER-Nelson.

O'Connor, A. R., Lever, C., & Moulin, C. J. A. (2010). Novel insights into false recollection: a model of déjà vécu. *Cognitive Neuropsychiatry, 15,* 118–144.

O'Connor, A. R., & Moulin, C. J. A. (2010). Recognition without identification, erroneous familiarity, and déjà vu. *Current Psychiatry Reports, 12*, 165–173.

Pisani, A., Marra, C., & Silveri, M. C. (2000). Anatomical and psychological mechanism of reduplicative misidentification syndromes. *Neurological Sciences, 21(5)*, 324-328.

Reitan, R. M. (1958). The validity of the trail making test as an indicator of organic brain damage. *Perceptual and Motor Skills, 8*, 271–276.

Schacter, D. L., & Addis, D. R. (2007). The cognitive neuroscience of constructive memory: remembering the past and imagining the future. *Philosophical Transactions of the Royal Society B: Biological Sciences, 362(1481)*, 773–786.

Tulving, E. (1985). Memory and consciousness. *Canadian Psychology-Psychologie Canadian, 26*, 1–12.

Tulving, E., Markowitsch, H. J., Craik, F. I., Habib, R., & Houle, S. (1996). Novelty and familiarity activations in PET studies of memory encoding and retrieval. *Cerebral Cortex, 6(1)*, 71–79.

Wells, C. E., Moulin, C. J. A., Ethridge, P., Illman, N. A., Davies, E., & Zeman, A. (2014). Persistent psychogenic déjà vu: a case report. *Journal of Medical Case Reports, 8*, 414.

Wilding, E. L. (2000). In what way does the parietal ERP old/new effect index recollection? *International Journal of Psychophysiology, 35(1)*, 81–87.

Wojcik, D. Z., Moulin, C. J., & Souchay, C. (2013). Metamemory in children with autism: exploring "feeling-of-knowing" in episodic and semantic memory. *Neuropsychology, 27(1)*, 19–27.

Yonelinas, A. P. (2002). The nature of recollection and familiarity: a review of 30 years of research. *Journal of Memory and Language, 46(3)*, 441–517.

8
CASE KC (KENT COCHRANE) AND HIS CONTRIBUTIONS TO RESEARCH AND THEORY ON MEMORY AND RELATED, NON-MEMORY FUNCTIONS

R. Shayna Rosenbaum and Morris Moscovitch

Kent Cochrane, known in the scientific literature by the initials KC, has a special status in the archives of memory research. He had been investigated extensively for nearly 30 years since a motorcycle accident left him with widespread brain damage that included large bilateral hippocampal lesions, resulting in a sharp dissociation between intact semantic memory and impaired episodic memory (Rosenbaum et al., 2005; Tulving, 1985, 2002; Tulving, Schacter, McLachlan & Moscovitch, 1988). In displaying such "episodic amnesia," which encompasses an entire lifetime of personal experiences, KC differs from many other amnesic patients in severity but not the pattern of spared and impaired function. He acted as a primary participant in over 25 published studies, many of which include multiple experiments, collectively cited at least 2,500 times, and has been tested as a member of a group of participants in many others. Countless reviews and book chapters mention KC or were influenced by his case. KC's and his family's long-standing involvement in psychological science has changed the way we think about memory and the brain, greatly influencing memory theory and clinical practice. It is remarkable that in an age when the field is driven by technological advances, close examination of a single person can still contribute a great deal to our understanding of brain-behaviour relations (Rosenbaum, Gilboa & Moscovitch, 2014). KC died unexpectedly of unknown cause at the age of 62, on March 30, 2014, but the wealth of data that he had provided continues to influence the field.

Case KC, whom you have assessed for over two decades, provides strong evidence supporting Tulving's dissociation between episodic and semantic memory. First of all, can you provide us with some background information about KC?

KC was a right-handed man with 16 years of formal education. Born prematurely in 1951 into a loving family, KC's development was reported as normal. He was the eldest of five children, and he spent his childhood and early adolescence in a suburban neighbourhood near Toronto. He completed high school and a three-year degree in business administration at a community college. At the age of 27, he became employed at an engineering and manufacturing plant, where he was responsible for delivery and pickup, and quality control of products. With a relatively mundane job, he sought excitement in other aspects of his life. Carefree and boisterous in his late adolescence and early adulthood, he was described by family and friends as the ringleader in mischief. He spent late nights at bars, travelled to Mardi Gras with fraternity brothers, and engaged in adventurous but risky behaviours that defined his colourful personality. This also likely contributed to the many mishaps that he had prior to the motorcycle accident that left him with a severe traumatic brain injury that had a dramatic, lasting effect on his memory and personality. No longer boisterous, he became placid and his life constrained.

In October of 1981, at the age of 30, he suffered his latest and most devastating head injury when he rode his motorcycle off an exit ramp on the stretch of highway from the plant to his nearby house. Upon arrival at a regional hospital, he was unconscious with dilated fixed pupils and was noted to have clonic seizures. Due to the severity of his neurological condition, he was soon transferred to a larger hospital where he underwent neurosurgery for the removal of a left-sided subdural hematoma. His return to consciousness at 72 hours post-trauma took place in an intensive care unit where he was to remain for one month until stable enough to be transferred to a rehabilitation hospital for a six-month stay. At around seven days, he appeared to recognize his mother. A follow-up CT scan performed during week three showed a chronic bilateral frontal subdural hematoma, slightly enlarged ventricles and sulci, and left occipital lobe infarction presumed to be secondary to compression of the left posterior cerebral artery from increased intracranial pressure.

Upon his transfer to the rehabilitation hospital, KC was noted to be reading and conversing quite well and began to recognize friends but showed slowed mentation as well as hemiplegia and a homonymous hemianopia, both affecting the right side. When he finally returned home in July 1982, the severity of his inability to commit new information of any type to memory became more evident, forewarning what was to remain apparent on later MRI scans: widespread brain damage that included severe injury to his medial temporal lobes, with almost complete hippocampal loss bilaterally (Rosenbaum et al., 2005; Tulving et al., 1988). It also became increasingly clear, especially to those who knew KC from before his injury, that any details of past personal happenings—episodic memories—that they had shared with him, however meaningful at the time of occurrence, had ceased to exist in KC's mind. Not even an intact corpus of mental faculties such as perception, language, and reasoning skills would enable KC to relive a personal episodic past or imagine possible future events in which he might participate.

It was in 1983 that KC was brought to the attention of one of us (MM) by an undergraduate student at Erindale College of the University of Toronto. The student had met KC at a sheltered workshop, where the student had worked part time, and was convinced that KC was "just like HM." KC was assessed on standard neuropsychological tests and, like HM, was found to exhibit a pattern of severely impaired anterograde memory and relatively preserved retrograde memory. However, upon referral to Endel Tulving, Daniel Schacter, and Elizabeth Glisky at the newly established Unit for Memory Disorders at the university, it was soon realized that KC, though exhibiting severe anterograde amnesia, was not quite like HM in that he did not seem to recall any personal happenings from his own life. At that time, HM was thought to be able to remember some of his life experiences up to five years or so before his surgery (Milner, Corkin & Teuber, 1968). However, it was later demonstrated, as a result of our theoretical and empirical work with KC and other amnesic patients (Nadel & Moscovitch, 1997; Moscovitch et al., 2005, 2006; Rosenbaum et al., 2008), that HM also could not recollect any personal happenings from any period in his life, other than an isolated occurrence in his childhood (Corkin, 2002; Steinvorth, Levine & Corkin, 2006). Work with KC contributed to our understanding not only of episodic and semantic memory but also to the development of other aspects of memory theory. These include the distinction between explicit memory (memory with conscious awareness) and implicit memory (memory without conscious awareness); the prospect of new learning in amnesia; the fate of recent and remote memory for autobiographical and public events, people, and spatial locations; the relationship between memory, time, and the self; and contributions of episodic memory to financial, social, and moral decisions.

How did you first realize that this case was interesting?

KC arrived at a fortuitous time when a memory disorders clinic was established at the University of Toronto and the field was trying to understand the nature of memory structures that do not depend on the hippocampus. KC was like HM and other amnesic cases reported in the literature in that he displayed anterograde amnesia for material encountered post-injury despite relatively preserved intelligence, language, and reasoning ability. However, unlike other amnesic cases that had been studied, his retrograde memory was also severely affected by his closed head injury, consistent with the multiple loci of damage amply demonstrated by his MRI scans (Rosenbaum et al., 2005; Tulving et al., 1988). This added complexity was especially problematic in terms of attributing a particular deficit to a single lesion site. However, it was KC's deficits against a background of preserved function that made him remarkable to study. The sharp contrast between his impaired episodic memory for personal life events and intact semantic memory for factual knowledge was noted from the start and was responsible for drawing our attention to his case. As a result, work with KC contributed to the eventual crumbling of the neat and tidy single-memory, single-locus model of amnesia, and helped to reveal at a biological level what had been earlier suspected at a theoretical level of multiple declarative memory systems (e.g., Tulving, 1972, 1983; Tulving & Schacter, 1990).

Interestingly, the majority of initial studies involving KC focused on the distinction between explicit and implicit memory, which were the questions du jour. Our initial hunch that KC would contribute in meaningful ways to memory theory was confirmed very early on in studies showing that, even without a functional hippocampus, priming can occur for pre-existing and self-generated novel word associates (Schacter, 1985; Schacter & Graf, 1986); is modality specific (Köhler et al., 1997); can last on the order of 30 minutes in some cases (Goshen-Gottstein, Moscovitch & Melo, 2000) and up to one year in others; and is possible following a single study exposure (Goshen-Gottstein et al., 2000; McAndrews, Glisky & Schacter, 1987). Early work with KC also demonstrated considerable procedural or complex learning, again in the absence of hippocampal support, such as the acquisition of computer-related knowledge through the "method of vanishing cues" (Glisky, Schacter & Tulving, 1986a, 1986b; Glisky & Schacter, 1988). This finding alone prompted rehabilitation efforts that are still in practice today (e.g., Kapur, Glisky & Wilson, 2002; Svoboda, Richards, Leach & Mertens, 2012; Svoboda, Richards, Yao & Leach, 2015). Also notable is evidence of limited learning of semantic facts relating to the self (trait self-knowledge, familiarity with family and friends; Tulving, 1993; Westmacott, Leach, Freedman & Moscovitch, 2001) and the world (famous people, vocabulary terms; Westmacott & Moscovitch, 2001, 2002) and a very limited amount of information that may be regarded as episodic (i.e., mnemonic precedence; Schacter, Moscovitch, Tulving, McLachlan & Freedman, 1986). For the most part, however, such learning depends heavily on repeated exposure of meaningful study material under conditions in which associative interference is kept to a minimum, and the contents of learning are almost always inflexible, inaccessible in novel situations, or impoverished in some way (Hayman, Macdonald & Tulving, 1993; Tulving, Hayman & MacDonald, 1991).

Another interesting observation that was made early on by Tulving and Schacter was that KC's ability to imagine a personal future appeared to be as compromised as his ability to describe personal events from his past. Inspired by Ingvar's theory relating episodic memory to future thinking and planning, Tulving and Schacter confirmed this relationship in extensive interviews with KC (Tulving, 1985), which laid the groundwork for future theories and research on autonoetic consciousness and future thinking (e.g., Clayton, Bussey & Dickinson, 2003; Craver, Kwan, Steindam & Rosenbaum, 2014; Klein, 2013; Schacter et al., 2012; Suddendorf & Corballis, 2007; Tulving, 2002).

Can you summarize the main neuroanatomical and neuropsychological features of this case?

MRI scanning and formal neuropsychological testing were conducted to provide a neural basis for, and to systematically assess, the remarkable pattern of functional dissociations observed in KC, with a primary focus on explaining severely impaired episodic memory in the face of seemingly intact semantic memory. MRI scans acquired in 1990 (Tulving et al., 1991) and in 1996 and 2002 (Rosenbaum et al., 2005) showed evidence of mild diffuse cortical atrophy, which reflected thinning of the cortical rims and underlying white matter in all lobes and coincided with bilateral ventricular enlargement. Throughout the brain, the left hemisphere was affected to a greater extent than the right hemisphere. Focal signal abnormalities were also observed predominantly in the left hemisphere, including a posterior lesion in occipitotemporal cortex and an anterior lesion in frontoparietal cortex and underlying white matter. The left-sided posterior hypointensity on the MR images reflected a lesion that appeared to be an occipital-temporal infarction, likely resulting from posterior cerebral artery compression secondary to the increased intracranial pressure caused by the head trauma. A contiguous volume of encephalomalacia (softening of the brain tissue) was seen in the lingual gyrus, fusiform gyrus, cuneus, precuneus, and parts of superior, middle, and inferior occipital gyri. Rostrally, medial aspects of the lesion extended into retrosplenial cortex. The left anterior hypointensity may have reflected sequelae of the subdural hematoma that was diagnosed and removed in the hospital immediately following KC's head trauma. Encephalomalacia was observable primarily in the white matter superior to the lateral ventricles, undercutting adjacent gray matter. From there, it extended into the white matter that underlies the superior precentral gyrus, affecting large portions of the pyramidal tract. Further rostrally, the lesion undercut superior premotor cortex and large aspects of the middle and superior frontal gyri (dorsolateral prefrontal cortex).

Especially prominent was extensive volume loss in medial temporal lobe structures, most notably the hippocampal formation along the entire rostrocaudal extent (i.e., longitudinal axis) and surrounding parahippocampal gyrus, bilaterally (Figure 8.1).

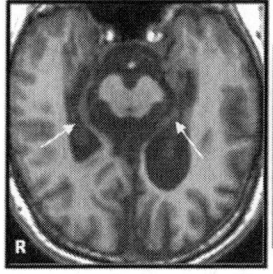

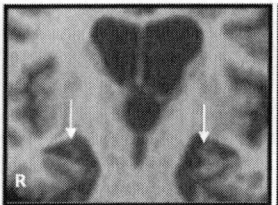

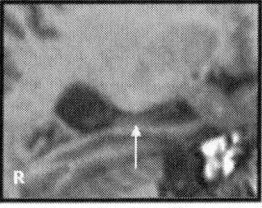

FIGURE 8.1 MRI displaying extensive damage to patient KC's MTL/hippocampus (arrows) in axial (left image) and coronal (middle image) and sagittal (right image) views as a result of a severe closed head injury. Reprinted from *Learning and Memory: A Comprehensive Reference*, Rosenbaum, Kim, & Baker, Semantic and episodic memory, 87–118, Copyright (2017), with permission from Elsevier.

Lateral temporal cortex appeared to have been spared from focal damage. Additional areas known to be involved in memory that were affected included the septal area, posterior thalamus, and caudate nucleus, bilaterally, as well as his left amygdala, mammillary bodies, and anterior thalamus. Quantification of tissue loss in these areas is provided in Table 8.1 and elaborated in Rosenbaum et al. (2005).

Overall, KC's severe head injury and related posterior cerebral artery compression resulted in brain damage that was diffuse and multifocal. What is unique about this double pathology is that the medial temporal lobes were effectively "hit" from both directions, affecting the anterior portion in the right hemisphere from the head injury and the posterior portion in the left hemisphere from a large occipital infarction.

KC underwent a detailed neuropsychological examination across multiple sessions in the late 1980s and 1996, and was re-examined in 2003, 2009, and 2011 on abridged versions of the test battery. Testing across the decades showed that KC's intellectual and cognitive function outside the domain of episodic memory were largely, although not completely, preserved. Performance on mental status screening tests administered in 1994 and 2003 was above the cut-off for dementia, with most points lost on the memory subscale. His verbal, performance, and full-scale IQ on the Wechsler Adult Intelligence Scale (WAIS; Wechsler, 1999) were in the average range.

The pattern of damaged and spared tissue seen on MRI may help account for some of KC's neuropsychological test profile, presented in Table 8.2. Damage to occipitotemporal structures, largely in the left hemisphere, from cuneus and through lingual and parahippocampal gyri is consistent with difficulties in perception of colour on the City University Color Vision Test (Fletcher, 1980) and

TABLE 8.1 Comparison of volumes for medial temporal lobe and related limbic structures in KC and control participants. Reprinted from Neuropsychologia, 43, Rosenbaum et al., The case of K.C.: contributions of a memory-impaired person to memory theory, 989–1021, Copyright (2005), with permission from Elsevier.

Brain Structure	Controls volume, mm^3 (SD)		KC Volume, mm^3 (z-score)	
	Left	Right	Left	Right
hippocampus	3974.01 (413.13)	4020.28 (356.94)	**749.12 (−7.8)**	**533.55 (−9.8)**
parahippocampal gyrus	1871.68 (73.05)	2009.95 (241.86)	**476.40 (−19.1)**	**857.48 (−4.8)**
amygdala	1564.09 (309.97)	1326.81 (396.13)	**512.46 (−3.4)**	452.29 (−2.2)
mammillary bodies	49.19 (9.33)	50.67 (10.01)	**15.03 (−3.7)**	25.55 (−2.5)
septal area	351.63 (76.18)	339.14 (69.73)	**68.67 (−3.7)**	**59.65 (−4.0)**
basal forebrain	199.19 (94.60)	206.38 (88.96)	69.22 (−1.4)	81.25 (−1.4)
hypothalamus	295.81 (82.54)	304.22 (107.26)	116.85 (−2.2)	172.46 (−1.2)
anterior thalamus	991.56 (118.29)	1072.87 (144.93)	**252.68 (−6.2)**	**617.78 (−3.1)**
posterior thalamus	4864.96 (327.17)	4794.41 (302.44)	**2619.51 (−6.9)**	**2876.23 (−6.3)**
caudate nucleus	1901.14 (70.40)	1830.32 (96.65)	**1424.07 (−6.8)**	**1191.41 (−6.6)**
anterior cingulate cortex	4827.40 (1831.43)	4288.69 (1550.68)	4415.09 (−0.2)	4061.62 (−0.1)
middle cingulate cortex	2509.00 (593.56)	2455.43 (421.35)	2324.19 (−0.3)	1925.48 (−1.3)
posterior cingulate cortex	3834.90 (793.29)	3524.72 (568.19)	2617.50 (−1.5)	2389.30 (−2.0)
orbitofrontal cortex	14133.63 (3793.92)	14658.61 (3608.29)	9143.69 (−1.3)	9371.85 (−1.5)

Note. Z-scores shown in bold typeface reflect disproportionate volume loss in KC (see text for details). Volumes were corrected for variations in head size.

Farnsworth-Munsell 100-hue test (Farnsworth, 1957) and face matching under degraded conditions on the Benton Facial Recognition Test (Benton, Hamsher, Varney & Spreen, 1983). Importantly, other aspects of his perception and recognition were preserved, including tasks requiring basic visual feature analysis such as line orientation and form discrimination on the Judgement of Line Orientation and Visual Form Discrimination tests, respectively (Benton et al.), as well as more complex processes such as reading and recognition of objects and familiar faces. He was also unimpaired in visuospatial reproduction of the Rey Osterrieth Complex Figure (ROCF; Osterrieth, 1944) and reconstruction of designs with blocks (WASI Block Design subtest; Wechsler, 1999). The possibility that damage to posterior neocortical areas contributed to KC's autobiographical episodic memory loss by affecting his visual imagery (Rubin & Greenberg, 1998) was tested and deemed unlikely (Rosenbaum et al., 2004a).

TABLE 8.2 Neuropsychological profile of patient KC. Reprinted from Neuropsychologia, 43, Rosenbaum et al., The case of K.C.: contributions of a memory-impaired person to memory theory, 989–1021, Copyright (2005), with permission from Elsevier.

Mental Status		
DRS (/144)[1]		125
	Attention (/37)	37
	Initiation/Persevation (/37)	34
	Construction (/6)	6
	Conceptualization (/39)	34
	Memory (/25)	14
General Intellectual Function		
WASI (standard score)	FSIQ	99
VIQ		99
PIQ		99
AM-NART (standard score)		102
Language		
Western Aphasia Battery (/100)		98.2 (unimpaired)
WAIS-R Vocabulary (scaled score)		9
Boston Naming (/60)		57 (unimpaired)
Semantic fluency[2] (scaled score)		10
Anterograde Memory		
WMS-R	General Memory (standard score)	61
	Verbal Memory (standard score)	67
	Visual Memory (standard score)	69
	Logical Memory I (%ile)	5th
	Logical Memory II (%ile)	<1st
	Visual Reproduction I (%ile)	13th
	Visual Reproduction II (%ile)	<1st
WRMT (/50)	Words	26
	Faces	25
CVLT	Acquisition (T-score)	12
	Short delay free (Z-score)	−5
	Long delay free (Z-score)	−5
	Recog. Discrim. (Z-score)	−5
ROCF (/36)	Immediate recall	4
	Delayed recall	0
Retrograde Memory		
AMI Autobiographical (/9)	Childhood	2
	Early Adult Life	3
	Recent Life	1
AMI Personal Semantics (/21)	Childhood	16
	Early Adult Life	13.5
	Recent Life	8

(*Continued*)

TABLE 8.2 (Continued)

Visuospatial Function		
Judgement of Line Orientation (/30)		23[3] (unimpaired)
Benton Visual Discrimination Test (%ile)		>95th
ROCF Copy (/36)		36
WASI Block Design		9
Hooper Visual Organization (T-score)		79[3]
Benton Face Recognition Test (%ile)		2–16th
Executive Function		
Letter fluency[4] (scaled score)		6
WAIS-R Digit Span (scaled score)		12
WASI Similarities (scaled score)		11
WASI Matrix Reasoning (scaled score)		11
WCST	Categories (/6)	6 (unimpaired)
	Persev. Resp. (Z-score)	−0.9
Trail Making Test	Part A	(raw score = 138 s)
	Part B	(raw score = 291 s)
Concept Generation Test Groupings		4 (unimpaired)

Note. DRS, Dementia Rating Scale; WASI, Wechsler Abbreviated Scale of Intelligence; WAIS-R, Wechsler Adult Intelligence Scale—Revised; AM-NART, American National Adult Reading Test; WMS-R, Wechsler Memory Scale—Revised; CVLT, California Verbal Learning Test; ROCF, Rey Osterrieth Complex Figure; AMI, Autobiographical Memory Interview; WCST, Wisconsin Card Sorting Test.

Damage to regions of frontal cortex was limited to dorsolateral and premotor areas. As a result, KC exhibited a markedly reduced fluency for spontaneous verbal output, including poor performance on the FAS phonemic fluency task (Spreen & Strauss, 1998). No other deficits were observed on tests of executive function, including the Wisconsin Card Sorting Test, the ratio of Trails B to Trails A, working memory and tests of abstract reasoning. Nonetheless, because frontal functions contribute to strategic retrieval on tests of recent and remote memory, it was important to test the possibility that frontal deficits may relate to loss of autobiographical memory, but this too, was deemed unlikely (Rosenbaum et al., 2004a). Sparing of ventrolateral prefrontal cortex and lateral temporal cortex likely accounts for his preserved language and semantic memory on the Western Aphasia Battery (Kertesz, 1982), Boston Naming Test (BNT; Kaplan, Goodglass & Weintraub, 1983), category (semantic) fluency, and vocabulary subtest of WAIS. Sparing of occipital lobe structures likely accounts for his preserved performance on implicit tests of visual learning.

The extent of damage to KC's medial temporal lobes, particularly to his hippocampus and parahippocampus, and associated diencephalic and basal forebrain structures, was in line with his profound impairment on all explicit tests of new learning and memory, whether the material was verbal or non-verbal. This included the Wechsler Memory Scale-Revised (WMS-R; Wechsler, 1987), California Verbal Learning Test (CVLT; Delis, Kramer, Kaplan & Ober, 1987), Warrington Recognition Memory test for words and faces (WRMT; Warrington, 1984), and recall of the ROCF. Less clear is whether this pattern of neurological damage also accounted for KC's severe remote autobiographical episodic memory loss on the Autobiographical Memory Interview (AMI; Kopelman, Wilson & Baddeley, 1990), the Galton-Crovitz word-cue task for autobiographical information (Crovitz & Schiffman, 1974), and the Autobiographical Interview (Levine, Svoboda, Hay, Winocur & Moscovitch, 2002) in the context of spared personal and general semantic memory (Moscovitch & Melo, 1997; Rosenbaum et al., 2004a, 2005). His performance improved only minimally when he was provided with additional prompts aimed at facilitating recall, and he was not prone to confabulating. Additional damage to KC's amygdala may have accounted for his blunted affect and personality changes.

Do you think this case contributes to our understanding of how the normal mind works?

When we began working with KC, functional neuroimaging was in its infancy, with the advent of PET and fMRI still a few years off. Unless the lesions were highly circumscribed, the focus of studies with patients with brain damage was to reveal the workings of the mind and to test psychological theories and models, as much, if not more so, than to reveal the workings of the brain. Our studies with KC were no different, especially since his lesions, caused by a closed head injury, were not restricted to a single structure. Despite this, however, his functional deficits were remarkably circumscribed, primarily affecting episodic memory while leaving many other cognitive and perceptual functions relatively intact, much as one would expect of patients with lesions confined to the medial temporal lobes. In this regard, KC was not different from many other amnesic patients. His store of semantic facts about himself and the world, procedural skills that were acquired in the first 30 years of his life, and his effortless functioning in his everyday environment was comparable to most amnesic cases.

What made KC exceptional, though not unique, with respect to many amnesic cases studied at the time was the severity and extent of his episodic memory loss: he could not recollect any specific event in which he himself participated or any happening that he himself witnessed, though he sometimes knew that those events occurred. In short, personal episodic memories were virtually absent, whereas personal semantic memory was relatively preserved. Given the nature of his brain damage, finding additional functional deficits would not be especially illuminating, but finding relatively preserved abilities in some functional domains in the face of such severe deficits in episodic memory would provide strong evidence for or against psychological theories in which the role of episodic memory and its status is clearly defined.

It is important to distinguish theories that have to do with mind and those that have to do with brain function. KC was an ideal participant to test predictions from psychological theories in which episodic memory was conflated with other memory and cognitive functions, and difficult to disentangle. We briefly review the contributions that KC made to such theories.

Dissociations Between Episodic and Semantic Memory, and Explicit and Implicit Memory

In the late 1970s, psychologists began distinguishing between different types of memory, each of which operated according to its own principles and was presumed to be mediated by different neurological structures. One such distinction was between episodic and semantic memory, and another was between explicit and implicit memory. The latter could itself be subdivided into a number of subtypes, including perceptual and conceptual priming, and procedural memory, which involves perceptual and motor learning (Squire, 1992). A bone of contention in these studies, and the theories they were meant to test, was whether participants used episodic memory, knowingly or unwittingly, to contribute to performance on non-episodic memory tasks, including semantic memory, and all forms of implicit memory.

It was in these studies that KC left an indelible mark on the field (see Rosenbaum et al., 2005 for review). Despite his profound episodic memory loss, his semantic memory, whether tested for general or personal knowledge, was relatively well preserved. Remarkably, he also performed as well as healthy controls on a variety of implicit memory tests, including perceptual and conceptual priming, implicit memory of associations, procedural memory that included learning to read transformed script and to write simple computer programs, acquiring conceptual knowledge, and solving riddles. His performance supported a class of dissociable memory theories, as opposed to unitary memory theories, that emerged at that time. Amongst these were memory systems theory (Tulving & Schacter, 1990), transfer appropriate processing theory (Roediger, Srinivas & Rajaram, 1998), and component process theory (Moscovitch, 1992; see review by Roediger, Buckner & McDermott, 1999), though his data alone could not adjudicate amongst them.

Dissociations Between Different Types of Spatial Memory

Space is a crucial component of many theories of episodic memory, and even constitutes one of its defining features: where an event occurred. Some neurobiological theories of memory even argue that allocentric spatial representations

(O'Keefe & Nadel, 1978; Burgess, Maguire & O'Keefe, 2002; Bird & Burgess, 2008) or scenes (Hassabis & Maguire, 2007; Maguire & Mullally, 2013) provide the foundation on which episodic memory is built and the scaffolding onto which memory for events are constructed. If true, people like KC with severe episodic memory loss, but sparing of semantic memory, should show comparable deficits in spatial memory. Our findings only partially supported this prediction.

In a series of experiments, we tested KC's spatial memory for a highly familiar neighbourhood where he lived for years before his accident and continued to live afterwards (Rosenbaum et al., 2000). We had him imagine navigating the neighbourhood and answer questions that assessed the representations he had of it, and the operations he could perform on them. He performed normally on all allocentric tests of spatial memory, including order judgements (the order in which landmarks are encountered on a route), finding alternate routes between two points when the typical route is blocked, and by vector mapping which tested the distance and direction between two points as the crow flies. He also was able to identify major landmarks, from pictures, that are used as anchors in navigation, but was impaired at identifying incidental buildings or houses, though he knew them well. When asked to sketch a map of his neighbourhood, KC provided fewer streets and landmarks than controls, though his configuration of them was accurate. Last, though he could identify the major landmarks, and know how to navigate from one to the other, he could not describe the perceptual details he may encounter on the way, or, in real life, when facing a landmark, what was behind him. His ability to acquire new spatial memories by learning a new environment was very compromised and as poor as his ability to acquire new episodic memories.

On the basis of these findings, we concluded that as semantic memory is preserved relative to episodic memory, so are schematic representations of highly familiar, premorbid environments, relative to rich, perceptual ones (Rosenbaum et al., 2001; Winocur & Moscovitch, 2011). The schematic representations retain allocentric information of the environment and support navigation in it. It is, in many respects, a relatively preserved cognitive map of the environment, but like all maps, lacks the rich detail that enables re-experiencing that environment from memory. In short, detailed episodic-like information is absent. Learning new environments and forming new schematic representations, however, is extremely impaired, much as is KC's ability to form new episodic memories. These findings have received support from studies of other cases of hippocampal amnesia (Herdman, Calarco, Moscovitch, Hirshhorn & Rosenbaum, 2015; Maguire, Nannery & Spiers, 2006; Rosenbaum et al., 2005; Rosenbaum, Cassidy & Herdman, 2015), rodents with bilateral hippocampal lesions (Winocur, Moscovitch, Fogel, Rosenbaum & Sekeres, 2005; Winocur, Moscovitch, Rosenbaum & Sekeres, 2010a), typical aging (Rosenbaum et al., 2012; Winocur, Moscovitch, Rosenbaum & Sekeres,

2010b), and neuroimaging (Hirshhorn, Grady, Rosenbaum, Winocur & Moscovitch, 2012; Rosenbaum et al., 2004b, 2007b).

With respect to "mind" models of spatial memory, the data from KC, and other patients with severe episodic memory loss, suggest that the models need to consider (at least) two types of representations: schematic representations that preserve configural (allocentric) information sufficient for navigation between major landmarks and along major routes, and more detailed representations that capture the rich perceptual landscape that enable re-experiencing the environment (Moscovitch, Cabeza, Winocur & Nadel, 2016).

A question one can ask, therefore, is whether these preserved schematic representations can serve as scaffolds on which to construct new episodic memories or recover old ones. Although we did not test this prediction directly, a number of studies with KC, and amnesic patients with more restricted medial temporal lobe lesions, suggests that these schematic representations cannot support rich event memories or scenes, whether veridical or fictitious (e.g., Hassabis, Kumaran, Vann & Maguire, 2007; Rosenbaum, Gilboa, Levine, Winocur & Moscovitch, 2009). This conclusion is supported by studies on healthy young and old participants that found that there is a close relationship between the perceptual richness and vividness of an event at a particular location, and how detailed one's representation of that location is (Robin & Moscovitch, 2017; Robin, Wynn & Moscovitch, 2016).

Having helped establish that memory is not unitary and that different memory functions can exist independently of one another, more recent work with KC has shown how such memory functions interact with one another. We will discuss those shortly.

Consolidation and Transformation

Memory theories, dating to the turn of the 20th century, included consolidation as a necessary process for retaining information after encoding so that it became relatively immune from interference, whether on the behavioural or neurological level. How long it took to consolidate memories depended on both physiological and psychological processes, including the extent of prior knowledge, both semantic and episodic, to which these new memories could be assimilated (Burnham, 1903; Dudai, 2012).

If episodic memory loss arises from damage to a consolidation process, then only recent memories should be affected. If, however, episodic memory loss results from damage to an underlying process inherent to episodic memory, then deficits in episodic memory should be observed no matter how long ago the memory was initially formed. Studies of KC support the latter conclusion since his episodic memory deficits extend encompass his entire lifetime. As noted previously, one can argue that recent and remote memory loss result from different causes related to extensive damage KC has to structures that are not implicated primarily in episodic memory (Bright et al., 2006; Bayley, Gold, Hopkins & Squire, 2005). Indeed, one of us (MM) argued as much when he first considered data from KC and from other patients with extensive retrograde amnesia (Moscovitch, 1982).

There is still a vigorous debate as to whether lesions restricted to structures restricted to the medial temporal lobe that cause profound anterograde episodic amnesia also cause an extensive retrograde amnesia or whether extensive retrograde amnesia results from damage to additional structures that mediate other processes (Squire & Wixted, 2011; Moscovitch et al., 2016; Dede, Wixted, Hopkins & Squire, 2016).

What is clear, however, is that semantic memory does not show this extensive memory loss either in KC or in other patients with amnesia. These findings led a number of investigators, including Penfield and Milner (1958), to argue, consistent with Bartlett (1932) that memories are transformed with time and experience from highly detailed episodic memories, to more gist-like or schematic memories of past events, or to frankly semantic memories (Winocur & Moscovitch, 2011; Sekeres et al., 2016). Such memories are fundamentally different from episodic memory and depend on different psychological processes mediated by different structures. For these reasons, these memories are spared in people with episodic memory loss, if they had had time to be transformed before the loss occurred. These observations in KC, and other patients like him, support dynamic theories of memory, in which memories are transformed and reconstructed, rather than static ones in which memories are reproduced in the manner they were encoded.

Mental Time Travel to the Past and the Future

Prominent theories of episodic memory, dating at least from James (1890), but given greater prominence by Tulving (1985) and others (Mandler, 1980; Jacoby, 1991; Yonelinas, 2002; Eichenbaum, Yonelinas & Ranganath, 2007), distinguish between recollection and familiarity. The former depends on (or is associated with) autonoetic consciousness, a consciousness with the self in it that enables one to re-experience the past from a personal perspective. Familiarity, by contrast, like semantic memory, depends on noetic consciousness, a feeling or knowledge that one has encountered a stimulus before without re-experiencing the past event in which the encounter occurred.

Tulving based his ideas, in part, on his interactions with KC. Tulving reasoned that any mental experience that depends on autonoetic consciousness, including imagining the future or planning for it, should be equally impaired. Once you are travelling mentally in time, it should not matter in what direction you are going (Tulving, 1988, 2002). Indeed, that was the case for KC (Kwan et al., 2012; Rosenbaum et al., 2005). His ability to imagine the future in detail was no better than his ability to remember the past, no matter how remote it was (Rosenbaum et al., 2008, 2009), a point which we will take up later.

As we noted earlier, however, given the extent of KC's brain damage, it is difficult to know to what to attribute the associated deficits. Are they related to the same impaired psychological processes that underlie his episodic memory loss, or are they related to other impaired processes that resulted from damage to areas that are not implicated in episodic memory? Studies on KC alone cannot distinguish clearly between these alternatives. It is important to note, however, that it is these observations in KC (Tulving et al., 1988) that served as the inspiration for an entire field of study on the relationship between past and future thought at both the psychological and neurological level (see Schacter et al., 2012, for review). In general, they confirm that performance on tests of past, episodic memories is highly correlated with performance on tests of future imagining, whether related to real plans or fictitious events, and are mediated by overlapping brain regions (Addis, Wong & Schacter, 2007; Schacter et al., 2012; Spreng, Mar & Kim, 2009). Ironically, the autonoetic consciousness hypothesis that gave rise to this research is not fully confirmed, as similar deficits are observed when people have to construct scenes or events in which they are not present (e.g., Hassabis et al., 2007), leading some investigators to argue that scene construction (Hassabis & Maguire, 2007; Maguire & Mullally, 2013) or relational processing (Olsen, Moses, Riggs & Ryan, 2012) are the determining processes that underlie these abilities.

Theory of Mind

By some theoretical accounts, episodic memory is considered to be inextricably linked to theory of mind. Amongst such accounts, simulation theories state that in order to imagine and make sense of other people's thoughts, feelings, intentions, and actions, we must rely, at least in part, on our autobiographical recollections (Buckner & Carroll, 2007; Schacter et al., 2012). This idea is bolstered by observation that both episodic memory and theory of mind emerge close in time during development (Perner & Ruffman, 1995) and that both rely on overlapping neural substrates (Spreng et al., 2009).

If these simulation models are correct, KC should perform very poorly on theory of mind tasks since his episodic memory is virtually absent. Contrary to this prediction, KC performed normally (Rosenbaum et al., 2007a). These findings are at variance with the idea that the ability to simulate or reconstruct one's own past mental states is necessary to imagine the contents of other people's minds. Both KC and ML, another patient with similar episodic memory loss, had no apparent difficulty in taking other persons' perspectives and inferring other people's thoughts, feelings, and intentions, as revealed by the theory of mind tests. The findings imply that KC's and ML's theory of mind ability may depend on semantic memory and general knowledge abilities that are largely preserved in both cases (Levine et al., 1998; Rosenbaum et al., 2005).

These studies, however, did not test predictions of simulation models which state that individuals are better at inferring another person's state of mind if that person and the participant resemble one another along dimensions related to the self, than if they do not (e.g., Jenkins, Macrae & Mitchell, 2008). If KC and other people with episodic memory loss perform poorly on those tasks, they would confirm that, insofar as the simulation hypothesis applies, it is the general semantic, rather than the episodic or personal semantic, aspects of one's sense of self that underlies the effects. This was confirmed in the case HC, a person with developmental amnesia in relation to early compromise of the hippocampus and extended hippocampal system (Rabin, Braverman, Gilboa, Stuss & Rosenbaum, 2012; Rabin, Carson, Gilboa, Stuss & Rosenbaum, 2013) but has yet to be investigated in patients with adult-onset amnesia.

Problem Solving and Temporal Discounting

It is clear from the previous discussion that past and future thinking are closely related. If it were not for KC, in the normal mind, we might have thought that the two are handled by different cognitive operations. The results of subsequent patient and fMRI studies were taken to suggest that the medial temporal lobes serve a flexible role, not only in retrieving details but also in relating elements of one's episodic memories in novel ways to create representations that may be used when making plans and decisions for oneself and for others. This is supported by very recent evidence from studies of amnesic patients with compromised performance on tests of open-ended problem solving (Sheldon, McAndrews & Moscovitch, 2011; Vandermorris, Sheldon, Winocur & Moscovitch, 2013), free association (Sheldon, Romero & Moscovitch, 2013), and verbal and figural creativity (Duff, Kurczek, Rubin, Cohen & Tranel, 2013) that place heavy demands on (re)constructive processes and require flexibility in relating disparate details. These findings contributed to a shift from viewing episodic memory as a distinct system to viewing it as a fluid process that shares properties with episodic future thinking (Craver et al., 2014; Rosenbaum, Gilboa & Moscovitch, 2014), whether in pure imagination or in problem solving.

One property is a subjective sense of time that gives rise to the mental experience or simulation of an event as taking place in the near or more distant past or future. Another property involves the construction, separation, and associative binding of details into personal narratives of unique events. Whether or not KC's deficit in imagining the future in detail is related to his episodic memory loss, his impairments in both domains are real. Nevertheless, these co-occurring deficits may reflect a failure to subjectively orient in time or to construct details of event narratives. We wondered if KC's impaired episodic future thinking might influence his ability to think and reason objectively about events or outcomes occurring at different times without the need to construct narratives of those events, such as the value attached to rewards that one can hope to receive in the near or distant future. Inter-temporal choice, which involves choosing between a smaller, immediate reward and a larger, delayed reward, typically results in a systematic reduction in the subjective value of the future reward as the value of the immediate reward or delay until receipt of the future reward increases (Green & Myerson, 2004; Lempert & Phelps, 2016).

Inter-temporal choice also has to do with the mind. It was assumed that people with poor episodic memory would not be able to normally discount future rewards because they cannot imagine the future (Boyer, 2008). Despite his episodic amnesia, KC was able to forgo smaller, immediate rewards for a larger future payoff at a rate similar to that of healthy controls, suggesting that the ability to value the future can occur in the absence of the ability to construct imagined future events (Kwan et al., 2012; Kwan, Craver, Green, Myerson & Rosenbaum, 2013; Kwan et al., 2015). Moreover, KC further showed a "magnitude effect" (shallower discounting of a larger compared to smaller delayed amount), a standard finding in the delay discounting literature that appears to be typical of humans (Green & Myerson, 2004). Without KC, we might not have known that there are dissociations within future thinking. Still, it is possible that in the absence of the ability to imagine using future rewards, KC's decision making was qualitatively different from that of controls.

Overall, work with KC has refined and broadened our understanding of memory and its many components at a functional level. For us and our colleagues, his case served as a touchstone for many of the theories of normal memory that were developed, from issues of priming to those relating to new semantic learning and the organizational structure of remote memory. KC has played a critical role in the evolution and development of concepts and ideas such as episodic memory, multiple memory systems, autonoetic and noetic consciousness, the "remember/know" paradigm, the serial-parallel-independent (SPI) model of the relations between episodic and semantic memory, and chronesthesia, an individual's conscious awareness of subjective time (Tulving, 1985, 2005). Beyond the individual studies in which he participated, KC was a source of inspiration for countless studies due to the theories that he helped shape, including the Multiple-Trace/Transformation Theory of systems consolidation and hippocampal-neocortical interactions.

KC informed us not only of what the hippocampus does but, perhaps more importantly, what the hippocampus does not do, which is difficult, if not impossible, to capture with current neuroimaging methods. In the more typical patient case with extensive brain damage, preservation of memory may be more informative from a neurobiological perspective than impairment of memory. Above all, KC's case allowed for exceptional theoretical clarity, not only because of the selective nature of his deficit, which nevertheless allows for stronger inferences to be made about the limits of hippocampal function in the presence of intact performance but also because of the personal interactions and long-term relationships that are not possible with a larger group and that informed us about his capabilities.

Do you think that there is anything unique that the reports of this case added to our knowledge?

We would argue that although KC was special, there was nothing unique about KC in the annals of memory. In his case, it is the severity of episodic memory that can be considered the hallmark of his amnesia, but he was no more unique than HM in that regard, and in fact, resembled many other patients, which is why KC was often included in group studies. In many ways, KC was like other amnesic cases and even any other healthy individual. His store of semantic facts about himself and the world, procedural skills that were acquired in the first 30 years of his life, and his effortless functioning in his everyday environment were comparable to most amnesic cases. What made him stand out from many amnesic cases studied at the time was his inability to recollect any specific event in which he himself participated or any happening that he himself witnessed. This impaired ability to relive a personal episodic past extended to inventing possible future events in which he might participate. As we illustrated in the previous sections, the complete absence of episodic memory provided us with the rare opportunity to investigate other abilities for which episodic memory may be needed, including some aspects of remote spatial memory (Rosenbaum et al., 2000, 2007b), decision making based on future scenarios (Kwan et al., 2012; Kwan et al., 2013) and ethical dilemmas (Craver et al., 2016), and theory of mind (Rosenbaum et al., 2007a). Findings of preserved performance in KC helped constrain theories of medial temporal lobe involvement in these domains.

Some of these findings may have been viewed as unique in KC in that they had yet to be investigated in other amnesic patients, but we believe that once investigated, these patients will show the same pattern as KC showed. In other patients with less extensive lesions, one might find that they try to rely on a damaged system to solve a problem, and then it might give the false impression that the impairment arises because of the partially damaged region when, in fact, if it were completely damaged, the person would revert to a different strategy or another brain system to enable intact performance. Partially intact regions could produce interference (the patients rely on the neural resources that are available, but such compensation may result in suboptimal processing).

Were there any relevant data that you did not manage to publish on this case?

In recognizing the valuable contributions that research with KC has made to our understanding of memory and the meaning that it added to his own life,

KC's family donated his brain as a lasting gift to the scientific community. Post-mortem MRI together with neuropathological autopsy will help to confirm the true extent of damage to the medial temporal lobes and to other brain regions that may have contributed to KC's profound memory impairment, damage that might not have been detected with ex-vivo neuroimaging. It may seem futile to conduct a post-mortem examination when brain damage is so widely and unevenly distributed in order to determine how a particular deficit corresponds to a specific lesion site. But what it can do is provide a unique window into how a severe brain injury that left in its wake few, if any, brain structures and connections between them untouched could result in preserved function in multiple cognitive domains, and within memory itself. Precise measurement of his hippocampus and surrounding entorhinal cortex, for example, would address the long-standing criticism that residual tissue within these brain regions supported areas of intact memory, such as aspects of remote spatial memory.

Neuropathological autopsy findings are also relevant to the widespread attention given in the scientific literature and in the media to individuals who have developed Alzheimer's disease or chronic traumatic encephalopathy after sustaining multiple, severe, closed head injuries, particularly in football and hockey athletes. But what about a person who does not experience the haunting memories of uncomfortable past events or the uncertainty of future plans? Is he protected against tauopathy or tangle pathologies? Analyses are underway, and we will attempt to answer these interesting questions in what we hope will result in a worthy swan song.

What are the shortcomings of this case?

Methodological and theoretical challenges associated with single case contributions to understanding mind-brain relations have been extensively debated for decades (Caramazza, 1992; Coltheart, 2011; Rosenbaum et al., 2014; Shallice, 1988). In the case of KC, it is difficult to draw strong conclusions about the role of the hippocampus from findings of impaired performance due to his extensive brain pathology. In a 2002 paper, Bayley and Squire (2002, p. 5747) commented that KC is "unlikely to illuminate the function of the hippocampus or other medial temporal lobe structures." KC's head injury resulted in brain damage that is multifocal and diffuse and therefore not readily mapped onto his behavioural/cognitive profile. His lesions affected his hippocampus bilaterally but also included a number of other structures, some of which are closely connected to the hippocampus within the medial temporal lobe and known for their role in memory, such as parahippocampal cortex and mammillothalamic tract. Other lesions may have also contributed to his memory deficits, including a large lateral fronto-temporo-occipital lesion. Indeed, on one occasion, we had been asked to remove any claims or speculation about the role of hippocampal damage in KC contributing to impaired constructive and reconstructive memory.

Because of the nature of KC's brain damage, we did not anticipate that he would contribute as much as he did. However, independent of the nature and extent of his lesions, the behavioural regularities that he exhibited were real and reliable, allowing important theoretical and functional distinctions to be made and parallels drawn. The primary purpose of much of our work with KC was not to determine the role of the hippocampus in various cognitive abilities that were assessed, but to gain insight into the requirement of episodic memory for those abilities to better understand the nature of severe episodic memory impairment. Studying a functional dissociation should not be viewed as a lesser pursuit in comparison to a neural one.

We also felt justified in speculating on hippocampal function based on consistencies across various patients described in the literature and based on the patterns of preserved and impaired performance observed in KC himself. Even in neurologically "clean" cases, it has been argued that it is not possible to map deficits onto specific lesion sites due to "hidden pathology" (e.g., Squire & Bayley, 2006). A similar line of reasoning was offered by Hassabis et al. (2007) in their study of scene construction in amnesic cases:

> It is notoriously difficult, if not impossible, to be certain in vivo that lesions are selective to a particular brain region. Even scrupulous measurements or ratings of tissue volume from MRI scans cannot provide a definitive indication as to whether the tissue is functioning or not (43, 45, 46) (see also SI Text) or the functional effect of a lesion on wider brain systems. In the patients we tested, the primary area of damage in every case seemed restricted to the hippocampi, which was the only area of overlap. Their neuropsychological profiles suggested an isolated memory impairment, and their performance on the experimental task was remarkably homogenous (excluding P01; see Results, Discussion, and SI Text). Notwithstanding the difficulties inherent in the field, we therefore feel that our data permit conclusions to be drawn regarding the hippocampus.
>
> *(Hassabis et al., 2007 p. 1730)*

A related challenge in research that we had conducted with KC was how to interpret functional neuroimaging data based on a single case. Non-surgical lesions do not always respect the boundaries of a brain region: some tissue within the region may be left intact, and adjacent brain regions may also be affected. It is difficult to know if intact performance in a patient is due to compensatory recruitment of intact brain regions or to activation of any remaining tissue within the otherwise damaged region (Mullally, Hassabis & Maguire, 2012; Rabin et al., 2016). fMRI presented to us the possibility of determining the functionality of KC's hippocampus in possibly supporting his intact remote spatial memory. In scanning KC, we found that the same network of brain regions recruited in control participants was also recruited by KC, as he performed tasks that assessed his ability to judge distances and directions between familiar landmarks and choose the most direct route between them. Importantly, this network did not include the hippocampus (Rosenbaum et al., 2007b).

Are there any interpretations of major findings that you would now reconsider?

As we noted, the Zeitgeist in memory research when KC first came to our attention, and for many years afterwards, was to show how different types of memory, such as semantic and episodic, could be dissociated one from the other. Indeed, KC was enlisted in this campaign and served admirably, especially in providing evidence for the existence of separable explicit and implicit memory systems, functionally and structurally. Based on studies with KC and other amnesic patients, it was concluded that the hippocampus is needed to support explicit memory whereas implicit memory is supported by other structures independently of the hippocampus (Moscovitch, 1992; Squire, 1992; Tulving & Schacter, 1990, 1994; Schacter, 1987).

Early indications that these conclusions may have overstated the case came from studies showing that in some instances, patients with medial temporal lesions and severe anterograde amnesia, performed worse than controls on some tests of implicit memory, suggesting a hippocampal contribution to implicit memory (Graf & Schacter, 1985). At the time, these findings were interpreted as being indicative of the inadvertent infiltration of episodic memory into performance on tests implicit memory in controls; their performance benefited from their intact episodic memory in a way that the performance of amnesic patients could not. It was argued that when the tests were immune to contamination by episodic memory, the control advantage would disappear (Bowers & Schacter, 1990).

Recent studies have challenged the "contamination" interpretation and indicate that the hippocampus can contribute to performance on implicit tests when there is no evidence of "contamination." Using recollection as a marker of hippocampal involvement (Eichenbaum et al., 2007), Sheldon and Moscovitch (2010) showed that in healthy, neurologically intact people, implicit memory for words, as measured by speeded stem completion and lexical decision, is better for words that participants subsequently classify as recollected than merely familiar. Performance on the latter is equivalent to that on words that had been studied but that the participant classified as new. Likewise, Hannula and Ranganath (2009) used eye movements to show that participants looked at old items, in a relational context, more quickly than at new ones, even when they claimed that they could not recognize the old items. Importantly, hippocampal activation was related to their eye-movement performance in those instances.

Indeed, using both functional neuroimaging and amnesic patients, investigators showed that performance on implicit tests of relational memory is associated with hippocampal activation, and is reduced in amnesic patients. In a series of elegant studies, Henke and her collaborators (Henke, 2010; Reber et al., 2016; Duss et al., 2014) showed that even when stimuli are presented subliminally, they are encoded by the hippocampus if they are relational, and then they can influence performance on implicit tests of memory, problem solving and decision making.

These findings have led investigators to modify their initial position regarding the role of the hippocampus in implicit and explicit memory, and the importance of conscious awareness as a pre-requisite for hippocampal processing. Moscovitch (2008; Sheldon & Moscovitch, 2010; Moscovitch et al., 2016) proposed a *two-stage model of recollection* that involves reactivation at retrieval of the hippocampal-neocortical ensemble that constitutes the memory trace or engram of an event. The first stage involves

> a rapid and unconscious interaction between the cue and hippocampus (ecphory), which in turn reactivates the neocortical traces bound with it. The process may end here or proceed to the second stage. In the second stage, which is slower and conscious, cortical processes operate on the output of the first stage to reinstate the conscious experience of the episode.
> *(Moscovitch, 2016, pp. 107–108)*

To accommodate the findings by Henke and her collaborators, one can assume that access to the hippocampally mediated (relational) memory trace can also occur without conscious awareness. That access leads to non-conscious reactivation of the memory trace which then can influence performance.

Do you believe that serendipity was involved in your assessment?

When one considers the challenges in drawing conclusions based on a single case, especially one who has widespread brain damage, it seems that a certain amount of serendipity is at play in bringing together memory theory with a functionally interesting case. KC's acceptance within the scientific community occurred at a time when theoretical developments in memory research were ripe for a case with a clean pattern of spared and impaired abilities. What was needed was a keen eye to observe functional dissociations, guided by clear theories to illuminate what we had observed. But none of this would have been possible without the support of a family who truly appreciated the value of scientific study.

KC was an interesting case from a scientific point of view because his cognitive functions other than episodic memory and future imagining seemed to be relatively well preserved in the face of extensive brain damage. However, he was also interesting from a personal perspective because he and his family were not only cooperative but dedicated, as they realized that scientific investigation gave meaning to a life that was otherwise very limited. Unlike other amnesic people who usually stay hidden from the public eye, KC and his family chose to participate openly in the study of his case, and were comfortable putting a human face to a memory disorder (see Figure 8.2). This helped to demystify an otherwise difficult-to-understand concept of amnesia. They did so without any expectation that investigations with KC would improve KC's lot, but realized that it would help the whole world better understand the complexities of the human mind. Because of the privileged access that they allowed us, we were able to test many hypotheses and generate new ones based on casual and systematic observation.

Though we, ourselves, have always been excited about what we have discovered from working with KC, we never quite realized how much of an impact this work would have on the scientific community at large. We also did not dare to

FIGURE 8.2 Recent photograph of KC and his mother looking through an album of photos from KC's young adulthood. KC's descriptions of the photos were limited for the most part to identifying people and places, with no sign that these elements triggered any feeling of re-experiencing. KC was unable to go beyond what he perceived in the photo to convey any sequence of events or to relate the photo to other life experiences; any narratives that he managed to produce lacked the subjective re-evoking of the emotional and contextual details that distinguish an episodic memory from a personal semantic memory. Photo of Patient KC by Galit Rodin.

Copyright © Galit Rodin, 2012, with permission.

expect that KC would be recognized by many as a psychological marvel, which he has now turned out to be, as attested by the sheer number of studies published on KC and the citations that they continue to receive.

References

Addis, D. R., Wong, A. T., & Schacter, D. L. (2007). Remembering the past and imagining the future: common and distinct neural substrates during event construction and elaboration. *Neuropsychologia, 45*, 1363–1377.

Bartlett, E. C. (1932). *Remembering. A Study in Experimental and Social Psychology*. London: Cambridge University Press.

Bayley, P. J., Gold, J. J., Hopkins, R. O., & Squire, L. R. (2005). The neuroanatomy of remote memory. *Neuron, 46*, 799–810.

Bayley, P. J., & Squire, L. R. (2002). Medial temporal lobe amnesia: gradual acquisition of factual information by nondeclarative memory. *Journal of Neuroscience, 22*, 5741–5748.

Benton, A. L., Hamsher, K., Varney, K. de S., & Spreen, O. (1983). *Contributions to Neuropsychological Assessment*. New York: Oxford University Press.

Bird, C. M., & Burgess, N. (2008). The hippocampus and memory: insights from spatial processing. *Nature Reviews: Neuroscience, 9*, 182–194.

Boyer, P. (2008). Evolutionary economics of mental time travel? *Trends in Cognitive Sciences, 12*, 219–224.

Bowers, J., & Schacter, D. L. (1990). Implicit memory and test awareness. *Journal of Experimental Psychology: Learning, Memory, & Cognition, 16*, 404–416.

Bright, P., Buckman, J., Fradera, A., Yoshimasu, H., Colchester, A. C., & Kopelman, M. D. (2006). Retrograde amnesia in patients with hippocampal, medial temporal, temporal lobe, or frontal pathology. *Learning and Memory, 13*, 545–557.

Buckner, R. L., & Carroll, D. C. (2007). Self-projection and the brain. *Trends in Cognitive Sciences, 11*, 49–57.

Burgess, N., Maguire, E. A., & O'Keefe, J. (2002). The human hippocampus and spatial and episodic memory. *Neuron, 35*, 625–641.

Burnham, W. H. (1903). Retroactive amnesia: illustrative cases and a tentative explanation. *American Journal of Psychology, 14*, 382–396.

Caramazza, A. (1992). Is cognitive neuropsychology possible? *Journal of Cognitive Neuroscience, 4*, 80–95.

Clayton, N. S., Bussey, T. J., & Dickinson, A. (2003). Can animals recall the past and plan for the future? *Nature Reviews: Neuroscience, 4*, 685–691.

Coltheart, M. (2011). Methods for modular modelling: additive factors and cognitive neuropsychology. *Cognitive Neuropsychology, 28(3–4)*, 224–240.

Corkin, S. (2002). What's new with the amnesic patient H.M.? *Nature Reviews: Neuroscience, 3*, 153–160.

Craver, C. F., Keven, N., Kwan, D., Kurczek, J., Duff, M., & Rosenbaum, R. S. (2016). Moral judgment in episodic amnesia. *Hippocampus, 26*, 975–979.

Craver, C., Kwan, D., Steindam, C., & Rosenbaum, R. S. (2014). Individuals with episodic amnesia are not stuck in time. *Neuropsychologia, 57*, 191–195.

Crovitz, H. F., & Schiffman, H. (1974). Frequency of episodic memories as a function of their age. *Bulletin of the Psychonomic Society, 4*, 519–521.

Dede, A. J., Wixted, J. T., Hopkins, R. O., & Squire, L. R. (2016). Autobiographical memory, future imagining, and the medial temporal lobe. *Proceedings of the National Academy of Sciences USA, 113*, 13474–13479.

Delis, D. C., Kramer, J. H., Kaplan, E., & Ober, B. A. (1987). *California Verbal Learning Test: Adult Version Manual.* San Antonio, TX: The Psychological Corporation.

Dudai, Y. (2012). The restless engram: consolidations never end. *Annual Review of Neuroscience, 35*, 227–247.

Duff, M. C., Kurczek, J., Rubin, R., Cohen, N. J., & Tranel, D. (2013). Hippocampal amnesia disrupts creative thinking. *Hippocampus, 23*, 1143–1149.

Duss, S. B., Reber, T. P., Hänggi, J., Schwab, S., Wiest, R., Müri, R. M., Brugger, P., Gutbrod, K., & Henke, K. (2014). Unconscious relational encoding depends on hippocampus. *Brain, 137*, 3355–3370.

Eichenbaum, H., Yonelinas, A. P., & Ranganath, C. (2007). The medial temporal lobe and recognition memory. *Annual Review of Neuroscience, 30*, 123–152.

Farnsworth, D. (1957). *The Farnsworth-Munsell 100-Hue Test for the Examination of Color Discrimination.* Maryland: Munsell Color Company, Inc.

Fletcher, R. (1980). *The City University Color Vision Test* (2nd ed.). London: Keeler.

Glisky, E. L., & Schacter, D. L. (1988). Long-term retention of computer learning by patients with memory disorders. *Neuropsychologia, 26*, 173–178.

Glisky, E. L., Schacter, D. L., & Tulving, E. (1986a). Learning and retention of computer related vocabulary in memory-impaired patients: method of vanishing cues. *Journal of Clinical and Experimental Neuropsychology, 8*, 292–312.

Glisky, E. L., Schacter, D. L., & Tulving, E. (1986b). Computer learning by memory-impaired patients: acquisition and retention of complex knowledge. *Neuropsychologia, 24*, 313–328.

Goshen-Gottstein, Y., Moscovitch, M., & Melo, B. (2000). Intact implicit memory for newly formed verbal associations in amnesic patients following single study trials. *Neuropsychology, 14*, 570–578.

Graf, P., & Schacter, D. L. (1985). Implicit and explicit memory for new associations in normal and amnesic subjects. *Journal of Experimental Psychology: Learning, Memory and Cognition, 11*, 501–518.

Green, L., & Myerson, J. (2004). A discounting framework for choice with delayed and probabilistic rewards. *Psychological Bulletin, 130*, 769–792.

Hannula, D. E., & Ranganath, C. (2009). The eyes have it: hippocampal activity predicts expression of memory in eye movements. *Neuron, 63*, 592–599.

Hassabis, D., Kumaran, D., Vann, S. D., & Maguire, E. A. (2007). Patients with hippocampal amnesia cannot imagine new experiences. *Proceedings of the National Academy of Sciences, USA, 104*, 1726–1731.

Hassabis, D., & Maguire, E. A. (2007). Deconstructing episodic memory with construction. *Trends in Cognitive Sciences, 11*, 299–306.

Hayman, C. A. G., Macdonald, C. A., & Tulving, E. (1993). The role of repetition and associative interference in new semantic learning in amnesia—a case experiment. *Journal of Cognitive Neuroscience, 5*, 375–389.

Henke, K. (2010). A model for memory systems based on processing modes rather than consciousness. *Nature Reviews: Neuroscience, 11*, 523–532.

Herdman, K. A., Calarco, N., Moscovitch, M., Hirshhorn, M., & Rosenbaum, R. S. (2015). Impoverished descriptions of familiar routes in three cases of hippocampal amnesia. *Cortex, 71*, 248–263.

Hirshhorn, M., Grady, C. L., Rosenbaum, R. S., Winocur, G., & Moscovitch, M. (2012). The hippocampus is involved in mental navigation for a recently learned, but not a highly familiar environment: a longitudinal fMRI study. *Hippocampus, 22*, 842–852.

Jacoby, L. L. (1991). A process dissociation framework: separating automatic from intentional uses of memory. *Journal of Memory and Language, 30*, 513–541.

James, W. (1890; 1918 edition). *The Principles of Psychology*. New York: Holt.

Jenkins, A. C., Macrae, C. N., & Mitchell, J. P. (2008). Repetition suppression of ventromedial prefrontal activity during judgments of self and others. *Proceedings of the National Academy of Sciences USA, 105*, 4507–4512.

Kaplan, E. F., Goodglass, H., & Weintraub, S. (1983). *The Boston Naming Test*. Philadelphia: Lea & Febiger.

Kapur, N., Glisky, E. L., & Wilson, B. A. (2002). External memory aids and computers in memory rehabilitation. In A. D. Baddeley, M. D. Kopelman & B. A. Wilson (Eds.), *The Handbook of Memory Disorders* (2nd ed.). West Sussex, UK: John Wiley and Sons, Ltd, pp. 757–783.

Kertesz, A. (1982). *Western Aphasia Battery*. San Antonio, TX: The Psychological Corporation.

Klein, S. B. (2013). The complex act of projecting oneself into the future. *Wiley Interdisciplinary Reviews: Cognitive Science, 4*, 63–79.

Köhler, S., Habib, R., Black, S. E., Szekely, C., Sinden, M., & Tulving, E. (1997). Cross-modal priming in the densely amnesic subject K.C. *Brain and Cognition, 35*, 420–423.

Kopelman, M. D., Wilson, B. A., & Baddeley, A. D. (1990). *The Autobiographical Memory Interview*. Suffolk, England: Thames Valley Test Company.

Kwan, D., Craver, C., Green, L., Myerson, J., Boyer, P., & Rosenbaum, R. S. (2012). Future decision-making without episodic mental time travel. *Hippocampus, 22*, 1215–1219.

Kwan, D., Craver, C. F., Green, L., Myerson, J., Gao, F., Black, S. E., & Rosenbaum, R. S. (2015). Cueing the personal future to reduce discounting in intertemporal choice: is episodic prospection necessary? *Hippocampus, 25*, 432–443.

Kwan, D., Craver, C., Green, L., Myerson, J., & Rosenbaum, R. S. (2013). Dissociations in future thinking following hippocampal damage: evidence from discounting and time perspective in episodic amnesia. *Journal of Experimental Psychology: General, 142*, 1355–1369.

Lempert, K. M., & Phelps, E. A. (2016). The malleability of intertemporal choice. *Trends in Cognitive Sciences, 20*, 64–74.

Levine, B., Black, S. E., Cabeza, R., Sinden, M., Mcintosh, A. R., Toth, J. P., Tulving, E., & Stuss, D. T. (1998). Episodic memory and the self in a case of isolated retrograde amnesia. *Brain, 121*, 1951–1973.

Levine, B., Svoboda, E., Hay, J. F., Winocur, G., & Moscovitch, M. (2002). Aging and autobiographical memory: dissociating episodic from semantic retrieval. *Psychology and Aging, 17*, 677–689.

Mandler, G. (1980). Recognizing: the judgment of previous occurrence. *Psychological Review, 87*, 252–271.

Maguire, E. A., & Mullally, S. L. (2013). The hippocampus: a manifesto for change. *Journal of Experimental Psychology: General, 142*, 1180–1189.

Maguire, E. A., Nannery, R., & Spiers, H. J. (2006). Navigation around London by a taxi driver with bilateral hippocampal lesions. *Brain, 129*, 2894–2907.

McAndrews, M. P., Glisky, E. L., & Schacter, D. L. (1987). When priming persists: long-lasting implicit memory for a single episode in amnesic patients. *Neuropsychologia, 25,* 497–506.
Milner, B., Corkin, S., & Teuber, H. L. (1968). Further analysis of the hippocampal amnesic syndrome: 14-year follow-up study of H. M. *Neuropsychologia, 6,* 215–234.
Moscovitch, M. (1982). Multiple dissociations of function in amnesia. In L. S. Cermak (Ed.), *Human Memory and Amnesia.* Hillsdale: Erlbaum, pp. 337–370.
Moscovitch, M. (2008). The hippocampus as a "stupid," domain-specific module: implications for theories of recent and remote memory, and of imagination. *Canadian Journal of Experimental Psychology, 62,* 62–79.
Moscovitch, M. (1992). Memory and working-with-memory: a component process model based on modules and central systems. *Journal of Cognitive Neuroscience, 4,* 257–267.
Moscovitch, M., Cabeza, R., Winocur, G., & Nadel, L. (2016). Episodic memory and beyond: the hippocampus and neocortex in transformation. *Annual Review of Psychology, 67,* 105–134.
Moscovitch, M., & Melo, B. (1997). Strategic retrieval and the frontal lobes: evidence from confabulation and amnesia. *Neuropsychologia, 35,* 1017–1034.
Moscovitch, M., Nadel, L., Winocur, G., Gilboa, A., & Rosenbaum, R. S. (2006). The cognitive neuroscience of remote episodic, semantic, and spatial memory. *Current Opinion in Neurobiology, 16,* 179–190.
Moscovitch, M., Rosenbaum, R. S., Gilboa, A., Addis, D. R., Westmacott, R., Grady, C. L., McAndrews, M. P., Winocur, G., & Nadel, L. (2005). Functional neuroanatomy of remote episodic, semantic, and spatial memory: a unified account based on multiple trace theory. *Journal of Anatomy, 207,* 35–66.
Mullally, S. L., Hassabis, D., & Maguire, E. A. (2012). Scene construction in amnesia: an fMRI study. *Journal of Neuroscience, 32,* 5646–5653.
Nadel, L., & Moscovitch, M. (1997). Memory consolidation, retrograde amnesia and the hippocampal complex. *Current Opinion in Neurobiology, 7,* 217–227.
O'Keefe, J., & Nadel, L. (1978). *The Hippocampus as a Cognitive Map.* Oxford: Clarendon Press.
Olsen, R. K., Moses, S. N., Riggs, L., & Ryan, J. D. (2012). The hippocampus supports multiple cognitive processes through relational binding and comparison. *Frontiers in Human Neuroscience, 6,* 146.
Osterrieth, P. A. (1944). Le test de copie d'une figure complexe: contribution à l'étude de la perception et de la mémoire [A test of copying a complex figure: a contribution to the study of perception and memory]. *Archives de Psychologie, Geneva, 30,* 205–220.
Penfield, W., & Milner, B. (1958). Memory deficit produced by bilateral lesions in the hippocampal zone. *Archives of Neurology and Psychiatry, 79,* 475–497.
Perner, J., & Ruffman, T. (1995). Episodic memory and autonoetic consciousness: developmental evidence and a theory of childhood amnesia. *Journal of Experimental Child Psychology, 59,* 516–548.
Rabin, J. S., Braverman, A., Gilboa, A., Stuss, D. T., & Rosenbaum, R. S. (2012). Theory of mind development can withstand compromised episodic memory development. *Neuropsychologia, 50,* 3781–3785.
Rabin, J. S., Carson, N., Gilboa, A., Stuss, D. T., & Rosenbaum, R. S. (2013). Imagining other people's experiences in a person with impaired episodic memory: the role of personal familiarity. *Frontiers in Psychology, 3,* 588.

Rajaram, S., Srinivas, K., & Roediger, H. L. (1998). A transfer-appropriate processing account of context effects in word fragment completion. *Journal of Experimental Psychology: Learning, Memory and Cognition, 24,* 993–1004.

Reber, T. P., Do Lam, A. T., Axmacher, N., Elger, C. E., Helmstaedter, C., Henke, K., & Fell, J. (2016). Intracranial EEG correlates of implicit relational inference within the hippocampus. *Hippocampus, 26,* 54–66.

Robin, J., & Moscovitch, M. (2017). Familiar real-world spatial cues provide memory benefits in older and younger adults. *Psychology and Aging, 32(3),* 210–219.

Robin, J., Wynn, J., & Moscovitch, M. (2016). The spatial scaffold: the effects of spatial context on memory for events. *Journal of Experimental Psychology: Learning, Memory, and Cognition, 42,* 308–315.

Roediger, H. L., Buckner, R. L., & McDermott, K. B. (1999). Components of processing. In J. K. Foster & M. Jelicic (Eds.), *Memory: Systems, Process or Function?.* Oxford: Oxford University Press, pp. 31–65.

Rosenbaum, R. S., Cassidy, B. N., & Herdman, K. A. (2015). Patterns of preserved and impaired spatial memory in developmental amnesia. *Frontiers in Human Neuroscience, 9,* 196.

Rosenbaum, R. S., Gilboa, A., Levine, B., Winocur, G., & Moscovitch, M. (2009). Amnesia as an impairment of detail generation and binding: evidence from personal, fictional, and semantic narratives in K.C. *Neuropsychologia, 47,* 2181–2187.

Rosenbaum, R. S., Gilboa, A., & Moscovitch, M. (2014). Case studies continue to illuminate the cognitive neuroscience of memory. The year in cognitive neuroscience, *Annals of the New York Academy of Sciences, 1316,* 105–133.

Rosenbaum, R. S., Köhler, S., Schacter, D. L., Moscovitch, M., Westmacott, R., Black, S. E., Gao, F., & Tulving, E. (2005). The case of K.C.: contributions of a memory-impaired person to memory theory. *Neuropsychologia, 43,* 989–1021.

Rosenbaum, R. S., McKinnon, M., Levine, B., & Moscovitch, M. (2004a). Visual imagery deficits, impaired strategic retrieval, or memory loss: disentangling the nature of an amnesic person's autobiographical memory deficit. *Neuropsychologia, 42,* 1619–1635.

Rosenbaum, R. S., Moscovitch, M., Foster, J. K., Schnyer, D. M., Gao, F. Q., Kovacevic, N., Verfaellie, M., Black, S. E., & Levine, B. (2008). Patterns of autobiographical memory loss in medial temporal lobe amnesic patients. *Journal of Cognitive Neuroscience, 20,* 1490–1506.

Rosenbaum, R. S., Priselac, S., Köhler, S., Black, S. E., Gao, F. Q., Nadel, L., & Moscovitch, M. (2000). Remote spatial memory in an amnesic person with extensive bilateral hippocampal lesions. *Nature Neuroscience, 3(10),* 1044–1048.

Rosenbaum, R. S., Stuss, D. T., Levine, B., & Tulving, E. (2007a). Theory of mind is independent of episodic memory. *Science, 318,* 1257.

Rosenbaum, R. S., Winocur, G., Binns, M., & Moscovitch, M. (2012). Remote spatial memory in aging: all is not lost. *Frontiers in Aging Neuroscience, 4,* 25.

Rosenbaum, R. S., Winocur, G., Grady, C. L., Ziegler, M., & Moscovitch, M. (2007b). Memory for familiar environments learned in the remote past: fMRI studies of healthy people and an amnesic person with extensive bilateral hippocampal lesions. *Hippocampus, 17,* 1241–1251.

Rosenbaum, R. S., Winocur, G., & Moscovitch, M. (2001). New views on old memories: re-evaluating the role of the hippocampal complex. *Behavioural Brain Research, 127,* 183–197.

Rosenbaum, R. S., Ziegler, M., Winocur, G., Grady, C. L., & Moscovitch, M. (2004b). "I have often walked down this street before:" fMRI studies on the hippocampus and other structures during mental navigation of an old environment. *Hippocampus, 14*, 826–835.

Rubin, D. C., & Greenberg, D. L. (1998). Visual memory-deficit amnesia: a distinct amnesia presentation and etiology. *Proceedings of the National Academy of Sciences, USA, 95*, 5413–5416.

Schacter, D. L. (1985). Priming of old and new knowledge in amnesic patients and normal subjects. *Annals of the New York Academy of Sciences, 444*, 41–53.

Schacter, D. L. (1987). Implicit memory: history and current status. *Journal of Experimental Psychology: Learning, Memory, and Cognition, 13*, 501–518.

Schacter, D. L., Addis, D. R., Hassabis, D., Martin, V. C., Spreng, R. N., & Szpunar, K. K. (2012). The future of memory: remembering, imagining, and the brain. *Neuron, 76*, 677–694.

Schacter, D. L., & Graf, P. (1986). Preserved learning in amnesic patients: perspectives from research on direct priming. *Journal of Clinical and Experimental Neuropsychology, 8*, 727–743.

Schacter, D. L., Moscovitch, M., Tulving, E., McLachlan, D. R., & Freedman, M. (1986). Mnemonic precedence in amnesic patients: an analogue of the AB error in infants? *Child Development, 57*, 816–823.

Schacter, D. L., & Tulving, E. (1994). What are the memory systems of 1994? In D. L. Schacter & E. Tulving (Eds.), *Memory Systems 1994*. Cambridge, MA: MIT Press, pp. 1–38.

Sekeres, M. J., Bonasia, K., St-Laurent, M., Pishdadian, S., Winocur, G., Grady, C., & Moscovitch, M. (2016). Recovering and preventing loss of detailed memory: differential rates of forgetting for detail types in episodic memory. *Learning and Memory, 23*, 72–82.

Shallice, T. (1988). *From Neuropsychology to Mental Structure*. New York: Cambridge University Press.

Sheldon, S., McAndrews, M. P., & Moscovitch, M. (2011). Episodic memory processes mediated by the medial temporal lobes contribute to open-ended problem solving. *Neuropsychologia, 49*, 2439–2447.

Sheldon, S., Romero, K., & Moscovitch, M. (2013). Medial temporal lobe amnesia impairs performance on a free association task. *Hippocampus, 23*, 405–412.

Sheldon, S. A., & Moscovitch, M. (2010). Recollective performance advantages for implicit memory tasks. *Memory, 18*, 681–697.

Spreen, O., & Strauss, E. (1998). *A Compendium of Neuropsychological Tests* (2nd ed.). New York: Oxford University Press.

Spreng, R. N., Mar, R. A., & Kim, A. S. (2009). The common neural basis of autobiographical memory, prospection, navigation, theory of mind and the default mode: a quantitative meta-analysis. *Journal of Cognitive Neuroscience, 21*, 489–510.

Squire, L. R. (1992). Memory and the hippocampus: a synthesis from findings with rats, monkeys and humans. *Psychological Review, 99*, 195–231.

Squire, L. R., & Bayley, P. J. (2006). The neuroanatomy of very remote memory. *Lancet Neurology, 5*, 112–113.

Squire, L. R., & Wixted, J. T. (2011). The cognitive neuroscience of human memory since H.M. *Annual Review of Neuroscience, 34*, 259–288.

Steinvorth, S., Levine, B., & Corkin, S. (2006). Medial temporal lobe structures are needed to re-experience remote autobiographical memories: evidence from H.M. and W.R. *Neuropsychologia, 43*, 479–496.

Suddendorf, T., & Corballis, M. C. (2007). The evolution of foresight: what is mental time travel, and is it unique to humans? *Behavioural Brain Sciences, 30*, 299–313.
Svoboda, E., Richards, B., Leach, L., & Mertens, V. (2012). PDA and smartphone use by individuals with moderate-to-severe memory impairment: application of a theory-driven training programme. *Neuropsychological Rehabilitation, 22*, 408–427.
Svoboda, E., Richards, B., Yao, C., & Leach, L. (2015). Long-term maintenance of smartphone and PDA use in individuals with moderate to severe memory impairment. *Neuropsychological Rehabilitation, 25*, 353–373.
Tulving, E. (1972). Episodic and semantic memory. In E. Tulving & W. Donalson (Eds.), *Organization of Memory*. New York: Academic Press, pp. 381–403.
Tulving, E. (1983). *Elements of Episodic Memory*. Oxford Oxfordshire: Oxford University Press.
Tulving, E. (1985). Memory and consciousness. *Canadian Psychologist, 25*, 1–12.
Tulving, E. (1993). Self-knowledge of an amnesic individual is represented abstractly. In T. K. Sdrull & R. S. Wyer, Jr., (Eds.), *The Mental Representation of Trait and Autobiographical Knowledge About the Self*. Hillsdale, NJ: Lawrence Erlbaum Associates, pp. 147–156.
Tulving, E. (2002). Episodic memory: from mind to brain. *Annual Review of Psychology, 53*, 1–25.
Tulving, E. (2005). Episodic memory and autonoesis: uniquely human? In H. Terrace & J. Metcalfe (Eds.), *The Missing Link in Cognition: Evolution of Self-Knowing Consciousness*. Oxford: Oxford University Press.
Tulving, E., Hayman, C. A., & MacDonald, C. A. (1991). Long-lasting perceptual priming and semantic learning in amnesia: a case experiment. *Journal of Experimental Psychology: Learning, Memory, and Cognition, 17*, 595–617.
Tulving, E., & Schacter, D. L. (1990). Priming and human memory systems. *Science, 247*, 301–306.
Tulving, E., Schacter, D. L., McLachlan, D. R., & Moscovitch, M. (1988). Priming of semantic autobiographical knowledge: a case study of retrograde amnesia. *Brain and Cognition, 8*, 3–20.
Vandermorris, S., Sheldon, S., Winocur, G., & Moscovitch, M. (2013). Differential contributions of executive and episodic memory functions to problem solving in younger and older adults. *Journal of the International Neuropsychological Society, 19*, 1087–1096.
Warrington, E. K. (1984). *Recognition Memory Test*. Windsor, England: NFER-Nelson.
Wechsler, D. (1987). *Wechsler Memory Scale—Revised*. San Antonio, TX: Psychological Corporation.
Wechsler, D. (1999). *The Wechsler Abbreviated Scale of Intelligence*. New York: The Psychological Corporation.
Westmacott, R., Leach, L., Freedman, M., & Moscovitch, M. (2001). Different patterns of autobiographical memory loss in semantic dementia and medial temporal lobe amnesia: a challenge to consolidation theory. *Neurocase, 7*, 37–55.
Westmacott, R., & Moscovitch, M. (2001). Names and words without meaning: incidental postmorbid semantic learning in a person with extensive bilateral medial temporal damage. *Neuropsychology, 15*, 586–596.
Westmacott, R., & Moscovitch, M. (2002). Temporally-graded retrograde memory loss for famous names and vocabulary terms in amnesia and semantic dementia: further evidence for opposite gradients using implicit memory tasks. *Cognitive Neuropsychology, 19*, 135–163.
Winocur, G., & Moscovitch, M. (2011). Memory transformation and systems consolidation. *Journal of the International Neuropsychological Society, 17*, 766–780.

Winocur, G., Moscovitch, M., Fogel, S., Rosenbaum, R. S., & Sekeres, M. (2005). Preserved spatial memory after hippocampal lesions: effects of extensive experience in a complex environment. *Nature Neuroscience, 8*, 273–275.

Winocur, G., Moscovitch, M., Rosenbaum, R. S., & Sekeres, M. (2010a). An investigation of the effects of hippocampal lesions in rats on pre- and post-operatively acquired spatial memory in a complex environment. *Hippocampus, 20*, 1350–1365.

Winocur, G., Moscovitch, M., Rosenbaum, R. S., & Sekeres, M. (2010b). A study of remote spatial memory in aged rats. *Neurobiology of Aging, 31*, 143–150.

Yonelinas, A. P., Kroll, N. E., Quamme, J. R., Lazzara, M. M., Sauvé, M. J., Widaman, K. F., & Knight, R. T. (2002). Effects of extensive temporal lobe damage or mild hypoxia on recollection and familiarity. *Nature Neuroscience, 5*, 1236–1241.

9

RIGHT IS RIGHT FOR EPISODIC MEMORIES IN TWO CONTRASTING CASE STUDIES, CH AND JR

Focal Retrograde Amnesia and Public Semantic Amnesia

Liliann Manning

Fifteen years ago, you described the case of CH, who presented with pure retrograde amnesia particularly affecting her autobiographical memory. More recently, you reported on case JR, who showed the curious dissociation between impaired recalling and future imagining of public events coupled with preserved past and future autobiographical episodic memory. Can you provide us with some background information about these cases?

To provide you with some background information about CH and JR, I would not only like to tell you about their neurological conditions and the theoretical context but also about the people behind the patients. Let me start with CH. Born in 1932, this right-handed interior decorator suffered a cerebral hypoxia during a surgical intervention, at age 65. She remained in a coma for 24 hours, and her EEG showed epileptic activity alternating with burst suppression. A few days later, her husband noted that she was unable to remember, for example, whether her husband had been with her a few hours earlier or not. These anterograde memory difficulties lasted for approximately eight days. Formal neuropsychological assessment, carried out for the first time four months post-onset, revealed a case of focal retrograde amnesia (Kapur, 1999; Kapur, Young, Bateman & Kennedy, 1989). Given CH's cognitive profile, she was tested again 18 and 24 months after her cerebral accident. It is worth noting that the scores obtained at her last assessment did not show any significant recovery from her focal retrograde amnesia.

From a theoretical standpoint, the crucial difficulty with cases of focal retrograde amnesia—and their hypothetical interest—is to account for retrieval mechanisms that are functional and efficient in retrieving post-onset encoded memories but fail to retrieve autobiographical memories stored before the brain pathology. When I investigated the case of CH, I relied on Damasio's model (1989; Damasio & Damasio, 1994) to suggest how to theoretically interpret her selectively impaired access to autobiographical incidents. Damasio postulated that encoding autobiographical incidents involved the formation of multiple neural configurations, which are located in separate primary sensory and motor cortices. The patterns of neural activity of feature fragments located at that level have combinatorial arrangements, which occur synchronously during the experience of the event. These patterns of activity are transmitted through downstream neurons to association cortices once they have also been encoded in modality-specific cortical areas. Feed-forward projections towards convergence zones and feedback projections from convergence zones interlock the neural configurations. The model (see Figure 9.1) proposes that the recall of experiences depends on time-locked neural configuration activations: information stored within the primary cortices is accessed by the activity of the binding codes stored in the amodal convergence zones (association cortices).

To describe the person behind the patient, CH is a delightful, intelligent, very active and determined woman, despite the fact that in the 1970s, she suffered from a malignant tumour, which required removal of part of her tongue. She had had serious difficulties with eating and talking, but after years of effort, she managed to speak almost normally. Aged 60, she started her own floral art centre and ran it successfully, winning international prizes for her floral arrangements.

The other patient, JR, was born in 1950; he is a right-handed man with 14 years of education, who was working as a technician at the time of his referral.

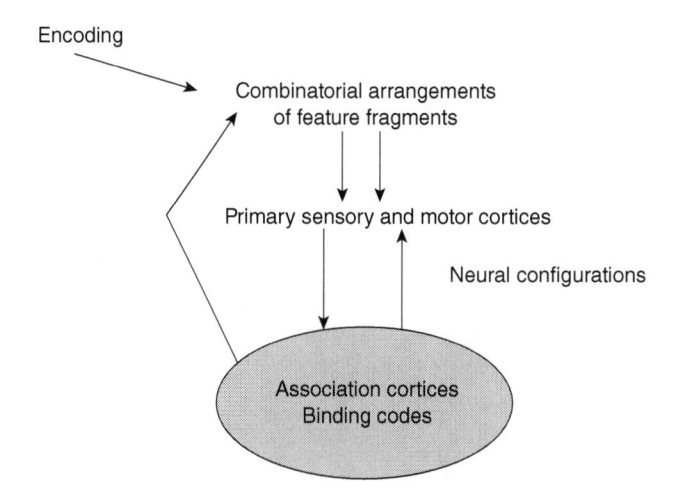

FIGURE 9.1 Schematic rendering of Damasio's (1989) Time-locked Multiregional Retroactivation Model

JR experienced his first epileptic seizure in 1963 and, a few years later, he was diagnosed with drug-resistant medial temporal lobe epilepsy. Unilateral localisation of epileptogenic focus was achieved by combining diagnostic information from video-electroencephalography (EEG) telemetry, structural MRI and single-photon emission computed tomography (SPECT) scanning. Significant preoperative left hippocampal volume loss was found while the right medial temporal lobe appeared normal. In 2002, a left anteromedial temporal lobectomy was performed, including complete removal of the hippocampus, amygdala, parahippocampal gyrus and the anterior 5 cm of the mid inferior temporal gyrus and the occipito-temporal lateral gyrus. Histological examination of resect specimens showed hippocampal sclerosis with severe neuronal loss of pyramidal cells in the hippocampal fields CA1 and CA2. The operation was successful, not only JR was seizure free, but after one year of reduced medication, he was also medication free. His first neuropsychological assessment took place two days before his neurosurgical intervention. This routine examination showed a counterintuitive dissociation between intact episodic autobiographical memory, and impaired semantic public events memory. This finding was largely corroborated by a wide range of examinations after the temporal lobectomy.

The patient's preservation of episodic autobiographical memory was thought to reflect, at least partially, normal functioning of structures in the right temporal lobe. This assumption is in accord with—to our knowledge—the two published works, involving medial temporal lobe epilepsy, and which reported spared right hippocampal formation in patients who presented with preserved episodic autobiographical memory coupled with impaired public semantic memory. The first was a transient epileptic amnesic patient studied by Kapur et al. in 1989, and the second work comprised a group study of medial temporal lobe epileptic patients studied by Barr et al. in 1990. The latter reported a disproportionate loss of public semantic memory compared with episodic autobiographical memory in left but not in right temporal lobe epileptic patients. With regard to non-epileptic patients, three cases, to our knowledge, presented with a similar cognitive profile (De Renzi, Liotti & Nichelli, 1989; Markowitsch, Calabrese, Neufeld, Gehlen & Durwen, 1999; Yasuda, Watanabe & Ono, 1997). Importantly, regardless of the aetiology, in every case, the brain damage involved only or predominantly the left medial and/or lateral temporal lobe. Of particular note, in relation to this issue, were Markowitsch et al.'s (2000) Positron Emission Tomography (PET) scan findings, showing that the amygdala, uncus and temporal pole in the right hemisphere are specifically activated during episodic autobiographical memory recollection in the intact brain.

In terms of JR's non-medical story, he managed to obtain some scholastic achievements as a technician, but he struggled most of the time to perform even at a modest level in his job. He became increasingly isolated in his workplace, owing to his difficulties in mastering new techniques, and the seizures he underwent, even if they were not very frequent. Notwithstanding these limitations, JR has always been a pleasant person, with a good sense of humour and who has learned to value the positive side of life in relation to his illness. One example that nicely illustrates what Morris (2004) calls the "redemption" process or "benefit finding", i.e., uncovering positive aspects to a negative life situation, is his conviction that it was "thanks to the epilepsy" that he had met "some wonderful people". He is married and a father of four but his family relationships became difficult during the first post-operative months where he was "so euphoric that nothing was a problem". It was all but easy for his wife to adjust to the fact that JR refused to be assisted in his everyday life activities, and most particularly, in the management of his salary.

How did you first realise that these cases were interesting?

In both cases, I realised fairly rapidly that they were different from the patients we usually examine in routine clinical settings. I remember CH saying that she realised when looking at pictures of herself in her front room, she felt unable to know where and when some of them had been taken, let alone who else, not seen in the picture, was there or what she was doing there. She also complained of serious difficulties finding her way to familiar places, most particularly the flower markets where she used to go several times a week, as a part of her working life. At odds with these comments, her performance on anterograde memory tests was excellent. In due time, the potential psychogenic factors that could have substantiated her complaints were ruled out. Once I was persuaded that CH presented with an organic deficit, I asked her and her husband to cooperate in what would be a long neuropsychological assessment period. They were very happy to accept my suggestion and both cooperated exceptionally well.

With regard to JR, I realised that he presented with a rather uncommon deficit when he was asked to carry out the Famous Faces test, as part of a routine neuropsychological assessment, before his surgical intervention. He failed to recognise Elvis Presley and Marilyn Monroe amongst several other less conspicuous celebrities. However, he was able to recognise and accurately name John F. Kennedy. JR vividly remembered the evening when his father shared with him the news of the President's assassination and how deeply affected he felt. JR was 13 years old at the time. If he could remember that event so well, could he also remember other events in his 20s and 30s? I gave him some cue-words, like "letter, tree, train", and asked him to retrieve memories involving these cue-words. The memories had to be of events that happened only once and lasted no longer than 24 hours. He did this easily, bringing to mind as many details as he could, the number of which was largely in the normal range (scores of autobiographical memory tests are usually based on the number and vividness of episodic details). Moreover, since this assessment took place in May 2002, I was very surprised when he said after a moment of hesitation that 11 September 2001 likely evoked an important football event. Taken together, his performance suggested an extraordinary pattern: I was to follow-up this case for the next ten years.

What were these cases' patterns of spared and impaired abilities?

CH's scores on a variety of cognitive tests, administered on three different occasions, did not show any significant changes. Her performance two years after her hypoxic accident showed her verbal and performance IQ were in the high average and average range respectively. Her performance was very good in naming as well as visuo-perceptual and visuo-spatial capacities. Her scores on executive tasks were also very good, however, the moderate level of difficulty of the tests presented, did not allow me to draw firm conclusions on her performance. Importantly, as mentioned earlier, her anterograde memory was excellent on tests exacting verbal and nonverbal memory. Likewise, her personal semantics were preserved, and she had no difficulties whatsoever in visual imagery.

In contrast with these results, when assessed using the modified Crovitz test (Crovitz & Schiffman, 1974; Graham & Hodges, 1997), CH's episodic autobiographical memory was deficient for events that took place approximately 15 years before onset. Her episodic autobiographical memory was well preserved for the remaining periods of life, including the time after her surgical intervention. This was observed across a large range of tests, comprising matched tasks that compared pre- and post-illness episodic recollections, using, amongst others, her own photographs, provided by her husband, and not seen by the patient after her brain hypoxia. It was also observed that her semantic knowledge for public events was impaired, compared to matched controls, for a period of approximately five years before her hypoxia.

JR's pattern of spared and impaired performance involved a series of tasks very similar to those mentioned in CH's cognitive baseline. Likewise, JR's anterograde memory was preserved. Importantly, his episodic autobiographical memory, general semantic memory and personal semantics were intact. In this context, his remarkably selective impairment on semantic public events memory tasks had led us to deepen our investigation and search for eventual theoretical implications. To that end, the follow-up study was designed, tackling three related aspects:

(i) The relationships between the two memory systems, which involved investigating how personal experiences interacted with memory for public events. This refers to the concept of *autobiographical significance*, put forward by Westmacott and Moscovitch (2003). Functional MRI was carried out while the patient performed the Famous Faces recognition task, using three possible responses: R: "I remember the person", K: "S/he is familiar" or "I don't know". The results showed the absence of brain activation for famous faces devoid of *autobiographical significance*, and activation of the episodic autobiographical memory cerebral network for personally significant famous people. In other words, JR's right-lateralised cerebral activations showed no differences whatsoever between famous people lacking personally experienced events and unknown people. Complementarily, the few public semantic memories having *autobiographical significance* appeared to be preserved and involved cerebral activations in the undamaged medial temporal lobe and posterior neocortical structures. These regions are consistently associated with retrieval of episodic autobiographical memories, including the recollection of sensory-perceptual details linked to personal memories (Conway, 2001; Moscovitch et al., 2005).

(ii) The future temporal dimension, as part of mental time travel (Suddendorf & Corballis, 1997), not only related to episodic autobiographical memory but also to semantic public events memory. Impersonal future has been remarkably less investigated than episodic future thinking. To my knowledge, there are only two studies: Klein, Loftus and Kihlstrom (2002) amnesic patient DB, who had great difficulty imagining his personal future, while his performance in evoking future public events was comparable to that of control subjects, and the group study carried out by Irish, Addis, Hodges and Piguet (2012). Using the same tests as Klein et al., Irish and colleagues explored the contribution of semantic memory to episodic future thinking in two neurological conditions, semantic dementia and Alzheimer's disease. The authors reported differential patterns of past and future performance contingent on the dementia group.

(iii) The influence of autobiographical significance in both past and future directions. Westmacott and Moscovitch (2003) demonstrated that some semantic concepts were more likely to be associated with specific personal memories than others and that such autobiographical significance gave those concepts *special status* in long-term memory.

Taking together these three lines of investigation, JR's "extended" pattern of performance is as follows: selective and coexisting impairment in the ability to recall past and imagine future public events, along with preserved functioning of past and future episodic autobiographical memory. Remarkably, autobiographically significant public *past* knowledge relied exclusively on the patient's spared episodic autobiographical memory. Remember the example involving John F Kennedy: JR's public events knowledge concerning President Kennedy was intact. But this was possible only because this famous personage had very strong *autobiographical significance* for JR. On the contrary, his public events *future* thinking was impaired, regardless of any potential help from his preserved episodic autobiographical memory. In other words, his preserved autobiographical significance seemed to be functional only for past public events. A further example showing this conclusion is as follows: JR being a practicing Catholic, recognised very well and commented upon a picture showing the funeral of Pope John Paul II. However, when a further image of an unknown Pope was shown together with the instruction to imagine and describe a new Pope, and imagine how he could have come to know him, JR was unable to respond.

Can you summarise the main features of these cases?

Although CH recovered from a period of global amnesia after eight days, she continued to suffer from focal retrograde amnesia and, two years post-onset, she did not show any significant recovery. Given the paucity of cases presenting a genuine focal retrograde amnesia and the counterintuitive nature of the syndrome, it could be said that CH's main features are related to her organic condition. In the first place, her retrograde amnesia spared the most difficult events of her medical history, while covering a period, which her husband and colleagues considered as being non-stressful and even rewarding for the patient. It was a time when she was in good health, she was doing exceptionally well in her career, winning international recognition for her floral arrangements, she and her husband travelled around the world, and her only son obtained an excellent job. Moreover, despite the fact that her medical file indicated that intubation should not take place due to an allergy, she was intubated during relatively minor surgery to extract a foreign body from the right lobar bronchus. Intubation caused massive tracheal lesions, which in turn provoked the cardiac arrest and cerebral hypoxia. Yet, CH decided not to take the medical staff to court, which strongly suggested that she was not motivated by any financial gain. More generally, she never manifested any psychiatric disorders and never suffered from depression despite major stressful events in her 40s. In the same vein, it is worth noting that a Positron Emission Tomography (PET) scan carried out one year post-onset showed a marked reduction in metabolism in the right occipito-temporo-parietal region (i.e., in the brain regions relevant for processing episodic autobiographical memories). This was observed together with normal medial temporal lobes on MRI. Moreover, MRI scanning on two different occasions revealed mild frontal changes mainly affecting white matter areas.

Cognitively, JR's main feature was his selective impairment in the ability to recall past and imagine future public events. More precisely, he had impaired scores on the Famous Scenes Test, regardless of the period tested (1980–1990 and 2000–2010), the Famous Faces Test, involving both remote (1970–1990) and recent (1990–2009) celebrities, and the New Word Questionnaire for words coined between 1996–1997 and 2006–2007. How could we account for this massive and ungraded deficit? Memory for public events is associated with media exposure (Kapur, Young, Bateman & Kennedy, 1998), which is a part of everyday life. Though most news events are rapidly forgotten, there are a few important facts that remain, and shape our stored public events memory. This affects an important part of our awareness of the surrounding world and allows us to share cultural community interests (Brown, 1990). On these bases, JR was, very likely, never able to fully share that kind of collective interests. Moreover, his results would be readily accounted for by a deficit in the encoding/storage of public semantic memory. An important factor provoking the patient's ungraded deficit is likely his age at illness onset. The age of acquisition of public events memory starts in adolescence. A study by Howes and Katz (1988) showed an increasing acquisition curve until late teens. Likewise, Holmes and Conway (1999) suggested that news events are retained because they are related to the formation of a "generation identity", whose peak recall for public news items was found in the period when participants were aged 10–19 years. It is possible that JR's epilepsy onset at age 13 hindered his launch of the process of integrating news events. In other words, it is very likely that JR could not learn "the basis" of public events that can be abstract, at least to some extent.

Are these two cases complementary to one another?

First of all, with regard to their baseline assessments, both patients showed preserved performance in verbal and performance IQ, verbal and nonverbal anterograde memory, naming and executive functions within the limits of the tests used in our studies. On these bases, the two cases may be seen as a double dissociation between the autobiographical and semantic public events memory systems. However, it is necessary to bear in mind that, while JR had intact episodic autobiographical memory, CH's autobiographical amnesia was "only" temporally graded. Complementarily, regarding the public events semantic system, the caveat is that while JR's deficit is ungraded, CH's preservation is not flawless, since her scores on some of the tests were poor for a period of approximately five years pre-onset.

From a neurological standpoint, CH's marked cerebral hypometabolism was shown in the posterior regions of the right hemisphere, with bilateral white matter changes in the frontal regions. JR's epileptogenic focus and, consequently, the temporal lobectomy, were localised in the left hemisphere. In other words, CH's autobiographical temporally graded amnesia was, at least partially, provoked by her right hemisphere hypometabolism, and JR's preserved episodic autobiographical memory was due, very likely, to a functional reorganisation in the right hemisphere. However, neurocognitive considerations of the episodic autobiographical memory system show that it engages predominantly *left* lateralised medial and cortical regions (see Svoboda, McKinnon & Levine, 2006 for a meta-analysis). It is interesting, in that context, that several cases besides CH and JR, have revealed that when the right predominates over the left hemisphere to support episodic autobiographical memory, a counterintuitive and therefore, case study pattern of performance, is described (either showing reorganisation of function, for example, De Renzi, Liotti & Nichelli, 1989; Manning, Denkova & Unterberger, 2013; Markowitsch, Calabrese, Neufeld, Gehlen & Durwen, 1999; Yasuda et al., 1997; or impairment in the episodic autobiographical memory system due to right-lateralised dysfunction, Hunkin et al., 1995; Manning, 2002; O'Connor, Butters, Miliotis, Eslinger & Cermak et al., 1992).

Do you think these cases contribute to our understanding of how the normal mind works?

CH and JR have a pattern of cognitive performance that differs from people with intact brains, but they had the same cognitive systems (at least potentially in the case of JR's public events memory), before their neurological conditions. On these bases, the two cases might contribute to our understanding of how the normal mind works. More to the point, CH and JR show two instances of how a brain lesion can selectively alter a given memory system. Perhaps a direct way to answer this question is to start by stating the obvious, that is, we would have been unable to uncover these detailed memory deficits on the bases of a patient group study. Having said that, interesting as the single case results may be, are they of any use? In *principle*, they are potentially useful. In *actual* terms, the answer is much more complicated, since the actual usefulness depends on whether and how the data are used by other clinicians. Be that as it may, CH and JR allowed us to suggest that the interactions between the functional lateralisation of cortical (temporo-parietal region) and sub-cortical (hippocampus) structures and the aetiology may show an almost mirror-image of deficits as discussed earlier.

With regard to CH, it is worth reminding the reader that Kapur (2000) and Kopelman (2000) put forward the possibility that anterograde amnesia may be mild, but still present, and that performance on memory tests may be normal at short delays but impaired at longer delays. However, CH's performance rendered neither of these possibilities likely, since she showed normal anterograde memory even at very long delays. The same can be said about patient JM, tested by Evans et al. in 1996 and re-assessed in 2003. JM's focal retrograde amnesia did not show significant changes after several years and, as the authors showed in their latter study, this selective impairment was not due to accelerated forgetting of episodic memories. In summary, the usefulness of CH's case seems to have been demonstrated, *in principle*, in that she suggested a new pattern of cognitive deficits, all the more so, that it was then corroborated by another single case (Evans, Graham, Pratt & Hodges, 2003).

In JR's case, it should be mentioned again that we demonstrated (using clinical tests) that his personal semantics, as well as his "general" semantic memory, were not affected. These may have been preserved because the anterior temporal regions were functional, bilaterally. In that context, JR's contribution could be to suggest that damage to the left mid-temporal lobe provoked massive impairments in public events memory due, at least partially, to the fact that the defining characteristics of public events generalise (from concrete to abstract), probably less obviously than do entities like "horse" or "tree", and to the comparatively late formation of cerebral networks sustaining public events memory (Holmes & Conway, 1999; Howes & Katz, 1988). JR's performance seems to indicate that the semantic public events memory system is either relatively or entirely independent from the "general" semantic system and that its construction in the human mind is probably one of the latest cognitive acquisitions during development.

The further potentially important contribution regarding JR's, reorganisation of episodic autobiographical memory in the right hemisphere, was observed using functional MRI. It should be specified that the medial temporal lobe structures, the mid inferior temporal gyrus and the occipito-temporal gyrus, which were surgically removed, most likely showed subclinical dysfunctions, before the formal diagnosis of temporal lobe epilepsy. Speculating on this result, it is tempting to wonder if—given the context of functional reorganisation—the episodic autobiographical memory system enjoys a privileged, "dominant" role over semantic public events memory (similar to the reorganisation of language in cases of early left hemisphere damage, for example, Tivarus, Starling, Newport & Langfitt, 2012).

Do you think that there is anything unique that the report of these cases added to our knowledge?

The case of CH, considered in terms of her central clinical results, that is, her focal retrograde amnesia, is not unique. In fact, focal retrograde amnesia or at least disproportionate retrograde amnesia has been reported in different neurological diseases (the excellent review by Kapur, 1999, is still relevant). However, CH's specificity, which was the clear-cut preserved anterograde—temporally impaired retrograde memory performance, is almost unique, since strictly speaking, only one other case, JM, as commented on before, was cognitively (though not neurologically) similar to CH (Evans, Breen, Antoun & Hodges, 1996; Evans et al., 2003). It seems therefore useful to remind the reader of how I accounted for this fairly unique pattern of performance. The apparent dissociation between retrograde and anterograde retrieval mechanisms would be more appropriately expressed in terms of *threshold* of impairment, which will determine the practicability of multi-level synchronous activation in the context of Damasio's (1989) model (briefly commented on when answering the first question). Indeed, the transitory patterns of multimodal activations formed before CH's brain accident may have become inaccessible after the hypoxia due to a failure of the binding codes to activate synchronously the ensemble of fragments, making up a memory, in the same neural conditions in which they were encoded. Encoding processes of post-accident autobiographical memories were intact due to the mildness of the brain lesions, which spared interconnectivity, thus allowing the formation of new neural configurations. By the same token, it should be possible to activate synchronously the fragments composing an autobiographical memory formed after the accident, however different their quality may be in comparison to pre-morbid autobiographical memories (Hunkin et al., 1995). More specifically, CH's mild neocortical dysfunction would have blocked access to premorbid memories because those neural subsystems responsible for the original encoding were no longer present, but the existence of other intact pathways allowed encoding and retrieval of new memories. This view points to the flexibility with which new memories can be stored.

JR's case viewed from his central clinical characteristics, that is, the counterintuitive dissociation between memory systems is not unique; at least four patients (see my response to the first question) have been reported in the literature. Likewise, exploring the ability to imagine one's impersonal future, although very rarely carried out, is also not unique since Klein, Loftus and Kihlstrom, 2002 and Irish et al., ten years later, have investigated that topic. Regarding autobiographical significance, it has been studied in neuropsychology, in clinical groups in the context of dementia, and amnesia by Westmacott et al. in 2004, and in healthy participants by means of functional MRI by Denkova et al. in 2006. However, to my knowledge, it has never been investigated in both neuropsychological and functional neuroimaging settings. This uniqueness in JR's case is interesting given the results that nicely confirmed the "takeover" of the episodic autobiographical memory by the right hemisphere. So, JR's contribution could be seen as the illustration of one way in which neural mechanisms responded to early neural dysfunction (clinical and very likely subclinical) limited to the left hemisphere.

Can you specify why these cases were relevant in relation to the knowledge at the time and would they still be relevant to the knowledge of today?

Very briefly and to avoid repetition, CH and JR's cases seemed relevant at the time and may still be so today on at least one account: both patients corroborate very sparse evidence in neuropsychological research. With regard to CH, she illustrates what Kapur (1997) stated about focal retrograde amnesia being the neurological condition that provides a test to assess one of the key questions in neuropsychology of memory, how is information stored in the brain? In JR's case, the past, and maybe still present, relevance is to show new ways of accounting for autobiographical significance.

More generally, the two cases might still be informative today in suggesting different, selective effects of the interactions of epileptic activity with individual factors. With regard to JR, his clinical observations are the consequences of his left medial temporal lobe refractory epileptic condition. In relation to CH, we have to bear in mind that she presented with evidence of epileptic activity during the early recovery period. It is then possible, as Kapur (2000) has argued, that subclinical epileptic activity played a predominant role in disrupting connections in the cortex and white matter, affecting past recollections but with no major impact on the consolidation of new memories. That point of view could provide some present relevance to CH and JR if we consider together their respective cognitive performance.

What are the shortcomings of these cases?

The most obvious shortcoming in relation to CH is the lack of more exacting tests to probe executive functions. With regard to JR, I had implemented a rehabilitation programme which proved its efficacy (Manning et al., 2006). However, it lasted only a few months. To be useful and exploitable, the programme should have lasted much longer.

Do you remember whether you had difficulty publishing your work with CH and JR? If so, what was this difficulty?

I had some difficulties publishing these cases, but they were very mild compared to other papers! I remember that there were doubts that CH's amnesia was the result of an organic condition. Therefore, I consulted her very old medical files and obtained permission to use her PET scan, amongst other things. I realised immediately that having confirmation that her amnesia was due to cerebral hypoxia did, in fact, strengthen the write-up of CH's case.

A first write-up of JR's case, which did not include the fMRI results, was submitted to the case report section of a journal that had a strict word limit. The journal rejected the manuscript with very little, if any, constructive suggestions. The second much longer version of our manuscript, which included the fMRI study, was submitted to a journal with a greater word limit. More importantly, we had excellent Reviewers. The paper improved thanks to their comments and it was accepted fairly rapidly.

Do you remember whether there were any issues that reviewers were particularly blunt about?

The sole reviewer, who had assessed JR's first rejected version with a limited number of words, was not familiar with the concept of autobiographical significance, which I had failed to explain properly. The reviewer's comments were that I should "cut out the twaddle".

Are there any assessments/paradigms that you would administer now to these individuals if they were available?

If I were to investigate these two cases today, I could certainly improve CH's case by using fMRI while performing two autobiographical memory tasks. One of them would include events that happened during the 12–15 year period affected by her episodic retrograde amnesia, while the second task would tackle postoperative recollections. In an fMRI study of a 38-year-old psychogenic patient, who was unable to access most of her autobiographical memories from her childhood up to 16 years of age (Botzung, Denkova & Manning, 2008), we showed a series of functional changes supporting the notion of common mechanisms involved in both organic and psychogenic amnesias. It would be interesting to compare in detail those psychogenic functional changes in our 2008 patient with the mechanisms involved in CH's also temporally graded forgotten period but organically caused focal retrograde amnesia.

Likewise, we could complete and improve the interpretation of JR's reorganisation of episodic autobiographical memory in the right hemisphere, by using fMRI functional connectivity. Comparisons between normal participants' and JR's right hemisphere functional connectivity during episodic memory tasks would perhaps bring to light some interesting data.

Do you think these cases have been considered by people who develop theories of the normal mind? If yes, how? If no, should they?

Not to my knowledge. It is possible that some theoreticians would find JR's case of some interest for normal mind theories when normal cerebral mechanisms sustaining the development of semantic public events memory is more systematically studied. CH's case would likely be more useful in theories of the normal mind when further similar cases, besides that reported by Evans et al. (2003), are available and studied by means of functional neuroimaging as well as detailed neuropsychological assessment.

In general, do you think that neuropsychology cases could contribute to our understanding of the normal mind? Should this data be considered and if so why?

Yes, single case studies that meet the demanding conditions required for publication, normally contribute to the understanding of the normal mind. It is one of the basics that cognitive neuropsychology students know nearly as an axiom. Far from wanting to expose any theoretical views of cognitive neuropsychology, I have nevertheless to mention some very general principles. In a few lines, the more we analyse the symptoms, the more useful questions about the theoretical account will emerge. Symptoms could not be studied in groups of patients; we seem to need single case studies to obtain detailed symptom characteristics, capable of shaking up theories. Without going into the intricacies of the "universality assumption" (Caramazza, 1986), suffice it to say that single cases tell us that the interactions of different factors resulting in a given pattern of performance are actual manifestations of 1, 2 or 20 of the hundreds of ways in which the normal mind disintegrates due to neurological injury. Each actual clinical manifestation (or the configuration of scores of a single case), derives from a universally shared architecture and is constrained and bound by this architecture. After a brain lesion, no patient ever started chirping or behaving in a way that is not represented in the original cognitive architecture. Each clinical manifestation is carefully considered in terms of how our normal cognitive or neurocognitive mechanisms work. Let's imagine that case studies are banned from the literature, and clinicians stop following-up cases for clinical research purposes. How would we manage to understand the cognitive processes of the normal mind on the bases of statistical data about a person, who never existed and will never do? Functional neuroimaging is undoubtedly useful in neurosciences, however, could we understand the normal mind by *localising* cerebral activations?

We are now living in an era where ethics committees would like to foresee every step. How much serendipity was involved in your assessment?

If I had to study CH and JR today, the ethics committees would have the role they had in 2002 and 2013, respectively. Serendipity was present in both cases, but nothing that would need today a different deontological procedure.

References

Barr, W., Goldberg, E., Wasserstein, J., & Novelly, R. A. (1990). Retrograde amnesia following unilateral temporal lobectomy. *Neuropsychologia, 28*, 243–255.

Botzung, A., Denkova, E., & Manning, L. (2008) Psychogenic memory deficits associated with functional cerebral changes: an fMRI study *Neurocase, 13*, 378–384.

Brown, N. (1990). Organization of public events in long-term memory. *Journal of Experimental Psychology General, 119*, 297–304.

Caramazza, A. (1986). On drawing inferences about the structure of normal cognitive systems from the analysis of patterns of impaired performance: the case for single-patient studies. *Brain & Cognition, 5*, 41–66.

Conway, M. A. (2001). Sensory-perceptual episodic memory and its context: autobiographical memory. *Philosophical Transactions of the Royal Society London B Biological Sciences, 356*, 1375–1384.

Crovitz, H., & Schiffman, H. (1974). Frequency of episodic memories as a function of their age. *Bulletin of the Psychonomic Society, 4*, 517–518.

Damasio, A. (1989). Time-locked multiregional retroactivation: a systems-level proposal for the neural substrates of recall and recognition. *Cognition, 3*, 25–62.

Damasio, A. R., & Damasio, H. (1994). Cortical systems underlying knowledge retrieval: evidence from human lesions studies. In T. A. Poggio & D. A. Glaser (Eds.), *Exploring Brain Functions: Models in Neuroscience*. New York: John Wiley.

Denkova, E., Botzung, A., & Manning, L. (2006). Neural correlates of remembering/knowing famous people: an event-related fMRI study. *Neuropsychologia, 44*, 2783–2791.

De Renzi, E., Liotti, M., & Nichelli, P. (1989). Semantic amnesia with preservation of autobiographic memory. a case report. *Cortex, 23*, 575–597.

Evans, J., Breen, K., Antoun, N., & Hodges, J. (1996). Focal retrograde amnesia for autobiographical events following cerebral vasculitis: a connectionist account. *Neurocase, 2*, 1–11.

Evans, J., Graham, K., Pratt, K., & Hodges, J. (2003). The impact of disrupted cortico-cortico connectivity: a long-term follow-up of a case of focal retrograde amnesia. *Cortex*, *39*, 767–790.

Graham, K., & Hodges, J. (1997). Differentiating the role of the hippocampal complex and neocortex in long-term memory storage: evidence from the study of semantic dementia and Alzheimer disease. *Neuropsychology*, *11*, 77–89.

Holmes, A., & Conway, M. (1999). Generation identity and the reminiscence bump: memory for public and private events. *Journal of Adult Development*, *6*, 21–34.

Howes, J. L., & Katz, A. N. (1988). Assessing remote memory with an improved public events questionnaire. *Psychology and Aging*, *3*, 142–150.

Hunkin, N., Parkin, A., Bradley, V., Burrows, E., Aldrich, E., Jansari, F., & Burdon-Cooper, A. (1995). Focal retrograde amnesia following closed head injury: a case study and theoretical account. *Neuropsychologia*, *4*, 509–523.

Irish, M., Addis, D., Hodges, J., & Piguet, O. (2012). Considering the role of semantic memory in episodic future thinking: evidence from semantic dementia. *Brain*, *135*, 2178–2191.

Kapur, N. (1997). How can we best explain retrograde amnesia in human memory disorder? *Memory*, *5*, 115–129.

Kapur, N. (1999). Syndromes of retrograde amnesia: a conceptual and empirical synthesis. *Psychological Bulletin*, *125*, 800–825.

Kapur, N. (2000). Focal retrograde amnesia and the attribution of causality—an exceptionally benign commentary. *Cognitive Neuropsychology*, *17*, 623–637.

Kapur, N., Young, A., Bateman, D., & Kennedy, P. (1989). Focal retrograde amnesia: a long-term clinical and neuropsychological follow-up. *Cortex*, *25*, 387–402.

Klein, S. B., Loftus, J., & Kihlstrom, J. F. (2002). Memory and temporal experience: the effects of episodic memory loss on an amnesic patient's ability to remember the past and imagine the future. *Social Cognition*, *20*, 353–379.

Kopelman, M. (2000). Focal retrograde amnesia and the attribution of causality—an exceptionally critical review. *Cognitive Neuropsychology*, *17*, 585–621.

Manning, L. (2002). Focal retrograde amnesia documented with matching anterograde and retrograde procedures. *Neuropsychologia*, *40*, 28–38.

Manning, L., Denkova, E., & Unterberger, L. (2013). Autobiographical significance in past and future public semantic memory: a case-study. *Cortex*, *49*, 207–220.

Manning, L., Voltzenlogel, V., Chassagnon, S., Hirsch, E. et al. (2006). Déficit sélectif de la mémoire des faits publics associés à un oubli accéléré chez un patient atteint d'épilepsie du lobe temporal gauche, *Revue Neurologique Paris*, *16*, 222–228.

Markowitsch, H. J., Calabrese, P., Neufeld, H., Gehlen, W., & Durwen, H. F. (1999). Retrograde amnesia for world knowledge and preserved memory for autobiographic events. A case report. *Cortex*, *35*, 243–252.

Markowitsch, H. J., Thiel, A., Reinkemeier, M., Kessler, J., Koyuncu, A., & Heiss, W. D. (2000). Right amygdalar and temporofrontal activation during autobiographic, but not during fictitious memory retrieval. *Behavioral Neurology*, *12*, 181–190.

Morris, D. (2004). Rebuilding identity through narrative following traumatic brain injury. *The Journal of Cognitive Rehabilitation*, *15*, 15–21.

Moscovitch, M., Rosenbaum, R. S., Gilboa, A., Addis, D. R., Westmacott, R., Grady, C., et al. (2005). Functional neuroanatomy of remote episodic, semantic and spatial memory: a unified account based on multiple trace theory. *Journal of Anatomy*, *207*, 35–66.

O'Connor, M., Butters, N., Miliotis, P., Eslinger, P., & Cermak, L. (1992). The dissociation of anterograde and retrograde amnesia in a patient with herpes encephalitis. *Journal of Clinical and Experimental Neuropsychology, 14,* 159–178.

Suddendorf, T., & Corballis, M. C. (1997). Mental time travel and the evolution of the human mind. *Genetic, Social and General Psychology Monographs, 123,* 133–167.

Svoboda, E., McKinnon, M. C., & Levine, B. (2006). The functional neuroanatomy of autobiographical memory: a meta-analysis. *Neuropsychologia, 44,* 2189–2208.

Tivarus, M. E., Starling, S. J., Newport, E. L., & Langfitt, J. T. (2012). Homotopic language reorganization in the right hemisphere after early left hemisphere injury. *Brain & Language, 123,* 1–10.

Westmacott, R., Black, S. E., Freedman, M., & Moscovitch, M. (2004). The contribution of autobiographical significance to semantic memory: evidence from Alzheimer's disease, semantic dementia, and amnesia. *Neuropsychologia, 42,* 25–48.

Westmacott, R., & Moscovitch, M. (2003). The contribution of autobiographical significance to semantic memory. *Memory and Cognition, 31,* 761–774.

Yasuda, K., Watanabe, O., & Ono, Y. (1997). Dissociation between semantic and autobiographic memory: a case report. *Cortex, 33,* 623–638.

10

SENSORY-SPECIFIC VISUAL AMNESIA (CASES 1 AND 2)

An Acquired Visual-Limbic Disconnection Syndrome

Elliott D. Ross

In 1980, you described two cases of isolated visual memory loss. Can you provide us with some background information about these cases?

The index case for this publication (Ross, 1980a) was Case 1, whom I first evaluated in November 1976. It turned out that one of my Neurology Residents, John Cella, was dating a woman who was very concerned about her brother's medical condition. He had been in the US Navy and suffered an ischemic stroke at age 34, probably related to a complicated migraine. He was admitted to the Great Lakes Naval Hospital in February 1974 because of the sudden loss of the ability to read, recognize objects, and perceive colors, although he was able to see. Initially, his symptoms were thought to be "hysterical" but within 12 hours, he had onset of a left hemiparesis with left hemianopsia and was diagnosed as having suffered a stroke. His admission physical examination was normal, but he was described as being confused with an anomic aphasia. On formal neurological examination, he had a left homonymous hemianopsia with left-sided ataxic hemiparesis and left-sided sensory extinction to bilateral simultaneous stimulation. Although his EEG showed right posterior slowing, his nuclide brain scan, lumbar puncture, cerebral angiography, and pneumoencephalography were normal (note: his stroke occurred before CT scanners were widely available as a diagnostic tool). After his hospital discharge, his confusional state, anomia and alexia resolved. He was discharged from the Navy and began attending a local college in Indiana. He noted that he was completely unable to recognize faces and had severe spatial disorientation.

In order to find his way around the college campus or to walk to and from school, he was constantly forced to consult maps and written notes or to "verbally memorize" routes. When he was assigned to a particular seat in a classroom, he would record its row and rank; otherwise, he could never find it again. Despite these difficulties, he was able to maintain a "C" average.

(Ross, 1980a, p. 193)

When the patient's sister voiced her concerns about her brother's residual symptoms and that no one had been able to explain what they were due to, my Resident thought that because my academic specialty was behavioral neurology, I might be able to help clarify his neurological condition. To accomplish this, John Cella arranged for the patient to be admitted to the Dallas VA Medical Center for evaluation. Fortunately, this was at a time when the VA had no length of stay requirements, which allowed me to assess the patient for approximately one month. At that time, my primary faculty appointment was Assistant Professor of Neurology at the University of Texas Health Sciences Center in Dallas, located approximately 20 miles (30-minute commute without traffic) from the VA. In addition, I had ~70% protected time to engage in academic-research activities as part of my employment. Thus, over the course of the month, I was able to spend over 60 hours evaluating his neurologic condition.

Case 2 was evaluated in May 1978. He was not an index Case in that I had already figured out how to diagnose and formally assess for isolated loss of visual recent memory, i.e. sensory-specific visual amnesia, from my previous encounter with Case 1. Thus, in this chapter, I will focus my comments on Case 1.

How did you first realize that these cases were interesting?

When I initially began to assess Case 1 and gather history from both the patient (Case 1) and his sister regarding his symptoms of spatial disorientation, it was readily apparent that he did not, from a behavioral perspective, fit any of the known causes for spatial disorientation (Benton, 1969; Brain, 1941; Meyer, 1900; Patterson & Zangwill, 1944; Holmes, 1918; Scotti, 1968), such as visual neglect, loss of topographical memory with or without visual agnosia or prosopagnosia, or the traditional Korsakoff syndrome, which is a multimodal amnestic disorder (Ross, 1980a, 2008). In addition, very early on, both he and his sister reported that he did not experience spatial disorientation in old environments, the disorientation only occurred in new environments following his 1974 stroke. For example, even though he verbally knew that he was currently living in an apartment with four separate areas (kitchen, living room, bedroom and bathroom) he had no idea of the actual topography of the floor plan other than it contained four separate living areas (see Figure 10.1). His sister reported that if they were sitting in his living room and the patient wished to use the toilet, he would wander around the apartment until he found the bathroom rather than take a direct route to the toilet. In contrast, when they visited their parents for Thanksgiving, his sister observed

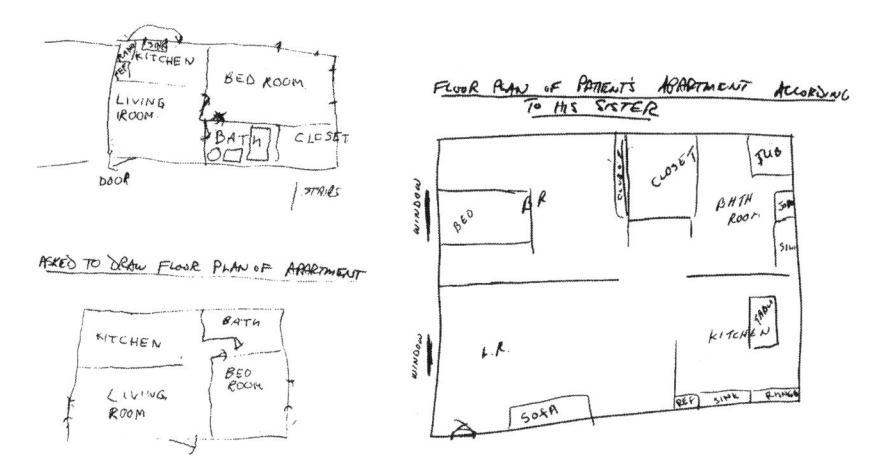

FIGURE 10.1 Two drafts by Case 1 depicting the floor plan of his apartment (left) versus accurate floor plan drawn by his sister (right) for comparison. Reproduced with permission from *Archives of Neurology*, 1980a, 37: 193–200.

Copyright © (1980) American Medical Association. All rights reserved.

that he was fully oriented in the house. In fact, when I asked the patient to draw the floor plan of his parent's house in which he was raised, he drew it accurately, as confirmed by his sister, including the placement of various windows and the cardinal (north, south, east, west) orientation of the house (see Figure 10.2). Thus, it became readily apparent that his spatial disorientation was most likely related to some sort of amnestic deficit because it appeared to affect recent but not remote topographical memory. However, he did not have any symptoms of a traditional, multimodal, amnestic syndrome (Ross, 1980a, 2008). He was able to give me an accurate history of what had transpired and was able to maintain a C average in college, suggesting that he did not have an amnestic disturbance, at least from a verbal-auditory perspective. When I formally screened him for memory loss using standard bedside techniques, no deficits were apparent. He was fully oriented and attentive with normal immediate recall. There were no aphasic deficits or anomia. Recent and remote memory, tested *verbally*, were completely intact. When I asked him to remember a story with 15 pieces of information, he was able to recite the story *verbatim* after a three-minute distracted delay and continued to do so over the entire course of his Dallas VA hospitalization. In addition, similarities, proverb interpretations, right/left orientation, map directions, map reading, geographic knowledge, two and three-dimensional constructions, calculations, dressing and finger recognition were normal. The only deficits found on testing of higher cortical function were: (1) a total inability to recognize the faces of family, friends, and famous people, with preserved ability to match pictures of the same face

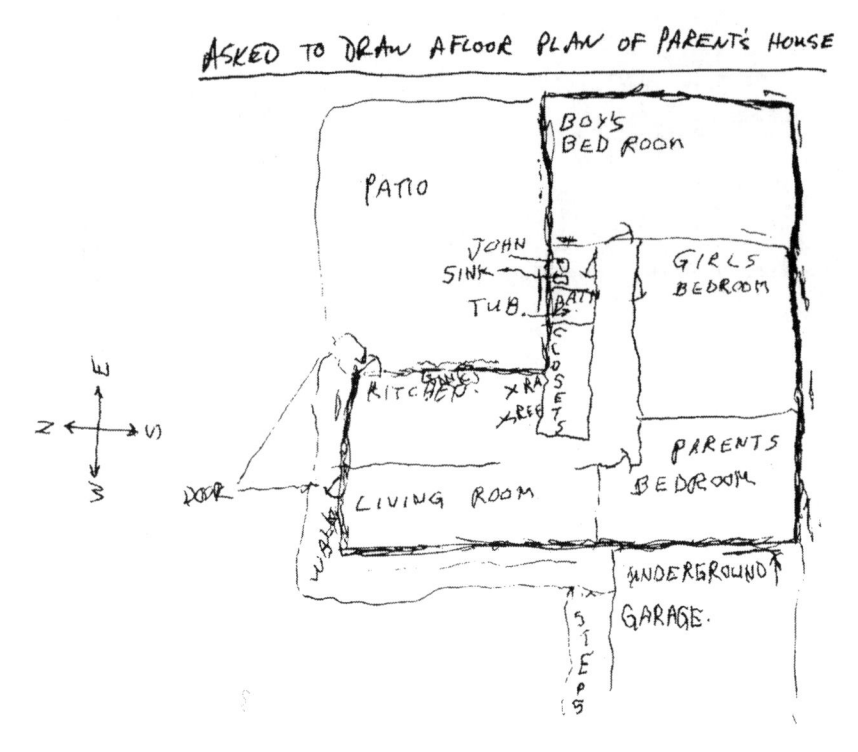

FIGURE 10.2 Draft by Case 1 depicting the floor plan of his parent's house. According to his sister, the drawing was accurate, including the north, west, east and south orientation of the house. Reproduced with permission from *Archives of Neurology*, 1980a, 37: 193–200.

Copyright © (1980) American Medical Association. All rights reserved.

taken at different photographic angles, (2) a severe inability to recognize and name colors that could not be explained by the patient's congenital color blindness, (3) a complete inability to sort colors that varied only in hue and (4) severe spatial disorientation that proved to be secondary to a profound loss of recent visual memory. Examination for elementary neurological deficits demonstrated a left hemianopsia with a partial right superior quadrantanopsia. There was mild loss of left facial sensation without weakness and he had normal motor strength throughout despite hyperreflexia and ataxia of his left limbs and a left-sided Babinski sign. No sensory neglect was present, and his station and gait were normal.

In order to determine if the cause of his spatial disorientation was due to an isolated loss of visual recent memory, I had to develop special tests. As stated earlier, he did not evince any deficits in verbal memory, which was and still is the traditional means to screen for the presence of amnesia (Ross, 2008). Non-verbal auditory recent memory, tested with noises and melodies, and tactile recent memory, tested in both hands while blindfolded (see companion paper for details; Ross, 1980b), were completely intact. Also, no deficits in immediate visual recall were detected using the Graham-Kendall Memory-for-Designs Test with the patient scoring a perfect 15 out of 15. To assess for remote visual memory, I asked him to draw the Statue of Liberty, Eiffel Tower, a map of Indiana and a face (see Figure 10.4 in Ross, 1980a) and a floor plan of his parents' house (see Figure 10.2). All of these drawings were done reasonably well for someone with no artistic talent. He had no trouble in naming or identifying visually a multitude of objects presented to him. When assessing his recent visual memory by presenting relatively non-verbalizable objects or line drawings (see Figure 10.3), he was totally unable to visually identify the object or line drawing from an array of similar objects or line drawings after a three-minute distracted delay. The reason for presenting relatively non-verbalizable stimuli was to prevent the patient from remembering the stimuli using his fully intact verbal memory. For example, if he was shown a ballpoint pen and the post-distraction array included the pen, a pencil, a comb and a piece of chalk, he would always choose the pen. However, if he was shown a ballpoint pen and the post-distraction array displayed the original pen with three other ballpoint pens that were visually dissimilar, he was not able to choose the correct pen. Thus, I was able to conclude that his spatial disorientation was due to an isolated, sensory-specific, loss of visual recent memory, i.e., a sensory-specific visual amnesia.

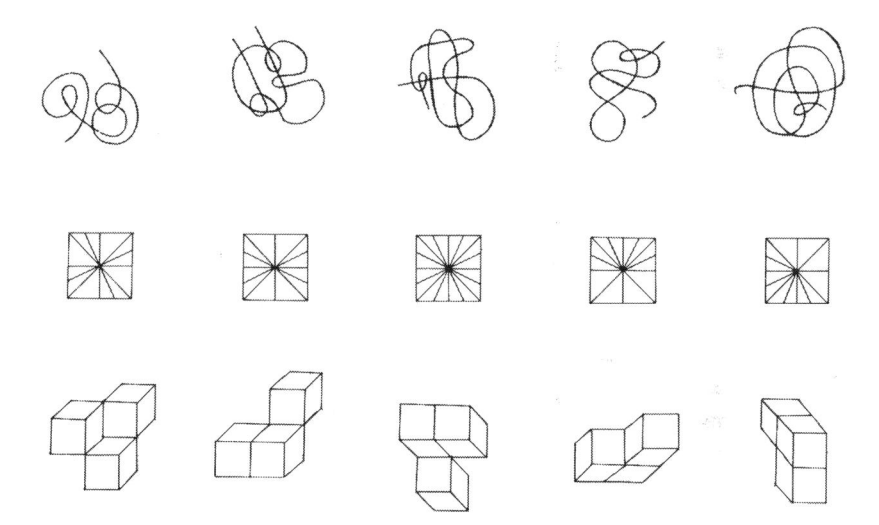

FIGURE 10.3 Three examples of the line drawings (five per set) used to assess visual recent memory and immediate visual recall. Reproduced with permission from *Archives of Neurology*, 1980b, 37: 267–272.

Copyright © (1980) American Medical Association. All rights reserved.

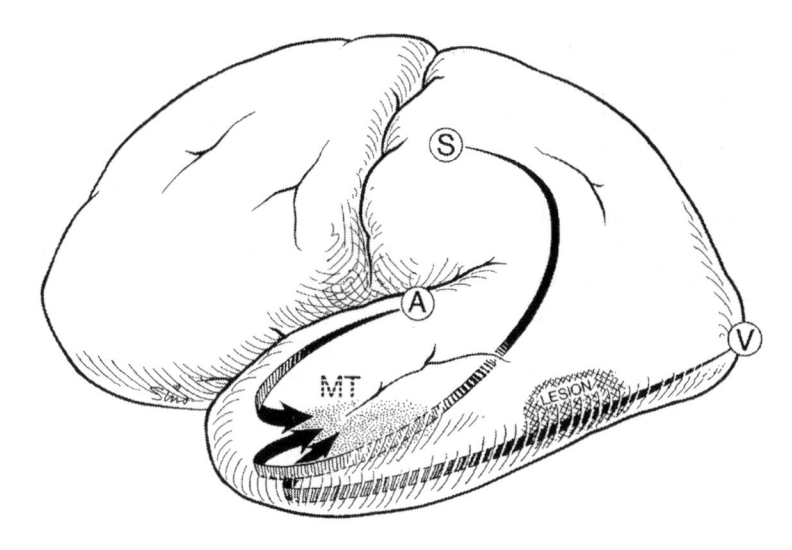

FIGURE 10.4 Highly schematic illustration depicting the separate anatomical routes taken by the somatosensory (**S**), auditory (**A**) and visual (**V**) information when coursing to the medial temporal (**MT**) lobe for processing into a recent memory by the hippocampal formation. Although the routes are depicted as solid lines, the pathways are multisynaptic in monkeys (Jones & Powell, 1970). However, recent MRI tractography has shown that in humans, there is both a multisynaptic and a direct visual pathway to the anterior temporal region via the inferior longitudinal fasciculus (Catani et al., 2003). If a bilateral lesion disconnects the visual cortices from sending information to the medial temporal region, specifically the hippocampal formation, isolated (sensory-specific) loss of visual recent memory occurs. Similarly, if strategic bilateral lesions disconnect the somatosensory or auditory cortices from sending information to the medial temporal region, then isolated (sensory-specific) tactile or auditory recent memory loss should occur, respectively. To date, sensory-specific tactile or auditory recent memory loss has not been described in humans but has been produced experimentally in monkeys (Wilson, 1957; Pribram & Barry, 1958; Stepién, Cordeau & Rasmussen, 1960; Ross, 1980a). Reproduced with permission from *Archives of Neurology*, 1980a, 37: 193–200.

Copyright © (1980) American Medical Association. All rights reserved.

The next issue that needed addressing was the neuroanatomical basis for his syndrome. When I obtained a CT scan of the patient's brain it demonstrated an old ischemic infarction involving most of the right occipital lobe and the left inferior occipital region. The lesion spared the medial temporal limbic regions bilaterally (see Figure 7 in Ross, 1980a). This was of great interest because at that time lesions producing amnestic syndromes involved either the medial temporal limbic region (hippocampal formation) or deep structures, such as the mamillary bodies or dorsal medial thalamus (Milner, 1966; Stepién & Sierpiński, 1960; Zangwill, 1966; Scoville & Milner, 1957; Brierley, 1966; Whitty & Lishman, 1966; Victor, Adams & Collins, 1971; Benson, Marsden & Meadows, 1974). However, I was very fortunate to have received my post-graduate Neurology training (1972–1975) under the mentorship of Norman Geschwind when he was the Putnam Professor of Neurology at Harvard Medical School and Director of the Neurological Unit at Boston City Hospital. Thus, I had read his seminal publication on disconnection syndromes (Geschwind, 1965) multiple times and, based on this publication and personal interactions with him, was well aware of the animal research that had been done to dissect out the neuroanatomical relationships involving the various behavioral components of Kluver-Bucy syndrome. Of particular interest was the discovery by Chow (1951), confirmed by Mishkin (1954) and Mishkin and Pribram (1954), that bilateral lesions of the inferotemporal cortex in monkeys caused a profound loss of their ability to learn new visual discriminations without impairing their ability to learn new tactile (Wilson, 1957) or auditory (Weiskrantz & Mishkin, 1958) discriminations. Most importantly, it was shown that the visual discrimination deficit was due to a loss of visual recent memory (Stepién, Cordeau & Rasmussen, 1960; Dean & Weiskrantz, 1974). In his disconnection paper, Geschwind (1965) had proposed that the loss of visual discrimination was not due to destruction of the inferotemporal cortex per se but rather to the lesion causing a disconnection between the visual cortex and the rhinencephalon, in particular the hippocampal formation, thus producing an "isolated visual recent memory deficit" (p. 252). Based on Geschwind's proposal, Horel and Misantone (1974) placed bilateral coronal white matter cuts in the basolateral portions of the posterior temporal lobes of monkeys, presumably to disrupt the inferior longitudinal fasciculi (Ross, 1980a, 2008; Catani, Jones, Donato & Ffytche, 2003) and found that their ability to learn new visual discrimination was lost similar to monkeys with bilateral lesions of the inferotemporal cortex, thus supporting Geschwind's disconnection proposal and my interpretation of the cases (see Figure 10.4).

Can you summarize the main features of these cases?

Both Cases 1 and 2 were unique in that they provided clinical evidence that amnestic memory loss, depending on the location of the lesion, could be sensory-specific rather than multimodal, in support of the experimental animal literature discussed earlier. Furthermore, it highlighted the deficiency of screening for amnesic syndromes by relying on strictly verbal assessments.

What were these cases' patterns of spared and impaired abilities?

The patients demonstrated that verbal and non-verbal auditory and right and left tactile recent memory functions could be preserved when there was loss of visual recent memory functions. Both patients also had other behavioral and elementary neurological deficits related to the lesion location, but none could explain their sensory-specific visual amnesia. Case 1 exhibited severe prosopagnosia and color agnosia, a left hemianopsia with a partial right superior quadrantanopsia and mild left-sided weakness with limb ataxia. Case 2 exhibited left-sided visual neglect with a dense left inferior quadrantanopsia and a partial left superior quadrantanopsia. In contrast to Case 1, he did not have prosopagnosia, color agnosia or left-sided weakness, suggesting that these deficits are not a necessary requirement for the syndrome of sensory-specific visual amnesia.

Why is this particular fractionation of the memory system relevant?

The discovery of patients with sensory-specific visual amnesia led to the companion paper (Ross, 1980b) in which I described patients with fractional disorders of memory due to unilateral posterior cerebral artery lesions that involved the medial temporo-occipital region. Patients with left-sided lesions had right but not left tactile amnesia and verbal but not non-verbal auditory amnesia. Patients with right-sided lesions had left but not right tactile amnesia and non-verbal but not verbal-auditory amnesia. Because all the patients had a dense contralateral hemianopsia, I was not able to determine if they had fractional loss of visual recent memory in their hemianopic visual field. As expected, none of the patients displayed loss visual of recent memory in their preserved visual field. The sensory-specific visual amnesia paper (Ross, 1980a) also contributed to the publication by Russ Bauer (personal communication, 1980) of a patient who had sensory-specific visual hypoemotionality in addition to sensory-specific visual amnesia (Bauer, 1982). Both conditions are the result of bilateral lesions that disconnect the visual cortex from interacting with temporal limbic structures, specifically the amygdala for emotional elaboration of stimuli and the hippocampal formation for mnestic elaboration of stimuli (Ross, 2008). Based on the papers describing sensory-specific and fractional loss of recent memory (Ross, 1980a, b) and sensory-specific visual hypoemotionality (Bauer, 1982) coupled with Geschwind's disconnection paper (1965) and Carl Wernicke's papers on language being a distributed left hemisphere neural network (Eggert, 1977; Margolin, 1991; Ross, 1993; Ross, 2010), I was able to develop an integrated neural network model for understanding the neurological basis of agnosias, emotions, memory and remembering and language and communication that includes both the left hemisphere (linguistic-verbal) and right hemisphere (affective-prosodic) contributions (Ross, 1997, 2008, 2010).

Do you think that there is anything unique that the report of these cases added to our knowledge?

The cases reported by Ross (1980a, b) and Bauer (1982) were all unique in that the syndromes had never been reported before in the clinical literature and, thus, led to a much deeper understanding of the neurological basis of agnosia, emotions, language, memory and remembering (Ross, 1997, 2008, 2010).

Can you specify why these cases were relevant in relation to the knowledge at the time and would they still be relevant to the knowledge of today?

These cases expanded our notions concerning the neurology of recent memory by demonstrating that focal lesions could produce sensory-specific and fractional amnestic disorders that would be missed by clinicians if patients' recent memory functions were assessed strictly using verbal probes. At the time, it was assumed that amnestic disorders were multimodal (Ross, 1980a), thus using verbal probes would be sufficient to identify patients with amnestic deficits. Unfortunately, we still screen and assess for memory deficits clinically using verbal probes both at the bedside and when using standard neuropsychological testing instruments, such as the Mini-Mental State Exam (Folstein, Folstein & McHugh, 1975), the Wechsler Adult Intelligence Scale-Revised (Wechsler, 1981), the California Verbal Learning Test (Delis, Kramer, Kaplan & Ober, 1987), the Rey Auditory Verbal Learning Test (Schmidt, 1996), the Repeatable Battery for the Assessment of Neuropsychological Status (Randolph, Tierney, Mohr and Chase, 1998) and the Montreal Cognitive Assessment (Nasreddine et al., 2005). There are a few formal tests that assess visual memory (Butters, Delis & Lucas, 1995) but none that formally assess tactile memory. To fully test memory functions one has to assess, at minimum, verbal and non-verbal memory, right and left tactile memory, and right and left visual memory. A complete multimodal test of memory functions would also have to include olfaction and taste. Because testing recent memory functions requires a distracted delay of one to three minutes between the presentation and identification of the test stimulus in order to force the stimulus out of the immediate recall and into the recent memory system, complete multimodal testing of memory functions is, perforce, extremely time consuming and difficult on both the examiner and subject, something I can attest to when I was assessing patients with sensory-specific and fractional amnesias (Ross, 1980a, b). Thus, it is highly unlikely to become a standard testing procedure in this day and age when clinicians in the USA are expected to see patients efficiently and as quickly as possible because of billing codes and reimbursement rates.

What are the shortcomings of these cases?

The imaging of the brain lesions was of meager quality because CT scanning at the time had poor resolution and MRI scanning had not yet become available.

Do you remember whether you had difficulty publishing this report? If so, what was this difficulty?

There were no problems publishing this report and the companion paper (Ross, 1980a, b). At the time, the Editor of the Archives of Neurology was Maurice Van Allen, Professor and Chair of Neurology at the University of Iowa Medical School. Dr. Van Allen was very interested in the behavioral aspects of Neurology (Joynt, 1986), thus the Archives of Neurology and the reviewers were receptive to my submissions and they received excellent critiques.

Are there any assessments/paradigms that you would administer now to these individuals if they were available?

No, other than obtaining an MRI rather than a CT scan to better delineate the exact location of the patients' ischemic infarctions and, perhaps, a tractography assessment using MRI diffusion tensor imaging to visualize the integrity of their inferior longitudinal fasciculi (Catani et al., 2003; Catani & Thiebaut de Schotten, 2008).

These cases were reported in 1980. Do you think these cases are still informative now? Are we now better able to interpret these patterns of spared and impaired abilities? If so, in what way?

These cases are very informative in that they led to a deeper understanding of how sensory and affective information is processed, stored and retrieved for cognitive-emotional activities, including working memory and affective communication (Ross, 1997, 2008, 2010). This in turn allows for a more detailed description of behavioral syndromes encountered clinically and why certain functions are spared while others are not.

Do you think these cases have been considered by people who develop theories of the normal mind? If yes, how? If no, should they?

Based on a review of the literature citing Ross (1980a), using the Web of Science, it is clear that the cases have not been incorporated into current neuropsychological theories of the normal mind, including memory and remembering, other than individual researchers interested in the neurobiology of disconnection syndromes or the neuroanatomical basis of clinical syndromes. Most theories of the normal mind are driven by deductive reasoning (see the following) and do not incorporate the powerful brain-behavioral relationships uncovered by clinicians over the last 150 years based on case studies that were initiated by the pivotal publications of Paul Broca (1861, 1865) and Carl Wernicke (1874). These publications established that the propositional aspects of language are a dominant and lateralized function of the left hemisphere and that language functions are localized in the brain as a large-scale, parallel-distributed, neural network rather than in discrete cortical regions (Wernicke, 1874; Geschwind, 1967; Eggert, 1977; Margolin, 1991; Ross, 1993, 2010).

We are now living in an era where ethics committees would like to foresee every step. How much serendipity was involved in your assessment?

Serendipity coupled with a "prepared mind" played a huge role in the assessment of patients with sensory-specific and fractional amnesias (Ross, 1980a, b). When I was a senior student at Boston University School of Medicine in 1967, I was drawn to a possible career in Psychiatry because I found the behavioral syndromes fascinating. However, in the 1960s, Psychiatry in the United States was overwhelmingly psychoanalytic, and the attending physicians had no interest or training in the Neurology of behavior. Whenever I asked questions about what was wrong with the patient's brain to cause such extraordinary behavioral deficits, I received only a blank look. Thus, I rapidly became very disillusioned about pursuing an academic career in Psychiatry. Near the end of the rotation, Norman Geschwind was invited to give Psychiatry grand rounds (serendipity) on the relationship between temporal lobe epilepsy and psychiatric illness. The lecture was so inspiring that I decided to pursue an academic career in Behavioral Neurology and to train under Professor Geschwind. A medical school classmate, who also was interested in Neurology, gave me a copy of Dr. Geschwind's seminal disconnection paper (Geschwind, 1965), which I read and re-read multiple times. After two years of training in Internal Medicine and two years of service in the US Navy, I finally started my Neurology Residency at Boston City Hospital in 1972 under the tutelage of Dr. Geschwind. After my Neurology Residency, I was fortunate to be hired as an Assistant Professor of Neurology the University of Texas Health Sciences Center in Dallas. If my Neurology Resident, John Cella, was not dating a woman whose brother had suffered a stroke causing strange behavioral problems, I would not have had the opportunity to evaluate the initial patient with sensory-specific visual amnesia (serendipity).

The currently accepted standard for scientific inquiry is the deductive rather than the inductive research model which is essentially what ethics committees and institutional review boards attempt to regulate and what funding agencies rely on to award grants, i.e., one generates a hypothesis (often a belief based on little or sparse data to explain a phenomenon; Schermer, 2011) and develop methods for testing the hypothesis through rational scientific experiments that are often self-serving. Inductive clinical research, such as case reports, that often rely on one or two subjects does not generate enough data for the results to undergo statistical analysis. In contrast, deductive research generates enough data to undergo statistical analysis using tests that generate p-values: t-tests, χ^2 analyses, ANOVAs, correlations, regression analyses, etc. In their zest to prove their hypotheses, researchers focus on whether or not the p-value is significant, usually with alpha set at 0.05 or 0.01. Unfortunately, p-values only tell you if the differences are *statistically* significant, i.e., the chance that the differences could be due to sampling error, which does not necessarily establish that the results are biologically significant (Kirk, 1996). For example, a p-value of 0.01 indicates that there is a one in a hundred chance that the differences are due to sampling errors, as embodied in the null hypothesis, rather than indicating a biologically significant difference. Statistical tests of significance, such as t, χ^2, r, F and R from which a p-value is derived, are confounded indices because they are the product of effect size (magnitude of the mean difference between variables that takes into account the degree of variance overlap) multiplied by the study or sample size (Rosenthal & Rosnow, 1991; Thompson, 1999; Ellis, 2010). As the number of data points or participants increase in a given experiment, the ease for showing statistical significance increases *exponentially* when the effect size is held constant (Cohen, 1992; Freeman, 1993). Thus, miniscule mean differences that are not biologically relevant may become statistically significant when the sample size is large even though the data variances, measured by the standard deviations, are almost completely overlapping. One of the ways to statistically address if the differences may be biologically relevant is to determine the effect size of statistically significant results (Kirk, 1996; Ellis, 2010). Strength of association effect size statistics, such as r^2 for two parametric variables (t-tests, correlations), ϕ^2 for non-parametric χ^2 analyses of 2 × 2 contingency tables, R^2 for multivariate (more than two) parametric variables (ANOVAs, regression analyses) and V^2 for χ^2 analyses of contingency tables greater than 2 × 2, range from 0, or complete data overlap, to 1, or no data overlap. By multiplying the strength of association statistic by 100 yields a percent approximation of the data overlap. For example, an r^2 of 0.18 means that approximately 18% of the data variance is explained by the independent variables whereas 82% of the data are overlapping. When doing research in an area of clinical dispute (Ross, Hansel, Orbelo & Monnot, 2005; Ross, Prodan & Monnot, 2007; Ross, Gupta, Adnan, Holden, Havlicek & Radhakrishnan, 2016) or reviewing submissions for publication in peer-reviewed journals, I have found that the average strength of association is usually less than 0.05, meaning that less than 5% of the data variance is explained by the independent variables. Yet, researchers will claim that their deductive hypotheses are biologically valid and advance scientific knowledge based solely on the results being *statistically significant*. Thus, as pointed out by Schermer (2011), deductive (hypothesis-driven) research is often self-serving, especially when using *p*-values rather than effect sizes (Kirk, 1996; Ross, 2005; Ellis, 2010) to judge biological significance, that often impedes rather than advances scientific knowledge by promoting false results with low rates of replication (Ioannidis, 2005).

In contrast, the inductive research model makes observations, often initially serendipitous, and from these observations determines the underlying mechanism that ultimately initiates a novel line of deductive research. Because inductive research is serendipitous and often based on a single observation that cannot be assessed by traditional statistical analyses, it is not amenable to what ethics committees and institutional review boards attempt to regulate and what funding agencies rely on to award grants. A striking example of inductive research is the serendipitous discovery of penicillin by Alexander Fleming (Fleming, 1929, 1945; Diggins, 1999, 2000) who had previously discovered the antibacterial properties of the lysozyme enzyme, a chemical found in tears and egg whites (prepared mind). The discovery was initiated by a chance observation (serendipity) that one of the petri dishes containing bacterial cultures of staphylococcus aureus was contaminated by the mold Penicillium notatum. Around the mold, there was a graded ring from no, to sparse, to degraded bacterial growth, which suggested to Fleming that the mold was excreting an antibacterial chemical, that he called penicillin. Until Fleming made his inductive discovery that initiated a line of deductive research, which ultimately led to the identification and commercial development of penicillin, investigators, including Fleming, threw away their "contaminated" petri dishes. In my estimation, it is inductive research (serendipity coupled with a prepared mind) that is the engine for major advances in science.

As such, individual case reports are a form of inductive research that may lead to major advances in the clinical sciences. For example, my line of research involving the right hemisphere's contribution to language and communication (Ross, 2010; Ross & Monnot, 2008), was initiated by a serendipitous observation in a patient with a right, superior-division, middle cerebral artery ischemic stroke who had lost the ability to impart affect in her speech and body language (Ross, 1982). This lead led to a case report, published with Marsel Mesulam, who had a similar clinical experience when evaluating a patient with a right, superior-division, middle cerebral artery ischemic stroke (Ross & Mesulam, 1979). Previous to our case report, Kenneth Heilman and colleagues had published a traditional deductive-type research paper describing a series of patients with right posterior-Sylvian stokes who had lost their ability to comprehend emotions in speech (Heilman, Scholes & Watson, 1975). However, in his book, *Matter of Mind: A Neurologist's View of Brain-Behavior Relationships* (Heilman, 2002), Ken recounts that it was a serendipitous clinical experience involving a single patient that ultimately lead to the deductive research presented in the 1975 paper. Thus, I suspect that some research presented in the literature as deductive has its roots, usually not included in the original publication, as an inductive discovery. Hopefully, the other contributors to this book will confirm this conjecture.

References

Bauer, R. M. (1982). Visual hypoemotionality as a symptom of visual—limbic disconnection in man. *Archives of Neurology, 39*, 702–708.

Benson, D. F., Marsden, C. D., & Meadows, J. C. (1974). The amnesic syndrome of posterior cerebral artery occlusion. *Acta Neurologica Scandinavica, 50*, 133–145.

Benton, A. L. (1969). Disorders of spatial orientation. In P. J. Vinken & G. W. Bruyn (Eds.), *Handbook of Clinical Neurology*, Vol. 3. Amsterdam: North-Holland, pp. 212–228.

Brain, L. (1941). Visual disorientation with special reference to lesions of the right cerebral hemisphere. *Brain, 64*, 244–272.

Broca, P. (1861). Remarques sur le siege de la faculte du langage articule, suives d'une observation d'aphemie. *Bulletin Société Anatomique* (Paris), *6*, 330–337; 398–407 [translated by von Bonin, G. (1960). *The Cerebral Cortex*. Springfield: Thomas, pp. 49–72].

Broca, P. (1865). Sur le siege de la faculte du langage articule. *Bulletin Société d'Anthropologie* (Paris), *6*, 337–393 [translated by Berker, E. A., Berker, A. H., & Smith, A. (1986). *Archives of Neurology, 43*, 1065–1072].

Brierley, J. B. (1966). The neuropathology of amnesic states. In C. W. M. Whitty & O. L. Zangwill (Eds.), *Amnesia*. London: Butterworth, pp. 150–180.

Butters, N., Delis, D. C., & Lucas, J. A. (1995). Clinical assessment of memory disorders in amnesia and dementia. *Annual Review of Psychology, 46*, 493–523.

Catani, M., Jones, D. K., Donato, R., & Ffytche, D. H. (2003). Occipito-temporal connections in the human brain. *Brain, 126*, 2093–2107.

Catani, M., & Thiebaut de Schotten, M. (2008). A diffusion tensor tractography atlas for virtual in vivo dissections. *Cortex, 44*, 1105–1132.

Chow, K. L. (1951). Effects of partial extirpation of posterior association cortex on visually mediated behavior in monkeys. *Comparative Psychology Monographs, 20*, 187–217.

Cohen, J. (1992). A power primer. *Psychological Bulletin, 11*, 155–159.

Dean, P., & Weiskrantz, L. (1974). Loss of preoperative habits in Rhesus monkeys with inferotemporal lesions: recognition failure or re-learning deficit? *Neuropsychologia, 12*, 299–311.

Delis, D. C., Kramer, J. H., Kaplan, E., & Ober, B. A. (1987). *California Verbal Learning Test*. San Antonio: Psychological Corporation.

Diggins, F. W. (1999). The true history of the discovery of penicillin, with refutation of the misinformation in the literature. *British Journal of Biomedical Science, 56*, 83–93.

Diggins, F. W. (2000). The discovery of penicillin: so many get it wrong. *Biologist (London), 47*, 115–119.

Eggert, G. H. (1977). *Wernicke's Works on Aphasia: A Sourcebook and Review*. The Hague: Mouton Publishers.

Ellis, P. D. (2010). *The Essential Guide to Effect Sizes*. Cambridge: Cambridge University Press.

Fleming, A. (1929). On the antibacterial action of cultures of a penicillium, with special reference to their use in the isolation of B. influenzae. *British Journal of Experimental Pathology, 10*, 226–236.

Fleming, A. (1945). *Penicillin* (Nobel Lecture, December 11, 1945). Available at www.nobelprize.org/nobel_prizes/medicine/laureates/1945/fleming-lecture.pdf.

Folstein, M. F., Folstein, S. E., & McHugh, P. R. (1975). "Mini-mental status". A practical method for grading the cognitive state of patients for the clinician. *Journal of Psychiatric Research, 12,* 189–198.

Freeman, P. R. (1993). The role of p-values in analyzing trial results. *Statistics in Medicine, 12,* 1443–1452.

Geschwind, N. (1965). Disconnexion syndromes in animals and man. *Brain, 88,* 237–294 & 585–644.

Geschwind, N. (1967). Wernicke's contribution to the study of aphasia. *Cortex, 3,* 449–463.

Heilman, K. M. (2002). *Matter of Mind: A Neurologist's View of Brain-Behavior Relationships.* New York: Oxford University Press, pp. 53–63.

Heilman, K. M., Scholes, R., & Watson, R. T. (1975). Auditory affective agnosia. Disturbed comprehension of affective speech. *Journal of Neurology, Neurosurgery & Psychiatry, 38,* 69–72.

Holmes, G. (1918). Disturbances of visual orientation. *British Journal of Ophthalmology, 2,* 449–468 & 506–516.

Horel, J. A., & Misantone, L. J. (1974). The Klüver-Bucy syndrome produced by partial isolation of the temporal lobe. *Experimental Neurology, 42,* 101–112.

Ioannidis, J. P. (2005). Why most published research findings are false. *PLoS Medicine, 2(8),* e124.

Jones, E. G., & Powell, T. P. S. (1970). An anatomical study of converging sensory pathways within the cerebral cortex of the monkey. *Brain, 93,* 793–820.

Joynt, R. J. (1986). Maurice Van Allen (1918–1986). *Archives of Neurology, 43,* 1183.

Kirk, R. (1996). Practical significance: a concept whose time has come. *Education and Psychological Measurement, 56,* 746–759.

Margolin, D. I. (1991). Cognitive neuropsychology. Resolving enigmas about Wernicke's aphasia and other higher cortical disorders. *Archives of Neurology, 48,* 751–765.

Meyer, O. (1900). Ein-und doppelseitige homonyme Hemianopsie mit Orientierungssttörungen. *Monatsschrift für Psychiatrie und Neurologie, 8,* 440–456.

Milner, B. (1966). Amnesia following operation on the temporal lobes. In C. W. M. Whitty & O. L. Zangwill (Eds.), *Amnesia.* London: Butterworth, pp. 109–135.

Mishkin, M. (1954). Visual discrimination performance following partial ablations of the temporal lobe: II. Ventral surface vs hippocampus. *Journal of Comparative and Physiological Psychology, 47,* 187–193.

Mishkin, M., & Pribram, K. H. (1954). Visual discrimination performance following partial ablations of the temporal lobe: I. Ventral vs lateral. *Journal of Comparative and Physiological Psychology, 47,* 14–20.

Nasreddine, Z. S., Phillips, N., Bédirian, V., Charbonneau, S., Whitehead, V., Collin, I., Cummings, J. L., & Chertkow, H. (2005). The Montreal Cognitive Assessment, MoCA: a brief screening tool for mild cognitive impairment. *Journal of the American Geriatrics Society, 53,* 695–699.

Patterson, A., & Zangwill, O. L. (1944). Recovery of spatial orientation in the posttraumatic confusional state. *Brain, 67,* 54–68.

Pribram, H. B., & Barry, J. (1958). Further behavioral analysis of parieto-temporo-preoccipital cortex. *Journal of Neurophysiology, 19,* 99–106.

Randolph, C., Tierney, M. C., Mohr, E., & Chase, T. N. (1998). The Repeatable Battery for the Assessment of Neuropsychological Status (RBANS): preliminary clinical validity. *Journal of Clinical and Experimental Neuropsychology, 20,* 310–319.

Rosenthal, R., & Rosnow, R. L. (1991). *Essentials of Behavioral Research.* Boston: McGraw-Hill.

Ross, E. D. (1980a). Sensory specific and fractional disorders of recent memory in man: I. Isolated loss of visual recent memory. *Archives of Neurology, 37*, 193–200.

Ross, E. D. (1980b). Sensory-specific and fractional disorders of recent memory in man II. unilateral loss of tactile recent memory. *Archives of Neurology, 37*, 267–272.

Ross, E. D. (1982). The divided self. *The Sciences, 22*, 8–12.

Ross, E. D. (1993). Intellectual origins and theoretical framework of behavioral neurology: a response to Dr. Trimble. *Neuropsychiatry, Neuropsychology, and Behavioral Neurology, 6*, 65–67.

Ross, E. D. (1997). Cortical representation of the emotions. In M. R. Trimble & J. L. Cummings (Eds.), *Contemporary Behavioral Neurology* (chap. 5). Boston: Butterworth-Heineman.

Ross, E. D. (2008). Sensory-specific amnesia and hypoemotionality in humans and monkeys: gateway for developing a hodology of memory. *Cortex, 44*, 1010–1022.

Ross, E. D. (2010). Cerebral Localization of functions and the neurology of language: fact versus fiction or is it something else? *Neuroscientist, 16*, 222–243.

Ross, E. D., Gupta, S. S., Adnan, A. M., Holden, T. L., Havlicek, J., & Radhakrishnan, S. (2016). Neurophysiology of spontaneous facial expressions: I. motor control of the upper and lower face is behaviorally independent in adults. *Cortex, 76*, 28–42.

Ross, E. D., Hansel, S. L., Orbelo, D. M., & Monnot, M. (2005). Relationship of leukoaraiosis to cognitive decline and cognitive aging. *Cognitive and Behavioral Neurology, 18*, 89–97.

Ross, E. D., & Mesulam, M. M. (1979). Dominant language functions of the right hemisphere? Prosody and emotional gesturing. *Archives of Neurology, 36*, 144–148.

Ross, E. D., & Monnot, M. (2008). Neurology of affective prosody and its functional-anatomic organization in right hemisphere. *Brain and Language, 104*, 51–74.

Ross, E. D., Prodan, C. I., & Monnot, M. (2007). Human facial expressions are organized functionally across the upper-lower facial axis. *Neuroscientist, 13*, 433–446.

Schmidt, M. (1996). *Rey Auditory Verbal Learning Test: A Handbook*. Los Angeles: Western Psychological Services.

Scotti, G. (1968). La perdita della memoria topographica: Descrizione di un caso. *Sistema Nervoso, 20*, 352–361.

Scoville, W. B., & Milner, B. (1957). Loss of recent memory after bilateral hippocampal lesions. *Journal of Neurology, Neurosurgery, and Psychiatry, 20*, 11–21.

Schermer, M. (2011). *The Believing Brain* (chap. 13). New York: Holt, pp. 280–303.

Stepién, L. S., & Cordeau, J. P., & Rasmussen, T. (1960). The effect of temporal lobe and hippocampal lesions on auditory and visual recent memory in monkeys. *Brain, 83*, 470–489.

Stepién, L., & Sierpiński, S. (1960). The effect of focal lesions of the brain upon auditory and visual recent memory in man. *Journal of Neurology, Neurosurgery, and Psychiatry, 23*, 334–340.

Thompson, B. (1999). If statistical significance tests are broken/misused, what practices should supplement or replace them? *Theory & Psychology, 9*, 165–181.

Victor, M., Adams, R. D., & Collins, G. H. (1971). *The Wernicke-Korsakoff Syndrome*. Philadelphia: F. A. Davis.

Wechsler, D. (1981). *Wechsler Adult Intelligence Scale-Revised*. New York: Psychological Corporation.

Weiskrantz, L., & Mishkin, M. (1958). Effects of temporal and frontal cortical lesions on auditory discrimination in monkeys. *Brain, 81*, 406–414.

Wernicke, C. (1874). *Der Aphasische Symptomencomplex: Eine psychologische Studie auf anatomischer Basis*. Breslau: Cohn & Weigert [translated by Eggert, G. H. (1977). *Wernicke's Works on Aphasia*. The Hague: Mouton, pp. 91–145].

Whitty, C. W. M., & Lishman, W. A. (1966). Amnesia in cerebral disease, In C. W. M. Whitty & O. L. Zangwill (Eds.), *Amnesia*. London: Butterworth, pp. 36–91.

Wilson, M. (1957). Effects of circumscribed cortical lesions upon somesthetic and visual discrimination in the monkey. *Journal of Comparative and Physiological Psychology, 50*, 630–635.

Zangwill, O. L. (1966). The amnesic syndrome. In C. W. M. Whitty & O. L. Zangwill (Eds.), *Amnesia*. London: Butterworth, pp. 109–135.

11

'YES, I REMEMBER'—APPARENT CONSOLIDATION UNDER CONDITIONS OF MINIMAL SENSORY INPUT IN A CASE OF SEVERE ANTEROGRADE AMNESIA

Case PB

Michaela Dewar

You have studied the case of PB, who was a dense anterograde and retrograde amnesic due to limbic encephalitis. PB has contributed to group studies but has never formally been reported as a single case. This case may add to our understanding of memory processing and forgetting, and in particular to the role of retroactive interference as a possible cause of amnesia.

Yes indeed. PB showed a remarkable capacity to retain *new episodic long-term memories*, provided that *sensory input was minimal after acquisition*. This finding challenges the traditional model of amnesia and has led to the novel hypothesis that some types of amnesia might be caused by an *interruption of memory consolidation via ongoing sensory input*. Together, this finding and hypothesis have contributed to the recent re-emergence of consolidation theory within neuropsychology/psychology. Specifically, they suggest that new memories need to strengthen immediately after acquisition and that the healthy mind might be rather adept at doing so, even in the presence of ongoing sensory input.

As a science graduate, PB was extremely eager to contribute to new knowledge by participating in my research, and I am sure that he would be delighted to know about his contribution to this very timely book. My sincerest thanks go to PB and his wife who both endured numerous testing sessions over the course of two years. I would like to dedicate this chapter to them.

First of all, can you provide us with some background information about PB?

I first met and tested PB in 2005. PB was a charming and articulate 72-year-old man with 17 years of formal education, including a university degree in zoology and subsequent teacher training. He had been teaching science at a senior school throughout his working life, retiring approximately 12 years before we met. One morning, in 2003, PB woke with acute vertigo, confusion, and severe anterograde and retrograde amnesia. Although his vertigo and confusion resolved with occasional recurrences of vertigo, his severe amnesia persisted. He also had brief seizures disrupting his attention for seconds. An MRI scan of the brain showed volume loss of the medial temporal lobes and hippocampi bilaterally. PB was eventually diagnosed with autoimmune limbic encephalitis, in which a person's antibodies attack specific regions of the brain, in particular the hippocampus. This disease is sometimes responsive to immunosuppressant treatments, which suppress the body's immune response (Vincent et al., 2004). Unfortunately, PB was unresponsive to this treatment (potentially due to a late start in his treatment regime), and his amnesia remained unchangeably severe: although PB was very articulate and focused at any one moment, he failed to hang on to any new information, seemingly forgetting this within minutes or even seconds. The severity of his anterograde amnesia is perhaps best illustrated by a couple of anecdotes: when we first met, PB's wife reported that a close family friend from abroad had recently been staying with them for several days. However, within minutes of the friend's departure, PB had no recollection of the friend's visit. More strikingly, after an hour of interviews and neuropsychological assessments, I left the room for a couple of seconds and then re-entered to examine informally PB's ability to remember me after a brief delay. When I returned, PB had no recollection of ever having met me before.

PB's retrograde amnesia appeared to be temporally graded. Although he was able to recall several memories pertaining to his remote past (corroborated by his wife where possible), he appeared to have lost recent pre-morbid memories.

What was this case's pattern of spared and impaired abilities in neuropsychological/experimental testing?

In keeping with the earlier case history and anecdotes, PB showed clear evidence of severe anterograde amnesia, as indicated by below cut-off scores on standardised tests of verbal and visual long-term memory (see Table 11.1). He completed the Selective Reminding Test, in which a list of 20 words has to be learned over multiple learning trials and recalled after a filled delay of 30 minutes (Buschke, 1973). Even though PB was able to recall a few words on each test of immediate recall, he showed no evidence of learning, and his total immediate recall score

TABLE 11.1 Selected demographic, anatomical and neuropsychological measures for Case PB

	PB	Test Reference
Age	72	
Education (years)	17	
Sex	M	
Aetiology	Autoimmune Limbic Encephalitis	
Known lesion sites	MTL, Including hippocampus (L + R)	
Years(y)/months(m) since onset	2y 2m	
Word-list learning—Total Immediate	53★	(1) ^
Word-list learning—Delayed Recall	0★	(1) #
Rey Figure Copy	34	(2) ^
Rey Figure Delayed	0★	(2) ^
Paired Associates—Total Immediate	0★	(3) #
Paired Associates—Delayed Recall	0★	(3) #
Digit span	5	(3) #
Corsi span	4	(3) #
Frenchay Aphasia Screening Test	30	(4) #
Verbal reasoning	30	(5) #
Non-verbal reasoning	35	(6) #
Trail Making (B-A)	275★	(7) ^
Modified Card Sorting Test	/	(8) could not complete task

MTL = medial temporal lobe
★ Abnormal—score below/above cut-off; ^data corrected for age and education, #raw data
(1) Buschke, 1973; (2) Caffarra et al., 2002; (3) Wechsler, 1997b; (4) Enderby et al., 1986;
(5) Wechsler, 1997a; (6) Basso et al., 1987; (7) Giovagnoli et al., 1996; (8) Nelson, 1976.

was well below the cut-off score for his age and education. Moreover, he could not recall any words following the delay. PB also completed the Paired Associative Learning test, in which a list of eight word pairs (e.g., 'truck-arrow') should be learned over multiple learning trials and recalled after a filled delay of ten minutes (Wechsler, 1997b). PB could not recall a single associate during the immediate recall testing or after the delay. Finally, PB completed the Rey Osterrieth Figure delayed recall test, in which a previously copied figure should be drawn from memory after a filled delay of ten minutes (Caffarra, Vezzadini, Dieci, Zonato & Venneri, 2002; Osterreith & Rey, 1944). PB could not remember having copied a figure ten minutes earlier. Even when shown his own copy, he did not recognise the figure, and he was surprised that the drawing was his.

PB also performed more poorly than expected on the Trail Making Test (Tombaugh, Kozak & Rees, 1999), hinting at mild deficits in some aspects of executive function. However, given his severe amnesia, it is difficult to rule out a memory-related basis of this impairment. PB's amnesia certainly prevented him from completing the Modified Card Sorting Task (Nelson, 1976), another test of executive function. It is of note that a profound problem in card sorting was also reported in patient EP (Insausti, Annese, Amaral & Squire, 2013), who had severe medial temporal lobe amnesia as a result of viral encephalitis.

In contrast to his severe deficits in anterograde memory function and his potential mild executive function deficit, PB performed normally on a range of tests assessing other cognitive functions (see Table 11.1). PB's ability to maintain simple information (digit and spatial span) over very short delays (i.e., seconds) was within the normal range (Wechsler, 1997b), and his language function was also entirely normal according to the Frenchay Aphasia Screening Test (FAST; Enderby, Wood, Wade & Hewer, 1986). Moreover, PB's very good performance on the Raven's Progressive Matrices (Basso, Capitani & Laiacona, 1987) and the Rey Osterrieth Figure copy test (Caffarra et al., 2002; Osterreith & Rey, 1944) suggested normal attentional/visuospatial function. His high performance on the Raven's Progressive Matrices (35/36) also suggested high intelligence, which was further supported by his high score on a test of verbal reasoning—the WAIS-III similarities (Wechsler, 1997a)—and was consistent with his high level of education.

These spared (and impaired) abilities in standard neuropsychological assessments were very much in keeping with those reported in similar cases of severe amnesia, including the much-reported temporal lobectomy patient HM (Milner, Corkin & Teuber, 1968; Scoville & Milner, 1957), and the viral encephalitis patients EP (Insausti et al., 2013; Stefanacci, Buffalo, Schmolck & Squire, 2000) and CW (Wilson, Baddeley & Kapur, 1995). However, novel experimental testing revealed a very interesting spared ability in PB that had not been reported previously in a patient with severe amnesia.

What was this spared ability and how did you reveal it?

In a nutshell, PB appeared to have a *spared ability to retain new explicit long-term memories under conditions of reduced sensory input*. I revealed this spared ability while running an experiment inspired by a fascinating finding by Cowan, Beschin and Della Sala (2004).

Let me start by providing some key background: in their initial study, Cowan et al. (2004) examined word-list retention in patients with severe anterograde amnesia associated with brain injury. They observed that four out of their six patients could retain word lists significantly better over a 10-minute delay if the patients rested quietly during the delay (49% retention) than if they engaged in cognitive tests (14% retention) (Cowan et al., 2004). Even more striking effects were revealed when the delay period was extended to one hour, and when prose passages were used instead of word lists: when the patients engaged in cognitive tests during the one-hour delay, one patient retained a meagre 27% of the prose passage material, and the other five patients retained nothing. However, when the patients rested quietly during the 1-hour delay, the patient who had retained 27% over the filled delay condition now retained 63%. What was more remarkable was that three patients who had retained 0% over the filled delay now retained 85%, 90%, and 78% in the absence of cognitive tests. On average, these four patients (the same four as in the word-list trials) went from 7% retention over a task-filled hour to an astounding 79% retention over an hour when no tasks were performed.

I was both excited and perplexed by these findings! How was it possible for people with severe anterograde amnesia to be able to retain so much new information over periods of up to one hour? Prior work in single cases and groups had revealed intriguing spared abilities in amnesic patients to form and retain new (i) *procedural* long-term memory—e.g., mirror drawing in patient HM (Milner, 1962), and (ii) *implicit* verbal and visual long-term memory—e.g., priming of pictures and words (Warrington & Weiskrantz, 1974), including in patient HM (Milner et al., 1968)—and *declarative* visual long-term memory via *recognition testing* (Freed, Corkin & Cohen, 1987). Notwithstanding these striking effects and their potential implications for rehabilitation, *numerous learning trials were necessary* in order for performance to improve in these paradigms in amnesic patients. Moreover, retention could only be demonstrated via *implicit and/or recognition tests*. This was not the case in the 'rest' study reported by Cowan et al. (2004), in which retention of *declarative memories* was demonstrated via paradigms that required *1-trial learning* and *free recall*. Somehow rest allowed severely amnesic patients to *freely recall* new *episodic memories* after a delay, but how?

One possibility was that the rest period simply allowed patients to think continuously about the learned material until the time of the test, without any involvement of long-term memory. This possibility resonated with the early report by Scoville and Milner (1957) that patients with severe anterograde amnesia, including patient HM, could '*retain a three-figure number of a pair of unrelated words for several minutes*' (p. 15) if they were not distracted during this period. However, their patients '*forgot the instant attention was diverted to a new topic*'. These classic findings contributed substantially to the traditional view that although patients with amnesia cannot *transfer* new declarative memories from short-term memory to long-term memory, i.e., they fail to consolidate new memories (Milner, 1966), they can maintain new information within their spared short-term memory until they cease to attend to the information. Several findings speak against a simple short-term memory account of the rest-related memory improvement in the amnesic patients tested by Cowan et al. (2004): first, the initial delayed recall came as a surprise, meaning that patients and controls had little incentive to think continuously about the learned material for up to an hour. Nonetheless, they did not perform more poorly on this trial than on subsequent trials. Second, two patients appeared to be napping for some of the rest delay, yet they benefitted from rest as much as on other trials, and as much as other patients. However, this was not sufficient evidence to debunk the pure short-term memory account of the rest-related memory improvement. Any conclusive debunking of this account hinged upon one critical demonstration: a *benefit of rest that survived a period of post-rest distraction*. In other words, one would need to be able to show that, unlike Scoville and Milner's (1957) patients, a patient did not forget '*the instant attention was diverted to a new topic*' after the rest period. If so, then the implication would be that, at least in some patients, a period of rest benefits *long-term memory processing*, and therefore that some capacity for new long-term memory processing remains. Since Cowan et al.'s (2004) patients were only tested immediately after the rest period, the jury was still out as to whether or not the benefit of rest could survive a period of post-rest distraction.

Patient PB provided the critical data, albeit in a somewhat unforeseen manner, as I had not planned to put this specific prediction to the test until the completion of some other studies. The study I was running when I first encountered PB was a group study assessing the effect of different types of filler tasks on memory retention (Dewar, Della Sala, Beschin & Cowan, 2010). As part of this group study, I presented PB with a short prose passage, which he had to recall in as much detail as possible immediately afterwards. This immediate recall stage was followed by a 10-minute delay period, during which I asked PB either to rest quietly in the testing room or take part in a cognitive task, in which he had to attend to and respond to tones embedded in background noise. As PB was staying at the hospital for a 7-day treatment regime, I tested him in a quiet hospital clinic room. Unfortunately, shortly after commencing the rest delay there was a problem with PB's IV drip, resulting in loud beeping, and the need for medical staff to enter the testing room (so much for a quiet rest!). Therefore, what should have been a period of rest had become a period abundant with sensory input, which led to my having to abort the rest condition and repeat the trial at the end of the study. However, the running of the rest trial at the end of the study was in fact advantageous as it permitted me the opportunity to expand on this final trial and probe PB's prose retention after his attention had been diverted post-resting. PB's performance on the main trial was rather striking: whereas he retained nothing over the task-filled delay, he retained 75% (of what he had recalled at immediate recall) over the rest delay (see Figure 11.1a). After PB had rested for ten minutes and recalled the prose (delayed recall 1), I engaged him in a conversation for five minutes so as to divert his attention. I then probed his memory of the prose a second time (delayed recall 2—'DR2'). As noted earlier, if the prior rest period had merely allowed PB to maintain the story material within short-term memory, with no additional long-term memory processing, then this material should have been forgotten rapidly from short-term memory as a result of the distracting five-minute conversation. If, on the other hand, the rest period had supported long-term memory, then PB should still be able to recall some of the material he had recalled initially.

What did I find? Well, despite the five-minute distraction that followed the rest delay, PB could still tell me half of the details that he had recounted verbatim

226 Michaela Dewar

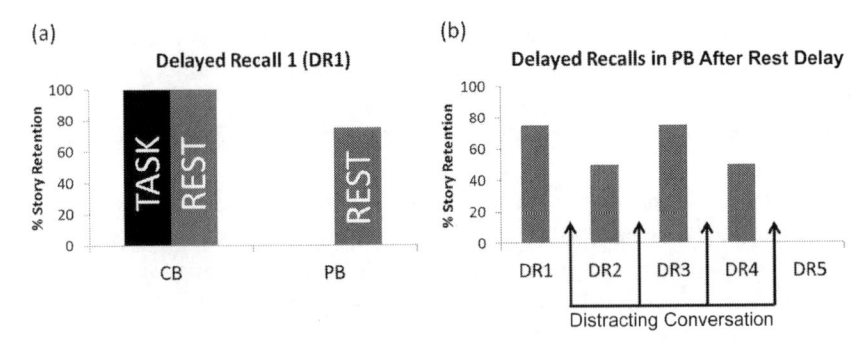

FIGURE 11.1 (a) Percentage retention (verbatim delayed/immediate) in PB and age- and education-matched control CB, after a 10-minute tone detection task (PB = 0%) and after a 10-minute rest period. (b) Percentage retention (verbatim delayed/immediate) in PB after (i) the 10-minute rest period (DR1), (ii) a subsequent 5-minute (post-rest) distraction period, during which PB was engaged in a conversation (DR2), and (iii) three further short distraction periods (DR3, DR4 and DR5). DR5 took place around 30 minutes after the original story presentation. Note that while PB could remember some gist of the prose at DR5, his recall did not qualify as verbatim recall and was thus scored as 0. CB was not tested further after DR1 as he was tested prior to PB (and thus according to the planned protocol).

at immediate recall (50% retention, see Figure 11.1b). Given his complete lack of retention under usual filled conditions in this experiment, in a range of standard memory tests and in day-to-day life, this finding struck me as rather fascinating, and almost impossible. Therefore, I decided to engage PB in several more such sequences of a short conservation, followed by prose recall, to ascertain if the finding would replicate. PB's verbatim prose retention on three further delayed recall tests was as follows: 75%, 50%, 0%. It should be noted that although PB could not recall any of the story units verbatim on the final test, he did remember the relevant gist of the story even at this point, i.e., around 30 minutes after hearing the story.

So, how did you interpret this apparent spared ability in PB, and how does this interpretation relate to previous accounts of amnesia?

PB's ability to recall new information following a post-rest distraction indicated that not all patients with severe anterograde amnesia forget '*the instant attention*' is '*diverted to a new topic*', to use the words of Scoville and Milner (1957). Since the beneficial effect of rest persisted *after distraction*, the rest period must have facilitated PB's explicit long-term memory rather than merely his short-term memory maintenance. In other words, at least in PB, the traditional account of amnesia could not explain the rest-related memory boost observed. This, in turn, demonstrated that, at least in PB, there was more spared long-term memory function than previously assumed. Of course, there is always a slim possibility that a single patient represents an anomaly within the patient population, and thus that a finding is not representative of the wider patient population. With this in mind, I sought to examine if the finding in PB replicated in other patients with severe amnesia. The benefit of rest survived a five-minute post-rest distraction in two out of three further cases (42% and 33% retention) (Dewar et al., 2010), thus strengthening the validity of the key demonstration in patient PB.

Having found strong evidence against a short-term memory account of the rest-related memory benefit in PB (and two other cases), an obvious question was: which *long-term memory* process does rest support in amnesia? The main processes implicated in long-term memory are encoding, consolidation and retrieval. Given that the initial encoding of long-term memory is assumed to take place rapidly and thus prior to the rest delay, it is unlikely that rest supported long-term memory encoding in PB. Could the rest delay have supported PB's long-term memory retrieval? Back in the 1970s, Warrington and Weiskrantz (1974) hypothesised that amnesic patients could in fact consolidate new memories but that they were unable to access (i.e., retrieve) these memories in the presence of competing memories. With this in mind, might the rest period have facilitated PB's access to the prose material by keeping at bay the formation of new competing memories? Several findings speak against this possibility. First, research by Warrington and Weiskrantz (1978) themselves showed that minimization of competing (i.e., very similar) responses did not in fact improve retention in their amnesic patients. In our study, the delay task consisted of a non-specific tone detection task. Therefore, both the rest and the task delay conditions were devoid of similar (competing) material. Nonetheless, PB (and six other patients in the group study) performed better following the rest delay than the task delay. Moreover, research on retrieval competition suggests that such competition is highest if competing memories are formed either immediately after the encoding of the to-be-retrieved memory or immediately preceding the retrieval of to-be-retrieved memory (Postman & Alper, 1946; Newton & Wickens, 1956; see Wixted, 2004 for a review). In the case of PB, the five-minute conversation following the rest immediately preceded the retrieval of the prose passage, and thus the effect of rest should have been reduced markedly as a consequence. However, as discussed earlier, PB was able to recall a substantial amount of information despite this pre-retrieval conversation. Therefore, it is unlikely that the rest-related memory enhancement in PB was the result of reduced retrieval competition.

Although the survival of the rest effect post-conversation poses a substantial problem for the short-term memory account and for the long-term memory retrieval account of the rest-related memory enhancement, this is not the case for the consolidation account, which could readily explain PB's data. Consolidation is the process that strengthens recently formed memories over time so that they can be remembered over the long-term. During consolidation, new fragile memories become increasingly resistant to disruptions. Evidence for this process comes from pharmacological work in animals examining the effects of protein synthesis inhibitors—toxins and antibiotics—on the persistence of new memories (see Dudai, 2004). Such protein synthesis inhibitors hamper memory consolidation. If they are introduced shortly after learning, the new memory remains in a very weak state due to a lack of consolidation, resulting in no or very poor recall after a delay. However, recall increases steadily with augmenting delay in the introduction of the protein synthesis inhibitor. This finding of a 'temporal gradient of interference' indicates that the longer a memory has to consolidate after initial acquisition, the less it is affected by conditions that hamper the consolidation process. It is possible therefore that in PB, and in the other patients showing a persistent benefit of rest, rest supported the consolidation of the prose memory, thus making it somewhat resistant to any deleterious effects of the subsequent five-minute conversation. It was beyond the scope of this case study to test this consolidation hypothesis in further detail. However, one of the key outcomes of this case study was that it paved the way for an important follow-up study to examine this question specifically (Dewar, Garcia, Cowan & Della Sala, 2009). This study was a behavioural analogue of the earlier work on protein synthesis in animals described earlier. In our study, 12 patients with amnesia due to amnestic Mild Cognitive Impairment and 12 age and IQ-matched controls were presented with a list of 15 words, which they had to recall immediately after presentation, and, unbeknown to them, after a 9-minute delay period. Critically, we manipulated the temporal onset of a 3-minute cognitive filler task within the otherwise unfilled delay (see Figure 11.2a). The cognitive task (picture naming, see Figure 11.2b), which also blocked short-term memory maintenance, either occurred during the first (early interference), the middle (mid-interference) or the final (late interference) three minutes of the delay period. We hypothesised that, if rest indeed supports memory consolidation in amnesic patients, then word-list retention should increase with augmenting delay in the cognitive filler task. The rationale for this prediction was that, as highlighted earlier, the word-list memories should stabilize progressively over time, and this stabilization would render them less and less susceptible to disruptions of consolidation by the cognitive filler task. In line with this hypothesis we found that the amnesic patients' word list retention was significantly better when the cognitive task was delayed by six minutes (late interference condition) than when it was delayed by three minutes (mid-interference condition), or when it occurred at the very beginning of the delay period (early interference condition) (see Figure 11.2c). These findings were very robust indeed, as evinced by a case-by-case analysis: all 12 patients showed the improvement from the early interference to the late interference conditions, and 8 patients showed the improvement from the mid-interference to the late interference conditions. In fact, although 8 of the 12 patients recalled nothing in

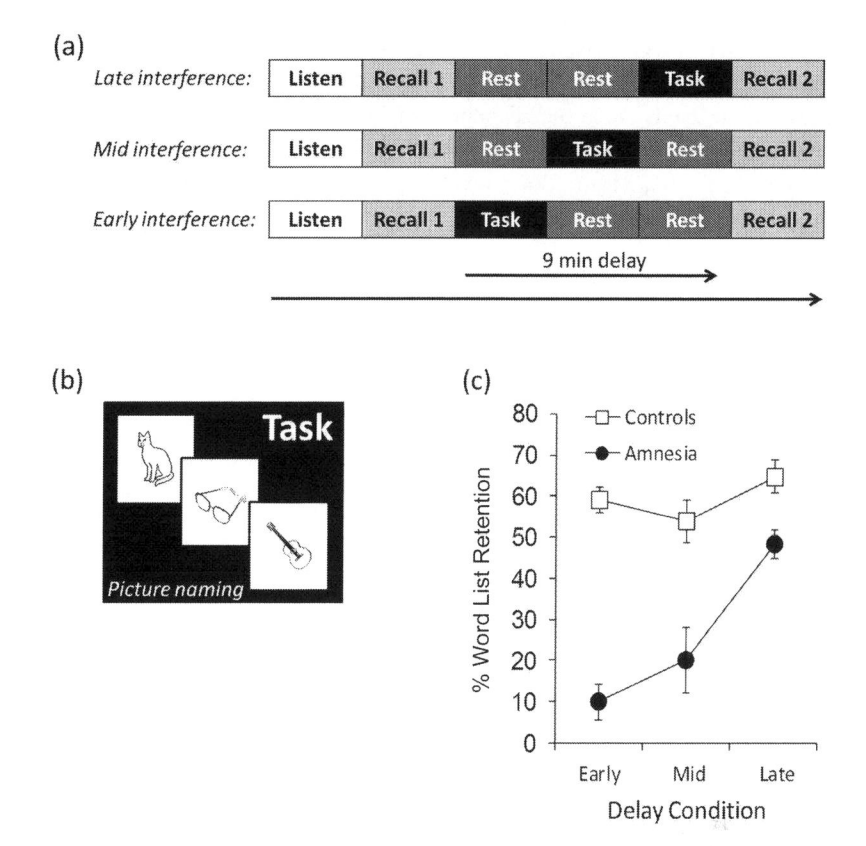

FIGURE 11.2 Testing the consolidation hypothesis in 12 patients with amnesia due to amnestic Mild Cognitive Impairment and 12 controls. **(a)** Outline of the study design. Participants were presented with a list of 15 words, which they had to recall immediately after presentation (Recall 1), and, unbeknown to them, after a 9-minute delay period (Recall 2). The critical manipulation occurred during the nine-minute delay period, during which we manipulated the temporal onset of a three-minute cognitive filler task within the otherwise unfilled rest delay. The cognitive task either occurred during the first (early interference), the middle (mid-interference) or the final (late interference) three minutes of the delay period. **(b)** The cognitive task consisted of a picture naming test. **(c)** Results of the study. Percentage retention ((Recall 2/Recall 1) × 100)) in the amnesic group and controls in the early interference, mid-interference and late interference conditions. In line with the consolidation hypothesis, the amnesic patients retained significantly more word-list material in the late interference condition than in the mid-interference condition or in the early interference condition. Error bars represent standard errors of the mean.

the early interference condition, all of them recalled between 30% and 70% when the cognitive task was delayed by six minutes.

These data were in keeping with PB's data. First, they provided further evidence against the short-term memory account of the rest-related memory enhancement in amnesia. If rest simply allowed patients to maintain new information within short-term memory, with no long-term memory processing, then delayed recall should have been equally poor in the three conditions, as short-term memory maintenance would have been blocked prior to delayed recall in all delay conditions. Moreover, a retrieval account also seemed unlikely given that we revealed a temporal gradient of 'interference' rather than an inverted U-curve (see the aforementioned). Instead, the finding of a temporal gradient of interference in amnesic patients supported the consolidation account of the rest-related memory enhancement, first suggested by PB's data.

So, if rest supports memory consolidation of new memories in PB, can he remember these memories for longer than 30 minutes?

This is an interesting question and one that I examined only very informally in PB. Ten months after the study described earlier, I saw PB again for some neuropsychological testing, and I took the opportunity to test his retention of the prose that he had been able to remember ten months before. PB showed no apparent retention of this prose, and in fact, he did not even remember me, or having been at that particular hospital before. Of course, ten months was quite a long 'delay', and without any respective data from control participants, it is difficult to know to what extent PB's inability to remember the contents of the prose was grossly abnormal or within the normal range for someone of his age. It is worth pointing out that one of the other patients included in the group study did show some apparent recollection of the study session after a year. This patient freely recalled that there had been an "English doctor" during previous testing. This memory was clearly not a mere intelligent guess. The patient was Italian and tested at his local Italian hospital where "English doctors" are not often found. However, on the day of testing, the team of experimenters had indeed included a visiting U.K. psychologist (myself). Whether or not this instance of enhanced memory was the result of the initial rest period or some entirely unrelated factor can, of course, not be deduced from this anecdote. Therefore, motivated by the extended retention over at least 30 minutes in PB, the anecdotal finding in the other case, and the caveats highlighted earlier, my collaborators and I carried out a controlled study to examine whether or not a period of rest can boost prose memory over 7 days in amnesia (Alber, Della Sala & Dewar, 2014). In our study, 15 patients with amnesia (associated with amnestic Mild Cognitive Impairment/ mild Alzheimer's disease) and 15 age and IQ-matched controls were presented with a prose passage, which they had to recall immediately after presentation, and,

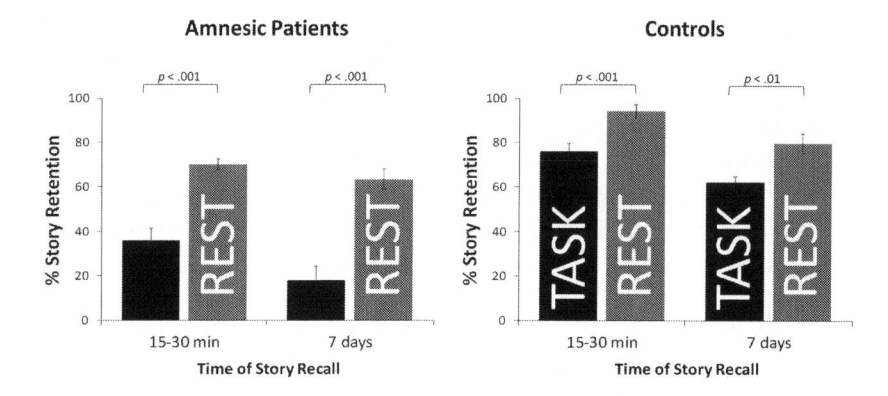

FIGURE 11.3 Mean percentage story retention ((Delayed recall/Immediate recall) × 100)) as a function of group (amnesic patients vs. controls), delay condition (task vs. rest) and time of recall (after 15–30 min. vs. after 7 days). During the task delay, participants engaged in a visual spot the difference game. Participants recalled significantly more story material when story learning was followed immediately by the 10-minute rest delay than by the 10-minute task delay. This rest-induced memory improvement persisted for at least seven days, both in amnesic patients and controls. Error bars represent standard errors of the mean.

unbeknown to them, after a 15–30-minute delay period and after a 7-day delay period. Prose presentation was followed either by a 10-minute period of rest or by a 10-minute period filled with a cognitive task (a spot-the-difference game). The rest period increased prose retention markedly in the patients over 15–30 minutes *and* 7 days (see Figure 11.3). In fact, after 7 days, all 15 patients retained more than 30% of the prose that had been learned prior to the rest period. In contrast, after seven days, only four patients retained more than 30% of the prose that had been learned prior to the spot-the-difference period. This persistence of the rest-related memory improvement over at least 7 days in patients with severe amnesia was remarkable and indicates that the beneficial effect of rest on memory can survive for even longer than 30 minutes, at least in patients with degenerative forms of amnesia.

So what do these findings in PB (and your follow-up studies) tell us about the cognitive basis of amnesia? Why do amnesic patients fail to remember new information after filled delays?

If we assume that the cause of some patients' memory deficit is indeed a consolidation deficit, then there are a couple of possibilities as to why these patients do not appear to retain new memories after filled delays, i.e., in everyday life and in standard clinical tests. First, there could be a general malfunction in the *automatic consolidation* of recently formed memories. Animal studies and human neuroimaging work suggests that consolidation occurs automatically and spontaneously within the healthy memory system following a new experience (e.g., Carr, Jadhav & Frank, 2011; Deuker et al., 2013; Foster & Wilson, 2006). In some patients, including PB, the memory system might fail to trigger vital consolidation runs intrinsically. If so, new memories might only become consolidated if this process is initiated *intentionally*, i.e., via intentional rehearsal processes. Rest periods would undoubtedly provide more opportunities for such 'compensatory' rehearsal than would task periods, and this difference in rehearsal opportunities could account for the discrepancy between PB's performance following a rest delay and task delay. While this automatic consolidation deficit account cannot be ruled out by the data to hand, PB's performance in two standard memory tests—the Selective Reminding Test and the Paired Associates Test—speaks against it. Both tests include multiple learning and retrieval trials, which benefit healthy people, in as much as learning ensues. However, PB did not benefit at all from these forms of rehearsal/repetition (see the section on PB's spared and impaired abilities earlier).

It is more likely that the stark contrast between PB's (and other cases') retention following a rest and task delay is the result of a disruption of memory consolidation by new sensory input/task engagement during the task delay. In short, it is possible that faults within the memory system in PB (and other patients) render the memory consolidation process highly susceptible to interference from ongoing sensory input/tasks.

Do you think that there is anything unique that a report of this case adds to our knowledge?

What we have learned from PB specifically is that, at least in some patients with amnesia, an unfilled delay (rest) can benefit *long-term memory processing* rather than simply allowing short-term memory maintenance. This could not be inferred from previous studies, which lacked the critical post-rest distraction trial. PB's specific data, and the follow-up data, also paved the way for a novel hypothesis of amnesia—the consolidation interference hypothesis. Of course, this is not to say that the finding of a persistent rest-related memory enhancement was unique to PB (as evinced by the various replications and follow-up studies mentioned earlier), or that PB provided a unique opportunity (e.g., due to a rare lesion) to falsify the short-term memory hypothesis of the rest-related memory enhancement.

Do you think this case also contributes to our understanding of how the normal mind works?

Yes. Assuming that PB's amnesia is the result of a disruption of memory consolidation via ongoing sensory input/tasks, the implication of this case (and the follow-up studies) would be that the normal memory system can consolidate new memories without substantial interference from ongoing sensory input/tasks. This in turn could indicate that the normal memory system is equipped with processes or resources to reduce interference during consolidation. This said, the normal memory system might not be wholly immune to such interference, as evinced by follow-up research in healthy people. This research, which was inspired by the earlier findings in PB and other patients, shows a modest boost in memory when healthy people rest in the period after learning as opposed to when they engage in a task (Craig, Della Sala & Dewar, 2014; Craig, Dewar, Della Sala & Wolbers, 2015; Craig, Dewar, Harris, Della Sala & Wolbers, 2016; Dewar, Alber, Butler, Cowan & Della Sala, 2012; Dewar, Alber, Cowan & Della Sala, 2014). These studies suggest that the activities that we engage in after learning effect how well the new memory will be retained, and therefore that some states (i.e., rest/sleep) are more conducive to consolidation than others.

Until recently, consolidation rarely featured in models of memory within psychology. Psychologists working within the domain of long-term memory mainly manipulated memory encoding and retrieval to establish the critical conditions for memory persistence, e.g., context dependency and depth of encoding. Hardly anyone had manipulated the interval *between* encoding and retrieval (i.e., the consolidation window), with the exception of Müller and Pilzecker (1900), who coined the term consolidation (Dewar et al., 2007), and researchers examining the effect of sleep on memory. The research on PB and other patients has changed the status quo to some extent, by reigniting the interest in consolidation sparked by a psychologist 117 years ago, and by fuelling novel, cross-disciplinary research on memory consolidation.

What are the shortcomings of this case?

It is unclear whether or not PB's poor performance on two tests of executive function was the result of an actual deficit in executive function or of his severe amnesia. Therefore, one cannot rule out the possibility that a deficit in executive function contributed to his poor performance in this experiment, e.g., due to heightened levels of retrieval competition/interference. However, we found no significant correlation between performance on the Trail Making Test (Part B-Part A) and performance on any of the measures of the experimental memory test in our group study (Dewar et al., 2010). Indeed, PB's performance was very similar to that of patients without any apparent deficits of executive function (according to the tests applied). Moreover, as discussed earlier, PB's data were not in keeping with the predictions of a retrieval interference account.

Another shortcoming of the case study reported here is the lack of control data for the additional delayed recall trials. The data for PB's matched control (CB) were collected prior to PB's testing session, and therefore the additional trial data could not be added retrospectively. This notwithstanding, I am of the opinion that the spared long-term memory ability in the rest condition in a severely amnesic patient speaks for itself, and that it would remain noteworthy even if accompanied by potential ceiling effects in a matched control.

Are there any assessments/paradigms that you would administer now to this individual if he was available?

Yes, sure. Since testing PB, I have conducted many collaborative follow-up studies, both in amnesic patients and healthy people. Doing so has resulted in many robust paradigms to examine memory consolidation and memory interference. If the opportunity arose, I would administer some of these to PB. In particular, I would examine his ability to remember material that cannot be rehearsed straightforwardly, e.g., non-words (Dewar et al., 2014) or complex spatial material (Craig, Wolbers, et al., 2016; Craig, Dewar, et al., 2016), in an attempt to falsify the hypothesis that rest benefits PB's long-term memory by facilitating compensatory, intentional rehearsal. The ensuing results would provide more conclusive insight into the specific cognitive basis of the apparent consolidation deficit in PB and other patients.

You first reported this case in 2010 as part of a group study. Do you think this case is still informative now? Are we now better able to interpret his pattern of spared and impaired abilities? If so, in what way?

Yes, the case is still informative today, and the associated group study and follow-up group study continue to be cited within empirical papers and theory/review papers, both within psychology, human neuroscience and animal neuroscience. The follow-up research in patients described earlier (Alber et al., 2014; Dewar et al., 2009), as well as behavioural (Craig, Wolbers et al., 2016; Craig et al., 2014; Craig, Dewar et al., 2016; Dewar et al., 2014) and neuroimaging studies (Deuker et al., 2013; Tambini, Ketz & Davachi, 2010) in healthy people are very much in keeping with the initial interpretation of the case's impaired and spared memory abilities, i.e., that the rest period allows patients like PB to consolidate new information better, likely due to reduced interference during the very early stages of consolidation. Of course, this is my current interpretation, based on the data to hand, and future research or theories might result in more compelling interpretations.

Do you think this case has been considered by people who develop theories of the normal mind? If yes, how? If no, should he?

To my knowledge, no such people have considered case PB specifically. This is not too surprising given that PB was reported as part of a group study. The group study and the follow-up study on consolidation have however been considered (and modelled) by several people who develop theories of the normal mind, including experimental psychologists advocating temporal distinctiveness theory of memory (and dismissing consolidation theory) (Brown & Lewandowsky, 2010), cognitive neuroscientists advocating consolidation theory (Mednick, Cai, Shuman, Anagnostaras & Wixted, 2011) or decay/interference-based forgetting theories (Hardt, Nader & Nadel, 2013; Sadeh, Ozubko, Winocur & Moscovitch, 2014).

In general, do you think that neuropsychology cases could contribute to our understanding of the normal mind? Should these data be considered and if so why?

Absolutely! Over the past 150 years or so, neuropsychological cases have contributed enormously to our understanding of the normal mind, both with regards to functional neuroanatomy and the architecture of the cognitive system. What makes neuropsychological cases especially powerful is their ability to reveal which areas of the normal brain are necessary for specific functions, and which functions are dissociated (and associated) within the normal mind. For example, by examining patient HM's spared and impaired abilities and his brain lesion, neuropsychologists revealed (i) the importance of the medial temporal lobes for declarative memory, and (ii) the fractionation of the memory system into independent (i.e., dissociable) declarative and non-declarative memory systems. Even more evidence for the latter comes from 'double dissociations' where two patients show opposing spared and impaired functions (e.g., Case 1: function A spared, function B impaired; Case 2: function A impaired, function B spared). Such inferences about necessity and functional independence cannot be made from functional neuroimaging in healthy people, as this method 'only' reveals which brain areas are sufficient for (i.e., associated with) a specific function. If there is increased activity in brain region A while a person completes task A, and increased activity in region B when a person completes task B, one cannot conclude that regions A and B are necessary for tasks A and B respectively, nor that these tasks tap into two functionally independent cognitive systems. Novel brain stimulation techniques such as transcranial magnetic stimulation (TMS) or transcranial direct current stimulation (tDCS) are much more akin to the traditional lesion method in that they provide powerful means for examining necessity and functional independence, albeit in healthy people. These techniques do reduce some of the limitations inherent to neuropsychological cases—the issue of small sample sizes, potential confounds due to additional lesions/cognitive deficits and requirement for between-subject control conditions. However, they cannot (currently) be used to create 'virtual lesions' in subcortical structures such as the hippocampus. Therefore, notwithstanding the power of these transient 'virtual lesions', I do believe that the study of neuropsychological patients will continue to play an important role in understanding the normal mind, by (i) revealing unique insight into the effect of brain damage on cognition and behaviour, and (ii) allowing for the generation of hypotheses that can be tested both within and beyond the domain of neuropsychology.

When debating the contribution of neuropsychological cases to the understanding of the mind, there appear to be three types of people: those who don't think that we need to study the brain at all in order to understand the mind, those who believe the case study/lesion study approach is old-fashioned, and those who do not see much merit in the modern techniques, perhaps due to a resistance to change or technophobia. In my opinion, we should definitely continue to study interesting neuropsychological cases and consider their data. I do however believe that we should also embrace the novel techniques available to us, and indeed that we should, where feasible, apply whatever method can provide us with the most scientifically sound answer to our research question. In some cases, a combination of techniques undoubtedly produces more compelling results and inferences than the neuropsychological case method alone, e.g., the use of fMRI to examine if there is (i) residual activity in a structurally damaged region (e.g., Maguire, Vargha-Khadem & Mishkin, 2001), (ii) potential compensatory activity elsewhere in the brain that might explain an unusual spared capacity in a patient, or (iii) reduced activity in a structurally intact region (e.g., Caulo et al., 2005), e.g., due to a potential disconnection of a core brain region implicated in a particular function.

Thus, I believe that the traditional neuropsychology case approach should remain firmly engrained within neuropsychology and cognitive neuroscience, but, that we should, where appropriate and relevant, marry this approach with more modern approaches so as to pave the way for future exciting discoveries!

We are now living in an era where ethics committees would like to foresee every step. How much serendipity was involved in your assessment?

Quite a lot of serendipity was involved in my assessment and key finding in fact! As highlighted earlier, I had not planned to include the additional post-rest distraction trials and recall tests. However, I took advantage of the unforeseen technical problems and added these extra trials at the end of the experiment. I reasoned that it would be perfectly acceptable to engage the patient in some unscripted conversation as well as to repeat the delayed recall several times, as both had been approved independently by the ethics panel as part of the overall assessment protocol. Had I first sought the opinion of the ethics panel, I might not have had a chance to test the patient again as he did not live locally. As a consequence, I might not have discovered that a short rest could boost his *long-term memory* function.

Acknowledgements

I am grateful to Professors Adam Zeman and Robert Will for referring PB to my research study.

References

Alber, J., Della Sala, S., & Dewar, M. (2014). Minimizing interference with early consolidation boosts 7-day retention in amnesic patients. *Neuropsychology, 28(5)*, 667–675.

Basso, A., Capitani, E., & Laiacona, M. (1987). Raven's coloured progressive matrices: normative values on 305 adult normal controls. *Functional Neurology, 2(2)*, 189–194.

Brown, G. D. A., & Lewandowsky, S. (2010). Forgetting in memory models. Arguments against trace decay and consolidation failure. In S. Della Sala (Ed.), *Forgetting*. Hove, East Sussex: Psychology Press, pp. 49–75.

Buschke, H. (1973). Selective reminding for analysis of memory and learning. *Journal of Verbal Learning and Verbal Behavior, 12(5)*, 543–550.

Caffarra, P., Vezzadini, G., Dieci, F., Zonato, F., & Venneri, A. (2002). Rey Osterrieth complex figure: normative values in an Italian population sample. *Neurological Sciences, 22(6)*, 443–447.

Carr, M. F., Jadhav, S. P., & Frank, L. M. (2011). Hippocampal replay in the awake state: a potential substrate for memory consolidation and retrieval. *Nature Neuroscience, 14(2)*, 147–153.

Caulo, M., Van Hecke, J., Toma, L., Ferretti, A., Tartaro, A., Colosimo, C., . . . Uncini, A (2005). Functional MRI study of diencephalic amnesia in Wernicke-Korsakoff syndrome. *Brain, 128*, 1584–1594.

Cowan, N., Beschin, N., & Della Sala, S. (2004). Verbal recall in amnesiacs under conditions of diminished retroactive interference. *Brain, 127*, 825–834.

Craig, M., Della Sala, S., & Dewar, M. (2014). Autobiographical thinking interferes with episodic memory consolidation. *PloS One, 9(4)*, e93915.

Craig, M., Dewar, M., Della Sala, S., & Wolbers, T. (2015). Rest boosts the long-term retention of spatial associative and temporal order information. *Hippocampus, 25(9)*, 1017–1027.

Craig, M., Dewar, M., Harris, M. A., Della Sala, S., & Wolbers, T. (2016). Wakeful rest promotes the integration of spatial memories into accurate cognitive maps. *Hippocampus, 26(2)*, 185–193.

Craig, M., Wolbers, T., Harris, M., Hauff, P., Della Sala, S., & Dewar, M. (2016). Comparable rest-related enhancement in cognitive map accuracy in younger and older adults. *Neurobiology of Aging, 48*, 143–152.

Deuker, L., Olligs, J., Fell, J., Kranz, T. A., Mormann, F., Montag, C., . . . Axmacher, N. (2013). Memory consolidation by replay of stimulus-specific neural activity. *Journal of Neuroscience, 33(49)*, 19373–19383.

Dewar, M., Alber, J., Butler, C., Cowan, N., & Della Sala, S. (2012). Brief wakeful resting boosts new memories over the long term. *Psychological Science, 23(9)*, 955–960.

Dewar, M., Alber, J., Cowan, N., & Della Sala, S. (2014). Boosting long-term memory via wakeful rest: intentional rehearsal is not necessary, consolidation is sufficient. *PLoS ONE, 9(10)*, e109542.

Dewar, M. T., Cowan, N., & Della Sala, S. (2007). Forgetting due to retroactive interference: a fusion of Müller and Pilzecker's (1900) early insights into everyday forgetting and recent research on anterograde amnesia. *Cortex, 43(5)*, 616–634.

Dewar, M., Della Sala, S., Beschin, N., & Cowan, N. (2010). Profound retroactive interference in anterograde amnesia: what interferes? *Neuropsychology, 24(3)*, 357–367.

Dewar, M., Garcia, Y. F., Cowan, N., & Della Sala, S. (2009). Delaying interference enhances memory consolidation in amnesic patients. *Neuropsychology, 23(5)*, 627–634.

Dudai, Y. (2004). The neurobiology of consolidations, or, how stable is the engram? *Annual Review of Psychology, 55(1)*, 51–86.

Enderby, P. M., Wood, V. A., Wade, D. T., & Hewer, R. L. (1986). The Frenchay Aphasia Screening Test: a short, simple test for aphasia appropriate for non-specialists. *International Rehabilitation Medicine, 8(4)*, 166–170.

Foster, D. J., & Wilson, M. A. (2006). Reverse replay of behavioural sequences in hippocampal place cells during the awake state. *Nature, 440(7084)*, 680–683.

Freed, D. M., Corkin, S., & Cohen, N. J. (1987). Forgetting in H.M.: a second look. *Neuropsychologia, 25(3)*, 461–471.

Giovagnoli, A. R., Del Pesce, M., Mascheroni, S., Simoncelli, M., Laiacono, M., & Capitani, E. (1996). Trail making test: normative values from 287 normal adult controls. *Italian Journal of Neurological Sciences, 17*, 305–309.

Hardt, O., Nader, K., & Nadel, L. (2013). Decay happens: the role of active forgetting in memory. *Trends in Cognitive Sciences, 17(3)*, 111–120.

Insausti, R., Annese, J., Amaral, D. G., & Squire, L. R. (2013). Human amnesia and the medial temporal lobe illuminated by neuropsychological and neurohistological findings for patient E.P. *Proceedings of the National Academy of Sciences of the United States of America, 110(21)*, E1953–E1962.

Maguire, E. A., Vargha-Khadem, F., & Mishkin, M. (2001). The effects of bilateral hippocampal damage on fMRI regional activations and interactions during memory retrieval. *Brain, 124*, 1156–1170.

Mednick, S. C., Cai, D. J., Shuman, T., Anagnostaras, S., & Wixted, J. T. (2011). An opportunistic theory of cellular and systems consolidation. *Trends in Neurosciences, 34(10)*, 504–514.

Milner, B. (1962). Les troubles de la mémoire accompagnant des lésions hippocampiques bilatérales. In P. Passouant (Ed.), *Physiologie de l'hippocampe*. Paris: Centre National de la Recherche Scientifique, pp. 257–272.

Milner, B. (1966). Amnesia following operations on the medial temporal lobes. In C. W. M. Whitty & O. L. Zangwill (Eds.), *Amnesia*. London: Butterworths, pp. 109–133.

Milner, B., Corkin, S., & Teuber, H.-L. (1968). Further analysis of the hippocampal amnesic syndrome: 14-year follow-up study of H.M. *Neuropsychologia, 6(3)*, 215–234.

Müller, G. E., & Pilzecker, A. (1900). Experimentelle Beiträge zur Lehrevom Gedächtnis [Experimental contributions on the theory of memory]. *Zeitschrift für Psychologie Ergänzungsband, 1*, 1–300.

Nelson, H. (1976). A modified card sorting test sensitive to frontal-lobe defects. *Cortex, 12*, 313–324.

Newton, J. M., & Wickens, D. D. (1956). Retroactive inhibition as a function of the temporal position of the interpolated learning. *Journal of Experimental Psychology, 51*, 149–154.

Osterreith, P., & Rey, A. (1944). Le copie d'une figure complexe. *Archiv Für Psychologie, 30*, 205–220.

Postman, L., & Alper, T. G. (1946). Retroactive inhibition as a function of the time of interpolation of the inhibitor between learning and recall. *The American Journal of Psychology, 59(3)*, 439–449.

Sadeh, T., Ozubko, J. D., Winocur, G., & Moscovitch, M. (2014). How we forget may depend on how we remember. *Trends in Cognitive Sciences, 18(1)*, 26–36.

Scoville, W. B., & Milner, B. (1957). Loss of recent memory after bilateral hippocampal lesions. *Journal of Neurology, Neurosurgery, and Psychiatry, 20(1)*, 11–21.

Stefanacci, L., Buffalo, E. A, Schmolck, H., & Squire, L. R. (2000). Profound amnesia after damage to the medial temporal lobe: a neuroanatomical and neuropsychological profile of patient E. P. *The Journal of Neuroscience, 20(18)*, 7024–7036.

Tambini, A., Ketz, N., & Davachi, L. (2010). Article enhanced brain correlations during rest are related to memory for recent experiences. *Neuron, 65(2)*, 280–290.

Tombaugh, T., Kozak, J., & Rees, L. (1999). Normative data stratified by age and education for two measures of verbal fluency FAS and animal naming. *Archives of Clinical Neuropsychology, 14(2)*, 167–177.

Vincent, A., Buckley, C., Schott, J. M., Baker, I., Dewar, B.-K., Detert, N., . . . Palace, J. (2004). Potassium channel antibody-associated encephalopathy: a potentially immunotherapy-responsive form of limbic encephalitis. *Brain, 127*(Pt 3), 701–712.

Warrington, E. K., & Weiskrantz, L. (1974). The effect of prior learning on subsequent retention in amnesic patients. *Neuropsychologia, 12(4)*, 419–428.

Warrington, E. K., & Weiskrantz, L. (1978). Further analysis of the prior learning effect in amnesic patients. *Neuropsychologia, 16(2)*, 169–177.

Wechsler, D. (1997a). *Wechsler Adult Intelligence Scale—3rd Edition* (WAIS-3). San Antonio, TX: Harcourt Assessment.

Wechsler, D. (1997b). *Wechsler Memory Scale III*. San Antonio, TX: The Psychological Corporation.

Wilson, B. A., Baddeley, A. D., & Kapur, N. (1995). Dense amnesia in a professional musician following herpes simplex virus encephalitis. *Journal of Clinical and Experimental Neuropsychology, 17(5)*, 668–681.

Wixted, J. T. (2004). The psychology and neuroscience of forgetting. *Annual Review of Psychology, 55*, 235–269.

12

VA

A Case Report of Transient Epileptic Amnesia

John Baker, Sharon Savage and Adam Zeman

In 2013, a 59-year-old, right-handed aircraft engineer, VA, was referred to the cognitive neurology clinic. He described a two-year history of transient episodes of memory impairment. The first of these occurred whilst on a motorcycle holiday with his wife. One morning, he woke up, unsure of where he was or what he had been doing on the previous day. He did not ask repetitive questions, and within a few minutes, he had returned to normal. As they were in the middle of their holiday, his wife attributed his disorientation to their travels and thought nothing more of it. VA himself does not recall this episode.

Approximately one month later, VA awoke unsure of where he was. He was unable to recollect his son's wedding which had taken place four days previously. Once again, this lasted for only a few minutes before resolving. His amnesia for this episode was incomplete: he is able to remember not being able to remember.

One month after that, a further episode occurred whilst visiting his daughter in her new house. VA's wife reports that she saw him walking to the bedroom window and asking, 'Where are we?' He could not recall the previous day, or that they were staying with their daughter.

At around this time, VA's wife noticed that these early morning amnesic episodes would be preceded by 'mouthing movements'. VA himself would notice a strange taste or smell, which was sometimes pleasant and sometimes unpleasant, at the time of these episodes.

In addition to these transient episodes of memory impairment, VA reported some interictal memory disturbances. He described 'blanks' for salient events over the last five years. These included holidays, weddings and other events which he felt that he should have been able to remember. He felt that memories 'faded' more rapidly than he would have expected. For example, if he was to read a book, he could pick it up again a week later, with no recollection that he had read it before. Although he reported that his memory for routes had never been particularly good, he was also aware that this had deteriorated over the same period. In particular, he found it difficult to visualize familiar routes.

He described being more emotional than he was previously; he could be moved more easily by something on radio or television. Furthermore, he reported that he was more irritable than he had been prior to the start of these episodes.

His past medical history is notable only for previous sinus surgery which had affected his sense of smell, and two episodes of what he referred to as 'burn-out' in 1989 and 1999. Although he has never satisfied the criteria for major depression, he met criteria for current and past generalized anxiety disorder. He is a non-smoker, with no history of excess alcohol consumption.

His neurological examination was entirely normal as was an MRI brain scan. An EEG showed occasional bursts of low voltage discrete spike and slow wave activity maximal over the right centro-temporal region. An example of this abnormality is shown next (see Figure 12.1). Given the clinical history and evidence provided by the EEG, it was felt that VA's amnesic events were epileptic seizures. VA was started on lamotrigine which was increased up to 100mg. He has had no further episodes since commencing treatment in December 2013.

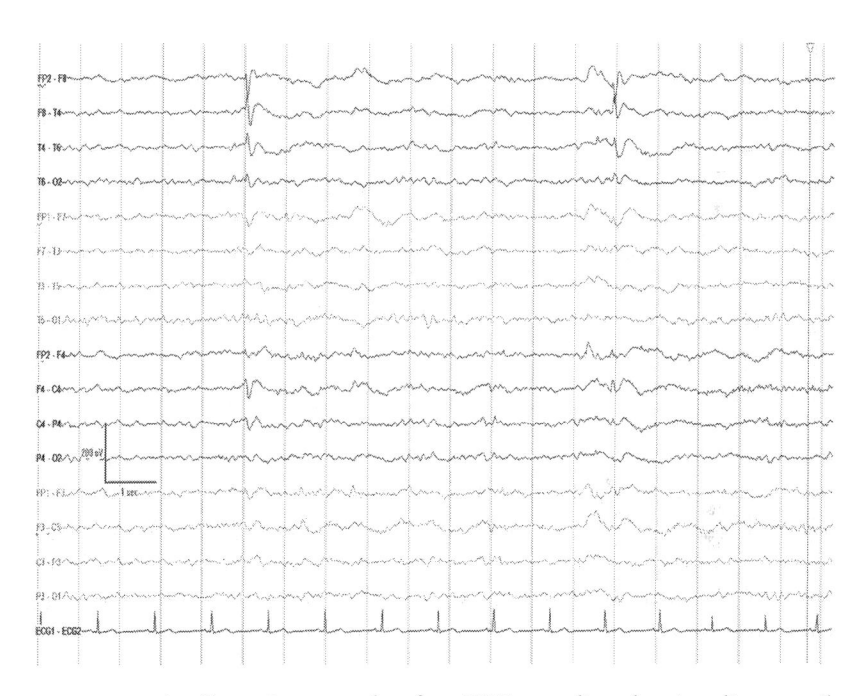

FIGURE 12.1 An illustrative example of an EEG recording showing discrete spike and slow wave activity maximal over the right centro-temporal region (F8-T4, T4-T6).

Following his initial interview, VA was recruited to the TIME (The Impairment of Memory in Epilepsy) study (http://projects.exeter.ac.uk/time/) and underwent a formal neuropsychological evaluation (see Table 12.1). The battery comprised standard tasks to estimate premorbid and current general cognitive ability, visual and verbal anterograde memory tests, a semantic memory test, and tests of executive function. Episodic autobiographical memory across the lifespan was assessed via the Modified Autobiographical Memory Interview. Finally, to assess forgetting over time, VA completed a modified version of a word learning task, the Rey Auditory Verbal Learning Test (RAVLT). Here he was required to repeat learning trials until he could recall at least 80% (12 words) of the list, with delayed recall assessed at 30 minutes and at one week.

Overall, VA's general cognitive abilities were rated within the high average range for his age. There was no evidence of impairment in his visuo-constructional abilities, executive function or semantic memory (although his approach to drawing the Rey Complex Figure task was somewhat unusual and fragmented). He performed variably on tests of anterograde memory. He showed good verbal recognition memory (words), and his learning over the standard five trials of the RAVLT was within the average range for his age. He was, however, less efficient in reaching the 80% learning criterion when compared with IQ-matched healthy controls, but did well to maintain his learning after a 30-minute delay. VA's immediate recall of a story was low average, while his 30-minute recall was poor. Visual memory was generally weaker. He showed disproportionally poorer visual recognition (for faces versus words) to a level observed in only 5%–10% of his peer group. His recall of the complex figure was distorted and below the first percentile for his age.

When retention of information was assessed over a longer period (one week), clear difficulties emerged. VA was unable to freely recall any of the words correctly from the list (recalling he had done the task, but confabulating four incorrect responses). Although he correctly recognized 13 of the 15 words when cued, he also endorsed having learned 5 words that were not on the list.

Assessment of his autobiographic memory revealed that while VA could recall specific events from each of the decades of his life, these often lacked rich episodic detail. In one instance, he could recall facts regarding his son's wedding which he attended in 2005, but was unable to describe any part of the event.

You are reporting here a new case of transient epileptic amnesia (TEA). First of all, can you provide us with an account of TEA and its link with accelerated forgetting and focal retrograde amnesia?

Our case highlights many of the key features of transient epileptic amnesia (TEA). This condition is now well described in a number of case series (Zeman, Boniface & Hodges, 1998; Butler et al., 2007; Lapenta et al., 2014; Mosbah et al., 2014).

TEA is a syndrome of temporal lobe epilepsy in which the principal manifestation of a seizure is a brief episode of amnesia during which other mental functions

TABLE 12.1 Neuropsychological test results for VA

Neuropsychological Test	Raw Score	Interpretation
General Cognitive Ability		
ACE-R (100)	94	WNL
NART (50)	11; IQ: 117	High Average
WASI—FSIQ (4 subtest)	119	High Average
WASI—Similarities (48)	38	Average
WASI—Matrix Reasoning (32)	28	Superior
WASI—Vocabulary (80)	71	Superior
WASI—Block Design (32)	45	Average
Visuospatial Skills		
RCFT—Copy (36)	33	WNL
Executive Function		
DKEFS Letter fluency	50	Superior
DKEFS Semantic fluency	47	Superior
DKEFS Switching Total	14	Average
DKEFS—TMT—visual scanning	20"	Average
DKEFS—TMT—number sequencing	33"	Average
DKEFS—TMT—letter sequencing	23"	Superior
DKEFS—TMT—number-letter switching	62"	Average
DKEFS—TMT—motor speed	22"	Average
Standard Memory Tests		
Logical Memory[a]★—Story 1—Immediate Recall (25)	11	Low average
Logical Memory[a]★—Story 1—Delayed Recall (25)	6	Extremely low
Logical Memory[a]★—Story 1—Recognition (15)	12	Low average
RCFT—30-minute delay (36)	7	Extremely low
RMT—Words	47	Above average
RMT—Faces	38	Low average
Graded Naming Test (30)	21	Average
Research Memory Tasks		
MAMI★—average episodic recall (10)	7.75	Below expectation
RAVLT LOT ((Sum Trials 1–5)–5★Trial 1)[b]	(5,7,7,9,10)–25	Average
RAVLT Trials to criterion (10)	8	Below expectation
RAVLT 40-second recall (15)	11	WNL
RAVLT 30-minute delay (15)	11	WNL
RAVLT 1-week recall (15)	0	Reduced
RAVLT 1-week recognition (15)	13 (+4 false pos)	

Notes: ACE = Addenbrooke's Cognitive Examination; NART = National Adult Reading Test; WASI = Wechsler Abbreviated Scale of Intelligence; RCFT = Rey Complex Figure Test; DKEFS = Delis Kaplan Executive Function System; TMT = Trail Making Test; RMT = Warrington Recognition Memory Test; MAMI = Modified Autobiographical Memory Interview; RAVLT = Rey Auditory Verbal Learning Test (LOT = Learning Over Trials); WNL = within normal limits; [a] from Wechsler Memory Scale, 3rd edition, but performance compared with control subjects from Butler et al., 2007; [b] Performance compared with MOANS norms from (Ivnik, Malec et al., 1992). Reduced: >1 but <2 SDs below mean. Below expectation: <2 SDs below mean are predominantly or entirely preserved. Unlike transient global amnesia, where a single episode of 2–24 hours is the norm (Bartsch & Butler, 2013), patients with TEA typically report recurrent, brief attacks which last less than one hour and often only a few minutes (Asadi-Pooya, 2014; Felician, Tramoni & Bartolomei, 2015). Episodes typically occur at roughly monthly intervals.

Approximately two-thirds of patients with TEA describe other phenomena associated with temporal lobe epilepsy, including olfactory and gustatory hallucinations and oroalimentary automatisms, occurring in some or all attacks (Butler & Zeman, 2011). Interictal routine or sleep-deprived EEGs show focal epileptiform abnormalities which help to confirm the diagnosis in around 1/3 of cases. Patients are usually sensitive to anticonvulsant treatment, which typically obliterate the attacks completely. Ictal records indicate that the amnesic episodes in TEA can be either ictal or immediately post-ictal manifestations (Zeman & Butler, 2010).

Although structural MRI is typically normal in TEA, imaging investigations in TEA patients have pointed to a seizure source in the medial temporal lobes. If structural abnormalities are present, they usually lie in the medial temporal lobes. A case report of a TEA patient with frequent seizures identified a high signal in the hippocampus, accompanied by hypermetabolism on PET, which resolved with successful treatment of his epilepsy (Butler & Zeman, 2008) (see Figure 12.2).

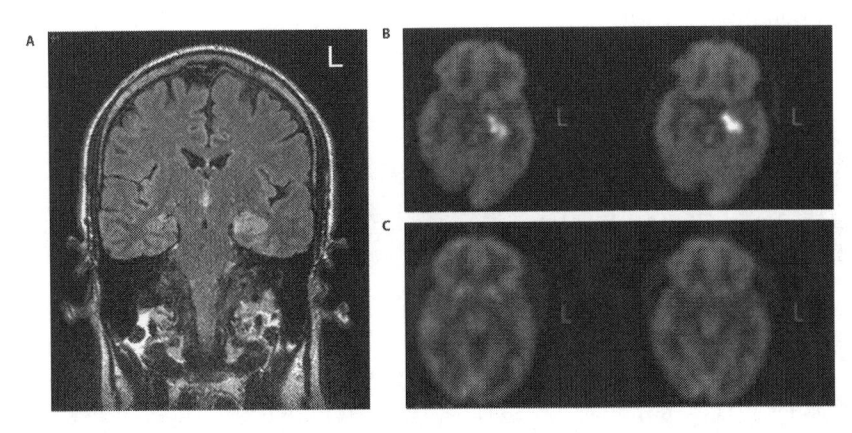

FIGURE 12.2   Brain scans from a patient with transient epileptic amnesia. (A) Fluid-attenuated inversion-recovery MRI scanning during a prolonged amnestic episode reveals hyperintensity in the left hippocampus. (B) 2-Fluoro-2-[18F]-deoxy-D-glucose PET scanning during the same episode shows hypermetabolism localized to the left anterior hippocampus. (C) Metabolism in the left anterior hippocampus returned to normal 1 month later. Abbreviation: L, left. Reprinted from *Nature Clinical Practice Neurology*, 4(9), Butler & Zeman, A case of transient epileptic amnesia with radiological localization, 516–521,

Copyright (2008), with permission from Springer Nature.

A group study of patients with TEA revealed subtle, bilateral hippocampal atrophy with volume loss of 8% (Butler et al., 2009). Automated measurement of cerebral regions identified additional atrophy of perirhinal and orbitofrontal cortices (Butler et al., 2013). A functional imaging study of autobiographical recollection in patients with TEA revealed reduced activation in the posterior right parahippocampal gyrus (Milton, Butler, Benattayallah & Zeman, 2012). Hypometabolism of the bilateral middle frontal gyri (BA6), left medial, superior, precentral and paracentral gyri (BA6, BA31) has been identified on FDG-PET studies. Additional areas of Hypometabolism within the right posterior hippocampus (BA36) and left uncus (BA28) have also been confirmed with use of a medial temporal mask (Mosbah et al., 2014).

The following diagnostic criteria for TEA have been widely used (Zeman et al., 1998):

1. A history of recurrent witnessed episodes of transient amnesia;
2. Cognitive functions other than memory are intact during typical episodes, as observed by a reliable witness;
3. Other evidence for a diagnosis of epilepsy. This evidence could be either:
   (a) Epileptiform abnormalities in EEG,
   (b) The concurrent onset of other clinical features of an epileptic seizure (e.g., lip-smacking and olfactory hallucinations), or
   (c) A clear-cut response to antiepileptic drugs,
   Or any combination of these three.

In addition to their ictal amnesia, patients with TEA often complain of interictal memory impairments. As we saw in our case, these include a feeling that new information learned may fade more rapidly than they would expect. This phenomenon has been termed accelerated long-term forgetting (Butler & Zeman, 2008). These patients can show good acquisition of new information, performing within the normal range on standard neuropsychological tests which measure immediate recall and at an interval of 30 minutes after learning, but exhibit a more rapid rate of forgetting than usual over longer delays (Manes, Graham, Zeman, de Lujan Calcagno & Hodges, 2005; Hoefeijzers, Dewar, Della Sala, Zeman & Butler, 2013; Elliott, Isaac & Muhlert, 2014). Studies show, despite normal acquisition, forgetting begins within hours (Hoefeijzers, Dewar, Della Sala, Butler & Zeman, 2015) and is most pronounced during the first 24 hours of retention (Muhlert, Milton, Butler, Kapur & Zeman, 2010). In keeping with this, our case demonstrated good initial retention of the word list, but was unable to recall any words after one week.

As well as a more rapid rate of forgetting for recently acquired information, these patients report what *might* be described as a patchy 'focal retrograde amnesia'. This characteristically involves a loss of memory for salient personal events and is sometimes described as 'holiday amnesia' as it often comes to light when discussing these memorable, discrete, autobiographical events (such as a friend's wedding, as in this case). It can extend across most or all of the lifespan, affecting memories formed well before the onset of seizures. Personal and public semantic memories are also affected but less severely (Milton et al., 2010). Describing this amnesia as 'focal' and 'retrograde' is controversial (Kopelman, 2000). As we have just seen, many patients with TEA have accelerated long-term forgetting, an atypical form of anterograde amnesia which would be expected to cause a cumulative amnesia for past events over time. We believe the term 'focal retrograde amnesia', is defensible, however, given the contrast between the relatively normal performance often demonstrated on standard measures of anterograde memory, and the patients' marked difficulties when they contemplate remote events, often ones they could previously recall.

As exemplified by the case described earlier, patients with TEA also commonly report a topographical amnesia. This will typically manifest as difficulty in remembering familiar routes as well as in recognizing familiar landmarks (Zeman, Butler, Muhlert & Milton, 2013).

These interictal memory impairments appear to be less responsive to anticonvulsant medications than the ictal episodes themselves (Bilo, Meo, Ruosi, de Leva & Striano, 2009; Felician et al., 2015). There are single case reports of improvement in interictal memory, including accelerated long-term forgetting, with treatment in patients with TEA and temporal lobe epilepsy (Goldstein, Patel, Aspinall & Lishman, 1992; O'Connor, Sieggreen, Ahern, Schomer & Mesulam, 1997; Walstra & Overweg, 2002; Tombini et al., 2005; Midorikawa & Kawamura, 2007; Razavi, Barrash & Paradiso, 2010), though this is not always found (Jansari, Davis, McGibbon, Firminger & Kapur, 2010). However in general, once established, autobiographical memory impairment appears not to improve (though for an interesting exception, see Milton, Butler & Zeman, 2011). We have recently embarked on a prospective study looking at the effects of treatment in TEA patients to shed further light on these questions.

The accelerated forgetting shown by patients with TEA seems counterintuitive; can it be accounted for by the current models of memory?

The two-compartment model of memory, which postulates distinct 'short-term' and 'long-term' memory stores, is supported by the double dissociation in patient studies between short-term or working memory, operating over seconds, and long-term memory operating over minutes to decades. There has been a working assumption in human neuropsychology, based on this model, that intact delayed recall after a delay of around half an hour implies successful acquisition of long-term memories. The phenomenon of accelerated long-term forgetting appears to call this into question: patients with accelerated long-term forgetting can perform normally at a standard half-hour interval yet fail to recall or recognize material at extended delays of days to weeks. This has been identified in both individual case reports and in case series of TEA (Butler et al., 2007; Butler & Zeman, 2008) (see Figure 12.3). It is tempting to infer that this phenomenon reflects an impairment of the complex processes of memory consolidation and transformation, involving cellular, synaptic and network mechanisms, revealed by neuroscience, but it is controversial whether this inference is correct.

It is helpful, in thinking this through, to distinguish a clinical and a theoretical question. On the clinical plane, there is no doubt that some patients with TEA and other forms of epilepsy perform normally on tests of memory administered at standard intervals and yet underperform at longer delays. This delayed underperformance accounts for some memory complaints which have previously been difficult to explain and creates a practical reason to consider the use of delayed tests in some patients or patient groups (Muhlert & Zeman, 2012; Witt et al., 2015).

On the theoretical plane, it could be, but is not necessarily the case, that accelerated long-term forgetting is the result of an impairment of an extended process of memory consolidation. It is not necessarily the case because subtle impairment at the point of memory acquisition might be undetectable at short delays, emerging at long delays essentially because these provide a harder test. The evidence on this question is conflicting. For example, Hoefeijzers et al. (2013) showed that in a word learning task undertaken by patients with TEA and controls, words that were presented and retrieved the same number of times at acquisition and recalled with the same reliability at standard delays by both groups were recalled less well by the patients at one week. Thus, even under precisely matched conditions of learning and 30-minute recall, patients displayed accelerated long-term forgetting, suggesting that the underlying cause relates to consolidation rather than acquisition. However, it is very difficult, on the basis of behavioural data alone, to exclude the possibility of a subtle acquisition defect. In contrast, Cassel, Morris, Koutroumanidis and Kopelman (2016) have recently provided evidence that the forgetting seen in patients with temporal lobe epilepsy is typically a continuous process, evident from soon after memory acquisition, implicating an impairment of 'early' processes, rather than a delayed one affecting later phases of consolidation.

This controversy will probably be resolved as we improve our ability to track the time course of memory processing in the human brain using, for example, advanced functional brain imaging methods. The impairments in patients with conditions like TEA may well turn out to affect both earlier and later processes: indeed, given that there is strong evidence for the importance of iterative processes of 'replay' in memory formation, there are very likely to be complex interactions between earlier and later processes. In our case, VA, this theory may provide the best explanation for his results. While his accelerated long-term forgetting of information (a word list), which had been successfully learned and retained in the short term, suggests impairment in later processes, he did also demonstrate inefficiency during encoding when compared to his IQ-matched peers. Here,

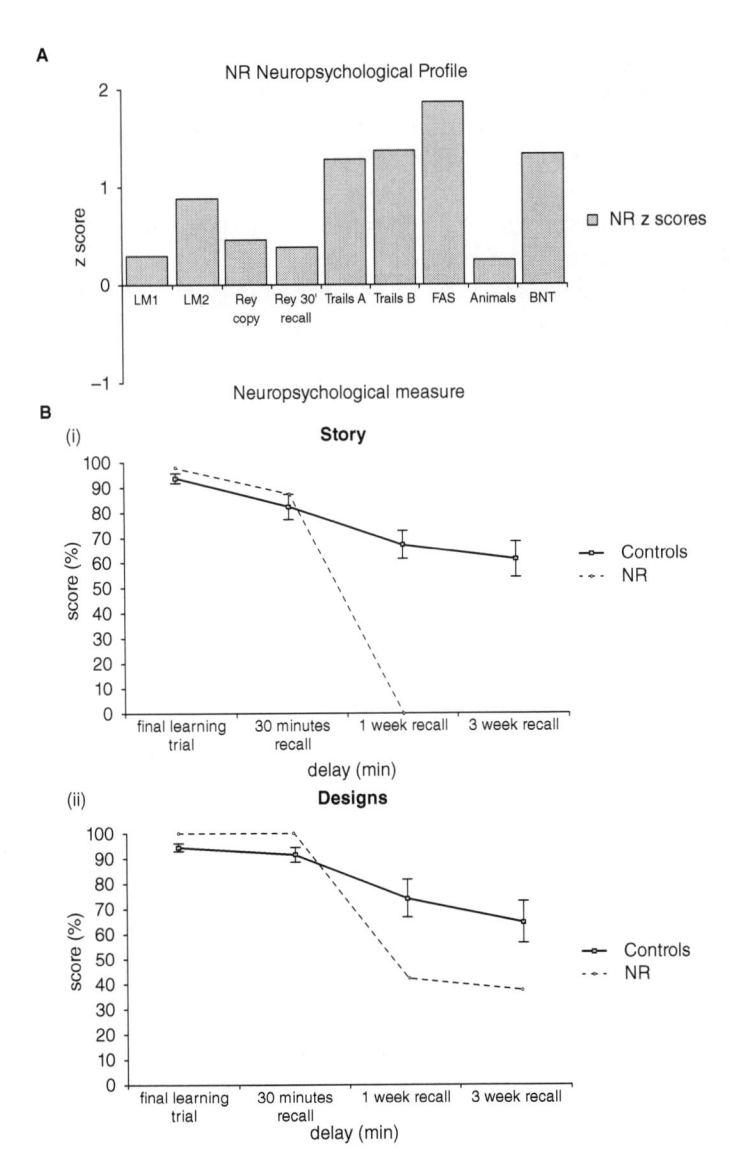

FIGURE 12.3 The patient's long-term recall of a learned word list and set of designs was compared with the performance of normal controls. Despite normal learning and 30-minute retention, the patient demonstrated accelerated forgetting over longer intervals; error bars indicate 2 SEs of the mean. Reprinted from *Nature Clinical Practice Neurology*, 4(9), Butler & Zeman, A case of transient epileptic amnesia with radiological localization, 516–521.

Copyright (2008), with permission from Springer Nature.

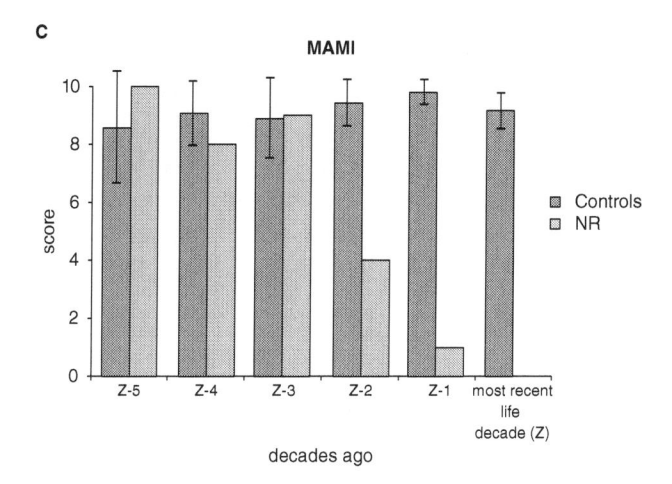

FIGURE 12.3 Continued.

he needed greater repetition of information in order to perform at the expected level, suggesting that earlier processes were also affected.

What is this case's pattern of spared and impaired abilities?

The diagnostic criteria for TEA require that cognition should be intact during typical attacks, with the exception of memory impairment. Indeed, patients with TEA are often able to perform complex activities in their amnesic state, for example, in another patient we have seen, completing a translation of a passage from one language to another. In some episodes, VA was able to lay down a memory for his amnesia, so that he was subsequently able to 'remember not being able to remember'. This indicates at least some sparing of anterograde memory processes during the event, in contrast to transient global amnesia where it is typical that episodes are not recalled at all.

Formal assessment of VA's cognitive abilities showed the expected pattern in TEA of preserved general intellect, semantic memory and executive function. Indeed, the average IQ in our previous series of patients with TEA was 118, indicating a tendency towards individuals with above-average cognitive ability, a puzzling finding. This could suggest that people of high IQ are at greater risk of the condition. However, we suspect, that these individuals are easier to diagnose, both because they can give an articulate account of their puzzling symptoms and because of the sharp contrast between their premorbid functioning and the disruption caused by the onset of memory difficulties.

With respect to memory skills, VA demonstrated a mixed pattern of results. His recognition memory for words was normal, and he could recall details of a story immediately after the presentation. While we did not test this in VA, we would have expected him to show preserved procedural learning, which we observed in a previous group study of patients with TEA (Muhlert et al., 2010).

By contrast, VA demonstrated particular difficulties with visual memory, retention of new information over longer periods (1 week), and episodic autobiographical memory. A disproportionate reduction in visual recognition memory has been reported in other TEA cases (Kapur, Young, Bateman & Kennedy, 1989; Kapur, 1993). His poor recall of the Rey figure is not a typical finding within TEA, and is likely to have been a result of his fragmented approach to the copy, leading to poorer encoding.

Despite some evidence of inefficiency when encoding new information, with sufficient repetition VA showed the ability to learn, store and retrieve a word list over half an hour, but over a period of one week, he demonstrated accelerated long-term forgetting. His semantic knowledge of autobiographical events remained well preserved, in that he could produce facts about a variety of events over the different decades of his life. By contrast, his episodic recall of life events was significantly reduced compared with his age-matched peers, with certain, salient events either completely forgotten or substantially degraded.

How did you first realize that this case was interesting?

We have chosen VA as an exemplary rather than a unique case. His story illustrates all the key features of this distinctive syndrome: recurrent, brief, amnesic attacks, with some sparing of anterograde memory, occurring especially on waking; occasional associated automatisms and olfactory/gustatory hallucinations; interictal memory disturbance with 'fading' of memories over days to weeks, autobiographical memory gaps, topographical memory disturbance; somewhat increased emotionality; rapid resolution of the amnesic episodes on treatment.

When one of the authors, AZ, encountered a patient with this constellation of features for the first time, in 1995, he found it so unfamiliar that he wondered whether it was psychogenic, making the mistake identified by the 17th century physician and father of neurology, Thomas Willis, who described the diagnosis of hysteria as the 'subterfuge of ignorance'. Having now seen well over 100 cases, he continues to find this presentation fascinating (how do these very varied but typically associated features hang together?) and rewarding, as treatment is reliably effective, and patients who are often concerned about the possibility of dementia or stroke can be reassured.

The first author, JB, encountered this case in 2016 as he reviewed the records of the TIME study, which has been recruiting cases of this kind since 2003. Following a description of the condition in a series of 50 patients in 2007 (Butler et al., 2007), we have continued to enrol new cases and learn more about the disorder. JB's review of this case series (in preparation) is broadly confirming the key findings of our previous description. The opportunity for prolonged follow-up of up to 20 years in some cases has provided reassuring evidence that the syndrome is non-progressive, and not, as a rule, a harbinger of dementia. In choosing a case for this chapter, we were keen to identify a story, which is both representative of TEA in general and shows the particular and idiosyncratic ways in which these impairments present, and their impact on the lives of those affected.

What does this particular case add to our understanding of TEA, of memory processing and forgetting?

The cardinal features of VA's case, summarized at the start of the previous section, suggest a series of conclusions and hypotheses.

They illustrate, first, that memory can be selectively disabled by an epileptic seizure. This is a remarkably focal seizure manifestation. It perhaps appears less surprising when one considers that déjà vu, a 'positive' distortion of memory and in a sense the converse of transient amnesia, is a well-recognized, subtle, manifestation of temporal lobe epilepsy (Warren-Gash & Zeman, 2014).

Second, given the prominent amnestic features in conjunction with olfactory hallucinations and emotionality, VA's case suggests that there must be an anatomical or functional relationship in the brain between olfaction, emotion and memory. We know, of course, that the processes underlying these functions in the brain are indeed closely associated in the medial temporal lobes and regions to which these project. Olfactory hallucinations are a recognized accompaniment of temporal lobe epilepsy, though they appear exceptionally common in TEA, occurring in 42% of cases (Butler & Zeman, 2008). Recently, we have further investigated olfactory abnormalities in the TEA cohort (Savage, Butler, Milton, Han & Zeman, 2017). Although olfactory hallucinations are not associated with impaired olfactory ability, an association has been identified between olfactory disturbances and topographical memory. The persistent and somewhat distinctive hyper-emotionality is an intriguing feature of TEA in need of more systematic study.

Thirdly, his case suggests a relationship between the occurrence of amnestic seizures and the persistent forms of memory disturbance accompanying these: accelerated long-term forgetting, autobiographical amnesia and topographical amnesia. Their association does not prove a causal relationship. But anecdotal reports of improvement in these deficits on treatment, combined with some evidence from single case studies (Goldstein et al., 1992; O'Connor et al., 1997; Walstra & Overweg, 2002; Tombini et al., 2005; Midorikawa & Kawamura, 2007; Razavi et al., 2010), supports the conjecture that epileptic activity in the medial temporal lobes is disruptive to these forms of memory. Structural change, either resulting from or giving rise to epilepsy, may well also contribute.

Can you specify why this case is relevant in relation to our knowledge of memory?

This case provides a good illustration of TEA and the associated pattern of interictal memory disruption. Work on TEA has expanded our understanding of the diagnostic possibilities amongst patients who present to hospital with one or several episodes of transient amnesia. The archetypal example of acute onset transient amnesia and the one of which hospital staff are most aware is transient global amnesia. It is defined by the following criteria (Bartsch & Butler, 2013):

- Presence of an anterograde amnesia that is witnessed by an observer
- No clouding of consciousness or loss of personal identity
- Cognitive impairment limited to amnesia
- No focal neurological or epileptic signs
- No recent history of head trauma or seizures
- Resolution of symptoms within 24 hours
- Mild vegetative symptoms (headache, nausea, dizziness) might be present during the acute phase

TEA is typically distinguished from transient global amnesia by the brevity of the attacks—typically less than an hour in TEA, several hours in transient global amnesia—and their frequency—typically around one per month in TEA, usually a single episode or very infrequent in transient global amnesia. The similarities and differences between transient global amnesia, TEA, and a third common cause of transient amnesia, psychogenic amnesia, are outlined in Table 12.2.

In addition to these three common causes, a number of other diagnoses should be considered in a patient who presents with transient amnesia. These include transient ischaemic attacks and stroke (Gupta, Kantor, Tung, Zhang &

TABLE 12.2 Distinguishing clinical features of the transient amnesic syndromes

Feature	Transient Epileptic Amnesia	Transient Global Amnesia	Psychogenic Amnesia
Typical age of onset	50–70 years	50–70 years	Any age
Past medical history	None	Migraine	'Organic' transient amnesia; substance abuse; psychiatric illness
Precipitants	Waking	Cold water; physical exertion; psychological stress	Minor head injury; stress; depression

Feature	Transient Epileptic Amnesia	Transient Global Amnesia	Psychogenic Amnesia
Ictal memory profile	Anterograde and retrograde amnesia showing within-patient variation; patient might later partially recall attack; retrograde procedural memory intact	Profound anterograde amnesia including repetitive questioning; variable retrograde amnesia; intact non-declarative memory	Highly variable; often profound retrograde amnesia with loss of personal identity; relatively preserved anterograde memory; variable procedural memory
Duration of amnestic episode	Usually <1hr but can last much longer (days)	Typically 4–10hr	Days or months
Recurrence	Mean frequency 13 attacks/yr	Rare	Rare
Postictal and interictal memory	Accelerated forgetting; remote autobiographical memory loss; topographical amnesia	Grossly intact, but subtle deficits persist for several months	Variable; patient might be able to 'relearn' the past
Other features	Olfactory hallucinations; oroalimentary automatisms; brief loss of responsiveness	Headache and/or nausea	Focal 'neurological' symptoms or signs, such as hemiparesis

Albers, 2014; Amuluru, Filippi & Lignelli, 2015), head injury, infective and autoimmune encephalitis (Garcia Garcia et al., 2013; Navarro et al., 2016), and the effects of drugs and sleep inertia (Ferguson, Paterson, Hall, Jay & Aisbett, 2016; Hilditch et al., 2016). Clues obtained from the history, neurological examination and appropriate investigations usually make it possible to differentiate between these causes.

Do you think this or similar cases contribute to our understanding of how the normal mind works?

The case of VA and the approximately 130 similar cases that our team has by now encountered shed light primarily on a form of neurological *dys*function, worthy of wider recognition than it has so far received, as it is a treatable cause of amnesia. But these cases also hint at some concealed features of the workings of the normal mind, several of them mentioned earlier in this chapter. We will briefly highlight three such areas here:

Rhythmic Processing in the Normal Mind Brain

TEA displays two forms of rhythmicity, one infradian, and the other circadian. The infradian cycle is evident in the striking rhythmicity of seizures in TEA which commonly, though not exclusively, occur at monthly intervals. This is a puzzling finding in a disorder which primarily affects middle-aged men, but a similar pattern has been described in other work on focal seizures (Cook et al., 2014; Cook et al., 2016). Whether this pattern reflects an environmental cycle or an endogenous rhythm, either present in the healthy brain or only in the presence of epilepsy, remains unclear.

A circadian cycle is in evidence in the tendency, again not exclusive, for seizures to occur on or close to awakening. In one case series (Butler et al., 2007), 74% of patients experienced seizures occurring on waking. 22% of these patients *only* experienced seizures on waking, and at no other time. This predilection for seizures to occur early in the morning, in the period soon after waking, has been recognized as a common phenomenon in epilepsy generally (van Campen, Valentijn, Jansen, Joels & Braun, 2015; van Campen et al., 2016). In humans, cortisol is released in ultradian pulses every one to two hours. The amplitude of these pulses peaks in the early morning hours and steadily declines during the day. Cortisol levels seem to be particularly related to seizure frequency in patients who report that stress is a likely precipitant for them (van Campen, Jansen, de Graan, Braun & Joels, 2014). Corticosteroid receptors are abundant in the medial temporal lobes: we conjecture that the circadian rhythmicity of the amnesic episodes in TEA reflects the circadian rhythm of cortisol secretion.

Memory Consolidation and Memory Maintenance in the Healthy Brain

As discussed earlier, the accelerated long-term forgetting seen in many patients with TEA certainly points to the value of testing memory at long delays in some patients with memory complaints and may reflect disturbance of 'later' stages of memory consolidation. Given the immense complexity and protracted course of the neural processes that subserve memory, such disturbances would be expected to occur on theoretical grounds, whether or not, as we suspect, TEA provides a genuine example.

The frequent though not invariable association of accelerated long-term forgetting with the apparent loss of autobiographical memories in patients with TEA, and with topographical memory loss, is intriguing. At present, unfortunately, too many questions about these deficits remain unanswered to interpret this association with any confidence. Just as it is uncertain whether accelerated long-term forgetting reflects a disorder of earlier or later phases of memory consolidation, it is unclear whether the autobiographical amnesia seen in patients with TEA primarily reflects a loss of memories or a retrieval failure. Similarly, as we have discussed, while there is some evidence the accelerated long-term forgetting is due to a functional disturbance, which can be rectified by anticonvulsant treatment, structural changes in the medial temporal lobes or their connections may be playing a part: a similar uncertainty surrounds the neural basis of autobiographical amnesia which could be due either to the effects on individual memories of epileptic activity propagating through the memory network or to structural change.

The association between autobiographical amnesia and topographical amnesia appears more likely to reflect a shared anatomical basis. Our functional imaging study of autobiographical recollection in patients with TEA identified the right posterior parahippocampal gyrus as the medial temporal lobe site at which activity was most markedly depressed amongst patients—with autobiographical amnesia impairment—by comparison with controls. This region is classically associated with spatial navigation, helping to explain the frequent association, in our patients' histories, between autobiographical and topographical memory complaints.

Memory and Emotion

Many patients with TEA report a tendency to increased emotionality following the onset of their amnesic episodes. In our previous large series, 18% of patients report this feature, as opposed to none in the control group (Butler et al., 2007). In our subsequent experience, accounts have repeatedly emerged of patients more easily moved to tears by films, books and television, or quicker to become emotional in circumstances where this would previously not have occurred. We presume that this reflects instability of emotional processing in the limbic system, leading to a disinhibition of emotion and emotional expression.

The relationship between emotion and epilepsy appears to be bidirectional. Emotional distress is a commonly reported seizure precipitant amongst patients with epilepsy (Lanteaume, Bartolomei & Bastien-Toniazzo, 2009; Galtrey, Mula & Cock, 2016) and there is evidence that depression is an independent risk factor for epilepsy (Hesdorffer et al., 2012). While the persistent interictal hyperemotionality reported by patients in the TEA cohort does not appear to be associated with an increased seizure frequency, we are investigating the possibility that mood disorder and adverse life events may be risk factors for TEA.

What are the shortcomings of this case?

A single case can refute a false generalization—for example, the generalization that normal performance on a memory test performed at a standard delay of 30 minutes establishes that long-term retention will be normal. A single case can also be a potent source of hypotheses: in the case of VA, for example, that limbic epilepsy gives rise to emotionality.

Single cases are, however, prone to the misleading play of chance: a putative link like the one just cited, between limbic epilepsy and emotionality, requires a group study to establish whether the relationship is robust, and to begin to probe the variables that might influence it; seizure frequency, say, or hippocampal volume. Similarly, disentangling the associations between transient amnestic seizures, accelerated long-term forgetting, autobiographical amnesia and topographical amnesia requires, at the least, a large group study and, probably, something more: a mechanistic understanding of the processes involved that behavioural measures alone will be hard-pressed to provide.

Clinical observations can, however, provide invaluable clues for mechanistic study. We hope to pursue the insight, from our recent detailed single case study of another patient, that modulating GABAergic processing in the brain can reproduce all the key manifestations of TEA (Zeman et al., 2016). In a patient who had suffered around 200 amnestic episodes during treatment with the GABA(B) receptor agonist, Baclofen, withdrawal of the drug led to the cessation of amnestic episodes and accelerated long-term forgetting. However, the autobiographical amnesia that had developed during the period of amnestic attacks persisted. This case points to a key role for the GABA(B) receptor in memory processing, suggests a close relationship between intermittent transient amnesia and accelerated long-term forgetting, such that preventing one prevents the other, but hints that autobiographical amnesia may be a cumulative and irreversible result of frequent transient amnesic episodes.

In general, do you think that neuropsychology cases could contribute to our understanding of the normal mind? Should these data be considered and if so why?

When part of the brain is damaged, injured, or even removed, neuropsychological testing is able to identify the deficits and abnormalities caused by this injury. These tests can thereby inform our understanding of what this damaged region does in the normal brain. The archetypal model for this process is, of course, patient HM (Scoville & Milner, 1957). In this case, bilateral medial temporal lobotomies led to the development of anterograde amnesia: careful neuropsychological assessment of this and related cases transformed our understanding of the role of the medial temporal lobe in the normal mind.

Neuropsychology has played a central role in our understanding of TEA. Three aspects of the neuropsychological study of TEA are particularly relevant to the normal mind. First, as we have discussed earlier, this work has produced some suggestive insights into normal memory processing; hinting, for example, at an extended process of consolidation that may be relevant to understanding accelerated long-term forgetting.

Second, the neuropsychological study of TEA and related work by other groups, illustrates the process by which introspection can be validated. This is a feature of neuropsychological work on both normal and abnormal behaviour. Thus, the use of memory tests at longer than standard intervals and the use of measures of autobiographical memory have quantified the genuine memory difficulties of individuals with TEA, whose problems were not captured by standard tests, and were sometimes denied as a result. Work in neuropsychology, and its close relative cognitive neuroscience, suggests that, while not entirely reliable, we are often accurate observers of what is happening in our own minds.

Third, the neuropsychological analysis of any condition requires robust normative data, obtained from participants with 'normal minds'. The process of obtaining these data can be revealing in itself, pointing, for example, to considerable individual variation in long-term retention of memories which may have interesting explanations and implications. Such normative work also reminds us that what constitutes a 'normal' mind varies with multiple factors including age, educational history, and cultural background. Extensive neuropsychological testing on these 'normal' cohorts has helped to define what is normal and what is not normal and how the border between these two territories can change.

We are now living in an era where ethics committees would like to foresee every step of experimental studies. How much serendipity was involved in your assessment?

Our assessment of VA, a representative case of the condition we study, was programmed from the outset by our research protocol and the corresponding ethical approval. However, the operation of research governance, both by ethics committees and—in the UK—by the recently established national Health Research Authority (HRA) and the numerous local Research and Development offices is very much at the front of our minds. Understandably, this complex system was devised primarily to regulate potentially injurious research, involving a range of medical interventions. But it was not designed for the kinds of scientifically important but medically innocuous observational studies that comprise the bulk of work in neuropsychology—and it is not appropriate for them. Our experienced research fellow (SS) has recently spent more than two full months of funded research time dealing with the labyrinthine complexities of the multiple local systems that will, if all goes well, allow us to identify small numbers of patients at sites scattered around the UK for just such an observational study. Ethical approval for this work had been in place for some time. We cannot discern any genuine value to patients whatsoever in this intricate process. Some projects will fail altogether as a result of this excessively burdensome regulation and most will be depleted by it. We strongly support the efforts of the British Neuropsychological Society to review and bring about change in a governance system that threatens to strangle our community's low risk yet intellectually worthwhile research.

References

Amuluru, K., Filippi, C. G., & Lignelli, A. (2015). Acute amnesia due to isolated mammillary body infarct. *Journal of Stroke and Cerebrovascular Diseases, 24(10)*, e303–305.

Asadi-Pooya, A. A. (2014). Transient epileptic amnesia: a concise review. *Epilepsy & Behavior, 31*, 243–245.

Bartsch, T., & Butler, C. (2013). Transient amnesic syndromes. *Nature Reviews Neurology, 9(2)*, 86–97.

Bilo, L., Meo, R., Ruosi, P., de Leva, M. F., & Striano, S. (2009). Transient epileptic amnesia: an emerging late-onset epileptic syndrome. *Epilepsia, 50, Suppl 5*, 58–61.

Butler, C., van Erp, W., Bhaduri, A., Hammers, A., Heckemann, R., & Zeman, A. (2013). Magnetic resonance volumetry reveals focal brain atrophy in transient epileptic amnesia. *Epilepsy & Behavior, 28(3)*, 363–369.

Butler, C. R., Bhaduri, A., Acosta-Cabronero, J., Nestor, P. J., Kapur, N., Graham, K. S., Hodges, J. R., Zeman, A. Z. (2009). Transient epileptic amnesia: regional brain atrophy and its relationship to memory deficits. *Brain, 132(Pt 2)*, 357–368.

Butler, C. R., Graham, K. S., Hodges, J. R., Kapur, N., Wardlaw, J. M., & Zeman, A. Z. (2007). The syndrome of transient epileptic amnesia. *Annals of Neurology, 61(6)*, 587–598.

Butler, C. R., & Zeman, A. (2008a). A case of transient epileptic amnesia with radiological localization. *Nature Clinical Practice Neurology, 4(9)*, 516–521.

Butler, C. R., & Zeman, A. (2008b). Recent insights into the impairment of memory in epilepsy: transient epileptic amnesia, accelerated long-term forgetting and remote memory impairment. *Brain, 131(Pt 9)*, 2243–2263. Cassel, A., Morris, R., Koutroumanidis, M., & Kopelman, M. (2016). Forgetting in temporal lobe epilepsy: when does it become accelerated? *Cortex, 78*, 70–84.

Butler, C. R., & Zeman, A. (2011). The causes and consequences of transient epileptic amnesia. *Behavioral Neurology, 24(4)*, 299–305.

Cook, M. J., Karoly, P. J., Freestone, D. R., Himes, D., Leyde, K., Berkovic, S., O'Brien, T., Grayden, D. B., & Boston, R. (2016). Human focal seizures are characterized by populations of fixed duration and interval. *Epilepsia, 57(3)*, 359–368.

Cook, M. J., Varsavsky, A., Himes, D., Leyde, K., Berkovic, S. F., O'Brien, T., & Mareels, I. (2014). The dynamics of the epileptic brain reveal long-memory processes. *Frontiers in Neurology, 5*, 217.

Elliott, G., Isaac, C. L., & Muhlert, N. (2014). Measuring forgetting: a critical review of accelerated long-term forgetting studies. *Cortex, 54*, 16–32.

Felician, O., Tramoni, E., & Bartolomei, F. (2015). Transient epileptic amnesia: update on a slowly emerging epileptic syndrome. *Revue Neurologique (Paris), 171(3)*, 289–297.

Ferguson, S. A., Paterson, J. L., Hall, S. J., Jay, S. M., & Aisbett, B. (2016). On-call work: to sleep or not to sleep? It depends. *Chronobiology International, 33(6)*, 678–684.

Galtrey, C. M., Mula, M., & Cock, H. R. (2016). Stress and epilepsy: fact or fiction, and what can we do about it? *Practical Neurology, 16(4)*, 270–278.

Garcia Garcia, M. E., Castrillo, S. M., Morales, I. G., Di Capua Sacoto, D., & Dolado, A. M. (2013). Acute amnesia and seizures in a young female. *Epileptic Disorders, 15(4)*, 455–460.

Goldstein, L. H., Patel, V., Aspinall, P., & Lishman, W. A. (1992). The effect of anticonvulsants on cognitive functioning following a probable encephalitic illness. *British Journal of Psychiatry, 160*, 546–549.

Gupta, M., Kantor, M. A., Tung, C. E., Zhang, N., & Albers, G. W. (2014). Transient global amnesia associated with a unilateral infarction of the fornix: case report and review of the literature. *Frontiers in Neurology, 5*, 291.

Hesdorffer, D. C., Ishihara, L., Mynepalli, L., Webb, D. J., Weil, J., & Hauser, W. A. (2012). Epilepsy, suicidality, and psychiatric disorders: a bidirectional association. *Annals of Neurology, 72(2)*, 184–191.

Hilditch, C. J., Short, M., Van Dongen, H. P., Centofanti, S. A., Dorrian, J., Köhler, M., & Banks, S. (2016). Sleep inertia during a simulated 6-h on/6-h off fixed split duty schedule. *Chronobiology International, 33(6)*, 685–696.

Hoefeijzers, S., Dewar, M., Della Sala, S., Butler, C., & Zeman, A. (2015). Accelerated long-term forgetting can become apparent within 3–8 hours of wakefulness in patients with transient epileptic amnesia. *Neuropsychology, 29(1)*, 117–125.

Hoefeijzers, S., Dewar, M., Della Sala, S., Zeman, A., & Butler, C. (2013). Accelerated long-term forgetting in transient epileptic amnesia: an acquisition or consolidation deficit? *Neuropsychologia, 51(8)*, 1549–1555.

Ivnik, R. J., Malec, J. F., Smith, G. E., Tangalos, E. G., Petersen, R. C., Kokmen, E., & Kurland, L. T. (1992). Mayo's older americans normative studies: updated AVLT norms for ages 56 to 97. *Clinical Neuropsychologist, 6(sup001)*, 83–104.

Jansari, A. S., Davis, K., McGibbon, T., Firminger, S., & Kapur, N. (2010). When "long-term memory" no longer means "forever": analysis of ascceletared long-term forgetting in a patient with temporal lobe epilepsy. *Neuropsychologia, 48(6)*, 1707–1715.

Kapur, N. (1993). Transient epileptic amnesia—a clinical update and a reformulation. *Journal of Neurology, Neurosurgery, and Psychiatry, 56(11)*, 1184–1190.

Kapur, N., Young, A., Bateman, D., & Kennedy, P. (1989). Focal retrograde amnesia: a long term clinical and neuropsychological follow-up. *Cortex, 25(3)*, 387–402.

Kopelman, M. D. (2000). Focal retrograde amnesia and the attribution of causality: an exceptionally critical view. *Cognitive Neuropsychology, 17(7)*, 585–621.

Lanteaume, L., Bartolomei, F., & Bastien-Toniazzo, M. (2009). How do cognition, emotion, and epileptogenesis meet? A study of emotional cognitive bias in temporal lobe epilepsy. *Epilepsy & Behavior, 15(2)*, 218–224.

Lapenta, L., Brunetti, V., Losurdo, A., Testani, E., Giannantoni, N. M., Quaranta, D., Di Lazzaro, V., & Della Marca, G. (2014). Transient epileptic amnesia: clinical report of a cohort of patients. *Clinical EEG and Neuroscience, 45(3)*, 179–183.

Manes, F., Graham, K. S., Zeman, A., de Lujan Calcagno, M., & Hodges, J. R. (2005). Autobiographical amnesia and accelerated forgetting in transient epileptic amnesia. *Journal of Neurology, Neurosurgery, and Psychiatry, 76(10)*, 1387–1391.

Midorikawa, A., & Kawamura, M. (2007). Recovery of long-term anterograde amnesia, but not retrograde amnesia, after initiation of an anti-epileptic drug in a case of transient epileptic amnesia. *Neurocase, 13(5)*, 385–389.

Milton, F., Butler, C. R., Benattayallah, A., & Zeman, A. Z. (2012). The neural basis of autobiographical memory deficits in transient epileptic amnesia. *Neuropsychologia, 50(14)*, 3528–3541.

Milton, F., Butler, C. R., & Zeman, A. Z. (2011). Transient epileptic amnesia: déjà vu heralding recovery of lost memories. *Journal of Neurology, Neurosurgery, and Psychiatry, 82(10)*, 1178–1179.

Milton, F., Muhlert, N., Pindus, D. M., Butler, C. R., Kapur, N., Graham, K. S., & Zeman, A. Z. (2010). Remote memory deficits in transient epileptic amnesia. *Brain, 133(Pt 5)*, 1368–1379.

Mosbah, A., Tramoni, E. Guedj, E., Aubert, S., Daquin, G., Ceccaldi, M., Felician, O., & Bartolomei, F. (2014). Clinical, neuropsychological, and metabolic characteristics of transient epileptic amnesia syndrome. *Epilepsia, 55(5)*, 699–706.

Muhlert, N., Milton, F., Butler, C. R., Kapur, N., & Zeman, A. Z. (2010). Accelerated forgetting of real-life events in transient epileptic amnesia. *Neuropsychologia, 48(11)*, 3235–3244.

Muhlert, N., & Zeman, A. (2012). The enigma of long-term forgetting. *Seizure, 21(2)*, 77–78.

Navarro, V., Kas, A., Apartis, E., Chami, L., Rogemond, V., Levy, P., Psimaras, D., Habert, M. O., Baulac, M., Delattre, J.Y., & Honnorat, J. (2016). Motor cortex and hippocampus are the two main cortical targets in LGI1-antibody encephalitis. *Brain, 139(Pt 4)*, 1079–1093.

O'Connor, M., Sieggreen, M. A., Ahern, G., Schomer, D., & Mesulam, M. (1997). Accelerated forgetting in association with temporal lobe epilepsy and paraneoplastic encephalitis. *Brain and Cognition, 35(1)*, 71–84.

Razavi, M., Barrash, J., & Paradiso, S. (2010). A longitudinal study of transient epileptic amnesia. *Cognitive and Behavioral Neurology, 23(2)*, 142–145.

Savage, S. A., Butler, C. R., Milton, F., Han, Y., & Zeman, A. Z. (2017). On the nose: olfactory disturbances in patients with transient epileptic amnesia. *Epilepsy & Behavior, 66*, 113–119.

Scoville, W. B., & Milner, B. (1957). Loss of recent memory after bilateral hippocampal lesions. *Journal of Neurology, Neurosurgery, and Psychiatry, 20(1)*, 11–21.

Tombini, M., Koch, G., Placidi, F., Sancesario, G., Marciani, M. G., & Bernardi, G. (2005). Temporal lobe epileptic activity mimicking dementia: a case report. *European Journal of Neurology, 12(10)*, 805–806.

van Campen, J. S., Hompe, E. L., Jansen, F. E., Velis, D. N., Otte, W. M., van de Berg, F., Braun, K. P., Visser, G. H., Sander, J. W., Joels, M., & Zijlmans, M. (2016). Cortisol fluctuations relate to interictal epileptiform discharges in stress sensitive epilepsy. *Brain, 139(Pt 6)*, 1673–1679.

van Campen, J. S., Jansen, F. E., de Graan, P. N., Braun, K. P., & Joels, M. (2014). Early life stress in epilepsy: a seizure precipitant and risk factor for epileptogenesis. *Epilepsy & Behavior, 38*, 160–171.

van Campen, J. S., Valentijn, F. A., Jansen, F. E., Joels, M., & Braun, K. P. (2015). Seizure occurrence and the circadian rhythm of cortisol: a systematic review. *Epilepsy & Behavior, 47*, 132–137.

Walstra, G. J., & Overweg, J. (2002). Amnesia treated successfully. *Age and Ageing, 31(1)*, 76–77.

Warren-Gash, C., & Zeman, A. (2014). Is there anything distinctive about epileptic déjà vu? *Journal of Neurology, Neurosurgery, and Psychiatry, 85(2)*, 143–147.

Witt, J. A., Vogt, V. L., Widman, G., Langen, K. J., Elger, C. E., & Helmstaedter, C. (2015). Loss of autonoetic awareness of recent autobiographical episodes and accelerated long-term forgetting in a patient with previously unrecognized glutamic acid decarboxylase antibody related limbic encephalitis. *Frontiers in Neurology, 6*, 130.

Zeman, A., & Butler, C. (2010). Transient epileptic amnesia. *Current Opinion in Neurology, 23(6)*, 610–616.

Zeman, A., Butler, C., Muhlert, N., & Milton, F. (2013). Novel forms of forgetting in temporal lobe epilepsy. *Epilepsy & Behavior, 26(3)*, 335–342.

Zeman, A., Hoefeijzers, S., Milton, F., Dewar, M., Carr, M., & Streatfield, C. (2016). The GABAB receptor agonist, baclofen, contributes to three distinct varieties of amnesia in the human brain—a detailed case report. *Cortex, 74*, 9–19.

Zeman, A. Z., Boniface, S. J., & Hodges, J. R. (1998). Transient epileptic amnesia: a description of the clinical and neuropsychological features in 10 cases and a review of the literature. *Journal of Neurology, Neurosurgery, & Psychiatry, 64(4)*, 435–443.

13
A "PUREST" IMPAIRMENT OF VERBAL SHORT-TERM MEMORY. THE CASE OF PV AND THE PHONOLOGICAL SHORT-TERM INPUT STORE

Giuseppe Vallar

In the '80s, you and your colleagues reported in a series of papers the performance of PV, a patient presenting with a selective impairment of auditory memory span. First of all, can you provide us with some background information about PV?

When we first assessed PV, she was a 28-year-old woman with 11 years of schooling. PV was fully right-handed on the Edinburgh Handedness Inventory (Oldfield, 1971), and had two right-handed sons, though a cousin was left-handed. In February 1977, PV, at the age of 26, suffered a stroke with a transient loss of consciousness. When admitted to hospital, PV presented with a right hemiparesis, which cleared in one month, and with slight, unspecified aphasic disturbances. No neuropsychological examination was performed at that time. The occurrence of a stroke at such a young age was probably due to PV's heart disease (a stenosis of the mitral valve). In April 1977, PV underwent a successful surgical operation of mitral commissurotomy. During the acute stage of her disease, PV was supported by her parents, but, as soon as her physical recovery was complete, she lived on her own with her two children (Basso, Spinnler, Vallar & Zanobio, 1982; Papagno & Vallar, 1995).

I first met PV seven months later, in November 1977, when she was referred to the Neuropsychology Centre of the University of Milano for a general evaluation of her dysphasic disturbances. PV lived in a town in the North of Italy. At that time, PV was completely autonomous in her everyday life and was going to set up as a dealer in pottery painted by herself; she had attended courses on the making and painting of pottery. A few years later, PV gave up this small business, to be able to spend as much time as possible with her two sons. Travelling by car from her town to Milan took about two hours. When PV came to Milan for the first visit, she travelled alone, driving her own car. In November 1977, PV spent three full days in the laboratory in Milan, during which she underwent a neurological and neuropsychological assessment. Every day in the late afternoon, when the examination was over, PV drove back home, because she wished to spend the evening with her children. The third day of this first study was extremely foggy, and driving in the motorway might have been dangerous, due to the low visibility, and the frequent accidents. We warned PV, but she could not be persuaded and returned home safely. I realized later that PV was a skilled and fast driver, when sometimes she drove me to the railway station of her town, coping with the traffic with great ability.

Can you summarize the main features of this case?

In the November 1977 assessment and study reported by Basso et al. (1982), PV was first given the Standard Language Examination of the Aphasia Unit of the University of Milano (Basso, Capitani & Vignolo, 1979). This showed a few phonemic paraphasias, and difficulties in finding the appropriate word, within a fluent expression. Specifically, in spontaneous speech, PV made a few phonological errors (misproduction of words, which typically involved omitted, extraneous, or duplicated sounds). Sometimes PV made dysgraphic errors in spontaneous writing. PV was severely and disproportionately impaired in the repetition of auditorily presented sentences. Also, comprehension of auditorily presented sentences was defective: on a shortened version of the Token Test (De Renzi & Faglioni, 1978), PV's score, adjusted for educational level, was 20 out of 36 (cut-off ≥ 29). On the Raven Progressive Matrices 47 (Basso, Capitani & Laiacona, 1987), PV scored 32 out of 36 (cut-off ≥ 24.2). The neurological examination was negative. This finding was somewhat surprising, considering the extensive CT-assessed perisylvian fronto-temporo-parietal lesion, that involved the whole of the language regions in the left hemisphere. The Language Examination was repeated twice, 14 and 23 months after the stroke. The only disorders revealed by the Language Exam were: 1) very poor repetition of sentences (the patient was unable to repeat phrases longer than eight syllables), while the repetition of single polysyllabic words was normal; and 2) poor performance on the Token Test (adjusted score 23, at the second assessment). The neurological exam was still negative. The only subjective and reported disturbance was PV's inability to "understand" (this was the term she used) even short sequences of digits spoken to her (e.g., prices of goods, telephone numbers), whereas she had no problems when the same sequences were presented visually.

How did you first realize that this case was interesting?

To reply appropriately to this question, two points are relevant. Firstly, I had started my research on short-term memory (STM) for verbal and nonverbal material in neurologically unimpaired participants (Berrini, Della Sala, Spinnler, Sterzi & Vallar, 1982; Spinnler, Sterzi, Tobaldini & Vallar, 1982), and in brain-damaged patients

(Capitani, Spinnler, Sterzi & Vallar, 1980). This was under the tutorship of Hans Spinnler (for Spinnler's contribution to Italian neuropsychology, see Boller, Gainotti, Grossi & Vallar, 2016), who had also been the supervisor of my MD thesis, titled "*L'importanza sulla memoria delle lesioni extra-limbiche degli emisferi cerebrali*" (*The role on memory of extra-limbic lesions of the cerebral hemispheres*). With Spinnler and my colleague Roberto Sterzi, I had written a review book in Italian on memory and amnesia (Spinnler, Sterzi & Vallar, 1977). I was then, in some way, "prepared" to study patients with such deficits. Secondly, the late 1970s and early 1980s were a period when the quantitative and statistically supported investigation of individual patients was becoming an increasingly adopted research approach, both in Europe and in the US. Illustrative examples include the first single case reports of imaginal unilateral spatial neglect—the renowned Piazza del Duomo study (Bisiach & Luzzatti, 1978) —, studies of dyslexia (Nolan & Caramazza, 1982; Warrington & Shallice, 1979), and of deficits of auditory-verbal STM (Caramazza, Basili, Koller & Berndt, 1981; Warrington & Shallice, 1969). This resurgence of the single case approach followed the 1960s-1970s in which, particularly in Italy, group studies, with standardized testing and sophisticated statistical analyses, had been the largely prevailing approach (Boller et al., 2016; Vallar, 2000).

This cultural climate in Italian neuropsychology, together with my own starting with neuropsychological research in STM, allowed me to realize the relevance of a patient such as PV, for investigating the patterns of impairment, and the functional organization of memory. PV as an important case was discovered by Anna "Mimi" Basso, who was in the Seventies the Head of the Service for the Rehabilitation of Aphasia of the Clinica Neurologica of the University of Milan, at the Ospedale Policlinico. PV had been referred to Professor Basso for an evaluation of her language disturbances. Mimi told me that she was assessing an interesting patient, who might have suffered from a selective deficit of verbal STM. I went through a baseline neuropsychological assessment, and I soon realized how selective, hence potentially interesting, studying that patient could be. A similar case had been reported a few years earlier, JB, who had a very similar, and selective, deficit of auditory-verbal span, with no other aphasic disorders (Case #2, Warrington, Logue & Pratt, 1971). Mimi passed away a few months ago (August 2018). On October 12th 2018, a one day Memorial Conference ("Giornata in ricordo della Professoressa Anna Basso") was held in Milano. There, in my talk, I recalled Mimi's clinical skills and cognitive neuropsychological expertise, that made her able to immediately and precisely detect the selective pattern of impairment of PV, and its potential interest.

What was this case's pattern of spared and impaired abilities?

PV had a selective impairment of auditory-verbal span, that was between two and three items (digits: 3.1; letters: 1.6; words: 2.5) with auditory presentation. With visual presentation, PV's span was higher (digits: 3.9; letters: 4.0; words: 4.8).

Furthermore, PV's defective pattern of performance, as to the effects of serial position, was compatible with an interpretation in terms of defective auditory-verbal STM (Warrington & Shallice, 1969). PV showed no recency effect in serial recall of auditory-verbal stimuli (i.e., span), with a most defective recall performance with the last and penultimate positions in the list (see Figure 2 of Basso et al., 1982). When given the task to freely recall ten supra-span lists of ten words, which PV was required to produce orally immediately after presentation, without any order constraint, no recency effect was present, and in 60% of her recall attempts, the first produced item came from the first two serial positions of the presented lists (see Figure 13.1). This pattern differs from the typical free recall of supra-span lists of verbal items, that is characterized by the better recall of the last, and of the two to three penultimate items of the list (the recency effect), and by a comparatively minor advantage of the first, and of the second, initial items

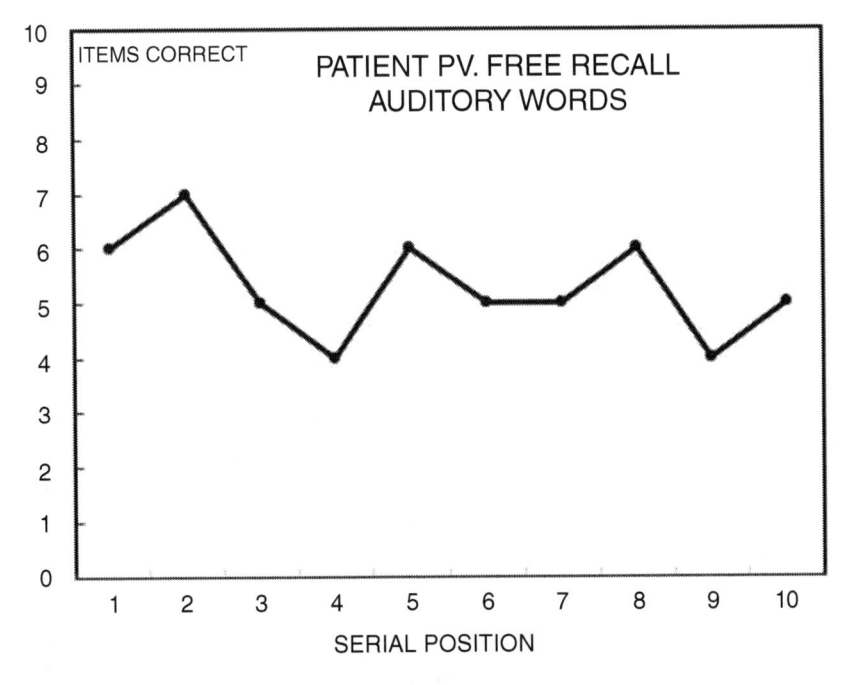

FIGURE 13.1 Free recall of ten auditorily presented lists, each including ten concrete two-syllable high-frequency words: number of correct responses by serial position at presentation. PV did not show any recency effect, with performance in the beginning and middle positions of the curve being remarkably good. In 60% of her attempts, the first items came from the first two serial positions of the list. Data collected in February 1980 and reported in part by Basso et al. (1982), and fully by Vallar and Papagno (1986).

(the primacy effect). The recency effect in immediate free recall, that also features the initial recall of final items, was considered to represent the output of STM systems, while the initial and beginning items of the list were assumed to be based on retention in long-term memory (LTM) (Glanzer, 1972; Glanzer & Cunitz, 1966). Other patients with a disproportionate reduction of auditory-verbal span had been reported with a reduced recency effect, that was definitely present only for the last item (Warrington et al., 1971). PV's deficit (see Figure 13.1) was more dramatic, with no recency effect at all.

The impairment of STM of auditory-verbal material was very selective. Verbal long-term episodic memory, as assessed by learning of meaningful material (free recall learning; paired-associate learning; learning of a short story), and visuo-spatial STM, and long-term visuo-spatial episodic learning and retention (spatial memory span, and learning of a supra-span sequence in Corsi's Block Tapping Test; visual maze learning; memory for a complex visual pattern, Rey's figure) were entirely preserved.

The selectivity of the STM impairment of PV is anecdotally illustrated by a postcard she sent to me some years later, from a village on the Ligurian sea, Cervo (see Figure 13.2).

Due to the selectivity of this impairment of auditory-verbal STM, a case study was submitted to *Neuropsychologia*, at that time edited by Henry Hècaen (Boller, 2006). The refereeing process was rapid, and the manuscript was published, with the only suggestion by Hècaen to reduce the number of figures. Accordingly, the present Figure 13.1 was not published in Basso et al. (1982), and the serial position data were later reported in a tabular format by Vallar and Papagno (1986), in an article specifically concerned with PV's defective recency effect in free recall of lists of words with auditory presentation.

Do you think this case contributes to our understanding of how the normal mind works?

The initial study by Basso et al. (1982) represented a replication of a pattern of impairment previously reported by Warrington and Shallice (1969), in a patient with an especially selective deficit, with no associated disorders of other components of memory, general intelligence, and language. Amongst the published patients at that time, a similarly "pure" pattern of impairment of auditory-verbal STM had been reported only in patient JB (Warrington et al., 1971).

In 1980, I worked for about three months at the Applied Psychology Unit of the Medical Research Council, in Cambridge, UK, at that time directed by Alan D. Baddeley (www.mrc-cbu.cam.ac.uk/history/overview/). There, in neurologically unimpaired participants, I performed a set of experiments exploring the functional architecture of verbal STM, within the theoretical framework of Alan Baddeley's Working Memory model (Baddeley, 1976; Baddeley & Hitch, 1974). In a study concerning the effects on short-term retention of interference using

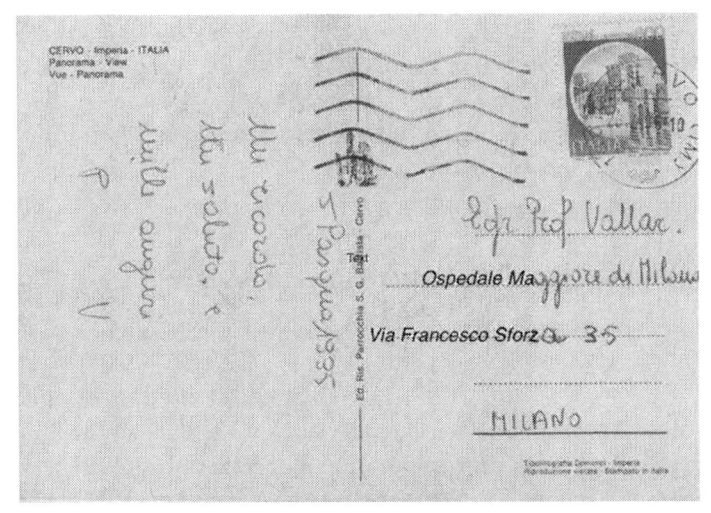

FIGURE 13.2 Postcard sent by PV to the author for Easter 1995 from a holiday location in the Ligurian seaside: "Un ricordo, un saluto, mille auguri" ("A memory, a greeting, thousand wishes"). The address has been partly cancelled by time. Only the initials of the patient's signature (PV) are shown.

subvocal articulatory rehearsal by the concurrent task of articulatory suppression (namely, the uttering of a speech sound irrelevant to the memory task, such as "the, the, the" while retaining a visually presented consonant trigram), we found that suppression produced minimal forgetting, and only at the longest retention interval of 15 seconds (Vallar & Baddeley, 1982). Conversely, the usual Peterson and Peterson (1959) interfering task of counting backwards by threes had the expected effects of dramatically disrupting short-term retention in the same time intervals. Having failed to find any major disruptive effect of a selective interference with articulatory coding (namely, covert or subvocal speech), such as that brought about by articulatory suppression, Vallar and Baddeley (1982, p. 53) concluded that "These results suggest that covert speech is not necessary for rehearsal in short-term verbal memory. As such they call for a re-evaluation of the nature and function of rehearsal." These findings suggested that, since immediate retention was minimally affected by articulatory suppression, the component disrupted by the counting backwards task, that caused the dramatic forgetting typically found in the Peterson task, was unlikely to be the *verbal STM store-Rehearsal system* or a *Phonological Output Buffer* (Caramazza, Miceli & Villa, 1986), and did not involve articulatory coding. Vallar and Baddeley (1982) concluded that the dramatically disruptive effects of counting backwards could take place in the central executive (Baddeley & Hitch, 1974), the limited capacity system responsible for selecting and operating the various control processes used in both the STM and more general information processing tasks. Other possible loci of interference included a visual short-term store (see for neuropsychological evidence, Warrington & Shallice, 1972), whose operation could have been disrupted by counting backwards (Phillips & Christie, 1977), but not by articulatory suppression. In sum, the results of Vallar and Baddeley (1982) suggested the existence of non-articulatory (auditory, visual) short-term storage and rehearsal systems.

The second study, performed by Baddeley, Lewis and Vallar (1984), was particularly relevant to the case of PV. We provided evidence for a fractionation of Baddeley and Hitch's (1974) verbal short-term retention system, the *Articulatory Loop* (a rehearsal buffer that was able to maintain verbal material through subvocal rehearsal). Specifically, we found that the *phonological similarity effect*, namely the phenomenon whereby sequences of acoustically or phonologically similar items, such as letters or words, are recalled worse than sequences of dissimilar ones (e.g., *can, cad, cat,* vs. *cow, day, bar*; B, C, D, vs. F, K, Q), in immediate serial recall, such as in the memory span paradigm, was not abolished by articulatory suppression, when the lists were presented auditorily. Conversely, the *word length effect*, namely the phenomenon whereby lists of long words are recalled worse than lists of short ones (e.g., *Stoat, Mumps, School,* vs. *Hippopotamus, Tuberculosis, University*) was abolished by articulatory suppression. These findings, together with the previous observations that both the phonological similarity effect (Murray, 1968), and the word length effect (Baddeley, Thomson & Buchanan,

1975) were abolished by suppression when the lists were presented visually, suggested a fractionation of the *articulatory loop*, using the terminology of Baddeley, Lewis and Vallar (1984), into an input *Phonological Short-Term Store (PhSTS)* and a process of *Rehearsal*.

These findings suggested that auditory-verbal material has direct access to a phonologically based input storage system, the *PhSTS*, that does not involve articulatory coding since the phonological similarity effect is not abolished by articulatory suppression. Conversely, the word length effect, being abolished by suppression with both visual and auditory presentation of the lists, was taken as an indicator of the operation of *Rehearsal*. The conclusion was that the *PhSTS* provides the main storage capacity for *Phonological STM*, while *Rehearsal*, on the one hand, revives the phonological trace held in the *PhSTS*, preventing its decay, and on the other hand, provides access of visually presented material to the *PhSTS*, after recoding from a visual to a phonological format. The main storage role of the input component (the *PhSTS*) was suggested by the observation that articulatory suppression impairs span (Murray, 1968), but does not reduce it so dramatically as brain damage does in patients with a defective *Phonological STM*: auditory digit span 2.38, according to a meta-analysis of 25 patients with a deficit of *Phonological STM*, made by Vallar and Papagno (2002). Converging evidence had been provided by Salamè and Baddeley (1982), who had found that unattended speech impairs immediate memory for visually presented digits, with the disrupting effect being directly related to the phonological similarity between the speech and the digits, and articulatory suppression abolishing the disrupting effect of speech. These findings were too interpreted as an indication of the existence of a phonological non-articulatory store (the *PhSTS*), to which auditory material had direct and obligatory access, and of an articulatory process *(Rehearsal)*, disrupted by suppression, that conveyed visual-verbal material to the *PhSTS*.

More generally, in the wider perspective of considering verbal STM systems as contributing to aspects of language, or being part of the language system, the *PhSTS* might have been involved in aspects of language comprehension (see Clark & Clark, 1977), while the process of *Rehearsal* might have been conceived as a *Phonological Output Buffer*, a temporary storage system for the assembling of phonology at a sub-lexical level (Caramazza, Miceli & Villa, 1986), contributing to the smooth production of articulated speech.

Patient PV had preserved speech production, with no paraphasias, and articulatory disorders, as assessed by a clinical examination of spontaneous speech (Basso et al., 1982). Also, the previously reported patient JB had preserved spontaneous speech, as indicated by a quantitative analysis of pausing and paraphasic errors (Shallice & Butterworth, 1977). The prediction could be made therefore that the functional locus of PV's STM deficit was to be placed in the input *PhSTS*, rather than in the process of articulatory *Rehearsal*.

The Functional Architecture of Auditory-Verbal STM

With these predictions in mind, Alan Baddeley and I prepared a set of experiments, aimed at assessing whether PV's functional impairment involved the *PhSTS*, articulatory *Rehearsal*, or both components of verbal STM. The one day testing program (see Figure 13.3) included: the effects of phonological similarity on span for sequences of letters (phonologically dissimilar set: *F, K, Q, R, X, W, Z*; phonologically similar set: *B, C, D, G, P, V, T*), with auditory and visual presentation, in which, in the latter input modality, the effects of articulatory suppression were also assessed; the word length effect with auditory presentation; an assessment of articulation rate, asking PV to count forward from 1 to 10 five successive

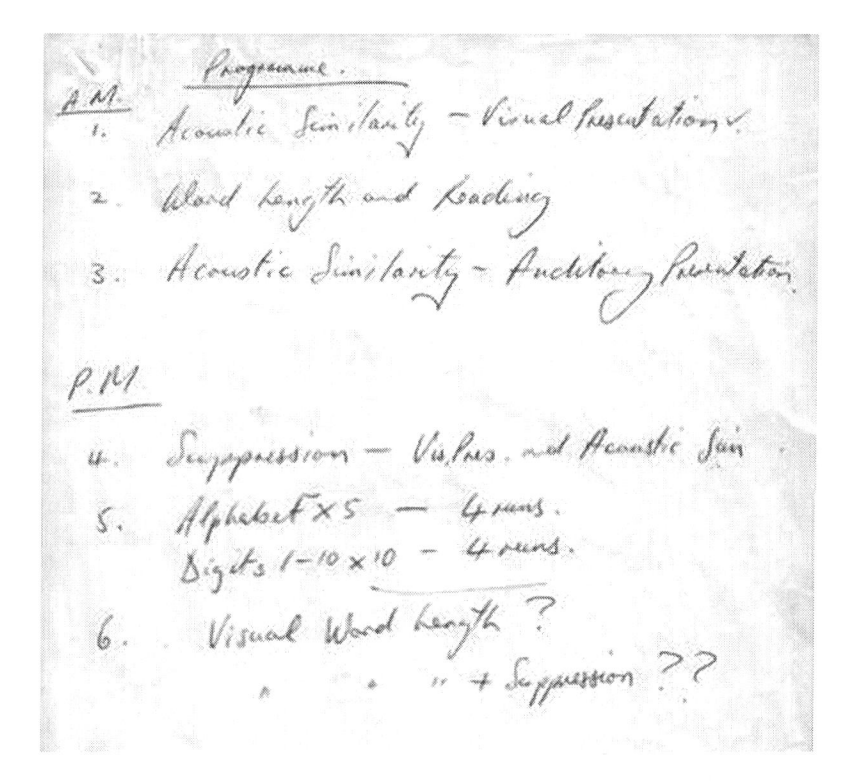

FIGURE 13.3 Program of the testing session with PV, handwritten by Alan D. Baddeley. Morning: (1) acoustic similarity-visual presentation; (2) word length and reading; (3) acoustic similarity-visual presentation. Afternoon: (4) suppression-visual presentation and acoustic similarity; (5) alphabet × 5, digits 1–10 × 5 (uttering); (6) visual word length + suppression. The last section (6) of the program (tentatively planned, and marked by the?) was not performed, due to the time of the day (late afternoon). The permission of Alan D. Baddeley to publish this note is gratefully acknowledged.

times on each trial, for a total of 10 trials, and to say the letters of the Italian alphabet from A to Z (20 trials). The experiments were performed on February 21, 1982: it was a Sunday, since PV was working in her pottery shop during the week, and was available for testing only on that day. The experiments were subdivided in a morning and an early afternoon session, with a pleasant light lunch with PV, Alan and I in a restaurant nearby.

PV showed the effects of phonological similarity with auditory, but not with visual, presentation of the letter strings. In the visual modality, PV's recall performance of phonologically similar and dissimilar lists was better than with auditory input, as typically shown by patients with a defective auditory-verbal STM (see review in Vallar & Papagno, 2002), and unaffected by concurrent articulatory suppression. Finally, PV did not show any effect of word length, although her rate of articulation was within the range of that of control participants.

Neurologically unimpaired participants show a detrimental effect of phonological similarity with both visual and auditory presentation of the stimuli, and their performance is slightly, but significantly, reduced by articulatory suppression, which also abolishes the effect of phonological similarity with visual input. Unimpaired participants also show a detrimental effect of word length with both auditory and visual presentation, and this effect is abolished by articulatory suppression in both input modalities (Baddeley et al., 1984, 1975; Murray, 1968). In serial recall, the level of performance is higher with auditory than with visual input, with a *modality effect* (see e.g., Watkins & Watkins, 1980).

Our conclusion that the functional locus of PV's impairment was to be located in the *PhSTS* component of STM was based on the following arguments:

1. PV showed the effect of phonological similarity with auditory presentation: this indicated that a) auditory-verbal material had access to PV's *PhSTS* and was then encoded phonologically, and b) PV's *PhSTS* had minimal residual capacity (PV was always able to repeat a single item with no errors).
2. PV a) did not show any effect of phonological similarity with visual presentation, and b) her memory performance was unaffected by articulatory suppression: this pattern indicated that she did not make use of the process of *Rehearsal*, for a) conveying visual-verbal material to the *PhSTS*, and b) refreshing a phonological memory trace held in the *PhSTS*.
3. PV did not show any effect of word length with auditory presentation of the stimuli, confirming the lack of use of *Rehearsal*.
4. PV's articulation rate was within the normal range, making implausible the hypothesis that the lack of use of the process of articulatory *Rehearsal* was due to its primary damage.

We concluded that articulatory *Rehearsal* was not used by PV, though *per se* unimpaired, due to damage (i.e., the disproportionately reduced capacity) to the *PhSTS*. This made the process of *Rehearsal* useless, or unavailable, as support for the damaged *PhSTS*, both for conveying, after recoding, visual items to PV's *PhSTS*, or for refreshing auditory items that had entered that damaged store. In sum, the absence of indicators of *Rehearsal* by PV in span tasks was interpreted by Vallar and Baddeley (1984a) to reflect a strategic choice. To what extent this strategy by PV, namely of not to use *Rehearsal* for immediate retention, was characterized by awareness, remains unexplored. In terms of subjective experience, PV repeatedly noted that she was unable to "keep in mind" items to be remembered for a short amount of time, within seconds, as in immediate repetition span.

This pattern of effects of phonological similarity and word length with visual and auditory presentation, found in PV, has been reported in most patients with a selective deficit of auditory-verbal span, although not all effects were assessed in all patients (see Table 3 of Vallar & Papagno, 2002).

The fractionation of Phonological STM into input (PhSTS) and output (Phonological Output Buffer) systems, with articulatory Rehearsal being conceived as a recirculation and transfer of stored material between "acoustic" and "planned articulatory" phonological representations appears to be still relevant today, with a role of these components of Phonological STM also in speech comprehension and production (in this latter case, mainly the Phonological Output Buffer, see review in Jacquemot & Scott, 2006).

The PhSTS and Sentence Comprehension

A second study we performed in the same period concerned the role of the *PhSTS* in language comprehension. Preliminarily, we verified that PV's phonological processing performance was within the normal range, as measured by phonological discrimination of auditory stimuli [discrimination of phonemes contrasting in voicing only (e.g., "*ba*" vs "*pa*"), in place only (e.g., "*pa*" vs "*ta*"), and in both distinctive features (e.g., "*pa*" vs "*ga*")], the assignment of stress to words [e.g., "*mèdico*" vs. "*soldàto*" (physician, soldier)], presented auditorily and visually, and rhyme judgements (also patient JB has preserved phonological skills, see Paulesu et al., 2017). Comprehension of individual words and short sentences was preserved. In a sentence verification task, in which we used syntactically correct sentences, PV proved to be entirely able to decide about the trueness of sentences such as "*Slippers are sold in pairs*" and "*Architects design buildings*," vs. "*Bishops may be bought in shops*," and "*Prime ministers are mountainous*" (A-type sentences). She was also unimpaired with longer sentences of this type, such as "*There is no doubt that champagne is something that can certainly be bought in shops*," and "*A creature such as the rabbit falls within the class of the animals that have four legs*" vs. "*Lettuce is the kind of person that one rarely meets in a schoolroom*," and "*It is true that physicians comprise a profession that is manufactured in factories from time to time*" (B-type sentences). PV, however, proved to be impaired with long sentences such as, "*It is fortunate that most rivers are able to be crossed by bridges, that are strong enough for cars*," and "*Many people know that often books contain pictures of various kinds, which are sometimes printed in colours,"* vs. "*One could reasonably claim that sailors are often lived on by ships of various kind,"* and "*The world divides the equator into two hemispheres, the northern and the southern*" (C-type sentences). The C-type sentences differed from the previous ones in that word order was crucial for deciding about the trueness *vs.* falseness of the item. We argued that PV's defective *PhSTS*, with the C-type sentences, was unable to provide the temporary storage of their verbatim sequential content, in a phonological format, necessary for extracting meaning, under conditions in which the lexical and semantic content of the sentence (at variance from the A- and the B-types of sentences) was not sufficient to allow comprehension, such as in the verification task we used (Vallar & Baddeley, 1984b). The relationship between sentence comprehension and Phonological STM (see for review Jacquemot & Scott, 2006) has been subsequently investigated by a number of researchers, with this conclusion by Papagno and Cecchetto (2018) "In our opinion, data from the literature suggest that both components of the phonological loop are involved in the comprehension of some type of sentence, namely syntactically complex sentences that load on memory, such as center-embedded object relative clauses". On the other hand, the suggestion has been also made (Martin, 2006, p. 74) that "working memory is still considered to provide critical constraints on sentence comprehension, but the capacity involved appears to be largely independent of the phonological storage involved in word list recall."

The PhSTS and the Recency Effect

Patients with a deficit of auditory-verbal STM in free recall show a reduced recency effect, confined to the last item of the list, with auditory presentation of the stimuli (Shallice & Warrington, 1970; Warrington et al., 1971). In neurologically unimpaired participants, the recency effect in immediate free recall involves the last four to five items of the list (Glanzer, 1972; Glanzer & Cunitz, 1966). PV, as shown in Figure 13.1, did not show any recency effect in free recall of lists presented auditorily (Basso et al., 1982; see Table 1 of Vallar & Papagno, 1986), data collected during the first assessment of PV's STM, in February 1980). Furthermore, in 60% of PV's recall attempts, the first items came from the first two serial positions, while neurologically unimpaired participants typically produce first and best the last items of the free recall list (Postman & Phillips, 1965). Neurologically unimpaired participants show a recency effect with both visual and auditory presentation of the stimuli, with the effect being larger with auditory stimuli (modality effect: review in Crowder, 1976; Watkins & Watkins, 1980). Patients with a defective auditory-verbal STM show a defective recency effect also in immediate serial recall (Basso et al., 1982; Saffran & Marin, 1975).

Recency effects had been also found in free recall after a delay filled by distracting activity (Bjork & Whitten, 1974). These findings suggested that recency phenomena in memory may result from the application of retrieval strategies, that may also include information about the temporal sequence of events, to different storage systems, be they short or long-term, giving rise to short- and long-term recency effects (Davelaar, Goshen-Gottstein, Ashkenazi, Haarmann & Usher, 2005).

We confirmed that PV did not show a recency effect in free recall when the word lists were presented auditorily; conversely, with visual presentation, PV's recency was within the normal range (Vallar & Papagno, 1986). PV, unlike neurologically unimpaired participants, started her recall attempts with items presented in the first half of the list, namely in pre-recency positions. PV was, however, able to start her recall from the end of the list ("recall from end"), under specific instructions: under these conditions, with auditory presentation of the lists, a recency effect occurred, but her performance level in the final positions remained defective. With visual presentation, both in free recall and in the recall from end conditions, PV's recency was within the normal range. These findings show a dissociation between recall strategies, based on serial position and temporal order, preserved in PV, and defective *vs.* preserved memory storage systems. Recency phenomena may reflect the application of retrieval strategies to the content of specific stores. In the case of PV, the absence of a recency effect in immediate free recall of auditory lists reflected the disproportionately reduced capacity of the *PhSTS*, due to brain damage. With visual lists, the items were likely to be stored in PV's preserved visual STM system (Warrington & Shallice, 1972), and a recency effect within the normal range took place. In accord with these findings and account of recency phenomena, a few years later we found that PV showed both a recall performance level and a long-term recency effect comparable to those of the control group in a task requiring the delayed free recall of a list of anagram solutions (Vallar, Papagno & Baddeley, 1991). These findings dissociated long and short-term recency phenomena, as reflecting the operation of different memory components.

PhSTS and Long-Term Learning

One important aspect of the selectivity of the memory impairment of patients with a reduced capacity of the *PhSTS* is that they are unimpaired in tasks assessing learning and retention of verbal information, such as a short story, paired-associate learning, learning of a list of words (Basso et al., 1982; Warrington & Shallice, 1969). PV had preserved memory performance for the initial and middle positions of a free recall list of auditory words, that reflect LTM processes (Vallar & Papagno, 1986). All these studies used, however, stimuli such as words, known to the patient, that therefore had lexical and semantic representations in PV's LTM systems. What could happen, however, when the verbal stimuli to be learned did not possess such representations, namely they were nonwords, or foreign words, unknown to the patient, transliterated into Italian? Under these conditions, no or minimal support from LTM lexical-semantic memory was to be expected, with the acquisition relying only on the preserved general learning strategies, that in

PV's case had proven to be effective for memorizing verbal material in the long-term. Accordingly, we asked PV to learn words or nonwords (i.e., Russian words, unknown to the patient, transliterated into Italian) by a paired-associate paradigm (e.g., *rosa*(rose)-*svieti*). The results were clear-cut. PV's capacity to learn pairs of meaningful words was within the normal range. However, when her capacity to learn to associate a familiar word with an unfamiliar item from another language was assessed, with auditory presentation she was completely unable to perform this task. With visual presentation, PV showed some evidence of learning but was clearly impaired (Baddeley et al., 1988). Findings about PV's impairment in learning novel phonological strings (new words, such as in second language acquisition) remain relevant (Kroll & De Groot, 2005; Perani, 2005).

The relevance of the results from patient PV for our understanding of the operation and functional architecture of the normal system, in that specific case, STM, was readily acknowledged by one of the two referees of the article by Vallar and Baddeley (1984a), published in the *Journal of Verbal Learning and Verbal Behavior* (*JVLVB*). Actually, one referee, Bob Crowder (see e.g., Crowder, 1976), wrote in his comments, "I am on record as endorsing the use of sharply defined pathologies to shed light on normal functioning. This case seems to present cleanly dissociated symptoms, readily amenable to interpretation in terms of currently theoretical models." This opinion was shared by the Editor, Fergus Craik, who wrote in his letter, "For JVLVB readers, you should stress the implications for normal memory (as you do, of course), but leave the more neuropsychologically slanted material for discussion elsewhere."

Some years later, Nadine Martin (2003) had a similar opinion about the implications of data from patient PV—and from patient JB (e.g., see Shallice & Butterworth, 1977)—for our understanding of the unimpaired system. Some of her comments on PV are reported next.

> PV is a noteworthy case in part because of the sheer number of empirical investigations of her STM and language processing abilities. More important, these studies, in total, provide an outstanding example of the use of neuropsychological data to test assumptions of a cognitive model of working memory.
>
> (Loc. cit. pp. 19–20)

> PV was the subject of many investigations and was studied over a fairly long period of time. This history is impressive in its own right. What makes the case studies of PV exceptional is that they systematically address assumptions and characteristics of an established and fairly well-articulated model of working memory. Working closely within such a model has both advantages and disadvantages. The phenomenon under study (impaired *Phonological STM*) was only recently identified and not understood very well. The advantage of Vallar and Baddeley's approach was that the working memory

model provided an empirically supported logical framework within which to make predictions about PV's performance on span tasks. This enabled a characterisation of PV's deficit within a model and subsequently led to the use of data from PV to test the assumptions of the working memory model (for example, the recency effect). A potential disadvantage of this approach is that exploration of a poorly understood phenomenon may be restricted by the assumptions of a model.

(loc. cit. p. 27)

PV and JB were similar cases in that both subjects evolved from a profile of mild language impairment accompanied by auditory STM deficits to one of primarily an auditory STM deficit. Both were subjects of thorough investigations to pinpoint their deficits within a model of verbal STM (although PV's investigation is more explicitly directed towards this end). In this respect, both PV and JB are prominent examples of the cognitive case study approach that uses a cognitive model to guide the investigation of a neuropsychological impairment. Moreover, these cases were relevant, indeed central, to a debate in cognitive neuropsychology that has paved the way for what is currently an active and productive line of research, discerning the mechanisms linking language, STM and learning. In these two respects, PV and JB can be considered classic cases who have contributed to both the empirical and theoretical development of cognitive neuropsychology.

(loc. cit., p. 36)

Retrospectively, the investigations performed with patient PV corroborated, from the neuropsychological perspective of the study of a patient with acquired brain damage, the functional architecture of auditory-verbal (Warrington & Shallice, 1969) or *Phonological STM* (Vallar & Baddeley, 1984a), as a system including two components:

1. The main storage component was a limited capacity input system, the *PhSTS*, to which auditory-verbal material had a direct, automatic and obligatory access, and where stored information was coded phonologically, as indexed by the *phonological similarity effect*.
2. Visually presented verbal (written) material, to gain access to the PhSTS, after *grapheme-to-phoneme (phonological) recoding*, needed to enter the process of Rehearsal, where information was coded in a phonological output format, that was conceived in terms of planned (premotor) articulatory sequences. Rehearsal was also assumed to revive or refresh the phonological trace stored in the *PhSTS*, preventing its corruption or decay.

Figure 13.4 (Vallar, 2015) summarizes the functional architecture of the system, as proposed by Vallar and Baddeley (1984a). The figure also indicates the main

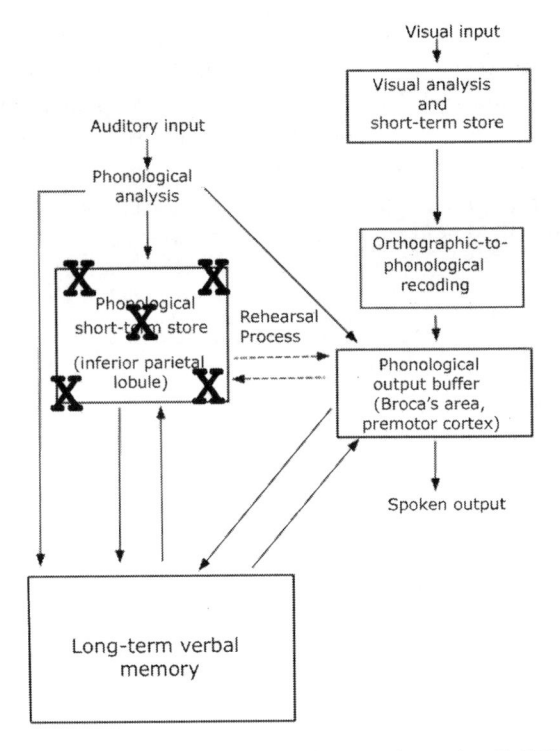

FIGURE 13.4 A model of *Phonological STM* distinguishing the *PhSTS*—damaged in PV, as indicated by X X X,—and the process of *Rehearsal*, that involves the recirculation of phonologically coded material between the input non-articulatory *PhSTS* and the *Phonological Output Buffer*, where phonological material is coded in an articulatory format, as planned sequences of impending speech (modified from Vallar, 2015).

neural underpinnings of these two components of *Phonological STM*: the inferior parietal lobule, particularly the supramarginal gyrus in the left hemisphere for the *PhSTS*, and the left premotor cortex (Broca's area) for *Rehearsal*. Rehearsal was conceived by Baddeley and me, in terms of a process consisting in the "recirculation" of material between the *PhSTS*, where information was stored in a phonological non-articulatory format (as indexed by the finding that articulatory suppression did not abolish the effect of phonological similarity, when the stimuli were presented auditorily), and a *Phonological Output Buffer*, where information was represented in a phonological articulatory (planned phonological sequences of impending speech) format (as indexed by the finding that articulatory suppression abolished the effect of phonological similarity when the stimuli were presented visually, since, to gain access to the *PhSTS*, they needed to enter *Rehearsal*).

The Phonological STM Input Store

Do you think that there is anything unique that the reports of this case added to our knowledge?

The study of patient PV provided novel results concerning aspects of STM function:

1. The complete pattern of functional impairment of the *PhSTS*, with *Rehearsal* and *Phonological Recoding* being preserved, was defined by the study of patient PV (Vallar & Baddeley, 1984a, b). This pattern is summarized in Table 13.1 (see also Vallar, 2017). Previous studies of patient KF, who suffered from a similar functional pattern of impairment of auditory-verbal (*Phonological*) *STM* (Warrington & Shallice, 1969), had provided converging evidence for the absence of phonological coding of visually presented verbal material in immediate retention span tasks. Visual material was not conveyed to the *PhSTS*, being possibly stored in visual STM instead (Warrington & Shallice, 1972).

2. The functional properties of the recency effect in immediate free recall of auditory-verbal material were characterized as the output of the *PhSTS*, defective in PV (Vallar & Papagno, 1986). More generally, the defective recency of patient PV in immediate serial (Basso et al., 1982; see also Saffran & Marin, 1975), and free (Basso et al., 1982; Vallar & Papagno, 1986; see

TABLE 13.1 Patterns of preserved/defective performance and present/absent effects found in brain-damaged patients following damage to:

1. Phonological STM's two components
   a. Phonological Short-Term Store (PhSTS), damaged in patient PV
   b. Articulatory Rehearsal (ArtReh)
2. Phonological recoding (PhRec)

Task	Span		PhSE		WLE		PhJ	RE		A-R
	A	V	A	V	A	V	V	A	V	
Damaged Component										
1. PhSTM										
a. PhSTS [PV]	XX§	(√)§	√§	X^§	X§	X°	√§	XX§	√§	√§
b. ArtReh	X	(√)	√	X	X	X	X	(√)	(√)	XX
2. PhRec	√	(√)	√	X	√	X	X	#	#	XX

A/V = Auditory/Visual input. PhS/WL/E = Phonological Similarity/Word Length Effect. PhJ-V = Phonological Judgements on Visual stimuli. RE = Recency Effect. A-R = Articulation Rate. √ = performance preserved/effect present. X = performance defective/effect absent. XX = maximal deficit. () = performance level reduced as compared with healthy participants. # = not assessed. § = assessed in PV; ^= assessed in PV also during articulatory suppression. °= not assessed in PV.

also Warrington et al., 1971) recall of auditorily presented verbal material, together with the preserved recency effect in free recall of visually presented verbal material (Vallar & Papagno, 1986) indicated that recency effects in immediate free recall of material presented in different modalities may result from the output of different stores. Previous studies in left-brain-damaged patients (KF, JB, WH) with a defective auditory-verbal STM had shown disproportionately reduced, but not entirely absent as in PV, recency effects in immediate free recall of auditory-verbal lists (Warrington et al., 1971). Furthermore, PV's preserved ability to recall the items' lists according to instructions requiring the explicit processing of temporal order (namely, "recall from end," "recall from beginning," in addition to "recall in any order you wish") draw a distinction between recall strategies, based on processing of temporal order (unimpaired in PV), and the specific stores to which they were applied (Vallar & Papagno, 1986). This conclusion was further corroborated by the finding that PV showed preserved long-term recency effects, in the free recall of anagram solutions (Vallar et al., 1991). Overall, these findings indicated that recency phenomena may occur in both STM and LTM retention conditions, and result from the application of ordinal retrieval strategies to the content of different stores. This, in case of brain damage, may bring about selective patterns of impairment, resulting from a deficit of specific storage systems, in patient PV's *PhSTS*, or of other stores or strategies (see Greene, 1986, for review).

3. Considering *Phonological STM*, and particularly the *PhSTS*, in the context of the language system, PV provided evidence for a role of this system in at least two main domains: a) sentence comprehension; and b) the acquisition of novel phonological entries, such as learning non-(new)words, unfamiliar to the patient.

   a. As for sentence comprehension, findings on patient PV by Vallar, Baddeley and Basso qualified the role of the input *PhSTS* in speech comprehension, for specific types of long sentences. On the one hand exceeding the disproportionately reduced capacity of the *PhSTS*, on the other hand requiring the preservation of their verbatim sequential content, in a phonological format, namely the linear arrangement of function and content words, since the mere lexical and semantic processing of elements of the sentence was not adequate to derive their meaning. This had been initially suggested by PV's (Basso et al., 1982) defective performance mainly in the last part (six) of the Token Test (De Renzi & Faglioni, 1978), that included the more complex instructions, and where word/item order was crucial for the appropriate comprehension of the command, in addition to lexical-semantic processing (e.g., "*Metta il cerchio rosso tra il quadrato giallo e quello verde*," "Put the red circle between the yellow square and that green one"). Furthermore, as visual presentation of the stimuli systematically evoked better memory performance than auditory presentation, the Token Test was administered to PV visually, with the commands being written on cards, and with an exposure time equal to the time necessary to present these commands orally. PV improved her performance from 23 (auditory presentation) to 28 out of 36, only marginally below the cut-off score (Basso et al., 1982). Since PV's visual STM was spared, this finding was compatible with the hypothesis of a possible role of a deficit of the *PhSTS* in PV's impairment in sentence comprehension, as revealed by her defective performance on the Token Test with auditory presentation. The successive studies by Vallar and Baddeley further elucidated these aspects. PV's comprehension of individual words and of short sentences was preserved, the latter tested both by sentence-picture matching and by the detection of syntactic or semantic anomalies. PV retained an intact capacity to detect semantic anomalies also when tested using long sentences, or prose passages. She retained some capacity for detecting syntactic anomalies even in long sentences, provided these were tested under conditions where such mismatches were very frequent; when they were embedded in more varied material, however, her performance deteriorated (Vallar & Baddeley, 1987, 1984b). Comprehension of long sentences was defective, whether presented visually or auditorily, when preservation of the specific wording was essential for understanding (Vallar & Baddeley, 1984b). Finally, when the syntactic anomaly involved an anaphoric mismatch across sentences, her performance dropped to chance level (Vallar & Baddeley, 1987).

b. As for the learning of novel words, such as words in a foreign language, that were actually nonwords, namely strings of letters, with no representation in PV's lexical-semantic system, her severe deficit in this type of learning indicated a role of *Phonological STM*, and specifically of the *PhSTS*, in language acquisition (Baddeley et al., 1998; Papagno et al., 1991; Papagno & Vallar, 1992). This was particularly in the building up of the phonological aspects of the lexicon (Jackendoff, 2002), such as in the acquisition of the first language by children (Gathercole et al., 1997), and of a second foreign language (Service, 1992). Finally, the role of *Phonological STM* in the acquisition of novel phonological strings qualified the view that material to be retained gains independent access to STM and LTM systems, that operate in a parallel fashion (Shallice & Warrington, 1970). This parallel architecture appears to be confined, as far as verbal stimuli are concerned, to words that have an available pre-existing representation in the lexical-semantic system. A similar pattern of impairment, with poor learning and memory for visual material confined to unfamiliar faces and objects (Hanley et al., 1990), was reported in a right-brain-damaged patient, ELD, who had a deficit in visuo-spatial STM, with a preserved *Phonological STM* (Hanley et al., 1991).

The evidence from patients PV and ELD indicated that, when unfamiliar material was to be learned, storage in the appropriate STM temporary retention systems was a first necessary stage for the learning and more stable storage in LTM systems to occur, supporting, in this case, a serial functional organization of STM and LTM (Atkinson & Shiffrin, 1971; Waugh & Norman, 1965). Taken together, the evidence from the learning of familiar (preserved) and unfamiliar (defective) items by patients with impaired verbal and visuo-spatial STM suggests that these systems come into play for learning and storage in LTM, when pre-existing representations of the material to be learned are not available in LTM. This overcomes the debate about serial *vs.* parallel organization of STM and LTM systems, favouring instead more flexible relationships.

Were there any relevant data that you did not manage to publish on this case?

We had no relevant unpublished data, except for the finding that PV's speech production appears to be completely normal as assessed by the distribution of pauses in spontaneous speech (Vallar, Vagges, Magno Caldognetto & Bottini, unpublished data).

Do you remember whether there were any issues that reviewers were particularly blunt about?

We had no major issues with the referees. In the following, I summarize some important suggestions made by the reviewers for three manuscripts, eventually published.

1. For the first study by Vallar and Baddeley (1984a), in the first submitted version of the manuscript we did not provide control data, considering that the available evidence from the literature about the effects of phonological similarity and word length in immediate serial recall was clear-cut enough (Baddeley et al., 1984, 1975). However, one referee wrote: "My most important misgiving about the paper is that no data are gathered from control subjects; rather, the authors compare the results obtained from a single patient with the pattern of results that is typically found in investigations in normal memory. Comparisons of this sort are potentially hazardous since factors that are idiosyncratic to a particular set of materials or procedures can be important, changing the pattern of results that would be found with normal..... It is here that a control subject that received the same lists would be useful." The Editor, Fergus Craik, strongly recommended that we collected such data from comparable Italian subjects (6–8 people). And we did so.

2. For the second study by Vallar and Baddeley (1984b), the referees and the Editor (Max Coltheart) asked that we discussed and argued in more detail our interpretation that PV's primary and only deficit involved the *PhSTS*, with the lack of use of a *per se* unimpaired *Rehearsal* being a strategy effect, contingent on the impairment of the *PhSTS*. Alternatively, PV could have suffered also from a primary deficit of *Rehearsal*, rather than from a strategic lack of use of it. Secondly, Coltheart asked us to explain PV's advantage in repeating words in a heard sentence (up to six items), as compared to span for unrelated words (less than three). Finally, the reviewers asked us to discuss in more detail the role of the *PhSTS* in sentence comprehension. In the revised and published version of the study, we discussed in detail our conclusion that PV did not have a deficit of subvocal *Rehearsal*:

   a. The span of unimpaired participants under conditions of articulatory suppression, that prevented the operation of *Rehearsal*, was much higher (about 5.75 digits) than that of PV (less than three digits).
   b. PV, as published STM patients (Warrington et al., 1971), and unlike neurologically unimpaired participants (e.g., Watkins & Watkins, 1977), had a higher visual-verbal span: this auditory-verbal, input-related, dissociation could be hardly traced back to the impairment of an output-related process such as *Rehearsal*.
   c. We lastly argued: "Finally, an interpretation of PV's disorder in terms of a subvocal rehearsal deficit requires an assumption as to the relationships between overt and covert articulation. In normal subjects there is a correlation between articulation rate, either silent or whispered, and memory span; accordingly, articulation rate may be used as a predictor of span (Baddeley et al., 1975; Standing et al., 1980). PV and three matched control subjects have comparable articulatory rates (Vallar & Baddeley, 1984a), but dramatically different digit spans-[PV: 2.0; controls: 6.67 (SD 0.58)]. Hence, an interpretation in terms of a subvocal rehearsal deficit has to assume a dissociation between a normal overt articulation and a grossly impaired covert articulation."
   d. As to the second issue raised by Max Coltheart, we argued that "PV's repetition defect involves different verbal items, ranging from sequences of digits, letters and words to sentences. As with normals, her sentence span (six words, eight syllables) is greater than her digit, letter or word span (two-three items). The three matched controls show the same pattern, but at a higher level of performance, sentence and digit span being 16.67 and 6.67 items respectively. These results may be interpreted by assuming that PV, like normal subjects, is able to use semantic coding to supplement her performance on a sentence repetition task, while semantics is likely to be less effective in the case of sequences of unrelated items. Similarly, Glanzer and Razel (1974) showed that more verbal items may

be retained in STM if they are organized in a sentence, as compared with sequences of unrelated words." Glanzer and Razel (1974) identified the verbal STS as a sentence processing unit.

e. While the finding of a defective *PhSTS* and an impairment of sentence comprehension is admittedly intrinsically weaker evidence than a dissociation (Vallar, 2000), regarding the causal relationships between these two deficits, we noted, "It is usually maintained that some form of short-term memory is important for comprehending speech (Baddeley & Hitch, 1974; Glanzer, 1972). Psycholinguists such as Clark and Clark (1977) proposed that a 'phonological working memory' retains the surface representation of a sentence for the time necessary to build its underlying representation [see Clark & Clark (1977) for a detailed discussion of the comprehension processes]. This is consistent with evidence that the verbatim content of sentences is retained in a short-term store (e.g., Sachs, 1967)." (*loc. cit.*, p. 125). Finally, in the conclusion of our study, also summarizing our results, we argued that: "This storage system may be impaired independently of the processes which provide phonological analysis of incoming auditory and visual information. A substantial deficit of the *PhSTS* does not affect comprehension of individual words and short sentences. Such a system becomes important for comprehending long sentences, whenever the temporary preservation of their verbatim content is necessary for extracting meaning. When the gist may be derived without retaining the specific wording, the importance of the *PhSTS* appears to be considerably less. This probably accounts for the observation that the STM patients usually show little evidence of comprehension deficit during ordinary conversation." (*loc. cit.*, p. 139). Since the link between impairments of the *PhSTS* (namely, a disproportionately reduced capacity of the system) and sentence comprehension deficits is that of an association between these deficits, that, furthermore, have been most investigated within the frame of separate theoretical domains (namely, memory, on the one hand, and language and aphasia research, on the other hand), it is not surprising that this area of PV's impairment raised discussions as to the more or less causal nature of this association of deficits (Caplan & Waters, 1999, and the discussion of this target article). Campbell and Butterworth (1985) reported a developmental deficit of phonological processing and STM in a female subject (RE) with no clearly definite neurological disorder ("At 6 years she may or may not have suffered a single petit-mal episode while she slept," p. 440, *loc. cit.*), who did not show any deficit of sentence comprehension, being however impaired on span and sentence repetition tasks (Butterworth et al., 1986). Vallar and Baddeley (1987) considered the evidence from this developmental case as dubiously relevant to the understanding of the functional architecture and operation of a normal system.

RE's development of the cognitive system might have been divergent in some aspects from an adult subject with no developmental deficits, but who instead (like PV) has a specific pattern of impairment after an acquired disorder, such as a stroke. A rejoinder (Howard & Butterworth, 1989), and a response (Vallar & Baddeley, 1989) followed. The available evidence from adult brain-damaged patients is mainly in support of a role of *Phonological STM* in aspects of sentence comprehension; there are however differences as to the precise type of sentential material whose comprehension is defective, although there is some agreement that these are complex and long, exceeding sentence span (Caramazza et al., 1981; see however Harris et al., 2014; McCarthy & Warrington, 1987; Papagno et al., 2007; Vallar & Baddeley, 1987, 1984b).

3. For the Vallar and Papagno (1986) manuscript about the effects of modality of input and strategies in free recall, and their relationships with the recency effect, the first submission, to the *Journal of Verbal Learning and Verbal Behavior*, was unsuccessful. While one referee did not raise any major problem ("The study is interesting and worth publishing"), the other one wrote: "Free recall is an inherently uncontrolled experimental procedure, and therefore not very useful as an analytic tool. There is just no good way to unconfound encoding strategies (which can vary even within subjects, by modality and/or serial position), retrieval strategies (which place retention intervals of individual items under the subject's control), and who knows what else. I think this was a poor idea in the first place. There are plenty of well-controlled methodologies for studying memory; if you want to figure it out what is wrong with P.V., use them in combination or invent new ones, but don't use free recall." The manuscript was then submitted to *Brain and Cognition*: here the opinions of two reviewers were positive, asking for more information and details about the functional model of reference, and the manuscript was accepted by the Editor, Alfonso Caramazza, with minor revisions.

Are there any assessments/paradigms that you would administer now to this individual if she was available?

At the behavioural level, I would probably investigate in further detail sentence comprehension, since this, as noted in the response to the previous questions, has proven to be a controversial issue, mainly arising from the fact that our finding was one of an *association* between two deficits (i.e., severely reduced auditory-verbal span *and* defective comprehension of certain long and complex sentences).

At the neural level, I would attempt to obtain better imaging, both structural (MRI, DTI) and functional (fMRI) (Passaro et al., 2016; Stamatakis et al., 2015), of PV's lesion and her residual neural activity during STM tasks (patient JB; Paulesu et al., 2017). Her lesion, as assessed by CT scan, was very extensive perisylvian damage (Basso et al., 1982).

In addition to the CT images, we had obtained evidence from an experiment in which, immediately after the central fixation-point, the memory stimulus was to the left or to the right of fixation. PV had no visual half-field deficits, and could, therefore, perform the task, that required her to recall the presented stimuli at various filled or unfilled retention intervals. The lateral presentation of the stimuli, with a short exposure time, prevented gaze movements to bring the stimulus into central fixation and, therefore, allowing processing by both hemispheres. Under these conditions, stimuli presented in the right visual half-field are first processed by the left hemisphere, stimuli presented in the left visual half-field by the right hemisphere (Bryden, 1982). PV could recall a single consonant for an unfilled delay of up to 15 sec with no errors, and with 90% to 100% of correct responses when the retention interval was filled by counting back in threes from a two-digit number at the rate of one per sec. With two and three consonants, PV showed an overall advantage for the right visual-half field/left hemisphere over the left visual-half field/right hemisphere, as unimpaired participants do with visually presented verbal material in a Brown-Peterson paradigm (Parravicini et al., 1981; Peterson & Peterson, 1959, for the original description of the paradigm). With two consonants, in the unfilled delay condition, PV recalled 57 out of 60 digrams presented in the right visual half-field, and 46 out of 60 digrams presented in the left visual half-field ($\chi 2 = 8.29$, d.f. $= 1$, $P < 0.004$). In May 1980, Tim Shallice and I administered this test to patient JB (Shallice & Butterworth, 1977; Warrington et al., 1971), in the Neuropsychology Laboratory of The National Hospital for Nervous and Mental Diseases, Queen Square, London, UK. JB was willing to take part in the study; JB, as PV, showed a right visual half-field/left hemisphere advantage (Basso et al., 1982, see note on p. 272), recalling 46 out of 60 digrams presented in the right visual half-field, and 31 out of 60 in the left visual-half field ($\chi 2 = 8.15$, d.f. $= 1$, $P < 0.005$), as shown in Figure 13.5. We concluded that processing and STM retention of visual-verbal material by PV, as by JB, was supported by the left hemisphere, as in neurologically unimpaired right-handed participants (Basso et al., 1982). We also speculated, based on the discrepancy between PV's extensive perisylvian lesion, involving the language area (Cappa & Vignolo, 1999) and her mild deficits, basically confined to the *PhSTS* component of Phonological STM, that PV might have had a bilateral representation of language function, finding (admittedly weak) support for this conclusion in the fact that, although PV and her two sons were right-handed, a cousin was left-handed. We concluded that

> all these considerations however must be regarded with great caution: as due to ethical reasons P.V. did not undergo a Wada Test or a unilateral ECT Test (Pratt and Warrington, 1972), we cannot rule out the possibility that functional reorganization of language occurred within the left hemisphere or that both hemispheres are involved in the residual speech performance.
>
> *(loc. cit., p. 273)*

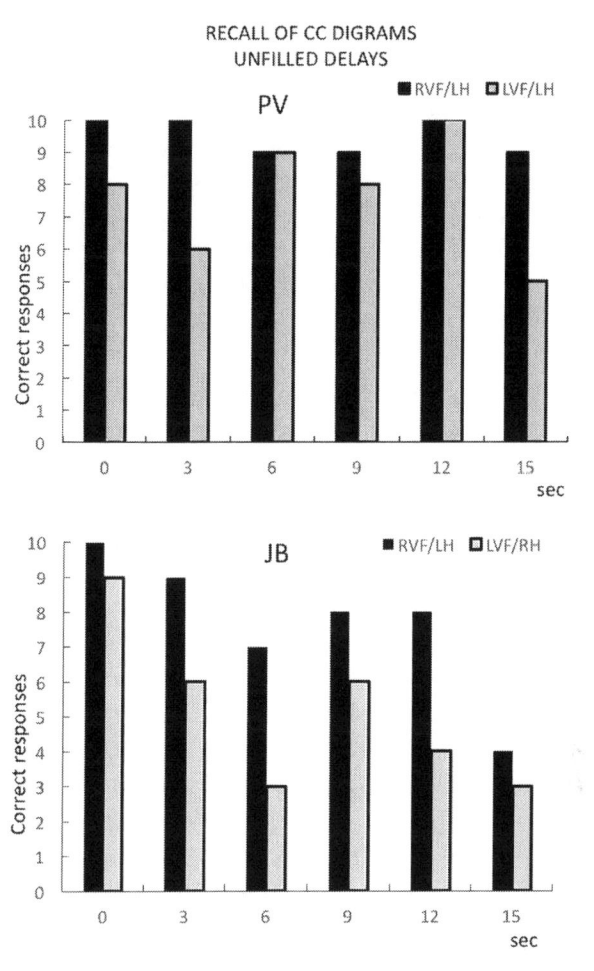

FIGURE 13.5 Short-term recall of two-consonant (CC) digrams by patients PV (data from Basso et al., 1982), and JB (see Basso et al., 1982, p. 272, footnote, with permission of Tim Shallice). Immediately after a central fixation-point (a black dot) had been exposed for 1500 msec, a CC digram was shown for 100 msec 3.5° to the left or to the right of the fixation-point. At each memory delay (0, 3, 6, 9, 12 and 15 seconds), 10 CC stimuli (10 in the left visual-half field/right hemisphere, and 10 in the right visual-half field/left hemisphere) were presented. The patients' task was to recall at the different retention intervals the CC presented in each half-field, in a random fixed order. The permission of Tim Shallice to publish this note is gratefully acknowledged.

You first reported this case in the 1980s. Do you think this case is still informative now? Are we now better able to interpret her pattern of spared and impaired abilities? If so, in what way?

My view is that the case of PV is still informative as to the effects of a selective deficit in a specific component of memory. Considering the subsequent publications on these topics, I would maintain the interpretation offered by Basso et al. (1982) and subsequently refined by Vallar and Baddeley (1984a, b). Within this framework (Baddeley, 2003; Vallar, 2006), also deficits of *Rehearsal* (Vallar et al., 1997) and of *Phonological Recoding* (Vallar & Cappa, 1987) have been analysed and interpreted.

Do you think this case has been considered by people who develop theories of the normal mind? If yes, how? If no, should she?

I have extensively given a positive response ("yes!") in the previous questions. The case of PV was acknowledged as relevant to our understanding of human memory, and to the relationships of specific components of it (*Phonological STM*) and other cognitive processes such as language. This is demonstrated in my response to previous questions, where I discuss the comments made by some referees, students of normal human memory, such as Robert Crowder, and a chapter on PV as a classic case in neuropsychology (Martin, 2003).

In general, do you think that neuropsychology single cases could contribute to our understanding of the normal mind? Should this data be considered and if so why?

My view, as witnessed by my own work is: "yes"! But with a *proviso*. They should be "pure" cases, as PV was. Basso et al. (1982, p. 272) wrote: "To the best of our knowledge, the present case, together with case J. B., is the only published case where a "pure" (i.e., with nearly no associated language disorders) STM defect was shown." "Pure" cases, namely patients with discrete and specific patterns of functional impairment, allow shedding of a more definite beam of light on the deranged function of damaged systems, and, by implication, on the function, normally operating, of the undamaged systems. The cognitive system is very complex and includes many interactive components (Shallice, 1988; Vallar, 2000). The more selective the functional deficit is, the less confounding effects due to damage to other components of the cognitive system need to be teased apart, so the results are the clearest they can be. Also, selective and pure deficits may allow better control, and understanding, of compensatory strategies, as, for instance, in PV's case, of the role of retrieval strategies in the recency effect and free recall (Vallar & Papagno, 1986).

We are now living in an era where ethics committees would like to foresee every step. How much serendipity was involved in your assessment?

Our investigations were not invasive at all, only behavioural. In the 1980s, no Ethics Committees were involved in this type of study. However, each experiment was planned in detail in advance, based on specific memory models and available paradigms we considered appropriate and suitable for PV (see Figure 13.3 for an example of such planning). We asked for consent from PV before each testing session. We explained that the experiments were mainly performed to elucidate the architecture of the memory systems, and, in the future, to possibly develop better diagnostic and rehabilitation procedures, although they might prove to be useful for her as behavioural training. No physical or psychological harm or risk for PV was predicted. PV agreed with these explanations and was always happy to take part in the experiments. PV was aware of her deficit, although not in terms of the specific damaged component of STM (namely, the *PhSTS*) until this was explained to her in plain words. I take advantage of this interview to express my gratitude to PV for her participation in our studies with such commitment, understanding and goodwill.

References

Atkinson, R. C., & Shiffrin, R. M. (1971). The control of short-term memory. *Scientific American*, *225*, 82–90.
Baddeley, A. D. (1976). *The Psychology of Memory*. New York: Basic Books Inc.
Baddeley, A. D. (2003). Working memory: looking back and looking forward. *Nature Reviews Neuroscience*, *4*, 829–839.
Baddeley, A. D., Gathercole, S. E., & Papagno, C. (1998). The phonological loop as a language learning device. *Psychological Review*, *105*, 158–173.
Baddeley, A. D., & Hitch, G. J. (1974). Working memory. In G. H. Bower (Ed.), *The Psychology of Learning and Motivation. Advances in Research and Theory*, Vol. 8. New York: Academic Press, pp. 47–89.
Baddeley, A. D., Lewis, V., & Vallar, G. (1984). Exploring the articulatory loop. *Quarterly Journal of Experimental Psychology*, *36A*, 233–252.
Baddeley, A. D., Papagno, C., & Vallar, G. (1988). When long-term learning depends on short-term storage. *Journal of Memory and Language*, *27*, 586–595.
Baddeley, A. D., Thomson, N., & Buchanan, M. (1975). Word length and the structure of short-term memory. *Journal of Verbal Learning and Verbal Behavior*, *14*, 575–589.
Basso, A., Capitani, E., & Laiacona, M. (1987). Raven's coloured progressive matrices: normative values on 305 adult normal controls. *Functional Neurology*, *2*, 189–194.
Basso, A., Capitani, E., & Vignolo, L. A. (1979). Influence of rehabilitation on language skills in aphasic patients. A controlled study. *Archives of Neurology*, *36*, 190–196.

Basso, A., Spinnler, H., Vallar, G., & Zanobio, M. E. (1982). Left hemisphere damage and selective impairment of auditory verbal short-term memory. A case study. *Neuropsychologia, 20,* 263–274.

Berrini, R., Della Sala, S., Spinnler, H., Sterzi, R., & Vallar, G. (1982). In eliciting hemisphere asymmetries which is more important: the stimulus input side or the recognition side? A tachistoscopic study on normals. *Neuropsychologia, 20,* 91–94.

Bisiach, E., & Luzzatti, C. (1978). Unilateral neglect of representational space. *Cortex, 14,* 129–133.

Bjork, R. A., & Whitten, W. B. (1974). Recency-sensitive retrieval processes in long-term free recall. *Cognitive Psychology, 6,* 173–189.

Boller, F. (2006). Modern neuropsychology in France: Henry Hècaen (1912–1983) and the Sainte-Anne Hospital. *Cortex, 42,* 1061–1063.

Boller, F., Gainotti, G., Grossi, D., & Vallar, G. (2016). History of Italian Neuropsychology. In W. Barr & L. A. Bielauskas (Eds.), *The Oxford Handbook of History of Clinical Neuropsychology,* pp. 1–59. Oxford, UK: Oxford University Press.

Bryden, M. P. (1982). *Laterality. Functional Asymmetry in the Intact Brain.* New York: Academic Press.

Butterworth, B., Campbell, R., & Howard, D. (1986). The uses of short-term memory: a case study. *Quarterly Journal of Experimental Psychology, 38A,* 705–737.

Campbell, R., & Butterworth, B. (1985). Phonological dyslexia and dysgraphia in a highly literate subject: a developmental case with associated deficits of phonemic processing and awareness. *Quarterly Journal of Experimental Psychology, 37A,* 435–475.

Capitani, E., Spinnler, H. R., Sterzi, R., & Vallar, G. (1980). The hemispheric side of neocortical damage does not affect memory for unidimensional position. An experiment with Posner and Konick's test. *Cortex, 16,* 295–304.

Caplan, D., & Waters, G. S. (1999). Verbal working memory and sentence comprehension. *The Behavioral and Brain Sciences, 22,* 77–94.

Cappa, S. F., & Vignolo, L. A. (1999). The neurological foundations of language. In G. Denes & L. Pizzamiglio (Eds.), *Handbook of Clinical and Experimental Neuropsychology.* Hove, East Sussex: Psychology Press, pp. 155–179.

Caramazza, A., Basili, A. G., Koller, J. J., & Berndt, R. S. (1981). An investigation of repetition and language processing in a case of conduction aphasia. *Brain and Language, 14,* 235–271.

Caramazza, A., Miceli, G., & Villa, G. (1986). The role of the (output) phonological buffer in reading, writing, and repetition. *Cognitive Neuropsychology, 3,* 37–76.

Clark, H. H., & Clark, E. (1977). *Psychology and Language. An Introduction to Psycholinguistics.* New York: Harcourt Brace Jovanovich.

Crowder, R. G. (1976). *Principles of Learning and Memory.* Hillsdale, NJ: Lawrence Erlbaum.

Davelaar, E. J., Goshen-Gottstein, Y., Ashkenazi, A., Haarmann, H. J., & Usher, M. (2005). The demise of short-term memory revisited: empirical and computational investigations of recency effects. *Psychological Review, 112,* 3–42.

De Renzi, E., & Faglioni, P. (1978). Normative data and screening power of a shortened version of the Token Test. *Cortex, 14,* 41–49.

Gathercole, S. E., Hitch, G. J., Service, E., & Martin, A. J. (1997). Phonological short-term memory and new word learning in children. *Developmental Psychology, 33,* 966–979.

Glanzer, M. (1972). Storage mechanisms in recall. In G. H. Bower (Ed.), *The Psychology of Learning and Motivation. Advances in Research and Theory,* Vol. 5. New York: Academic Press, pp. 129–193.

Glanzer, M., & Cunitz, A. R. (1966). Two storage mechanisms in free recall. *Journal of Verbal Learning and Verbal Behavior, 5*, 351–360.

Glanzer, M., & Razel, M. (1974). The size of the unit in short-term storage. *Journal of Verbal Learning and Verbal Behavior, 13*, 114–131.

Greene, R. L. (1986). Sources of recency effects in free recall. *Psychological Bulletin, 99*, 221–228.

Hanley, J. R., Pearson, N. A., & Young, A. W. (1990). Impaired memory for new visual forms. *Brain, 113*, 1131–1148.

Hanley, J. R., Young, A. W., & Pearson, N. A. (1991). Impairment of the visuo-spatial sketch pad. *The Quarterly Journal of Experimental Psychology, 43A*, 101–125.

Harris, L., Olson, A., & Humphreys, G. (2014). The link between STM and sentence comprehension: a neuropsychological rehabilitation study. *Neuropsychological Rehabilitation, 24*, 678–720.

Howard, D., & Butterworth, B. (1989). Short-term memory and sentence comprehension: a reply to Vallar and Baddeley, 1987. *Cognitive Neuropsychology, 6*, 455–463.

Jackendoff, R. S. (2002). *Foundations of Language: Brain, Meaning, Grammar, and Evolution.* Oxford: Oxford University Press.

Jacquemot, C., & Scott, S. K. (2006). What is the relationship between phonological short-term memory and speech processing? *Trends in Cognitive Sciences, 10*, 480–486.

Kroll, J. F., & De Groot, A. M. B. (2005). *Handbook of Bilingualism: Psycholinguistic Approaches.* Oxford: Oxford University Press.

Martin, N. (2003). PV and JB: two cognitive neuropsychological studies of phonological STM impairment and their impact on theories of language and memory. In C. Code, C.-W. Wallesch, Y. Joanette, & A. R. Lecours (Eds.), *Classic Cases in Neuropsychology. Vol. II.* Hove and New York: Psychology Press. Taylor & Francis Group, pp. 19–36.

Martin, R. C. (2006). The neuropsychology of sentence processing: where do we stand? *Cognitive Neuropsychology, 23(1)*, 74–95.

McCarthy, R. A., & Warrington, E. K. (1987). Understanding: a function of short-term memory? *Brain, 110*, 1565–1578.

Murray, D. J. (1968). Articulation and acoustic confusability in short-term memory. *Journal of Experimental Psychology, 78*, 679–684.

Nolan, K. A., & Caramazza, A. (1982). Modality-independent impairments in word processing in a deep dyslexic patient. *Brain and Language, 16*, 237–264.

Oldfield, R. C. (1971). The assessment and analysis of handedness: the Edinburgh inventory. *Neuropsychologia, 9*, 97–113.

Papagno, C., & Cecchetto, C. (2018). Is STM involved in sentence comprehension? *Cortex*, in press.

Papagno, C., Cecchetto, C., Reati, F., & Bello, L. (2007). Processing of syntactically complex sentences relies on verbal short-term memory: evidence from a short-term memory patient. *Cognitive Neuropsychology, 24*, 292–311.

Papagno, C., Valentine, T., & Baddeley, A. D. (1991). Phonological short-term memory and foreign language vocabulary learning. *Journal of Memory and Language, 30*, 331–347.

Papagno, C., & Vallar, G. (1992). Phonological short-term memory and the learning of novel words: the effect of phonological similarity and item length. *Quarterly Journal of Experimental Psychology, 44A*, 47–67.

Papagno, C., & Vallar, G. (1995). To learn or not to learn vocabulary in foreign languages: the problem with phonological memory. In R. Campbell & M. Conway (Eds.), *Broken Memories*. Oxford: Basil Blackwell, pp. 334–343.

Parravicini, C., Spinnler, H., Sterzi, R., & Vallar, G. (1981). Counting back from a visually presented digit increases recall asymmetries between hemispheres: a Brown-Peterson experiment with lateral projection of trigrams. *Cortex, 17,* 279–289.

Passaro, A., Christidi, F., Tsirka, V., & Papanicolaou, A. C. (2016). In A. C. Papanicolau (Ed.), *The Oxford Handbook of Functional Brain Imaging in Neuropsychology and Cognitive Neurosciences*. Oxford: Oxford University Press, pp. 1–88.

Paulesu, E., Shallice, T., Danelli, L., Sberna, M., Frackowiak, R. S. J., & Frith, C. D. (2017). Anatomical modularity of verbal working memory? Functional anatomical evidence from a famous patient with short-term memory deficits. *Frontiers in Human Neuroscience, 11(231),* 1–16.

Perani, D. (2005). The neural basis of language talent in bilinguals. *Trends in Cognitive Sciences, 9(5),* 211–213.

Peterson, L. R., & Peterson, M. J. (1959). Short-term retention of individual verbal items. *Journal of Experimental Psychology, 58,* 193–198.

Phillips, W. A., & Christie, D. F. (1977). Interference with visualization. *Quarterly Journal of Experimental Psychology, 29,* 637–650.

Postman, L., & Phillips, L. W. (1965). Short-term temporal changes in free recall. *Quarterly Journal of Experimental Psychology, 17,* 132–138.

Pratt, R. T. C., & Warrington, E. K. (1972). The assessment of cerebral dominance with unilateral ECT. *The British Journal of Psychiatry, 121,* 327–328.

Sachs, J. S. (1967). Recopition memory for syntactic and semantic aspects of connected discourse. *Perception & Psychophysics, 2,* 437–442.

Saffran, E. M., & Marin, O. S. M. (1975). Immediate memory for word lists and sentences in a patient with deficient auditory short-term memory. *Brain and Language, 2,* 420–433.

Salamè, P., & Baddeley, A. D. (1982). Disruption of short-term memory by unattended speech: implications for the structure of working memory. *Journal of Verbal Learning and Verbal Behavior, 21,* 150–164.

Service, E. (1992). Phonology, working memory, and foreign-language learning. *The Quarterly Journal of Experimental Psychology, 45A,* 21–50.

Shallice, T. (1988). *From Neuropsychology to Mental Structure*. Cambridge: Cambridge University Press.

Shallice, T., & Butterworth, B. (1977). Short-term memory impairment and spontaneous speech. *Neuropsychologia, 15,* 729–735.

Shallice, T., & Warrington, E. K. (1970). Independent functioning of verbal memory stores: a neuropsychological study. *Quarterly Journal of Experimental Psychology, 22,* 261–273.

Spinnler, H. R., Sterzi, R., Tobaldini, L., & Vallar, G. (1982). Dissociation between normal hemispheres in delayed recognition of verbal and spatial cues of the same visual pattern. *Behavioural Brain Research, 6,* 227–236.

Spinnler, H. R., Sterzi, R., & Vallar, G. (1977). *Le Amnesie*. Milano: Franco Angeli.

Stamatakis, E. A., Orfanidou, E., & Papanicolaou, A. C. (2015). Functional magnetic resonance imaging. In A. C. Papanicolaou (Ed.), *The Oxford Handbook of Functional Brain Imaging in Neuropsychology and Cognitive Neurosciences*. Oxford: Oxford University Press, pp. 1–27.

Standing, L., Bond, B., Smith, P., & Isely, C. (1980). Is the immediate memory span determined by subvocalization rate? *British Journal of Psychology, 71,* 525.

Vallar, G. (2000). The methodological foundations of human neuropsychology: studies in brain-damaged patients. In F. Boller, J. Grafman & G. Rizzolatti (Eds.), *Handbook of Neuropsychology,* Vol. 1. Amsterdam, The Netherlands: Elsevier, pp. 305–344.

Vallar, G. (2006). Memory systems: the case of phonological short-term memory. A festschrift for cognitive neuropsychology. *Cognitive Neuropsychology, 23*, 135–155.
Vallar, G. (2015). Short-term memory: psychological and neural aspects. In J. D. Wright (Ed.), *International Encyclopedia of the Social & Behavioral Sciences. Vol. 21*, (2nd ed.). Oxford: Elsevier, pp. 909–916.
Vallar, G. (2017). Short-term memory. In E. Rolls (Ed.), *Reference Module in Neuroscience and Biobehavioral Psychology*. Amsterdam: Elsevier.
Vallar, G., & Baddeley, A. D. (1982). Short-term forgetting and the articulatory loop. *Quarterly Journal of Experimental Psychology, 34*, 53–60.
Vallar, G., & Baddeley, A. D. (1984a). Fractionation of working memory: neuropsychological evidence for a phonological short-term store. *Journal of Verbal Learning and Verbal Behavior, 23*, 151–161.
Vallar, G., & Baddeley, A. D. (1984b). Phonological short-term store, phonological processing and sentence comprehension. *Cognitive Neuropsychology, 1*, 121–141.
Vallar, G., & Baddeley, A. D. (1987). Phonological short-term store and sentence processing. *Cognitive Neuropsychology, 4*, 417–438.
Vallar, G., & Baddeley, A. D. (1989). Developmental disorders of verbal short-term memory and their relation to sentence comprehension: a reply to Howard and Butterworth. *Cognitive Neuropsychology, 6*, 465–473.
Vallar, G., & Cappa, S. F. (1987). Articulation and verbal short-term memory. Evidence from anarthria. *Cognitive Neuropsychology, 4*, 55–78.
Vallar, G., Di Betta, A. M., & Silveri, M. C. (1997). The phonological short-term store-rehearsal system: patterns of impairment and neural correlates. *Neuropsychologia, 35*, 795–812.
Vallar, G., & Papagno, C. (1986). Phonological short-term store and the nature of the recency effect: evidence from neuropsychology. *Brain and Cognition, 5*, 428–442.
Vallar, G., & Papagno, C. (2002). Neuropsychological impairments of verbal short-term memory. In A. Baddeley, B. Wilson & M. Kopelman (Eds.), *Handbook of Memory Disorders*. Chichester, England: Wiley, pp. 249–270.
Vallar, G., Papagno, C., & Baddeley, A. D. (1991). Long-term recency effects and phonological short-term memory. A neuropsychological case study. *Cortex, 27*, 323–326.
Warrington, E. K., Logue, V., & Pratt, R. T. C. (1971). The anatomical localisation of selective impairment of auditory verbal short-term memory. *Neuropsychologia, 9*, 377–387.
Warrington, E. K., & Shallice, T. (1969). The selective impairment of auditory-verbal short-term memory. *Brain, 92*, 885–896.
Warrington, E. K., & Shallice, T. (1972). Neuropsychological evidence of visual storage in short-term memory tasks. *Quarterly Journal of Experimental Psychology, 24*, 30–40.
Warrington, E. K., & Shallice, T. (1979). Semantic access dyslexia. *Brain, 102*, 43–63.
Watkins, O. C., & Watkins, M. J. (1977). Serial recall and the modality effect: effects of word frequency. *Journal of Experimental Psychology: Human Learning and Memory, 3*, 712–718.
Watkins, O. C., & Watkins, M. J. (1980). The modality effect and echoic persistence. *Journal of Experimental Psychology: General, 109*, 251–278.
Waugh, N., & Norman, D. A. (1965). Primary memory. *Psychological Review, 72*, 89–1104.

14
SEMANTIC SHORT-TERM MEMORY AND ITS ROLE IN SENTENCE PROCESSING AND LONG-TERM MEMORY

Evidence From Cases AB and ML

Randi C. Martin

In 1994, you and your colleagues first discuss the case of AB who showed evidence of a short-term memory deficit for maintaining semantic information. In 1996, you reported another case, ML, who showed a similar STM pattern. Firstly, can you provide us with some background information about AB and ML?

AB was referred to my lab in the late 1980s and ML in the early 1990s by speech pathologists at local hospitals to participate in my ongoing studies on sentence comprehension deficits in aphasia. AB had completed a law degree and was a practicing lawyer when in 1979, at the age of 59, he began to experience intermittent right hemiparesis and slurring of speech. He was operated on for a left frontal hematoma. Following the operation, he had a dense global aphasia which later resolved to mildly nonfluent speech and a mild comprehension deficit on clinical assessment. In 1990, at the age of 50, ML had a left hemisphere stroke. Following the stroke, his clinical assessment indicated he had generally good language comprehension but a slowed speech rate. He had completed two years of college and had been employed as a draftsman. For both, clinical CT scans indicated damage to left posterior inferior frontal regions and to the adjacent parietal cortex. It should be noted that a later research MRI scan for ML indicated more extensive left frontal and parietal damage, though a general sparing of the temporal lobe.

Both men were functioning at a high level when they began participating in my research studies, living on their own, doing their own shopping, and arranging their own transportation, though neither had been able to continue in his profession. Both were a pleasure to work with as they were generally pleasant and optimistic and worked hard to do their best on the testing. ML particularly enjoyed being part of the research and would sometimes show up at the lab unannounced, asking if any study was in progress that he could take part in. He liked to stay in contact with the members of the lab, mailing us newspaper clippings, usually on topics related to the brain and brain disorders. After his participation in what he thought was a particularly challenging grammaticality judgement task, he mailed us a cartoon showing Tweety Bird being corrected by a teacher for an error in his sentence diagram for "I tawt I taw a puddy tat."

How did you first realize that these cases were interesting?

In my research program at the time, I was interested in studying the relation between short-term memory (STM) and sentence comprehension. All participants were given a battery of STM tests manipulating variables previously demonstrated to be relevant to verbal memory span—that is, phonological similarity, word length, lexical status (word vs. nonwords), and visual vs. auditory presentation, with the goal of determining whether any deficits could be attributed to disruptions of phonological storage or articulatory rehearsal. The principal question was whether these two sources of a STM deficit might have differential effects on sentence comprehension (Martin, 1987). Previously, patients had been reported from other labs who showed evidence of a deficit in phonological storage, demonstrating very reduced span, an absence of standard phonological similarity and word length effects (at least with visual presentation), and better performance with visual than auditory input (see Shallice & Vallar, 1990, for a review). Patient EA from our lab demonstrated this pattern (Martin, Shelton & Yaffee, 1994). In addition, she showed very poor recall of nonword lists relative to word lists. In fact, she had difficulty repeating a single nonword if it had contained more than three phonemes, though her single word repetition was excellent for words of varying lengths.

AB's pattern of performance on this set of memory span tasks was hard to interpret within this framework of possible damage to phonological storage and articulatory components. His memory span was similar to that of EA, but he showed phonological similarity and word length effects with both auditory and visual presentation, and better performance with auditory than visual lists, suggesting that he was able to retain phonological codes. An unusual and striking feature of his performance was that he showed no advantage for word over nonwords lists (Martin et al., 1994). This last finding suggested that he did not benefit from the semantic information in the words. ML demonstrated a very similar pattern as AB on span tasks (Martin & He, 2004). (See Figure 14.1) Thus, these patients were interesting in that their pattern of performance did not fit with models of verbal STM that focused on phonological retention. The lack of advantage for words over nonwords suggested instead that they had difficulty

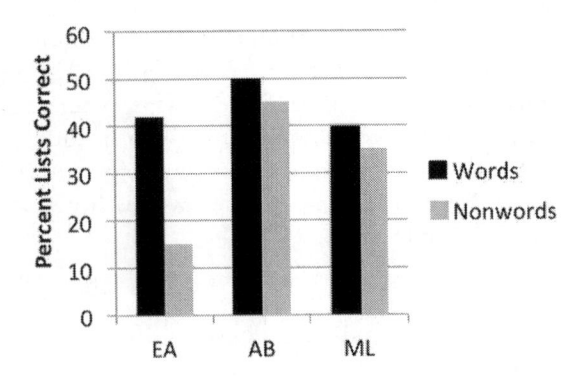

FIGURE 14.1 Percent lists correct for two- and three-item word and nonword lists. Based on data reported in Martin and He (2004).

maintaining semantic information, while their ability to maintain phonological information was relatively preserved.

Can you summarize the main features of these cases?

Both AB and ML performed at a normal level on standardized picture naming tests and above the mean for controls on standardized measures of word comprehension (Martin et al., 1994). Thus, their hypothesized deficits in maintaining semantic information could not be readily attributed to impaired semantic knowledge per se. We devised category probe vs. rhyme probe tasks as another means of providing evidence about their semantic vs. phonological STM abilities. In the category probe task, individuals heard a list of words and judged whether the probe was in the same category as any list item. On the rhyme probe task, they judged whether a probe word rhymed with any list item. In line with the supposition that AB had a deficit in semantic retention whereas EA had a phonological STM deficit, AB performed better than EA on the rhyme probe task and EA performed better than AB on the category probe task (Martin et al., 1994). ML basically replicated the pattern of STM performance exhibited by AB (Martin & He, 2004).

What were these cases' patterns of spared and impaired abilities?

The pattern of spared and impaired abilities for verbal STM for AB and ML relative to EA was described in answer to the preceding questions. Here I will focus on their sentence processing abilities, including sentence repetition, comprehension, and production. On a sentence repetition task for complex sentences, AB showed much better verbatim repetition than did EA, making generally single word omission or substitution errors. In contrast, patient EA, with the phonological STM deficit, often paraphrased the sentences, preserving meaning but changing the wording considerably (Martin et al., 1994). To assess sentence comprehension, we administered an attribute judgement task similar to one developed by Warrington and McCarthy (1987), which employed spoken questions such as "Which is quiet, a concert or a library?" AB was dramatically impaired on this task (Martin et al., 1994). He provided a correct answer on only 20% of the trials and produced no answer on the rest, refusing to guess when he was unsure. In contrast, patient EA's performance on the same materials was 100% correct. AB's poor performance could not be attributed to a lack of knowledge of the nouns and their attributes. When the questions were shortened slightly to include only one of the nouns (e.g., "Is a library quiet?"), he performed at 100% correct. With the original questions presented visually with unlimited viewing time to minimize STM load, he also obtained 100% correct. ML performed similarly to AB, though doing somewhat better on the original spoken questions, scoring 65% correct (Martin & He, 2004). He scored 88% correct on the shortened auditory questions and 100% on the written longer questions. Thus, both AB and ML had great difficulty maintaining the meanings of one adjective and two nouns in order to answer the spoken questions. Their difficulty could not be attributed to generally reduced span, as EA performed perfectly on this task. Her severe phonological STM deficit did not prevent her from being able to maintain these meanings in order to make the appropriate comparisons and answer the questions.

A subsequent sentence comprehension test specifically manipulated the amount of lexical-semantic information that had to be maintained prior to integration of word meanings during sentence comprehension (Martin & Romani, 1994). The sentences either had from one to three adjectives appearing before or after a noun (e.g., "The rusty, old, red, swimsuit" vs. "the swimsuit was old, red, and rusty") or from one to three nouns appearing before or after a verb (e.g., "Rugs, vases, and mirrors cracked during the move" vs. "The movers cracked the vases, mirrors, and rugs"). The motivation for these manipulations was that in the "before" condition, as the number of adjectives or number of nouns increased, an increasing number of unintegrated word meanings would have to be retained whereas in the "after" condition, each word could be integrated immediately. That is, for the adjectives, individual adjective meanings would have to be maintained in the "before" until the noun was processed, whereas in the "after" condition, each adjective could be integrated with the noun as it was heard. Similarly for the nouns, in the "before" condition, the role of the nouns with respect to the verb (e.g., agent, theme, location) could not be determined until the verb was processed, whereas in the "after" condition the role of each noun could be determined immediately. If sentence comprehension deficits caused by a semantic STM deficit related solely to the number of content words in a sentence, no difference between the before and after conditions should be found. On the other hand, if it is the number of unintegrated words meanings that is important, then performance should be worse in the before than the after condition. We found that the latter was the case. Relative to controls, both AB and ML performed close to chance for two to three adjectives before the noun or two to three nouns before the verb, but at a high level with only one adjective or one noun. In the "after condition," they also performed at a high level and showed little effect of the number of adjectives. EA, in contrast, showed an effect of the "before–after" manipulation that was within the range of controls. (See Figure 14.2) These results suggested that prior to integration, retention of word meanings depended on the STM capacity that was damaged for AB and ML. However, once the information could be chunked, the load on semantic STM was reduced. Interestingly, on grammaticality judgement tests that manipulated the distance intervening between two words signalling a grammatical error on several different sentence types (e.g., "The hopeful young contestants didn't win and neither ★was their rather aggressive competitor" vs. "Susan didn't leave despite many hints from her tired hosts and neither ★was Mary"), neither AB or ML showed a significant effect of distance. Thus, the retention of syntactic information across intervening words did not appear to be affected by their semantic STM deficit.

Later studies examined the effects of these patients' semantic STM deficit on language production (e.g., Martin & Freedman, 2001; Martin, Miller & Vu, 2004; Freedman, Martin & Biegler, 2004). Martin and Freedman assessed their ability to produce adjective-noun phrases, manipulating the number of adjectives to be produced in an adjective-noun phrase (e.g., blonde hair, curly blonde hair) or

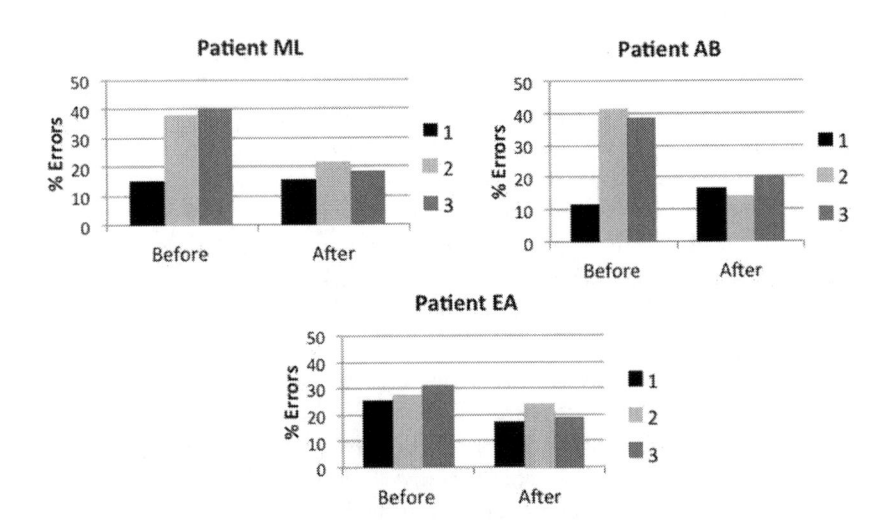

FIGURE 14.2   Percent errors on sentence anomaly judgement task for delayed (before) vs. immediate (after) integration with 1–3 adjectives before or after a noun or 1–3 nouns before or after a verb. Based on data reported in Martin and Romani (1994) and Martin and He (2004).

FIGURE 14.3 Picture stimuli for eliciting adjective-adjective N phrases ("long, curly hair"). Short-term retention of lexical-semantic representations: Implications for speech production. Martin, R. C., & Freedman, M. L. (2001). Taylor & Francis Ltd, reprinted by permission of Taylor & Francis Ltd (www.tandfonline.com).

in a sentence (e.g., the hair is blonde, the hair is curly and blonde). (See Figure 14.3 for example stimuli for eliciting adjective-adjective noun production.) As shown in Table 14.1, we found that AB and ML struggled to produce the phrases, even with a single adjective, often producing parts of the utterance separately. For example, when attempting to produce "small leaf," AB said, "It's a leaf. It's small." ML often worked his way towards the correct utterance. When attempting to produce "small rough leaf," he said, "small, . . . small . . . rough, rough leaf . . . small, rough leaf." Both patients did significantly better in producing the sentences than the phrases. EA performed within the normal range for both phrases and sentences. We interpreted these findings as suggesting that advance planning during production occurs at a phrasal level and that semantic STM is used to plan the content words in phrases prior to articulation. Sentences could be more easily produced because each phrase had fewer content words. The good performance for patient EA suggested either that advance planning at the phonological level has a much smaller scope (e.g., see Wheeldon & Lahiri, 2002) or there are

TABLE 14.1 Percent correct producing single adjectives and nouns and adjective-noun phrases. (Numbers in parentheses are percent correct after self-correction). Short-term retention of lexical-semantic representations: Implications for speech production. Martin, R. C., & Freedman, M. L. (2001). Taylor & Francis Ltd, reprinted by permission of Taylor & Francis Ltd (www.tandfonline.com).

	Adj.	N.	Ajd. N	AAN
Controls (n = 6)	100	88 (93)	92 (97)	77 (82)
Phon. STM				
EA	100	90 (90)	90 (100)	70 (80)
Semantic STM				
AB	100	100	30 (30)	0 (0)
ML	100	100	20 (80)	10 (40)

separate phonological capacities on the input and output sides and EA's deficit only affected the input side (Martin, Lesch & Bartha, 1999).

A final area of exploration examined the consequences of these patients' STM deficits for long-term learning. According to traditional models, information has to be held in STM to be transferred to long-term memory (LTM; e.g., Atkinson & Shiffrin, 1968). Evidence from the well-known patient KF, reported by Shallice and Warrington (1970), was taken as evidence against this claim, as he had very reduced span but performed normally on a number of long-term memory tasks. However, assuming that KF's deficit was one of phonological retention, whereas most verbal LTM tasks appear to rely on semantic encoding, it is possible that he had preserved semantic STM, which supported his long-term learning. We reasoned that a patient like AB might show greater impairment on LTM tasks, given his semantic STM deficit and the assumption that maintenance in semantic STM is necessary for the learning of semantic information. Romani and Martin (1999) showed that this was the case for standard word-list materials, where AB's performance was very impaired and at the level of a severely amnesic patient. In contrast, though, his memory for stories, tested with multiple-choice and true/false questions, was at the level of controls and much better than the amnesic patient's. Again, it seemed that when the semantic information from individual words could be integrated into larger chunks of meaning—in this case, integrated into meaningful sentences and further integrated into story schemas—he could remember the information very well. A second study, which included ML and EA amongst other patients with semantic and phonological STM deficits, provided more direct evidence of a domain-specific relation between STM and LTM (Freedman & Martin, 2001). That is, as shown in Figure 14.4, EA was more

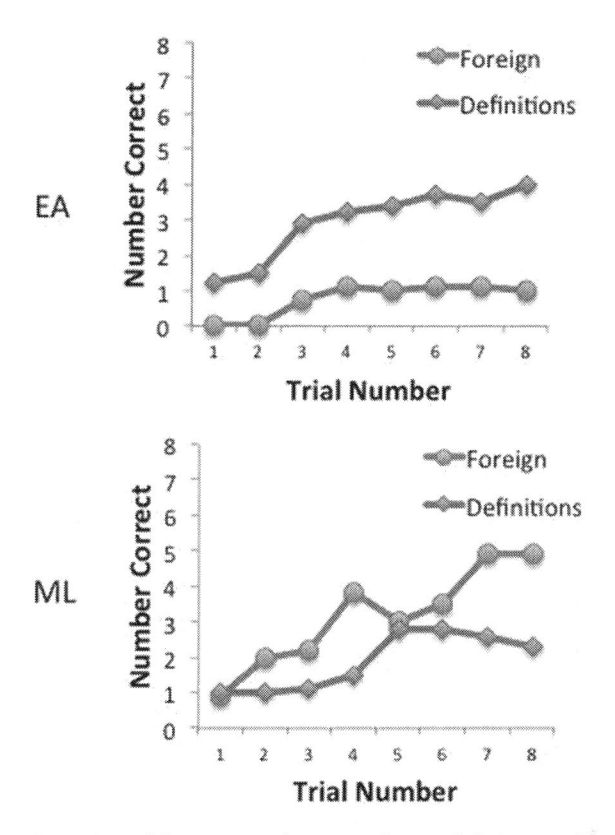

FIGURE 14.4 Learning of foreign translations and new definitions of known words for a patient EA (phonological STM deficit) and patient ML (semantic STM deficit) across paired-associate learning trials. Based on data from Freedman and Martin (2001).

impaired on learning new phonological forms (i.e., Spanish translations of English words) than in learning new meanings for known words (e.g., rye: gypsy man). ML, in contrast, was better at learning new translations than in learning new meanings.

An important issue that is often raised with regard to whether a separate semantic STM store should be postulated is whether the semantic STM deficits for these patients could be attributed to slowed or disrupted access to semantic information. As indicated earlier, both AB and ML performed at or above control level on standardized picture naming and word comprehension tasks. Even though their accuracy was high, it remained possible that they might show deficits on speeded tasks. Martin et al. (1994) addressed this issue comparing AB and EA on three timed tasks: property verification ("belt has buckle": yes/no), category judgements (city: Paris), and living-nonliving judgements for single words. On the property verification task, both AB and EA had longer RTs and somewhat more errors than controls, but there was no difference between AB and EA's performance. Thus, it seems unlikely that AB's very impaired performance on the attribute judgement task (e.g., "which is loud—a concert or a library") relative to EAs perfect performance could be attributed to slowed semantic access. On the other two tasks, though, AB did perform more slowly than EA and on the category judgement task, he made more errors than she did. In a later study with ML (Martin & He, 2004), his mean RT on the living-nonliving judgement task was just outside the range of controls and his accuracy was within the control range. Given that his baseline RTs on simple and choice reaction times were also longer than controls, it seems that the longer time could be attributed to some degree of motor slowing. His reaction times on the category judgements were substantially longer (and thus less likely to be due solely to motor slowing), but his error rate was within the normal range. We suggested that the design of the category judgement task did put some load on semantic working memory, with the category being presented auditorily, followed by visual presentation of the exemplar. Thus, his longer RTs might be attributed to there being some load on semantic STM for this task. Overall, the results, particularly for ML, suggested that these patients' semantic STM deficits could not readily be attributed to slowed semantic access.

Were there any relevant data that you did not manage to publish on these cases?

As another means of addressing the speed of semantic access for ML, a former graduate student of mine, An Hong, assessed semantic priming for ML with varying delays between prime and target in his master's thesis (Hong, 2007). He found that ML showed semantic priming within the control range under conditions favouring automatic priming (i.e., a short SOA of 350 ms and a low proportion of related trials; Neely, 1991; Shelton & Martin, 1992). We also found that his priming at longer SOAs was within the control range under conditions that discouraged the strategy used by controls. Thus, it appeared that ML showed preserved and rapid access to semantics for single words and a normal rate of decay of spreading activation over time. These findings provided further evidence that his semantic STM deficit did not derive from abnormal processing in the semantic system per se.

Do you think these cases contribute to our understanding of how the normal mind works?

These cases reveal the importance of a capacity for maintaining multiple semantic representations in mind that have been neglected in typical approaches to STM that focus on phonological retention. We interpreted these findings within a language-based model of STM—that is, assuming that verbal STM depends on the levels of representation in language processing on both the input and output side, with buffers to maintain these levels of representations at the semantic and input and output phonological levels (Martin et al., 1999). It should be noted that a similar approach has been put forward by Nadine Martin and colleagues based on data from brain-damaged patients, starting with a paper in 1997 (N. Martin & Saffran, 1997; see also Martin, Saffran & Dell, 1996; Martin & Ayala, 2004). Their approach, like ours, is to see STM as deriving from fundamental processes of the language system rather than as a system independent of it. The major difference between our approaches is that they argue that decay of representations is an intrinsic property of processing in the lexical system that leads to consequences for STM whereas we argue for buffers that may be damaged independent of the lexical system.

Our findings and the language-based STM model based on these findings have inspired us and others to look for converging evidence from healthy young and old individuals for a role for semantic retention in sentence processing. For instance, we have demonstrated the importance of a capacity for semantic retention in healthy individuals in comprehending the delayed vs. immediate integration sentences that were first reported for AB (Martin & Romani, 1994) and ML (Martin & He, 2004). That is, as shown in Figure 14.5, control subjects showed increasing reaction times for detecting the anomaly as the number of adjectives before a noun or the number of nouns before a verb increased, but showed no difference in reaction times or even faster reaction times as the number of adjectives after a noun or nouns after a verb increased. We have also shown in an fMRI study with healthy young subjects that inferior frontal regions show an increasing load effect for holding unintegrated semantic information in mind relative to materials with the same content but where immediate integration is possible (Hamilton Martin & Burton, 2009). Regions thought to be involved in phonological

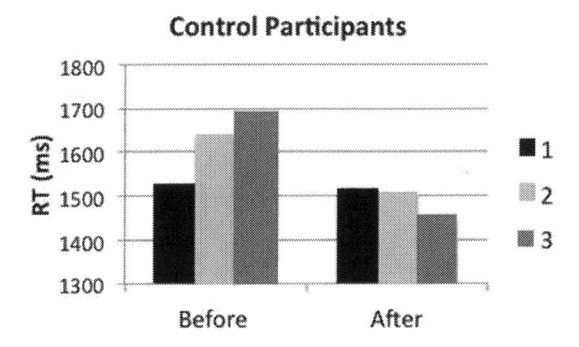

FIGURE 14.5 RT results for control participants for sentence anomaly judgement task for delayed (before) vs. immediate (after) integration with 1–3 adjectives before or after a noun or 1–3 nouns before or after a verb. Based on data reported in Martin and Romani (1994).

retention did not show this effect. We have also demonstrated that a semantic capacity as tapped by the category probe task first reported by Martin et al. (1994) for AB and EA relates to the ability to resolve semantic interference during sentence comprehension for healthy young subjects (Tan, Martin & Van Dyke, 2016). A measure of phonological retention ability (digit span) was found to be unrelated to individuals' ability to resolve either semantic or syntactic interference during comprehension. The answer to a later question addresses how these findings have influenced others' research and theorizing about normal cognition.

Do you think that there is anything unique that the reports of these cases added to our knowledge?

Of course. These were the first cases to be reported which provided evidence for a semantic retention capacity that was separable from a phonological retention capacity, where the semantic retention deficit could not be attributed to a deficit in semantic knowledge per se.

Can you specify why these cases were relevant in relation to the knowledge at the time and would they still be relevant to the knowledge of today?

At the time, the supposition of different storage capacities was limited to phonological and visual-spatial capacities, as in Baddeley and colleagues' approach (e.g., Baddeley & Hitch, 1974; Baddeley, 1986). It was unclear from such a model how sentence comprehension proceeded. That is, how did one hold onto the semantic and syntactic information derived from hearing a sentence, in order to integrate early parts of the sentence with later parts? Early evidence argued against a critical role for phonological retention, given that the retention of three unrelated words had little effect on sentence comprehension (Baddeley & Hitch, 1974). On logical grounds, it is unclear how phonological retention by itself would be of use. For instance, when a comprehender hears a verb and needs to integrate it with its subject, which may have occurred several words earlier in the sentence, phonological information is not going to be of help in locating the word corresponding to the subject. It is the semantic and syntactic properties of the preceding words that are relevant, not their sounds. Thus, there was a gaping hole in the discussion of verbal STM and how it fit into language processing at the sentence level—the level that most would intuitively consider to draw on putative verbal STM resources.

Today, there is a much more expansive notion of temporary storage of various types of representation, with much of the evidence coming from neuroimaging findings. That is, researchers have examined WM for faces (Gazzaley, Rissman & D'Esposito, 2004), visual word representations (Fiebach, Rissman & D'Esposito, 2006), orthographic information used in spelling (Rapp & Dufor, 2011), visual motion (Riggall & Postle, 2012), and odours (Dade, Zatorre,

Evans & Jones-Gotman, 2001). Some studies in the neuroimaging literature take for granted that retention of semantics involves brain regions that are separable from those involving the retention of phonology (e.g., Crosson et al., 1999; Lewis-Peacock, Drysdale, Oberauer & Postle, 2012). Much of this work does not assume the existence of a semantic buffer but instead takes an embedded processes view in which working memory is seen as the activated portion of LTM (Cowan, 1999). For example, the fusiform face area, which is involved in recognizing faces, has been shown to be activated in a face STM task during the delay period between list presentation and the presentation of a recognition probe (Gazzaley et al., 2004). Similarly, the visual word-form area, which has been argued to be a key region in word recognition, has been shown to be activated during retention of written words in a STM task (Fiebach et al., 2006). Activated regions outside of those supporting the processing and recognition of faces and words—specifically, frontal and parietal regions—are assumed to be involved in directing attention towards the relevant information to be maintained, rather than serving as buffers for maintaining the information. There is considerable controversy on the interpretation of these findings, however, with a growing literature in the visual STM domain debating the relationship between processing and storage in this domain (e.g., Bettencourt & Xu, 2016; Fougnie & Marois, 2006). Our patient findings still seem relevant in that they provide evidence that seems difficult to accommodate by the embedded processes view—specifically, the demonstration that patients may show processing within a given domain that is at a high level (as for ML) but show very restricted STM in that domain (see Martin & Breedin, 1992, for evidence with respect to the phonological domain).

An alternative explanation for the patient findings that would fit with the embedded processes account is that their STM deficits result from an attentional deficit that prevents them from being able to bring information into the focus of attention or from inhibiting distraction from irrelevant information. Some explanations along these lines have been suggested in the literature (e.g., Ravizza, Hazeltine, Ruiz & Zhu, 2011), but then one would have to explain why their STM deficit is limited to a specific domain. That is, why would a patient show preserved visual-spatial memory (as on the Corsi blocks task) but very impaired phonological STM? One might argue that there are highly specific attentional capacities—e.g., one for phonology, one for semantics, one for orthography—and that patients have selective damage to one of these. Allowing such a possibility, though, would seem to undermine claims that the embedded processes approach is more parsimonious than theories that assume multiple working memory buffers (Kintsch, Healy, Hegarty & Pennington, 1999; Ruchkin, Grafman, Cameron & Berndt, 2003).

It is the case, nonetheless, that domain-specific attentional capacities have been proposed. A program of research by Beth Jefferies and Matt Lambon Ralph and their colleagues have suggested that multi-modal semantic deficits (i.e., semantic deficits for verbal and nonverbal information) for individuals with aphasia derive from a deficit in "semantic control"—specifically, the ability to access appropriate semantic representations in the face of conflict and the ability to manipulate these representations (e.g., Jefferies & Lambon Ralph, 2006; Jefferies, Baker, Doran & Lambon Ralph, 2007; Jefferies, Rogers, Hopper & Lambon Ralph, 2010). Although some of the work coming out of their labs has seemed to suggest general executive function deficits as the source of the semantic deficits (e.g., Jefferies & Lambon Ralph, 2006), other more recent findings suggest control problems may be specific to semantics (Hoffman, Jefferies, Haffey, Littlejohns & Lambon Ralph, 2013). These researchers have argued that patients with semantic STM deficits are those with mild semantic control deficits, as they perform at a high level of accuracy on many single word semantic tasks, but may show abnormal reaction time effects (Hoffman, Jefferies, Ehsan, Hopper & Ralph, 2009). Their STM deficit is argued to be evident even though single word processing is relatively preserved because semantic STM tasks like category probe put a higher demand on semantic control.

A related line of work comes from Sharon Thompson-Schill and colleagues (e.g., Thompson-Schill, D'Esposito, Aguirre & Farah, 1997; Thompson-Schill et al., 2002). These researchers have focused on the role of the left inferior frontal gyrus (LIFG) in cognitive processing, arguing that this region is critically involved in cognitive control—that is, in biasing processing towards task-relevant information and away from irrelevant information (Thompson-Schill, Bedny & Goldberg, 2005). Both AB and ML had damage to the LIFG. Thus, both the theoretical positions of Jefferies and Lambon Ralph and Thompson-Schill and colleagues raise the possibility that the STM deficits and the associated deficits in sentence processing observed for AB and ML derive from control deficits rather than semantic storage deficits per se.

In fact, some of our later studies with ML were directed at assessing whether he had an impairment in cognitive control (specifically, in inhibiting irrelevant verbal information). Some of the STM findings with him had suggested that might be the case. For instance, he demonstrated a high number of intrusions from prior lists during short-term recall (Martin & Lesch, 1996). Hamilton and Martin (2005, 2007) demonstrated that, relative to controls, ML had a greatly exaggerated Stroop effect and greatly exaggerated difficulty in rejecting recognition probes in a recent negatives task (i.e., where some probes match an item in the preceding list but not the current list; Monsell, 1978). In contrast, he performed at the level of controls on two tasks tapping cognitive control for nonverbal materials (e.g., the anti-saccade task and a nonverbal analogue to the Stroop task). Vuong and Martin (2011, 2014) demonstrated that ML had difficulty in comprehending sentences with lexical or syntactic ambiguities, where a strongly preferred interpretation had to be overridden. While a deficit in inhibiting irrelevant verbal information might account for some of the findings (e.g., difficulty in comprehending garden path sentences), it is hard to see how it could account for the sentence comprehension difficulties on the attribute judgement task or on sentences requiring the retention of several unintegrated semantic representations or the difficulties in producing phrases with several lexical-semantic representations (Martin & He, 2004). While I made some attempts to integrate these findings into an inhibition deficit account (Martin, 2007), the account was not compelling (even to me). A study we did of 20 individuals with aphasia showed no significant correlation between performance on a composite semantic STM measure and on simple or complex executive function tasks, including tasks tapping inhibition (Allen, Martin & Martin, 2012). Thus, these findings suggest that ML may have had two deficits (one in semantic STM capacity and another in cognitive control for verbal information). Clearly, further work is required to both spell out the relation between attentional or cognitive control processes and STM in various domains and to determine the extent to which each of these deficits may contribute to sentence comprehension and production deficits. Some current work along this line is being carried out in our lab in a large-scale study of individuals with acute stroke (for preliminary findings, see Martin, Schnur & Anderson, 2016). With an anticipated sample size of 90 individuals, we should be able to determine if dissociations between semantic STM and attentional control exist and which of these predicts the sentence processing abilities we had attributed to semantic STM deficits.

What are the shortcomings of these cases?

As noted earlier, AB did show some semantic processing deficits on speeded tasks, particularly on the category judgements. Also, as just discussed, there remains a question of the extent to which semantic STM deficits vs. cognitive control in the semantic domain might best characterize the deficits of AB and ML.

Do you remember whether you had difficulty publishing your work with AB and ML? If so, what was this difficulty?

I had some degree of difficulty publishing the first paper on AB's semantic STM deficit and its contrast with EA's phonological STM deficit, though it was eventually accepted after a rather lengthy revision process in the first journal to which we had submitted it (i.e., Martin et al., 1994, *Journal of Memory and Language*). One difficulty was that at least one of the reviewers required that I address the issue of whether AB, relative to EA, had a deficit in speed of processing in the semantic domain, which was quite difficult to do as EA was located about 1600 miles away and additional testing was hard to carry out. These data were eventually collected, and I have to admit that it was valuable to have those findings, which could be later amplified with testing of patient ML. The paper reporting the replication of many findings of AB for patient ML appeared in a journal that published many neuropsychological findings (i.e., Martin & He, 2004, *Brain and Language*) and I had a much easier time in the review process there.

Do you remember whether there were any issues that reviewers were particularly blunt about?

One of the reviewers of the first paper on AB (Martin et al., 1994) thought that the paper would be more appropriate for a specifically neuropsychological journal rather than one that typically published papers on healthy (young) individuals. This reviewer seemed resistant to using neuropsychological data for addressing basic issues in cognition. Luckily, the editor and other reviewers thought otherwise.

Are there any assessments/paradigms that you would administer now to these individuals if they were available?

Given Jefferies and Lambon Ralph's claims about the relation between semantic STM deficits and general semantic control deficits, it would be important to test the patients thoroughly on single word semantic tests requiring inhibition of strong distractors—e.g., a synonym matching task where distractors are strongly associated (Hoffman, Jefferies & Lambon Ralph, 2011). Also, given Thompson-Schill and colleagues' (Thompson-Schill & Botvinick, 2006) related claims about the role of LIFG regions in biasing processing towards relevant information and away from irrelevant, it would be important to try to determine if patients show dissociations between semantic STM and such biasing abilities, and examine which of these deficits is critical for the sentence processing patterns that were observed.

It would also be valuable to obtain eye-tracking or ERP measures of sentence processing so that more online processing could be observed. Such methods could be used to obtain evidence regarding the time course of the detection of, for instance, semantic anomalies depending on the number of intervening unintegrated elements, without requiring RT measures that may be slowed due to motor control issues. The time course of detection should be similar to that of controls when there are minimal demands on STM. They could also be used to address the patients' ability to generate expectancies for upcoming words in a sentence based on semantic information, which should be preserved in the face of semantic STM deficits.

You first reported these cases in 1994 and 2004. Do you think these cases are still informative now? Are we now better able to interpret their patterns of spared and impaired abilities? If so, in what way?

I believe these cases are still relevant as they address the issue of how working memory becomes involved in language production and comprehension, given the need to maintain more than one semantic representation simultaneously in both. Our findings and myriad others suggest that phonological STM does not support this critical function (e.g., Butterworth, Campbell & Howard, 1986; Caplan &

Waters, 1999; Tan et al., 2017). In fact, it is hard to see how it could. Retaining a phonological representation of prior words does not tell you how the appropriate word can be identified when, for instance, needing to integrate a verb with its preceding subject across several intervening words. It is not clear that a better interpretation of these patients' patterns of performance can be given at present.

Do you think these cases have been considered by people who develop theories of the normal mind? If yes, how? If no, should they be?

To some extent, these findings have been considered. They have been cited as part of the inspiration for investigating the role of semantic retention in the STM performance of healthy individuals in a substantial number of studies (e.g., Acheson, MacDonald & Postle, 2011; Campoy, Castella, Provencio, Hitch & Baddeley, 2015; Davelaar, Goshen-Gottstein, Ashkenazi, Haarmann & Usher, 2005; Haarmann & Usher, 2001; Nishiyama, 2013, 2014; Poirier, Saint-Aubin, Mair, Tehan & Tolan, 2015; Shivde & Anderson, 2011). As indicated earlier, neuroimaging studies refer to these findings, but often interpret them in terms of support for an embedded processes approach (e.g., Lewis-Peacock et al., 2012; Ruchkin et al., 2003).

In contrast, only a few studies have depended heavily on our work with respect to the testing and development of theories of sentence comprehension. One such study was that of Haarmann, Davelaar and Usher (2003), who demonstrated that individual differences in their own measure of semantic STM capacity predicted healthy subjects' sentence comprehension. A variety of sentence processing studies have made more passing reference to our studies with respect to the notion that phonological retention may not be critical in the comprehension domain and separable semantic and syntactic capacities may exist (e.g., Kielar et al., 2015; Grossman, Cooke et al., 2002; Manenti, Cappa, Rossini & Miniussi, 2008). A recent theoretical proposal concerning the need for rapid integration of elements during sentence processing (Christiansen & Chater, 2016) refers to our findings of the effects on comprehension and production when maintenance of phonological and sematic information is impaired. The lesser impact in the sentence comprehension domain is no doubt due to several factors, but one important one may have been the existence of the large body of work that has focused on relating the comprehension of sentences of varying difficulty to complex measures of span (such as reading span, which requires subjects to read a set of sentence aloud and recall the last word of each at the end of the set). This work grows out of the original findings of Daneman and Carpenter (1980) showing that simple STM measures like digit span, reflecting mainly phonological STM, were not highly predictive of comprehension performance whereas the complex reading span measure was. Just and Carpenter (1992) put forward a theory about a general verbal working memory capacity (tapped by the reading span task) that could be allocated to both processing and retention at all levels of representation (e.g., lexical, semantic, syntactic, pragmatic) during comprehension. Simple span measures did not tap the processing component sufficiently to be predictive of comprehension ability. Thus, with respect to the Just and Carpenter position, our findings of good comprehension with poor phonological STM were not very newsworthy. In the comprehension literature focusing on the relation to complex span, there has been no attempt to sort out whether a specific contribution of semantic retention could be demonstrated that was distinct from whatever was tapped by the measures like reading span. A recent study from my lab (Tan, Martin & Van Dyke, 2017) did, however, find a specific contribution of semantic retention for healthy young individuals in resolving semantic interference in sentence comprehension independent of the capacity tapped by complex span measures.

Our neuropsychological findings appear to have had more influence on theories of sentence production than comprehension, with studies of healthy individuals taking into account our findings suggesting a phrasal scope of advance planning at the lexical-semantic level (e.g., Allum & Wheeldon, 2007, 2009; Belke & Meyer, 2007; Ferreira & Slevc, 2007; Gillespie, James, Federmeier & Watson, 2014; Miller & Johnson, 2010; Schweppe & Rummer, 2007; Slevc, 2011). Perhaps our findings were more easily accommodated by existing theories in this domain, as influential models of production assume a level at which lexical-semantic representations are maintained prior to phonological access (Bock & Levelt, 1994; Garrett, 1980). Also, some findings suggested a difference in the scope of planning at lexical-semantic and phonological levels (Garrett, 1980; Meyer, 1996), with a greater scope at the lexical-semantic level, which would make greater demands on a working memory capacity. Of course, there has not been unanimous support for our position on the scope of planning in production, with several studies arguing against our claims (e.g., Griffin & Spieler, 2006; Wagner, Jescheniak & Schriefers, 2010), or arguing that the semantic STM deficits are really at a non-verbal conceptual level (Griffin, 2004). Nonetheless, the neuropsychological findings have been used as a motivation for examining scope of planning at semantic and phonological levels and for relating production ability to different types of STM capacity.

In general, do you think that neuropsychology cases are still relevant to our understanding of the normal mind? If so, why?

Since the advent of functional neuroimaging, many have questioned whether the study of neuropsychological cases is still valuable, given the uncontrolled location of lesions and the variety of functions that may be impacted in any one individual. Many researchers who started their careers doing neuropsychological work have moved solely or mainly into neuroimaging work. Some of the critiques of the neuropsychological approach focus on the difficulties in determining the neural basis of a cognitive function from lesion data (though some have argued that advantages still exist; Rorden & Karnath, 2004). Nonetheless, as has been discussed at length elsewhere, cognitive neuropsychological studies may focus solely on the organization of cognitive processing from a functional perspective without consideration of the neural basis (e.g., Coltheart, 2001). This functional approach is the approach that has been taken for the most part in my lab, focusing on the pattern of spared and impaired performance and their implications for cognitive theory. I would argue that cognitive neuropsychological findings are data that need to be considered in theoretical formulations, along with data from other sources. There are certainly many existing findings in the neuropsychological literature that have yet to be explained adequately by existing theories—for instance, the range of domain-specific STM deficits that are observed in the absence of processing deficits within those domains. Attributing such deficits to possible attentional impairments is just so much hand-waving at present. Beyond the body of findings already available, there is, no doubt, an endless supply of theoretically challenging findings yet to be uncovered by the study of neuropsychological cases. Most who work in the field will agree that much of the attraction of carrying out this work derives from the surprising findings that pop up that do not seem to fit within current cognitive theorizing. For the cases AB and ML reported here, such surprising findings included the lack of advantage for words over nonwords in list recall, their difficulty in responding to simple attribute questions given their seemingly good comprehension in everyday conversation, and their difficulty producing "small leaf" when they could produce "small" and "leaf" separately. Our account of these findings can certainly be challenged, but that is true for any theoretical interpretation of data, irrespective of whether the conclusions were derived from behavioural or imaging studies of healthy individuals or from neuropsychological findings.

I would acknowledge, though, that given the current excitement and interest in neuroimaging approaches, it is a challenge to bring the neuropsychological findings to the attention of those in the field. Recently, however, Krakauer, Ghazanfar, Gomez-Marin, MacIver and Poeppel (2017) published an article in the prominent neuroscience journal *Neuron*, arguing that greater emphasis on behaviour is needed in neuroscience studies. Further technological improvements in imaging alone will not suffice to improve our understanding of the neural basis of behaviour. Understanding the neural basis depends on a thorough understanding of the behaviour itself, which can only be obtained from a detailed and theoretically motivated examination. Let us hope that volumes like the present one will help to ensure that this crucial study of behaviour will be seen as benefitting from the convergence of findings from healthy individuals and neuropsychological cases.

Author Notes

Preparation of this manuscript was supported in part by NIH grant DC014976 to Baylor College of Medicine, Houston, Texas, with a subcontract to Rice University. The author would like to acknowledge Hao Yan and Heather Dial for their help in editing this chapter.

References

Acheson, D. J., MacDonald, M. C., & Postle, B. R. (2011). The effect of concurrent semantic categorization on delayed serial recall. *Journal of Experimental Psychology: Learning, Memory, and Cognition, 37*, 44–59.

Allen, C. M., Martin, R. C., & Martin, N. (2012). Relations between short-term memory deficits, semantic processing and executive function. *Aphasiology, 26*, 428–461.

Allum, P. H., & Wheeldon, L. R. (2007). Planning scope in spoken sentence production: the role of grammatical units. *Journal of Experimental Psychology: Learning, Memory, and Cognition, 33*, 791–810.

Allum, P. H., & Wheeldon, L. (2009). Scope of lexical access in spoken sentence production: implications for the conceptual—syntactic interface. *Journal of Experimental Psychology: Learning, Memory, and Cognition, 35*, 1240–1255.

Atkinson, R. C., & Shiffrin, R. M. (1968). Human memory: a proposed system and its control processes. In K. W. Spence & J. T. Spence (Eds.), *The Psychology of Learning and Memory: Advances in Research and Theory*. New York: Academic Press, pp. 89–195.

Baddeley, A. D. (1986). *Oxford psychology series, No. 11. Working memory*. New York NY, US: Clarendon Press/Oxford Univeristy Press.

Baddeley, A. D., & Hitch, G. (1974). Working memory. *Psychology of Learning and Motivation, 8*, 47–89.

Belke, E., & Meyer, A. S. (2007). Single and multiple object naming in healthy ageing. *Language and Cognitive Processes, 22*, 1178–1211.

Bettencourt, K. C., & Xu, Y. (2016). Decoding the content of visual short-term memory under distraction in occipital and parietal areas. *Nature Neuroscience, 19*, 150–157.

Bock, J. K., & Levelt, W. (1994). Language production: grammatical encoding. In M. A. Gernsbacher (Ed.), *Handbook of Psycholinguistics*. San Diego, CA: Academic Press, Inc, pp. 945–984.

Butterworth, B., Campbell, R., & Howard, D. (1986). The uses of short-term memory: a case study. *The Quarterly Journal of Experimental Psychology, 38*, 705–737.

Campoy, G., Castellà, J., Provencio, V., Hitch, G. J., & Baddeley, A. D. (2015). Automatic semantic encoding in verbal short-term memory: evidence from the concreteness effect. *The Quarterly Journal of Experimental Psychology, 68*, 759–778.

Caplan, D., & Waters, G. S. (1999). Verbal working memory and sentence comprehension. *Behavioral and Brain Sciences, 22*, 77–94.

Christiansen, M. H., & Chater, N. (2016). The Now-or-never bottleneck: a fundamental constraint on language. *Behavioral and Brain Sciences, 39*, e62. doi:10.1017/S0140525X1500031.

Coltheart, M. (2001). Assumptions and methods in cognitive neuropsychology. In B. Rapp (Ed.), *Handbook of Cognitive Neuropsychology: What Deficits Reveal about the Human Mind*. New York: Psychology Press, pp. 3–21.

Cowan, N. (1999). An embedded-processes model of working memory. In A. Miyake & P. Shah (Eds.), *Models of working memory*. Cambrige, UK: Cambridge U. Press, pp. 62–101.

Crosson, B., Rao, S. M., Woodley, S. J., Rosen, A. C., Bobholz, J. A., Mayer, A., Stein, E. A. (1999). Mapping of semantic, phonological, and orthographic verbal working memory in normal adults with functional magnetic resonance imaging. *Neuropsychology, 13*, 171–187.

Dade, L. A., Zatorre, R. J., Evans, A. C., & Jones-Gotman, M. (2001). Working memory in another dimension: functional imaging of human olfactory working memory. *Neuroimage, 14*, 650–660.

Daneman, M., & Carpenter, P. A. (1980). Individual differences in working memory and reading. *Journal of Verbal Learning and Verbal Behavior, 19*, 450–466.

Davelaar, E. J., Goshen-Gottstein, Y., Ashkenazi, A., Haarmann, H. J., & Usher, M. (2005). The demise of short-term memory revisited: empirical and computational investigations of recency effects. *Psychological Review, 112*, 3–42.

Ferreira, V. S., & Slevc, L. R. (2007). Language production: grammatical encoding. In M. G. Gaskell (Ed.), *The Oxford Handbook of Psycholinguistics*. New York: Oxford University Press, Inc, pp. 453–469.

Fiebach, C. J., Rissman, J., & D'Esposito, M. (2006). Modulation of inferotemporal cortex activation during verbal working memory maintenance. *Neuron, 51*, 251–261.

Fougnie, D., & Marois, R. (2006). Distinct capacity limits for attention and working memory: evidence from attentive tracking and visual working memory paradigms. *Psychological Science, 17*, 526–534.

Freedman, M., & Martin, R. (2001). Dissociable components of short-term memory and their relation to long-term learning. *Cognitive Neuropsychology, 18*, 193–226.

Freedman, M., Martin, R. C., & Biegler, K. (2004). Semantic relatedness effects in conjoined noun phrase production: implications for the role of short-term memory. *Cognitive Neuropsychology, 21*, 245–265.

Gazzaley, A., Rissman, J., & D'Esposito, M. (2004). Functional connectivity during working memory maintenance. *Cognitive, Affective, & Behavioral Neuroscience, 4*, 580–599.

Garrett, M. (1980). Levels of processing in sentence production. In B. Butterworth (Ed.), *Language Production Vol. 1: Speech and Talk*. London: Academic Press, pp. 177–220.

Gillespie, M., James, A. N., Federmeier, K. D., & Watson, D. G. (2014). Verbal working memory predicts co-speech gesture: evidence from individual differences. *Cognition, 132*, 174–180.

Griffin, Z. M. (2004). Why look? Reasons for speech-related eye movements. *The Integration of Language, Vision, and Action: Eye Movements and the Visual World*, 191–211.

Griffin, Z. M., & Spieler, D. H. (2006). Observing the what and when of language production for different age groups by monitoring speakers' eye movements. *Brain and Language, 99*, 272–288.

Grossman, M., Cooke, A., DeVita, C., Alsop, D., Detre, J., Chen, W., & Gee, J. (2002). Age-related changes in working memory during sentence comprehension: an fMRI study. *Neuroimage, 15*, 302–317.

Haarmann, H. J., Davelaar, E. J., & Usher, M. (2003). Individual differences in semantic short-term memory capacity and reading comprehension. *Journal of Memory and Language, 48*, 320–345.

Haarmann, H. J., & Usher, M. (2001). Maintenance of semantic information in capacity limited item short-term memory. *Psychonomic Bulletin & Review, 8*, 568–578.

Hamilton, A. C., & Martin, R. C. (2005). Dissociations among tasks involving inhibition: a single case study. *Cognitive, Affective, & Behavioral Neuroscience, 5*, 1–13.

Hamilton, A., & Martin, R. C. (2007). Proactive interference in a semantic short-term memory deficit: role of semantic and phonological relatedness. *Cortex, 43*, 112–123.

Hamilton, A. C., Martin, R. C., & Burton, P. (2009). Converging functional magnetic resonance imaging evidence for a role of the left inferior frontal lobe in semantic retention during language comprehension. *Cognitive Neuropsychology, 26*, 685–704.

Hoffman, P., Jefferies, E., Ehsan, S., Hopper, S., & Ralph, M. A. L. (2009). Selective short-term memory deficits arise from impaired domain-general semantic control mechanisms. *Journal of Experimental Psychology: Learning, Memory, and Cognition, 35*, 137–156.

Hoffman, P., Jefferies, E., Haffey, A., Littlejohns, T., & Lambon Ralph, M. A. (2013). Domain-specific control of semantic cognition: a dissociation within patients with semantic working memory deficits. *Aphasiology, 27*, 740–764.

Hoffman, P., Jefferies, E., & Ralph, M.A.L. (2011). Explaining semantic short-term memory deficits: evidence for the critical role of semantic control. *Neuropsychologia, 49*, 368–381.

Hong, A. (2007). Semantic priming effects in a patient with a semantic short-term memory deficit. Unpublished master's thesis, Rice University, Houston, TX.

Jefferies, E., Baker, S. S., Doran, M, & Lambon Ralph, M. A. (2007). Refractory effects in stroke aphasia: a consequence of semantic control. *Neuropsychologia, 45*, 1065–1079.

Jefferies, E., & Lambon Ralph, M.A. (2006). Semantic impairment in stroke aphasia versus semantic dementia: a case-series comparison. *Brain, 129*, 2132–2147.

Jefferies, E., Rogers, T.T., Hopper, S., & Lambon Ralph, M.A. (2010)."Pre-semantic" cognition revisited: crticial differences between semantic aphasia and semantic dementia. *Neuropsychologia, 48*, 248–261.

Just, M.A., & Carpenter, P.A. (1992). A capacity theory of comprehension: individual differences in working memory. *Psychological Review, 99*, 122–149.

Krakauer, J. W., Ghazanfar, A. A., Gomez-Marin, A., MacIver, M. A., Poeppel, D. (2017). Neuroscience needs behavior: correcting a reductionist bias. *Neuron, 93*, 480–490.

Kielar, A., Panamsky, L., Links, K., Meltzer, J.A. (2015). Localization of electrophysiological responses to semantic and syntactic anomalies in language comprehension with MEG. *Neuroimage, 105*, 507–524.

Kintsch, W., Healy, A. F., Hegarty, M., & Pennington, B. F. (1999). Models of working memory. In A. Miyake & P. Shah (Eds.), *Models of Working Memory: Mechanisms of Active Maintenance and Executive Control.* Cambridge, UK: Cambridge University Press, pp. 412–437.

Lewis-Peacock, J.A., Drysdale, A.T., Oberauer, K., & Postle, B. R. (2012). Neural evidence for a distinction between short-term memory and the focus of attention. *Journal of Cognitive Neuroscience, 24*, 61–79.

Manenti, R., Cappa, S. F., Rossini, P. M., & Miniussi, C. (2008). The role of the prefrontal cortex in sentence comprehension: an rTMS study. *Cortex, 44*, 337–344.

Martin, N., & Ayala, J. (2004). Measurement of auditory-verbal STM span in aphasia: effects of item, task, and lexical impairment. *Brain and Language, 3*, 464–483.

Martin, N., & Saffran, E. M. (1997). Language and auditory-verbal short-term memory impairment: evidence for common underlying processes. *Cognitive Neuropsychology, 14*, 641–682.

Martin, N., Saffran, E. M., & Dell, G. S. (1996). Recovery in deep dysphasia: evidence for a relation between auditory-verbal STM capacity and lexical errors in repetition. *Brain and Language, 52*, 83–113.

Martin, R. C. (1987). Articulatory and phonological deficits in short-term memory and their relation to syntactic processing. *Brain and Language, 32*, 137–158.

Martin, R. C., & Breedin, S. (1992). Dissociations between speech perception and phonological short-term memory. *Cognitive Neuropsychology, 9*, 509–534.

Martin, R. C., & Freedman, M. L. (2001). Short-term retention of lexical-semantic representations: implications for speech production. *Memory, 9*, 261–280.

Martin, R. C., & He, T. (2004). Semantic short-term memory deficit and language processing: a replication, *Brain and Language, 89*, 76–82.

Martin, R. C., & Lesch, M. (1996). Associations and dissociations between language processing and list recall: implications for models of short-term memory. In S. Gathercole (Ed.), *Models of Short-term Memory.* Hove, England: Erlbaum, pp. 149–178.

Martin, R. C., Lesch, M., & Bartha, M. (1999). Independence of input and output phonology in word processing and short-term memory. *Journal of Memory and Language, 41,* 3–29.

Martin, R. C., Miller, M., & Vu, H. (2004). Working memory and sentence production: evidence for a phrasal scope of planning at a lexical-semantic level. *Cognitive Neuropsychology, 21,* 625–644.

Martin, R. C., & Romani, C. (1994). Verbal working memory and sentence processing: a multiple components view. *Neuropsychology, 8,* 506–523.

Martin, R. C., Schnur, T and Anderson, J. (2016). Semantic but not phonological short-term memory supports sentence elaboration in narrative production: evidence from left hemisphere acute stroke. *Front. Psychol. Conference Abstract: 54th Annual Academy of Aphasia Meeting.* doi: 10.3389/conf.fpsyg.2016.68.00056.

Martin, R. C., Shelton, J., & Yaffee, L. (1994). Language processing and working memory: neuropsychological evidence for separate phonological and semantic capacities. *Journal of Memory and Language, 33,* 83–111.

Meyer, A. (1996). Lexical access in phrase and sentence production: results form picture-word interference paradigms. *Journal of Memory and Language, 35,* 477–496.

Miller, M. D., & Johnson, J. S. (2010). Phonological and lexical-semantic short-term memory and their relationship to sentence production in older adults. *Aging, Neuropsychology, and Cognition, 11,* 395–415.

Monsell, S. (1978). Recency, immediate recognition memory, and reaction time. *Cognitive Psychology, 10,* 465–501.

Neely, J. H. (1991). Semantic priming effects in visual word recognition: a selective review of current findings and theories. In D. Besner & G. W. Humphreys (Eds.), *Basic Processes in Reading: Visual Word Recognition.* Hillsdale, NJ: Erlbaum, pp. 264–336.

Nishiyama, R. (2013). Dissociative contributions of semantic and lexical—phonological information to immediate recognition. *Journal of Experimental Psychology: Learning, Memory, and Cognition, 39,* 642–648.

Nishiyama, R. (2014). Active maintenance of semantic representations. *Psychonomic Bulletin & Review, 21,* 1583–1589.

Poirier, M., Saint-Aubin, J., Mair, A., Tehan, G., & Tolan, A. (2015). Order recall in verbal short-term memory: the role of semantic networks. *Memory & Cognition, 43,* 489–499.

Rapp, B., & Dufor, O. (2011). The neurotopography of written word production: an fMRI investigation of the distribution of sensitivity to length and frequency. *Journal of Cognitive Neuroscience, 23,* 4067–4081.

Ravizza, S. M., Hazeltine, E., Ruiz, S., & Zhu, D. C. (2011). Left TPJ activity in verbal working memory: implications for storage-and sensory-specific models of short-term memory. *Neuroimage, 55,* 1836–1846.

Riggall, A. C., & Postle, B. R. (2012). The relationship between working memory storage and elevated activity as measured with functional magnetic resonance imaging. *Journal of Neuroscience, 32,* 12990–12998.

Romani, C., & Martin, R. (1999). A deficit in the short-term retention of lexical-semantic information: forgetting words but remembering a story. *Journal of Experimental Psychology: General, 128,* 56–77.

Rorden, C., & Karnath, H. (2004). Using human brain lesions to infer function: a relic from a past era in the fMRI age? *Nature Reviews Neuroscience, 5,* 812–819.

Ruchkin, D. S., Grafman, J., Cameron, K., & Berndt, R. S. (2003). Working memory retention systems: a state of activated long-term memory. *Behavioral and Brain Sciences, 26,* 709–728.

Shallice, T., & Vallar, G. (1990). The impairment of auditory-verbal short-term storage. *Neuropsychological Impairments of Short-Term Memory*, 11–53.

Shallice, T., & Warrington, E. K. (1970). Independent functioning of verbal memory stores: a neuropsychological study. *The Quarterly Journal of Experimental Psychology, 22*, 261–273.

Shelton, J. R., & Martin, R. C. (1992). How semantic is automatic "semantic" priming? *Journal of Experimental Psychology: Learning, Memory, and Cognition, 18*, 1191–1210.

Shivde, G., & Anderson, M. C. (2011). On the existence of semantic working memory: evidence for direct semantic maintenance. *Journal of Experimental Psychology: Learning, Memory, and Cognition, 37*, 1342–1370.

Schweppe, J., & Rummer, R. (2007). Shared representations in language processing and verbal short-term memory: the case of grammatical gender. *Journal of Memory and Language, 56*, 336–356.

Slevc, L. R. (2011). Saying what's on your mind: working memory effects on sentence production. *Journal of Experimental Psychology: Learning, Memory, and Cognition, 37*, 1503–1514.

Tan, Y., Martin, R. C., Van Dyke, J. A. (2017). Semantic and syntactic interference in sentence comprehension: a comparison of working memory models. *Frontiers in Psychology*, 8:198, doi: 10.3389/fpsyg.2017.00198.

Thompson-Schill, S. L., Bedny, M., & Goldberg, R. F. (2005). The frontal lobes and the regulation of mental activity. *Current Opinion in Neurobiology, 15*, 219–224.

Thompson-Schill, S. L., & Botvinick, M. M. (2006). Resolving conflict: a response to Martin and Cheng (2006). *Psychonomic Bulletin & Review, 13*, 402–408.

Thompson-Schill., S. L., D'Esposito, M., Guirre, G. K., & Faraha, M. J. (1997). Role of left inferior prefrontal cortex in retrieval of semantic knowledge: a reevaluation. *Proceedings of the National Academy of Sciences, 94*, 14792–14797.

Thompson-Shill, S. L., Jonides, J., Marshuetz, C., Smith, E. E., D'Esposito, M., & Kan, I. P. (2002). Effects of frontal lobe damage on interference effects in working memory. *Cognitive, Affective, and Behavioral Neuroscience, 2*, 109–120.

Vuong, L. C., & Martin, R. C. (2011). LIFG-based attentional control and the resolution of lexical ambiguities in sentence context. *Brain and Language, 116*, 22–32.

Vuong, L. C., & Martin, R. C. (2014). Domain-specific executive control and the revision of misinterpretations in sentence comprehension. *Language and Cognitive Processes, 29*, 312–325.

Wagner, V., Jescheniak, J. D., & Schriefers, H. (2010). On the flexibility of grammatical advance planning during sentence production effects of cognitive load on multiple lexical access. *Journal of Experimental Psychology: Learning, Memory, and Cognition, 36*, 423–440.

Warrington, E. K., & McCarthy, R. A. (1987). Categories of knowledge. *Brain, 110(5)*, 1273–1296.

Wheeldon, L. R., & Lahiri, A. (2002). The minimal unit of phonological encoding: prosodic or lexical word. *Cognition, 85*, B31–B41.

15

INTERRELATIONSHIP BETWEEN SEMANTIC MEMORY AND PERSONAL EXPERIENCE

Evidence From Semantic Dementia Patients KE and WM

Julie Snowden

In the mid-90s, you described the cases of patients KE and WM affected by semantic dementia who demonstrated impaired semantic memory but spared autobiographical memory. Can you provide us with some background information about these cases?

Both patients were referred to the multidisciplinary clinical neuroscience unit where I work for diagnostic assessment of suspected neurodegenerative disease. KE was a 56-year-old school assistant at the time of her referral. Over the previous seven years, she had developed increasing difficulty remembering the names of people, places and things and remembering what objects were for. Her husband reported that she could no longer relay telephone messages, as she could not remember the name of the person who had telephoned or what had been said. When shopping, she did not recognize goods in the supermarket. To compensate, she had developed a strategy of taking empty cartons with her to match up with items on the supermarket shelf. There were some changes in her behaviour too. She had become more routine-bound and had a fixed weekly routine. She would cook the same meal on the same day of each week. She watched the same television programmes repeatedly. Despite her difficulties, she was independent in activities of daily living. She continued to drive, to find her way around her locality, and to carry out without assistance all household tasks such as shopping and cooking. She had no physical symptoms. There was no relevant previous medical history or family history of dementia. We were asked to establish the basis for KE's symptoms.

WM, a high school deputy head teacher, was referred for assessment when she was 55 years old. She had begun to develop symptoms six years earlier, at 49 years.

Relatives and friends noticed that she had difficulties in naming and understanding words and she would use wrong words (e.g., "flies" for birds). These difficulties had become increasingly pronounced over time. The problem was not just with words. She also had problems recognizing acquaintances. Like KE, she had adopted a rigid daily routine, carrying out specific activities at particular times of the day. She had taken to reading the dictionary to try to learn words that she did not know, suggesting a degree of insight. Nevertheless, she ascribed her problems to a failure to keep up with 'new' words that were being added to the dictionary, which suggested a lack of full appreciation of her disorder. WM lived alone, having separated from her husband, and, like KE, was fully independent in all activities of daily living. She continued to drive and had never become lost. She remembered appointments without prompting. Like KE, WM was physically well, and she had no relevant previous medical or family history.

Our neurologist examined KE and WM and found no neurological abnormality. Brain scans showed severe temporal lobe atrophy, affecting both temporal lobes equally in KE and more prominent in the left temporal lobe in WM. I was part of the clinical diagnostic team and was responsible for the neuropsychological work-up of both patients.

How did you first realize that these cases were interesting?

Both KE and WM struck me as interesting as soon as I met them and heard the clinical history and even more so once I had carried out the initial neuropsychological assessment. At the time of their initial assessments in 1991 and 1992, there was still little awareness of different forms of dementia. The prevailing assumption was that degenerative dementia equates with Alzheimer's disease, especially when patients' complaints involve memory. In the case of KE, many of her symptoms were framed in terms of 'remembering' things, and this had raised the usual initial suspicion of a memory disorder linked to Alzheimer's disease. Yet it was apparent from the clinical history that this was not a conventional memory disorder. Her husband reported that KE took empty cartons to the supermarket to match up with items on the supermarket shelf, yet she had no difficulty remembering to go to the supermarket in the first place and she did so unprompted. She had no difficulty finding her way there and had never become lost. She remembered which shelf to go to in order to find the required item. She did not forget to bring the empty carton with her when shopping. In her home, she remembered the time that her husband returned from work and ensured that meals were ready at precisely the right time. She did not behave at all like a person with a conventional amnesia. It was evident that this was a specific type of 'memory' disorder. WM also complained of difficulty 'remembering things'. Yet, it was clear that this difficulty in 'remembering' was specifically in remembering the names for things, not events as in classical amnesia.

So, the first point of interest was that this was a different form of memory disorder. My neuropsychological assessment revealed in both patients a severe, yet remarkably selective disorder of semantic memory. Elizabeth Warrington had described three similar patients back in 1975 (Warrington, 1975). The aetiology was unknown. We had reported three cases in 1989 (Snowden, Goulding & Neary, 1989), and coined the term 'semantic dementia' on the basis of the multi-modal nature of the semantic disorder. We argued that this was a form of dementia distinct from Alzheimer's disease, although at the time had no proof. This would come later. We described a further six patients in the context of progressive aphasia: a fluent aphasia characterized by impairments in naming and word comprehension, accompanied by an associative form of agnosia (Snowden et al., 1992). In the same year, John Hodges reported five patients with semantic dementia (Hodges, Patterson, Oxbury & Funnell, 1992). Despite these cases, the disorder, in 1991 and 1992, was still very novel, and a cause of curiosity and excitement for neuropsychologists. The profile appeared to provide confirmatory evidence of the distinction between semantic and episodic memory: the complement or double dissociation of classical amnesia.

It was not just the fact of the patients' relatively circumscribed semantic memory disorder that was of interest. I was struck by its magnitude. The severity of impairment, which became apparent on neuropsychological testing, seemed at odds with the reports of these patients' high level of functional independence. I wondered how patients managed so well in daily life when they showed such profound difficulties in the clinic. I discovered that KE could not recognize the meaning of even common household objects and food items when they were presented to her in the clinic. How then could she manage her home? How could she prepare meals unassisted using the right ingredients?

One thing that particularly intrigued me was the apparent disparity between patients' conversational and test vocabulary. In general conversation, both patients conversed fluently and effortlessly. In fact, both were decidedly garrulous. Their sentences included nominal terms, which, for the most part, were used appropriately. In the case of WM, her vocabulary was sufficiently rich that it was not apparent to the attending physician that she had a problem with language at all. Yet, when I came to test the patients, I discovered that their naming performance was at or approached floor level. I wondered how it could be that WM was unable to name common objects such as tie, comb and watch, yet in conversation, produced utterances such as "I am church warden. I help prepare the chalice for the Eucharist. Afterwards, I put the chalice back in the vestry"; "my daughter is catering manager at the agricultural college"; "I need to talk to my solicitor about my driving licence". Test modality did not provide an explanation. Formal naming performance was just as poor when WM was asked to name an object from a verbal description (e.g., What do you use to do your hair?) as from a picture or from the object itself. The findings seemed counter-intuitive. A reasonable assumption, in a degraded semantic system, is that factors such as word frequency, concept familiarity and typicality would be predictors of performance. Common vocabulary such as 'dog' and 'cat' should be better retained than less common vocabulary such as 'penguin' and 'leopard'. There is now robust evidence, in the context of performance on formal naming tests, that this is so (Lambon Ralph, Graham, Ellis & Hodges, 1998; Woollams, Lambon Ralph, Plaut & Patterson, 2008). Yet, KE and WM's conversational vocabulary, which included remarkably low-frequency terms, seemed to fly in the face of that general principle. I was keen to understand the basis for such anomalies.

Did you have any clues?

Yes. I noticed that patients' conversation invariably centred around their daily lives. The patients never conversed about non-personal topics. I wondered whether patients' experiential memory, which seemed to be so remarkably well preserved, might be helping to maintain or invest meaning in vocabulary that would otherwise be lost. That is, direct personal experience might be a more relevant determinant of performance than abstract measures of familiarity as defined by population norms. The investigations that I carried out were designed to examine the influence of personal experience on the patients' knowledge.

Can you summarise the main features of these cases? What were these cases' patterns of spared and impaired abilities?

To place the findings of more directed tests in context, it is perhaps first worth summarizing the background neuropsychological findings. Both patients showed problems in language that were consistent with a circumscribed semantic disorder. They spoke in grammatical sentences with no problems in phonology or articulation. By contrast, they showed very profound difficulties in naming and word comprehension. I have already provided examples of WM's difficulties. The problems were even more marked in KE. Her naming was nil and her understanding, as measured by word-picture and word-object matching tests, was at chance level. She could not, for example, match the word "rabbit" with one of four pictures of animals, "sock" with one of four pictures of clothing or "comb", "glasses" and "pen" with the corresponding object presented in an array. The results were the same regardless of whether words were presented in spoken or written form. KE showed virtually no understanding of even the most common nominal terms.

In both patients, performance was entirely consistent. Words that were not recognized on one occasion would not be recognized on another. This is a core feature of degraded semantic knowledge, as opposed to a problem in semantic access (Shallice, 1988).

In keeping with their impaired word comprehension, both patients made 'regularisation' errors in word reading (e.g., 'glove' to rhyme with 'rove; 'pint' to rhyme with 'mint') consistent with surface dyslexia, a feature now recognized to be strongly associated with semantic dementia (Woollams et al., 2007). The patients made parallel, regularisation errors in writing (e.g., 'cort' for 'caught'), consistent with surface dysgraphia.

In both KE and WM, the semantic disorder extended beyond the verbal domain. They had difficulties recognizing pictures of famous people and famous buildings, sorting pictures of dogs, cats, birds and fish into the relevant category, separating real fruits and vegetables according to the context in which they would be eaten (e.g., cooked/uncooked, main course/dessert) and matching tastes of fruit juices with the appropriate fruit. KE was unable to demonstrate through gesture the function of common objects and reported that she did not know what the objects were.

By contrast, KE and WM performed well on perceptual, spatial and constructional tasks provided these made no semantic demands. They performed normally on visual matching tasks involving subtle perceptual discrimination, such as the Benton face-matching test (Levin, Hamsher & Benton, 1975). They could copy line drawings of objects that they did not recognize. Both patients performed poorly on formal memory tests, which involved words that they did not understand. Nevertheless, they were fully oriented in time and place and they gave an accurate account of recent autobiographical events, within the confines of their vocabulary, which was corroborated by their respective husbands.

In short, both patients showed the characteristic profile of strengths and weaknesses that we now associate with semantic dementia.

What about the experimental test findings?

My studies of KE and WM (Snowden, Griffiths & Neary, 1994, 1995, 1996) explored the relationship between personal experience and patients' understanding of concepts. There were three key findings. Firstly, KE and WM both showed a strongly significant autobiographical effect. Their understanding was better for personally relevant than non-personal material. Secondly, their understanding was better for material relevant to their current life as opposed to relevant in the past. Thirdly, their understanding of 'known' concepts was not normal but limited to that aspect of information related to their personal experience.

I'll give some information about the studies on which these findings are based. The patients' respective husbands provided me with names of acquaintances that had *current* relevance for the patient, such as a current neighbour or local shopkeeper, and names that were relevant in the *past*, such as a former work colleague. For comparison, I selected current and past high-profile famous names (e.g., Elvis Presley, Winston Churchill), which the patients' husbands confirmed would have been well known to the patient in the past. I asked the patient to i) match a surname with one of three first-names (e.g., PRESLEY: Cliff Elvis Adam; CHURCHILL: Winston Vincent Lester) and ii) provide identifying information ("Who is. . .?").

KE and WM, like three other patients with semantic dementia, showed the same pattern. They recognized names of acquaintances significantly better than famous names, and *currently* relevant names better than those from the past, both when measured by surname-first name matching and by explicit identifying information (Figure 15.1). These differences could not be explained by task difficulty or general familiarity. Four amnesic patients with Alzheimer disease showed no differences in performance for personal, famous, current and past names. To underscore the autobiographical effect, KE sometimes interpreted famous names within a personal context (e.g., "Margaret Thatcher, is that Margaret and Reg who we go for a drink with?").

A repeat test in WM, using a different set of personal and famous names, showed the same pattern: better understanding of personal than famous names and better understanding of names of current relevance than names from the past. Notably, she reported 100% of current personal names to be subjectively familiar but 0% of past famous names.

The autobiographical effect extended to place names. I compared patients' recognition of autobiographically relevant place names (e.g., where the patient

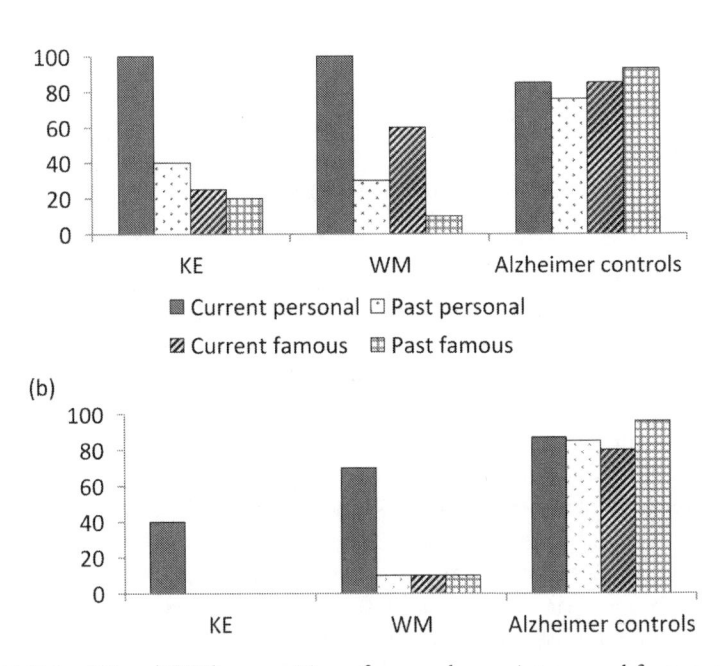

FIGURE 15.1 KE and WM's recognition of personal acquaintance and famous names, as measured by (a) surname—first name matching (chance = 33%) and (b) provision of explicit identifying information.

Semantic Memory and Personal Experience 321

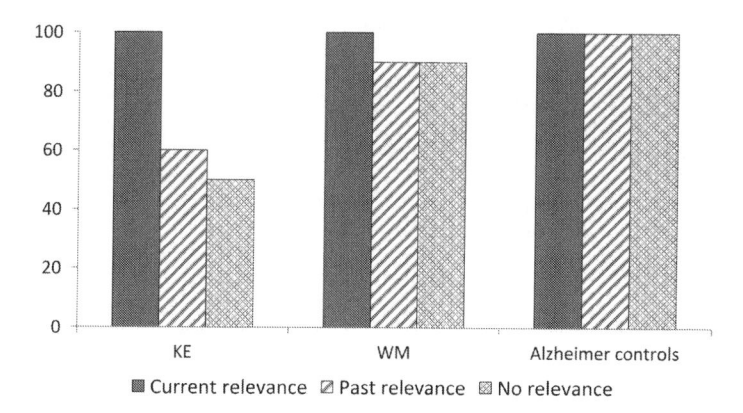

[Bar chart showing percentages for KE, WM, and Alzheimer controls with three bars each for Current relevance, Past relevance, and No relevance. KE: 100, 60, 50. WM: 100, 90, 90. Alzheimer controls: ~100, ~100, ~100.]

FIGURE 15.2 KE and WM's recognition that a place name (e.g., London) is 'a place' as a function of personal autobiographical relevance.

shops, visits her daughter or has been on holiday) with high-profile place names (e.g., London, Paris) that had no personal relevance for the patient. The 'personally relevant' place names (e.g., Knaresborough, Gozo) were generally less well-known/semantically salient than the impersonal place names. To test understanding, I interspersed the place names amongst a list of non-place words (e.g., shirt, potato) and asked the patients to give the meaning of each word. I was interested to know simply whether the patient recognized the place name as signifying a place. WM recognized all current, personally relevant place names as a place, but was less than perfect for other place names. KE showed an even more marked disparity. She recognized 100% of places of current relevance, but only 50% impersonal place names (Figure 15.2). Alzheimer patients recognized all place names as places.

The severity of KE's semantic impairment precluded further exploration of place knowledge. She did not understand localizing distinctions such as "this country or abroad" and she did not recognize maps. WM's milder disorder offered more scope. She provided more detailed information about personally relevant than impersonal place names. She located more personally relevant towns on an outline map of UK and countries and regions on an outline map of the countries of Europe (Figure 15.3). There were striking differences in the quality of her responses. For example, when offered the name "Auvergne", a region of France that she had visited on holiday, she immediately pointed to the correct part of France on the map of Europe, accompanied by the comment "It's in France, here by the Dordogne. We used to go there in the caravanette". By contrast, she denied familiarity with "Portugal", a country that she had never visited. Her response, "What's Portugal?", indicated that she did not recognize it as the name of a place.

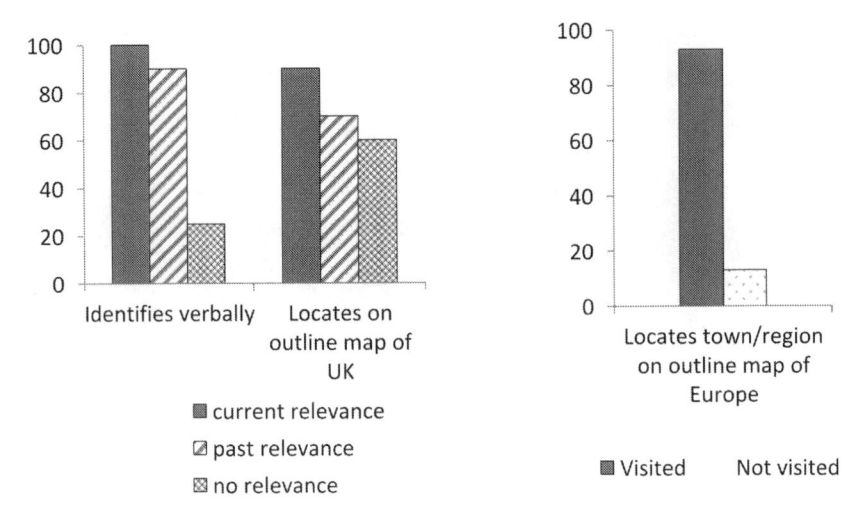

FIGURE 15.3 Place knowledge in WM, measured by her verbal definitions and location on outline maps, as a function of personal relevance.

Was there an autobiographical influence also on recognition of non-verbal material?

Yes. I could explore this particularly with KE because she showed severe object recognition problems. I carried out the study in her home. I showed her 30 of her own household objects (e.g., kettle, comb, spoon) and 30 examples of the same objects brought from my own home. She saw each object three times a) once in the object's usual context (e.g., kettle in the kitchen), b) once in an incongruous context (e.g., comb in the refrigerator) and c) once in a neutral context, on a table in an array. As KE could name no objects, I judged her ability to recognize the objects based on her verbal descriptions and pantomimes of the object's function. I found a dramatic effect of personal ownership. She recognized her own objects significantly better than my objects (Figure 15.4), and objects presented in their usual location better than in an incongruous or neutral location. For example, she had no difficulty recognizing a coat hanger when it was hanging in the wardrobe but was unable to do so when it was placed in the bath. I showed KE line drawings of 24 of the objects used in the main task. Her recognition of the line drawings was similar to that for my objects presented in a neutral array. Thus, the quality of perceptual information (real object versus line drawing) was less important in determining recognition than personal ownership and topographical context.

I found some aspects of KE's performance particularly intriguing. KE recognized and gave an elaborate account of her electric toaster, even though her husband had bought the toaster only the week before (at which time she did not understand what it was for) and she had never previously owned a toaster. Thus,

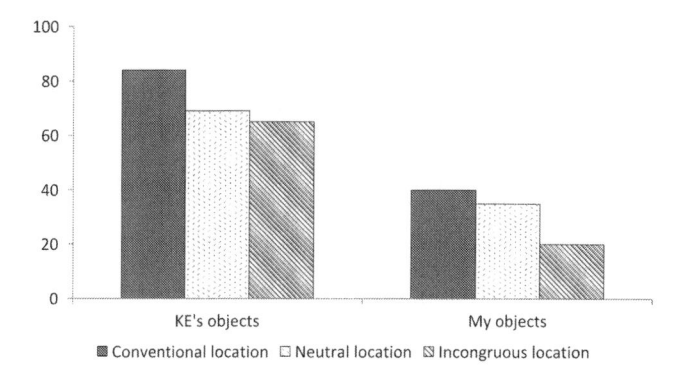

FIGURE 15.4 KE's object recognition as a function of personal ownership and topographical context in which the object was presented.

her recognition could not be attributed to cumulative familiarity, as defined by frequency of exposure. Moreover, some of her responses were idiosyncratic. For example, she recognized her jug as a receptacle for flowers, consistent with her own personal usage, but she had no knowledge of its canonical function.

What about object recognition in WM?

WM showed only mild difficulties recognizing household objects (in a study mirroring that in KE she recognized 100% of her objects and 93% of my objects). Nevertheless, I had the opportunity to examine in WM the relative influence of current and past experience on object recognition through a study of coins. In the early 1990s, only two decades had passed since a change in the British monetary system from imperial (1 pound = 20 shillings; 1 shilling = 12 pence) to decimal (1 pound = 100 pence). WM would have spent the first 34 years of her life being exposed to imperial coinage and the second 21 years to the decimal system, so she would have been highly familiar with both systems. WM identified current coins by name but showed no recognition of pre-decimal coins. Similarly, she had good knowledge of the value of current coins: how many of one would be equivalent to another, achieving a score of 100%, but she scored at floor level (0%) for pre-decimal coins. By contrast, a group of age-matched amnesic Alzheimer patients showed no significant differences between current and past coinage. Thus, WM's performance provided further evidence that relevance to *current* personal experience is the critical factor in facilitating understanding. I found too that WM showed a reversed temporal gradient on the Autobiographical Memory Interview (Kopelman, Wilson & Baddeley, 1990), the opposite of that shown by a group of amnesic Alzheimer patients (Figure 15.5). I was particularly struck by the fact too that whilst she had no difficulty recognizing and naming current photos of her grandchildren, she showed no recognition at all of past photos of herself or

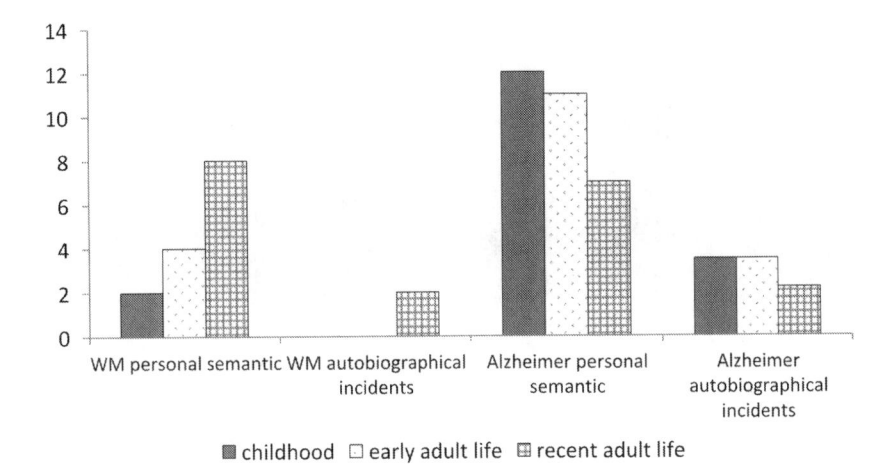

FIGURE 15.5 WM's performance on the Autobiographical Memory Interview. Mean scores for a reference group of amnesic Alzheimer patients are shown for comparison.

her parents, now deceased. Again, *current* autobiographical relevance seemed more important in influencing WM's knowledge than frequency of exposure or cumulative familiarity or indeed affective valence.

These data showed that the 'autobiographical' effect was robust, being demonstrable for a variety of semantic tasks involving both verbal and non-verbal material, and that current experience is particularly crucial. Yet, it begged the question as to the status of apparently 'preserved' concepts. When, for example, WM referred to "driving licence" in conversation, did she have full understanding of the meaning of the word 'licence' or was her understanding limited to the specific context of her personal experience? To address this question I identified, from transcripts of recorded speech, nouns and noun phrases that WM used (appropriately) in conversation. I re-combined these to form noun phrases and compound words that I had not heard her use. For example:

driving licence, dog → dog licence;
church warden, traffic → traffic warden;
oil, field → oil field;
sales, man → salesman

WM had no difficulty defining nouns and noun phrases that were drawn from her conversational vocabulary (Figure 15.6). By contrast, when these 'known' words were re-combined to form new noun phrases or compound words (e.g., dog licence, salesman), she could generally offer no definition at all. Similarly, she denied understanding constituent words (e.g., licence) of 'known' noun phrases

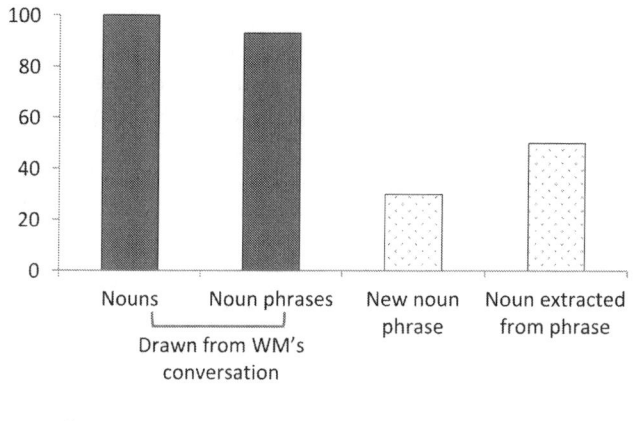

FIGURE 15.6 WM's definitions of noun and noun phrases.

(driving licence), when taken out of their noun-phrase context. She frequently reported that she had never heard the words before. Her understanding appeared limited to her own highly specific usage of terms. Indeed, all her definitions of 'known' words and phrases were entirely autobiographical in nature. For example:

DRIVING LICENCE: "I have the driving licence for driving cars, caravanettes and minibuses. I get it from the DVLC. It's labelled with my name".
DOG: "They're out there (referring to dogs barking outside). I take the vicar's dog for a walk at two o'clock".
OIL: "I store it in the outhouse. It goes in the radiators in winter to keep me warm".

The findings suggested that WM's understanding of words that she used in conversation was not normal. It was personalized and constrained by autobiographical context.

Do you think these cases contribute to our understanding of how the normal mind works?

I do. I think they give us cause for thought. A child must inevitably acquire knowledge of the world through experience, either direct (through sensory experience) or indirect (what is taught at school, read in books etc). Yet, there is a common presumption that once that knowledge is acquired, it is represented in an abstracted form independent of personal experience. Thus, we recognize the names of people and places, and understand the meaning of words and objects without recourse to our particular direct experiences of those things. The findings in KE and WM suggest that this formulation may be an over-simplification. KE and WM both have an understanding of the world sufficient to enable them to function relatively independently. Yet, what they know is strongly influenced by their direct personal experience. There may be a closer interaction and continuing interrelationship between concept knowledge and experience than is often thought.

We have proposed (Julien, Thompson, Neary & Snowden, 2008; Julien, Neary & Snowden, 2010), in line with Funnell (2001), that conceptual knowledge can be represented at different levels of abstraction, from information that is embedded in specific contexts, relating to personal experience, to information that is relatively context-free. In KE and WM, the most abstracted levels of knowledge are compromised, and the patients are increasingly reliant on meaning that is grounded in personal everyday experience.

Why might direct experience be helpful to KE and WM? We know from their neuropsychological performance that spatial skills are well preserved. So too is their understanding of time and temporal relationships. I have argued (Snowden et al., 1999) that personal experience links an object with a meaningful temporal and spatial context (e.g., taking the vicar's dog for a walk in the fields each afternoon at two o'clock). Experiential memories, subserved by hippocampal function, would draw together weak neocortical information about percepts (words and objects) and relatively strong spatial and sequential information, the latter providing a support or conceptual reference for the latter.

Do you think that there is anything unique that the report of these cases added to our knowledge?

A fundamental general point was the demonstration of the interdependence between experiential and semantic memory. There were some specific findings that seemed particularly unique. Firstly, there was evidence that KE and WM's knowledge about the world was personalized and influenced by the way concepts impinged on their experience. KE recognized a jug as a receptacle for flowers but not a container for liquids. WM understood 'oil' as a commodity that goes in her radiators but had no understanding beyond her personal usage. It would be reasonable to suppose *a priori*, that patients with a degraded semantic system would retain knowledge of core characteristics and canonical function (e.g., a jug holds liquid, enables pouring) better than less common functions (e.g., a jug can be used as a vase). KE and WM's idiosyncratic knowledge highlights the importance of direct personal experience as distinct from frequency of encounter or generic markers of familiarity.

Another finding that was unique at the time related to the disproportionate effect of *current* experience and the documentation in these patients of an inverse temporal gradient of retrograde memory. The findings, which have subsequently been demonstrated by others (Hodges & Graham, 1998), forced us to re-evaluate the nature of semantic memory and its relationship with autobiographical and episodic memory.

Can you specify why these cases were relevant in relation to the knowledge at the time and would they still be relevant to the knowledge of today?

They were relevant for a number of reasons. On the one hand, the patients' severe yet relatively circumscribed disorder of semantic memory provided a validation of the theoretical distinction between semantic and episodic memory, which had been advanced two decades earlier (Tulving, 1972, 1983). On the other hand, these cases provided challenges to existing accounts of semantic memory. In Tulving's original formulation, semantic memory was defined as information that is i) acquired early in life, ii) culturally shared and iii) not tied to a particular temporal or spatial context. The implication was that semantic knowledge of words and objects, once acquired, represents an essentially stable knowledge base that is independent of autobiographical experience. Language-based models of semantic memory, construed in terms of a hierarchical network (Collins & Quillian, 1969) or a set of defining and characteristic features (Smith, Shoben & Ripps, 1974), also supposed a relatively static storehouse of concepts, divorced from experience. Yet, the findings in KE and WM suggested a more complex and dynamic interplay between semantic memory and personal experience.

To a certain extent, there is now much greater appreciation of the interdependence between aspects of memory. The finding of an effect of personal experience on knowledge has been replicated by independent studies of semantic dementia (Péron et al., 2015; Westmacott, Leach, Freedman & Moscovitch, 2004). Péron et al. controlled for frequency of encounter, reinforcing our own findings that the experiential effect is a direct effect that is not equivalent to cumulative frequency of occurrence or overall familiarity. Other studies have reported an impact of semantic memory impairment on autobiographical and episodic memories (Graham, Simons, Pratt, Patterson & Hodges, 2000; Irish, Addis, Hodges & Piguet, 2012; Maguire, Kumaran, Hassabis & Kopelman, 2010; Westmacott et al., 2001) and conversely an impact of episodic memory impairment on semantic memory (Greenberg & Verfaellie, 2010).

Nevertheless, theories of semantic memory still pay scant attention to the interrelationship. There is nowadays a general consensus that semantic memory involves distributed brain networks. There is evidence that the brain regions involved in representing sensory and motor properties of object concepts (colour, taste, form, movement etc) correspond to those involved in sensory perception and action (Martin, 2007; Pulvermüller, 2012). Thus, object concepts are grounded in and emerge from activity within property-based brain regions—although whether there need also be an amodal level of representation, which abstracts away from modality-specific attributes, remains an area of contention (Patterson, Nestor & Rogers, 2007). I find these studies impressive and the data arising from them hugely illuminating. They are crucial for our understanding of how the brain represents knowledge about objects. Yet, I think KE and WM serve as a reminder that semantic memory is more than an assemblage of properties of objects. It encompasses all that we know and how we function in and interact with the wider world. To my mind, this broader conception of semantic memory is the major challenge for semantic memory theorists.

Back in the 1970s, there was a school of thought that recognized that semantic memory must encompass more than simple word or object concepts defined by properties or attributes. This group of scientists framed knowledge in terms of schema or scripts. Schank and Abelson (1977) proposed that people build up schema/scripts that represent commonly experienced activities and events. I think this kind of notion has potential relevance for helping to understand why KE and WM might understand a word or object within one context but not another. In any event, the fact that the findings in these two patients are not readily accommodated by contemporary accounts of semantic memory demonstrates why they are still relevant today.

The striking effect of *current* experience and demonstration of an inverse temporal gradient of memory in KE and WM was highly relevant at the time because it was the opposite of that found in classical amnesia. The traditional interpretation of the temporal graded memory loss in amnesia was that memories become more embedded over time and hence less vulnerable to disruption (Ribot's law). Such an explanation would clearly have difficulty accounting for the obverse finding in our patients. The findings continue to have implications for the understanding of retrograde memory function.

Were there any relevant data that you did not manage to publish on these cases?

There were no directly relevant data. I had tried to explore factors underpinning KE's idiosyncratic use of verbs. She appeared to apply 'twisting' to all actions involving movement and 'banging' to all actions involving sound!

What are the shortcomings of these cases?

KE was severely affected at the time she was seen. The scope for investigation was limited by her profound inability to name or understand words. It would have been helpful to have seen her in the early stages of the disease, when more vocabulary was available to her. In both patients, longitudinal investigations would have been valuable because it would have permitted closer examination of the relationship between knowledge and ongoing experience. More sophisticated neuroimaging that allowed better evaluation of structure and function of temporal neocortices and medial temporal lobe structures would certainly have assisted in the interpretation of the data.

Do you remember whether you had difficulty publishing this report? If so, what was this difficulty?

There was no difficulty in publication. As far as I can recall the reviews were positive and enthusiastic. One reviewer requested clarification of the precise role of autobiographical experience in supporting meaning: specifically, whether I thought experiences were *integral* to the meaning of a concept or whether they served merely to *refresh memory for meaning*, by virtue of repetition of exposure. This was a relevant and perceptive question. If experience merely had a general facilitatory role, in activating a concept and hence preventing it from being eroded, then knowledge of a concept ought to be preserved in its entirety. Moreover, overall familiarity—or frequency of encounter—ought to be a predictor of performance. Such an account would not explain the patients' partial or idiosyncratic understanding, their recognition in one context but not another and their ability to learn new information such as the meaning of an electric toaster. Far from having a general effect in maintaining the integrity of a concept direct experience appeared to have an effect of imbuing a sometimes highly personalised significance to an object. The distinction raised by the reviewer was to prove relevant to a controversy that arose later.

What was the controversy?

A few years after the reports on KE and WM, colleagues in Cambridge published an article rejecting the notion of an autobiographical effect on semantic memory (Graham et al., 1997). In actual fact, their findings in two semantic dementia patients were not fundamentally dissimilar to our own. Current personal relevance influenced surname-first name matching, just as it did in KE and WM. The controversy arose less from differences in data and more from interpretation. Graham et al. had expected experience to maintain *all* aspects of knowledge about a concept, that is, maintain a concept's integrity, presumably in line with an interpretation of the autobiographical effect as one of "refreshing memory for meaning through exposure". They expected semantic knowledge for the sports in which their patients participated to be preserved and generally superior to knowledge for other sports. This was not the case. Their patients continued to play golf and bowls, but their explicit semantic knowledge of these sports was far from normal. These authors proposed that ostensibly preserved knowledge might not be semantic at all. They argued that the preserved abilities in their patients (playing sports) had a strong procedural component.

So could KE and WM's ability to function relatively well in the confines of their daily routine likewise be attributed to preserved procedural memory? I argued that it could not (Snowden et al., 1999). It would have difficulty accounting for the dramatic difference in recognition of KE's own and my objects when they were both presented in their usual topographical context. An incident brought this point into sharp focus. After the object recognition task, KE invited me to have a cup of tea. She discovered my kettle in the place where her own kettle normally resides. She exclaimed, "What's that?", moved it aside and went to retrieve her own kettle from the bedroom, where she recalled having seen it last (in its incongruous context). She then proceeded to brew tea in the normal way. If KE had available only general procedures or well-rehearsed action routines, then she ought to have implemented the tea-making routine regardless of which kettle was available to her. Instead, she carried out a novel set of actions, entirely outside the remit of her daily routine.

The most fundamental challenge put forward by Graham and colleagues, centred on the definition of semantic memory. For them, semantic memory was abstract, decontextualized knowledge, as defined by Tulving (1972). Thus, if the factual information available to KE and WM is underpinned by autobiographical memories then, by definition, it cannot be semantic. Yet, in my view, WM's explicit knowledge that the Auvergne is a part of France by the Dordogne (Snowden et al., 1994) is not rendered less semantic just because that knowledge was enabled by virtue of her recall of a previous visit to that region of France and was autobiographically constrained. Rather it forces us to re-evaluate our notions of semantic memory.

Some years later, the Cambridge group demonstrated a 'personal familiarity' effect on object recognition in two semantic dementia patients (Bozeat, Lambon Ralph, Patterson & Hodges, 2002). Again, those authors rejected an explanation in terms of semantic memory on the basis that the patients' recognition did not generalize to other examples of the same object and so did not conform to traditional definitions of semantic memory. They favoured the explanation that repeated use of a specific object establishes a set of automatic, stereotyped responses, which are triggered by that particular object without activation of, or reliance on, semantic knowledge. This explanation made me wonder—would automatic object usage without semantics reduce the patient to an automaton? KE's entirely novel actions with respect to her kettle, her learning of new objects with minimal exposure and her ability to provide an explicit verbal commentary about an object's function suggest that she is not merely exhibiting a set of automatic, stereotyped responses. I think the findings challenge our notions about what constitutes semantic memory.

Are there any assessments/paradigms that you would administer now to these individuals if they were available?

I would have liked to explore more systematically the constraints on WM's understanding and use of vocabulary. I noticed that WM, during the process of moving house, referred spontaneously to the prospective buyers and to her solicitor by name, but three months after the house move, she showed no recognition of their names. I would have liked to carry out a systematic, longitudinal investigation of her vocabulary in relation to its continuing relevance to her life and explored in more detail the extent of her knowledge of 'known' concepts.

These cases were reported in the '90s. Do you think these cases are still informative now? Are we now better able to interpret these patterns of spared and impaired abilities? If so, in what way?

Semantic dementia is now very well recognized. Performance is remarkably consistent and predictable from one patient to another. Thus, the overall pattern of these patients' strengths (non-semantic aspects of function) and weaknesses (semantic functions), which seemed so remarkable in the early 90s, is no longer a surprise. Moreover, neuroimaging is now a readily available resource. It has helped to clarify the underlying anatomical changes—the marked degenerative change in temporal neocortices and the loss of white matter connectivity throughout ventral pathways (Acosta-Cabronero et al., 2011; Agosta et al., 2010).

Nevertheless, in other respects, I think these cases are just as informative—and puzzling—as in the 1990s. Despite accumulating evidence of the role of personal experience in supporting semantic knowledge (Julien et al., 2010; Péron et al., 2015; Westmacott et al., 2001; Westmacott, Black, Freedman & Moscovitch, 2004), there is still no full, principled account of the autobiographical effect. I do not think the effect can be dismissed as products of procedural memory or artefacts of general effects of frequency or familiarity.

Do you think these cases have been considered by people who develop theories of the normal mind? If yes, how? If no, should they?

This is a good question. Theorists have certainly taken note of the broad phenomena of semantic dementia and recognize its theoretical significance. I think they neglect the minutiae of the disorder.

I have intimated earlier that research into semantic memory typically focuses on words and objects. This is perhaps unsurprising because it is easier to control and manipulate variables under investigation. Yet, KE and WM show us that semantic memory is much more than that. I think models of semantic memory need to take a broader approach.

In general, do you think that neuropsychology cases could contribute to our understanding of the normal mind? Should these data be considered and if so why?

To my mind neuropsychology cases are crucial. That is because the data that they elicit are so often counter-intuitive. They challenge prior conceptions and force us to re-evaluate models that we may have taken for granted. To take one example in the field of aphasia: one might not expect *a priori* that, in the absence of a motor speech impairment, an anomic patient would be able to write down the name of an object correctly (e.g., cat) yet be totally unable to retrieve that same object name in its spoken form. Yet, we do see dissociations between spoken and written naming in patients with neurological disease. One traditional model of language argued that in order to spell a word, it is necessary first to have access to its sound. Yet, a single neuropsychology case is sufficient to counter the notion that access to the orthographic form of a word inevitably requires prior access to its phonological form.

In recent years, technological advances have opened up a variety of avenues for investigating the normal mind, for example, though functional imaging, transcranial magnetic stimulation or computer modelling. But I consider these approaches to be complementary. They do not supersede the neuropsychological data. Models, derived from studies of healthy individuals or computer modelling, will always need to account for what patients actually do.

We are now living in an era where ethics committees would like to foresee every step. How much serendipity was involved in your assessment?

There was a great deal of serendipity. I was, at the time, in a fortunate—and fairly unusual—position of having a combined clinical and research role. The boundaries between those roles were blurred. There was no clear dividing line between what constituted a clinical diagnostic assessment and what constituted research. The aim was simply to understand the patient's disorder as fully as possible. Clinically, the desired effect was to optimize accuracy of diagnosis, and hence likely prognosis, and to enable the most appropriate advice to be given to the patients and their families on dealing with their condition. The evaluation also yielded research data of theoretical relevance. The blurred clinical/research distinction meant that it was not difficult, following patients' initial diagnostic assessment, to arrange extra assessment sessions and home visits, subject to approval and informed consent from patients and families. Moreover, it offered the opportunity to get to know the patients' well, and hence notice aspects of their condition that might otherwise have been overlooked.

From a contemporary perspective, where health service time is costed, and work activity needs to conform precisely to an agreed job plan, this flexibility seems a luxury. There is now an implicit assumption that research and clinical activity are—and should be—totally separate activities. In many spheres, this assumption is, of course, justified and an appropriate safeguard for patients. It is essential, for example, that the conduct of an ethically approved clinical trial of a new medication is separated from the routine medical prescription of a licenced therapy. Yet, neuropsychology is rather different. Patients' performance on neuropsychological tests can raise questions that are relevant both to theory and to the patient's individual clinical care and management. There is not a clear dividing line.

It goes without saying that it would have been difficult to carry out the studies of KE and WM within the confines either of a time-limited clinical neuropsychological assessment or a prescribed research study involving a pre-defined battery of tests. KE and WM exemplify the fact that neuropsychological questions and insights can be patient-driven as well as theory-driven.

References

Acosta-Cabronero, J., Patterson, K., Fryer, T. D., Hodges, J. R., Williams, G. B., & Nestor, P. J. (2011). Atrophy, hypometabolism and white matter abnormalities in semantic dementia tell a coherent story. *Brain, 134,* 2025–2035.

Agosta, F., Henry, R., Migliaccio, R., Neuhaus, J., Miller, B. L., Dronkers, N., Brambati, S. M., Filippi, M., Ogar, J. M., Wilson, S. M., Gorno-Tempini, M. L. (2010). Language networks in semantic dementia. *Brain, 133,* 286–299.

Bozeat, S., Lambon Ralph, M. A., Patterson, K., & Hodges, J. R. (2002). The influence of personal familiarity and context on object use in semantic dementia. *Neurocase, 8(1–2),* 127–134.

Collins, A. M., & Quillian, M. R. (1969). Retrieval time from semantic memory. *Journal of Verbal Learning and Verbal Behaviour, 8,* 240–247.

Funnell, E. (2001). Evidence for scripts in semantic dementia: implications for theories of semantic memory. *Cognitive Neuropsychology, 18(4),* 323–341.

Graham, K. S., Lambon Ralph, M. A., & Hodges, J. R. (1997). Determining the impact of autobiographical experience on "meaning": new insights from investigating sport-related vocabulary and knowledge in two cases with semantic dementia. *Cognitive Neuropsychology, 14(6),* 801–837.

Graham, K. S., Simons, J. S., Pratt, K. H., Patterson, K., & Hodges, J. R. (2000). Insights from semantic dementia on the relationship between episodic and semantic memory. *Neuropsychologia, 38(3),* 313–324.

Greenberg, D. L., & Verfaellie, M. (2010). Interdependence of episodic and semantic memory: evidence from neuropsychology. *Journal of the International Neuropsychological Society, 16(5),* 748–753.

Hodges, J. R., & Graham, K. (1998). A reversal of the temporal gradient for famous person knowledge in semantic dementia: implications for the neural organisation of long-term memory. *Neuropsychologia, 36(8),* 803–825.

Hodges, J. R., Patterson, K., Oxbury, S., & Funnell, E. (1992). Semantic dementia. Progressive fluent aphasia with temporal lobe atrophy. *Brain, 115(6),* 1783–1806.

Irish, M., Addis, D. R., Hodges, J. R., & Piguet, O. (2012). Considering the role of semantic memory in episodic future thinking: evidence from semantic dementia. *Brain, 135(7),* 2178–2191.

Julien, C. L., Neary, D., & Snowden, J. S. (2010). Personal experience and arithmetic meaning in semantic dementia. *Neuropsychologia, 48(1),* 278–287.

Julien, C. L., Thompson, J. C., Neary, D., & Snowden, J. S. (2008). Arithmetic knowledge in semantic dementia: is it invariably preserved? *Neuropsychologia, 46,* 2732–2744.

Kopelman, M. D., Wilson, B. A., & Baddeley, A. D. (1990). *The Autobiographical Memory Interview*. Oxford: Pearson Assessment.

Lambon Ralph, M. A., Graham, K. S., Ellis, A. W., & Hodges, J. R. (1998). Naming in semantic dementia—what matters? *Neuropsychologia, 36(8),* 775–784.

Levin, H. S., Hamsher, K. D., & Benton, A. L. (1975). A short form of facial recognition for clinical use. *Journal of Psychology, 91,* 223–228.

Maguire, E. A., Kumaran, D., Hassabis, D., & Kopelman, M. D. (2010). Autobiographical memory in semantic dementia: a longitudinal fMRI study. *Neuropsychologia, 48(1),* 123–136.

Martin, A. (2007). The representation of object concepts in the brain. *Annual Review of Psychology, 58,* 25–45.

Patterson, K., Nestor, P. J., & Rogers, T. T. (2007). Where do you know what you know? The representation of semantic knowledge in the human brain. *Nature Reviews Neuroscience, 8(12),* 976–987.

Péron, J. A., Piolino, P., Le Moal-Boursiquot, S., Biseul, I., Leray, E., Bon, L., Desgranges, B., Eustache, F., & Belliard, S. (2015). Preservation of person-specific semantic knowledge in semantic dementia: does direct personal experience have a specific role? *Frontiers in Human Neuroscience, 9,* 625.

Pulvermüller, F. (2012). Meaning and the brain: the neurosemantics of referential, interactive and combinatorial knowledge. *Journal of Neurolinguistics, 25(5),* 423–459.

Schank, R. C., & Abelson, R. (1977). *Scripts, Plans, Goals and Understanding*. Hillsdale, NJ: Lawrence Erlbaum Associates.

Shallice, T. (1988). *From Neuropsychology to Mental Structure*. Cambridge: Cambridge University Press.

Smith, E. E., Shoben, E. L., & Ripps, L. J. (1974). Structure and process in semantic memory: a featural model for semantic decisions. *Psychological Review, 81,* 214–241.

Snowden, J. S., Goulding, P. J., & Neary, D. (1989). Semantic dementia: a form of circumscribed atrophy. *Behavioural Neurology, 2,* 167–182.

Snowden, J. S., Griffiths, H., & Neary, D. (1994). Semantic dementia: autobiographical contribution to preservation of meaning. *Cognitive Neuropsychology, 11(3),* 265–288.

Snowden, J. S., Griffiths, H.L., & Neary, D. (1995). Autobiographical experience and word meaning. *Memory, 3(3/4),* 225–246.

Snowden, J. S., Griffiths, H., & Neary, D. (1996). Semantic-episodic memory interactions in semantic dementia: implications for retrograde memory function. *Cognitive Neuropsychology, 13(8),* 1101–1137.

Snowden, J. S., Griffiths, H. L., & Neary, D. (1999). The impact of autobiographical experience on meaning: reply to Graham, Lambon Ralph and Hodges. *Cognitive Neuropsychology, 16(7),* 673–687.

Snowden, J. S., Neary, D., Mann, D. M. A. et al. (1992). Progressive language disorder due to lobar atrophy. *Annals of Neurology, 31(2),* 174–183.

Tulving, E. (1972). Episodic and semantic memory. In E. Tulving & W. Donaldson (Eds.), *Organization of Memory*. New York: Academic Press, pp. 381–403.

Tulving, E. (1983). *Elements of Episodic Memory*. Oxford: Oxford University Press.

Warrington, E. K. (1975). The selective impairment of semantic memory. *The Quarterly Journal of Experimental Psychology, 27,* 635–637.

Westmacott, R., Black, S. E., Freedman, M., & Moscovitch, M. (2004). The contribution of autobiographical significance to semantic memory: evidence from Alzheimer's disease, semantic dementia and amnesia. *Neuropsychologia, 42(1),* 25–48.

Westmacott, R., Leach, L., Freedman, M., & Moscovitch, M. (2001). Different patterns of autobiographical memory loss in semantic dementia and medial temporal lobe amnesia: a challenge to consolidation theory. *Neurocase, 7(1)*, 37–55.

Woollams, A. M., Cooper-Pye, E., Hodges, J. R., & Patterson, K. (2008). Anomia: a doubly typical signature of semantic dementia. *Neuropsychologia, 46(10)*, 2503–2514.

Woollams, A. M., Lambon Ralph, M. A., Plaut, D. C., & Patterson, K. (2007). SD-squared: on the association between semantic dementia and surface dyslexia. *Psychological Review, 114(2)*, 316–339.

16

IRIS MURDOCH

Days Without Writing[1]

Peter Garrard, John R. Hodges, Vijeya Ganesan and Karalyn Patterson

In 2005, you published a report examining changes in the writing of the author Iris Murdoch from the start of her career, the peak of her career and finally the end of her career when she was considered to be in the early stages of Alzheimer's disease. This case may be relevant to our understanding of memory processes and deficits in Alzheimer's disease. Can you provide us with some background information about this case?

Jean Iris Murdoch (IM) was one of the most acclaimed novelists of the 20th century. Born in Dublin in 1919 into a middle-class protestant family, she was educated at Badminton School and then Somerville College Oxford, from where she graduated with a first in Greats (Ancient History and Philosophy) in 1942. Following wartime service in the Treasury and a post-war attachment to the United Nations, she returned to academic philosophy, first at Cambridge and later Oxford, where she became Fellow and Tutor at St. Anne's College in 1948.

IM wrote several short works of fiction (most of which she later destroyed) before the publication in 1953 of her first novel *Under the Net*, a first-person narrative that chronicles the adventures of a down-at-heel writer/philosopher in post-war London. Encouraged by the immediate success of this initial offering, IM carried on writing and her reputation as a novelist continued to grow, such that in 1963 she was able to retire from teaching philosophy and devote herself exclusively to writing.

Her creative method was highly individual: for up to eight months, she would concentrate on carefully working out the cast of characters together with their interrelationships and roles in the plot, before spending six months writing out the text of the book, in longhand, working from beginning to end. To enquiries about progress during the planning stage, she would often reply, 'The book is finished. All I have to do now is write it'.[2] She never used a typewriter and never owned a computer. There is no evidence that she agonised over the choice of words or made extensive use of dictionaries or thesauri, and an examination of her handwritten manuscript pages confirms that she seldom indulged in large-scale or repeated revisions of passages. Her publishers would be sent longhand manuscripts, which they often complained they could not read, but she eschewed any editorial interference. In consequence, and as illustrated in the manuscript and published versions of a passage from Chapter 17 of IM's 1956 novel *The Flight from the Enchanter* reproduced in Figure 16.1, the texts that appear in the print editions of her novels are, more or less, identical to the spontaneous output of IM's creative mind.

IM's work attracted outstanding critical acclaim. Reviewing *Under the Net* in 1953, Kingsley Amis hailed its author's 'brilliant talent'. Three years later, *The Flight from the Enchanter* was praised for its 'double and deceptive quality: crystal clear, but reflecting darkness'. *The Nice and the Good* (1968) was shortlisted for the Booker Prize in 1969, as were *The Black Prince* (1973), *The Sea, The Sea* (the 1978 winner), *The Good Apprentice* (1985), and *The Book and the Brotherhood* (1987). In 1987, IM was created by Dame Commander of the British Empire in recognition of her contribution to British literary life.

Over the following decade (1987–97), IM produced two philosophical works—*Metaphysics as a Guide to Morals* (1992) and *Existentialists and Mystics* (1997)—as

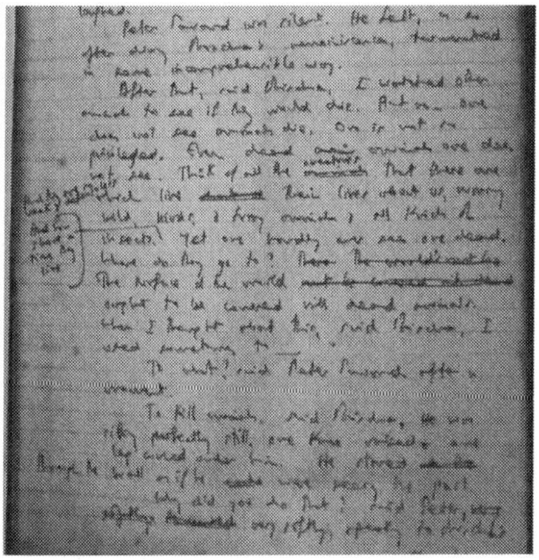

Peter Saward was silent. He felt, as he so frequently did during Mischa's reminiscences, tormented in some incomprehensible way.

'After that,' said Mischa, 'I watched other animals to see if they would die. But no – one does not see animals die. One is not so privileged. Even dead animals one does not see. Think of all the creatures that there are which live their lives about us, birds and animals and all kinds of insects. Helpless creatures and who do not live for long. Yet one hardly ever sees one dead. Where do they go to? The surface of the world ought to be covered with dead animals. When I thought about this,' said Mischa, 'I used sometimes to – '

'To what?' said Peter Saward after a moment.

'To kill animals,' said Mischa. He was sitting perfectly still, one knee raised and one leg curled under him. He stared through the wall as if he were seeing the past.

'Why did you do that?' asked Peter, very softly, speaking to Mischa's thought.

FIGURE 16.1 Manuscript (left) and text (right) of a passage from *The Flight from the Enchanter* (1956), illustrating the finality of the former in the creative process.

well as three further novels, the last of which (*Jackson's Dilemma*) came out in 1995. *Jackson's Dilemma* tells of the lives and love affairs of a group of friends, with the manservant Jackson as a shadowy, behind-the-scenes protagonist. The novel was received 'respectfully' but without enthusiasm, and IM would later reveal that she had been dogged by an intense and distressing 'writer's block' while working on it. A year earlier, she had become uncharacteristically inarticulate while taking part in an unscripted question-and-answer session about her work at a conference (Bayley, 1998), and diary entries from as early as 1993 are noted by her biographer as already being reduced to 'heart-rending simplicity' (Conradi, 2001).

As is often the case in more conventional clinical situations, the possible significance of these changes went unremarked until much later. Yet in retrospect, they can be seen as deeply ominous, clearly presaging the later decline in her intellectual abilities. She did undergo a specialist review at the Radcliffe Infirmary, Oxford, where she was reassured that there was nothing wrong, but her difficulties, particularly with words, persisted. A diagnosis of probable Alzheimer's disease was made after a further clinical assessment by JRH who found her to be profoundly amnesic as well as significantly anomic. JRH and KP assessed her again in November 1996 and June 1997, her condition deteriorating markedly even over this seven-month interval: in early November 1996, she achieved 20/30 on the Mini-Mental State Examination (Folstein et al., 1975), with points lost mainly on tests of attention and orientation. By the following summer, she could identify her surroundings only by the name of the city (Oxford), was unable to perform serial subtraction or reverse spelling, and could register but not recall a three-item word list, yielding a mini-mental score of 10/30.

The controversially candid three-volume memoir written by her husband, John Bayley, describes IM's rapid decline into dependency over the following year, her need for increasing supervision and her fascination with children's daytime television. The final weeks of her life were spent in an Oxford nursing home, where she 'declined food and drink for some time' before her death on February 8, 1999.

IM had granted permission for her brain to be examined by a pathologist after death, and changes characteristic of Alzheimer's disease were shown to be both present and widespread, confirming that the clinical diagnosis made during life had been correct.

How did you first realise that this case was interesting?

When *Jackson's Dilemma* was first published in 1995, many readers (us included) found the experience of reading it less than satisfactory. It was clearly different from any of IM's earlier works: admittedly, its characters were true to type in their detachment from the inconveniences of life and their capacity for prolix discussions about love and metaphysics, but the world in which they moved seemed immaterial and unconvincing, while the narrative was simple almost to the point of banality. The critics showed a similar lack of enthusiasm. Even though many of them were Murdoch's contemporaries, admirers and friends, most managed to remain vague enough to preserve a fitting respectfulness. A.S. Byatt, for instance, compared the structure of the novel to 'an Indian Rope Trick . . . in which all the people have no selves and therefore there is no story and no novel', while Penelope Fitzgerald noted that the economy of the writing made it appear 'as though Murdoch had let her fiction wear through almost to transparency'. Kate Kellaway found *Jackson's Dilemma* 'not a perfect novel: the narrative itself is, at times, a little distrait: like Jackson [a central character], it often moves with scant explanation'. Hugo Barnacle, though, was more outspoken, comparing the book to 'the work of a 13-year-old schoolgirl who doesn't get out enough'.

IM herself, in a post-publication interview for *The Guardian*, described the difficulties that she had experienced while writing the book, claiming that for the first time in her life she had suffered from 'writer's block', and that these and other unfamiliar difficulties had taken her to a 'very, very bad, quiet place' (Coles, 1996).

At the time this interview was published, we were working together at the MRC Cognition and Brain Sciences Unit (CBU) in Cambridge, studying the effects of Alzheimer's disease and other dementias on the brain's ability to process different aspects of language. Our colleague, Matt Lambon Ralph, brought a cutting of the interview to one of our Thursday morning research meetings and pointed out the remarkable similarity between the words IM had used to describe her difficulties, and those often used by patients with early onset dementia when they presented to our clinic for diagnosis. There were a multitude of clues: the hesitancy and lack of confidence in some of her utterances; the generic and repetitive vocabulary; the subtle deviations from syntactic propriety; and most poignantly of all the underlying melancholy in the way she comes across to the reader. The following extracts from the interview are particularly illustrative:

> *Did she find it difficult to live up to her reputation?* 'Well, the books I've written in the past I've done quite quickly, and known what to do and been geared up by them. But I'm afraid at the moment that I'm just falling, falling . . . just falling as it were. But I may get better. I hope so'.
> *There is a copy of Conversations with Isiah Berlin lying open at her feet. What else is she reading at the moment?* 'Um, well, quite a lot of things, but I haven't found anything which would be really useful to me. I find I haven't got anything at the moment, and this is really rather startling to me. I feel as though maybe the whole thing has packed up. But I hope, I really do believe actually, I could get on and find myself in a happier state, but I don't think so at the very moment. I'm just wandering. I think of things and then they go away forever.'

And later,

> 'I've slipped out of the university now,' says Iris. 'But I do every day try and collect something or other to myself.' Then she gives me a beautiful, generous smile. 'Your arrival may help me.'

At the end of the interview, John Bayley confides in the interviewer that

> we've been to see doctors you know, and they say the old brain's very crafty. It can come up against a block, and for a bit, things seem a bit strange, but then it finds its way around these things again.

Can you summarise the main features of this case?

IM agreed to be examined at her home in Oxford by a research team from the CBU in November 1996, and soon afterwards travelled to London for a volumetric MRI scan at the Institute of Neurology. The latter revealed established atrophy, with a posterior emphasis and undoubted hippocampal involvement, though—unusually for Alzheimer's—the volume loss was somewhat asymmetric (see Figure 16.2). The neuropsychological deficits were also highly characteristic of AD:

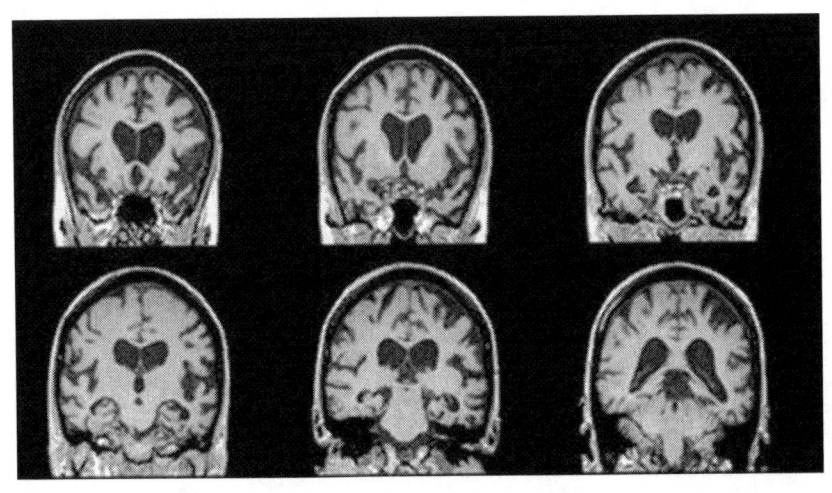

FIGURE 16.2   Sample T1-weighted images from IM's MRI (left hemisphere on right) showing bilateral hippocampal atrophy, moderate to severe global volume loss, with a temporal and parietal predominance. Reprinted from Garrard, Maloney, Hodges, & Patterson, The effects of very early Alzheimer's disease on the characteristics of writing by a renowned author, *Brain*, 2005, 128(Pt 2), 250–260, by permission of Oxford University Press.

she displayed scant knowledge of current events (a point to which we will return) and had extreme difficulty committing lists of objects to memory. Her copy of the Rey complex figure is shown in Figure 16.3, and she was unable to reproduce any elements of it from memory. IM was unable to produce the names of many familiar objects and animals when presented with line drawings, her responses suggesting an underlying loss of semantic knowledge, with descriptive or circumlocutory errors (a kangaroo was 'a beautiful creature that jumps'; a squirrel 'a dear little creature'), and deficiencies in attribute knowledge (an owl was 'about two feet' in size, and a violin played by having its strings 'picked'). A transcription of IM's Cookie Theft picture description is reproduced in Box 16.1.

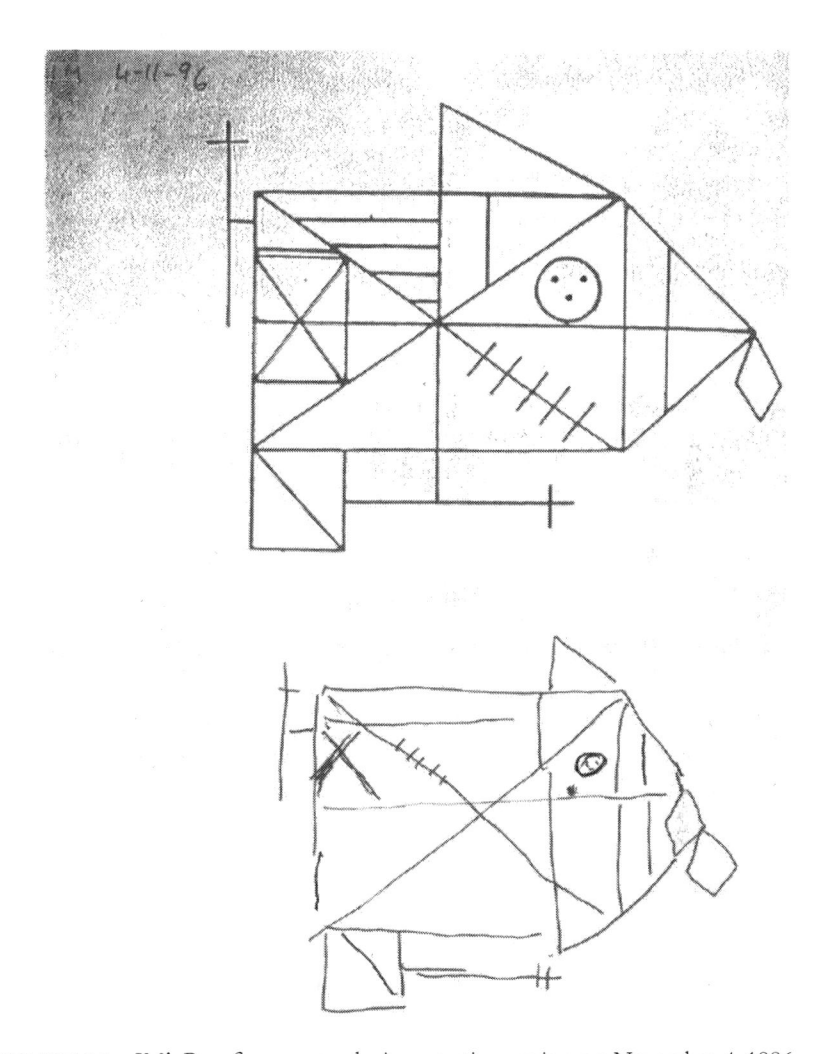

FIGURE 16.3 IM's Rey figure copy during a testing session on November 4, 1996.

> **BOX 16.1**
>
> The little girl is looking up to her brother. She holds up her left hand and puts her other hand into her mouth to help him. The boy had picked up . . . a cookie or something—says so on the jar. Going to give it to the girl balancing in an [illegible] way. The girl is just holding a plate and various pieces of . . . well . . . something useful. Standing at a window. Whether the window is open is not quite clear to me. The thing where the water is running out. The girl doesn't bother. The window is open. Plate and two cups.

IM's clinical profile could, therefore, be summarised as a mixed picture of verbal and nonverbal memory deficits coupled with profound semantic and visuospatial impairments—a profile entirely compatible with the early-to-middle stages of an Alzheimer type dementia. In itself, this was an unexceptional presentation of a common disease, but unlike the majority of patients with the condition, IM also had a detailed and extensive record that reflected her cognitive activity over a period spanning more than four decades of her life. The similarities with the Nun Study (Snowdon et al., 1996; Snowdon, Greiner & Markesbery, 2000) did not escape our attention at the time, nor later when, like the Minnesota sisters, our single case gave permission for her brain to be examined histologically after death. Unlike the Nun Study participants, however, IM had been a prolific writer for the whole duration of her adult life, which meant that we not only had access to large volumes of text from her early thirties, but from the entire lifespan right up to the earliest symptomatic period, including the normally silent 'presymptomatic' phase of the illness, during which the damage caused by plaque and tangle build-up appears to be compensated for by the patient's 'cognitive reserve'.

What was this case's patterns of spared and impaired abilities?

The idea of a detailed analysis of the 'odd-ball' novel *Jackson's Dilemma* arose from the fact that IM's dementia had been diagnosed less than a year after she had finished the work, implying that physical degenerative changes would have been accumulating in her brain throughout the 18-month period between conceiving the ideas behind the novel and delivering the finished manuscript to her publisher. It was possible, therefore, that by subjecting the language of the book to the same kinds of analyses as we had been using in Cambridge to examine the breakdown of speech in patients with early Alzheimer's disease, we might reveal similar changes in the writing. If these changes were to appear, then the much-discussed 'unusual character' of the work would be open to fresh interpretation.

Furthermore, if it were to be informative, the retrospective language analysis technique might also prove useful to the problem of how to study the elusive 'silent' presymptomatic phase of early Alzheimer's disease.

Alzheimer's sufferers experience linguistic difficulties in both spoken and written modalities (Forbes, Shanks & Venneri, 2004). Although there are obvious differences between these two modes of production—not least the greater degree of cognitive control that is available while writing than while speaking—both ultimately depend on a functioning language system. There had been little previous work on changes in the linguistic aspects of writing in Alzheimer's disease, so it was from studies of spoken discourse that we derived predictions of changes that could also be looked for in written texts. Three major candidate markers emerged: the extent of the vocabulary (how repetitious was the text?); the frequency of the words used (how unusual was the language of the work?); and the syntactic structure of the sentences (how complex were the sentences used to express the ideas of the book?). If the language used in *Jackson's Dilemma* had been influenced by the neurodegenerative process, then a comparison with the findings of identical analyses in a selection of IM's earlier novels would be expected to reveal systematic linguistic changes along one or more of these dimensions.

IM's fiction reached the height of its popularity well before the era of electronic texts, and none of them was commercially available in this format in 2004 when we started to assemble the material for analysis. Approaches to IM's publisher (Chatto & Windus) with requests for the electronic versions used in typesetting some of the texts were unsuccessful, yet in order to carry out our analyses within an acceptable time frame (i.e., weeks, rather than years), electronic versions of three texts (*Under the Net*, *The Sea The Sea*, and *Jackson's Dilemma*) were essential. Eventually, these were acquired using a document scanner and commercial optical character recognition (OCR) software. The texts in question were chosen as representing not only the early and late phases of IM's writing career but also the period when she was at the height of her powers, winning the Booker Prize and other public plaudits. In fact, we wondered whether, in addition to a deterioration culminating in *Jackson's Dilemma*, we might also find a *positive* development between IM's early and mid-career writings.

The Concordance software developed by Dr. Rob Watt of the Department of English at the University of Dundee *www.concordancesoftware.co.uk* proved to be another invaluable electronic tool: one of Concordance's basic functions was the transformation of a text into an alphabetical word list, complete with occurrence counts, line references, and contexts. This made possible the analyses that confirmed many of our predictions: one of the most striking results came from an examination of the rate at which words are re-used. Figure 16.4 plots the ratio of the total number of words (word tokens) to unique usages (word types) in successive thousand-word chunks of the three texts. A steeper curve indicates a greater number of types-per-token, and thus a more innovative, less repetitive use of vocabulary. Clearly, given that the number of words available in a language

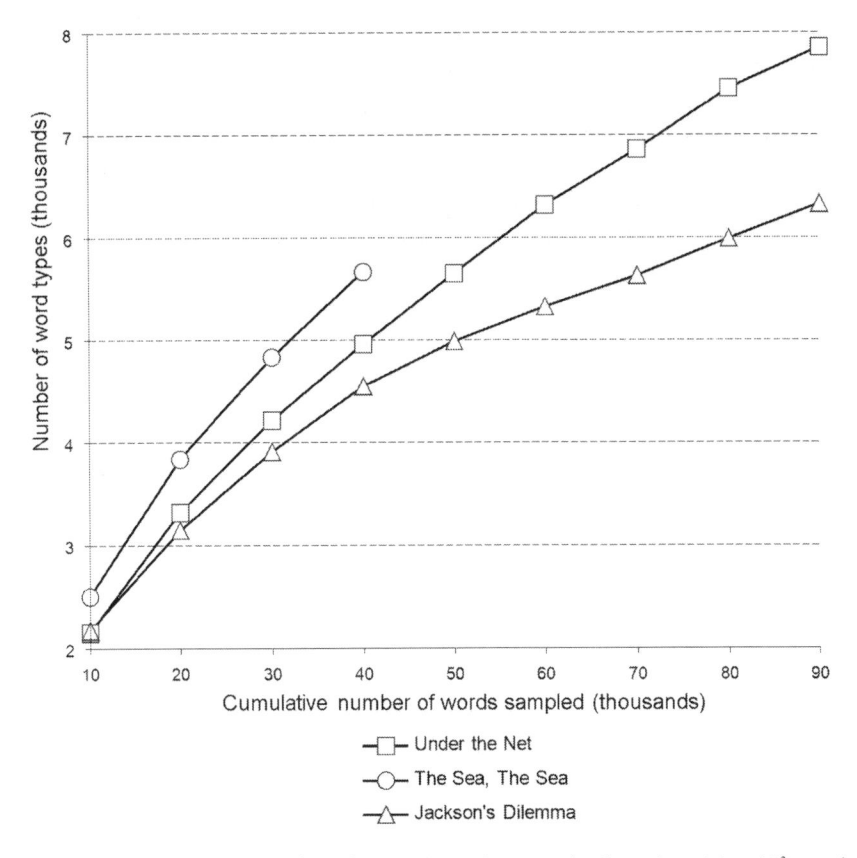

FIGURE 16.4 Proportions of word types (y-axis) to word tokens (x-axis) at 10^3-word intervals in the texts of Under the Net, The Sea, The Sea and Jackson's Dilemma. Reprinted from Garrard, Maloney, Hodges & Patterson, The effects of very early Alzheimer's disease on the characteristics of writing by a renowned author, *Brain*, 2005, 128(Pt 2), 250–260, by permission of Oxford University Press.

is finite (English contains an estimated quarter-of-a-million word types), all texts will eventually have to 'recycle' words at some point, resulting in an inevitable flattening of its token-to-type ratio. The location of this point in a text will, however, depend on its lexical variety, and the figure clearly illustrates that it is reached earlier in *Jackson's Dilemma*, and later in *The Sea, The Sea* than in *Under the Net*. The technique thus accurately reflects an enrichment of IM's repertoire over the first two-and-a-half decades of her writing career and an impoverishment at the end of it.

A similar pattern emerged when we looked at the lexical frequency (usages per million words in samples of written and spoken language) of the vocabulary of the three books: *Jackson's Dilemma* was associated with the highest overall frequency of usage, and *The Sea, The Sea* with the lowest, suggesting that the unusual (low frequency) words had become less easily available while IM was writing her last novel—a well-established phenomenon in studies of spoken language in patients with Alzheimer's disease. In contrast, syntactic complexity (which was modelled using sentence length, clause length, and short-range repetition of grammatical function words) showed little or no variation. This pattern fits with some (though not all) previous studies of the syntactic aspects of language in early Alzheimer's disease. Differences may have been undetectable in our analyses because we could not implement the comparisons on as large a scale as we were able to do with the lexical measures. Le, Lancashire, Hirst and Jokel (2011) and Pakhomov, Chacon, Wicklund and Gundel (2011) later revisited the question of change at a syntactic level, modelling the emergence of differences across a larger selection of texts using diachronic computational methods. Both later studies did identify changes in grammatical complexity, while Le et al. also claimed to have found similar effects in the later works of another prolific 20th-century novelist, Agatha Christie.

Do you think this case contributes to our understanding of how the normal mind works?

Alzheimer's disease is a progressive condition caused by the accumulation of toxic protein species that affect the structure of nerve cells and their interconnections, leading to their eventual destruction. Once this degenerative process is established it is impossible to stop, let alone to reverse, and its cumulative effect over time is thus characterised by a progressive disappearance of neuronal elements, shrinkage of brain substance and gradual erosion of the intellectual abilities of the sufferer. Visible changes in behaviour and performance lag to a variable extent behind the onset of pathological change in the brain. This is because, like many other organs of the body, the brain has a reserve capacity built into it, meaning that information processing can continue at a constant level even after a proportion of the brain's physical constituents have been destroyed. It follows, therefore, that the beginnings of the destructive process caused by Alzheimer's disease will always predate the onset of intellectual difficulty. The length of this lead-time is almost certainly variable and, for obvious reasons, difficult to determine. Some investigators have argued that it may extend back over years, or even decades (Ohm, Muller, Braak & Bohl, 1995). More recently, evidence has begun to emerge that intellectual activity and/or occupational complexity may help to lengthen the silent, early phase of the disease, and thus delay the devastating effects of neural degeneration on patients and their families (the 'cognitive reserve' hypothesis; Alladi et al., 2013; Boots et al., 2015). A lifetime of thinking, teaching, and writing creatively about the most profound and difficult questions that can be asked concerning human existence, must surely have qualified IM to have benefited from this sort of 'protective' effect.

Do you think that there is anything unique that the report of this case added to our knowledge?

From a literary perspective, the changes that we found in *Jackson's Dilemma* showed that similar effects can certainly be sought in the writings of other authors. Those who were known to have suffered from neurodegenerative disease would be expected to show similar profiles, while others who died with all cognitive faculties intact should perhaps present a pattern of initial development that more closely resembles the findings from the first half of IM's career. As already noted, Le et al. (2011) documented analogous changes in the written output of Agatha Christie, supporting the long-held suspicion that her later years (and later works) were affected by cognitive decline. Le et al. also studied the writings of PD James who was still alive at the time and was not known to show signs of cognitive impairment. The absence of any change in the PD James corpus thus provides further support for the status of written language as a potential early disease biomarker. To determine whether the same changes might also be detected in the casual, unpublished writings of people who wrote for pleasure or out of necessity, rather than as a profession, PG was awarded grant funding by the Medical Research Council to develop the 'Cognitive Archaeology' project, to collect, archive, digitise and analyse informal writings (mainly letters and diaries). The project aimed to scale up the approaches used in the IM project for application to much larger and diverse datasets. Results of a preliminary survey of a set of 80 digital text archives, each spanning between 2 and 3 decades of an individual's life, is expected to be published in late 2018 or early 2019.

Can you specify why this case was relevant in relation to the knowledge at the time and would she still be relevant to the knowledge of today?

In 2004, the quest for inexpensive, easily detectable dementia biomarkers was just gaining momentum. Another 'Holy Grail' of the time was a means of detecting the emergence of the earliest stages of Alzheimer's and other degenerative dementias. It was, and remains, axiomatic that the most desirable time for 'switching off' progression of the condition with disease-modifying agents is while symptoms are still at a mild stage. Indeed, this was what motivated the first formal definition of the syndrome of mild cognitive impairment (Petersen et al., 1999) and its subsequent refinements (Dubois et al., 2007).

It is certainly arguable that the case has even more relevance to today's state of knowledge. As the decade of smartphone apps, online shopping, Twitter, Facebook and the gig economy draws to a close, the search for value in big data is in danger of becoming the new gold rush. The data on offer in the form of recorded language are amongst the most potentially valuable of all, with information about the affective state, consumer preferences, opinions and political allegiances of millions of people waiting to be unlocked (Garrard & Elvevag, 2014). Seen in this context, a corpus the size of IM's written work (an estimated five million words) is a data miner's dream, with the potential not only to reveal correlations between linguistic and cognitive change but also to support the rapid evaluation of new computational approaches to analysis in 'real-world' material. If, in the coming decade, patients in dementia disease-modifying drug trials can be regularly monitored for progression using a composite of measurements made on samples of spoken language (a sort of 'mental blood test'), perhaps obtained through the medium of an 'intelligent personal assistant'; and if, as a result, the duration of such trials shortens, and increasingly effective treatments begin to be licensed sooner, a small part of the credit will remain due to IM and her novels.

Were there any relevant data that you did not manage to publish on this case?

The late 1990s were an exciting time to be working in the dementia research group at the MRC Cognition and Brain Sciences Unit in Cambridge. Not only were we seeing patients with unusual constellations of deficits and game-changing neuropathological lesions, but we also had frequent opportunities to construct and administer bespoke cognitive assessments designed to probe areas of special relevance to individual cases. IM was one of these: we wondered whether memory for the products of one's own imagination could represent a unique type of material, on which performance might well differ from that observed using more conventional materials, such as words, stories and faces.

There is a scene in Richard Eyre's 2001 film *Iris* about IM's life, in which the heroine—still in the relatively early stages of her illness—is seen watching Tony Blair deliver his 1996 party conference speech. As Blair rhetorically asks what are his three main priorities for government and answers himself with the phrase 'education, education and education', IM turns haplessly to her husband John Bayley and asks, 'Why does he keep saying that?'

There is evidence both from John Bayley's account and from our own clinical assessment that IM did indeed have severe problems with this kind of material. The Addenbrooke's Cognitive Examination (Mathuranath, Nestor, Berrios, Rakowicz & Hodges, 2000) that was administered on 16/06/1996 included four 'Retrograde Memory' questions: the names of the current and previous Prime Ministers, the leader of the opposition and the American President. When we asked her the name of the Prime Minister, IM thought for a bit, then said 'I don't know'; but then reassured us 'It's all right, someone will know'. Later, we showed her a series of 106 pictures of faces, half of which were famous and half not. We first asked if the face looked famous, or familiar to her. If she said no, we moved on to the next face. If she said yes, we asked for the person's name. If she could not name the person (which was almost always the case), we asked why the person was famous.

IM's famous/not famous judgements were impaired, though well above chance level: 74% of the 53 famous faces were identified as famous, and 83% of the anonymous ones as not famous. By contrast, her ability to name famous faces was almost non-existent: fully correct responses were given only to pictures of the Queen and Hitler; the Queen Mother (still alive then) was named as 'The Queen', Prince Charles as 'Prince' and when prompted ('Prince of what?') 'Prince of Wales'. In some cases, she could provide a plausible approximation, such as 'The king of the other side of the world' for Bill Clinton (who was US President at the time) and 'The top of the . . . he's running England' for John Major (who was still the Prime Minister).

Sometimes she would give the impression of knowing more than she could say. For example, to a picture of Boris Yeltsin, she said 'a very powerful person' but answered a probe question ('Where is he powerful?') incorrectly—'America'. Another example was Marilyn Monroe, whom she described as being 'in the theatre, she was very famous. I'd know her name if I heard it'. Yet when KP probed with 'Greta Garbo?' IM responded 'YES!' as though that was the name she had been thinking of all along.

Instead of trying to name the person, IM would sometimes volunteer information about either their nationality or profession, both of which could sometimes be right (John F Kennedy: 'American'; David Steel: 'in England'; Luciano Pavarotti: 'something in the theatre') but just as likely to be wrong (Duke of Edinburgh: 'He's an American, he has a jolly time in America'; George Bush: 'He's a splendid chap and able to do lots of things; he's English'; Norman Lamont: 'On the stage'; Albert Einstein: 'In the theatre').

We wondered whether retrograde memory of the titles of and characters from her own books might show a contrasting preservation. KP, therefore, devised two tests of 'Iris Murdoch literary knowledge' and administered them in April 1997. The first was a two-alternative forced choice between the title of one of her books and a similar-sounding title of a real 20th-century book written by someone else: e.g., 'The Unicorn' [Iris Murdoch, 1963] vs. 'The Waves' [Virginia Woolf, 1931]. To the question 'which of these two books did you write?' IM scored 25 out of 29, making a single incorrect choice, and responding 'I don't know' or 'both' to the remaining three. In the second test, IM was presented with the title of one of her novels, together with the names of two of her fictional main characters—one from the book shown, and the other from one of her other 28 novels. On this latter test, IM made only 12 out of 18 correct choices, many of them after long deliberation. In contrast, her husband rapidly made 17 correct selections. When the year of the book was taken into consideration, no effect of chronology was evident.

What are the shortcomings of this case?

However clear-cut the differences that we detected in IM's texts, it goes without saying that examining data from only three time points in a series spanning more than 40 years meant that several opportunities were necessarily missed. The most important was the ability to look for the point in the series where critical variables began to turn from the levels that they had reached during the writing of *The Sea, The Sea* towards those documented in the final work. To have found evidence of a monotonic change in language characteristics beginning even before the subtlest and earliest behavioural manifestations would have been a stunning discovery. Change-point analysis (Taylor, 2000) provides a statistically robust method for detecting changes in time series of this nature and could have been implemented had the required volume of data been acquired. Later studies (such as those of Le et al. and Pakhomov et al., both cited earlier) were based on larger numbers of text samples, but both faced the same difficulties in acquiring the data accurately in digital format. Acquisition of the texts of all the novels was gradually completed using OCR between 2004 and 2007 by a series of temporary research assistants and interns working with PG at the Institute of Cognitive Science, but the painstaking task of error checking and standardisation is still only around 70% accomplished.

The other major shortcoming concerns the fact that the critical changes in IM's language were only demonstrated using an internal comparison (i.e., with IM's *own* language from other points in her life as a control sample). Although subsequent studies have demonstrated that the effects in question are seen in other writers affected by late-life cognitive disorders and absent from those who remain (ostensibly) cognitively intact throughout life (Van Velzen & Garrard, 2008; Le et al., 2011), the findings are still open to the explanation—which is either more or less prosaic, depending on your point of view—that the structure and properties of *Jackson's Dilemma* resulted from a deliberate decision on IM's part: a stylistic experimentation in novelistic form.

The Murdoch scholar Richard Todd put forward a reasoned case for such a literary interpretation, though he emphasised narrative rather than lexical aspects of the text, and showed that in places there appeared to be confusion about the temporal order of events and the authorial point of view (Todd, 2006). For example, at the beginning of *Jackson's Dilemma*, the author assumes the voice of the 'omniscient narrator', only to violate its assumptions briefly at least once in what follows. Todd argues (correctly) that it is unwise to conclude too hastily that such inconsistencies reflect IM's mental state at the time of writing, even if they were unprecedented in the whole of her preceding literary output. As Garrard (2010) pointed out, however, the changes found in IM's writing were exactly those predicted from aspects of language and cognitive function known to be vulnerable to AD. It remains possible, if unlikely, that this was coincidence, but a far greater one would have been that IM chose consciously to mimic the characteristics of a condition that she was unaware of having.

Do you remember whether there were any issues that reviewers were particularly blunt about?

Two anonymous referees reviewed the first version of the original manuscript for the editor of Brain. In this version, we had confined ourselves to the comparison between *Under the Net* and *Jackson's Dilemma*, which had revealed the striking differences outlined earlier. The reviewers, however, highlighted the confound between natural stylistic development and the effects of early Alzheimer's disease on the differences between IM's first and last novels as the major shortcoming of the study. One reviewer explicitly suggested that adding a novel written at the height of her career to create a three-way analysis would provide a more credible longitudinal dimension, as well as making the time course of IM's writing career somewhat easier to appreciate. We therefore rapidly acquired and cleaned a digital text of *The Sea, the Sea*, which we then subjected to the analyses that had been set up for the two-book comparison.

Are there any assessments/paradigms that you would administer now to this case if she was available?

One of the things that make IM unique as a single case is that she *is* still available: as long as her books remain accessible in some form, the products of her cognition will enable assessment by any researcher with ideas about the nature and time course of language change in Alzheimer's disease. Follow-up studies have indeed replicated and expanded on our original findings and sampled across larger numbers of texts from the entire duration of her writing career. The idea has also prompted application of the same textual analytic approach when large longitudinal samples of written discourse have been available from patients with other neurodegenerative syndromes.

You first reported this case in 2005. Do you think this case is still informative now? Are we now better able to interpret her pattern of spared and impaired abilities? If so, in what way?

It turns out that *Jackson's Dilemma* was not IM's final work after all. A couple of years ago, PG came across an archived BBC Radio broadcast by John Bailey's former undergraduate pupil and lifelong friend of IM, the novelist A.N. Wilson. Wilson had spent a great deal of time with IM both before and after she had received her clinical diagnosis, while she laboured over the completion of her collection of literary and philosophical essays entitled *Existentialists and Mystics*. Wilson said that she spent a full two years 'writing and rewriting that bloody book' and that it was the effort that 'precipitated her dementia; although' he added 'no doctor would agree with me'. So if it can be established which sections of *Existentialists and Mystics* she was working on during the years immediately before and immediately after Alzheimer's was diagnosed, it should be possible to i) trace a progression in the changes observed in *Jackson's Dilemma* (thus putting the relationship between these changes and the effects of the disease beyond reasonable doubt), and ii) identify other markers that may have been difficult to detect at earlier stages of the disease, and then go back to measure these same variables in pre-dementia texts.

We are now living in an era where ethics committees would like to foresee every step. How much serendipity was involved in your assessment?

The manner in which we learned about IM's early symptoms (i.e., via a newspaper interview) could scarcely have been more serendipitous, nor could the timing of our initial invitation to her to take part in our research, during a period (often, sadly, a long one) when she was still in 'diagnostic limbo'. It was also perhaps serendipitous that IM and her husband were both professional academics, steeped in learning, and with a deep-rooted love of scholarship. They seemed to understand instinctively the importance of scientific research into IM's condition, so it was perhaps not surprising that they both agreed so readily to participate in testing and scanning experiments, even travelling to London on one occasion to take part in structural MR imaging sessions at the Institute of Neurology. When, after IM's death, JRH wrote briefly to John Bailey to ask whether he would have any objections to a systematic examination of his late wife's texts and potential disclosure of details of her condition, he replied [emphases preserved from the original]:

Dear Dr Hodges—John that is—apologies!
 Of course, I should be only too pleased for you to include all the personal data on Iris you find useful. (That is a *V.* interesting point about Jackson's Dilemma. I find it <u>very</u> moving but *strange* in many ways. I'm sure Peter Garrard will find some interesting things there.)

After the paper was published, we sent a copy to Professor Bailey and he wrote back expressing great interest in meeting PG at his house in Charlbury Road, Oxford. I recall sitting opposite him at the large kitchen table, on which back issues of the Times Literary Supplement and pieces of junk mail served as coasters and writing surfaces. I vividly remember as he explained to me why Henry James would have found our work *particularly* fascinating, and showed me numerous piles of pebbles and sticks, which he and Iris had collected over a lifetime of Oxfordshire walks and never, at Iris's insistence, thrown away. What startled me the most, however, was his deep, almost morbid interest in his wife's condition:

his fascination with the MR images displayed in the copy of the paper, but most of all his earnest request to set eyes on the histology slides that we described in the case history. I think I muttered something about 'looking into that' but never followed it up.

Notes

1. In honour of her friend, A.N. Wilson's moving tribute to Iris's dedication as a writer: "Her patient, humble working life was an example to any writer. *Nulla dies sine linea*, as Erasmus decreed—not a day should pass without writing something. She was entirely without fuss in her approach to work. When JOB broke his ankle, she sat at the end of his hospital bed with a large pad, writing her novel. If she had an hour to kill waiting for a train, out would come the pad once more. There was no nonsense about need to write in a special place or with special nibs. She was humbly the servant of her craft" (Wilson, 2004, p. 263).
2. John Bailey—personal communication.

References

Alladi, S., Bak, T. H., Duggirala, V., Surampudi, B., Shailaja, M., Shukla, A. K., Chaudhuri, J. R., & Kaul, S. (2013). Bilingualism delays age at onset of dementia, independent of education and immigration status. *Neurology*, *81*, 1938–1944.

Bayley, J. (1998). *Iris: A Memoir of Iris Murdoch*. London: Gerald Duckworth & Co. Ltd.

Boots, E. A., Schultz, S. A., Almeida, R. P., Oh, J. M., Koscik, R. L., Dowling, M. N., Gallagher, C. L., Carlsson, C. M., Rowley, H. A., Bendlin, B. B., Asthana, S., Sager, M. A., Hermann, B. P., Johnson, S. C., & Okonkwo, O. C. (2015). Occupational complexity and cognitive reserve in a middle-aged cohort at risk for Alzheimer's disease. *Archives of Clinical Neuropsychogy*, *30*, 634–642.

Coles, J. (1996). Duet in perfect harmony. *The Guardian*.

Conradi, P. (2001). *Iris Murdoch—A Life*. New York: W.W. Norton & Company, Inc.

Dubois, B., Feldman, H. H., Jacova, C., Dekosky, S. T., Barberger-Gateau, P., Cummings, J., Delocourte, A., Galasko, D., Gauthier, S., Jicha, G., Meguro, K., O'Brien, J., Pasquier, F., Robert, P., Rossor, M., Solloway, S., Stern, Y., Visser, P. J., & Scheltens, P. (2007). Research criteria for the diagnosis of Alzheimer's disease: revising the NINCDS-ADRDA criteria. *Lancet Neurology*, *6*, 734–746.

Folstein, M. F., Folstein, S.E., & McHugh, P. R. (1975) 'Mini-mental state'. A practical method for grading the cognitive state of patients for the clinican. *Journal of Psychiatric Research*, *12*, 189–198.

Forbes, K. E., Shanks, M. F., & Venneri, A. (2004). The evolution of dysgraphia in Alzheimer's disease. *Brain Research Bulletin*, *63*, 19–24.

Garrard, P. (2010). Literature, history and biology. *The Psychologist*, *23*, 2–3.

Garrard, P., & Elvevag, B. (2014). Language, computers and cognitive neuroscience. *Cortex*, *55*, 1–4.

Garrard, P., Maloney, L. M., Hodges, J. R., & Patterson, K. (2005). The effects of very early Alzheimer's disease on the characteristics of writing by a renowned author. *Brain*, *128(Pt 2)*, 250–260.

Le, X., Lancashire, I., Hirst, G., & Jokel, R. (2011). Longitudinal detection of dementia through lexical and syntactic changes in writing: a case study of three British novelists. *Literary and Linguistic Computing*, *26*, 435–461.

Mathuranath, P. S., Nestor, P. J., Berrios, G. E., Rakowicz, W., & Hodges, J. R. (2000). A brief cognitive test battery to differentiate Alzheimer's disease and frontotemporal dementia. *Neurology, 55,* 1613–1620.

Ohm, T. G., Muller, H., Braak, H., & Bohl, J. (1995). Close-Meshed prevalence rates of different stages as a tool to uncover the rate of Alzheimers disease-related neurofibrillary changes. *Neuroscience, 64,* 209–217.

Pakhomov, S., Chacon, D., Wicklund, M., & Gundel, J. (2011). Computerized assessment of syntactic complexity in Alzheimer's disease: a case study of Iris Murdoch's writing. *Behavioural Research Methods, 43,* 136–144.

Petersen, R. C., Smith, G. E., Waring, S. C., Ivnik, R. J., Tangalos, E. G., & Kokmen, E. (1999). Mild cognitive impairment: clinical characterization and outcome. *Archives of Neurology, 56,* 303–308.

Snowdon, D. A., Greiner, L. H., & Markesbery, W. R. (2000). Linguistic ability in early life and the neuropathology of Alzheimer's disease and cerebrovascular disease—findings from the nun study. *Vascular Factors in Alzheimer's Disease, 903,* 34–38.

Snowdon, D. A., Kemper, S. J., Mortimer, J. A., Greiner, L. H., Wekstein, D. R., & Markesbery, W. R. (1996). Linguistic ability in early life and cognitive function and Alzheimer's disease in late life—findings from the Nun Study. *Jama—Journal of the American Medical Association, 275,* 528–532.

Taylor, W. (2000). *Change-Point Analyzer 2.0 Shareware Program.* Libertyville, IL: Taylor Enterprises.

Todd, R. (2006). What is Jackson's Dilemma? In *Third International Iris Murdoch Conference,* University of Kingston.

Van Velzen, M., & Garrard, P. (2008). From hindsight to insight—retrospective analysis of language written by a renowned Alzheimer's patient. *Interdisciplinary Science Reviews, 33,* 278–286.

Wilson, A. N. (2004). *Iris Murdoch As I Knew Her.* London: Arrow Books.

17

THE WEALTH OF EVIDENCE FROM BRAIN LESIONS AFFECTING MEMORY

How Should We Use It?

Nelson Cowan and Candice C. Morey

In this volume, perhaps more than any other, we learn about the discovery of individuals with the hapless situation of having received brain lesions of various sorts that result in distinctly different varieties of memory loss. The purposes of this chapter are (1) to foster an appreciation of the scope of the evidence and (2) to stimulate thought about the benefits and limitations of the evidence, as well as how that evidence might be put to best use.

Appreciating the Evidence: A House Tour

Considering the presented case studies together, through answers to questions that were posed to the original researchers, we get a grand tour through the memory system. It is somewhat as if one night a homeowner turned on all lights and electrical devices in the house and then went to the circuit-breaker box in the basement and flipped each switch one at a time so that the distinct areas of darkness and eerie silence could be observed in different rooms and hallways.

Let's take a similarly bewildering and thought-provoking tour of this book, from a subjective standpoint for maximum appreciation, with your mind as the house. MacKay (Chapter 2) has you in a state in which you are unable to learn any new combination of what, why, how and where so that, when addressed, you answer with familiarities and do not fully understand new arrangements of elements presented to you. In your personal history, time is frozen. Your language subtly suffers because you cannot remember enough to put together the parts in all their complexity. You are blind to puns and double entendres but remember something of the general topics recently discussed. Given your bewilderment with the passage of time, you cannot read aloud without skipping some of the words. For example, you read aloud the sentence, *I just don't feel like pleasing salesmen* as "I don't like pleasing salesmen" (no *just*, no *feel*); then on a second try when asked, as "I just don't like pleasing salesmen," and on a third try, as "I just don't feel like pleasing, yep."

Holdstock et al. (Chapter 3) has you unable to learn information such as whose face goes with whose name, or any association between different kinds of things. Somewhat oddly, you have no trouble finding certain faces and names familiar, as well as being able to learn to associate like pairs (such as remembering which people were sitting together).

Tudor-Sfetea and Cipolotti (Chapter 4) have you unable to form new semantic memories, but some things you can learn perfectly well; you can learn to recognize a new person's face, but cannot learn new facts.

Kopelman and Morton (Chapter 5) have you now as an actor by profession, old and growing slow, worse than other actors at repeating lines on first presentation but able to acquire them normally when repeated twice. It is also a world in which you have started smoking simply because you forgot that you gave it up.

Kapur and Kemp (Chapter 6) have you as someone who goes through waves of remembering and then waves of not remembering. You also go through waves of new experiences seeming familiar, that is, déjà vu.

Moulin (Chapter 7) has you as someone who perpetually experiences déjà vu but not only do new experiences seem familiar; you easily come up with fabulous explanations to support your odd feelings. *Of course*, this morning's newspaper has stories you have already read—the paper was delivered the evening before, this once only, and you read it and then put it back in the wrapping for others to unwrap!

Rosenbaum and Moscovitch (Chapter 8) have you doing just fine in a conversation, perhaps happily discussing how dogs and cats have different personalities, but then your conversational partner asks if you ever had a pet and you have no idea! In fact, you cannot remember anything about yourself, or anything that ever happened to you, save one isolated childhood memory. Nor can you figure out anything regarding what you are going to do in the near future, or in the far future for that matter.

Manning (Chapter 9) has you with two opposing problems in sequence. In one of them, you have problems with your self-knowledge like some of the situations we have discussed already, but then everything flips. Now your autobiography is as fully clear as in most people, but you have a different, somewhat bewildering, problem. You have lost any memory of anything that happened publicly, such as who became president or what kind of speech you heard in your former high school.

Ross (Chapter 10) has you remembering what you hear just fine, and your visual perception is fine, but your visual memory is quite impaired. If you want to use the toilet in your own home, you wander around as if you have never seen the house before until you find the right room.

Dewar (Chapter 11) has you once more in a world in which you remember only old, familiar things. When she presents a new story and then plunges you into quiet darkness for a few minutes, though, a memory of the recent story forms! You reminisce about this story, which is finally intruding into your past set of usual memories, as the first new thing you have learned in quite a long time.

Baker et al. (Chapter 12) have you awakening and unsure of where you are or what you have been up to recently. After a few minutes, this situation is then resolved as you remember where you are, and you continue to remember the trauma of not being able to remember. This happens to you recurrently.

Vallar (Chapter 13) has you able to remember most things and to function well in general, but there is a slight problem. Someone tells you a telephone number and you can only retain two or three of the digits at most. If you try to learn a new word, you are unable to do so. It is a world in which spoken communication must be rather terse unless you are able to get the drift of what is being said right away.

Martin (Chapter 14) has you unable to remember meanings even in a very short term. If you are asked to think about a chipmunk, an ant, and a robin, you may not be able to answer the question of whether there was a mammal in the set. In fact, surprisingly, your memory for these words is not substantially better than your memory of similar-sounding nonsense words like "a choopmank, an int, and a rebbin."

Snowden (Chapter 15) has you back in tune with your own personal experiences but myopic in memory, with little depth beyond your personal perspective. You have taken to reading the dictionary to compensate for words you cannot remember, but in your mind, you are just trying to keep up with the many new words that keep being added to the language! Your memory of France, where you often visit, is superb, yet when you are asked about a nearby country you have never visited but surely knew at one time, Portugal, you ask perplexed, "What's Portugal?"

Finally, Garrard et al. (Chapter 16) has you as a writer, which is scary to contemplate while writing this. Your writing is not so strange in its meaning, but the syntax and word choices have become more simplistic over the years. To no good effect, your style begins to become less and less like that of Faulkner and more and more like that of Hemingway.

We contend that the sum total of these case studies is profound. The human imagination as documented in fictional writings may not have allowed imagination of these fissions within the human mind, or anticipation of these humans who are in some ways stranger than fiction. Scientifically, what we learn is how the fabric of human experience can be torn in one way while remaining intact in other ways.

Exploring Scientific Issues About Memory Impairment

General Observations

There can be no doubt that there is something illuminating about the study of memory disorders caused by brain injuries and brain degradation. A main thought-provoking question addressed in this book is whether this kind of evidence has important implications for the study of normal memory. One way in which it seems to help is by providing existence proofs of various dissociations in memory. It is possible to have impairment in Function A without impairment in Function B; therefore, A and B are differently represented in the brain. Moreover, impairment in Function A is always accompanied by damage somewhere in the X-Y-Z neural network, whereas impairment in Function B is sometimes observed without damage to this particular network (and with damage to some other, perhaps yet unclear network).

Also of special interest is when the particular abnormality in behavior is counterintuitive. In Chapter 2, MacKay makes the case that the famous memory impairment case of HM (posthumously revealed as Henry Molaison) had abnormalities in language use, stemming from his inability to make new associations between ideas to form new explicit, episodic memories. Presumably, because he had a difficulty keeping track of the reference of pronouns, it was pointed out that he tended to use proper names more than the ordinary person did. Given that, for most of us, pronouns seem easier to remember than proper names, this finding is counterintuitive and sheds light on the issue of what makes a task difficult, and how it depends on the skills and limitations of the individual.

Despite the intense interest in brain damage and its relation to memory, it is clear that there are many impediments to the responsible scientific use of this evidence. Let us consider some of the impediments, and how they might be met in future work. This discussion is only partial; for example, it is clear that better methods of brain imaging can help, as many of the authors have pointed out, and we will not belabor that issue further. Instead, we focus on evaluating the quality and completeness of the available information, and considering ways to further encourage cooperation among investigators with opposing views.

Some Challenges to the Use of Memory-Disorder Case Studies

Here we discuss challenges facing the field of memory-disorder case studies, including dissociations as reflecting just half of the necessary equation, the possibility of non-modularity of processing making it difficult to find dissociations, inter- and intra-patient variability, the role of investigators' theoretical lenses with which they approach a case, the importance of undiscovered cases, and challenges with institutional review boards. In each case, we try to provide recommendations for dealing with the issue.

Dissociation as Just One-Half of the Equation

It is common to discuss dissociations between one sort of brain function and another, the most common being a breakdown of explicit memory for events but with preserved procedural learning, as in the case of HM. This kind of evidence, however, does not do enough to clarify the grain of the dissociation. Suppose it proved possible to dissociate any two kinds of memory: visual memory impairment without auditory impairment, impairment of memory for chairs accompanied by normal memory for tables, and so on. Such a pattern of evidence would suggest that the brain is diffusely distributed and connectionist in its operation, with little suggestion of any modularity or anatomical specialization. In order to establish specialization, it is important for theorists to spend more time discussing the opposite of dissociations. What functions do you assert must always occur together or be lost together (i.e., cannot be dissociated)? If that assertion is disproven, what are the implications for the functioning of the brain and mind? It seems as if this topic is the basis of a critically important but rarely held conversation.

Although these limitations must be kept in mind, the strongest case is a double dissociation. Clean examples of it are, however, difficult to find. As one possible example, whereas most researchers show the impairment of episodic memory with preserved semantic memory (as in the typical view of HM), Manning (Chapter 9) conversely showed a deficit in public semantic memory with preserved episodic memory. A skeptic might continue, however, to hold an account in which partial memory preservation occurs because the damage simply affects a cognitively more demanding function while leaving spared a less demanding function. The patient could remember public semantic knowledge (e.g., who famous people were) only if there was a personal, episodic connection and that might be a trend in normal individuals as well. The interpretation might be clarified by convergent neuroimaging evidence. In this particular situation, it is relevant that Hodgetts et al. (2017) recently found a neural dissociation that may mirror the brain lesion evidence. Among 27 normal adults, episodic but not semantic detail in autobiographical memories was predicted by the white matter microstructure of the major hippocampal input and output pathway, the fornix, whereas semantic but not episodic detail was predicted by the white matter microstructure of the inferior longitudinal fasciculus, which connects the occipitotemporal areas to the anterior temporal lobe. What we appear to have therefore is a pair of parallel double dissociations, with that of neural lesion case studies, taken together, parallel with that of structural neuroimaging individual differences.

Non-modularity in Processing

The finding of dissociations within memory impairment depends on the existence of several sorts of modularity. The first is brain modularity. If two functions are well-separated anatomically in the brain and depend on separate circulatory subsystems, the situation is fortunate for scientists; it is less fortunate to the extent that the two functions are functionally separate but are anatomically intermingled or dependent on the same circulatory subsystem and, for one of these reasons, tend to be damaged together. A clear example of that outside of memory is the co-morbidity of hearing and balance because they have evolved to share physiological mechanisms along the eighth cranial nerve.

The second kind of non-modularity is functional non-modularity. For example, we theoretically might want to view autobiographical and semantic memory as separate but Snowden (Chapter 15) described a patient for which semantic events were apparently retained only insofar as they linked into current personal relevance within autobiographical memory. We might want to think of memory for items and associations as separate but MacKay (Chapter 2) described how HM made omission errors, that is item failures, when he could not "conjoin words into the novel phrases and propositions that he wanted to express," an associative failure. We must explore methods to take into account these types of non-modularity in our thinking about brain damage.

Inter-patient Differences in Cognitive Style

In the future, we will have to be careful to take note of the possibly powerful role of individual differences in cognitive style stemming from the pre-lesion period of the patient's life. As a hypothetical example, suppose there are two individuals, one of whom has as a goal in life to learn as much knowledge and information about the world as possible, whereas the other has a goal of having fun. It is possible that the former individual incorporates semantic information richly into an episodic trace, keeping track of where each important fact was learned as a personal story of knowledge acquisition, whereas that information is hardly encoded in individuals who just wanna have fun. If both individuals later display mild cognitive impairment, the impairment of semantic memory could be much less noticeable (compared to group norms) in the individual for whom knowledge acquisition is a goal of daily living. We must try to consider individual differences in cognitive style to understand the effects of brain lesions on memory. If we accept that inter-patient differences in cognition and expertise may obscure or magnify evidence of a deficit, then this represents an inherent limit on the strength of evidence that a single patient case may yield, at least without considerable digging into the details of each case.

Patients' aspirations, knowledge and expertise may interact in important ways with their deficits. A patient may have an underlying impairment that is unobservable either because the patient had the exceptional pre-morbid ability in the area, i.e. cognitive reserve, or has pre-morbid knowledge that compensates for defective processing. For example, Kopelman and Morton (Chapter 5) had a patient who was an actor and recovered function in the area of acting much more than in everyday life. The discussion was about a residual resource that could somehow be allocated to the high-interest area of acting at the expense of other domains, or that the resource at least was not powerful enough to have the same effect in other domains. Similarly, the renowned author Iris Murdoch remained capable of writing at an expert level even after the onset of Alzheimer's dementia (Garrard et al.,

Chapter 16). With single cases, the most appropriate control comparison (i.e., to the patient's functioning before the onset of the illness) will not always be possible.

Intra-Patient Variability of Function

Some functions that an ordinary person can accomplish, a brain-damaged individual can too, though what is easy for the ordinary person can occur only with considerable effort in the brain-damaged individual. It is possible, therefore, that the behavior becomes more variable in brain-damaged individuals, as is often observed. There might also be physiological factors that vary or vacillate within a brain-damaged individual, such as the ability to use the fronto-parietal attention control network well when it is compromised; perhaps it works when the patient is feeling energetic, but not at other times. The dual-mechanisms of cognitive control framework (Braver, 2012) delineates one possibility for how this may work within the scope of healthy functioning.

We should give careful thought to how moment-to-moment or day-to-day variability would play out in particular cases. For example, MacKay (Chapter 2) indicated that HM's problem was not with memory storage or retrieval, but with memory encoding. From this point of view, one might think that variability in mental state should have minimal effects because it can only affect retrieval, not the original encoding of the event in question. Yet, more subtle aspects of HM's mental state that were discussed suggested that the act of retrieval can itself involve further encoding. For example, if he were asked, "Where did you live after [a particular residence]," the encoding of two residences in a row within the question might pose difficulties on one day but not on another. Although this hypothetical example may or may not fit the facts of this case, we hope that the general point is still clear; the possible effects of within-patient variability should be taken into account.

Suppose a patient has been tested on X but has not yet been tested on A, B, or C. In the rare opportunities to test the patient again, the last thing the investigator is eager to do is to test again on another version of X, but we advocate that this test-retest reliability is in fact not to be taken for granted and an important thing to establish, if neuropsychological investigation is to be well respected along with nomothetic methods.

Investigators' Theoretical Lenses

It is often lamented that a limitation of neuropsychology is that we are dealing with rare case studies rather than groups of individuals who all suffer from exactly the same lesion or malady, allowing a valid group examination. That is true, but the challenge is actually even greater. Specifically, given that different patients are examined by investigators with different theoretical views, it is often difficult to separate the effects of the patient's idiosyncrasies from the effects of the investigator's theoretical expectations and biases. MacKay's observations in Chapter 2 show dramatically that the same patient observed by different individuals can lead to different conclusions about how the mind works. Rosenbaum and Moscovitch (Chapter 8) make the point that when a theorist begins to expect a certain pattern of results, that theorist may go out of his or her way to examine data in a manner that is consistent with that expectation, and the theorist may be more willing to accept and consider evidence for which he or she can think of at least one explanation. For example, Rosenbaum and Moscovitch considered how even an indirect memory test question could be solved with the help of hippocampal function, even though the same problem might be solved by other individuals without help from hippocampal function.

Investigators' theoretical lenses influence which tests are run, because the tests are chosen so as to confirm the patient's functioning with respect to the investigators' beliefs about the nature of the malady and about their theoretical interpretation of that malady. Alternative explanations for a patient's functioning might extend to categorically different realms of cognition; see for example MacKay's extensive probing into patient HM's language functioning (Chapter 2), while other researchers working with HM insisted that his deficits were restricted to explicit recent memories. Had MacKay been unable to independently investigate HM, we might not know the extent of his deficits beyond explicit recent memory.

We wonder how much more we would understand about each of these unique patient cases if investigators with different theories about the presented dysfunction were routinely encouraged to design test batteries for patients. Nearly every contributor to this volume who was asked to imagine the chance to test the same patient again came up with additional measures he or she would like to collect. External observers would think of even more. Given the scarcity of such opportunities, soliciting proposals for tests broadly when the chance arises would provide us with even richer data about future cases. There could be a systematic way for expert readers with a different take on the impairment to request tests (experimental or standardized) that could confirm or falsify their hunches. For example, the journal editor could issue a call for proposals along with publication of a case report.

Perhaps we also need a network of regular visitations from one laboratory to another and permission to observe patients together by investigators differing in theoretical orientation to reduce this source of distortion of the field. This kind of methodological initiative would mirror one of the oldest in the field of psychology, when the astronomer Friedrich Bessel in the early 1800s visited various laboratories in Europe and concluded that basic astronomical observations could be interpreted only by taking into account the perceptual bias of the particular astronomer, what he ended up calling the "personal equation."

The opportunity for distortion is increased when a clinical case becomes textbook material. Many science teachers will tell you that what they need most for classroom teaching is clear evidence with straightforward interpretations. It is from this need that a patient like HM can quickly become a legend, after which many former students become resistant to a reinterpretation because the implication is that what they think they know most firmly they actually do not know; therefore, they cannot trust anything they think they know. For this problem to be solved, students must be encouraged and somehow incentivized to think like independent investigators early on in their academic careers, whether they intend to become researchers or not. For one thing, imagine how profoundly this approach would improve the field of medicine where, currently, exceptionally bright individuals learn to present absolute and unambiguous answers to their fearful patients who yearn for clarity. We would prefer that professors truly educate their students in the need to tolerate ambiguity and that doctors similarly try to educate their patients about the limitations as well as the achievements of our present scientific knowledge.

Undiscovered Cases

Given the theoretical lens effect we have discussed and given many practical constraints, we cannot take the absence of reporting of a certain kind of memory failure to indicate that such a case may never be found. If an individual had a selective memory deficit only for red objects, but with normal color vision, what are the chances that investigators would think to ask the right questions to detect the true nature of that deficit? What about memory impairment coupled with expressive language deficits as in the tragic but relatively common case of a patient who is not comatose but still has no way to communicate the contents of his or her conscious awareness? This is one area for which better brain imaging methods eventually could prove critical in providing clues to the nature of the memory disorder.

Permission to Conduct the Study and to Publish the Results

We are cautiously optimistic about the practical issues investigators face in this field.

Authors of the chapters in this volume almost uniformly held the opinion that the kinds of spontaneous investigations that led to their most important discoveries might not be possible with today's Institutional Review Board (IRB) constraints on experimentation. That might be, but, in fact, the authors reported few instances of actually having been turned down in the request for open-ended methods. Perhaps it is a matter of clarifying to the IRB committee the parameters and limits of the intended exploration, after which necessary freedom of exploration hopefully could be permitted. In support of this possibility, qualitative research often involves open-ended survey follow-up questions and we know of investigators who have gotten permission to do such questioning, without having had to provide a complete protocol of the intended questions.

Some, though not other, investigators have had trouble publishing results that flew in the face of established theories. This resistance to change is, alas, a deeply ingrained aspect of human nature but we believe that investigators can do something about it. In most cases, we believe that the resistant reviewers are not bad or selfish people but are motivated largely by the inability to make sense of the new results; this is a manifestation of the unfortunate discomfort with ambiguity we mentioned earlier. The best way to overcome this resistance is for authors to think hard about how to explain the new findings in light of existing theory, making the smallest necessary changes to theory. An example is the 2004 article in *Brain* by Cowan et al. cited by Dewar (Chapter 11). The article showed that many densely amnesic individuals could learn new information if it was followed by a quiet, dark hour-long period, revealed even after they slept (and snored) during some of that period. The resistance from reviewers was annoying; some reviewers said that the result was not believable, whereas others said that the result was not novel. The solution was to take reviewers seriously and, when their concern seemed out of line, to remain assertive and steadfast in communication with the editor of the journal (e.g., to insist that loud snoring was, of course, valid proof of sleeping); and when their concern seemed reasonable, to figure out how to communicate better (e.g., by realizing that the novelty of the finding becomes clearer if the result is described not just as "removal of interference" but more specifically as "removal of retroactive interference"). Editors and reviewers should also bear in mind that endorsing a paper for publication need not imply agreement with its interpretation. We suggest that getting soundly conducted research into the public record where it may be broadly scrutinized is more important than protecting the theoretical status quo from challenging data. As we stressed earlier, a tolerance for ambiguity, along with a willingness to re-evaluate prior conclusions, is needed while psychological theories develop.

Conclusion

The editors of this volume have inspired a great convening of observations from the eyes and hands of some of the best clinical scientists of memory disorders on the planet. These reflections bring new dimensions to these classic cases, adding details that will help readers interpret the available evidence. We have tried to compare the chapters in terms of both the different nature of the memory patients involved and the different viewpoints of the investigators involved. Memory is the substance of a person's identity and there is only a thin shield that physically protects that identity from dissolution. We hope that those who have suffered because they or a loved one has had a brain disorder may benefit from a better understanding of the disorder. They might encounter something that could lead to living with amnesia better, for example, by trying out the technique of a quiet, dark rest period after learning something of importance, or they might gain hope that the observations in this volume someday will be translated into treatments and cures as soon as that becomes feasible.

References

Braver, T. S. (2012). The variable nature of cognitive control: a dual-mechanisms framework. *Trends in Cognitive Science, 16*, 106–113.

Hodgetts, C. J., Postans, M., Warne, N., Varnava, A., Lawrence, A. D., & Graham, K. S. (2017). Distinct contributions of the fornix and inferior longitudinal fasciculus to episodic and semantic autobiographical memory. *Cortex, 94*, 1–14.

18
BIASES AND CONCERNS WITH THE SINGLE CASE APPROACH IN THE NEUROPSYCHOLOGY OF MEMORY

Roberto Cubelli

The interviews collected in the present volume compose a complete and intriguing picture of the modern neuropsychological investigation of memory and amnesia. They disclose three inter-related aspects: (1) the methodology of the single case study, which is the most representative and productive approach in cognitive neuropsychology; (2) the contribution of individual patients, who have always supported research by participating in numerous and sometime tedious experiments; and (3) the endeavour of researchers and neuroscientists in accruing knowledge regarding memory processes and brain functioning.

The history of neuropsychology is mainly a history of single case reports. The birth of the discipline is usually attributed to both Paul Broca, who first introduced the investigation of the cerebral bases of cognition by indicating the site for articulated speech (Benton, 1981), and Carl Wernicke, who proposed the first neuropsychological model based on the observation of different types of aphasia (Geschwind, 1967). After these pioneering studies, the single case approach was instrumental in advancing the discipline and increasing knowledge in all cognitive domains, including memory (e.g., Parkin, 1997; Rosenbaum et al., 2014). Single case reports of patients with amnesia have always been described (Mabille & Pitres, 1913; Beduschi, 1922), but it was the case series reported by Scoville and Milner (1957), which included HM, that was crucial in the development of the neuropsychology of memory.

The purpose of single case studies, regarding memory as well as other cognitive processes, is twofold: either descriptive or theoretical. Case studies may consist of meticulous clinical descriptions or insightful experimental investigations.

Firstly, publishing reports of single cases aims to share new data and observations and to solicit replication and interpretation attempts. Clinicians describe patients with amnesia in detail to underscore neat or unexpected neuroanatomical findings and behavioural phenomena. This kind of report provides exemplar cases or novel profiles of symptoms to be considered in future reviews or case series. As Lillian Manning has stated in the present volume, single patients "would likely be more useful in theories of the normal mind when further similar cases (...) are available and studied by means of functional neuroimaging and detailed neuropsychological assessment" (p. 199). The appropriateness of the employed methodology and the meticulousness of the clinical description are critical factors to make readers, as well as the entire scientific community, able to appreciate the single case's similarities and differences with previously reported patients and, hence, to encourage theoretical accounts and new questions.

Alternatively, single case studies can offer direct theoretical contributions, inasmuch as they provide relevant information to understand the working brain and the functional architecture of mental processes.

On the one hand (i.e., the neuro-anatomical point of view), the accurate description of damaged brain structures can suggest which neural networks and circuits underlie those particular cognitive functions and abilities. Following Holdstock et al. (this volume), "the study of a patient who has a selective and accurately localized lesion in a brain region of theoretical interest (...) aims to identify what the cognitive functions of the critical structure are when it is working properly" (p. 40). Yet, only group studies permit precise localisation of the cerebral regions most frequently associated with a given deficit and therefore can identify the cerebral regions directly involved in normal cognitive functioning (see Robertson, Knight, Rafal & Shimamura, 1993). Clinical categories such as 'hippocampal amnesia" and 'diencephalic amnesia', designating patients with the same lesion site, are useful to reveal the differential contribution of the damaged cerebral regions. Notwithstanding, the advantage of the single case approach is to appreciate the functional role of spared brain regions. As stated by Rosenbaum and Moscovitch, the patient they studied informed "not only of what the hippocampus does but, perhaps more importantly, what the hippocampus does not do, which is difficult, if not impossible, to capture with current neuroimaging methods" (present volume, p. 172).

On the other hand (i.e., the cognitive point of view), the accurate analysis of the pattern of impaired and intact cognitive performance observed in single patients permits individuals to develop models of normal cognitive function. According to McCloskey and Caramazza (1988), "single-patient studies represent the only appropriate methodology for drawing inferences about normal cognition in research involving brain-damaged patients" (p. 583). In the present volume, Kopelman and Morton underline the importance of single cases: "models of normal memory need to allow for the manner in which highly specific cognitive deficits unfold in brain damage (...) neuropsychological information, particularly from single cases, plays an important role in contributing to that understanding" (p. 107).

The single case approach in the assessment of patients with memory disorders has indeed proved to be very fruitful. Neuropsychological studies have documented a number of clear-cut dissociations between task performance, thus introducing or confirming important distinctions between memory type (episodic, procedural, semantic and autobiographic memories), processes (implicit vs. explicit, recall vs. recognition, familiarity vs. recollection) and structures (working memory and long-term memory). In investigating memory, however, three idiosyncrasies or biases should be avoided; they have even surfaced in some of the interviews included in the present volume.

1. For many authors, the 'purity, of the functional deficit is a required, sometimes indispensable, feature that should be reported in single cases. Vallar, for instance, claimed that, in cognitive neuropsychology, patients "should be 'pure' cases as PV was. (. . .) 'Pure' cases, namely patients with discrete and specific patterns of functional impairment, allow shedding of a more definite beam of light on the deranged function of damaged systems" (this volume p. 286). Here 'pure' is an ambiguous term. Defining a clinical picture or a given pattern of performance as 'pure' implies the presence of a single deficit (or a unique set of related signs) due to only one locus of functional impairment. It follows that all symptoms and phenomena should be interpreted as necessarily related and theoretically transparent (i.e., they are assumed to reflect (or reveal) all the properties attributed to the alleged damaged component of the impaired system). Both the behavioural and cognitive performance are described as the definitive confirmation of the chosen theoretical model and of its structure and internal coherency, as if empirical data and a pre-existing theory were logically linked. However, as suggested by Coltheart (2000), it is not possible to "claim that certain data logically require a particular architecture, because, of course, it is never the case that data logically require a particular theory. A theory is a reasonable interpretation of data, not a logical consequence of data" (p. 15).

    In clinical neuropsychology, 'pure' cases are very rare. PV was not a pure case. When first described (Basso, Spinnler, Vallar & Zanobio, 1982), PV presented with reduced span for digits, letters and words, no recency effect in free recall and an impaired score on the Token Test, with more defective performance when the items were auditorily presented than when they were visually presented. Furthermore, she showed phonemic paraphasias and word finding difficulties in oral expression and dysgraphic errors in spontaneous writing. Overall, this picture does not mean that only one deficit was present and that only one interpretation was admitted. Span and recency effect can double dissociate in both brain-damaged patients and neurologically unimpaired participants (Della Sala, Logie, Trivelli, Cubelli & Marchetti, 1998). Further, segmental errors in oral and written language may occur independently of short-term memory deficits (e.g., Shallice & Warrington, 1977).

Then, it is possible that PV, like almost all patients, suffered with multiple independent deficits.

In the first paper, PV's pattern of performance on short-term memory (STM) tasks was interpreted as consistent with "an auditory-verbal STM defect" (Basso et al., 1982, p. 272). Later, it was thought to reflect a selective impairment of the phonological loop, i.e., the verbal component of the working memory system (Vallar & Baddeley, 1984). Indeed, her behaviour mirrored that of normal participants under articulatory suppression: reduced span, an absence of the phonological similarity effect with visual presentation, and an absence of the word length effect with both auditory and visual input. Yet, PV did not show any articulatory disorders in spontaneous speech; her speech was fluent and effortless, thus contrasting with the relevant role attributed to articulation in rehearsing information held in short-term memory, as demonstrated by the correlation between STM accuracy and articulation time (Baddeley, Thomson & Buchanan, 1975). To account for PV's profile, one could assume that the articulation code involved in STM tasks is abstract in nature and that it can be impaired following a cerebral lesion without affecting spontaneous speech (Baddeley & Wilson, 1985). No independent evidence, however, supports this interpretation. Alternatively, one can maintain the hypothesis of a functional link between overt articulation and STM tasks, by considering the distinction between a phonological store and an articulatory rehearsal mechanism, proposed by Salamè and Baddeley (1982) to fractionate the phonological loop. PV might suffer from a reduced capacity of the phonological store and a subsequent functional disengagement (or disconnection) of the articulatory mechanism. Even this interpretation has no support from empirical data (for a discussion, see Caplan & Waters, 1990). Patients unable to articulate but who reproduce the pattern of STM effects shown by normal participants under articulatory suppression have never been described. Nonetheless, patients with anarthria do not behave normally. They have shown an abnormal pattern of experimental effects in STM tasks, which vary according to the cerebral lesion site (Vallar & Cappa, 1987; Cubelli & Nichelli, 1992; Papagno, Lucchelli & Vallar, 2008). Patients with pontine lesions have presented with the phonological similarity effect for both auditory and visual stimuli, but not the word length effect for either modality, revealing a deficit in rehearsing information within the phonological store. In contrast, patients with bilateral opercular lesions showed both phonological similarity and word length effects but only for auditory stimuli, revealing an inability to transfer visually presented stimuli into the phonological store. These results called for a revision of the structure of the rehearsal component the articulatory loop (Cubelli & Nichelli, 1992) and support the interpretation of PV's data. Whereas anarthric patients, who are unable to produce overt speech, present with selective deficits of the articulatory rehearsal mechanism components, PV should be attributed two separate impairments: one direct, affecting the phonological store and one indirect, preventing the use of preserved articulation to increase memory capacity.

In sum, the neuropsychological deficits in single patients are rarely 'pure', as they are neither so isolated to reflect damage limited to a single processing component, nor so transparent to reveal immediately the underlying locus of impairment.

2. Due to a misunderstanding of the principle of Occam's razor, some neuropsychologists prefer to interpret the entire set of signs and symptoms shown by a single patient as being related and, consequently, tend to elaborate on a unitary interpretation. The Occam's razor is a metaphor suggesting parsimony and simplicity (i.e., the razor eliminates all that is superfluous or redundant), but it does not imply that a single account is always preferable, as if all symptoms should constitute a coherent and meaningful picture. The metaphor means that, when competing hypotheses are available, the one with fewest assumptions should be preferred, not that if two or more phenomena can be accounted for by a single explanation, this is always preferable to an interpretation in which the same phenomena are accounted for in different ways.

In the present volume, Donald MacKay reported that the famous case of HM showed linguistic deficits in addition to his amnesia. In a series of studies, HM was impaired in terms of sentence comprehension and sentence reading; further, when required to describe unfamiliar pictures, he presented with word-retrieval problems and was more ungrammatical and incoherent than controls (for a different view and data, see Corkin, 2013). These observations led MacKay to suggest that memory and language are not separable cognitive functions because event and language memories have the same status.

The nosographic category 'amnesia', indicating a selective deficit of long-term memory, is consistent with the clinical data reported in the first paper describing HM: "On the Wechsler-Bellevue Intelligence Scale he achieved a full-scale IQ rating of 112 (. . .). An extensive test battery failed to reveal any deficits in perception, abstract thinking, or reasoning ability, and his motivation remained excellent throughout. On the Wechsler Memory Scale (he obtained) the low memory quotient of 67" (Scoville & Milner, 1957, pp. 16–17). Nevertheless, the label 'amnesia' assigned to a patient does not mean that memory is the only cognitive domain affected by the cerebral lesion and does not rule out the presence of associated disorders. It is possible that HM showed linguistic deficits but these deficits were not necessarily associated with his memory disorders or due to the same functional impairment causing amnesia. Yet, MacKay proposed a unitary account of the deficits shown by HM. He concluded that HM was unable to form new internal representations (new memories) and that this deficit impaired his ability in "comprehending new linguistic information, creating novel speech and action plans, and perceiving novel stimuli in the visual world, as well as to remembering personally experienced events" (present volume, p. 28). This interpretation aimed to explain the full range of symptoms and phenomena through an integrated view. The supposed single deficit is assumed to cause even the omission of familiar words in reading sentences aloud, as sentences by definition are always novel stimuli. Yet, no existing theory justifies such an account. No hypotheses linking impaired episodic memory and omission errors in reading aloud can be derived from acknowledged models.

In sum, neuropsychologists tend to propose *ad hoc* explanations to describe a supposed coherent and unified picture by providing a unitary account for all data and signs. In science, however, any account should derive from independent theories and models. Theoretical hypotheses are to explain empirical phenomena, not force them to meet in one unique combination. Models and theories require converging evidence, not a number of signs arising from a single source.

3. Beyond the philosophical controversy on dualism and reductionism, in exploring neuropsychological structures and processes, it is necessary to maintain the distinction of different levels of explanation: neurobiological (structural) and psychological (functional). Understanding how the brain works (from single neurons to complex circuits) is a completely different enterprise to exploring the functioning of mental and cognitive processes. In some cases, however, neuropsychologists fail to maintain a clear separation between the two epistemological levels and tend to use neurological constructs to explain psychological phenomena. For instance, Dewar (present volume) explained retroactive interference in amnesia as being due to "an interruption of memory consolidation", using a concept derived from pharmacological and neurobiological research. Consolidation of new memories is a process occurring at the molecular level, which depends on a key phase of protein synthesis (Alberini, 2005). Describing the difficulties in delayed free recall shown by amnesic patients as due to a defective mechanism in neural consolidation does not allow for the comprehension of the cognitive processes underlying rest-related memory enhancement in amnesia. To explain the long-term retention effect after post-rest distraction reported by Dewar and her co-workers, accounts at the psychological level are needed. One of them is the temporal distinctiveness theory, according to which the retrieval of items depends on their temporal isolation after the list presentation (e.g., Ecker, Brown & Lewandowsky, 2015).

The neuropsychological assessment of individual patients for either clinical or experimental aims is a very complex process (Cubelli, Pedrizzi & Della Sala, 2016). It requires explicit theoretical questions derived from models of normal cognitive functions. Motivated hypotheses should always guide neuropsychological assessment; at the same time, assessment should always aim to test, modify or develop existing models. Collecting empirical data and proposing in-depth explanations always entail the mediation of independent theoretical frameworks.

The overt use of models and theories is crucial to prevent biases and misinterpretations but also to circumvent the most frequent concerns. Many scientists have claimed that, given the uniqueness of each individual patient, the single case approach does not allow the replication of findings and the generalizability of the theoretical conclusions. This is not true. In the single case approach, what is to-be-replicated is not the whole clinical picture or the complete set of symptoms but the pattern of performance consistent with (or explained by) a given model. Neuropsychological models deriving from the single case approach do not imply the observation of patients with clinical pictures overlapping in every detail. Consider, for instance, the patients reviewed by Caplan and Waters (1990), who show a selective deficit of the phonological STM store. They shared the critical features predicted by the model of working memory (i.e., impaired performance on span tasks, both quantitatively and qualitatively) but differed in a number of other signs (e.g., divergent performance on tasks like sentence comprehension and reading aloud).

Theories should not only explain the similarities but also the differences amongst patients. Take, for instance, the temporal gradient in retrograde amnesia, which varies in the different syndromes. As groups, amnesics with Alzheimer's disease show better remote than recent memory, whereas patients with semantic dementia show the reverse pattern: better recent than remote memory (Nestor, Graham, Bozeat, Simons & Hodges, 2002). Nevertheless, individual patients may show different profiles: temporal gradient, no differences across time or lacunar deficits (Vallar, 1999, p. 332). It follows that any theory explaining retrograde amnesia should also explain why retrograde memory failures in individual patients may involve different temporal divisions.

Only the single case study can reveal different patterns of performance within a group of patients belonging to the same clinical category. This is why the single case study approach is a key methodology in cognitive neuropsychology.

References

Alberini, C. (2005). Mechanisms of memory stabilization: are consolidation and reconsolidation similar or distinct processes? *Trends in Neuroscience, 28*, 51–56.

Baddeley, A. D., Thomson, N., & Buchanan, M. (1975). Word length and the structure of short-term memory. *Journal of Verbal Learning & Verbal Behavior, 14*, 575–589.

Baddeley, A., & Wilson, B. A. (1985). Phonological coding and short-term memory in patients without speech. *Journal of Memory and Language, 24*, 490–502.

Basso, A., Spinnler, H., Vallar, G., & Zanobio, M. E. (1982). Left hemisphere damage and selective impairment of auditory verbal short-term memory. A case study. *Neuropsychologia, 20*, 263–274.

Beduschi, V. (1922). La sindrome d'amnesia post-apoplettica. *Il cervello, 1(2)*, 1–13.

Benton, A. (1981). Aphasia: historical perspectives. In M. T. Sarno (Ed.), *Acquired Aphasia*. New York: Academic Press.

Caplan, D., & Waters, G. (1990). Short-term memory and language comprehension: a critical review of the neuropsychological literature. In G. Vallar & T. Shallice (Eds.), *Neuropsychological Impairments of Short-term Memory*. Cambridge: Cambridge University Press.

Coltheart, M. (2000). Assumptions and methods in cognitive neuropsychology. In B. Rapp (Ed.), *The Handbook of Cognitive Neuropsychology: What Deficits Reveal about the Human Mind*. Philadelphia: Psychology Press.

Corkin, S. (2013). *Permanent Present Tense: The Unforgettable Life of the Amnesic Patient, H.M.* New York: Basic Books.

Cubelli, R., & Nichelli, P. (1992). Inner speech in anarthria: neuropsychological evidence of differential effects of cerebral lesions on subvocal articulation. *Journal of Clinical and Experimental Neuropsychology, 14*, 499–517.

Cubelli, R., Pedrizzi, S., & Della Sala, S. (2016). The role of cognitive neuropsychology in clinical settings: the example of a single case of deep dyslexia. In J. Macniven (Ed.), *Neuropsychological Formulation: A Clinical Casebook*. New York: Springer.

Della Sala, S., Logie, R. H., Trivelli, C., Cubelli, R., & Marchetti, C. (1998). Dissociation between recency and span: neuropsychological and experimental evidence. *Neuropsychology, 12*, 533–545.

Ecker, U. K., Brown, G. D., & Lewandowsky, S. (2015). Memory without consolidation: temporal distinctiveness explains retroactive interference. *Cognitive Science, 39*, 1570–1593.

Geschwind, N. (1967). Wernicke's contribution to the study of aphasia. *Cortex, 3*, 449–463.

Mabille, H., & Pitres, A. (1913). Sur un cas d'amnésie de fixation post-apoplectique ayant persisté pendant vingt-trois ans. *Revue de Médicine, 33*, 257–279.

McCloskey, M., & Caramazza, A. (1988). Theory and methodology in cognitive neuropsychology: a response to our critics. *Cognitive Neuropsychology, 5*, 583–623.

Nestor, P. J., Graham, K. S., Bozeat, S., Simons, J. S., & Hodges, J. R. (2002). Memory consolidation and the hippocampus: further evidence from studies of autobiographical memory in semantic dementia and frontal variant frontotemporal dementia. *Neuropsychologia, 40*, 633–654.

Papagno, C., Lucchelli, F., & Vallar, G. (2008). Phonological recoding, visual short-term store and the effect of unattended speech: evidence from a case of slowly progressive anarthria. *Cortex, 44*, 312–324.

Parkin, A. J. (1997). *Case Studies in the Neuropsychology of Memory*. Hove: Psychology Press.

Robertson, L. C., Knight, R. T., Rafal, R., & Shimamura, A. P. (1993). Cognitive neuropsychology is more than single-case studies. *Journal of Experimental Psychology: Learning, Memory, and Cognition, 19*, 710–717.

Rosenbaum, R. S., Gilboa, A., & Moscovitch, M. (2014). Case studies continue to illuminate the cognitive neuroscience of memory. *Annals of the New York Academy of Sciences, 1316*, 105–133.

Salamè, P., & Baddeley, A. D. (1982). Disruption of short-term memory by unattended speech: implications for the structure of working memory. *Journal of Verbal Learning and Verbal Behavior, 21*, 150–164.

Scoville, W.B., & Milner, B. (1957). Loss of recent memory after bilateral hippocampal lesions. *Journal of Neurology, Neurosurgery and Psychiatry, 20*, 11–21.

Shallice, T., & Warrington, E. K. (1977). Auditory-verbal short-term memory impairment and spontaneous speech. *Brain and Language. 4*, 479–491.

Vallar, G. (1999). The methodological foundations of neuropsychology. In G. Denes & L. Pizzamiglio (Eds.), *Handbook of Clinical and Experimental Neuropsychology*. Hove, East Sussex: Psychology Press.

Vallar, G., & Baddeley, A. D. (1984). Fractionation of working memory. Neuropsychological evidence of a phonological short-term store. *Journal of Verbal Learning and Verbal Behavior, 23*, 151–161.

Vallar, G., & Cappa, S. F. (1987). Articulation and verbal short-term memory. Evidence from anarthria. *Cognitive Neuropsychology, 4*, 55–78.

Notes to Chapter 18

Donald MacKay's Reply to Roberto Cubelli

I did not conclude that memory and language are *never* separable in *any* patient. I concluded that damage to hippocampal structures in Henry M's brain impaired his encoding of never-previously encountered facts, events and linguistic units. Other patients suffering less extensive damage to hippocampal structures than Henry can *in principle* experience *independent* deficits involving event versus language memories, *especially in everyday life*. This is because many words recur extremely frequently in normal language use, whereas an event experienced at a particular time is always new and never recurs: We cannot step into the same river of events twice.

The suggestion that data from Corkin (2013) contradict Henry's word-retrieval problems in my experiments is inaccurate. Even when Corkin's lab and my UCLA lab gave Henry the *identical* Boston Naming Test, we conducted different analyses and observed deficits in Henry's picture naming performance that Corkin *could not detect* (see MacKay & Hadley, 2009). Finally, binding theory (see MacKay, James & Hadley, 2008) is a widely acknowledged and empirically supported model (see e.g., Piaia et al., 2016; Meyer et al., 2005) that *does* link impaired episodic memory to omission errors in reading sentences aloud in case HM. My forthcoming book (MacKay, in press) elaborates on these points.

Roberto Cubelli's Reply to Donald MacKay

MacKay proposes a unitary account of HM's cognitive profile by suggesting a unique functional deficit for all the observed symptoms. I maintain that linguistic impairments were not necessarily due to the same impaired mechanisms responsible for anterograde amnesia. Making reference to neurophysiological evidence indicating that the hippocampus plays an important role in language comprehension (Meyer et al., 2005; Piaia et al., 2016) does not suffice to sustain the assumption that in HM one functional deficit only can account for both the inaccuracies in episodic memory tasks and the omissions in sentence reading tasks. I cannot ignore what Corkin wrote in her book (2013):

> We continued to study Henry's linguistic abilities until nearly the end of his life. We did not believe, as the UCLA researcher did, that his bilateral medial temporal-lobe lesions impaired his appreciation of linguistic ambiguity or any other speech-processing capacities. (...) The bulk of our research ultimately indicated that overall, Henry's language abilities were consistent with his socioeconomic status and likely the same as before his operation.
>
> *(Chapter 11, pp. 240–241)*

References

Corkin, S. (2013). *Permanent Present Tense: The Unforgettable Life of the Amnesic Patient, H.M.* New York: Basic Books.

MacKay, D. G. (in press). *Remembering: What Fifty Years of Research with Famous Amnesia Patient H.M. can Teach Us about Memory and How It Works.* New York: Prometheus Books.

MacKay, D. G., & Hadley, C. (2009). Supra-normal age-linked retrograde amnesia: lessons from an older amnesic (H.M.). *Hippocampus, 19,* 424–445.

MacKay, D. G., James, L. E., & Hadley, C. (2008). Amnesic H.M.'s performance on the test of language competence: parallel deficits in memory and sentence production. *Journal of Experimental and Clinical Neuropsychology, 30,* 280–300.

Meyer, P. et al. (2005). Language processing within the human medial temporal lobe. *Hippocampus, 15,* 451–459.

Piaia, V. et al. (2016). Direct brain recordings reveal hippocampal rhythm underpinnings of language processing. *Proceedings of the National Academy of Sciences, 113,* 11366–11371.

Giuseppe Vallar's Reply to Roberto Cubelli

I briefly argue against the claim that PV was not a 'pure' case, presenting with impairment of components other than the Phonological Short-Term Store.

PV's Speech Output Impairments

The only output disorder that PV showed 14 and 23 months after her stroke, when experiments were performed, was "very poor repetition of sentences (the patient was unable to repeat phrases longer than eight syllables), while the repetition of single polysyllabic words was normal" (Basso, Spinnler, Vallar & Zanobio, 1982).

Functional Models referred to in Experiments with PV

The reference model was that of Salamè and Baddeley (1982), who separated the original *Articulatory Loop* (Baddeley & Hitch, 1974) into two components: a *phonological store*, and a control process involving *articulatory rehearsal*. Since PV's articulation rate was within the normal range (Vallar & Baddeley, 1984), and articulation rate positively correlates with memory span (Hulme, Thomson, Muir & Lawrence, 1984; see also Smyth & Scholey, 1996), defective in PV, we concluded that the articulatory rehearsal component of the system was spared in PV. This argument was supported by the observation that, with visual stimuli, PV was able to assign stress to individual words, and to make rhyme judgements (Vallar & Baddeley, 1987). These tasks make use of rehearsal (Vallar, Di Betta & Silveri, 1997). In sum, the damaged functional component was the Phonological Short-Term Store.

Recency Effect in Immediate Serial Recall and Span

PV showed defective recency and span performance. One indication that a Phonological Short-Term Store deficit plays the main role in PV's impaired performance on both tasks comes from the finding that, not only in free recall (Vallar & Papagno, 1986) but also in span (where recall is serial), PV's performance was most defective in the final (recency) positions of the list (Basso et al., 1982).

I am nevertheless aware that arguing that PV had a single functional deficit, being therefore a 'pure' case, is based on the negative finding of NOT having detected other deficits.

Roberto Cubelli's Reply to Giuseppe Vallar

A series of defective performances within the same cognitive domain does not justify the claim that all the observed phenomena are due to the same mechanism represented as a single component within a theoretical model.

As confirmed by Giuseppe Vallar, the PV's cognitive picture was quite complex.

1. She had no articulatory impairment, but she showed no articulatory rehearsal activity in immediate serial recall: no word length effect with visually and auditorily presented stimuli and no phonological similarity effect with visual stimuli.
2. She behaved like neurologically unimpaired participants under articulatory suppression in verbal short-term memory tasks but was accurate oin phonological judgement tasks, which are sensitive to articulatory suppression (Burani, Vallar & Bottini, 1991; Norris, Sally Butterfield, Hall & Page, 2018).
3. She showed reduced verbal span and no recency effect in free recall, but span and recency can double dissociate in both brain-damaged people and normal participants (Della Sala, Logie, Trivelli, Cubelli & Marchetti, 1998).

References

Baddeley, A. D., & Hitch, G. J. (1974). Working memory. In G. H. Bower (Ed.), *The Psychology of Learning and Motivation. Advances in Research and Theory* (Vol. 8). New York: Academic Press, pp. 47–89.

Basso, A., Spinnler, H., Vallar, G., & Zanobio, M. E. (1982). Left hemisphere damage and selective impairment of auditory verbal short-term memory. A case study. *Neuropsychologia, 20(3)*, 263–274.

Burani, C., Vallar, G., & Bottini, M. G. (1991). Articulatory coding and phonological judgements on written words and pictures: the role of the output phonological buffer. *European Journal of Cognitive Psychology, 3*, 379–398.

Della Sala, S., Logie, R. H., Trivelli, C., Cubelli, R., & Marchetti, C. (1998). Dissociation between recency and span: neuropsychological and experimental evidence. *Neuropsychology, 12*, 533–545.

Hulme, C., Thomson, N., Muir, C., & Lawrence, A. (1984). Speech rate and the development of short-term memory span. *Journal of Experimental Child Psychology, 38(2)*, 241–253.

Norris, D., Sally Butterfield, S., Hall, J., & Page, M. P. A (2018). Phonological recoding under articulatory suppression. *Memory and Cognition, 46*, 173–180.

Salamè, P., & Baddeley, A. D. (1982). Disruption of short-term memory by unattended speech: implications for the structure of working memory. *Journal of Verbal Learning and Verbal Behavior, 21(2),* 150–164.

Smyth, M. M., & Scholey, K. A. (1996). The relationship between articulation time and memory performance in verbal and visuospatial tasks. *British Journal of Psychology, 87(2),* 179–191.

Vallar, G., & Baddeley, A. D. (1984). Fractionation of working memory: neuropsychological evidence for a phonological short-term store. *Journal of Verbal Learning and Verbal Behavior, 23(2),* 151–161.

Vallar, G., & Baddeley, A. D. (1987). Phonological short-term store and sentence processing. *Cognitive Neuropsychology, 4(4),* 417–438.

Vallar, G., Di Betta, A. M., & Silveri, M. C. (1997). The phonological short-term store-rehearsal system: patterns of impairment and neural correlates. *Neuropsychologia, 35(6),* 795–812.

Vallar, G., & Papagno, C. (1986). Phonological short-term store and the nature of the recency effect: evidence from neuropsychology. *Brain and Cognition, 5(4),* 428–442.

19
THE CASE FOR SINGLE CASE STUDIES IN MEMORY RESEARCH

Simon Fischer-Baum and Yingxue Tian

As the preceding chapters in this volume illustrate, our understanding of how human memory works has benefited from more than 125 years of careful investigation of individuals with brain damage. The chapters span descriptions of classic cases from the late 19th century (Chapter 6), to cases first described within the last five years, like AB (Chapter 5) and VA (Chapter 12). Each chapter provides a clear summary of how data from a specific patient has informed cognitive and neural theories of memory. The individual patterns of performance described are fascinating and taken together demonstrate the richness of the memory system. Beyond that, the informal format of the chapters provides a window into the sociology of case study investigations, including details rarely found in scientific articles, such as how the unique patterns were first observed and followed up on and anecdotal information about interacting with the patients.

All in all, the collection of interviews makes a strong argument for the benefits of single case approaches in the cognitive neuroscience of memory. This argument is timely, as there is a sense that single case cognitive neuropsychology as a mode of inquiry is in decline (e.g., Medina & Fischer-Baum, 2017; Shallice, 2015). Specifically, with the goal of determining what role, if any, single case cognitive neuropsychology should play in the future study of memory, we read the preceding chapters with the following questions in mind: First, have single cases provided insights into memory models? Second, is there any indication that the age of insights from single case studies has come to an end? Third, what are the barriers in the current scientific climate to doing this type of research? We take up the three questions in turn.

Have single cases provided insights into memory models?

To determine whether case study methodologies are currently useful for building memory models, it is important to demonstrate that they were ever useful. The answer is a clear and unequivocal yes. The preceding chapters report single case studies that are commonly taught in introductory psychology courses, like HM (Chapter 2), KC (Chapter 8) and PV (Chapter 13). The fact that the insights generated by these single cases are how we teach students about the organization of memory is perhaps the best demonstration of the historical value of neuropsychological data. Furthermore, the insights first provided by these single cases are frequently supported by converging evidence from different methodologies, for example, neuroimaging studies or behavioral experiments. Therefore, there is no doubt that our current understanding of how memory works has benefited extensively from these experiments of nature.

The clearest case of this is, of course, HM whose case report has been credited with the development of theories that localize the encoding of new episodic memories to specific medial temporal lobe structures like the hippocampus (Chapter 2; Eichenbaum, 2013). Much of the cognitive neuroscience research on long-term memory builds on these insights, investigating the function of the hippocampus and other medial temporal lobe structures in making memories (Eichenbaum et al., 2016). While only a small portion of this research continues to rely on the single case study method, MacKay is not exaggerating when he describes it as an "earthquake that forever reshaped the intellectual landscape of memory, mind and brain" (Chapter 2).

Focusing on HM's contribution to memory research provides a limited view of how case studies have contributed to the literature. It is common to think that the major contribution of case study research is limited to exploratory or inductive research, rather than hypothesis-driven or deductive research. Indeed, Ross (Chapter 10) links the decline in single case methods to contemporary attitudes toward science that favor deductive research over inductive research. Under this view, impactful case studies are those individuals whose pattern of performance is so unexpected that they force the field to rethink their basic assumptions and develop new theories that can then be tested with hypothesis-driven research. While this is clearly true for a case like HM, it is not true that all impactful case studies following this inductive model.

Take, for instance, case KC reported in Chapter 8. This case is discussed in psychology classrooms as some of the strongest evidence for a divide between semantic and episodic memory, and has contributed to our understanding of the divide between implicit and explicit memory. But theories that proposed dissociations between semantic and episodic memory (Tulving, 1972) predated KC's accident by approximately a decade. While it was serendipitous to find a patient whose impairments fit within this theoretical framework, the real value of KC was that the logic of neuropsychology provided a tool to test subtler hypotheses about the relationship between these two memory systems, for example in understanding the interaction between semantic and episodic memory in our autobiographical knowledge (Tulving, Schacter, McLachlan, & Moscovitch, 1988). Similarly, the fact that PV (Chapter 13) showed a selective impairment in verbal short-term memory was not the observation that led to the Baddeley-Hitch model of working memory, which predated PV's injury by more than a decade (Baddeley & Hitch, 1974). Instead, identifying a case with a particularly pure deficit provided an opportunity to test different predictions of the Baddeley-Hitch model, for example, predictions about the role that the phonological loop plays in language learning (e.g., Baddeley, Papagno, & Vallar, 1988). As these cases illustrate, the single case approach has made strong and long-lasting contributions to our understanding of memory in both the inductive, data-driven and deductive, hypothesis-driven research frameworks.

Has the age of insights from single case studies come to an end?

The cases described in the previous section are now decades old. In the intervening years, our theories of memory have become more precise and cognitive neuroscientific methods have become more sophisticated. Perhaps, then, historically single cases played an important role in developing theories of memory, but their contribution is more limited in contemporary cognitive science. To this claim, our answer is a resounding no. The major critique of single case cognitive neuropsychology is that contemporary methods—whether they be new neuroimaging techniques (Fellows et al., 2005), the availability of much larger samples of brain-damaged patients (Schwartz & Dell, 2010) or advances in computational modeling (Patterson & Plaut, 2009)—have made the careful analysis of single cases obsolete. Based on our reading of the preceding chapters, none of these reasons are particularly compelling to us. We go through them in turn.

While often not stated explicitly, the assumption that single case neuropsychology, or lesion studies more generally, are no longer relevant in this era of rapidly advancing neuroimaging techniques can be readily observed in the behavior of cognitive neuroscientists. Fellows and colleagues (2005) investigated the citation patterns for cognitive neuroscience papers that used either functional neuroimaging or lesion-based methods. Not only were functional neuroimaging papers cited more but also there was an asymmetry in the citation pattern whereby papers with lesion methods were more likely to cite both previous lesion studies and previous neuroimaging studies, while neuroimaging papers were more likely to primarily cite previous neuroimaging studies. This pattern of bias in citation, along with more explicit shifts like journals that previously published single case studies no longer accepting submissions that focus on single cases (Medina &

Fischer-Baum, 2017), magnifies the perception that advancing technologies may have made lesion studies in general, and single case neuropsychology more specifically, "a relic from a past era" (Rorden & Karnath, 2004).

This critique of neuropsychology assumes that, at best, cognitive neuropsychology can teach us exactly what these other methods can teach us, and more likely, these other methods can be used to answer more fine-grained questions of the exact same sort that can be addressed with individuals with brain damage. However, it is clear that neuroimaging and lesion methods address complementary questions. From the perspective of localizing cognitive functions, neuroimaging techniques are able to identify regions that have large populations of synchronously firing neurons whose activation is associated with the ability to perform a specific task. Lesion techniques can identify regions that contain neural populations that are necessary to perform a specific task (Rorden & Karnath, 2004). Neuroimaging and lesion methods can lead to different conclusions about functional localization because they are answering slightly different questions about the role the region plays in a specific task.

Consider the question of the role of the hippocampus in item and source recognition. As reviewed by Henson (2005), many early neuroimaging studies of recognition memory found increased activity in the hippocampus during encoding for items that are subsequently remembered than items that are subsequently forgotten, meaning that activity in the hippocampus is associated with successful encoding of items into memory. However, it is not clear from these imaging studies that the hippocampus is necessary for being able to encode items into memory. Lesion research, like the case study, YR, described in Chapter 3, provide a stronger test of whether having a hippocampus is necessary for these functions. Strikingly, YR had lesions that were selective to the hippocampus and was intact on item recognition tasks, while showing substantial impairments on recall and associative recognition. This pattern suggests that the hippocampus is necessary to encode some types of memories, but not necessary for item recognition, in particular, item recognition that can be based on a sense of familiarity. More recent neuroimaging studies have reached the same conclusions about the role that the hippocampus plays in memory (e.g., Ritchey, Libby & Ranganath, 2015), guided, in part, by these insights from brain-damaged patients. When lesion and neuroimaging methods build on each other toward providing converging evidence for the function of a specific region, as they have arguably with the role of the hippocampus in memory (Konkel & Cohen, 2009), this can be taken as particularly strong evidence that we understand the function of this region.

Perhaps this reciprocal relationship is even clearer in cases when there is no convergence across methods. For example, there is currently extensive debate over the neural correlates of semantic memory. Lesion evidence has pointed to the anterior temporal lobes (e.g., Mummery et al., 2000; Walker et al., 2011), but neuroimaging studies have typically not found activation in those regions during semantic processing tasks (see Binder & Desai, 2011 for discussion). In contrast, neuroimaging studies have identified the angular gyrus as being critical for semantic memory (Binder, Desai, Graves & Conant, 2009), but damage to this region is uncorrelated with semantic memory impairments (Hamilton, Martin & Schnur, 2013). Understanding this complex pattern of results across methods will provide a richer conception of the neural correlates of semantic memory than we would get if we focused only on one method (e.g., Mahon & Caramazza, 2009). It is not that lesion-based methods for localizing functions are inherently better than functional neuroimaging. Indeed, lesion-based methods have their own potential shortfalls, particularly in the study of individuals in the chronic state whose brains may have reorganized in response to damage (Fischer-Baum & Campana, 2017). All cognitive neuroscientific methods are imperfect, and it would be a loss to fully ignore the contributions that any method might play in furthering our understanding of how the mind is organized, particularly a method like single case neuropsychology that has proven itself to be so useful historically.

The earlier section makes the case for the importance of lesion methods generally. However, nearly all of the studies described earlier rely on large samples of individuals with brain damage. This is because brain damage in individual subjects rarely results in lesions that completely damage a particular region of interest while keeping the rest of the brain intact. For example, what was striking about the case of YR discussed earlier was that damage was limited to the hippocampus. Approximately 50% of her hippocampus remained intact, leading to heterogeneity between YR and patients with full hippocampus damage, as well as YR and patients with 50% hippocampus and other comorbid areas, and further limiting the types of conclusions that could be drawn from this individual. To address this concern, functional localization with lesion methods typically relies on large samples of patients with brain damage (e.g., Mummery et al., 2000; Walker et al., 2011) or studies comparing groups of patients whose damage is largely limited to one region of interest or another (e.g., Konkel, Warren, Duff, Tranel & Cohen, 2008). For researchers that are used to other methods in cognitive psychology and cognitive neuroscience, it is common to assume that with a larger sample, a more stable and consistent pattern with less noise will be obtained. This leads us to the second potential critique of single case cognitive neuropsychology. The fact that it is now possible to gather large samples of patients might suggest that the single case approach is no longer necessary.

In other areas of cognitive neuropsychology, largely in the cognitive neuropsychology of language, there has been extensive debate over whether averaging over a group of patients is statistically appropriate, or whether single case studies are the only legitimate approach in cognitive neuropsychology (for the single case only approach, see Caramazza, 1984, 1986; Coltheart, 2001; McCloskey & Caramazza, 1988, for a single case and group studies approach see Bub & Bub, 1988; Caplan, 1988; Robertson, Knight, Rafal & Shimamura, 1993). Briefly, the case against group studies is the following. Prior to damage, it is reasonable to assume that everyone's neural and cognitive system operates essentially the same way; hence, the same damage being introduced in the neural system would result in identical impairments in the cognitive system postmorbidly. It is this assumption that allows cognitive psychologists and neuroscientists to do group studies with neurotypical individuals. However, it is unlikely for organic brain damage to result in identical damage to the underlying cognitive and neural system. That is, there is extensive heterogeneity in the patterns of cognitive impairments that fall under a single clinical syndrome label. Because of this heterogeneity, it is statistically inappropriate to average across participants, as the pattern observed on average across the group may not true of any individual in the group.

Part of this problem with heterogeneity comes down to the fact that it is challenging to define appropriate inclusion criterion for a homogenous group. Available options are etiology, anatomical lesion loci, and neuropsychological profile. Etiology is not an efficient criterion, given that organic lesions are usually distributed and unpredictable, meaning that heterogeneity in cognitive deficits is likely. Anatomical inclusion criterion is the most commonly used one, although it is never the case that all members of the group have identical lesion locations. The regions that do not overlap likely result in heterogeneity in the group. Indeed, if the purpose is to claim homogeneity in the underlying cognitive deficit then neuropsychological profile presents the only reasonable inclusion criteria, but to what extent the neuropsychological profile should be consistent across patients is unclear. If a group of patients was recruited with the stringent criteria of almost identical behavioral patterns, there would be no more concerns about heterogeneity. However, if the research is able to truly demonstrate that each individual has the same underlying deficits, the additional benefit of averaging across the participants rather than just reporting each individual separately in a multiple case study approach is unclear.

If the primary reason to favor single case studies over group studies is concern about heterogeneity in the group, perhaps this concern is more relevant in some cognitive domains (like language) than other cognitive domains (like memory). That is, there may be a wide variety of language impairments following damage that includes either Broca's or Wernicke's area but all patients with damage to the hippocampus or the medial temporal lobe more broadly suffer the same memory impairments. However, the cases reported in the current volume provide a strong argument against this claim, as they repeatedly demonstrate how heterogeneous the underlying cognitive impairments in the single-memory cases are if enough attention is paid to truly understanding the deficit in each case. For example, both of the cases discussed by Manning in Chapter 9 had damage to similar cortical regions in a manner that they might have been included in the same group in a group study. However, they clearly have different patterns of memory impairments, with one patient showing pure retrograde amnesia for autobiographical memory and the other showing retrograde amnesia for semantic public events, but not autobiographical events. These different patterns of impairments provide novel insights into the organization of the memory system, and as Manning notes, "we would have been unable to uncover these detailed memory deficits on the bases of a patient group study" (Chapter 9). The heterogeneity of memory deficits observed in the patients contained within this volume, in terms of differences between memory tasks (e.g., recall and recognition), memory systems (e.g., episodic and semantic) and other factors, not only support the idea that it is still worth pursuing single case methods in memory research, they suggest that it is in fact better to investigate memory deficits from a single case approach rather than a group study approach.

A final critique of the role that single case neuropsychology plays in contemporary cognitive science has come from computational modelers, who claim that that data generated by these studies are too coarse-grained to inform the richer theories about cognition that computational models have provided (Patterson & Plaut, 2009). Much of this argument rests on the idea that single cases can only provide dissociations. A single dissociation is formed by intact performance on one task with impaired performance on the other, and a double dissociation is formed by two patients showing opposite patterns of performance, which is the best type of data that case studies can provide. We do not want to rehash the debate over whether or not double dissociations provide strong evidence for separable brain mechanisms (see Dunn & Kirsner, 2003 for a volume dedicated to this issue), though it is clear that there are many cases in the cognitive neuroscience of memory in which a surprising dissociation within a single case has provided a productive spark for theory development. Instead, we want to highlight the fact that this is an exceedingly narrow view of the type of data that single case cognitive neuropsychology can provide (see McCloskey, 2003 for a similar argument).

While it is certainly the case that the conclusions of many of the chapters in the current volume rely on dissociation logic, it is also clear that inferences are being drawn from patterns of association and from careful analyses of errors in these single cases as well. For example, in Chapter 2, MacKay describes very carefully run association studies demonstrating a link between the kinds of difficulties that HM had in memory processing with very specific kinds of errors that he made in language comprehension tasks. Similarly, in Chapter 14, Martin describes associations, within single participants, between the type of short-term memory deficit they suffer and performance on very specific types of sentence processing tasks. In both cases, it is associations within a single subject that provide a tool for understanding the role that different memory systems play in language processing. While it might be the case that very broad level dissociations are not always informative for computationally explicit cognitive theories, single case studies, especially with individuals like HM for whom an enormous amount of data have been collected, can provide a rich source of data that can be used to test very subtle predictions of cognitive theories.

In brief, we find no support for the claim that single case studies are no longer relevant despite being historically important in cognitive science. Cognitive neuropsychology methods complement neuroimaging methods for questions of functional localization. Heterogeneity in the underlying memory disorders that follow damage to even very similar regions indicates that we are better off studying cases individually than as groups. A richer conception of the types of data that single case neuropsychology can provide allows these studies to continue to be relevant even as cognitive theories become more computationally explicit.

What are the barriers in the current scientific climate?

Given that single case cognitive neuropsychology has historically been an important tool for theory development in cognitive science and there is no reason to think that it is not still useful in contemporary science, why is this approach on the decline? In the preceding chapters, a number of structural barriers are mentioned, from challenges with institutional review boards to issues in getting research published. In addition to those important concerns, we want to highlight a number of other ways that single case cognitive neuropsychology does not fit well with the incentive structure and current concerns in science.

Single case studies take a long time and can lead the researcher in unexpected directions. Based on the chapters in the volume and our own experience, it is not uncommon for a case study to take at least five to seven years from initial contact with the patient to eventual publication. During that time, the investigation can take unexpected turns, and the conclusions about the patient deficit at the end of the study may be very different than what was expected from initial observations. Indeed, it is possible that researchers can spend a long time studying an individual and eventually decide that there is nothing publishable about the case. These chapters report cases that made a clear contribution to the cognitive neuroscience of memory; who knows how many single case studies have been pursued for years and then dropped because no clear pattern emerged, or because the patient had another stroke or health event before the end of data completion. Single case studies are not a safe bet in a scientific climate that incentives maximizing the number of publications.

Even if researchers are willing to take the time to carefully study an interesting case, there are no guarantees that researchers will be able to recruit compelling cases to their labs. It is clear from the preceding chapters that many of these cases came to the researchers through serendipity, like a connection through the patient's son-in-law (Chapter 5) or the brother of researcher's resident's girlfriend (Chapter 10). Even for researchers who see many memory cases in a clinical setting, there is no standard path to finding these particularly interesting cases. Building a research program that depends on finding these interesting cases may not be worth the risk.

Single case methods are also not well suited to the competitive grant climate. It is unlikely to find grant funding for a project that simply proposes to find the next HM, whose pattern of dissociations will cause a major breakthrough in our understanding of how the mind and brain work. Even for deductive, hypothesis-driven single case neuropsychology, researchers cannot be certain that they will be able to find the appropriate case to investigate these questions, particularly when the type of deficit is relatively rare. Indeed, many of the researchers in this volume highlight how important being flexible about their research focus was to their use of single case methods. For example, Moulin (Chapter 7) describes how he did not set out to study déjà vu. Once he met the first case of an individual whose memory complaint was a constant feeling of already having experienced the current moment, he became interested in this phenomenon, which inspired a broader research program. Most advice for junior faculty is to build their career as an expert in a specific, focused, area rather than developing a CV that includes contributions to a scattered set of areas. The uncertainty inherent in the single case approach makes following this advice difficult.

These are only a few of the reasons that single case neuropsychology does not fit well with the current scientific climate. Given the arguments made in the previous sections, we think it is important to continue this empirical approach. This continuation requires students to be trained in this approach, hired as faculty and granted tenure. The current scientific climate places barriers on all of these things happening. Single case neuropsychology may be a declining methodology, but its decline has more to do with structural issues in contemporary science than with theoretical issues of how this method contributes to our understanding of how the mind and brain work.

Conclusions

The chapters in this volume make a strong case for single case cognitive neuropsychology in memory, both in terms of its historical importance and its value in the present day. The case for single case neuropsychology is made pragmatically, demonstrating time and time again how valuable these cases have actually been, not focusing on whether they could be valuable in theory.

Also contained within this volume are a number of important ideas about how we can do even better with single case neuropsychology. One major challenge in single case neuropsychology is drawing inferences from individuals following brain damage, given that we do not know how their memory worked premorbidly. Even though cognitive scientists assume that every neurotypical individual's memory system works essentially the same way, it is clear that there is extensive variation in the strength of different memory capacities and in the content of memory based on interests, social context and areas of expertise. When we do not know about what the patient's memory system was like before damage, we do not really know the cognitive consequences of the damage.

Several of the chapters in the book offer interesting ideas about dealing with this problem. Garrard and colleagues (Chapter 16) use longitudinal data from a public figure to be able to show changes in writing from her novels over time. While most patients in a memory clinic have probably not written dozens of novels, in our digital world, there may be methods for collecting information about the patient prior to the damage that could be used to assess where the patient fell on a continuum of memory ability premorbidly. Kopelman and Morton (Chapter 5) embrace the heterogeneity. The patient they describe, AB, was an actor whose profession required a special kind of memory skill, the ability to memorize lines that go beyond what is common. Because there was a record of AB's plays, they could study his memory for specific passages from these plays. By finding a very specific type of control participant, other actors without brain damage, they were able to take into account what AB was likely to remember from before the accident. Most patients we test are not Shakespearean actors, but with all single cases, we can learn about what kinds of memory strengths they might have premorbidly and carefully design tests that probe those memories after the damage.

Indeed, a real value of the single case approach that researchers should remember is that the careful investigation of one individual over many years provides us the opportunity to listen to the participants we test, including descriptions of how they experience the world. These descriptions can help guide our research. For example, Dr. Z (recounted in Chapter 6) provided a description of his own phenomenology of memory following seizure events and was studied more scientifically by Hughlings-Jackson. In single case cognitive neuropsychology, we can combine objective scientific measures with a personalized approach based on our patient's own experience of the world. Beyond the scientific impact of single case neuropsychology, it is notable how many of the researchers interviewed for this volume described just how much they enjoyed getting to know the participants they were testing over the years. This has been our experience as cognitive neuropsychologists as well, and the lovely, human side of this type of research is one last reason that we think that single case neuropsychology remains so valuable.

References

Baddeley, A. D., & Hitch, G. (1974). Working memory. In G. H. Bowers (Ed.), *Psychology of Learning and Motivation (Vol. 8)*. Cambridge, MA: Academic Press, pp. 47–89.

Baddeley, A., Papagno, C., & Vallar, G. (1988). When long-term learning depends on short-term storage. *Journal of Memory and Language, 27(5)*, 586–595.

Binder, J. R., & Desai, R. H. (2011). The neurobiology of semantic memory. *Trends in Cognitive Sciences, 15(11)*, 527–536.

Binder, J. R., Desai, R. H., Graves, W. W., & Conant, L. L. (2009). Where is the semantic system? A critical review and meta-analysis of 120 functional neuroimaging studies. *Cerebral Cortex, 19(12)*, 2767–2796.

Bub, J., & Bub, D. (1988). On the methodology of single-case studies in cognitive neuropsychology. *Cognitive Neuropsychology, 5(5)*, 565–582.

Caplan, D. (1988). On the role of group studies in neuropsychological and pathopsychological research. *Cognitive Neuropsychology, 5(5)*, 535–547.

Caramazza, A. (1984). The logic of neuropsychological research and the problem of patient classification in aphasia. *Brain and Language, 21(1)*, 9–20.

Caramazza, A. (1986). On drawing inferences about the structure of normal cognitive systems from the analysis of patterns of impaired performance: the case for single-patient studies. *Brain and Cognition, 5(1)*, 41–66.

Coltheart, M. (2001). Assumptions and methods in cognitive neuropsychology. In B. Rapp (Ed.), *The Handbook of Cognitive Neuropsychology: What Deficits Reveal About the Human Mind*. Philadelphia: Psychology Press, pp. 3–21.

Dunn, J. C., & Kirsner, K. (Eds). (2003). What can we infer from double dissociations? [Special Issue]. *Cortex, 39(1)*, 1–7.

Eichenbaum, H. (2013). What HM taught us. *Journal of Cognitive Neuroscience, 25(1)*, 14–21.

Eichenbaum, H., Amaral, D. G., Buffalo, E. A., Buzsáki, G., Cohen, N., Davachi, L., . . ., & Nadel, L. (2016). Hippocampus at 25. *Hippocampus, 26(10)*, 1238–1249.

Fellows, L. K., Heberlein, A. S., Morales, D. A., Shivde, G., Waller, S., & Wu, D. H. (2005). Method matters: an empirical study of impact in cognitive neuroscience. *Journal of Cognitive Neuroscience, 17(6)*, 850–858.

Fischer-Baum, S., & Campana, G. (2017). Neuroplasticity and the logic of cognitive neuropsychology. *Cognitive Neuropsychology, 34(7–8)*, 403–411.

Hamilton, A., Martin, R., & Schnur, T. (2013). A role for the angular gyrus in semantic processing? No evidence from chronic & acute stroke. *Procedia-Social and Behavioral Sciences, 94*, 90–91.

Henson, R. (2005). A mini-review of fMRI studies of human medial temporal lobe activity associated with recognition memory. *The Quarterly Journal of Experimental Psychology Section B, 58(3–4B)*, 340–360.

Konkel, A., & Cohen, N. J. (2009). Relational memory and the hippocampus: representations and methods. *Frontiers in Neuroscience, 3(2)*, 166–174.

Konkel, A., Warren, D. E., Duff, M. C., Tranel, D., & Cohen, N. J. (2008). Hippocampal amnesia impairs all manner of relational memory. *Frontiers in human neuroscience, 2*, 15.

Mahon, B. Z., & Caramazza, A. (2009). Concepts and categories: a cognitive neuropsychological perspective. *Annual Review of Psychology, 60*, 27–51.

McCloskey, M. (2003). Beyond task dissociation logic: a richer conception of cognitive neuropsychology. *Cortex, 39(1)*, 196–202.

McCloskey, M., & Caramazza, A. (1988). Theory and methodology in cognitive neuropsychology: a response to our critics. *Cognitive Neuropsychology, 5(5)*, 583–623.

Medina, J., & Fischer-Baum, S. (2017). Single-case cognitive neuropsychology in the age of big data. *Cognitive Neuropsychology, 34(7–8)*, 440–448.

Mummery, C. J., Patterson, K., Price, C. J., Ashburner, J., Frackowiak, R. S., & Hodges, J. R. (2000). A voxel-based morphometry study of semantic dementia: relationship between temporal lobe atrophy and semantic memory. *Annals of Neurology, 47(1)*, 36–45.

Patterson, K., & Plaut, D. C. (2009). "Shallow draughts intoxicate the brain": lessons from cognitive science for cognitive neuropsychology. *Topics in Cognitive Science, 1(1)*, 39–58.

Ritchey, M., Libby, L. A., & Ranganath, C. (2015). Cortico-hippocampal systems involved in memory and cognition: the PMAT framework. *Progress in Brain Research, 219*, 45–64.

Robertson, L. C., Knight, R. T., Rafal, R., & Shimamura, A. P. (1993). Cognitive neuropsychology is more than single-case studies. *Journal of Experimental Psychology: Learning, Memory, and Cognition, 19(3)*, 710–717.

Rorden, C., & Karnath, H. O. (2004). Using human brain lesions to infer function: a relic from a past era in the fMRI age? *Nature Reviews Neuroscience, 5(10)*, 812–819.

Schwartz, M. F., & Dell, G. S. (2010). Case series investigations in cognitive neuropsychology. *Cognitive Neuropsychology, 27(6)*, 477–494.
Shallice, T. (2015). Cognitive neuropsychology and its vicissitudes: the fate of Caramazza's axioms. *Cognitive Neuropsychology, 32(7–8)*, 385–411.
Tulving, E. (1972). Episodic and semantic memory. In E. Tulving & W. Donaldson (Eds.), *Organization of Memory*. New York: Academic Press, pp. 381–403.
Tulving, E., Schacter, D. L., McLachlan, D. R., & Moscovitch, M. (1988). Priming of semantic autobiographical knowledge: a case study of retrograde amnesia. *Brain and Cognition, 8(1)*, 3–20.
Walker, G. M., Schwartz, M. F., Kimberg, D. Y., Faseyitan, O., Brecher, A., Dell, G. S., & Coslett, H. B. (2011). Support for anterior temporal involvement in semantic error production in aphasia: new evidence from VLSM. *Brain and Language, 117(3)*, 110–122.

20

COMMENTS ON THE SINGLE CASE APPROACH TO THE STUDY OF MEMORY AND OTHER DOMAINS OF COGNITION

Max Coltheart

Two types of single case study

In their chapter in this book (Chapter 3), Juliet Holdstock and her colleagues begin by identifying two different kinds of neuropsychological single case study.

The first kind focuses on the brain: the aim of this kind of study, they say, is "to identify precisely what deficits relatively selective damage/dysfunction of a specific structure causes and, by appropriately qualified inference . . . to identify what the cognitive functions of the critical structure are when it is working properly."

The second kind of single case study focusses on cognition: for this kind of study, they say,

> the sole interest is to find behavioural dissociations in order to determine how the normal human mind is functionally organized. Knowledge of the precise location of brain damage is usually unnecessary and of little relevance for this second kind of single case study.

This distinction is echoed in Chapter 8 by Rosenbaum and Moscovitch, who say, "It is important to distinguish theories that have to do with mind and those that have to do with brain function," and they add, "Studying a functional dissociation should not be viewed as a lesser pursuit in comparison to a neural one."

The distinction between these two categories of single case study is fundamental, because they belong to different disciplines. Work which aims to discover the cognitive functions of particular brain structures (the first kind of case study) belongs to the discipline of cognitive neuroscience, which is a subfield of neuroscience ("theories that have to do with brain function," using the terms of Rosenbaum and Moscovitch). Since this category of single case study is about the brain, I will use the term SC-B to refer to it.

Work which aims to discover aspects of the functional organization of the human mind (the second kind of case study) belongs to the discipline of cognitive neuropsychology, which is a subfield of cognitive psychology ("theories that have to do with the mind," using the terms of Rosenbaum and Moscovitch). Since this category of single case study is about the mind, I will use the term SC-M to refer to it.

There are examples of both categories of single case study in this book. The SC-B category is represented by, for example, such chapters as those by Holdstock and colleagues in Chapter 3 (whose principal conclusion from their studies of patient YR was that the hippocampus does not play a role in certain memory tasks, specifically item recognition and recognition of associations between items) and by Tudor-Sfetea and Cipolotti in Chapter 4 (who concluded from their findings with patient VC that the hippocampus is critical for consolidating semantic information in other brain regions, and critical for recollection as opposed to familiarity judgement).

The SC-M category is represented by, for example, such chapters as those by MacKay in Chapter 2 (whose results with the amnesic patient HM suggest that the ability to make new associations between words (an ability which this patient lacked) plays a role in normal language use—for example, in keeping track of the reference of pronouns) and by Dewar in Chapter 11 (whose results with patient PB indicate that in cases of severe retrograde amnesia, new information can be stored relatively well in the absence of distraction before recall, and the effect of such distraction is to disrupt consolidation, rather than affecting encoding or retrieval processes).

As the Editors indicate in their Preface, it is the SC-M category of single case study with which this book is primarily concerned: there, the Editors say, "The present volume (...) hope[s] to reconstruct the link between neuropsychological single case observations of specific memory loss and their meaning in terms of the cognitive architecture of memory in the healthy brain."

Assumptions Needed for Making Inferences From Single Case Studies

If we are intending to make inferences about the functional architecture of some domain of cognition (e.g., memory) using data from an individual in whom cognitive processing in that domain has been impaired by brain damage, we are not of course doing this simply to make inferences about the functional organization of cognition *in that individual*. We are instead wanting to make inferences about the functional organization of cognition *in some population* of whom the individual is a representative specimen. That aim would make no sense unless it were the case that, in all members of that population, the functional organization of the relevant domain of cognition is the same. So, the SC-M approach must assume such cognitive homogeneity.

This assumption is one of the four fundamental assumptions of cognitive neuropsychology articulated by Caramazza (1984, 1986). Since these are four assumptions that the SC-M approach must make, I will list them here:

(a) The assumption of *cognitive modularity*: any cognitive system is composed of a number of independent processing units (cognitive subsystems);
(b) The assumption of *fractionation*: brain damage can impair some of the cognitive components in a cognitive system whilst sparing the remaining units;
(c) The assumption of *transparency*: the relationship between behaviour and a cognitive system is sufficiently transparent that one can infer from appropriate behavioural testing which of the cognitive components in a cognitive system are impaired and which spared, in any single case study. This assumption "essentially says that the cognitive system of a brain-damaged patient is fundamentally the same as that of a normal subject except for a 'local' modification of the system" (Caramazza, 1986, p. 52). Others (Saffran, 1982; Coltheart, 2001) have referred to this assumption as the assumption of *subtractivity* to emphasize that what is being assumed here is that pathology can subtract old cognitive subsystems but cannot add new ones.
(d) The assumption of *universality:* the assumption that a proposed functional architecture of cognition "is true of 'normal' human mind/brains in general and, therefore, of any individual normal mind/brain. Of course, it is clear that we are going to have to place some restrictions on what will count as 'normal human mind/brain,' but it is equally clear that if we were not to accept the assumption of universality, we would negate the possibility of scientifically investigating the mind/brain" (Caramazza, 1986, p. 49).

So, these four assumptions must be made by the SC-M approach when studying cognition in general and memory in particular.

Of course, the SC-B approach has to make assumptions too; for example, it too has to assume universality. To infer from a single case study of a person with damage to some specific brain structure what the cognitive functions of that brain structure are when it is working properly relies on the assumption that the cognitive functions of this structure in that person are also the cognitive functions of this structure in the brains of all of the members of some specified population (the population to which one wants to generalize one's conclusions).

Caramazza's choice of the term 'universality' to refer to his fourth assumption was perhaps a little risky, since it invites the misconception that he was making some claim about the universality of cognition itself. He intended no such claim. The transparency assumption assumes that the inferences drawn "will be assumed to be true of all individuals in the reference population. This argument is only valid if the assumption of universality is true" (Caramazza, 1986, pp. 49–50). To illustrate what he meant by 'reference population,' he gave the example of single case studies of acquired dyslexia in English. "It would not cross the mind of any reasonable investigator" (Caramazza, 1986, p. 51) to generalize any results from such studies to theories about how Chinese is read. The differences between the alphabetic writing system of English and the ideographic writing system of Chinese are so great that the functional organization of the reading system for English must be very different from the one for Chinese.

So, in the case of studying reading in English, SC-M investigators need to give thought as to what their reference population is—that is, to what population do they want to make inferences? Is it solely all readers of English? Or is it all readers of any language written in the Roman alphabet? Or is it all readers of any language written in *any* kind of alphabet (e.g., Roman, Greek Cyrillic)?

There is an intriguing contrast between reading and memory here. For the reason just given, generalization from SC-M studies of reading in English can only be to a very restricted reference population. But what about SC-M studies of memory? All the patients whose data are reported in this book were people from North America or Western Europe. Are the various forms of memory studied in these patients—short-term memory, working memory, semantic memory, episodic memory, autobiographical memory, topographical memory—all present in the memory systems of people from every culture, so that the reference population of the single case studies described in this book is all of (adult) humanity? I am too ignorant of the cross-cultural literature on memory to know whether this particular question has ever been directly studied. But this needs to be done if we are to decide how far we can generalize the theoretical conclusions reached from the SC-M studies described in this book.

One can ask the same question of the SC-B studies. If these studies have concluded what the role played in memory of a particular brain structure is when it is working properly, is that conclusion meant to apply to every adult brain in the world?

This issue about the intended reference population even arises within the confines of this book. Here, two patients are discussed who had abilities which very few people, even in these patients' own culture had: the distinguished actor AB studied by Kopelman and Morton in Chapter 5 (how many of the rest of us can memorize lines the way he was once able to?) and the distinguished author Iris Murdoch studied by Garrard and colleagues in Chapter 16 (how many of us can write novels in the way she was once able to?). Were their supranormal abilities due to their having memory systems qualitatively different from the memory systems of others around them (which would exclude them from the reference population)? Or were these due to the impact of experiences or practices that shaped the normal memory system in some quantitative way (which would allow them to be included in the reference population)?

Single Case Studies and Serendipity

As noted in several chapters in this book, one virtue of the single case approach is that it facilitates serendipitous discovery; indeed, Shallice goes so far as to say in his Introductory chapter, "the single case study . . . is a royal road to serendipity." I too have found this to be so and will offer an example.

I was once told by a clinical neuropsychologist about a patient of hers, DC, who had suffered a gunshot wound to the head and whose reading, she said, had been *entirely* abolished by this injury. I doubted this, so asked whether I could see him, and we tested him together. It was indeed the case that he was entirely unable to perform numerous reading tasks that I gave him, not even such elementary tasks as letter-naming or cross-case matching (responding 'Same' to Aa and 'Different' to Ae).

However, as I was completing a letter-naming test with him, I accidentally gave him an uppercase A with its apex pointed towards him, and **he rotated the card through 180 degrees.**

Now the letter A was correctly oriented with respect to him. Nevertheless, as before, he failed to name the letter. But of course, the fact that he had corrected its orientation suggested that he had retained *some* knowledge about letters. So, on the spot, I extemporized a new task: presenting single letters to him in various orientations and asking him to orient them correctly. He could do this easily. So, I had, serendipitously, made the discovery that a reader's knowledge about letters is not just confined to knowing their names (as tested by letter-naming) and their identities (as tested by cross-case matching). There is some other body of knowledge about letters which DC still possessed, and which is drawn upon by the letter orientation task. Such findings are unlikely to emerge from the limited testing of individual patients that is characteristic of the group study approach to neuropsychological testing.

The Future of the Single Case Study Approach

All of the contributors to this book exhibit enthusiasm for the study of single cases and none raise any fundamental criticisms for this approach. Nevertheless, Shallice, and Fischer-Baum and Tian, express a number of worries about the future prospects of this method. For example, in Chapter 19, Fischer-Baum and Tian, though they deny that the age of insights from single case studies has come to an end, do offer the view that this approach is currently "on the decline." They, and Shallice, offer a variety of reasons for their pessimism.

(a) Single case studies are time-intensive: often a researcher will spend many years seeing an individual patient. And as discussed earlier, these studies can lead the researcher in unexpected directions. But there is never any guarantee that something publishable will emerge. That happened with respect to the patient DC: I was never able to make sufficient theoretical sense of the dissociation between preservation of letter orientation ability and abolition of letter-naming and letter identification to arrive at something worth publishing. This has always been true for single case studies, yet in the past it has not prevented the approach from making great contributions to our understanding of cognition. But, as Fischer-Baum and Tian point out, these days "single case studies are not a safe bet in a scientific climate that incentivizes maximizing the number of publications."

(b) I might add a related point here. As many of the chapters in this book attest, it is common for friendships to develop between patient and scientist over the protracted course of a single case study. It can happen that at some point the scientist feels that there are no further investigations to be carried out with the patient that would be scientifically productive. Yet their meetings ought to continue because they are beneficial to the patient. This too might be considered, in the current research-administration climate, as a waste of resources and so a reason for frowning upon the single case study approach.

(c) Fischer-Baum and Tian identify another way in which the single case study approach is not well suited to the current scientific climate. One of the reasons that this approach is scientifically exciting is that patients lead scientists in unexpected and challenging directions. For example, the single case study of the patient KF carried out by Warrington and Shallice (1969) had a major impact on theories of memory (see Shallice's chapter in this book for further details); but KF also had an important form of acquired dyslexia called deep dyslexia (Coltheart, Patterson & Marshall, 1980) and the single case study of his impaired reading carried out by Shallice and Warrington (1975) was an early milestone in the cognitive neuropsychology of reading. So, when one is studying a patient with any acquired disorder of cognition, one can never predict which domain of cognition that patient will lead one into. And yet, as Fischer-Baum and Tian say, "Most advice for junior faculty is to build their career in a specific, focused, area rather than developing a CV that includes a contribution in a scattered set of areas."

(d) As Shallice points out, there are now some journals which will not consider publishing single case studies. For example, the Instructions for Authors of the journal *Brain*, a journal which published single case studies in the past (Warrington & Shallice, 1969, for example), currently say: "Preliminary reports of work in progress or single case studies are not considered. More detailed studies of single cases may—in rare instances—be considered as a Report (see the following) only when they resolve definitively an important problem in the field or when the data lead to a significant conceptual advance. Studies of single cases that can be readily performed on groups of patients will not be considered." The journal does not give any reason for taking this attitude to the single case study approach.

Universality Versus Atypicality

Shallice speculates that journals' adoption of this attitude towards single case studies may be a reflection of the argument that single cases may be 'atypical,' and gives an example of such an argument:

> The sheer rarity of the STM patient, for there are no more than 10 to 15 cases reported in the literature, might indicate that there is something out of the ordinary in the underlying neurobiology of these particular individuals. . . . Although the neuropsychological method emphasizes the value of "existence proofs" (i.e., the observation of a single white crow falsifies the assertion that all crows are black), it may be that the STM patient may be an example of an "exception that proves the rule."
> *(Buchsbaum & D'Esposito, 2008, p. 773)*

I find it impossible to see any coherence in this argument. If one accepts that the theory "all crows are black" is falsified by the observation of a single white crow, then one must accept that any cognitive theory of memory according to which the specific pattern of memory performance seen in STM patients cannot occur is falsified by the observation of a single such STM patient. Similarly, any theory about the neural basis of memory according to which a certain pattern of brain damage should not affect memory is falsified by the observation of just one patient in whom that pattern of brain damage does have the effect on memory that is not predicted by that theory.

Furthermore, there is an obvious circularity in this argument concerning atypicality. If a theorist responds to the fact that there are 10–15 patients whose data are inconsistent with one's theory by saying that the theory is not meant to apply to these patients because they are atypical, how could this theorist answer the question, "How do you know that they are atypical?" The answer could only be, "Because my theory does not predict their behaviour," which is obviously circular. In terms of Caramazza's assumption of universality and his concept of a reference population, what is being done here is defining "reference population" as "the population for which my theory makes the correct predictions." That's what is circular. The only way to escape such circularity is to define the "reference population" independently of one's theory.

Such attempts to defend one's theory by appealing to the rarity of patients whose data conflict with that theory are seen from time to time when data from single case studies that are inconsistent with that theory emerge. For example, consider the theory that acquired phonological dyslexia (i.e., the selective inability to read nonwords) is not a specific impairment of the reading system itself but is due to an impairment of the phonological processing system. Single case studies of patients with phonological dyslexia but no phonological impairments provide evidence against this theory. Such patients have been reported. Can they be ignored? This has been attempted:

> Patterson (2000, pp. 59–60) has proposed [that] "before concluding that phonological alexia can be interpreted as a specific reading impairment, we might like to see more than one or two documented cases without an accompanying non-reading phonological deficit." One is tempted to ask here: How many more than one or two?
>
> *(Coltheart, 2006, p. 105)*

It may well be that the principle of universality of functional architecture of cognition (suitably embellished with a definition of a reference population for one's theory defined independently of that theory) is false. If it is, then one cannot make generalizations from the results of single case studies to some theory of cognition that is meant to apply beyond that case. But if this is so, then:

(a) This would not be a problem specific to the single case approach. On the contrary, it would be a worse problem for the group study approach. Averaging across a group of subjects who were cognitively heterogeneous would obscure this unfortunate heterogeneity. Treating the subjects as individuals would at least reveal it. More generally, completely rejecting the assumption of suitably defined universality "would negate the possibility of scientifically investigating the mind/brain" (Caramazza, 1986, p. 49).

(b) Is the assumption of universality false (i.e., is subject/patient atypicality common)? Shallice in his chapter concludes not: "In the whole range of neuropsychological studies of individual cases, I know of only one example where theoretical inferences drawn from individual cases may not have been justified because the relevant patients were at the extremes of a distribution or otherwise atypical. This relates to the syndrome of 'reading without semantics' (Woollams, Ralph, Plaut & Patterson, 2007, but see also Coltheart, Tree & Saunders, 2010)". Even this single example of Shallice's does not challenge the universality assumption. To be at the extreme of a distribution is not the same as being atypical: to be at the extreme of a distribution is a quantitative matter, whereas being atypical is a qualitative matter. What Coltheart et al. (2010) showed was that a single model (i.e., one that was assumed universal to all readers of English, including those with reading impairments due to brain damage) could account for the data of *all* the patients with the "reading without semantics" syndrome; so none of these patients were atypical with respect to that model.

Conclusions

One could put Shallice's point a little differently. Suppose that as a matter of fact, Caramazza's assumption of universality was not true of cognition—that is, suppose there are appreciable qualitative differences between people in the functional architectures of their cognitive systems. In that case, the single case study approach to investigating cognition could not succeed. But the contributors to this book all believe that this approach has succeeded notably in the domain of memory. The successes of this approach in other cognitive domains—reading, spelling, object recognition, speech production and so on—are equally obvious. So the single case approach is scientifically valuable, which is why we should all be as worried about the future of this approach as Shallice, and Fischer-Baum and Tian, are.

References

Buchsbaum, B. R., & D'Esposito, M. (2008). The search for the phonological store: from loop to convolution. *Journal of Cognitive Neuroscience, 20*, 762–778.

Caramazza, A. (1984). The logic of neuropsychological research and the problem of patient classification in aphasia. *Brain and Language, 21*, 9–20.

Caramazza, A. (1986). On drawing inferences about the structure of normal cognitive systems from the analysis of patterns of impaired performance. *Brain and Cognition, 5*, 41–66.

Coltheart, M. (2001). Assumptions and methods in cognitive neuropsychology. In B. Rapp (Ed.), *Handbook of Cognitive Neuropsychology*. New York: Psychology Press.

Coltheart, M. (2006). Acquired dyslexias and the computational modelling of reading. *Cognitive Neuropsychology, 23*, 96–109.

Coltheart, M., Patterson, K., & Marshall, J. C. (Eds.) (1980). *Deep Dyslexia*. London: Routledge and Kegan Paul. Second edition 1987.

Coltheart, M., Tree, J., & Saunders, S. (2010). Computational modelling of reading in semantic dementia: comment on Woollams, Lambon Ralph, Plaut and Patterson (2007). *Psychological Review, 117*, 256–272.

Patterson, K. (2000). Phonological alexia: the case of the singing detective. In E. Funnell (Ed.), *Case Studies in the Neuropsychology of Reading*. Hove, UK: Lawrence Erlbaum Associates Ltd, pp. 57–83.

Saffran, E. (1982). Neuropsychological approaches to the study of language. *British Journal of Psychology, 73*, 317–337.

Shallice, T., & Warrington, E. K. (1975). Word recognition in a phonemic dyslexic patient. *Quarterly Journal of Experimental Psychology, 27*, 187–199.

Warrington, E. K., & Shallice, T. (1969). The selective impairment of auditory verbal short-term memory. *Brain, 92*, 885–896.

Woollams, A. M., Lambon Ralph, M. A., Plaut, D. C., & Patterson, K. (2007). SD-squared: on the association between semantic dementia and surface dyslexia. *Psychological Review, 114*, 316–339.

INDEX

Note: Page numbers in *italic* indicate a figure and page numbers in **bold** indicate a table on the corresponding page.

AB (patient) 92–98, 292–300, 386, 392; contribution to knowledge 102–105; impaired abilities of 98–100; and normal mind 107–108, 300–302, 307–309; and publications 105–107, 305–306; spared abilities of 101–102; testing of 302–305, 306–307
acquired sociopathy 81
actor 98–101, 104, 355
acyclovir 6
Addenbrooke's Cognitive Examination **243**, 347
Adult Memory and Information Processing Battery *68*, 134
AKP (patient) 131–134; and déjà vu 141–142, 144–145; and normal mind 140–141, 148–150; and reduplicative paramnesia 142–143; testing of 135–140
Alzheimer's disease 9, 371; and Iris Jean Murdoch 338–340; *vs.* semantic dementia 316, 320; and writing 342–343
American National Adult Reading Test (AM-NART) *164*
amygdala 43, 165, 189, 210
angular gyrus 381
anterior temporal lobes 6, 195, 358, 380
anterograde amnesia 29; dual-process theory of 43, 51, 72; and PB (patient) 226–232, 233–234

anterograde memory 65–68, 71–72
anteromedial temporal lobectomy 189
aphasia 292; and semantic memory 304–305; study of 2
articulatory loop 267, 374
articulatory rehearsal 268–271, 281, 286, 374–375
associations 52–56, 390; and hippocampus 59–60
associative recognition 49–50, 52
autobiographical amnesia 94, 96–102, 105
autobiographical memory 9, 188–191; and semantic public events memory 194; *see also* personal experiences
Autobiographical Memory Interview (AMI) 98, *164*, 165, 323–324
autobiographical significance 191–192, 198
autoimmune limbic encephalitis 221, 222
autonoetic consciousness 160, 169–170

baclofen 256
Baddeley-Hitch model 379
Bayesian Standardised Difference Test (BSDT) 106
Benton Face Recognition Test 162, *164*
Benton Visual Discrimination Test *164*
Black Prince, The 337
Book and the Brotherhood, The 337
Boston Naming Test *164*, 373

Broca, Paul 365
Broca's area *30*, 276, 382
Brown-Peterson paradigm 284

California Verbal Learning Test (CVLT) *164*, 165, 211
Cambridge Comprehension Test 70
Camel and Cactus Test 70
cardiac arrest 94
Case 1 (patient) 203–204; and ethics committees 213–216; and fractionation 210–212; and normal mind 212–213; and publications 212; testing of 204–210
Case 2 (patient) 204, 209–210
case studies 1–3, 10–11, 357–363, 365, 377–379, 382; future of 393–394; inferences from 390; limitations of 384–385; and serendipity 393; types of 389–390; and universality 395–397; value of 385–386
category specificity effect 6–7
cerebellum 25
cerebral hypoxia 187
CH (patient) 187–188; and normal mind 195–200; testing of 191–194
Christie, Agatha 346
City University Color Vision Test 161
Cochrane, Kent 156–160; and consolidation 168–169; and lesions 174–176; and normal mind 165–166, 170–171, 173–174; and problem solving 171–173; and spatial memory 166–168; testing of 160–165, 176–179; and time 169–170
Cognitive Archaeology project 346
Cognitive Estimates Test *67*
cognitive modularity 391
cognitive neuropsychology 381, 383–386; assumptions of 391; *vs.* cognitive neuroscience 390
cognitive neuroscience 389
cognitive psychology 3
cognitive reserve hypothesis 345
cognitive styles 359–360
confabulations 9–10, 93, 106
consolidation 168, 220, 370; and accelerated long-term forgetting 256; and rest-related memory enhancement 228–235
context confusions 10
Convergence, Recollection and Familiarity Theory (CRAFT) 54–55, 61
Corsi Span *222*

cortisol 254
CRAFT *see* Convergence, Recollection and Familiarity Theory (CRAFT)
creativity 35–36
Crovitz Test 191

Damasio's Time-locked Multiregional Retroactivation Model *188*
DC (patient) 393
declarative memory 224, 235
deductive research 213–216
Deese-Roediger-McDermott paradigm 119
déjà vécu *see* recollective confabulation
déjà vu 111–112, 113–114, 131–133; and epilepsy 251; media portrayal of 151–153; and recollective confabulation 141–142; types of 144
Delis Kaplan Executive Function System (DKEFS) *243*
dementia 142–143, 148
Dementia Rating Scale (DRS) *164*
developmental amnesia 78
diencephalon 1
diffusor-tensor imaging (DTI) 84
digit span 3, 307–308; Subtest 21–22, *68*, *69*, 134, *222*
disconnection syndromes 209
dissociable memory theories 166
dissociation 357
Doors and People Test 42, *69*, 106
Dr Z (patient) 386 *see* Myers, Anthony
DTI *see* diffusor-tensor imaging (DTI)
dysphasia 121

EA (patient) 305
ECT Test 284
emotions 255
encephalitis 6–7, 223; *see also* autoimmune limbic encephalitis; herpes simplex encephalitis
encephalomalacia 160
encoding categories 34–35
epilepsy 110, 197, 241; *see also* seizures; transient epileptic amnesia (TEA)
epilepsy surgery 125–126
epileptic amnesia 111–112, 115–119
episodic amnesia 156
episodic memory 5–6, 81–82, 96, 99, 112, 124, 158, 173; and autonoetic consciousness 169–170; and consolidation 168–169; and future thinking 171–172; and hippocampus

102; and non-episodic memory tasks 166; and posterior neocortical areas 162; and semantic memory 160; and spatial memory 166–167; and theory of mind 170–171; and VC 69–70
epistemic feelings 140
ethics committees 86, 108, 150–151, 200; and Case 1 (patient) 213–216; and PB (patient) 236; and PV (patient) 287; and VA (patient) 257
event memory 19–20, 34
Existentialists and Mystics 337, 350–351
experiential memory 326
explicit memory 158, 176

false recollections 111–112
familiarity 8, 43, 52; false 114; and recognition 46–47, 58–59; and recollection 138–139, 144, 147–149, 169
Famous Faces Test 71, 72, 190, 191, 193
Famous Public Events Questionnaire Test 71, 72
Famous Scenes Test 193
Farnsworth-Munsell 100-hue test 162
fast mapping 59
Flight from the Enchanter, The 337
fMRI *see* functional MRI (fMRI)
focal retrograde amnesia 187, 193
fornix 358
fractionation 41, 391
Frenchay Aphasia Screening Test 222, 223
frontal hematoma 292
functional MRI (fMRI) 75, 123, 236; *see also* structural MRI; volumetric MRI
future thinking 171–172, 192–193

GABA(B) receptor 256
Galton-Crovitz word-cue task 165
glucose uptake 94
Good Apprentice, The 337
Graded Difficulty Naming Test 67
Graded Synonyms Test 70
Graham-Kendall Memory-for-Designs Test 207
graphemic output buffer 5
Groundhog Day 151

Hayling Sentence Completion Test 67
herpes simplex encephalitis 6–7, 124
hippocampal sclerosis 122, 189
hippocampus 17, 20, 366, 380; and anterograde amnesia 51, 73; and associations 52–55, 159; atrophied 65–68, 145, 221, 245; and Convergence, Recollection and Familiarity Theory (CRAFT) 61; damage to 73–74, 161; and déjà vu 134; and episodic memory 102; and familiarity 77; and forgetting rates 60; and imagined experiences 84–85; and implicit and explicit memory 176–177; and internal representations 22–25, 29–33, 36; and language comprehension 373; lesions of 1, 8–9, 42, 43–44, 57–58, 59, 174–176, 381; and recollection 77, 140–141; and recollection/recall 56; and remote memory 76–77; and reorganization of function 57; and semantic memory 78, 80, 82; and spatial memory 50; and temporo-parietal region 195; and visual memory 77–78
HM (patient) *see* Molaison, Henry
Hooper Visual Organization Test 164
Hopkins Verbal Learning Test (HVLT) 134
Hub-and-Spokes model 6, 7
hypoemotionality 210
hypometabolism 245
hysteria 250

imagination 35–36
IM (patient) *see* Murdoch, Iris Jean
implicit memory 158, 176, 224
inductive research 213–215
inferior longitudinal fasciculi 209, 212, 358
inferior medial frontal lobe 10
inferotemporal cortex 209
intelligence quotient (IQ) *see* IQ
interictal memory 240–241, 246, 252
internal representations 21–23, 24–28; novel 29–32; preformed 35
inter-temporal choice 172
Intra-Individual Measure of Association (IIMA) 106
IQ: and anterograde amnesia 65; and autobiographical amnesia 92; and episodic memory 161, 191, 194; and recollective confabulation 134; and transient epileptic amnesia (TEA) 249
ischaemic infarctions 208, 212, 252

Jackson's Dilemma 338, 342, 343, 349–350, 351
James, Henry 351
JB (patient) 265
JR (patient) 188–190; and normal mind 195–200; testing of 191–194
Judgement of Line Orientation 162

Index **401**

KC (patient) *see* Cochrane, Kent
KE (patient) 315–319; and ethics committees 332–333; and normal mind 325–328, 331–332; and publications 328–330; testing of 319–320
KF (patient) 4, 298, 394
Kluver-Bucy syndrome 209

language memory 19, 33–34
lateral temporal cortex 164
lexical frequency 344–345
lexical variety 343–344
long-term memory (LTM) 265, 273–274, 279–280
LTM *see* long-term memory (LTM)

MA (patient) 132
mass action 2
medial temporal cortex 61
medial temporal lobes 16, *17*, 79, *95*, 147, *161,208*; atrophy of 106, 221; damage to 164–165; and declarative memory 235; and epilepsy 189; and language comprehension 373; volume loss of 160; volumes of 162
memory models 246–249
metaphors 23
Metaphysics as a Guide to Morals 337
Mini-Mental State Examination (MMSE) 134, 211
mirror neurons 28
ML (patient) 292–300; and normal mind 300–302, 307–309; and publications 305–306; testing of 302–305, 306–307
modality effect 270
Modified Autobiographical Memory Interview (MAMI) 242, **243**
Modified Card Sorting Task *222*, 223; Wisconsin Card Sorting Task 67
Molaison, Henry (HM) 2–3, 11, 16–20, *37*, 223, 224, 256, 357, 369, 378, 383; and case studies 365; and creativity 35–36; and encoding categories 34–35; and KC 158–159; and language impairment 25–27, 36; and memory impairments 28–31; and omission errors 32–33; and sentence comprehension 20–25; and word retrieval 373
Montreal Cognitive Assessment 211
MR spectroscopy 76
Multiple Trace Theory 76, 79, 81
Murdoch, Iris Jean 336–340, 360, 392; case features of 340–345; and ethics committees 351–352; and normal mind 345; and publications 347–348; testing of 346–347, 349–351
Murray, Bill 151, 152
Myers, Anthony 110–119

National Adult Reading Test 134, **243**
neuropsychological approach 85, 274–275, 365–367, 371, 377, 380; and normal mind 107–108, 126–127, 150, 235–236, 256, 308–309; and serendipity 333
Nice and the Good, The 337
normal mind 126, 140–141; and Case 1 (patient) 212–213; and PB (patient) 220–221; and PV (patient) 286–287; and semantic public events memory 199; and VA (patient) 253–257
Nun Study 342

object recognition 322–323; forced-choice object recognition test 47–48; yes/no object recognition 47–48, *48*
Occam's razor 369
occipital lobe 164
occipital lobe infarction 157
omission errors 32
ophthalmoplegia 133
opiates 41
organic amnesia 41, 42

paired associative learning: paradigm 274; test *68*, 222
parahippocampal cortex 54–55; atrophied 145
parietal cortex 292
Patient 1 120–121
Patient 2 120–121
PB (patient) 220–221; and anterograde amnesia 226–232, 233–234; and ethics committees 236; and normal mind 232–233, 234–236; testing of 221–226
penicillin 215
perirhinal cortex 54–55
perisylvian area 283
personal experiences 327–330; *see also* autobiographical memory
Personal Semantic/Autobiographical Memory Questionnaire 97
phonological dyslexia 395–396
phonological loop 379
phonological output buffer 5, 271, *276*
phonological recoding 275, *277*, 286
phonological short-term store (PhSTS) 268, 271–277, 374–375
phonological similarity effect 267, 275

Piazza del Duomo study 263
posterior inferior frontal regions 292
posterior parahippocampal gyrus 255
premotor cortex 276
procedural memory 112, 124; and anterograde amnesia 224
process dissociation procedure 146–147
protein synthesis 228, 370
psychogenic amnesia **252–253**
pure amnesia 66
PV (patient) 261–263, 368, 374–375, 379; and ethics committees 287; and normal mind 265–269, 286–287; and phonological short-term store (PhSTS) 271–277; and publication 280–283; and short-term memory 269–271, 277–280; testing of 263–265, 283–285

quadrantanopsia 210
Quaerens (patient) *see* Myers, Anthony
qualitative research 362

Raven's Progressive Matrices 223, 262
recall 8, 390; free recall 3–4, 272–273, 278, 283; and hippocampus 42; and recognition 42–43, 45, 51
recency effect 272–273, 277, 278, 367
recognition: and brain regions 58; false 135–137; immediate recognition test 47; item recognition; 42, 46–47
and familiarity 51; processes of 8; and recall 42–43, 45
Recognition Memory Test for Faces *68*
Recognition Memory Test for Words *68*
recollection 8–9; false 114; and familiarity 138–139, 144, 147–149, 169; and recognition 46–47, 51, 58–59; two-stage model of 177
recollective confabulation 131, 140–142; and dementia 148; media portrayal of 152
recollective experience paradigm 138
redemption process 190
reduplicative paramnesia 142–143
rehearsal *see* articulatory rehearsal
Remember/Know technique 46
remote memory 71, 124–125; and hippocampus 76–77
Repeatable Battery for the Assessment of Neuropsychological Status 211
rest-related memory enhancement 224–231
retrograde amnesia 29

retrograde memory: non-personal 69, 71; personal 71
retrosplenial cortex 106
Rey Auditory Verbal Learning Test (RAVLT) 211, 242, **243**
Rey Osterrieth Complex Figure (ROCF) *68*, 162, *164*, 242, **243**, 341; Delayed *222;* Test 84, 222, *222*, 223
rhinencephalon 209
Ribot's law 328

scenes 55
schemas 328
schematic representations 168
scripts 328
Sea, The Sea, The 337, 349, 350
seizures 113; *see also* epilepsy
Selective Reminding Test 221–222
semantic dementia 6, 9, 315–319; and normal mind 331–332; test findings of 319–325
semantic learning 102–105
semantic memory 5–7, 112, 158, 355; and cognitive styles 359; and episodic memory 166, 167; and hippocampus 78, 80; and personal experiences 327–330; and retention capacity 300–303, 307–308; short term 292–300; and VC 69
semantic public events memory 189, 191, 193–194, 199
sensory-specific amnesia 209–210, 211
sentence comprehension 20–24, 295–296; and short-term memory 293, 302, 304, 307–308
sentence processing 294–295, 304–307
Shakespeare, William 96–97, 102–104
short-term memory (STM) 3–5, 368; and PV (patient) 265–269, 277–280; and sentence comprehension 293; and universality 395; and VC 69
Short-term Topographical Memory Test **68**
spatial disorientation 204–205, 207
spatial position 50, 52
spatial representations 166–168
stages of processing framework 28
Standard Consolidation Theory 81, 85
Standard Language Examination 262
stroke 203, 215, 292; and PV (patient) 261
Stroop effect 304
structural MRI 73–74, *75; see also* functional MRI; volumetric MRI
subclinical amnesia 117

Index **403**

subdural hematoma 157
syntactic complexity 345

tactile memory 211
TEA *see* transient epileptic amnesia (TEA)
temporal discounting 171
temporal lobectomy 120–121, 123, 223
temporal lobes 134; and epilepsy 110–111, 114–115, 124, 133, 242; injury to 158
temporal memory 50, 52
temporal pole 189
Test of Language Competence (TLC) 23
thalamus 106
TIME (The Impairment of Memory in Epilepsy) study 242, 250
Token Test 262, 278–279, 367
topographical amnesia 246
Topographical Memory Test of outdoor scenes **68**
topographical recognition memory 73
Trail Making Test (TMT) **164**, 222, 233, **243**
transcranial direct current stimulation (tDCS) 235
transcranial magnetic stimulation (TMS) 235
Transformation Theory 76, 81
transient epileptic amnesia (TEA) 113, 114–119; description of 242–246; and memory models 246–249; and VA (patient) 240–242, 249–253; *see also* epilepsy
transient global amnesia 115, 244, 249, 252, **252–253**
traumatic brain injury 157

uncus 114; and autobiographical memory 189
Under the Net 336, 337, 350
Unicorn, The 348
universality 391, 395–396

VA (patient): and ethics committees 257; and normal mind 253–257; and transient epileptic amnesia (TEA) 240–242, 249–253
VC (patient) 65–68; imaging findings of 73–76; and normal mind 76–81, 85; and publications 81–83; testing of 68–73, 84–85, 86

verbal memory 73, 206, 265
ventrolateral prefrontal cortex 164
visual amnesia 207
visual cortex 30, *208*, 209
Visual Form Discrimination Test 162
visual imagery 162
visual memory 207, 211, 250, 355
Visual Object and Space Perception Battery **67**, 84
visual recall 207
volumetric MRI 74; *see also* functional MRI (fMRI); structural MRI
voxel-based morphometry 74–75

Wada Test 122–123, 284
Warrington Recognition Memory Test (RMT) 42, 58, 165, **243**
Waves, The 348
Wearing, Clive 124
Wechsler Abbreviated Scale of Intelligence (WASI) 69, **164**,**243;** Wechsler Abbreviated Scale of Intelligence—Revised (WASI-R) **67**,68, 69, *70;* Wechsler Adult Intelligence Scale 161; Wechsler Adult Intelligence Scale—Revised (WAIS-R) **164**,211
Wechsler-Bellevue Intelligence Scale 369
Wechsler Memory Scale—Revised (WMS-R) **164**,165, 369
Weigl Sorting Test **67**
Wernicke, Carl 365
Wernicke's area 382
Western Aphasia Battery 164
Willis, Thomas 250
Wisconsin Card Sorting Test 164
WM (patient) 315–319; and ethics committees 332–333; and normal mind 325–328, 331–332; and publications 328–330; testing of 319–322, 323–325
word length effect 267
word-list learning **222**
working memory 368; model of 5, 265
writer's block 339

YR (patient) 41–42; and associative recognition 49–50, 55–56; and hippocampal damage 57, 60–61; and recognition *vs.* recall 43–49; and spatiotemporal information 50–51